AYN RAND is the author of *Atlas Shrugged*, philosophically the most challenging best-seller of its time. Her first novel, *We the Living*, was published in 1936, followed by *Anthem*. With the publication of *The Fountainhead* in 1943, she achieved a spectacular and enduring success. Rand's unique philosophy, Objectivism, has gained a worldwide audience. The fundamentals of her philosophy are set forth in such books as *Introduction to Objectivist Epistemology*, *The Virtue of Selfishness*, *Capitalism: The Unknown Ideal*, and *The Romantic Manifesto*. Ayn Rand died in 1982.

LEONARD PEIKOFF is universally recognized as the preeminent Rand scholar writing today. He worked closely with her for thirty years and was designated by Rand as her intellectual heir and as heir to her estate. He has taught philosophy at Hunter College, Long Island University, and New York University, and lectures on Rand's philosophy throughout the country. Peikoff is the author of *Objectivism: The Philosophy of Ayn Rand*, and hosts the national radio talk show "Philosophy: Who Needs It?"

GARY HULL, who holds a Ph.D. in philosophy from Claremont, has taught philosophy at California State University, Fullerton, Whittier College, and is currently an adjunct professor at Duke University. He has lectured on Ayn Rand's philosophy throughout the country and teaches an annual seminar on Objectivism for the Ayn Rand Institute.

THE
AYN RAND
READER

Edited by Gary Hull
and Leonard Peikoff
Introduction by Leonard Peikoff

A PLUME BOOK

PLUME
Published by the Penguin Group
Penguin Putnam Inc., 375 Hudson Street, New York, New York 10014, U.S.A.
Penguin Books Ltd, 27 Wrights Lane, London W8 5TZ, England
Penguin Books Australia Ltd, Ringwood, Victoria, Australia
Penguin Books Canada Ltd, 10 Alcorn Avenue, Toronto, Ontario, Canada M4V 3B2
Penguin Books (N.Z.) Ltd, 182–190 Wairau Road, Auckland 10, New Zealand

Penguin Books Ltd, Registered Offices: Harmondsworth, Middlesex, England

First published by Plume, a member of Penguin Putnam Inc.

First Printing, January, 1999
10 9 8 7

ACKNOWLEDGMENTS
Excerpts from *The Fountainhead* reprinted with the permission of Simon & Schuster.
Copyright 1943 by The Bobbs-Merrill Company; copyright renewed © 1970 by Ayn Rand.

 REGISTERED TRADEMARK—MARCA REGISTRADA

Library of Congress Cataloging-in-Publication Data:

Rand, Ayn.
    The Ayn Rand reader / edited by Gary Hull and Leonard Peikoff.
      p.   cm.
    ISBN 0-452-28040-0
    I. Hull, Gary.   II. Peikoff, Leonard.   III. Title.
PS3535.A547A6   1999
813'.52—dc21   98-26698
                                                    CIP

Printed in the United States of America
Set in Transitional 521
Designed by Eve L. Kirch

PUBLISHER'S NOTE
Included are works of fiction. Names, characters, places, and incidents either are the
products of the author's imagination or are used fictitiously, and any resemblance to
actual persons, living or dead, events, or locales is entirely coincidental.

Contents

Contents

Part Three: Atlas Shrugged

Part Four: Basic Philosophy

Part Five: Early Novels and Politics

Part Six: Romanticism and the Benevolent Universe

INTRODUCTION

by Leonard Peikoff

AYN RAND'S body of work, including posthumous collections, now extends to twenty-two volumes. Her best-known and most philosophical novels, *The Fountainhead* and *Atlas Shrugged*, number respectively 727 and 1,168 pages (in hardcover). This abundance of material poses a problem for many time-pressed readers. They do not know where to plunge in or how to select a representative sample. The present book is designed to meet these needs.

The readers I have in mind probably read relatively little fiction or philosophy. But they have noticed that AR is known virtually everywhere—and that everyone seems to have an impassioned opinion about her. They have heard her books being extolled and denounced with equal intensity—often in quite unexpected quarters. Naturally enough, they are intrigued by the controversy.

Here is a chance for such individuals to explore her works briefly and reach a judgment of their own.

Although I hope it will be of value to previous readers of AR, this anthology is intended as an entrée for those who know little or nothing about her. Each of her four novels and every branch of philosophy are represented within its pages, even if only in brief excerpts. Whoever finishes the book, therefore, can say in all conscience that he knows the essence of AR—and that he knows it by means of actually having read her.

AR's philosophic ideas permeate each of her novels. In broad tendency, however, her early novels are devoted to social-political issues; *The Fountainhead* to ethical issues; and *Atlas Shrugged*, her magnum opus, to the fundamental branches of philosophy. This progression is the key to the present book's organization (see the Editor's Preface below).

Although the material has been organized in a definite structure, browsers who wish merely to dip in at random can profit from doing so. Those who wish to explore further will find that the selections are not only representative; they have been picked deliberately from a wide range of primary sources, and thereby suggest a fairly complete range of options for future reading.

As a mini-orientation for new readers, let me offer here a thumb-nail sketch of AR's Objectivist philosophy.

Metaphysics: The universe exists objectively, independent of consciousness. Its fundamental law is the law of identity, A is A.

Epistemology: Reason is man's only means of knowledge, both of facts and of values. "Reason" is the faculty of identifying and integrating, in conceptual form, the material provided by man's senses.

Ethics: The only scientific ethics is the ethics of rational self-interest, which holds that Man's Life is the standard of moral value and that rationality is the primary virtue. Each man, therefore, should live by his own mind and for his own sake, neither sacrificing himself to others nor others to himself.

Politics: The only social system consistent with the requirements of Man's Life is laissez-faire capitalism, the complete separation of state and economics. The proper function of government is to protect each individual's inalienable rights to life, liberty, property, and the pursuit of happiness.

Esthetics: "Art" is the re-creation of reality according to an artist's metaphysical value-judgments—and the greatest school in art history is Romanticism, whose art presents things not as they are, but as they might be and ought to be.

To put the above in negative terms, AR rejects, among many other kindred isms, every form of supernaturalism, subjectivism, mysticism, skepticism, altruism, relativism, collectivism, statism, and (in art) both Naturalism and "modernism."

As you may be starting to see, AR cannot be identified by using the conventional categories. She is neither a liberal nor a conservative. She admires Aristotle, but denies that "moderation" is the definition of virtue. She regards Libertarians as worse than Communists. She is a moralist who rejects religion, an individualist who dismisses Spencer, an egoist who denounces Nietzsche—and a philosopher who writes thrillers. How is all this possible? Read on and find out for yourself.

The Ayn Rand Reader represents the work of two editors. Gary Hull, a longtime teacher of Objectivism, had the painful job of making the preliminary selections; he also devised the book's structure and wrote the first draft of most of the editorial notes. As Executor of the Estate of AR, I myself then implemented a layer of suggestions, along with many editorial revisions.

Arnold Dolin, Associate Publisher of Dutton/Signet, had been urging me for years to prepare this kind of book. Unfortunately, the demands of other commitments always made it impossible. It is thanks to the labor of Dr. Hull that this anthology has finally become a reality. His work (which includes all the proofreading) was really the time-consuming part of the project.

I hope that *The Ayn Rand Reader* serves its purpose, and introduces AR to many readers who would otherwise be denied the pleasure and knowledge she has to offer.

Leonard Peikoff
Irvine, California
January 1998

EDITOR'S PREFACE

by Gary Hull

TO INTRODUCE new readers to the novels and philosophy of Ayn Rand, this anthology presents alternating fiction and nonfiction sections. Excerpts from a novel are followed by nonfiction passages elaborating on its theme.

I have chosen relatively self-contained excerpts from AR's four novels: *The Fountainhead* (in Part One), *Atlas Shrugged* (Part Three), *We the Living*, and *Anthem* (Part Five). These selections at least suggest the novels' themes, plots, and literary style, along with some leading characters.

Although *The Fountainhead* was published in 1943, seven years after *We the Living*, I have placed it at the beginning because the hero—Howard Roark—is the best known of AR's characters, and is her first fully developed depiction of the moral ideal. This led naturally to a nonfiction section on AR's ethics (Part Two), including her explanation of why man needs morality, her defense of selfishness, and her view of man's nature.

Next comes *Atlas Shrugged*, followed by a section on basic philosophy (Part Four). This section covers such issues as the axioms of Objectivism and the mind-body question, along with some more technical material on AR's view of concepts.

This left me with AR's early, directly political novels—followed by a section on her social-political convictions (Part Five). I have concluded with a section presenting both her theory of art—and, as a final overview, her benevolent-universe viewpoint (Part Six).

Given AR's voluminous writings, I have had to be extremely selective. For instance, if I had more space, I would have included all of

John Galt's speech in *Atlas Shrugged*—the briefest statement of her philosophy available. Other omissions include selections from her plays, early short stories, journals, and letters, as well as her views on education, psychology, economics and law, music and history, and on many vital current social issues. I hope that the bibliography of AR's complete works will serve as a resource for further reading.

The editor's notes provide, where necessary, minimal background information to orient a new reader. In a number of cases, a passage was deleted from an excerpt because, out of context, it would have confused or distracted a reader. Such deletions are indicated by ellipses in square brackets. Occasional explanatory words have been inserted in brackets. I have, of course, made no changes in AR's own words.

For twelve years of intellectual, financial, and emotional support I extend my sincerest appreciation to the Ayn Rand Institute. Lara Piper worked diligently to prepare the manuscript for the printer. Most of all, I want to thank Leonard Peikoff for the wonderful opportunity to work on this project, and for the insightful guidance he offered me throughout.

PART ONE

The Fountainhead

EDITOR'S NOTE: *The theme of* The Fountainhead *(published in 1943) is individualism versus collectivism, not in politics but in man's soul. In this excerpt, the first three chapters of the novel, we meet Ayn Rand's ideal man: the intransigent individualist Howard Roark. We also meet his antithesis, the man without a self, Peter Keating. This introduces the novel's basic conflict: independence versus dependence.*

Roark vs. Keating

HOWARD ROARK laughed.

He stood naked at the edge of a cliff. The lake lay far below him. A frozen explosion of granite burst in flight to the sky over motionless water. The water seemed immovable, the stone—flowing. The stone had the stillness of one brief moment in battle when thrust meets thrust and the currents are held in a pause more dynamic than motion. The stone glowed, wet with sunrays.

The lake below was only a thin steel ring that cut the rocks in half. The rocks went on into the depth, unchanged. They began and ended in the sky. So that the world seemed suspended in space, an island floating on nothing, anchored to the feet of the man on the cliff.

His body leaned back against the sky. It was a body of long straight lines and angles, each curve broken into planes. He stood, rigid, his hands hanging at his sides, palms out. He felt his shoulder blades drawn tight together, the curve of his neck, and the weight of the blood in his hands. He felt the wind behind him, in the hollow of his spine. The wind waved his hair against the sky. His hair was neither blond nor red, but the exact color of ripe orange rind.

He laughed at the thing which had happened to him that morning and at the things which now lay ahead.

He knew that the days ahead would be difficult. There were questions to be faced and a plan of action to be prepared. He knew that he should think about it. He knew also that he would not think, because everything was clear to him already, because the plan had been set long ago, and because he wanted to laugh.

He tried to consider it. But he forgot. He was looking at the granite.

He did not laugh as his eyes stopped in awareness of the earth around him. His face was like a law of nature—a thing one could not question, alter or implore. It had high cheekbones over gaunt, hollow cheeks; gray eyes, cold and steady; a contemptuous mouth shut tight, the mouth of an executioner or a saint.

He looked at the granite. To be cut, he thought, and made into walls. He looked at a tree. To be split and made into rafters. He looked at a streak of rust on the stone and thought of iron ore under the ground. To be melted and to emerge as girders against the sky.

These rocks, he thought, are here for me; waiting for the drill, the dynamite and my voice; waiting to be split, ripped, pounded, reborn; waiting for the shape my hands will give them.

Then he shook his head, because he remembered that morning and that there were many things to be done. He stepped to the edge, raised his arms, and dived down into the sky below.

He cut straight across the lake to the shore ahead. He reached the rocks where he had left his clothes. He looked regretfully about him. For three years, ever since he had lived in Stanton, he had come here for his only relaxation, to swim, to rest, to think, to be alone and alive, whenever he could find one hour to spare, which had not been often. In his new freedom the first thing he wanted to do was to come here, because he knew that he was coming for the last time. That morning he had been expelled from the Architectural School of the Stanton Institute of Technology.

He pulled his clothes on: old denim trousers, sandals, a shirt with short sleeves and most of its buttons missing. He swung down a narrow trail among the boulders, to a path running through a green slope, to the road below.

He walked swiftly, with a loose, lazy expertness of motion. He walked down the long road, in the sun. Far ahead Stanton lay sprawled on the coast of Massachusetts, a little town as a setting for the gem of its existence—the great institute rising on a hill beyond.

The township of Stanton began with a dump. A gray mound of refuse rose in the grass. It smoked faintly. Tin cans glittered in the sun. The road led past the first houses to a church. The church was a Gothic monument of shingles painted pigeon blue. It had stout wooden buttresses supporting nothing. It had stained-glass windows with heavy traceries of imitation stone. It opened the way into long

streets edged by tight, exhibitionist lawns. Behind the lawns stood
wooden piles tortured out of all shape: twisted into gables, turrets,
dormers; bulging with porches; crushed under huge, sloping roofs.
White curtains floated at the windows. A garbage can stood at a side
door, flowing over. An old Pekinese sat upon a cushion on a door step,
its mouth drooling. A line of diapers fluttered in the wind between
the columns of a porch.

People turned to look at Howard Roark as he passed. Some remained staring after him with sudden resentment. They could give
no reason for it: it was an instinct his presence awakened in most people. Howard Roark saw no one. For him, the streets were empty. He
could have walked there naked without concern.

He crossed the heart of Stanton, a broad green edged by shop windows. The windows displayed new placards announcing: WELCOME TO
THE CLASS OF '22! GOOD LUCK, CLASS OF '22! The Class of '22 of the
Stanton Institute of Technology was holding its commencement exercises that afternoon.

Roark swung into a side street, where at the end of a long row, on
a knoll over a green ravine, stood the house of Mrs. Keating. He had
boarded at that house for three years.

Mrs. Keating was out on the porch. She was feeding a couple of ca-
naries in a cage suspended over the railing. Her pudgy little hand
stopped in mid-air when she saw him. She watched him with curiosity. She tried to pull her mouth into a proper expression of sympathy;
she succeeded only in betraying that the process was an effort.

He was crossing the porch without noticing her. She stopped him.

"Mr. Roark!"

"Yes?"

"Mr. Roark, I'm so sorry about—" she hesitated demurely,
"—about what happened this morning."

"What?" he asked.

"Your being expelled from the Institute. I can't tell you how sorry
I am. I only want you to know that I feel for you."

He stood looking at her. She knew that he did not see her. No, she
thought, it was not that exactly. He always looked straight at people
and his damnable eyes never missed a thing, it was only that he made
people feel as if they did not exist. He just stood looking. He would
not answer.

"But what I say," she continued, "is that if one suffers in this world,
it's on account of error. Of course, you'll have to give up the architect

profession now, won't you? But then a young man can always earn a decent living clerking or selling or something."

He turned to go.

"Oh, Mr. Roark!" she called.

"Yes?"

"The Dean phoned for you while you were out."

For once, she expected some emotion from him; and an emotion would be the equivalent of seeing him broken. She did not know what it was about him that had always made her want to see him broken.

"Yes?" he asked.

"The Dean," she repeated uncertainly, trying to recapture her effect. "The Dean himself through his secretary."

"Well?"

"She said to tell you that the Dean wanted to see you immediately the moment you got back."

"Thank you."

"What do you suppose he can want *now?*"

"I don't know."

He had said: "I don't know." She had heard distinctly: "I don't give a damn." She stared at him incredulously.

"By the way," she said, "Petey is graduating today." She said it without apparent relevance.

"Today? Oh, yes."

"It's a great day for me. When I think of how I skimped and slaved to put my boy through school. Not that I'm complaining. I'm not one to complain. Petey's a brilliant boy."

She stood drawn up. Her stout little body was corseted so tightly under the starched folds of her cotton dress that it seemed to squeeze the fat out to her wrists and ankles.

"But of course," she went on rapidly, with the eagerness of her favorite subject, "I'm not one to boast. Some mothers are lucky and others just aren't. We're all in our rightful place. You just watch Petey from now on. I'm not one to want my boy to kill himself with work and I'll thank the Lord for any small success that comes his way. But if that boy isn't the greatest architect of this U.S.A., his mother will want to know the reason why!"

He moved to go.

"But what am I doing, gabbing with you like that!" she said brightly. "You've got to hurry and change and run along. The Dean's waiting for you."

She stood looking after him through the screen door, watching his gaunt figure move across the rigid neatness of her parlor. He always made her uncomfortable in the house, with a vague feeling of apprehension, as if she were waiting to see him swing out suddenly and smash her coffee tables, her Chinese vases, her framed photographs. He had never shown any inclination to do so. She kept expecting it, without knowing why.

Roark went up the stairs to his room. It was a large, bare room, made luminous by the clean glow of whitewash. Mrs. Keating had never had the feeling that Roark really lived there. He had not added a single object to the bare necessities of furniture which she had provided; no pictures, no pennants, no cheering human touch. He had brought nothing to the room but his clothes and his drawings; there were few clothes and too many drawings; they were stacked high in one corner; sometimes she thought that the drawings lived there, not the man.

Roark walked now to these drawings; they were the first things to be packed. He lifted one of them, then the next, then another. He stood looking at the broad sheets.

They were sketches of buildings such as had never stood on the face of the earth. They were as the first houses built by the first man born, who had never heard of others building before him. There was nothing to be said of them, except that each structure was inevitably what it had to be. It was not as if the draftsman had sat over them, pondering laboriously, piecing together doors, windows and columns, as his whim dictated and as the books prescribed. It was as if the buildings had sprung from the earth and from some living force, complete, unalterably right. The hand that had made the sharp pencil lines still had much to learn. But not a line seemed superfluous, not a needed plane was missing. The structures were austere and simple, until one looked at them and realized what work, what complexity of method, what tension of thought had achieved the simplicity. No laws had dictated a single detail. The buildings were not Classical, they were not Gothic, they were not Renaissance. They were only Howard Roark.

He stopped, looking at a sketch. It was one that had never satisfied him. He had designed it as an exercise he had given himself, apart from his schoolwork; he did that often when he found some particular site and stopped before it to think of what building it should bear. He had spent nights staring at this sketch, wondering what he had missed. Glancing at it now, unprepared, he saw the mistake he had made.

He flung the sketch down on the table, he bent over it, he slashed lines straight through his neat drawing. He stopped once in a while and stood looking at it, his fingertips pressed to the paper; as if his hands held the building. His hands had long fingers, hard veins, prominent joints and wristbones.

An hour later he heard a knock at his door.

"Come in!" he snapped, without stopping.

"Mr. Roark!" gasped Mrs. Keating, staring at him from the threshold. "What on earth are you doing?"

He turned and looked at her, trying to remember who she was.

"How about the Dean?" she moaned. "The Dean that's waiting for you?"

"Oh," said Roark. "Oh, yes. I forgot."

"You . . . *forgot?*"

"Yes." There was a note of wonder in his voice, astonished by her astonishment.

"Well, all I can say," she choked, "is that it serves you right! It just serves you right. And with the commencement beginning at four-thirty, how do you expect him to have time to see you?"

"I'll go at once, Mrs. Keating."

It was not her curiosity alone that prompted her to action; it was a secret fear that the sentence of the Board might be revoked. He went to the bathroom at the end of the hall; she watched him washing his hands, throwing his loose, straight hair back into a semblance of order. He came out again, he was on his way to the stairs before she realized that he was leaving.

"Mr. Roark!" she gasped, pointing at his clothes. "You're not going like *this?*"

"Why not?"

"But it's your *Dean!*"

"Not any more, Mrs. Keating."

She thought, aghast, that he said it as if he were actually happy.

The Stanton Institute of Technology stood on a hill, its crenelated walls raised as a crown over the city stretched below. It looked like a medieval fortress, with a Gothic cathedral grafted to its belly. The fortress was eminently suited to its purpose, with stout, brick walls, a few slits wide enough for sentries, ramparts behind which defending archers could hide, and corner turrets from which boiling oil could be poured upon the attacker—should such an emergency arise in an institute of learning. The cathedral rose over it in lace splendor, a fragile defense against two great enemies: light and air.

The Dean's office looked like a chapel, a pool of dreamy twilight fed by one tall window of stained glass. The twilight flowed in through the garments of stiff saints, their arms contorted at the elbows. A red spot of light and a purple one rested respectively upon two genuine gargoyles squatting at the corners of a fireplace that had never been used. A green spot stood in the center of a picture of the Parthenon, suspended over the fireplace.

When Roark entered the office, the outlines of the Dean's figure swam dimly behind his desk, which was carved like a confessional. He was a short, plumpish gentleman whose spreading flesh was held in check by an indomitable dignity.

"Ah, yes, Roark," he smiled. "Do sit down, please."

Roark sat down. The Dean entwined his fingers on his stomach and waited for the plea he expected. No plea came. The Dean cleared his throat.

"It will be unnecessary for me to express my regret at the unfortunate event of this morning," he began, "since I take it for granted that you have always known my sincere interest in your welfare."

"Quite unnecessary," said Roark.

The Dean looked at him dubiously, but continued:

"Needless to say, I did not vote against you. I abstained entirely. But you may be glad to know that you had quite a determined little group of defenders at the meeting. Small, but determined. Your professor of structural engineering acted quite the crusader on your behalf. So did your professor of mathematics. Unfortunately, those who felt it their duty to vote for your expulsion quite outnumbered the others. Professor Peterkin, your critic of design, made an issue of the matter. He went so far as to threaten us with his resignation unless you were expelled. You must realize that you have given Professor Peterkin great provocation."

"I do," said Roark.

"That, you see, was the trouble. I am speaking of your attitude towards the subject of architectural design. You have never given it the attention it deserves. And yet, you have been excellent in all the engineering sciences. Of course, no one denies the importance of structural engineering to a future architect, but why go to extremes? Why neglect what may be termed the artistic and inspirational side of your profession and concentrate on all those dry, technical, mathematical subjects? You intended to become an architect, not a civil engineer."

"Isn't this superfluous?" Roark asked. "It's past. There's no point in discussing my choice of subjects now."

"I am endeavoring to be helpful, Roark. You must be fair about this. You cannot say that you were not given many warnings before this happened."

"I was."

The Dean moved in his chair. Roark made him uncomfortable. Roark's eyes were fixed on him politely. The Dean thought, there's nothing wrong with the way he's looking at me, in fact it's quite correct, most properly attentive; only, it's as if I were not here.

"Every problem you were given," the Dean went on, "every project you had to design—what did you do with it? Every one of them done in that—well, I cannot call it a style—in that incredible manner of yours. It is contrary to every principle we have tried to teach you, contrary to all established precedents and traditions of Art. You may think you are what is called a modernist, but it isn't even that. It is . . . it is sheer insanity, if you don't mind."

"I don't mind."

"When you were given projects that left the choice of style up to you and you turned in one of your wild stunts—well, frankly, your teachers passed you because they did not know what to make of it. But, when you were given an exercise in the historical styles, a Tudor chapel or a French opera house to design—and you turned in something that looked like a lot of boxes piled together without rhyme or reason—would you say it was an answer to an assignment or plain insubordination?"

"It was insubordination," said Roark.

"We wanted to give you a chance—in view of your brilliant record in all other subjects. But when you turn in this—" the Dean slammed his fist down on a sheet spread before him—"*this* as a Renaissance villa for your final project of the year—really, my boy, it was too much!"

The sheet bore a drawing—a house of glass and concrete. In the corner there was a sharp, angular signature: Howard Roark.

"How do you expect us to pass you after this?"

"I don't."

"You left us no choice in the matter. Naturally, you would feel bitterness toward us at this moment, but . . ."

"I feel nothing of the kind," said Roark quietly. "I owe you an apology. I don't usually let things happen to me. I made a mistake this time. I shouldn't have waited for you to throw me out. I should have left long ago."

"Now, now, don't get discouraged. This is not the right attitude to take. Particularly in view of what I am going to tell you."

The Dean smiled and leaned forward confidentially, enjoying the overture to a good deed.

"Here is the real purpose of our interview. I was anxious to let you know as soon as possible. I did not wish to leave you disheartened. Oh, I did, personally, take a chance with the President's temper when I mentioned this to him, but . . . Mind you, he did not commit himself, but . . . Here is how things stand: now that you realize how serious it is, if you take a year off, to rest, to think it over—shall we say to grow up?—there might be a chance of our taking you back. Mind you, I cannot promise anything—this is strictly unofficial—it would be most unusual, but in view of the circumstances and of your brilliant record, there might be a very good chance."

Roark smiled. It was not a happy smile, it was not a grateful one. It was a simple, easy smile and it was amused.

"I don't think you understood me," said Roark. "What made you suppose that I want to come back?"

"Eh?"

"I won't be back. I have nothing further to learn here."

"I *don't* understand you," said the Dean stiffly.

"Is there any point in explaining? It's of no interest to you any longer."

"You will kindly explain yourself."

"If you wish. I want to be an architect, not an archeologist. I see no purpose in doing Renaissance villas. Why learn to design them, when I'll never build them?"

"My dear boy, the great style of the Renaissance is far from dead. Houses of that style are being erected every day."

"They are. And they will be. But not by me."

"Come, come, now, this is childish."

"I came here to learn about building. When I was given a project, its only value to me was to learn to solve it as I would solve a real one in the future. I did them the way I'll build them. I've learned all I could learn here—in the structural sciences of which you don't approve. One more year of drawing Italian post cards would give me nothing."

An hour ago the Dean had wished that this interview would proceed as calmly as possible. Now he wished that Roark would display some emotion; it seemed unnatural for him to be so quietly natural in the circumstances.

"Do you mean to tell me that you're thinking seriously of building *that way*, when and *if* you are an architect?"

"Yes."

"My dear fellow, who will let you?"

"That's not the point. The point is, who will stop me?"

"Look here, this is serious. I am sorry that I haven't had a long, earnest talk with you much earlier . . . I know, I know, I know, don't interrupt me, you've seen a modernistic building or two, and it gave you ideas. But do you realize what a passing fancy that whole so-called modern movement is? You must learn to understand—and it has been proved by all authorities—that everything beautiful in architecture has been done already. There is a treasure mine in every style of the past. We can only choose from the great masters. Who are we to improve upon them? We can only attempt, respectfully, to repeat."

"Why?" asked Howard Roark.

No, thought the Dean, no, he hasn't said anything else; it's a perfectly innocent word; he's not threatening me.

"But it's self-evident!" said the Dean.

"Look," said Roark evenly, and pointed at the window. "Can you see the campus and the town? Do you see how many men are walking and living down there? Well, I don't give a damn what any or all of them think about architecture—or about anything else, for that matter. Why should I consider what their grandfathers thought of it?"

"That is our sacred tradition."

"Why?"

"For heaven's sake, can't you stop being so naïve about it?"

"But I don't understand. Why do you want me to think that *this* is great architecture?" He pointed to the picture of the Parthenon.

"*That*," said the Dean, "is the Parthenon."

"So it is."

"I haven't the time to waste on silly questions."

"All right, then." Roark got up, he took a long ruler from the desk, he walked to the picture. "Shall I tell you what's rotten about it?"

"It's the *Parthenon*!" said the Dean.

"Yes, God damn it, the Parthenon!"

The ruler struck the glass over the picture.

"Look," said Roark. "The famous flutings on the famous

columns—what are they there for? To hide the joints in wood—when columns were made of wood, only these aren't, they're marble. The triglyphs, what are they? *Wood*. Wooden beams, the way they had to be laid when people began to build wooden shacks. Your Greeks took marble and they made copies of their wooden structures out of it, because others had done it that way. Then your masters of the Renaissance came along and made copies in plaster of copies in marble of copies in wood. Now here we are, making copies in steel and concrete of copies in plaster of copies in marble of copies in wood. Why?"

The Dean sat watching him curiously. Something puzzled him, not in the words, but in Roark's manner of saying them.

"Rules?" said Roark. "Here are my rules: what can be done with one substance must never be done with another. No two materials are alike. No two sites on earth are alike. No two buildings have the same purpose. The purpose, the site, the material determine the shape. Nothing can be reasonable or beautiful unless it's made by one central idea, and the idea sets every detail. A building is alive, like a man. Its integrity is to follow its own truth, its one single theme, and to serve its own single purpose. A man doesn't borrow pieces of his body. A building doesn't borrow hunks of its soul. Its maker gives it the soul and every wall, window and stairway to express it."

"But all the proper forms of expression have been discovered long ago."

"Expression—of what? The Parthenon did not serve the same purpose as its wooden ancestor. An airline terminal does not serve the same purpose as the Parthenon. Every form has its own meaning. Every man creates his meaning and form and goal. Why is it so important—what others have done? Why does it become sacred by the mere fact of not being your own? Why is anyone and everyone right—so long as it's not yourself? Why does the number of those others take the place of truth? Why is truth made a mere matter of arithmetic—and only of addition at that? Why is everything twisted out of all sense to fit everything else? There must be some reason. I don't know. I've never known it. I'd like to understand."

"For heaven's sake," said the Dean. "Sit down. . . . That's better. . . . Would you mind very much putting that ruler down? . . . Thank you. . . . Now listen to me. No one has ever denied the importance of modern technique to an architect. We must learn to adapt the beauty of the past to the needs of the present. The voice of the past is the voice of the people. Nothing has ever been invented by one man in architecture. The proper creative process is a slow, gradual, anonymous, collective one, in which each man collaborates with all the others and subordinates himself to the standards of the majority."

"But you see," said Roark quietly, "I have, let's say, sixty years to live. Most of that time will be spent working. I've chosen the work I want to do. If I find no joy in it, then I'm only condemning myself to sixty years of torture. And I can find the joy only if I do my work in the best way possible to me. But the best is a matter of standards— and I set my own standards. I inherit nothing. I stand at the end of no tradition. I may, perhaps, stand at the beginning of one."

"How old are you?" asked the Dean.

"Twenty-two," said Roark.

"Quite excusable," said the Dean; he seemed relieved. "You'll outgrow all that." He smiled. "The old standards have lived for thousands of years and nobody has been able to improve upon them. What are your modernists? A transient mode, exhibitionists trying to attract attention. Have you observed the course of their careers? Can you name one who has achieved any permanent distinction? Look at Henry Cameron. A great man, a leading architect twenty years ago. What is he today? Lucky if he gets—once a year—a garage to remodel. A bum and a drunkard, who . . ."

"We won't discuss Henry Cameron."

"Oh? Is he a friend of yours?"

"No. But I've seen his buildings."

"And you found them . . ."

"I said we won't discuss Henry Cameron."

"Very well. You must realize that I am allowing you a great deal of . . . shall we say, latitude? I am not accustomed to hold a discussion with a student who behaves in your manner. However, I am anxious to forestall, if possible, what appears to be a tragedy, the spectacle of a young man of your obvious mental gifts setting out deliberately to make a mess of his life."

The Dean wondered why he had promised the professor of mathematics to do all he could for this boy. Merely because the professor had said: "This," and pointed to Roark's project, "is a great man." A great man, thought the Dean, or a criminal. The Dean winced. He did not approve of either.

He thought of what he had heard about Roark's past. Roark's father had been a steel puddler somewhere in Ohio and had died long

ago. The boy's entrance papers showed no record of nearest relatives. When asked about it, Roark had said indifferently: "I don't
think I have any relatives. I may have. I don't know." He had seemed
astonished that he should be expected to have any interest in the
matter. He had not made or sought a single friend on the campus.
He had refused to join a fraternity. He had worked his way through
high school and through the three years here at the Institute. He
had worked as a common laborer in the building trades since childhood. He had done plastering, plumbing, steel work, anything he
could get, going from one small town to another, working his way
east, to the great cities. The Dean had seen him, last summer, on his
vacation, catching rivets on a skyscraper in construction in Boston;
his long body relaxed under greasy overalls, only his eyes intent, and
his right arm swinging forward, once in a while, expertly, without effort, to catch the flying ball of fire at the last moment, when it
seemed that the hot rivet would miss the bucket and strike him in
the face.

"Look here, Roark," said the Dean gently. "You have worked hard
for your education. You had only one year left to go. There is something important to consider, particularly for a boy in your position.
There's the *practical* side of an architect's career to think about. An
architect is not an end in himself. He is only a small part of a great social whole. *Co-operation* is the key word to our modern world and to
the profession of architecture in particular. Have you thought of your
potential clients?"

"Yes," said Roark.

"The *Client*," said the Dean. "The Client. Think of that above all.
He's the one to live in the house you build. Your only purpose is to
serve him. You must aspire to give the proper artistic expression to his
wishes. Isn't that all one can say on the subject?"

"Well, I could say that I must aspire to build for my client the most
comfortable, the most logical, the most beautiful house that can be
built. I could say that I must try to sell him the best I have and also
teach him to know the best. I could say it, but I won't. Because I don't
intend to build in order to serve or help anyone. I don't intend to
build in order to have clients. I intend to have clients in order to
build."

"How do you propose to force your ideas on them?"

"I don't propose to force or be forced. Those who want me will
come to me."

Then the Dean understood what had puzzled him in Roark's manner.

"You know," he said, "you would sound much more convincing if you spoke as if you cared whether I agreed with you or not."

"That's true," said Roark. "I don't care whether you agree with me or not." He said it so simply that it did not sound offensive, it sounded like the statement of a fact which he noticed, puzzled, for the first time.

"You don't care what others think—which might be understandable. But you don't care even to make them think as you do?"

"No."

"But that's . . . that's monstrous."

"Is it? Probably. I couldn't say."

"I'm glad of this interview," said the Dean, suddenly, too loudly. "It has relieved my conscience. I believe, as others stated at the meeting, that the profession of architecture is not for you. I have tried to help you. Now I agree with the Board. You are a man not to be encouraged. You are dangerous."

"To whom?" asked Roark.

But the Dean rose, indicating that the interview was over.

Roark left the room. He walked slowly through the long halls, down the stairs, out to the lawn below. He had met many men such as the Dean; he had never understood them. He knew only that there was some important difference between his actions and theirs. It had ceased to disturb him long ago. But he always looked for a central theme in buildings and he looked for a central impulse in men. He knew the source of his actions; he could not discover theirs. He did not care. He had never learned the process of thinking about other people. But he wondered, at times, what made them such as they were. He wondered again, thinking of the Dean. There was an important secret involved somewhere in that question, he thought. There was a principle which he must discover.

But he stopped. He saw the sunlight of late afternoon, held still in the moment before it was to fade, on the gray limestone of a string-course running along the brick wall of the Institute building. He forgot men, the Dean and the principle behind the Dean, which he wanted to discover. He thought only of how lovely the stone looked in the fragile light and of what he could have done with that stone.

He thought of a broad sheet of paper, and he saw, rising on the paper, bare walls of gray limestone with long bands of glass, admitting the glow of the sky into the classrooms. In the corner of the sheet stood a sharp, angular signature—HOWARD ROARK.

*　　*　　*

". . . ARCHITECTURE, my friends, is a great Art based on two cosmic principles: Beauty and Utility. In a broader sense, these are but part of the three eternal entities: Truth, Love and Beauty. Truth—to the traditions of our Art, Love—for our fellow men whom we are to serve, Beauty—ah, Beauty is a compelling goddess to all artists, be it in the shape of a lovely woman or a building. . . . Hm. . . . Yes. . . . In conclusion, I should like to say to you, who are about to embark upon your careers in architecture, that you are now the custodians of a sacred heritage. . . . Hm. . . . Yes. . . . So, go forth into the world, armed with the three eternal entities—armed with courage and vision, loyal to the standards this great school has represented for many years. May you all serve faithfully, neither as slaves to the past nor as those parvenus who preach originality for its own sake, which attitude is only ignorant vanity. May you all have many rich, active years before you and leave, as you depart from this world, your mark on the sands of time!"

Guy Francon ended with a flourish, raising his right arm in a sweeping salute; informal, but with an air, that gay, swaggering air which Guy Francon could always permit himself. The huge hall before him came to life in applause and approval.

A sea of faces, young, perspiring and eager, had been raised solemnly—for forty-five minutes—to the platform where Guy Francon had held forth as the speaker at the commencement exercises of the Stanton Institute of Technology, Guy Francon who had brought his own person from New York for the occasion; Guy Francon, of the illustrious firm of Francon & Heyer, vice-president of the Architects' Guild of America, member of the American Academy of Arts and Letters, member of the National Fine Arts Commission, Secretary of the Arts and Crafts League of New York, chairman of the Society for Architectural Enlightenment of the U.S.A.; Guy Francon, knight of the Legion of Honor of France, decorated by the governments of Great Britain, Belgium, Monaco and Siam; Guy Francon, Stanton's greatest alumnus, who had designed the famous Frink National Bank Building of New York City, on the top of which, twenty-five floors above the pavements, there burned in a miniature replica of the Hadrian Mausoleum a wind-blown torch made of glass and the best General Electric bulbs.

Guy Francon descended from the platform, fully conscious of his timing and movements. He was of medium height and not too heavy, with just an unfortunate tendency to stoutness. Nobody, he knew, would give him his real age, which was fifty-one. His face bore not a wrinkle nor a single straight line; it was an artful composition in globes, circles, arcs and ellipses, with bright little eyes twinkling wittily. His clothes displayed an artist's infinite attention to details. He wished, as he descended the steps, that this were a co-educational school.

The hall before him, he thought, was a splendid specimen of architecture, made a bit stuffy today by the crowd and by the neglected problem of ventilation. But it boasted green marble dadoes, Corinthian columns of cast iron painted gold, and garlands of gilded fruit on the walls; the pineapples particularly, thought Guy Francon, had stood the test of years very well. It is, thought Guy Francon, touching; it was I who built this annex and this very hall, twenty years ago; and here I am.

The hall was packed with bodies and faces, so tightly that one could not distinguish at a glance which faces belonged to which bodies. It was like a soft, shivering aspic made of mixed arms, shoulders, chests and stomachs. One of the heads, pale, dark haired and beautiful, belonged to Peter Keating.

He sat, well in front, trying to keep his eyes on the platform, because he knew that many people were looking at him and would look at him later. He did not glance back, but the consciousness of those centered glances never left him. His eyes were dark, alert, intelligent. His mouth, a small upturned crescent faultlessly traced, was gentle and generous, and warm with the faint promise of a smile. His head had a certain classical perfection in the shape of the skull, in the natural wave of black ringlets about finely hollowed temples. He held his head in the manner of one who takes his beauty for granted, but knows that others do not. He was Peter Keating, star student of Stanton, president of the student body, captain of the track team, member of the most important fraternity, voted the most popular man on the campus.

The crowd was there, thought Peter Keating, to see him graduate, and he tried to estimate the capacity of the hall. They knew of his scholastic record and no one would beat his record today. Oh, well, there was Shlinker. Shlinker had given him stiff competition, but he had beaten Shlinker this last year. He had worked like a dog, because he had wanted to beat Shlinker. He had no rivals today. . . . Then he felt suddenly as if something had fallen down, inside his throat, to his stomach, something cold and empty, a blank hole rolling down and leaving that feeling on its way: not a thought, just the hint of a question asking him whether he was really as great as this day would proclaim him to be. He looked for Shlinker in the crowd; he saw his yellow face and gold-rimmed glasses. He stared at Shlinker warmly, in relief, in reassurance, in gratitude. It was obvious that Shlinker could never hope to equal his own appearance or ability; he had nothing to doubt; he would always beat Shlinker and all the Shlinkers of the world; he would let no one achieve what he could not achieve. Let them all watch him. He would give them good reason to stare. He felt the hot breaths about him and the expectation, like a tonic. It was wonderful, thought Peter Keating, to be alive.

His head was beginning to reel a little. It was a pleasant feeling. The feeling carried him, unresisting and unremembering, to the platform in front of all those faces. He stood—slender, trim, athletic— and let the deluge break upon his head. He gathered from its roar that he had graduated with honors, that the Architects' Guild of America had presented him with a gold medal and that he had been awarded the Prix de Paris by the Society for Architectural Enlightenment of the U.S.A.—a four-year scholarship at the Ecole des Beaux Arts in Paris.

Then he was shaking hands, scratching the perspiration off his face with the end of a rolled parchment, nodding, smiling, suffocating in his black gown and hoping that people would not notice his mother sobbing with her arms about him. The President of the Institute shook his hand, booming: "Stanton will be proud of you, my boy." The Dean shook his hand, repeating: ". . . a glorious future . . . a glorious future . . . a glorious future . . ." Professor Peterkin shook his hand, and patted his shoulder, saying: ". . . and you'll find it absolutely essential; for example, I had the experience when I built the Peabody Post Office . . ." Keating did not listen to the rest, because he had heard the story of the Peabody Post Office many times. It was the only structure anyone had ever known Professor Peterkin to have erected, before he sacrificed his practice to the responsibilities of teaching. A great deal was said about Keating's final project—a Palace of Fine Arts. For the life of him, Keating could not remember at the moment what that project was.

Through all this, his eyes held the vision of Guy Francon shaking his hand, and his ears held the sounds of Francon's mellow voice: ". . . as I have told you, it is still open, my boy. Of course, now that you have this scholarship . . . you will have to decide . . . a Beaux-Arts diploma is very important to a young man . . . but I should be delighted to have you in our office. . . ."

The banquet of the Class of '22 was long and solemn. Keating listened to the speeches with interest; when he heard the endless sentences about "young men as the hope of American Architecture" and "the future opening its golden gates," he knew that he was the hope and his was the future, and it was pleasant to hear this confirmation from so many eminent lips. He looked at the gray-haired orators and thought of how much younger he would be when he reached their positions, theirs and beyond them.

Then he thought suddenly of Howard Roark. He was surprised to find that the flash of that name in his memory gave him a sharp little twinge of pleasure, before he could know why. Then he remembered: Howard Roark had been expelled this morning. He reproached himself silently; he made a determined effort to feel sorry. But the secret glow came back, whenever he thought of that expulsion. The event proved conclusively that he had been a fool to imagine Roark a dangerous rival; at one time, he had worried about Roark more than about Shlinker, even though Roark was two years younger and one class below him. If he had ever entertained any doubts on their respective gifts, hadn't this day settled it all? And, he remembered, Roark had been very nice to him, helping him whenever he was stuck on a problem . . . not stuck, really, just did not have the time to think it out, a plan or something. Christ! how Roark could untangle a plan, like pulling a string and it was open . . . well, what if he could? What did it get him? He was done for now. And knowing this, Peter Keating experienced, at last a satisfying pang of sympathy for Howard Roark.

When Keating was called upon to speak, he rose confidently. He could not show that he was terrified. He had nothing to say about architecture. But he spoke, his head high, as an equal among equals, just subtly diffident, so that no great name present could take offense. He remembered saying: "Architecture is a great art . . . with our eyes to the future and the reverence of the past in our hearts . . . of all the crafts, the most important one sociologically . . . and, as the man who is an inspiration to us all has said today, the three eternal entities are: Truth, Love and Beauty. . . ."

Then, in the corridors outside, in the noisy confusion of leave-taking, a boy had thrown an arm about Keating's shoulders and whispered: "Run on home and get out of the soup-and-fish, Pete, and it's Boston for us tonight, just our own gang; I'll pick you up in an hour." Ted Shlinker had urged: "Of course you're coming, Pete. No fun without you. And, by the way, congratulations and all that sort of thing. No hard feelings. May the best man win." Keating had thrown his arm about Shlinker's shoulders; Keating's eyes had glowed with an insistent kind of warmth, as if Shlinker were his most precious friend; Keating's eyes glowed like that on everybody. He had said: "Thanks, Ted, old man. I really do feel awful about the A.G.A. medal—I think you were the one for it, but you never can tell what possesses those old fogies." And now Keating was on his way home through the soft darkness, wondering how to get away from his mother for the night.

His mother, he thought, had done a great deal for him. As she pointed out frequently, she was a lady and had graduated from high school; yet she had worked hard, had taken boarders into their home, a concession unprecedented in her family.

His father had owned a stationery store in Stanton. Changing times had ended the business and a hernia had ended Peter Keating, Sr., twelve years ago. Louisa Keating had been left with the home that stood at the end of a respectable street, an annuity from an insurance kept up accurately—she had seen to that—and her son. The annuity was a modest one, but with the help of the boarders and of a tenacious purpose Mrs. Keating had managed. In the summers her son helped, clerking in hotels or posing for hat advertisements. Her son, Mrs. Keating had decided, would assume his rightful place in the world, and she had clung to this as softly, as inexorably as a leech. . . . It's funny, Keating remembered, at one time he had wanted to be an artist. It was his mother who had chosen a better field in which to exercise his talent for drawing. "Architecture," she had said, "is such a respectable profession. Besides, you meet the best people in it." She had pushed him into his career, he had never known when or how. It's funny, thought Keating, he had not remembered that youthful ambition of his for years. It's funny that it should hurt him now—to remember. Well, this was the night to remember it—and to forget it forever.

Architects, he thought, always made brilliant careers. And once on top, did they ever fail? Suddenly, he recalled Henry Cameron; builder of skyscrapers twenty years ago; old drunkard with offices on some waterfront today. Keating shuddered and walked faster.

He wondered, as he walked, whether people were looking at him. He watched the rectangles of lighted windows; when a curtain fluttered and a head leaned out, he tried to guess whether it had leaned to watch his passing; if it hadn't, some day it would; some day, they all would.

Howard Roark was sitting on the porch steps when Keating approached the house. He was leaning back against the steps, propped up on his elbows, his long legs stretched out. A morning-glory climbed over the porch pillars, as a curtain between the house and the light of a lamppost on the corner.

It was strange to see an electric globe in the air of a spring night. It made the street darker and softer; it hung alone, like a gap, and left nothing to be seen but a few branches heavy with leaves, standing still at the gap's edges. The small hint became immense, as if the darkness held nothing but a flood of leaves. The mechanical ball of glass made the leaves seem more living; it took away their color and gave the promise that in daylight they would be a brighter green than had ever existed; it took away one's sight and left a new sense instead, neither smell nor touch, yet both, a sense of spring and space.

Keating stopped when he recognized the preposterous orange hair in the darkness of the porch. It was the one person whom he had wanted to see tonight. He was glad to find Roark alone, and a little afraid of it.

"Congratulations, Peter," said Roark.

"Oh . . . Oh, thanks. . . ." Keating was surprised to find that he felt more pleasure than from any other compliment he had received today. He was timidly glad that Roark approved, and he called himself inwardly a fool for it. ". . . I mean . . . do you know or . . ." He added sharply: "Has Mother been telling you?"

"She has."

"She shouldn't have!"

"Why not?"

"Look, Howard, you know that I'm terribly sorry about your being . . ."

Roark threw his head back and looked up at him.

"Forget it," said Roark.

"I . . . there's something I want to speak to you about, Howard, to ask your advice. Mind if I sit down?"

"What is it?"

Keating sat down on the steps beside him. There was no part that he could ever play in Roark's presence. Besides, he did not feel like playing a part now. He heard a leaf rustling in its fall to the earth; it was a thin, glassy, spring sound.

He knew, for the moment, that he felt affection for Roark; an affection that held pain, astonishment and helplessness.

"You won't think," said Keating gently, in complete sincerity, "that it's awful of me to be asking about my business, when you've just been . . . ?"

"I said forget about that. What is it?"

"You know," said Keating honestly and unexpectedly even to himself, "I've often thought that you're crazy. But I know that you know many things about it—architecture, I mean—which those fools never knew. And I know that you love it as they never will."

"Well?"

"Well, I don't know why I should come to you, but—Howard, I've never said it before, but you see, I'd rather have your opinion on things than the Dean's—I'd probably follow the Dean's, but it's just that yours means more to me myself, I don't know why. I don't know why I'm saying this, either."

Roark turned over on his side, looked at him, and laughed. It was a young, kind, friendly laughter, a thing so rare to hear from Roark that Keating felt as if someone had taken his hand in reassurance; and he forgot that he had a party in Boston waiting for him.

"Come on," said Roark, "you're not being afraid of me, are you? What do you want to ask about?"

"It's about my scholarship. The Paris prize I got."

"Yes?"

"It's for four years. But, on the other hand, Guy Francon offered me a job with him some time ago. Today he said it's still open. And I don't know which to take."

Roark looked at him; Roark's fingers moved in slow rotation, beating against the steps.

"If you want my advice, Peter," he said at last, "you've made a mistake already. By asking me. By asking anyone. Never ask people. Not about your work. Don't you know what you want? How can you stand it, not to know?"

"You see, that's what I admire about you, Howard. You always know."

"Drop the compliments."

"But I mean it. How do you always manage to decide?"

"How can you let others decide for you?"

"But you see, I'm not sure, Howard. I'm never sure of myself. I don't know whether I'm as good as they all tell me I am. I wouldn't admit that to anyone but you. I think it's because you're always so sure that I . . ."

"Petey!" Mrs. Keating's voice exploded behind them. "Petey, sweetheart! What *are* you doing there?"

She stood in the doorway, in her best dress of burgundy taffeta, happy and angry.

"And here I've been sitting all alone, waiting for you! What on earth are you doing on those filthy steps in your dress suit? Get up this minute! Come on in the house, boys. I've got hot chocolate and cookies ready for you."

"But, Mother. I wanted to speak to Howard about something important," said Keating. But he rose to his feet.

She seemed not to have heard. She walked into the house. Keating followed.

Roark looked after them, shrugged, rose and went in also.

Mrs. Keating settled down in an armchair, her stiff skirt crackling. "Well?" she asked. "What were you two discussing out there?"

Keating fingered an ash tray, picked up a matchbox and dropped it, then, ignoring her, turned to Roark.

"Look, Howard, drop the pose," he said, his voice high. "Shall I junk the scholarship and go to work, or let Francon wait and grab the Beaux-Arts to impress the yokels? What do you think?"

Something was gone. The one moment was lost.

"Now, Petey, let me get this straight . . ." began Mrs. Keating.

"Oh, wait a minute, Mother! . . . Howard, I've got to weigh it carefully. It isn't everyone who can get a scholarship like that. You're pretty good when you rate that. A course at the Beaux-Arts—you know how important that is."

"I don't," said Roark.

"Oh, hell, I know your crazy ideas, but I'm speaking practically, for a man in *my* position. Ideals aside for a moment, it certainly is . . ."

"You don't want my advice," said Roark.

"Of course I do! I'm asking you!"

But Keating could never be the same when he had an audience, any audience. Something was gone. He did not know it, but he felt that Roark knew; Roark's eyes made him uncomfortable and that made him angry.

"I want to *practice* architecture," snapped Keating, "not talk about it! Gives you a great prestige—the old Ecole. Puts you above the rank and file of the ex-plumbers who think they can build. On the other hand, an opening with Francon—Guy Francon himself offering it!"

Roark turned away.

"How many boys will match that?" Keating went on blindly. "A year from now they'll be boasting they're working for Smith or Jones if they find work at all. While I'll be with *Francon & Heyer!*"

"You're quite right, Peter," said Mrs. Keating, rising. "On a question like that you don't want to consult your mother. It's too important. I'll leave you to settle it with Mr. Roark."

He looked at his mother. He did not want to hear what she thought of this; he knew that his only chance to decide was to make the decision before he heard her; she had stopped, looking at him, ready to turn and leave the room; he knew it was not a pose—she would leave if he wished it; he wanted her to go; he wanted it desperately. He said:

"Why, Mother, how can you say that? Of course I want your opinion. What . . . what do you think?"

She ignored the raw irritation in his voice. She smiled.

"Petey, I never think anything. It's up to you. It's always been up to you."

"Well . . ." he began hesitantly, watching her, "if I go to the Beaux-Arts . . ."

"Fine," said Mrs. Keating, "go to the Beaux-Arts. It's a grand place. A whole ocean away from your home. Of course, if you go, Mr. Francon will take somebody else. People will talk about that. Everybody knows that Mr. Francon picks out the best boy from Stanton every year for his office. I wonder how it'll look if some other boy gets the job? But I guess that doesn't matter."

"What . . . what will people say?"

"Nothing much, I guess. Only that the other boy was the best man of his class. I guess he'll take Shlinker."

"No!" he gulped furiously. "Not Shlinker!"

"Yes," she said sweetly. "Shlinker."

"But . . ."

"But why should you care what people will say? All you have to do is please yourself."

"And you think that Francon . . ."

"Why should I think of Mr. Francon? It's nothing to me."

"Mother, you want me to take the job with Francon?"

"I don't want anything, Petey. You're the boss."

He wondered whether he really liked his mother. But she was his mother and this fact was recognized by everybody as meaning automatically that he loved her, and so he took for granted that whatever he felt for her was love. He did not know whether there was any reason why he should respect her judgment. She was his mother; this was supposed to take the place of reasons.

"Yes, of course, Mother. . . . But . . . Yes, I know, but . . . Howard?"

It was a plea for help. Roark was there, on a davenport in the corner, half lying, sprawled limply like a kitten. It had often astonished Keating; he had seen Roark moving with the soundless tension, the control, the precision of a cat; he had seen him relaxed, like a cat, in shapeless ease, as if his body held no single solid bone. Roark glanced up at him. He said:

"Peter, you know how I feel about either one of your opportunities. Take your choice of the lesser evil. What will you learn at the Beaux-Arts? Only more Renaissance palaces and operetta settings. They'll kill everything you might have in you. You do good work, once in a while, when somebody lets you. If you really want to learn, go to work. Francon is a bastard and a fool, but you will be building. It will prepare you for going on your own that much sooner."

"Even Mr. Roark can talk sense sometimes," said Mrs. Keating, "even if he does talk like a truck driver."

"Do you really think that I do good work?" Keating looked at him, as if his eyes still held the reflection of that one sentence—and nothing else mattered.

"Occasionally," said Roark. "Not often."

"Now that it's all settled . . ." began Mrs. Keating.

"I . . . I'll have to think it over, Mother."

"Now that it's all settled, how about the hot chocolate? I'll have it out to you in a jiffy!"

She smiled at her son, an innocent smile that declared her obedience and gratitude, and she rustled out of the room.

Keating paced nervously, stopped, lighted a cigarette, stood spitting the smoke out in short jerks, then looked at Roark.

"What are you going to do now, Howard?"

"I?"

"Very thoughtless of me, I know, going on like that about myself. Mother means well, but she drives me crazy. . . . Well, to hell with that. What are you going to do?"

"I'm going to New York."

"Oh, swell. To get a job?"

"To get a job."

"In . . . in architecture?"

"In architecture, Peter."

"That's grand. I'm glad. Got any definite prospects?"

"I'm going to work for Henry Cameron."

"Oh, no, Howard!"

Roark smiled slowly, the corners of his mouth sharp, and said nothing.

"Oh, no, Howard!"

"Yes."

"But he's nothing, nobody any more! Oh, I know he has a name, but he's done for! He never gets any important buildings, hasn't had any for years! They say he's got a dump for an office. What kind of future will you get out of him? What will you learn?"

"Not much. Only how to build."

"For God's sake, you can't go on like that, deliberately ruining yourself! I thought . . . well, yes, I thought you'd learned something today!"

"I have."

"Look, Howard, if it's because you think that no one else will have you now, no one better, why, I'll help you. I'll work old Francon and I'll get connections and . . ."

"Thank you, Peter. But it won't be necessary. It's settled."

"What did he say?"

"Who?"

"Cameron."

"I've never met him."

Then a horn screamed outside. Keating remembered, started off to change his clothes, collided with his mother at the door and knocked a cup off her loaded tray.

"Petey!"

"Never mind, Mother!" He seized her elbows. "I'm in a hurry, sweetheart. A little party with the boys—now, now, don't say anything—I won't be late and—look! We'll celebrate my going with Francon & Heyer!"

He kissed her impulsively, with the gay exuberance that made him irresistible at times, and flew out of the room, up the stairs. Mrs. Keating shook her head, flustered, reproving and happy.

In his room, while flinging his clothes in all directions, Keating thought suddenly of a wire he would send to New York. That particular subject had not been in his mind all day, but it came to him with a sense of desperate urgency; he wanted to send that wire now, at once. He scribbled it down on a piece of paper:

"Katie dearest coming New York job Francon love ever
                                        "Peter"

That night Keating raced toward Boston, wedged in between two boys, the wind and the road whistling past him. And he thought that the world was opening to him now, like the darkness fleeing before the bobbing headlights. He was free. He was ready. In a few years—so very soon, for time did not exist in the speed of that car—his name would ring like a horn, ripping people out of sleep. He was ready to do great things, magnificent things, things unsurpassed in . . . in . . . oh, hell . . . in architecture.

*   *   *

PETER KEATING looked at the streets of New York. The people, he observed, were extremely well dressed.

He had stopped for a moment before the building on Fifth Avenue, where the office of Francon & Heyer and his first day of work awaited him. He looked at the men who hurried past. Smart, he thought, smart as hell. He glanced regretfully at his own clothes. He had a great deal to learn in New York.

When he could delay it no longer, he turned to the door. It was a miniature Doric portico, every inch of it scaled down to the exact proportions decreed by the artists who had worn flowing Grecian tunics; between the marble perfection of the columns a revolving door sparkled with nickel-plate, reflecting the streaks of automobiles flying past. Keating walked through the revolving door, through the lustrous marble lobby, to an elevator of gilt and red lacquer that brought him, thirty floors later, to a mahogany door. He saw a slender brass plate with delicate letters:

FRANCON & HEYER, ARCHITECTS.

The reception room of the office of Francon & Heyer, Architects, looked like a cool, intimate ballroom in a Colonial mansion. The silver white walls were paneled with flat pilasters; the pilasters were fluted and curved into Ionic snails; they supported little pediments broken in the middle to make room for half a Grecian urn plastered against the wall. Etchings of Greek temples adorned the panels, too small to be distinguished, but presenting the unmistakable columns, pediments and crumbling stone.

Quite incongruously, Keating felt as if a conveyor belt was under his feet, from the moment he crossed the threshold. It carried him to the reception clerk who sat at a telephone switchboard behind the white balustrade of a Florentine balcony. It transferred him to the threshold of a huge drafting room. He saw long, flat tables, a forest of twisted rods descending from the ceiling to end in green-shaded lamps, enormous blueprint files, towers of yellow drawers, papers, tin boxes, sample bricks, pots of glue and calendars from construction companies, most of them bearing pictures of naked women. The chief draftsman snapped at Keating, without quite seeing him. He was bored and crackling with purpose simultaneously. He jerked his thumb in the direction of a locker room, thrust his chin out toward the door of a locker, and stood, rocking from heels to toes, while Keating pulled a pearl-gray smock over his stiff, uncertain body. Francon had insisted on that smock. The conveyor belt stopped at a table in a corner of the drafting room, where Keating found himself with a set of plans to expand, the scraggy back of the chief draftsman retreating from him in the unmistakable manner of having forgotten his existence.

Keating bent over his task at once, his eyes fixed, his throat rigid. He saw nothing but the pearly shimmer of the paper before him. The steady lines he drew surprised him, for he felt certain that his hand was jerking an inch back and forth across the sheet. He followed the lines, not knowing where they led or why. He knew only that the plan was someone's tremendous achievement which he could neither question nor equal. He wondered why he had ever thought of himself as a potential architect.

Much later, he noticed the wrinkles of a gray smock sticking to a pair of shoulder blades over the next table. He glanced about him, cautiously at first, then with curiosity, then with pleasure, then with contempt. When he reached this last, Peter Keating became himself again and felt love for mankind. He noticed sallow cheeks, a funny nose, a wart on a receding chin, a stomach squashed against the edge of a table. He loved these sights. What these could do, he could do better. He smiled. Peter Keating needed his fellow men.

When he glanced at his plans again, he noticed the flaws glaring at him from the masterpiece. It was the floor of a private residence, and he noted the twisted hallways that sliced great hunks of space for no apparent reason, the long, rectangular sausages of rooms doomed to darkness. Jesus, he thought, they'd have flunked me for this in the first term. After which, he proceeded with his work swiftly, easily, expertly—and happily.

Before lunchtime. Keating had made friends in the room, not any definite friends, but a vague soil spread and ready from which friendship would spring. He had smiled at his neighbors and winked in understanding over nothing at all. He had used each trip to the water cooler to caress those he passed with the soft, cheering glow of his eyes, the brilliant eyes that seemed to pick each man in turn out of the room, out of the universe, as the most important specimen of humanity and as Keating's dearest friend. There goes—there seemed to be left in his wake—a smart boy and a hell of a good fellow.

Keating noticed that a tall blond youth at the next table was doing the elevation of an office building. Keating leaned with chummy respect against the boy's shoulder and looked at the laurel garlands entwined about fluted columns three floors high.

"Pretty good for the old man," said Keating with admiration.

"Who?" asked the boy.

"Why, Francon," said Keating.

"Francon hell," said the boy placidly. "He hasn't designed a doghouse in eight years." He jerked his thumb over his shoulder, at a glass door behind them. "Him."

"What?" asked Keating, turning.

"Him," said the boy. "Stengel. He does all these things."

Behind the glass door Keating saw a pair of bony shoulders above the edge of a desk, a small, triangular head bent intently, and two blank pools of light in the round frames of glasses.

It was late in the afternoon when a presence seemed to have passed beyond the closed door, and Keating learned from the rustle of whispers around him that Guy Francon had arrived and had risen to his office on the floor above. Half an hour later the glass door opened and Stengel came out, a huge piece of cardboard dangling between his fingers.

"Hey, you," he said, his glasses stopping on Keating's face. "You doing the plans for this?" He swung the cardboard forward. "Take this up to the boss for the okay. Try to listen to what he'll say and try to look intelligent. Neither of which matters anyway."

He was short and his arms seemed to hang down to his ankles; arms swinging like ropes in the long sleeves, with big, efficient hands. Keating's eyes froze, darkening, for one-tenth of a second, gathered in a tight stare at the blank lenses. Then Keating smiled and said pleasantly:

"Yes, sir."

He carried the cardboard on the tips of his ten fingers, up the crimson-plushed stairway to Guy Francon's office. The cardboard displayed a water-color perspective of a gray granite mansion with three tiers of dormers, five balconies, four bays, twelve columns, one flagpole and two lions at the entrance. In the corner, neatly printed by hand, stood: "Residence of Mr. and Mrs. James S. Whattles. Francon & Heyer, Architects." Keating whistled softly: James S. Whattles was the multimillionaire manufacturer of shaving lotions.

Guy Francon's office was polished. No, thought Keating, not polished, but shellacked; no, not shellacked, but liquid with mirrors melted and poured over every object. He saw splinters of his own reflection let loose like a swarm of butterflies, following him across the room, on the Chippendale cabinets, on the Jacobean chairs, on the Louis XV mantelpiece. He had time to note a genuine Roman statue in a corner, sepia photographs of the Parthenon, of Rheims Cathedral, of Versailles and of the Frink National Bank Building with the eternal torch.

He saw his own legs approaching him in the side of the massive mahogany desk. Guy Francon sat behind the desk. Guy Francon's face was yellow and his cheeks sagged. He looked at Keating for an instant as if he had never seen him before, then remembered and smiled expansively.

"Well, well, well, Kittredge, my boy, here we are, all set and at home! So glad to see you. Sit down, boy, sit down, what have you got there? Well, there's no hurry, no hurry at all. Sit down. How do you like it here?"

"I'm afraid, sir, that I'm a little too happy," said Keating, with an expression of frank, boyish helplessness. "I thought I could be businesslike on my first job, but starting in a place like this . . . I guess it knocked me out a little. . . . I'll get over it, sir," he promised.

"Of course," said Guy Francon. "It might be a bit overwhelming for a boy, just a bit. But don't you worry. I'm sure you'll make good."

"I'll do my best, sir."

"Of course you will. What's this they sent me?" Francon extended his hand to the drawing, but his fingers came to rest limply on his forehead instead. "It's so annoying, this headache. . . . No, no, nothing serious—" he smiled at Keating's prompt concern— "just a little *mal de tête*. One works so hard."

"Is there anything I can get for you, sir?"

"No, no, thank you. It's not anything you can get for me, it's if only you could take something away from me." He winked. "The champagne. *Entre nous*, that champagne of theirs wasn't worth a damn last night. I've never cared for champagne anyway. Let me tell you, Kittredge, it's very important to know about wines, for instance when you'll take a client out to dinner and will want to be sure of the proper thing to order. Now I'll tell you a professional secret. Take quail, for instance. Now most people would order Burgundy with it. What do you do? You call for Clos Vougeot 1904. See? Adds that certain touch. Correct, but original. One must always be original. . . . Who sent you up, by the way?"

"Mr. Stengel, sir."

"Oh, Stengel." The tone in which he pronounced the name clicked like a shutter in Keating's mind: it was a permission to be stored away for future use. "Too grand to bring his own stuff up, eh? Mind you, he's a great designer, the best designer in New York City, but he's just getting to be a bit too grand lately. He thinks he's the only one doing any work around here, just because he smudges at a board all day long. You'll learn, my boy, when you've been in the business longer, that the real work of an office is done beyond its walls. Take last night, for instance. Banquet of the Clarion Real Estate Association. Two hundred guests—dinner and champagne—oh, yes, champagne!" He wrinkled his nose fastidiously, in self-mockery. "A few words to say informally in a little after-dinner speech—you know, nothing blatant, no vulgar sales talk—only a few well-chosen thoughts on the responsibility of realtors to society, on the importance of selecting architects who are competent, respected and well established. You know, a few bright little slogans that will stick in the mind."

"Yes, sir, like 'Choose the builder of your home as carefully as you choose the bride to inhabit it.' "

"Not bad. Not bad at all, Kittredge. Mind if I jot it down?"

"My name is Keating, sir," said Keating firmly. "You are very welcome to the idea. I'm happy if it appeals to you."

"Keating, of course! Why, of course, Keating," said Francon with a disarming smile. "Dear me, one meets so many people. How did you say it? Choose the builder . . . it was very well put."

He made Keating repeat it and wrote it down on a pad, picking a pencil from an array before him, new, many-colored pencils, sharpened to a professional needle point, ready, unused.

Then he pushed the pad aside, sighed, patted the smooth waves of his hair and said wearily:

"Well, all right, I suppose I'll have to look at the thing."

Keating extended the drawing respectfully. Francon leaned back, held the cardboard out at arm's length and looked at it. He closed his left eye, then his right eye, then moved the cardboard an inch farther. Keating expected wildly to see him turn the drawing upside down. But Francon just held it and Keating knew suddenly that he had long since stopped seeing it. Francon was studying it for his, Keating's, benefit; and then Keating felt light, light as air, and he saw the road to his future, clear and open.

"Hm . . . yes," Francon was saying, rubbing his chin with the tips of two soft fingers. "Hm . . . yes . . ."

He turned to Keating.

"Not bad," said Francon. "Not bad at all. . . . Well . . . perhaps . . . it would have been more distinguished, you know, but . . . well, the drawing is done so neatly. . . . What do you think, Keating?"

Keating thought that four of the windows faced four mammoth granite columns. But he looked at Francon's fingers playing with a petunia-mauve necktie, and decided not to mention it. He said instead:

"If I may make a suggestion, sir, it seems to me that the cartouches between the fourth and fifth floors are somewhat too modest for so imposing a building. It would appear that an ornamented stringcourse would be so much more appropriate."

"That's it. I was just going to say it. An ornamented stringcourse. . . . But . . . but look, it would mean diminishing the fenestration, wouldn't it?"

"Yes," said Keating, a faint coating of diffidence over the tone he had used in discussions with his classmates, "but windows are less important than the dignity of a building's façade."

"That's right. Dignity. We must give our clients dignity above all. Yes, definitely, an ornamented stringcourse. . . . Only . . . look, I've approved the preliminary drawings, and Stengel has had this done up so neatly."

"Mr. Stengel will be delighted to change it if you advise him to."

Francon's eyes held Keating's for a moment. Then Francon's lashes dropped and he picked a piece of lint off his sleeve.

"Of course, of course . . ." he said vaguely. "But . . . do you think the stringcourse is really important?"

"I think," said Keating slowly, "it is more important to make changes you find necessary than to okay every drawing just as Mr. Stengel designed it."

Because Francon said nothing, but only looked straight at him, because Francon's eyes were focused and his hands limp, Keating knew that he had taken a terrible chance and won; he became frightened by the chance after he knew he had won.

They looked silently across the desk, and both saw that they were two men who could understand each other.

"We'll have an ornamented stringcourse," said Francon with calm, genuine authority. "Leave this here. Tell Stengel that I want to see him."

He had turned to go. Francon stopped him. Francon's voice was gay and warm:

"Oh, Keating, by the way, may I make a suggestion? Just between us, no offense intended, but a burgundy necktie would be so much better than blue with your gray smock, don't you think so?"

"Yes, sir," said Keating easily. "Thank you. You'll see it tomorrow."

He walked out and closed the door softly.

On his way back through the reception room, Keating saw a distinguished, gray-haired gentleman escorting a lady to the door. The gentleman wore no hat and obviously belonged to the office; the lady wore a mink cape, and was obviously a client.

The gentleman was not bowing to the ground, he was not unrolling a carpet, he was not waving a fan over her head; he was only holding the door for her. It merely seemed to Keating that the gentleman was doing all of that.

The Frink National Bank Building rose over Lower Manhattan, and its long shadow moved, as the sun traveled over the sky, like a huge clock hand across grimy tenements, from the Aquarium to Manhattan Bridge. When the sun was gone, the torch of Hadrian's Mausoleum flared up in its stead, and made glowing red smears on the glass of windows for miles around, on the top stories of buildings high enough to reflect it. The Frink National Bank Building displayed the entire history of Roman art in well-chosen specimens; for a long time it had been considered the best building of the city, because no other structure could boast a single Classical item which it did not possess.

It offered so many columns, pediments, friezes, tripods, gladiators, urns and volutes that it looked as if it had not been built of white marble, but squeezed out of a pastry tube. It was, however, built of white marble. No one knew that but the owners who had paid for it. It was now of a streaked, blotched, leprous color, neither brown nor green but the worst tones of both, the color of slow rot, the color of smoke, gas fumes and acids eating into a delicate stone intended for clean air and open country. The Frink National Bank Building, however, was a great success. It had been so great a success that it was the last structure Guy Francon ever designed; its prestige spared him the bother from then on.

Three blocks east of the Frink National Bank stood the Dana Building. It was some stories lower and without any prestige whatever. Its lines were hard and simple, revealing, emphasizing the harmony of the steel skeleton within, as a body reveals the perfection of its bones. It had no other ornament to offer. It displayed nothing but the precision of its sharp angles, the modeling of its planes, the long streaks of its windows like streams of ice running down from the roof to the pavements. New Yorkers seldom looked at the Dana Building. Sometimes, a rare country visitor would come upon it unexpectedly in the moonlight and stop and wonder from what dream that vision had come. But such visitors were rare. The tenants of the Dana Building said that they would not exchange it for any structure on earth; they appreciated the light, the air, the beautiful logic of the plan in their halls and offices. But the tenants of the Dana Building were not numerous; no prominent man wished his business to be located in a building that looked "like a warehouse."

The Dana Building had been designed by Henry Cameron.

In the eighteen-eighties, the architects of New York fought one another for second place in their profession. No one aspired to the first. The first was held by Henry Cameron. Henry Cameron was hard to get in those days. He had a waiting list two years in advance; he designed personally every structure that left his office. He chose what he wished to build. When he built, a client kept his mouth shut. He demanded of all people the one thing he had never granted anybody: obedience. He went through the years of his fame like a projectile flying to a goal no one could guess. People called him crazy. But they took what he gave them, whether they understood it or not, because it was a building "by Henry Cameron."

At first, his buildings were merely a little different, not enough to frighten anyone. He made startling experiments, once in a while, but people expected it and one did not argue with Henry Cameron. Something was growing in him with each new building, struggling, taking shape, rising dangerously to an explosion. The explosion came with the birth of the skyscraper. When structures began to rise not in tier on ponderous tier of masonry, but as arrows of steel shooting upward without weight or limit, Henry Cameron was among the first to understand this new miracle and to give it form. He was among the first and the few who accepted the truth that a tall building must look tall. While architects cursed, wondering how to make a twenty-story building look like an old brick mansion, while they used every horizontal device available in order to cheat it of its height, shrink it down to tradition, hide the shame of its steel, make it small, safe and ancient—Henry Cameron designed skyscrapers in straight, vertical lines, flaunting their steel and height. While architects drew friezes and pediments, Henry Cameron decided that the skyscraper must not copy the Greeks. Henry Cameron decided that no building must copy any other.

He was thirty-nine years old then, short, stocky, unkempt; he worked like a dog, missed his sleep and meals, drank seldom but then brutally, called his clients unprintable names, laughed at hatred and fanned it deliberately, behaved like a feudal lord and a longshoreman, and lived in a passionate tension that stung men in any room he entered, a fire neither they nor he could endure much longer. It was the year 1892.

The Columbian Exposition of Chicago opened in the year 1893.

The Rome of two thousand years ago rose on the shores of Lake Michigan, a Rome improved by pieces of France, Spain, Athens and every style that followed it. It was a "Dream City" of columns, triumphal arches, blue lagoons, crystal fountains and popcorn. Its architects competed on who could steal best, from the oldest source and from the most sources at once. It spread before the eyes of a new country every structural crime ever committed in all the old ones. It was white as a plague, and it spread as such.

People came, looked, were astounded, and carried away with them, to the cities of America, the seeds of what they had seen. The seeds sprouted into weeds; into shingled post offices with Doric porticos, brick mansions with iron pediments, lofts made of twelve Parthenons piled on top of one another. The weeds grew and choked everything else.

Henry Cameron had refused to work for the Columbian Exposition, and had called it names that were unprintable, but repeatable, though not in mixed company. They were repeated. It was repeated also that he had thrown an inkstand at the face of a distinguished banker who had asked him to design a railroad station in the shape of the temple of Diana at Ephesus. The banker never came back. There were others who never came back.

Just as he reached the goal of long, struggling years, just as he gave shape to the truth he had sought—the last barrier fell closed before him. A young country had watched him on his way, had wondered, had begun to accept the new grandeur of his work. A country flung two thousand years back in an orgy of Classicism could find no place for him and no use.

It was not necessary to design buildings any longer, only to photograph them; the architect with the best library was the best architect. Imitators copied imitations. To sanction it there was Culture; there were twenty centuries unrolling in moldering ruins; there was the great Exposition; there was every European post card in every family album.

Henry Cameron had nothing to offer against this; nothing but a faith he held merely because it was his own. He had nobody to quote and nothing of importance to say. He said only that the form of a building must follow its function; that the structure of a building is the key to its beauty; that new methods of construction demand new forms; that he wished to build as he wished and for that reason only. But people could not listen to him when they were discussing Vitruvius, Michelangelo and Sir Christopher Wren.

Men hate passion, any great passion. Henry Cameron made a mistake: he loved his work. That was why he fought. That was why he lost.

People said he never knew that he had lost. If he did, he never let them see it. As his clients became rarer, his manner to them grew more overbearing. The less the prestige of his name, the more arrogant the sound of his voice pronouncing it. He had had an astute business manager, a mild, self-effacing little man of iron who, in the days of his glory, faced quietly the storms of Cameron's temper and brought him clients; Cameron insulted the clients, but the little man made them accept it and come back. The little man died.

Cameron had never known how to face people. They did not matter to him, as his own life did not matter, as nothing mattered but buildings. He had never learned to give explanations, only orders. He had never been liked. He had been feared. No one feared him any longer.

He was allowed to live. He lived to loathe the streets of the city he had dreamed of rebuilding. He lived to sit at the desk in his empty office, motionless, idle, waiting. He lived to read in a well-meaning newspaper account a reference to "the late Henry Cameron." He lived to begin drinking, quietly, steadily, terribly, for days and nights at a time; and to hear those who had driven him to it say, when his name was mentioned for a commission: "Cameron? I should say not. He drinks like a fish. That's why he never gets any work." He lived to move from the offices that occupied three floors of a famous building to one floor on a less expensive street, then to a suite farther downtown, then to three rooms facing an air shaft, near the Battery. He chose these rooms because, by pressing his face to the window of his office, he could see, over a brick wall, the top of the Dana Building.

Howard Roark looked at the Dana Building beyond the windows, stopping at each landing, as he mounted the six flights of stairs to Henry Cameron's office; the elevator was out of order. The stairs had been painted a dirty file-green a long time ago; a little of the paint remained to grate under shoe soles in crumbling patches. Roark went up swiftly, as if he had an appointment, a folder of his drawings under his arm, his eyes on the Dana Building. He collided once with a man descending the stairs; this had happened to him often in the last two days; he had walked through the streets of the city, his head thrown back, noticing nothing but the buildings of New York.

In the dark cubbyhole of Cameron's anteroom stood a desk with a telephone and a typewriter. A gray-haired skeleton of a man sat at the desk, in his shirt sleeves, with a pair of limp suspenders over his shoulders. He was typing specifications intently, with two fingers and incredible speed. The light from a feeble bulb made a pool of yellow on his back, where the damp shirt stuck to his shoulder blades.

The man raised his head slowly, when Roark entered. He looked at Roark, said nothing and waited, his old eyes weary, unquestioning, incurious.

"I should like to see Mr. Cameron," said Roark.

"Yeah?" said the man, without challenge, offense or meaning. "About what?"

"About a job."

"What job?"

"Drafting."

The man sat looking at him blankly. It was a request that had not confronted him for a long time. He rose at last, without a word, shuffled to a door behind him and went in.

He left the door half open. Roark heard him drawling:

"Mr. Cameron, there's a fellow outside says he's looking for a job here."

Then a voice answered, a strong, clear voice that held no tones of age:

"Why, the damn fool! Throw him out . . . Wait! Send him in!"

The old man returned, held the door open and jerked his head at it silently. Roark went in. The door closed behind him.

Henry Cameron sat at his desk at the end of a long, bare room. He sat bent forward, his forearms on the desk, his two hands closed before him. His hair and his beard were coal black, with coarse threads of white. The muscles of his short, thick neck bulged like ropes. He wore a white shirt with the sleeves rolled above the elbows; the bare arms were hard, heavy and brown. The flesh of his broad face was rigid, as if it had aged by compression. The eyes were dark, young, living.

Roark stood on the threshold and they looked at each other across the long room.

The light from the air shaft was gray, and the dust on the drafting table, on the few green files, looked like fuzzy crystals deposited by the light. But on the wall, between the windows, Roark saw a picture. It was the only picture in the room. It was the drawing of a skyscraper that had never been erected.

Roark's eyes moved first and they moved to the drawing. He walked across the office, stopped before it and stood looking at it. Cameron's eyes followed him, a heavy glance, like a long, thin needle held fast at one end, describing a slow circle, its point piercing Roark's body, keeping it pinned firmly. Cameron looked at the orange hair, at the hand hanging by his side, its palm to the drawing, the fingers bent slightly, forgotten not in a gesture but in the overture to a gesture of asking or seizing something.

"Well?" said Cameron at last. "Did you come to see me or did you come to look at pictures?"

Roark turned to him.

"Both," said Roark.

He walked to the desk. People had always lost their sense of existence in Roark's presence; but Cameron felt suddenly that he had never been as real as in the awareness of the eyes now looking at him.

"What do you want?" snapped Cameron.

"I should like to work for you," said Roark quietly. The voice said: "I should like to work for you." The tone of the voice said: "I'm going to work for you."

"Are you?" said Cameron, not realizing that he answered the unpronounced sentence. "What's the matter? None of the bigger and better fellows will have you?"

"I have not applied to anyone else."

"Why not? Do you think this is the easiest place to begin? Think anybody can walk in here without trouble? Do you know who I am?"

"Yes. That's why I'm here."

"Who sent you?"

"No one."

"Why the hell should you pick me?"

"I think you know that."

"What infernal impudence made you presume that I'd want you? Have you decided that I'm so hard up that I'd throw the gates open for any punk who'd do me the honor? 'Old Cameron,' you've said to yourself, 'is a has-been, a drunken . . .' come on, you've said it! . . . 'a drunken failure who can't be particular!' Is that it? . . . Come on, answer me! Answer me, damn you! What are you staring at? Is that it? Go on! Deny it!"

"It's not necessary."

"Where have you worked before?"

"I'm just beginning."

"What have you done?"

"I've had three years at Stanton."

"Oh? The gentleman was too lazy to finish?"

"I have been expelled."

"Great!" Cameron slapped the desk with his fist and laughed. "Splendid! You're not good enough for the lice nest at Stanton, but you'll work for Henry Cameron! You've decided this is the place for refuse! What did they kick you out for? Drink? Women? What?"

"These," said Roark, and extended his drawings.

Cameron looked at the first one, then at the next, then at every one of them to the bottom. Roark heard the paper rustling as Cameron slipped one sheet behind another. Then Cameron raised his head.

"Sit down."

Roark obeyed. Cameron stared at him, his thick fingers drumming against the pile of drawings.

"So you think they're good?" said Cameron. "Well, they're awful. It's unspeakable. It's a crime. Look," he shoved a drawing at Roark's face, "look at that. What in Christ's name was your idea? What possessed you to indent that plan here? Did you just want to make it pretty, because you had to patch something together? Who do you think you are? Guy Francon, God help you? . . . Look at this building, you fool! You get an idea like this and you don't know what to do with it! You stumble on a magnificent thing and you have to ruin it! Do you know how much you've got to learn?"

"Yes. That's why I'm here."

"And look at that one! I wish I'd done that at your age! But why did you have to botch it? Do you know what I'd do with that? Look, to hell with your stairways and to hell with your furnace room! When you lay the foundations . . ."

He spoke furiously for a long time. He cursed. He did not find one sketch to satisfy him. But Roark noticed that he spoke as of buildings that were in construction.

He broke off abruptly, pushed the drawings aside, and put his fist over them. He asked:

"When did you decide to become an architect?"

"When I was ten years old."

"Men don't know what they want so early in life, if ever. You're lying."

"Am I?"

"Don't stare at me like that! Can't you look at something else? Why did you decide to be an architect?"

"I didn't know it then. But it's because I've never believed in God."

"Come on, talk sense."

"Because I love this earth. That's all I love. I don't like the shape of things on this earth. I want to change them."

"For whom?"

"For myself."

"How old are you?"

"Twenty-two."

"When did you hear all that?"

"I didn't."

"Men don't talk like that at twenty-two. You're abnormal."

"Probably."

"I didn't mean it as a compliment."

"I didn't either."

"Got any family?"

"No."

"Worked through school?"

"Yes."

"At what?"

"In the building trades."

"How much money have you got left?"

"Seventeen dollars and thirty cents."

"When did you come to New York?"

"Yesterday."

Cameron looked at the white pile under his fist.

"God damn you," said Cameron softly.

"God damn you!" roared Cameron suddenly, leaning forward. "I didn't ask you to come here! I don't need any draftsmen! There's nothing here to draft! I don't have enough work to keep myself and my men out of the Bowery Mission! I don't want any fool visionaries starving around here! I don't want the responsibility. I didn't ask for it. I never thought I'd see it again. I'm through with it. I was through with that many years ago. I'm perfectly happy with the drooling dolts I've got here, who never had anything and never will have and it makes no difference what becomes of them. That's all I want. Why did you have to come here? You're setting out to ruin yourself, you know that, don't you? And I'll help you to do it. I don't want to see you. I don't like you. I don't like your face. You look like an insufferable egotist. You're impertinent. You're too sure of yourself. Twenty years ago I'd have punched your face with the greatest of pleasure. You're coming to work here tomorrow at nine o'clock sharp."

"Yes," said Roark, rising.

"Fifteen dollars a week. That's all I can pay you."

"Yes."

"You're a damn fool. You should have gone to someone else. I'll kill you if you go to anyone else. What's your name?"

"Howard Roark."

"If you're late, I'll fire you."

"Yes."

Roark extended his hand for the drawings.

"Leave these here!" bellowed Cameron. "Now get out!"

EDITOR'S NOTE: *The following excerpt (150 pages later) depicts the first meeting between Howard Roark and the lovely Dominique Francon—and its consequences. Dominique worships greatness, but believes that Roark is doomed in a world ruled by mediocrity.*

Roark, rejected by the world, has closed his practice to work in a granite quarry. The quarry happens to be owned by Dominique's father, the architect Guy Francon. Dominique is spending the summer alone in her father's mansion a few miles from the quarry.

The Quarry Sequence

BECAUSE THE sun was too hot that morning, and she knew it would be hotter at the granite quarry, because she wanted to see no one and knew she would face a gang of workers, Dominique walked to the quarry. The thought of seeing it on that blazing day was revolting; she enjoyed the prospect.

When she came out of the woods to the edge of the great stone bowl, she felt as if she were thrust into an execution chamber filled with scalding steam. The heat did not come from the sun, but from that broken cut in the earth, from the reflectors of flat ridges. Her shoulders, her head, her back, exposed to the sky, seemed cool while she felt the hot breath of the stone rising up her legs, to her chin, to her nostrils. The air shimmered below, sparks of fire shot through the granite; she thought the stone was stirring, melting, running in white trickles of lava. Drills and hammers cracked the still weight of the air. It was obscene to see men on the shelves of the furnace. They did not look like workers, they looked like a chain gang serving an unspeakable penance for some unspeakable crime. She could not turn away.

She stood, as an insult to the place below. Her dress—the color of water, a pale green-blue, too simple and expensive, its pleats exact like edges of glass—her thin heels planted wide apart on the boulders, the smooth helmet of her hair, the exaggerated fragility of her body against the sky—flaunted the fastidious coolness of the gardens and drawing rooms from which she came.

She looked down. Her eyes stopped on the orange hair of a man who raised his head and looked at her.

She stood very still, because her first perception was not of sight, but of touch: the consciousness, not of a visual presence, but of a slap in the face. She held one hand awkwardly away from her body, the fingers spread wide on the air, as against a wall. She knew that she could not move until he permitted her to.

She saw his mouth and the silent contempt in the shape of his mouth; the planes of his gaunt, hollow cheeks; the cold, pure brilliance of the eyes that had no trace of pity. She knew it was the most beautiful face she would ever see, because it was the abstraction of strength made visible. She felt a convulsion of anger, of protest, of resistance—and of pleasure. He stood looking up at her; it was not a glance, but an act of ownership. She thought she must let her face give him the answer he deserved. But she was looking, instead, at the stone dust on his burned arms, the wet shirt clinging to his ribs, the lines of his long legs. She was thinking of those statues of men she had always sought; she was wondering what he would look like naked. She saw him looking at her as if he knew that. She thought she had found an aim in life—a sudden, sweeping hatred for that man.

She was first to move. She turned and walked away from him. She saw the superintendent of the quarry on the path ahead, and she waved. The superintendent rushed forward to meet her. "Why, Miss Francon!" he cried. "Why, how do you do, Miss Francon!"

She hoped the words were heard by the man below. For the first time in her life, she was glad of being Miss Francon, glad of her father's position and possessions, which she had always despised. She thought suddenly that the man below was only a common worker, owned by the owner of this place, and she was almost the owner of this place.

The superintendent stood before her respectfully. She smiled and said:

"I suppose I'll inherit the quarry some day, so I thought I should show some interest in it once in a while."

The superintendent preceded her down the path, displayed his domain to her, explained the work. She followed him far to the other side of the quarry; she descended to the dusty green dell of the work sheds; she inspected the bewildering machinery. She allowed a convincingly sufficient time to elapse. Then she walked back, alone, down the edge of the granite bowl.

She saw him from a distance as she approached. He was working.

She saw one strand of red hair that fell over his face and swayed with the trembling of the drill. She thought—hopefully—that the vibrations of the drill hurt him, hurt his body, everything inside his body.

When she was on the rocks above him, he raised his head and looked at her; she had not caught him noticing her approach; he looked up as if he expected her to be there, as if he knew she would be back. She saw the hint of a smile, more insulting than words. He sustained the insolence of looking straight at her, he would not move, he would not grant the concession of turning away—of acknowledging that he had no right to look at her in such manner. He had not merely taken that right, he was saying silently that she had given it to him.

She turned sharply and walked on, down the rocky slope, away from the quarry.

It was not his eyes, not his mouth that she remembered, but his hands. The meaning of that day seemed held in a single picture she had noted: the simple instant of his one hand resting against granite. She saw it again: his fingertips pressed to the stone, his long fingers continuing the straight lines of the tendons that spread in a fan from his wrist to his knuckles. She thought of him, but the vision present through all her thoughts was the picture of that hand on the granite. It frightened her; she could not understand it.

He's only a common worker, she thought, a hired man doing a convict's labor. She thought of that, sitting before the glass shelf of her dressing table. She looked at the crystal objects spread before her; they were like sculptures in ice—they proclaimed her own cold, luxurious fragility; and she thought of his strained body, of his clothes drenched in dust and sweat, of his hands. She stressed the contrast, because it degraded her. She leaned back, closing her eyes. She thought of the many distinguished men whom she had refused. She thought of the quarry worker. She thought of being broken—not by a man she admired, but by a man she loathed. She let her head fall down on her arm; the thought left her weak with pleasure.

For two days she made herself believe that she would escape from this place; she found old travel folders in her trunk, studied them, chose the resort, the hotel and the particular room in that hotel, selected the train she would take, the boat and the number of the stateroom. She found a vicious amusement in doing that, because she knew she would not take this trip she wanted; she would go back to the quarry.

She went back to the quarry three days later. She stopped over the ledge where he worked and she stood watching him openly. When he raised his head, she did not turn away. Her glance told him she knew the meaning of her action, but did not respect him enough to conceal it. His glance told her only that he had expected her to come. He bent over his drill and went on with his work. She waited. She wanted him to look up. She knew that he knew it. He would not look again.

She stood, watching his hands, waiting for the moments when he touched stone. She forgot the drill and the dynamite. She liked to think of the granite being broken by his hands.

She heard the superintendent calling her name, hurrying to her up the path. She turned to him when he approached.

"I like to watch the men working," she explained.

"Yes, quite a picture, isn't it?" the superintendent agreed. "There's the train starting over there with another load."

She was not watching the train. She saw the man below looking at her, she saw the insolent hint of amusement tell her that he knew she did not want him to look at her now. She turned her head away. The superintendent's eyes traveled over the pit and stopped on the man below them.

"Hey, you down there!" he shouted. "Are you paid to work or to gape?"

The man bent silently over his drill. Dominique laughed aloud.

The superintendent said: "It's a tough crew we got down here, Miss Francon . . . Some of 'em even with jail records."

"Has that man a jail record?" she asked, pointing down.

"Well, I couldn't say. Wouldn't know them all by sight."

She hoped he had. She wondered whether they whipped convicts nowadays. She hoped they did. At the thought of it, she felt a sinking gasp such as she had felt in childhood, in dreams of falling down a long stairway; but she felt the sinking in her stomach.

She turned brusquely and left the quarry.

She came back many days later. She saw him, unexpectedly, on a flat stretch of stone before her, by the side of the path. She stopped short. She did not want to come too close. It was strange to see him before her, without the defense and excuse of distance.

He stood looking straight at her. Their understanding was too offensively intimate, because they had never said a word to each other. She destroyed it by speaking to him.

"Why do you always stare at me?" she asked sharply.

She thought with relief that words were the best means of estrangement. She had denied everything they both knew by naming it. For a moment, he stood silently, looking at her. She felt terror at the thought that he would not answer, that he would let his silence tell her too clearly why no answer was necessary. But he answered. He said:

"For the same reason you've been staring at me."

"I don't know what you're talking about."

"If you didn't, you'd be much more astonished and much less angry, Miss Francon."

"So you know my name?"

"You've been advertising it loudly enough."

"You'd better not be insolent. I can have you fired at a moment's notice, you know."

He turned his head, looking for someone among the men below. He asked: "Shall I call the superintendent?"

She smiled contemptuously.

"No, of course not. It would be too simple. But since you know who I am, it would be better if you stopped looking at me when I come here. It might be misunderstood."

"I don't think so."

She turned away. She had to control her voice. She looked over the stone ledges. She asked: "Do you find it very hard to work here?"

"Yes. Terribly."

"Do you get tired?"

"Inhumanly."

"How does that feel?"

"I can hardly walk when the day's ended. I can't move my arms at night. When I lie in bed, I can count every muscle in my body to the number of separate, different pains."

She knew suddenly that he was not telling her about himself; he was speaking of her, he was saying the things she wanted to hear and telling her that he knew why she wanted to hear these particular sentences.

She felt anger, a satisfying anger because it was cold and certain. She felt also a desire to let her skin touch his; to let the length of her bare arm press against the length of his; just that; the desire went no further.

She was asking calmly:

"You don't belong here, do you? You don't talk like a worker. What were you before?"

"An electrician. A plumber. A plasterer. Many things."

"Why are you working here?"

"For the money you're paying me, Miss Francon."

She shrugged. She turned and walked away from him up the path. She knew that he was looking after her. She did not glance back. She continued on her way through the quarry, and she left it as soon as she could, but she did not go back down the path where she would have to see him again.

*   *   *

DOMINIQUE awakened each morning to the prospect of a day made significant by the existence of a goal to be reached: the goal of making it a day on which she would not go to the quarry.

She had lost the freedom she loved. She knew that a continuous struggle against the compulsion of a single desire was compulsion also, but it was the form she preferred to accept. It was the only manner in which she could let him motivate her life. She found a dark satisfaction in pain—because that pain came from him.

She went to call on her distant neighbors, a wealthy, gracious family who had bored her in New York; she had visited no one all summer. They were astonished and delighted to see her. She sat among a group of distinguished people at the edge of a swimming pool. She watched the air of fastidious elegance around her. She watched the deference of these people's manner when they spoke to her. She glanced at her own reflection in the pool: she looked more delicately austere than any among them.

And she thought, with a vicious thrill, of what these people would do if they read her mind in this moment; if they knew that she was thinking of a man in a quarry, thinking of his body with a sharp intimacy as one does not think of another's body but only of one's own. She smiled; the cold purity of her face prevented them from seeing the nature of that smile. She came back again to visit these people—for the same of such thoughts in the presence of their respect for her.

One evening, a guest offered to drive her back to her house. He was an eminent young poet. He was pale and slender; he had a soft, sensitive mouth, and eyes hurt by the whole universe. She had not noticed the wistful attention with which he had watched her for a long time. As they drove through the twilight she saw him leaning hesitantly closer to her. She heard his voice whispering the pleading, incoherent things she had heard from many men. He stopped the car. She felt his lips pressed to her shoulder.

She jerked away from him. She sat still for an instant, because she would have to brush against him if she moved and she could not bear to touch him. Then she flung the door open, she leaped out, she slammed the door behind her as if the crash of sound could wipe him out of existence, and she ran blindly. She stopped running after a while, and she walked on shivering, walked down the dark road until she saw the roof line of her own house.

She stopped, looking about her with her first coherent thought of astonishment. Such incidents had happened to her often in the past; only then she had been amused; she had felt no revulsion; she had felt nothing.

She walked slowly across the lawn, to the house. On the stairs to her room she stopped. She thought of the man in the quarry. She thought, in clear, formed words, that the man in the quarry wanted her. She had known it before; she had known it with his first glance at her. But she had never stated the knowledge to herself.

She laughed. She looked about her, at the silent splendor of her house. The house made the words preposterous. She knew that would never happen to her. And she knew the kind of suffering she could impose on him.

For days she walked with satisfaction through the rooms of her house. It was her defense. She heard the explosions of blasting from the quarry and smiled.

But she felt too certain and the house was too safe. She felt a desire to underscore the safety by challenging it.

She chose the marble slab in front of the fireplace in her bedroom. She wanted it broken. She knelt, hammer in hand, and tried to smash the marble. She pounded it, her thin arm sweeping high over her head, crashing down with ferocious helplessness. She felt the pain in the bones of her arms, in her shoulder sockets. She succeeded in making a long scratch across the marble.

She went to the quarry. She saw him from a distance and walked straight to him.

"Hello," she said casually.

He stopped the drill. He leaned against a stone shelf. He answered: "Hello."

"I have been thinking of you," she said softly, and stopped, then added, her voice flowing on in the same tone of compelling invitation, "because there's a bit of a dirty job to be done at my house. Would you like to make some extra money?"

"Certainly, Miss Francon."

"Will you come to my house tonight? The way to the servants' entrance is off Ridgewood Road. There's a marble piece at a fireplace that's broken and has to be replaced. I want you to take it out and order a new one made for me."

She expected anger and refusal. He asked:

"What time shall I come?"

"At seven o'clock. What are you paid here?"

"Sixty-two cents an hour."

"I'm sure you're worth that. I'm quite willing to pay you at the same rate. Do you know how to find my house?"

"No, Miss Francon."

"Just ask anyone in the village to direct you."

"Yes, Miss Francon."

She walked away, disappointed. She felt that their secret understanding was lost; he had spoken as if it were a simple job which she could have offered to any other workman. Then she felt the sinking gasp inside, that feeling of shame and pleasure which he always gave her: she realized that their understanding had been more intimate and flagrant than ever—in his natural acceptance of an unnatural offer; he had shown her how much he knew—by his lack of astonishment.

She asked her old caretaker and his wife to remain in the house that evening. Their diffident presence completed the picture of a feudal mansion. She heard the bell of the servants' entrance at seven o'clock. The old woman escorted him to the great front hall where Dominique stood on the landing of a broad stairway.

She watched him approaching, looking up at her. She held the pose long enough to let him suspect that it was a deliberate pose deliberately planned; she broke it at the exact moment before he could become certain of it. She said: "Good evening." Her voice was austerely quiet.

He did not answer, but inclined his head and walked on up the stairs toward her. He wore his work clothes and he carried a bag of tools. His movements had a swift, relaxed kind of energy that did not belong here, in her house, on the polished steps, between the delicate, rigid banisters. She had expected him to seem incongruous in her house; but it was the house that seemed incongruous around him.

She moved one hand, indicating the door of her bedroom. He followed obediently. He did not seem to notice the room when he entered. He entered it as if it were a workshop. He walked straight to the fireplace.

"There it is," she said, one finger pointing to the marble slab.

He said nothing. He knelt, took a thin metal wedge from his bag, held its point against the scratch on the slab, took a hammer and struck one blow. The marble split in a long, deep cut.

He glanced up at her. It was the look she dreaded, a look of laughter that could not be answered, because the laughter could not be seen, only felt. He said:

"Now it's broken and has to be replaced."

She asked calmly:

"Would you know what kind of marble this is and where to order another piece like it?"

"Yes, Miss Francon."

"Go ahead, then. Take it out."

"Yes, Miss Francon."

She stood watching him. It was strange to feel a senseless necessity to watch the mechanical process of the work as if her eyes were helping it. Then she knew that she was afraid to look at the room around them. She made herself raise her head.

She saw the shelf of her dressing table, its glass edge like a narrow green satin ribbon in the semidarkness, and the crystal containers; she saw a pair of white bedroom slippers, a pale blue towel on the floor by a mirror, a pair of stockings thrown over the arm of a chair; she saw the white satin cover of her bed. His shirt had damp stains and gray patches of stone dust; the dust made streaks on the skin of his arms. She felt as if each object in the room had been touched by him, as if the air were a heavy pool of water into which they had been plunged together, and the water that touched him carried the touch to her, to every object in the room. She wanted him to look up. He worked, without raising his head.

She approached him and stood silently over him. She had never stood so close to him before. She looked down at the smooth skin on the back of his neck; she could distinguish single threads of his hair. She glanced down at the tip of her sandal. It was there, on the floor, an inch away from his body; she needed but one movement, a very slight movement of her foot, to touch him. She made a step back.

He moved his head, but not to look up, only to pick another tool from the bag, and bent over his work again.

She laughed aloud. He stopped and glanced at her.

"Yes?" he asked.

Her face was grave, her voice gentle when she answered:

"Oh, I'm sorry. You might have thought that I was laughing at you. But I wasn't, of course."

She added:

"I didn't want to disturb you. I'm sure you're anxious to finish and get out of here. I mean, of course, because you must be tired. But then, on the other hand, I'm paying you by the hour, so it's quite all right if you stretch your time a little, if you want to make more out of it. There must be things you'd like to talk about."

"Oh, yes, Miss Francon."

"Well?"

"I think this is an atrocious fireplace."

"Really? This house was designed by my father."

"Yes, of course, Miss Francon."

"There's no point in your discussing the work of an architect."

"None at all."

"Surely we could choose some other subject."

"Yes, Miss Francon."

She moved away from him. She sat down on the bed, leaning back on straight arms, her legs crossed and pressed close together in a long, straight line. Her body, sagging limply from her shoulders, contradicted the inflexible precision of the legs; the cold austerity of her face contradicted the pose of her body.

He glanced at her occasionally, as he worked. He was speaking obediently. He was saying:

"I shall make certain to get a piece of marble of precisely the same quality, Miss Francon. It is very important to distinguish between the various kinds of marble. Generally speaking, there are three kinds. The white marbles, which are derived from the recrystallization of limestone, the onyx marbles which are chemical deposits of calcium carbonate, and the green marbles which consist mainly of hydrous magnesium silicate or serpentine. This last must not be considered as true marble. True marble is a metamorphic form of limestone, produced by heat and pressure. Pressure is a powerful factor. It leads to consequences which, once started, cannot be controlled."

"What consequences?" she asked, leaning forward.

"The recrystallization of the particles of limestone and the infiltration of foreign elements from the surrounding soil. These constitute the colored streaks which are to be found in most marbles. Pink marble is caused by the presence of manganese oxides, gray marble is due to carbonaceous matter, yellow marble is attributed to a hydrous oxide of iron. This piece here is, of course, white marble. There are a great many varieties of white marble. You should be very careful, Miss Francon . . ."

She sat leaning forward, gathered into a dim black huddle; the lamp light fell on one hand she had dropped limply on her knees, palm up, the fingers half-closed, a thin edge of fire outlining each finger, the dark cloth of her dress making the hand too naked and brilliant.

". . . to make certain that I order a new piece of precisely the same quality. It would not be advisable, for instance, to substitute a piece of white Georgia marble which is not as fine-grained as the white marble of Alabama. This is Alabama marble. Very high grade. Very expensive."

He saw her hand close and drop down, out of the light. He continued his work in silence.

When he had finished, he rose, asking:

"Where shall I put the stone?"

"Leave it there. I'll have it removed."

"I'll order a new piece cut to measure and delivered to you C.O.D. Do you wish me to set it?"

"Yes, certainly. I'll let you know when it comes. How much do I owe you?" She glanced at a clock on her bedside table. "Let me see, you've been here three quarters of an hour. That's forty-eight cents." She reached for her bag, she took out the dollar bill, she handed it to him. "Keep the change," she said.

She hoped he would throw it back in her face. He slipped the bill into his pocket. He said:

"Thank you, Miss Francon."

He saw the edge of her long black sleeve trembling over her closed fingers.

"Good night," she said, her voice hollow in anger.

He bowed: "Good night, Miss Francon."

He turned and walked down the stairs, out of the house.

*   *   *

She stopped thinking of him. She thought of the piece of marble he had ordered. She waited for it to come, with the feverish intensity of a sudden mania; she counted the days; she watched the rare trucks on the road beyond the lawn.

She told herself fiercely that she merely wanted the marble to come; just that; nothing else, no hidden reasons; no reasons at all. It was a last, hysterical aftermath; she was free of everything else. The stone would come and that would be the end.

When the stone came, she barely glanced at it. The delivery truck had not left the grounds, when she was at her desk, writing a note on a piece of exquisite stationery. She wrote:

"The marble is here. I want it set tonight."

She sent her caretaker with the note to the quarry. She ordered it delivered to: "I don't know his name. The redheaded workman who was here."

The caretaker came back and brought her a scrap torn from a brown paper bag, bearing in pencil:

"You'll have it set tonight."

She waited, in the suffocating emptiness of impatience, at the window of her bedroom. The servants' entrance bell rang at seven o'clock. There was a knock at her door. "Come in," she snapped—to hide the strange sound of her own voice. The door opened and the caretaker's wife entered, motioning for someone to follow. The person who followed was a short, squat, middle-aged Italian with bow legs, a gold hoop in one ear and a frayed hat held respectfully in both hands.

"The man sent from the quarry, Miss Francon," said the caretaker's wife.

Dominique asked, her voice not a scream and not a question:

"Who are you?"

"Pasquale Orsini," the man answered obediently, bewildered.

"What do you want?"

"Well, I . . . Well, Red down at the quarry said fireplace gotta be fixed, he said you wanta I fix her."

"Yes. Yes, of course," she said, rising. "I forgot. Go ahead."

She had to get out of the room. She had to run, not to be seen by anyone, not to be seen by herself if she could escape it.

She stopped somewhere in the garden and stood trembling, pressing her fists against her eyes. It was anger. It was a pure, single emotion that swept everything clean; everything but the terror under the anger; terror, because she knew that she could not go near the quarry now and that she would go.

It was early evening, many days later, when she went to the quarry. She returned on horseback from a long ride through the country, and she saw the shadows lengthening on the lawn; she knew that she could not live through another night. She had to get there before the workers left. She wheeled about. She rode to the quarry, flying, the wind cutting her cheeks.

He was not there when she reached the quarry. She knew at once that he was not there, even though the workers were just leaving and a great many of them were filing down the paths from the stone bowl. She stood, her lips tight, and she looked for him. But she knew that he had left.

She rode into the woods. She flew at random between walls of leaves that melted ahead in the gathering twilight. She stopped, broke a long, thin branch off a tree, tore the leaves off, and went on, using the flexible stick as a whip, lashing her horse to fly faster. She felt as if the speed would hasten the evening on, force the hours ahead to pass more quickly, let her leap across time to catch the coming morning before it came. And then she saw him walking alone on the path before her.

She tore ahead. She caught up with him and stopped sharply, the jolt throwing her forward then back like the release of a spring. He stopped.

They said nothing. They looked at each other. She thought that every silent instant passing was a betrayal; this wordless encounter was too eloquent, this recognition that no greeting was necessary.

She asked, her voice flat:

"Why didn't you come to set the marble?"

"I didn't think it would make any difference to you who came. Or did it, Miss Francon?"

She felt the words not as sounds, but as a blow flat against her mouth. The branch she held went up and slashed across his face. She started off in the sweep of the same motion.

*   *   *

Dominique sat at the dressing table in her bedroom. It was very late. There was no sound in the vast, empty house around her. The french windows of the bedroom were open on a terrace and there was no sound of leaves in the dark garden beyond.

The blankets on her bed were turned down, waiting for her, the pillow white against the tall, black windows. She thought she would try to sleep. She had not seen him for three days. She ran her hands over her head, the curves of her palms pressing against the smooth planes of hair. She pressed her fingertips, wet with perfume, to the hollows of her temples, and held them there for a moment; she felt relief in the cold, contracting bite of the liquid on her skin. A spilled drop of perfume remained on the glass of the dressing table, a drop sparkling like a gem and as expensive.

She did not hear the sound of steps in the garden. She heard them only when they rose up the stairs to the terrace. She sat up, frowning. She looked at the french windows.

He came in. He wore his work clothes, the dirty shirt with rolled sleeves, the trousers smeared with stone dust. He stood looking at her. There was no laughing understanding in his face. His face was drawn, austere in cruelty, ascetic in passion, the cheeks sunken, the lips pulled down, set tight. She jumped to her feet, she stood, her arms thrown back, her fingers spread apart. He did not move. She saw a vein of his neck rise, beating, and fall down again.

Then he walked to her. He held her as if his flesh had cut through hers and she felt the bones of his arms on the bones of her ribs, her legs jerked tight against his, his mouth on hers.

She did not know whether the jolt of terror shook her first and she thrust her elbows at his throat, twisting her body to escape, or whether she lay still in his arms, in the first instant, in the shock of feeling his skin against hers, the thing she had thought about, had expected, had never known to be like this, could not have known, because this was not part of living, but a thing one could not bear longer than a second.

She tried to tear herself away from him. The effort broke against his arms that had not felt it. Her fists beat against his shoulders, against his face. He moved one hand, took her two wrists, pinned them behind her, under his arm, wrenching her shoulder blades. She twisted her head back. She felt his lips on her breast. She tore herself free.

She fell back against the dressing table, she stood crouching, her hands clasping the edge behind her, her eyes wide, colorless, shapeless in terror. He was laughing. There was the movement of laughter on his face, but no sound. Perhaps he had released her intentionally. He stood, his legs apart, his arms hanging at his sides, letting her be more sharply aware of his body across the space between them than she had been in his arms. She looked at the door behind him, he saw the first hint of movement, no more than a thought of leaping toward that door. He extended his arm, not touching her, and fell back. Her shoulders moved faintly, rising. He took a step forward and her shoulders fell. She huddled lower, closer to the table. He let her wait. Then he approached. He lifted her without effort. She let her teeth sink into his hand and felt blood on the tip of her tongue. He pulled her head back and he forced her mouth open against his.

She fought like an animal. But she made no sound. She did not call for help. She heard the echoes of her blows in a gasp of his breath, and she knew that it was a gasp of pleasure. She reached for the lamp on the dressing table. He knocked the lamp out of her hand. The crystal burst to pieces in the darkness.

He had thrown her down on the bed and she felt the blood beating in her throat, in her eyes, the hatred, the helpless terror in her blood. She felt the hatred and his hands; his hands moving over her body, the hands that broke granite. She fought in a last convulsion. Then the sudden pain shot up, through her body, to her throat, and she screamed. Then she lay still.

It was an act that could be performed in tenderness, as a seal of love, or in contempt, as a symbol of humiliation and conquest. It could be the act of a lover or the act of a soldier violating an enemy woman. He did it as an act of scorn. Not as love, but as defilement. And this made her lie still and submit. One gesture of tenderness from him—and she would have remained cold, untouched by the thing done to her body. But the act of a master taking shameful, contemptuous possession of her was the kind of rapture she had wanted. Then she felt him shaking with the agony of a pleasure unbearable even to him, she knew that she had given that to him, that it came from her, from her body, and she bit her lips and she knew what he had wanted her to know.

He lay still across the bed, away from her, his head hanging back over the edge. She heard the slow, ending gasps of his breath. She lay on her back, as he had left her, not moving, her mouth open. She felt empty, light and flat.

She saw him get up. She saw his silhouette against the window. He went out, without a word or a glance at her. She noticed that, but it did not matter. She listened blankly to the sound of his steps moving away in the garden.

She lay still for a long time. Then she moved her tongue in her open mouth. She heard a sound that came from somewhere within her, and it was the dry, short, sickening sound of a sob, but she was not crying, her eyes were held paralyzed, dry and open. The sound became motion, a jolt running down her throat to her stomach. It flung her up, she stood awkwardly, bent over, her forearms pressed to her stomach. She heard the small table by the bed rattling in the darkness, and she looked at it, in empty astonishment that a table should move without reason. Then she understood that she was shaking. She was not frightened; it seemed foolish to shake like that, in short, separate jerks, like soundless hiccoughs. She thought she must take a bath. The need was unbearable, as if she had felt it for a long time. Nothing mattered, if only she would take a bath. She dragged her feet slowly to the door of her bathroom.

She turned the light on in the bathroom. She saw herself in a tall mirror. She saw the purple bruises left on her body by his mouth. She heard a moan muffled in her throat, not very loud. It was not the sight, but the sudden flash of knowledge. She knew that she would not take a bath. She knew that she wanted to keep the feeling of his body, the traces of his body on hers, knowing also what such a desire implied. She fell on her knees, clasping the edge of the bathtub. She could not make herself crawl over that edge. Her hands slipped, she lay still on the floor. The tiles were hard and cold under her body. She lay there till morning.

———

EDITOR'S NOTE: *In this section, Roark is on trial—having been sued by Hopton Stoddard, a client who had hired him to build a "Temple of the Human Spirit." Everyone considers the Temple blasphemous.*

Ellsworth Toohey—critic, "humanitarian," archenemy of Roark—foreseeing that Roark's revolutionary manner of building would antagonize people, had manipulated Stoddard into giving the commission to Roark and then into suing him.

*In the newspaper column "Sacrilege," which instigated the lawsuit,
Toohey had written: "Instead of being austerely enclosed, this alleged
temple is wide open, like a western saloon [. . .] Man's proper posture in
a house of God is on his knees. Nobody in his right mind would kneel
within Mr. Roark's temple. The place forbids it. The emotions it sug-
gests are of a different nature: arrogance, audacity, defiance, self-exaltation. It is not a house of God, but the cell of a megalomaniac."*

The Stoddard Trial

THE CASE of Hopton Stoddard versus Howard Roark opened in Feb-
ruary of 1931.

The courtroom was so full that mass reactions could be expressed
only by a slow motion running across the spread of heads, a sluggish
wave like the ripple under the tight-packed skin of a sea lion.

The crowd, brown and streaked with subdued color, looked like a
fruitcake of all the arts, with the cream of the A.G.A. rich and heavy
on top. There were distinguished men and well-dressed, tight-lipped
women; each woman seemed to feel an exclusive proprietorship of
the art practiced by her escort, a monopoly guarded by resentful
glances at the others. Almost everybody knew almost everybody else.
The room had the atmosphere of a convention, an opening night and
a family picnic. There was a feeling of "our bunch," "our boys," "our
show." [. . .]

Beyond the windows the sky was white and flat like frosted glass.
The light seemed to come from the banks of snow on roofs and
ledges, an unnatural light that made everything in the room look
naked.

The judge sat hunched on his high bench as if he were roosting.
He had a small face, wizened into virtue. He kept his hands upright
in front of his chest, the fingertips pressed together. Hopton Stoddard
was not present. He was represented by his attorney, a handsome gentleman, tall and grave as an ambassador.

Roark sat alone at the defense table. The crowd had stared at him
and given up angrily, finding no satisfaction. He did not look crushed
and he did not look defiant. He looked impersonal and calm. He was
not like a public figure in a public place; he was like a man alone in
his own room, listening to the radio. He took no notes; there were no

papers on the table before him, only a large brown envelope. The crowd would have forgiven anything, except a man who could remain normal under the vibrations of its enormous collective sneer. Some of them had come prepared to pity him; all of them hated him after the first few minutes.

The plaintiff's attorney stated his case in a simple opening address; it was true, he admitted, that Hopton Stoddard had given Roark full freedom to design and build the Temple; the point was, however, that Mr. Stoddard had clearly specified and expected *a temple*; the building in question could not be considered a temple by any known standards; as the plaintiff proposed to prove with the help of the best authorities in the field.

Roark waived his privilege to make an opening statement to the jury.

Ellsworth Monkton Toohey was the first witness called by the plaintiff. He sat on the edge of the witness chair and leaned back, resting on the end of his spine: he lifted one leg and placed it horizontally across the other. He looked amused—but managed to suggest that his amusement was a well-bred protection against looking bored.

The attorney went through a long list of questions about Mr. Toohey's professional qualifications, including the number of copies sold of his book *Sermons in Stone*. Then he read aloud Toohey's column "Sacrilege" and asked him to state whether he had written it. Toohey replied that he had. There followed a list of questions in erudite terms on the architectural merits of the Temple. Toohey proved that it had none. There followed an historical review. Toohey, speaking easily and casually, gave a brief sketch of all known civilizations and of their outstanding religious monuments—from the Incas to the Phoenicians to the Easter Islanders—including, whenever possible, the dates when these monuments were begun and the dates when they were completed, the number of workers employed in the construction and the approximate cost in modern American dollars. The audience listened punch-drunk.

Toohey proved that the Stoddard Temple contradicted every brick, stone and precept of history. "I have endeavored to show," he said in conclusion, "that the two essentials of the conception of a temple are a sense of awe and a sense of man's humility. We have noted the gigantic proportions of religious edifices, the soaring lines, the horrible grotesques of monster-like gods, or, later, gargoyles. All of it tends to impress upon man his essential insignificance, to crush him by sheer magnitude, to imbue him with that sacred terror which leads to the meekness of virtue. The Stoddard Temple is a brazen denial of our entire past, an insolent 'No' flung in the face of history. I may venture a guess as to the reason why this case has aroused such public interest. All of us have recognized instinctively that it involves a moral issue much beyond its legal aspects. This building is a monument to a profound hatred of humanity. It is one man's ego defying the most sacred impulses of all mankind, of every man on the street, of every man in this courtroom!"

This was not a witness in court, but Ellsworth Toohey addressing a meeting—and the reaction was inevitable: the audience burst into applause. The judge struck his gavel and made a threat to have the courtroom cleared. Order was restored, but not to the faces of the crowd: the faces remained lecherously self-righteous. It was pleasant to be singled out and brought into the case as an injured party. Three-fourths of them had never seen the Stoddard Temple.

"Thank you, Mr. Toohey," said the attorney, faintly suggesting a bow. Then he turned to Roark and said with delicate courtesy: "Your witness."

"No questions," said Roark.

Ellsworth Toohey raised one eyebrow and left the stand regretfully.

"Mr. Peter Keating!" called the attorney.

Peter Keating's face looked attractive and fresh, as if he had had a good night's sleep. He mounted the witness stand with a collegiate sort of gusto, swinging his shoulders and arms unnecessarily. He took the oath and answered the first questions gaily. His pose in the witness chair was strange: his torso slumped to one side with swaggering ease, an elbow on the chair's arm; but his feet were planted awkwardly straight, and his knees were pressed tight together. He never looked at Roark. [. . .]

"Now, Mr. Keating, you attended the Stanton Institute of Technology at the same period as Mr. Roark?"

"Yes."

"What can you tell us about Mr. Roark's record there?"

"He was expelled."

"He was expelled because he was unable to live up to the Institute's high standard of requirements?"

"Yes. Yes, that was it."

The judge glanced at Roark. A lawyer would have objected to this testimony as irrelevant. Roark made no objection.

"At that time, did you think that he showed any talent for the profession of architecture?"

"No."

"Will you please speak a little louder, Mr. Keating?"

"I didn't . . . think he had any talent."

Queer things were happening to Keating's verbal punctuation: some words came out crisply, as if he dropped an exclamation point after each; others ran together, as if he would not stop to let himself hear them. He did not look at the attorney. He kept his eyes on the audience. At times, he looked like a boy out on a lark, a boy who has just drawn a mustache on the face of a beautiful girl on a subway toothpaste ad. Then he looked as if he were begging the crowd for support—as if he were on trial before them.

"At one time you employed Mr. Roark in your office?"

"Yes."

"And you found yourself forced to fire him?"

"Yes . . . we did."

"For incompetence?"

"Yes."

"What can you tell us about Mr. Roark's subsequent career?"

"Well, you know, 'career' is a relative term. In volume of achievement any draftsman in our office has done more than Mr. Roark. We don't call one or two buildings a career. We put up that many every month or so."

"Will you give us your professional opinion of his work?"

"Well, I think it's immature. Very startling, even quite interesting at times, but essentially—adolescent."

"Then Mr. Roark cannot be called a full-fledged architect?"

"Not in the sense in which we speak of Mr. Ralston Holcombe, Mr. Guy Francon, Mr. Gordon Prescott—no. But, of course, I want to be fair. I think Mr. Roark had definite potentialities, particularly in problems of pure engineering. He could have made something of himself. I've tried to talk to him about it—I've tried to help him—I honestly did. But it was like talking to one of his pet pieces of reinforced concrete. I knew that he'd come to something like this. I wasn't surprised when I heard that a client had had to sue him at last."

"What can you tell us about Mr. Roark's attitude toward clients?"

"Well, that's the point. That's the whole point. He didn't care what the clients thought or wished, what anyone in the world thought or wished. He didn't even understand how other architects could care. He wouldn't even give you that, not even understanding, not even enough to . . . respect you a little just the same. I don't see what's so wrong with trying to please people. I don't see what's wrong with wanting to be friendly and liked and popular. Why is that a crime? Why should anyone sneer at you for that, sneer all the time, all the time, day and night, not giving you a moment's peace, like the Chinese water torture, you know where they drop water on your skull drop by drop?"

People in the audience began to realize that Peter Keating was drunk. The attorney frowned; the testimony had been rehearsed; but it was getting off the rails.

"Well, now, Mr. Keating, perhaps you'd better tell us about Mr. Roark's views on architecture."

"I'll tell you, if you want to know. He thinks you should take your shoes off and kneel, when you speak of architecture. That's what he thinks. Now why should you? Why? It's a business like any other, isn't it? What's so damn sacred about it? Why do we have to be all keyed up? We're only human. We want to make a living. Why can't things be simple and easy? Why do we have to be some sort of God-damn heroes?"

"Now, now, Mr. Keating, I think we're straying slightly from the subject. We're . . ."

"No, we're not. I know what I'm talking about. You do, too. They all do. Every one of them here. I'm talking about the Temple. Don't you see? Why pick a fiend to build a temple? Only a very human sort of man should be chosen to do that. A man who understands . . . and forgives. A man who forgives . . . That's what you go to church for— to be . . . forgiven . . ."

"Yes, Mr. Keating, but speaking of Mr. Roark . . ."

"Well, what about Mr. Roark? He's no architect. He's no good. Why should I be afraid to say that he's no good? Why are you all afraid of him?"

"Mr. Keating, if you're not well and wish to be dismissed . . . ?"

Keating looked at him, as if awakening. He tried to control himself. After a while he said, his voice flat, resigned:

"No. I'm all right. I'll tell you anything you want. What is it you want me to say?"

"Will you tell us—in professional terms—your opinion of the structure known as the Stoddard Temple?"

"Yes. Sure. The Stoddard Temple . . . The Stoddard Temple has an improperly articulated plan, which leads to spatial confusion. There is no balance of masses. It lacks a sense of symmetry. Its proportions are inept." He spoke in a monotone. His neck was stiff; he was making an effort not to let it drop forward. "It's out of scale. It contradicts the elementary principles of composition. The total effect is that of . . ."

"Louder please, Mr. Keating."

"The total effect is that of crudeness and architectural illiteracy. It shows . . . it shows no sense of structure, no instinct for beauty, no creative imagination, no . . ." he closed his eyes, ". . . artistic integrity . . ."

"Thank you, Mr. Keating. That is all."

The attorney turned to Roark and said nervously:

"Your witness."

"No questions," said Roark.

This concluded the first day of the trial. [. . .]

In the next two days a succession of witnesses testified for the plaintiff. Every examination began with questions that brought out the professional achievements of the witness. The attorney gave them leads like an expert press agent. Austen Heller remarked that architects must have fought for the privilege of being called to the witness stand, since it was the grandest spree of publicity in a usually silent profession.

None of the witnesses looked at Roark. He looked at them. He listened to the testimony. He said: "No questions," to each one.

Ralston Holcombe on the stand, with flowing tie and gold-headed cane, had the appearance of a Grand Duke or a beer-garden composer. His testimony was long and scholarly, but it came down to:

"It's all nonsense. It's all a lot of childish nonsense. I can't say that I feel much sympathy for Mr. Hopton Stoddard. He should have known better. It is a scientific fact that the architectural style of the Renaissance is the only one appropriate to our age. If our best people, like Mr. Stoddard, refuse to recognize this, what can you expect from all sorts of parvenus, would-be architects and the rabble in general? It has been proved that Renaissance is the only permissible style for all churches, temples and cathedrals. What about Sir Christopher Wren? Just laugh that off. And remember the greatest religious monument of all time—St. Peter's in Rome. Are you going to improve upon St. Peter's? And if Mr. Stoddard did not specifically insist on Renaissance, he got just exactly what he deserved. It serves him jolly well right."

Gordon L. Prescott wore a turtle-neck sweater under a plaid coat, tweed trousers and heavy golf shoes.

"The correlation of the transcendental to the purely spatial in the building under discussion is entirely screwy," he said. "If we take the horizontal as the one-dimensional, the vertical as the two-dimensional, the diagonal as the three-dimensional, and the interpenetration of spaces as the fourth-dimensional—architecture being a fourth-dimensional art—we can see quite simply that this building is homaloidal, or—in the language of the layman—flat. The flowing life which comes from the sense of order in chaos, or, if you prefer, from unity in diversity, as well as vice versa, which is the realization of the contradiction inherent in architecture, is here absolutely absent. I am really trying to express myself as clearly as I can, but it is impossible to present a dialectic state by covering it up with an old fig leaf of logic just for the sake of the mentally lazy layman."

John Erik Snyte testified modestly and unobtrusively that he had employed Roark in his office, that Roark had been an unreliable, disloyal and unscrupulous employee, and that Roark had started his career by stealing a client from him.

On the fourth day of the trial the plaintiff's attorney called his last witness.

"Miss Dominique Francon," he announced solemnly. [. . .]

The attorney had reserved Dominique for his climax, partly because he expected a great deal from her, and partly because he was worried; she was the only unrehearsed witness; she had refused to be coached. She had never mentioned the Stoddard Temple in her column; but he had looked up her earlier writings on Roark; and Ellsworth Toohey had advised him to call her.

Dominique stood for a moment on the elevation of the witness stand, looking slowly over the crowd. Her beauty was startling but too impersonal, as if it did not belong to her; it seemed present in the room as a separate entity. People thought of a vision that had not quite appeared, of a victim on a scaffold, of a person standing at night at the rail of an ocean liner.

"What is your name?"

"Dominique Francon."

"And your occupation, Miss Francon?"

"Newspaper woman."

"You are the author of the brilliant column 'Your House' appearing in the New York *Banner?*"

"I am the author of 'Your House.' "

"Your father is Guy Francon, the eminent architect?"

"Yes. My father was asked to come here to testify. He refused. He said he did not care for a building such as the Stoddard Temple, but he did not think that we were behaving like gentlemen."

"Well, now, Miss Francon, shall we confine our answers to our questions? We are indeed fortunate to have you with us, since you are our only woman witness, and women have always had the purest sense of religious faith. Being, in addition, an outstanding authority on architecture, you are eminently qualified to give us what I shall call, with all deference, the feminine angle on this case. Will you tell us in your own words what you think of the Stoddard Temple?"

"I think that Mr. Stoddard has made a mistake. There would have been no doubt about the justice of his case if he had sued, not for alteration costs, but for demolition costs."

The attorney looked relieved. "Will you explain your reasons, Miss Francon?"

"You have heard them from every witness at this trial."

"Then I take it that you agree with the preceding testimony?"

"Completely. Even more completely than the persons who testified. They were very convincing witnesses."

"Will you . . . clarify that, Miss Francon? Just what do you mean?"

"What Mr. Toohey said: that this temple is a threat to all of us."

"Oh, I see."

"Mr. Toohey understood the issue so well. Shall I clarify it—in my own words?"

"By all means."

"Howard Roark built a temple to the human spirit. He saw man as strong, proud, clean, wise and fearless. He saw man as a heroic being. And he built a temple to that. A temple is a place where man is to experience exaltation. He thought that exaltation comes from the consciousness of being guiltless, of seeing the truth and achieving it, of living up to one's highest possibility, of knowing no shame and having no cause for shame, of being able to stand naked in full sunlight. He thought that exaltation means joy and that joy is man's birthright. He thought that a place built as a setting for man is a sacred place. That is what Howard Roark thought of man and of exaltation. But Ellsworth Toohey said that this temple was a monument to a profound hatred of humanity. Ellsworth Toohey said that the essence of exaltation was to be scared out of your wits, to fall down and to grovel. Ellsworth Toohey said that man's highest act was to realize his own worthlessness and to beg forgiveness. Ellsworth Toohey said it was depraved not to take for granted that man is something which needs to be forgiven. Ellsworth Toohey saw that this building was of man and of the earth—and Ellsworth Toohey said that this building had its belly in the mud. To glorify man, said Ellsworth Toohey, was to glorify the gross pleasure of the flesh, for the realm of the spirit is beyond the grasp of man. To enter that realm, said Ellsworth Toohey, man must come as a beggar, on his knees. Ellsworth Toohey is a lover of mankind."

"Miss Francon, we are not really discussing Mr. Toohey, so if you will confine yourself to . . ."

"I do not condemn Ellsworth Toohey. I condemn Howard Roark. A building, they say, must be part of its site. In what kind of world did Roark build his temple? For what kind of men? Look around you. Can you see a shrine becoming sacred by serving as a setting for Mr. Hopton Stoddard? For Mr. Ralston Holcombe? For Mr. Peter Keating? When you look at them all, do you hate Ellsworth Toohey—or do you damn Howard Roark for the unspeakable indignity which he did commit? Ellsworth Toohey is right, that temple *is* a sacrilege, though not in the sense he meant. I think Mr. Toohey knows that, however. When you see a man casting pearls without getting even a pork chop in return—it is not against the swine that you feel indignation. It is against the man who valued his pearls so little that he was willing to fling them into the muck and to let them become the occasion for a whole concert of grunting, transcribed by the court stenographer."

"Miss Francon, I hardly think that this line of testimony is relevant or admissible . . ."

"The witness must be allowed to testify," the judge declared unexpectedly. He had been bored and he liked to watch Dominique's figure. Besides, he knew that the audience was enjoying it, in the sheer excitement of scandal, even though their sympathies were with Hopton Stoddard.

"Your Honor, some misunderstanding seems to have occurred," said the attorney. "Miss Francon, for whom are you testifying? For Mr. Roark or Mr. Stoddard?"

"For Mr. Stoddard, of course. I am stating the reasons why Mr. Stoddard should win this case. I have sworn to tell the truth."

"Proceed," said the judge.

"All the witnesses have told the truth. But not the whole truth. I am merely filling in the omissions. They spoke of a threat and of hatred. They were right. The Stoddard Temple is a threat to many things. If it were allowed to exist, nobody would dare to look at himself in the mirror. And that is a cruel thing to do to men. Ask anything of men. Ask them to achieve wealth, fame, love, brutality, murder, self-sacrifice. But don't ask them to achieve self-respect. They will hate your soul. Well, they know best. They must have their reasons. They won't say, of course, that they hate you. They will say that you hate them. It's near enough, I suppose. They know the emotion involved. Such are men as they are. So what is the use of being a martyr to the impossible? What is the use of building for a world that does not exist?"

"Your Honor, I don't see what possible bearing this can have on . . ."

"I am proving your case for you. I am proving why you must go with Ellsworth Toohey, as you will anyway. The Stoddard Temple must be destroyed. Not to save men from it, but to save it from men. What's the difference, however? Mr. Stoddard wins. I am in full agreement with everything that's being done here, except for one point. I didn't think we should be allowed to get away with that point. Let us destroy, but don't let us pretend that we are committing an act of virtue. Let us say that we are moles and we object to mountain peaks. Or, perhaps, that we are lemmings, the animals who cannot help swimming out to self-destruction. I realize fully that at this moment I am as futile as Howard Roark. *This* is my Stoddard Temple— my first and my last." She inclined her head to the judge. "That is all, Your Honor."

"Your witness," the attorney snapped to Roark.

"No questions," said Roark.

Dominique left the stand.

The attorney bowed to the bench and said: "The plaintiff rests."

The judge turned to Roark and made a vague gesture, inviting him to proceed.

Roark got up and walked to the bench, the brown envelope in hand. He took out of the envelope ten photographs of the Stoddard Temple and laid them on the judge's desk. He said:

"The defense rests."

PART TWO

Ethics

EDITOR'S NOTE: AR's *purpose in her novels was the projection of an ideal man. "The portrayal of a moral ideal," she wrote, is "my ultimate literary goal [. . .] to which any didactic, intellectual or philosophical values contained in [the] novel are only the means" ("The Goal of My Writing," Romantic Manifesto, 1975, p. 162).*

To create a hero such as Howard Roark, she had to identify in detail her view of moral perfection. "Since my purpose," she said, "is the presentation of an ideal man [. . .] I had to define and present a rational code of ethics" (Introduction to The Fountainhead, *50th anniversary edition, 1993, p. vii).*

In this section devoted to ethics, we begin with Roark's speech at the climax of The Fountainhead. *Roark had agreed to design Cortlandt, a government housing project, on definite terms—but a breach of contract by the government left him without legal recourse. His response was to dynamite the building while it was still under construction. Roark's courtroom speech, a moral defense of his actions, is an early statement of AR's ethics.*

1. Selfishness

From Roark's Speech

"THOUSANDS OF years ago, the first man discovered how to make fire. He was probably burned at the stake he had taught his brothers to light. He was considered an evildoer who had dealt with a demon mankind dreaded. But thereafter men had fire to keep them warm, to cook their food, to light their caves. He had left them a gift they had not conceived and he had lifted darkness off the earth. Centuries later, the first man invented the wheel. He was probably torn on the rack he had taught his brothers to build. He was considered a transgressor who ventured into forbidden territory. But thereafter, men could travel past any horizon. He had left them a gift they had not conceived and he had opened the roads of the world.

"That man, the unsubmissive and first, stands in the opening chapter of every legend mankind has recorded about its beginning. Prometheus was chained to a rock and torn by vultures—because he had stolen the fire of the gods. Adam was condemned to suffer—because he had eaten the fruit of the tree of knowledge. Whatever the legend, somewhere in the shadows of its memory mankind knew that its glory began with one and that that one paid for his courage.

"Throughout the centuries there were men who took first steps down new roads armed with nothing but their own vision. Their goals differed, but they all had this in common: that the step was first, the road new, the vision unborrowed, and the response they received—hatred. The great creators—the thinkers, the artists, the scientists, the inventors—stood alone against the men of their time. Every great new thought was opposed. Every great new invention was denounced. The first motor was considered foolish. The airplane was considered impossible. The power loom was considered vicious. Anesthesia was considered sinful. But the men of unborrowed vision went ahead. They fought, they suffered and they paid. But they won.

"No creator was prompted by a desire to serve his brothers, for his brothers rejected the gift he offered and that gift destroyed the slothful routine of their lives. His truth was his only motive. His own truth, and his own work to achieve it in his own way. A symphony, a book, an engine, a philosophy, an airplane or a building—that was his goal and his life. Not those who heard, read, operated, believed, flew or inhabited the thing he had created. The creation, not its users. The creation, not the benefits others derived from it. The creation which gave form to his truth. He held his truth above all things and against all men.

"His vision, his strength, his courage came from his own spirit. A man's spirit, however, is his self. That entity which is his consciousness. To think, to feel, to judge, to act are functions of the ego.

"The creators were not selfless. It is the whole secret of their power—that it was self-sufficient, self-motivated, self-generated. A first cause, a fount of energy, a life force, a Prime Mover. The creator served nothing and no one. He had lived for himself.

"And only by living for himself was he able to achieve the things which are the glory of mankind. Such is the nature of achievement.

"Man cannot survive except through his mind. He comes on earth unarmed. His brain is his only weapon. Animals obtain food by force. Man has no claws, no fangs, no horns, no great strength of muscle. He must plant his food or hunt it. To plant, he needs a process of thought. To hunt, he needs weapons, and to make weapons—a process of thought. From this simplest necessity to the highest religious abstraction, from the wheel to the skyscraper, everything we are and everything we have comes from a single attribute of man—the function of his reasoning mind.

"But the mind is an attribute of the individual. There is no such thing as a collective brain. There is no such thing as a collective thought. An agreement reached by a group of men is only a compromise or an average drawn upon many individual thoughts. It is a secondary consequence. The primary act—the process of reason—must be performed by each man alone. We can divide a meal among many men. We cannot digest it in a collective stomach. No man can use his lungs to breathe for another man. No man can use his brain to think for another. All the functions of body and spirit are private. They cannot be shared or transferred.

"We inherit the products of the thought of other men. We inherit the wheel. We make a cart. The cart becomes an automobile. The automobile becomes an airplane. But all through the process what we receive from others is only the end product of their thinking. The moving force is the creative faculty which takes this product as material, uses it and originates the next step. This creative faculty cannot be given or received, shared or borrowed. It belongs to single, individual men. That which it creates is the property of the creator. Men learn from one another. But all learning is only the exchange of material. No man can give another the capacity to think. Yet that capacity is our only means of survival.

"Nothing is given to man on earth. Everything he needs has to be produced. And here man faces his basic alternative: he can survive in only one of two ways—by the independent work of his own mind or as a parasite fed by the minds of others. The creator originates. The parasite borrows. The creator faces nature alone. The parasite faces nature through an intermediary.

"The creator's concern is the conquest of nature. The parasite's concern is the conquest of men.

"The creator lives for his work. He needs no other men. His primary goal is within himself. The parasite lives second-hand. He needs others. Others become his prime motive.

"The basic need of the creator is independence. The reasoning mind cannot work under any form of compulsion. It cannot be curbed, sacrificed or subordinated to any consideration whatsoever. It demands total independence in function and in motive. To a creator, all relations with men are secondary.

"The basic need of the second-hander is to secure his ties with men in order to be fed. He places relations first. He declares that man exists in order to serve others. He preaches altruism.

"Altruism is the doctrine which demands that man live for others and place others above self.

"No man can live for another. He cannot share his spirit just as he cannot share his body. But the second-hander has used altruism as a weapon of exploitation and reversed the base of mankind's moral principles. Men have been taught every precept that destroys the creator. Men have been taught dependence as a virtue.

"The man who attempts to live for others is a dependent. He is a parasite in motive and makes parasites of those he serves. The relationship produces nothing but mutual corruption. It is impossible in concept. The nearest approach to it in reality—the man who lives to serve others—is the slave. If physical slavery is repulsive, how much more repulsive is the concept of servility of the spirit? The conquered slave has a vestige of honor. He has the merit of having resisted and of considering his condition evil. But the man who enslaves himself voluntarily in the name of love is the basest of creatures. He degrades the dignity of man and he degrades the conception of love. But this is the essence of altruism.

"Men have been taught that the highest virtue is not to achieve, but to give. Yet one cannot give that which has not been created. Creation comes before distribution—or there will be nothing to distribute. The need of the creator comes before the need of any possible beneficiary. Yet we are taught to admire the second-hander who dispenses gifts he has not produced above the man who made the gifts possible. We praise an act of charity. We shrug at an act of achievement.

"Men have been taught that their first concern is to relieve the suffering of others. But suffering is a disease. Should one come upon it, one tries to give relief and assistance. To make that the highest test of virtue is to make suffering the most important part of life. Then man must wish to see others suffer—in order that he may be virtuous. Such is the nature of altruism. The creator is not concerned with disease, but with life. Yet the work of the creators has eliminated one form of disease after another, in man's body and spirit, and brought more relief from suffering than any altruist could ever conceive.

"Men have been taught that it is a virtue to agree with others. But the creator is the man who disagrees. Men have been taught that it is a virtue to swim with the current. But the creator is the man who goes against the current. Men have been taught that it is a virtue to stand together. But the creator is the man who stands alone.

"Men have been taught that the ego is the synonym of evil, and selflessness the ideal of virtue. But the creator is the egotist in the absolute sense, and the selfless man is the one who does not think, feel, judge, or act. These are functions of the self.

"Here the basic reversal is most deadly. The issue has been perverted and man has been left no alternative—and no freedom. As poles of good and evil, he was offered two conceptions: egotism and altruism. Egotism was held to mean the sacrifice of others to self. Altruism—the sacrifice of self to others. This tied man irrevocably to other men and left him nothing but a choice of pain: his own pain borne for the sake of others or pain inflicted upon others for the sake of self. When it was added that man must find joy in self-immolation, the trap was closed. Man was forced to accept masochism as his ideal—under the threat that sadism was his only alternative. This was the greatest fraud ever perpetrated on mankind.

"This was the device by which dependence and suffering were perpetuated as fundamentals of life.

"The choice is not self-sacrifice or domination. The choice is independence or dependence. The code of the creator or the code of the second-hander. This is the basic issue. It rests upon the alternative of life or death. The code of the creator is built on the needs of the reasoning mind which allows man to survive. The code of the second-hander is built on the needs of a mind incapable of survival. All that which proceeds from man's independent ego is good. All that which proceeds from man's dependence upon men is evil.

"The egotist in the absolute sense is not the man who sacrifices others. He is the man who stands above the need of using others in any manner. He does not function through them. He is not concerned with them in any primary matter. Not in his aim, not in his motive, not in his thinking, not in his desires, not in the source of his energy. He does not exist for any other man—and he asks no other man to exist for him. This is the only form of brotherhood and mutual respect possible between men.

"Degrees of ability vary, but the basic principle remains the same: the degree of a man's independence, initiative and personal love for his work determines his talent as a worker and his worth as a man. Independence is the only gauge of human virtue and value. What a man is and makes of himself; not what he has or hasn't done for others. There is no substitute for personal dignity. There is no standard of personal dignity except independence.

"In all proper relationships there is no sacrifice of anyone to anyone. An architect needs clients, but he does not subordinate his work to their wishes. They need him, but they do not order a house just to give him a commission. Men exchange their work by free, mutual consent to mutual advantage when their personal interests agree and they both desire the exchange. If they do not desire it, they are not forced to deal with each other. They seek further. This is the only possible form of relationship between equals. Anything else is a relation of slave to master, or victim to executioner.

"No work is ever done collectively, by a majority decision. Every creative job is achieved under the guidance of a single individual thought. An architect requires a great many men to erect his building. But he does not ask them to vote on his design. They work together by free agreement and each is free in his proper function. An architect uses steel, glass, concrete, produced by others. But the materials remain just so much steel, glass and concrete until he touches them. What he does with them is his individual product and his individual property. This is the only pattern for proper co-operation among men.

"The first right on earth is the right of the ego. Man's first duty is to himself. His moral law is never to place his prime goal within the persons of others. His moral obligation is to do what he wishes, provided his wish does not depend *primarily* upon other men. This includes the whole sphere of his creative faculty, his thinking, his work. But it does not include the sphere of the gangster, the altruist and the dictator.

"A man thinks and works alone. A man cannot rob, exploit or rule—alone. Robbery, exploitation and ruling presuppose victims. They imply dependence. They are the province of the second-hander.

"Rulers of men are not egotists. They create nothing. They exist entirely through the persons of others. Their goal is in their subjects, in the activity of enslaving. They are as dependent as the beggar, the social worker and the bandit. The form of dependence does not matter.

"But men were taught to regard second-handers—tyrants, emperors, dictators—as exponents of egotism. By this fraud they were made to destroy the ego, themselves and others. The purpose of the fraud was to destroy the creators. Or to harness them. Which is a synonym.

"From the beginning of history, the two antagonists have stood face to face: the creator and the second-hander. When the first creator invented the wheel, the first second-hander responded. He invented altruism.

"The creator—denied, opposed, persecuted, exploited—went on, moved forward and carried all humanity along on his energy. The second-hander contributed nothing to the process except the impediments. The contest has another name: the individual against the collective.

"The 'common good' of a collective—a race, a class, a state—was the claim and justification of every tyranny ever established over men. Every major horror of history was committed in the name of an altruistic motive. Has any act of selfishness ever equaled the carnage perpetrated by disciples of altruism? Does the fault lie in men's hypocrisy or in the nature of the principle? The most dreadful butchers were the most sincere. They believed in the perfect society reached through the guillotine and the firing squad. Nobody questioned their right to murder since they were murdering for an altruistic purpose. It was accepted that man must be sacrificed for other men. Actors change, but the course of the tragedy remains the same. A humanitarian who starts with declarations of love for mankind and ends with a sea of blood. It goes on and will go on so long as men believe that an action is good if it is unselfish. That permits the altruist to act and forces his victims to bear it. The leaders of collectivist movements ask nothing for themselves. But observe the results.

"The only good which men can do to one another and the only statement of their proper relationship is—Hands off!

"Now observe the results of a society built on the principle of individualism. This, our country. The noblest country in the history of men. The country of greatest achievement, greatest prosperity, greatest freedom. This country was not based on selfless service, sacrifice, renunciation or any precept of altruism. It was based on a man's right to the pursuit of happiness. His own happiness. Not anyone else's. A private, personal, selfish motive. Look at the results. Look into your own conscience.

"It is an ancient conflict. Men have come close to the truth, but it was destroyed each time and one civilization fell after another. Civilization is the progress toward a society of privacy. The savage's whole existence is public, ruled by the laws of his tribe. Civilization is the process of setting man free from men.

"Now, in our age, collectivism, the rule of the second-hander and second-rater, the ancient monster, has broken loose and is running amuck. It has brought men to a level of intellectual indecency never equaled on earth. It has reached a scale of horror without precedent. It has poisoned every mind. It has swallowed most of Europe. It is engulfing our country.

"I am an architect. I know what is to come by the principle on which it is built. We are approaching a world in which I cannot permit myself to live.

"Now you know why I dynamited Cortlandt.

"I designed Cortlandt. I gave it to you. I destroyed it.

"I destroyed it because I did not choose to let it exist. It was a double monster. In form and in implication. I had to blast both. The form was mutilated by two second-handers who assumed the right to improve upon that which they had not made and could not equal. They were permitted to do it by the general implication that the altruistic purpose of the building superseded all rights and that I had no claim to stand against it.

"I agreed to design Cortlandt for the purpose of seeing it erected as I designed it and for no other reason. That was the price I set for my work. I was not paid.

"I do not blame Peter Keating. He was helpless. He had a contract with his employers. It was ignored. He had a promise that the structure he offered would be built as designed. The promise was broken. The love of a man for the integrity of his work and his right to preserve it are now considered a vague intangible and an unessential. You have heard the prosecutor say that. Why was the building disfigured? For no reason. Such acts never have any reason, unless it's the vanity of some second-handers who feel they have a right to anyone's property, spiritual or material. Who permitted them to do it? No particular man among the dozens in authority. No one cared to permit it or to stop it. No one was responsible. No one can be held to account. Such is the nature of all collective action.

"I did not receive the payment I asked. But the owners of Cortlandt got what they needed from me. They wanted a scheme devised to build a structure as cheaply as possible. They found no one else who could do it to their satisfaction. I could and did. They took the benefit of my work and made me contribute it as a gift. But I am not an altruist. I do not contribute gifts of this nature.

"It is said that I have destroyed the home of the destitute. It is forgotten that but for me the destitute could not have had this particular home. Those who were concerned with the poor had to come to me, who have never been concerned, in order to help the poor. It is believed that the poverty of the future tenants gave them a right to my work. That their need constituted a claim on my life. That it was my duty to contribute anything demanded of me. This is the second-hander's credo now swallowing the world.

"I came here to say that I do not recognize anyone's right to one minute of my life. Nor to any part of my energy. Nor to any achievement of mine. No matter who makes the claim, how large their number or how great their need.

"I wished to come here and say that I am a man who does not exist for others.

"It had to be said. The world is perishing from an orgy of self-sacrificing.

"I wished to come here and say that the integrity of a man's creative work is of greater importance than any charitable endeavor. Those of you who do not understand this are the men who're destroying the world.

"I wished to come here and state my terms. I do not care to exist on any others.

"I recognize no obligations toward men except one: to respect their freedom and to take no part in a slave society. To my country, I wish to give the ten years which I will spend in jail if my country exists no longer. I will spend them in memory and in gratitude for what my country has been. It will be my act of loyalty, my refusal to live or work in what has taken its place.

"My act of loyalty to every creator who ever lived and was made to suffer by the force responsible for the Cortlandt I dynamited. To every tortured hour of loneliness, denial, frustration, abuse he was made to spend—and to the battles he won. To every creator whose name is known—and to every creator who lived, struggled and perished unrecognized before he could achieve. To every creator who was destroyed in body or in spirit. To Henry Cameron. To Steven Mallory. To a man who doesn't want to be named, but who is sitting in this courtroom and knows that I am speaking of him."

———

EDITOR'S NOTE: *This excerpt from* The Virtue of Selfishness *explains why AR called her ethics "selfishness."*

Why "Selfishness"?

THE TITLE of this book may evoke the kind of question that I hear once in a while: "Why do you use the word 'selfishness' to denote virtuous qualities of character, when that word antagonizes so many people to whom it does not mean the things you mean?"

To those who ask it, my answer is: "For the reason that makes you afraid of it."

But there are others, who would not ask that question, sensing the moral cowardice it implies, yet who are unable to formulate my actual reason or to identify the profound moral issue involved. It is to them that I will give a more explicit answer.

It is not a mere semantic issue nor a matter of arbitrary choice. The meaning ascribed in popular usage to the word "selfishness" is not merely wrong: it represents a devastating intellectual "package-deal," which is responsible, more than any other single factor, for the arrested moral development of mankind.

In popular usage, the word "selfishness" is a synonym of evil; the image it conjures is of a murderous brute who tramples over piles of corpses to achieve his own ends, who cares for no living being and pursues nothing but the gratification of the mindless whims of any immediate moment.

Yet the exact meaning and dictionary definition of the word "selfishness" is: *concern with one's own interests*.

This concept does *not* include a moral evaluation; it does not tell us whether concern with one's own interests is good or evil; nor does it tell us what constitutes man's actual interests. It is the task of ethics to answer such questions.

The ethics of altruism has created the image of the brute, as its answer, in order to make men accept two inhuman tenets: (a) that any concern with one's own interests is evil, regardless of what these interests might be, and (b) that the brute's activities are *in fact* to one's own interest (which altruism enjoins man to renounce for the sake of his neighbors).

For a view of the nature of altruism, its consequences and the enormity of the moral corruption it perpetrates, I shall refer you to *Atlas Shrugged*—or to any of today's newspaper headlines. What concerns us here is altruism's *default* in the field of ethical theory.

There are two moral questions which altruism lumps together into one "package-deal": (1) What are values? (2) Who should be the beneficiary of values? Altruism substitutes the second for the first; it evades the task of defining a code of moral values, thus leaving man, in fact, without moral guidance.

Altruism declares that any action taken for the benefit of others is good, and any action taken for one's own benefit is evil. Thus the *beneficiary* of an action is the only criterion of moral value—and so long as that beneficiary is anybody other than oneself, anything goes.

Hence the appalling immorality, the chronic injustice, the grotesque double standards, the insoluble conflicts and contradictions that have characterized human relationships and human societies throughout history, under all the variants of the altruist ethics.

Observe the indecency of what passes for moral judgments today. An industrialist who produces a fortune, and a gangster who robs a bank are regarded as equally immoral, since they both sought wealth for their own "selfish" benefit. A young man who gives up his career in order to support his parents and never rises beyond the rank of grocery clerk is regarded as morally superior to the young man who endures an excruciating struggle and achieves his personal ambition. A dictator is regarded as moral, since the unspeakable atrocities he committed were intended to benefit "the people," not himself.

Observe what this beneficiary-criterion of morality does to a man's life. The first thing he learns is that morality is his enemy; he has nothing to gain from it, he can only lose; self-inflicted loss, self-inflicted pain and the gray, debilitating pall of an incomprehensible duty is all that he can expect. He may hope that others might occasionally sacrifice themselves for his benefit, as he grudgingly sacrifices himself for theirs, but he knows that the relationship will bring mutual resentment, not pleasure—and that, morally, their pursuit of values will be like an exchange of unwanted, unchosen Christmas presents, which neither is morally permitted to buy for himself. Apart from such times as he manages to perform some act of self-sacrifice, he possesses no moral significance: morality takes no cognizance of him and has nothing to say to him for guidance in the crucial issues of his life; it is only his own personal, private, "selfish" life and, as such, it is regarded either as evil or, at best, *amoral.*

Since nature does not provide man with an automatic form of survival, since he has to support his life by his own effort, the doctrine that concern with one's own interests is evil means that man's desire to live is evil—that man's life, as such, is evil. No doctrine could be more evil than that.

Yet that is the meaning of altruism, implicit in such examples as the equation of an industrialist with a robber. There is a fundamental moral difference between a man who sees his self-interest in production and a man who sees it in robbery. The evil of a robber does *not* lie in the fact that he pursues his own interests, but in *what* he regards as to his own interest; *not* in the fact that he pursues his values, but in *what* he chose to value; *not* in the fact that he wants to live, but in the fact that he wants to live on a subhuman level (see "The Objectivist Ethics").

If it is true that what I mean by "selfishness" is not what is meant conventionally, then *this* is one of the worst indictments of altruism: it means that altruism *permits no concept* of a self-respecting, self-supporting man—a man who supports his life by his own effort and neither sacrifices himself nor others. It means that altruism permits no view of men except as sacrificial animals and profiteers-on-sacrifice, as victims and parasites—that it permits no concept of a benevolent co-existence among men—that it permits no concept of *justice*.

If you wonder about the reasons behind the ugly mixture of cynicism and guilt in which most men spend their lives, these are the reasons: cynicism, because they neither practice nor accept the altruist morality—guilt, because they dare not reject it.

To rebel against so devastating an evil, one has to rebel against its basic premise. To redeem both man and morality, it is the concept of *"selfishness"* that one has to redeem.

The first step is to assert *man's right to a moral existence*—that is: to recognize his need of a moral code to guide the course and the fulfillment of his own life.

For a brief outline of the nature and the validation of a rational morality, see my lecture on "The Objectivist Ethics" which follows. The reasons why man needs a moral code will tell you that the purpose of morality is to define man's proper values and interests, that *concern with his own interests* is the essence of a moral existence, and that *man must be the beneficiary of his own moral actions*.

Since all values have to be gained and/or kept by men's actions, any breach between actor and beneficiary necessitates an injustice: the sacrifice of some men to others, of the actors to the nonactors, of the moral to the immoral. Nothing could ever justify such a breach, and no one ever has.

The choice of the beneficiary of moral values is merely a preliminary or introductory issue in the field of morality. It is not a substitute for morality nor a criterion of moral value, as altruism has made it. Neither is it a moral *primary*: it has to be derived from and validated by the fundamental premises of a moral system.

The Objectivist ethics holds that the actor must always be the beneficiary of his action and that man must act for his own *rational* self-interest. But his right to do so is derived from his nature as man and from the function of moral values in human life—and, therefore, is applicable *only* in the context of a rational, objectively demonstrated and validated code of moral principles which define and determine his actual self-interest. It is not a license "to do as he pleases" and it is not applicable to the altruists' image of a "selfish" brute nor to any man motivated by irrational emotions, feelings, urges, wishes or whims.

This is said as a warning against the kind of "Nietzschean egoists" who, in fact, are a product of the altruist morality and represent the other side of the altruist coin: the men who believe that any action, regardless of its nature, is good if it is intended for one's own benefit. Just as the satisfaction of the irrational desires of others is *not* a criterion of moral value, neither is the satisfaction of one's own irrational desires. Morality is not a contest of whims.

A similar type of error is committed by the man who declares that since man must be guided by his own independent judgment, any action he chooses to take is moral if *he* chooses it. One's own independent judgment is the *means* by which one must choose one's actions, but it is not a moral criterion nor a moral validation: only reference to a demonstrable principle can validate one's choices.

Just as man cannot survive by any random means, but must discover and practice the principles which his survival requires, so man's self-interest cannot be determined by blind desires or random whims, but must be discovered and achieved by the guidance of rational principles. This is why the Objectivist ethics is a morality of *rational* self-interest—or of *rational selfishness*.

Since selfishness is "concern with one's own interests," the Objectivist ethics uses that concept in its exact and purest sense. It is not a concept that one can surrender to man's enemies, nor to the unthinking misconceptions, distortions, prejudices and fears of the ignorant and the irrational. The attack on "selfishness" is an attack on man's self-esteem; to surrender one, is to surrender the other. . . .

———————

EDITOR'S NOTE: *These selections from "The Objectivist Ethics," a talk given at the University of Wisconsin in 1961, discuss the fundamental issue of ethics: why man needs values at all—and, therefore, how ethics is grounded in the facts of reality.*

The Objectivist Ethics

SINCE I am to speak on the Objectivist Ethics, I shall begin by quoting its best representative—John Galt, in *Atlas Shrugged:*

"Through centuries of scourges and disasters, brought about by your code of morality, you have cried that your code had been broken, that the scourges were punishment for breaking it, that men were too weak and too selfish to spill all the blood it required. You damned man, you damned existence, you damned this earth, but never dared to question your code. . . . You went on crying that your code was noble, but human nature was not good enough to practice it. And no one rose to ask the question: Good?—by what standard?

"You wanted to know John Galt's identity. I am the man who has asked that question.

"Yes, this *is* an age of moral crisis. . . . Your moral code has reached its climax, the blind alley at the end of its course. And if you wish to go on living, what you now need is not to *return* to morality . . . but to *discover* it."

What is morality, or ethics? It is a code of values to guide man's choices and actions—the choices and actions that determine the purpose and the course of his life. Ethics, as a science, deals with discovering and defining such a code.

The first question that has to be answered, as a precondition of any attempt to define, to judge or to accept any specific system of ethics, is: *Why* does man need a code of values?

Let me stress this. The first question is not: What particular code of values should man accept? The first question is: Does man need values at all—and why?

Is the concept of *value*, of "good or evil" an arbitrary human invention, unrelated to, underived from and unsupported by any facts of reality—or is it based on a *metaphysical* fact, on an unalterable condition of man's existence? (I use the word "metaphysical" to mean: that which pertains to reality, to the nature of things, to existence.) Does an arbitrary human convention, a mere custom, decree that man must guide his actions by a set of principles—or is there a fact of reality that demands it? Is ethics the province of *whims*: of personal emotions, social edicts and mystic revelations—or is it the province of *reason*? Is ethics a subjective luxury—or an *objective* necessity?

In the sorry record of the history of mankind's ethics—with a few rare, and unsuccessful, exceptions—moralists have regarded ethics as the province of whims, that is: of the irrational. Some of them did so explicitly, by intention—others implicitly, by default. A "whim" is a desire experienced by a person who does not know and does not care to discover its cause.

No philosopher has given a rational, objectively demonstrable, scientific answer to the question of *why* man needs a code of values. So long as that question remained unanswered, no rational, scientific, *objective* code of ethics could be discovered or defined. The greatest of all philosophers, Aristotle, did not regard ethics as an exact science; he based his ethical system on observations of what the noble and wise men of his time chose to do, leaving unanswered the questions of: *why* they chose to do it and *why* he evaluated them as noble and wise.

Most philosophers took the existence of ethics for granted, as the given, as a historical fact, and were not concerned with discovering its metaphysical cause or objective validation. Many of them attempted to break the traditional monopoly of mysticism in the field of ethics and, allegedly, to define a rational, scientific, nonreligious morality. But their attempts consisted of trying to justify them on *social* grounds, merely substituting *society* for *God*.

The avowed mystics held the arbitrary, unaccountable "will of God" as the standard of the good and as the validation of their ethics. The neomystics replaced it with "the good of society," thus collapsing into the circularity of a definition such as "the standard of the good is that which is good for society." This meant, in logic—and, today, in worldwide practice—that "society" stands above any principles of ethics, since *it* is the source, standard and criterion of ethics, since "the good" is whatever *it* wills, whatever *it* happens to assert as its own welfare and pleasure. This meant that "society" may do anything it pleases, since "the good" is whatever it chooses to do *because* it chooses to do it. And—since there is no such entity as "society," since society is only a number of individual men—this meant that *some* men (the majority or any gang that claims to be its spokesman) are ethically entitled to pursue any whims (or any atrocities) they desire to pursue, while *other* men are ethically obliged to spend their lives in the service of that gang's desires.

This could hardly be called rational, yet most philosophers have now decided to declare that reason has failed, that ethics is outside the power of reason, that no rational ethics can ever be defined, and that in the field of ethics—in the choice of his values, of his actions, of his pursuits, of his life's goals—man must be guided by something other than reason. By what? Faith—instinct—intuition—revelation—feeling—taste—urge—wish—*whim*. Today, as in the past, most philosophers agree that the ultimate standard of ethics is *whim* (they call it "arbitrary postulate" or "subjective choice" or "emotional commitment")—and the battle is only over the question of *whose* whim: one's own or society's or the dictator's or God's. Whatever else they may disagree about, today's moralists agree that ethics is a *subjective* issue and that the three things barred from its field are: reason—mind—reality.

If you wonder why the world is now collapsing to a lower and ever lower rung of hell, *this* is the reason.

If you want to save civilization, it is *this* premise of modern ethics—and of all ethical history—that you must challenge.

To challenge the basic premise of any discipline, one must begin at the beginning. In ethics, one must begin by asking: What are *values?* Why does man need them?

"Value" is that which one acts to gain and/or keep. The concept "value" is not a primary; it presupposes an answer to the question: of value to *whom* and for *what?* It presupposes an entity capable of acting to achieve a goal in the face of an alternative. Where no alternative exists, no goals and no values are possible.

I quote from Galt's speech: "There is only one fundamental alternative in the universe: existence or nonexistence—and it pertains to a single class of entities: to living organisms. The existence of inanimate matter is unconditional, the existence of life is not: it depends on a specific course of action. Matter is indestructible, it changes its forms, but it cannot cease to exist. It is only a living organism that faces a constant alternative: the issue of life or death. Life is a process of self-sustaining and self-generated action. If an organism fails in that action, it dies; its chemical elements remain, but its life goes out of existence. It is only the concept of 'Life' that makes the concept of 'Value' possible. It is only to a living entity that things can be good or evil."

To make this point fully clear, try to imagine an immortal, indestructible robot, an entity which moves and acts, but which cannot be affected by anything, which cannot be changed in any respect, which cannot be damaged, injured or destroyed. Such an entity would not be able to have any values; it would have nothing to gain or to lose; it could not regard anything as *for* or *against* it, as serving or threatening its welfare, as fulfilling or frustrating its interests. It could have no interests and no goals.

Only a *living* entity can have goals or can originate them. And it is only a living organism that has the capacity for self-generated, goal-directed action. On the *physical* level, the functions of all living organisms, from the simplest to the most complex—from the nutritive function in the single cell of an amoeba to the blood circulation in the body of a man—are actions generated by the organism itself and directed to a single goal: the maintenance of the organism's life.*

An organism's life depends on two factors: the material or fuel which it needs from the outside, from its physical background, and the action of its own body, the action of using that fuel *properly*. What standard determines what is *proper* in this context? The standard is the organism's life, or: that which is required for the organism's survival.

No choice is open to an organism in this issue: that which is required for its survival is determined by its *nature*, by the kind of entity it *is*. Many variations, many forms of adaptation to its background are possible to an organism, including the possibility of existing for a while in a crippled, disabled or diseased condition, but the fundamental alternative of its existence remains the same: if an organism fails in the basic functions required by its nature—if an amoeba's protoplasm stops assimilating food, or if a man's heart stops beating—the organism dies. In a fundamental sense, stillness is the antithesis of life. Life can be kept in existence only by a constant process of self-sustaining action. The goal of that action, the ultimate *value* which, to be kept, must be gained through its every moment, is the organism's *life*.

An *ultimate* value is that final goal or end to which all lesser goals are the means—and it sets the standard by which all lesser goals are *evaluated*. An organism's life is its *standard of value*: that which furthers its life is the *good*, that which threatens it is the *evil*.

Without an ultimate goal or end, there can be no lesser goals or means: a series of means going off into an infinite progression toward a nonexistent end is a metaphysical and epistemological impossibil-

---

*When applied to physical phenomena, such as the automatic functions of an organism, the term "goal-directed" is not to be taken to mean "purposive" (a concept applicable only to the actions of a consciousness) and is not to imply the existence of any teleological principle operating in insentient nature. I use the term "goal-directed," in this context, to designate the fact that the automatic functions of living organisms are actions whose nature is such that they *result* in the preservation of an organism's life.

ity. It is only an ultimate goal, an *end in itself*, that makes the existence of values possible. Metaphysically, *life* is the only phenomenon that is an end in itself: a value gained and kept by a constant process of action. Epistemologically, the concept of "value" is genetically dependent upon and derived from the antecedent concept of "life." To speak of "value" as apart from "life" is worse than a contradiction in terms. "It is only the concept of 'Life' that makes the concept of 'Value' possible."

In answer to those philosophers who claim that no relation can be established between ultimate ends or values and the facts of reality, let me stress that the fact that living entities exist and function necessitates the existence of values and of an ultimate value which for any given living entity is its own life. Thus the validation of value judgments is to be achieved by reference to the facts of reality. The fact that a living entity *is*, determines what it *ought* to do. So much for the issue of the relation between "*is*" and "*ought*." [. . .]

Man has no automatic code of survival. He has no automatic course of action, no automatic set of values. His senses do not tell him automatically what is good for him or evil, what will benefit his life or endanger it, what goals he should pursue and what means will achieve them, what *values* his life depends on, what course of action it requires. His own consciousness has to discover the answers to all these questions—but his consciousness will not function *automatically*. Man, the highest living species on this earth—the being whose consciousness has a limitless capacity for gaining knowledge—man is the only living entity born without any guarantee of *remaining* conscious at all. Man's particular distinction from all other living species is the fact that *his* consciousness is *volitional*.

Just as the automatic values directing the functions of a plant's body are sufficient for its survival, but are not sufficient for an animal's—so the automatic values provided by the sensory-perceptual mechanism of its consciousness are sufficient to guide an animal, but are not sufficient for man. Man's actions and survival require the guidance of *conceptual* values derived from *conceptual* knowledge. But *conceptual* knowledge cannot be acquired *automatically*.

A "*concept*" is a mental integration of two or more perceptual concretes, which are isolated by a process of *abstraction* and united by means of a specific definition. Every word of man's language, with the exception of proper names, denotes a *concept*, an abstraction that stands for an unlimited number of concretes of a specific kind. It is by organizing his perceptual material into concepts, and his concepts into wider and still wider concepts that man is able to grasp and retain, to identify and integrate an unlimited amount of knowledge, a knowledge extending beyond the immediate perceptions of any given, immediate moment. Man's sense organs function automatically; man's brain integrates his sense data into percepts automatically; but the process of integrating percepts into concepts—the process of abstraction and of concept-formation—is *not* automatic.

The process of concept-formation does not consist merely of grasping a few simple abstractions, such as "chair," "table," "hot," "cold," and of learning to speak. It consists of a method of using one's consciousness, best designated by the term "conceptualizing." It is not a passive state of registering random impressions. It is an actively sustained process of identifying one's impressions in conceptual terms, of integrating every event and every observation into a conceptual context, of grasping relationships, differences, similarities in one's perceptual material and of abstracting them into new concepts, of drawing inferences, of making deductions, of reaching conclusions, of asking new questions and discovering new answers and expanding one's knowledge into an ever-growing sum. The faculty that directs this process, the faculty that works by means of concepts, is: *reason.* The process is *thinking*.

Reason is the faculty that identifies and integrates the material provided by man's senses. It is a faculty that man has to exercise *by choice*. Thinking is not an automatic function. In any hour and issue of his life, man is free to think or to evade that effort. Thinking requires a state of full, focused awareness. The act of focusing one's consciousness is volitional. Man can focus his mind to a full, active, purposefully directed awareness of reality—or he can unfocus it and let himself drift in a semiconscious daze, merely reacting to any chance stimulus of the immediate moment, at the mercy of his undirected sensory-perceptual mechanism and of any random, associational connections it might happen to make.

When man unfocuses his mind, he may be said to be conscious in a subhuman sense of the word, since he experiences sensations and perceptions. But in the sense of the word applicable to man—in the sense of a consciousness which is aware of reality and able to deal with it, a consciousness able to direct the actions and provide for the survival of a human being—an unfocused mind is *not* conscious.

Psychologically, the choice "to think or not" is the choice "to focus or not." Existentially, the choice "to focus or not" is the choice "to be conscious or not." Metaphysically, the choice "to be conscious or not" is the choice of life or death.

Consciousness—for those living organisms which possess it—is the basic means of survival. For man, the basic means of survival is *reason*. Man cannot survive, as animals do, by the guidance of mere percepts. A sensation of hunger will tell him that he needs food (if he has learned to identify it as "hunger"), but it will not tell him how to obtain his food and it will not tell him what food is good for him or poisonous. He cannot provide for his simplest physical needs without a process of thought. He needs a process of thought to discover how to plant and grow his food or how to make weapons for hunting. His percepts might lead him to a cave, if one is available—but to build the simplest shelter, he needs a process of thought. No percepts and no "instincts" will tell him how to light a fire, how to weave cloth, how to forge tools, how to make a wheel, how to make an airplane, how to perform an appendectomy, how to produce an electric light bulb or an electronic tube or a cyclotron or a box of matches. Yet his life depends on such knowledge—and only a volitional act of his consciousness, a process of thought, can provide it.

But man's responsibility goes still further: a process of thought is not automatic nor "instinctive" nor involuntary—nor *infalliable*. Man has to initiate it, to sustain it and to bear responsibility for its results. He has to discover how to tell what is true or false and how to correct his own errors; he has to discover how to validate his concepts, his conclusions, his knowledge; he has to discover the rules of thought, *the laws of logic*, to direct his thinking. Nature gives him no automatic guarantee of the efficacy of his mental effort.

Nothing is given to man on earth except a potential and the material on which to actualize it. The potential is a superlative machine: his consciousness; but it is a machine without a spark plug, a machine of which his own will has to be the spark plug, the self-starter and the driver; *he* has to discover how to use it and *he* has to keep it in constant action. The material is the whole of the universe, with no limits set to the knowledge he can acquire and to the enjoyment of life he can achieve. But everything he needs or desires has to be learned, discovered and produced by *him*—by his own choice, by his own effort, by his own mind.

A being who does not know automatically what is true or false, cannot know automatically what is right or wrong, what is good for him or evil. Yet he needs that knowledge in order to live. He is not exempt from the laws of reality, he is a specific organism of a specific nature that requires specific actions to sustain his life. He cannot achieve his survival by arbitrary means nor by random motions nor by blind urges nor by chance nor by whim. That which his survival requires is set by his nature and is not open to his choice. What *is* open to his choice is only whether he will discover it or not, whether he will choose the right goals and *values* or not. He is free to make the wrong choice, but not free to succeed with it. He is free to evade reality, he is free to unfocus his mind and stumble blindly down any road he pleases, but not free to avoid the abyss he refuses to see. Knowledge, for any conscious organism, is the means of survival; to a living consciousness, every *"is"* implies an *"ought."* Man is free to choose not to be conscious, but not free to escape the penalty of unconsciousness: destruction. Man is the only living species that has the power to act as his own destroyer—and that is the way he has acted through most of his history.

What, then, are the right goals for man to pursue? What are the values his survival requires? That is the question to be answered by the science of *ethics*. And *this*, ladies and gentlemen, is why man needs a code of ethics.

Now you can assess the meaning of the doctrines which tell you that ethics is the province of the irrational, that reason cannot guide man's life, that his goals and values should be chosen by vote or by whim—that ethics has nothing to do with reality, with existence, with one's practical actions and concerns—or that the goal of ethics is beyond the grave, that the dead need ethics, not the living.

Ethics is *not* a mystic fantasy—nor a social convention—nor a dispensable, subjective luxury, to be switched or discarded in any emergency. Ethics is an *objective, metaphysical necessity of man's survival*—not by the grace of the supernatural nor of your neighbors nor of your whims, but by the grace of reality and the nature of life.

I quote from Galt's speech: "Man has been called a rational being, but rationality is a matter of choice—and the alternative his nature offers him is: rational being or suicidal animal. Man has to be man—by choice; he has to hold his life as a value—by choice; he has to learn to sustain it—by choice; he has to discover the values it requires and practice his virtues—by choice. A code of values accepted by choice is a code of morality."

The standard of value of the Objectivist ethics—the standard by which one judges what is good or evil—is *man's life*, or: that which is required for man's survival *qua* man.

Since reason is man's basic means of survival, that which is proper to the life of a rational being is the good; that which negates, opposes or destroys it is the evil.

Since everything man needs has to be discovered by his own mind and produced by his own effort, the two essentials of the method of survival proper to a rational being are: thinking and productive work. [. . .]

[T]he Objectivist ethics is the morality of life—as against the three major schools of ethical theory, the mystic, the social, the subjective, which have brought the world to its present state and which represent the morality of death.

These three schools differ only in their method of approach, not in their content. In content, they are merely variants of altruism, the ethical theory which regards man as a sacrificial animal, which holds that man has no right to exist for his own sake, that service to others is the only justification of his existence, and that self-sacrifice is his highest moral duty, virtue and value. The differences occur only over the question of who is to be sacrificed to whom. Altruism holds *death* as its ultimate goal and standard of value—and it is logical that renunciation, resignation, self-denial, and every other form of suffering, including self-destruction, are the virtues it advocates. And, logically, these are the only things that the practitioners of altruism have achieved and are achieving now.

Observe that these three schools of ethical theory are anti-life, not merely in content, but also in their method of approach.

The mystic theory of ethics is explicitly based on the premise that the standard of value of man's ethics is set beyond the grave, by the laws or requirements of another, supernatural dimension, that ethics is impossible for man to practice, that it is unsuited for and opposed to man's life on earth, and that man must take the blame for it and suffer through the whole of his earthly existence, to atone for the guilt of being unable to practice the impracticable. The Dark Ages and the Middle Ages are the existential monument to *this* theory of ethics.

The social theory of ethics substitutes "society" for God—and although it claims that its chief concern is life on earth, it is *not* the life of man, not the life of an individual, but the life of a disembodied entity, *the collective*, which, in relation to every individual, consists of everybody except himself. As far as the individual is concerned, *his* ethical duty is to be the selfless, voiceless, rightless slave of any need, claim or demand asserted by others. The motto "dog eat dog"—which is *not* applicable to capitalism nor to dogs—*is* applicable to the social theory of ethics. The existential monuments to *this* theory are Nazi Germany and Soviet Russia.

The subjectivist theory of ethics is, strictly speaking, not a theory, but a negation of ethics. And more: it is a negation of reality, a negation not merely of man's existence, but of *all* existence. Only the concept of a fluid, plastic, indeterminate, Heraclitean universe could permit anyone to think or to preach that man needs no *objective* principles of action—that reality gives him a blank check on values—that anything he cares to pick as the good or the evil, will do—that a man's whim is a valid moral standard, and that the only question is how to get away with it. The existential monument to *this* theory is the present state of our culture.

It is not men's *immorality* that is responsible for the collapse now threatening to destroy the civilized world, but the kind of *moralities* men have been asked to practice. The responsibility belongs to the philosophers of altruism. They have no cause to be shocked by the spectacle of their own success, and no right to damn human nature: men have obeyed them and have brought their moral ideals into full reality.

It is philosophy that sets men's goals and determines their course; it is only philosophy that can save them now. Today, the world is facing a choice: if civilization is to survive, it is the altruist morality that men have to reject.

I will close with the words of John Galt, which I address, as he did, to all the moralists of altruism, past or present:

"You have been using fear as your weapon and have been bringing death to man as his punishment for rejecting your morality. We offer him life as his reward for accepting ours."

2. Anti-Altruism

This selection from Atlas Shrugged *(published in 1957) is a more detailed discussion, by the novel's hero, John Galt, of the meaning and consequences of altruism.*

From Galt's Speech

"WHOEVER IS now within reach of my voice, whoever is man the victim, not man the killer, I am speaking at the deathbed of your mind, at the brink of that darkness in which you're drowning, and if there still remains within you the power to struggle to hold on to those fading sparks which had been yourself—use it now. The word that has destroyed you is '*sacrifice*.' Use the last of your strength to understand its meaning. You're still alive. You have a chance.

" 'Sacrifice' does not mean the rejection of the worthless, but of the precious. 'Sacrifice' does not mean the rejection of the evil for the sake of the good, but of the good for the sake of the evil. 'Sacrifice' is the surrender of that which you value in favor of that which you don't.

"If you exchange a penny for a dollar, it is *not* a sacrifice; if you exchange a dollar for a penny, it *is*. If you achieve a career you wanted, after years of struggle, it is *not* a sacrifice; if you then renounce it for the sake of a rival, it *is*. If you own a bottle of milk and gave it to your starving child, it is *not* a sacrifice; if you give it to your neighbor's child and let your own die, it *is*.

"If you give money to help a friend, it is *not* a sacrifice; if you give it to a worthless stranger, it *is*. If you give your friend a sum you can afford, it is *not* a sacrifice; if you give him money at the cost of your own discomfort, it is only a partial virtue, according to this sort of moral standard; if you give him money at the cost of disaster to yourself—*that* is the virtue of sacrifice in full.

"If you renounce all personal desire and dedicate your life to those you love, you do not achieve full virtue: you still retain a value of your own, which is your love. If you devote your life to random strangers, it is an act of greater virtue. If you devote your life to serving men you hate—*that* is the greatest of the virtues you can practice.

"A sacrifice is the surrender of a value. Full sacrifice is full surrender of all values. If you wish to achieve full virtue, you must seek no gratitude in return for your sacrifice, no praise, no love, no admiration, no self-esteem, not even the pride of being virtuous; the faintest trace of any gain dilutes your virtue. If you pursue a course of action that does not taint your life by any joy, that brings you no value in matter, no value in spirit, no gain, no profit, no reward—if you achieve this state of total zero, you have achieved the ideal of moral perfection.

"You are told that moral perfection is impossible to man—and, by this standard, it is. You cannot achieve it so long as you live, but the value of your life and of your persons is gauged by how closely you succeed in approaching that ideal zero which is *death*.

"If you start, however, as a passionless blank, as a vegetable seeking to be eaten, with no values to reject and no wishes to renounce, you will not win the crown of sacrifice. It is not a sacrifice to renounce the unwanted. It is not a sacrifice to give your life for others, if death is your personal desire. To achieve the virtue of sacrifice, you must want to live, you must love it, you must burn with passion for this earth and for all the splendor it can give you—you must feel the twist of every knife as it slashes your desires away from your reach and drains your love out of your body. It is not mere death that the morality of sacrifice holds out to you as an ideal, but death by slow torture.

"Do not remind me that it pertains only to this life on earth. I am concerned with no other. Neither are you.

"If you wish to save the last of your dignity, do not call your best actions a 'sacrifice': that term brands you as immoral. If a mother buys food for her hungry child rather than a hat for herself, it is *not* a sacrifice: she values the child higher than the hat; but it is a sacrifice to the kind of mother whose higher value is the hat, who would prefer her child to starve and feeds him only from a sense of duty. If a man dies fighting for his own freedom, it is *not* a sacrifice: he is not willing to live as a slave; but it *is* a sacrifice to the kind of man who's willing. If a man refuses to sell his convictions, it is *not* a sacrifice, unless he is the sort of man who has no convictions.

"Sacrifice could be proper only for those who have nothing to sacrifice—no values, no standards, no judgment—those whose desires are irrational whims, blindly conceived and lightly surrendered. For a man of moral stature, whose desires are born of rational values, sacrifice is the surrender of the right to the wrong, of the good to the evil.

"The creed of sacrifice is a morality for the immoral—a morality that declares its own bankruptcy by confessing that it can't impart to men any personal stake in virtues or value, and that their souls are sewers of depravity, which they must be taught to sacrifice. By his own confession, it is impotent to teach men to be good and can only subject them to constant punishment.

"Are you thinking, in some foggy stupor, that it's only *material* values that your morality requires you to sacrifice? And *what* do you think are material values? Matter has no value except as a means for the satisfaction of human desires. Matter is only a tool of human values. To what service are you asked to give the material tools your virtue has produced? To the service of that which *you* regard as evil: to a principle you do not share, to a person you do not respect, to the achievement of a purpose opposed to your own—else your gift is *not* a sacrifice.

"Your morality tells you to renounce the material world and to divorce your values from matter. A man whose values are given no expression in material form, whose existence is unrelated to his ideals, whose actions contradict his convictions, is a cheap little hypocrite—yet *that* is the man who obeys your morality and divorces his values from matter. The man who loves one woman, but sleeps with another—the man who admires the talent of a worker, but hires another—the man who considers one cause to be just, but donates his money to the support of another—the man who holds high standards of craftsmanship, but devotes his effort to the production of trash—*these* are the men who have renounced matter, the men who believe that the values of their spirit cannot be brought into material reality.

"Do you say it is the spirit that such men have renounced? Yes, of course. You cannot have one without the other. You are an indivisible entity of matter and consciousness. Renounce your consciousness and you become a brute. Renounce your body and you become a fake. Renounce the material world and you surrender it to evil.

"And *that* is precisely the goal of your morality, the duty that your code demands of you. Give to that which you do not enjoy, serve that which you do not admire, submit to that which you consider evil—surrender the world to the values of others, deny, reject, renounce your *self*. Your self is your *mind*: renounce it and you become a chunk of meat ready for any cannibal to swallow.

"It is your *mind* that they want you to surrender—all those who preach the creed of sacrifice, whatever their tags or their motives, whether they demand it for the sake of your soul or of your body, whether they promise you another life in heaven or a full stomach on this earth. Those who start by saying: 'It is selfish to pursue your own wishes, you must sacrifice them to the wishes of others'—end up by saying: 'It is selfish to uphold your convictions, you must sacrifice them to the convictions of others.'

"This much is true: the most *selfish* of all things is the independent mind that recognizes no authority higher than its own and no value higher than its judgment of truth. You are asked to sacrifice your intellectual integrity, your logic, your reason, your standard of truth—in favor of becoming a prostitute whose standard is the greatest good for the greatest number.

"If you search your code for guidance, for an answer to the question: 'What *is* the good?'—the only answer you will find is *'The good of others.'* The good is whatever others wish, whatever you feel they feel they wish, or whatever you feel they ought to feel. 'The good of others' is a magic formula that transforms anything into gold, a formula to be recited as a guarantee of moral glory and as a fumigator for any action, even the slaughter of a continent. Your standard of virtue is not an object, not an act, not a principle, but an *intention*. You need no proof, no reasons, no success, you need not achieve *in fact* the good of others—all you need to know is that your motive was the good of others, *not* your own. Your only definition of the good is a negation: the good is the 'non-good for me.'

"Your code—which boasts that it upholds eternal, absolute, objective moral values and scorns the conditional, the relative and the subjective—your code hands out, as its version of the absolute, the following rule of moral conduct: If *you* wish it, it's evil; if others wish it, it's good; if the motive of your action is *your* welfare, don't do it; if the motive is the welfare of others, then anything goes.

"As this double-jointed, double-standard morality splits you in half, so it splits mankind into two enemy camps: one is *you*, the other is all the rest of humanity. *You* are the only outcast who has no right to wish to live. *You* are the only servant, the rest are the masters, *you* are the only giver, the rest are the takers, *you* are the eternal debtor, the rest are the creditors never to be paid off. You must not question their right to your sacrifice, or the nature of their wishes and their needs: their right is conferred upon them by a negative, by the fact that they are 'non-you.'

"For those of you who might ask questions, your code provides a consolation prize and booby-trap: it is for your own happiness, it says, that you must serve the happiness of others, the only way to achieve your joy is to give it up to others, the only way to achieve your prosperity is to surrender your wealth to others, the only way to protect your life is to protect all men except yourself—and if you find no joy in this procedure, it is your own fault and the proof of your evil; if you were good, you would find your happiness in providing a banquet for others, and your dignity in existing on such crumbs as *they* might care to toss you.

"You who have no standard of self-esteem, accept the guilt and dare not ask the questions. But you know the unadmitted answer, refusing to acknowledge what you see, what hidden premise moves your world. You know it, not in honest statement, but as a dark uneasiness within you, while you flounder between guilty cheating and grudgingly practicing a principle too vicious to name.

"I, who do not accept the unearned, neither in values nor in *guilt*, am here to ask the questions you evaded. Why is it moral to serve the happiness of others, but not your own? If enjoyment is a value, why is it moral when experienced by others, but immoral when experienced by you? If the sensation of eating a cake is a value, why is it an immoral indulgence in your stomach, but a moral goal for you to achieve in the stomach of others? Why is it immoral for you to desire, but moral for others to do so? Why is it immoral to produce a value and keep it, but moral to give it away? And if it is not moral for you to keep a value, why is it moral for others to accept it? If you are selfless and virtuous when you give it, are they not selfish and vicious when they take it? Does virtue consist of serving vice? Is the moral purpose of those who are good, self-immolation for the sake of those who are evil?

"The answer you evade, the monstrous answer is: No, the takers are not evil, provided they did not *earn* the value you gave them. It is not immoral for them to accept it, provided they are unable to produce it, unable to deserve it, unable to give you any value in return. It is not immoral for them to enjoy it, provided they do not obtain it *by right*.

"Such is the secret core of your creed, the other half of your double standard: it is immoral to live by your own effort, but moral to live by the effort of others—it is immoral to consume your own product, but moral to consume the products of others—it is immoral to earn, but moral to mooch—it is the parasites who are the moral justification for the existence of the producers, but the existence of the parasites is an end in itself—it is evil to profit by achievement, but good to profit by sacrifice—it is evil to create your own happiness, but good to enjoy it at the price of the blood of others.

"Your code divides mankind into two castes and commands them to live by opposite rules: those who may desire anything and those who may desire nothing, the chosen and the damned, the riders and the carriers, the eaters and the eaten. What standard determines your caste? What passkey admits you to the moral elite? The passkey is *lack of value*.

"Whatever the value involved, it is your lack of it that gives you a claim upon those who don't lack it. It is your *need* that gives you a claim to rewards. If you are able to satisfy your need, your ability annuls your right to satisfy it. But a need you are *unable* to satisfy gives you first right to the lives of mankind.

"If you succeed, any man who fails is your master; if you fail, any man who succeeds is your serf. Whether your failure is just or not whether your wishes are rational or not, whether your misfortune is undeserved or the result of your vices, it is *misfortune* that gives you a right to rewards. It is *pain*, regardless of its nature or cause, pain as a primary absolute, that gives you a mortgage on all of existence.

"If you heal your pain by your own effort, you receive no moral credit: your code regards it scornfully as an act of self-interest. Whatever value you seek to acquire, be it wealth or food or love or rights, if you acquire it by means of your virtue, your code does not regard it as a moral acquisition: you occasion no loss to anyone, it is a trade, not alms; a payment, not a sacrifice. The *deserved* belongs in the selfish, commercial realm of mutual profit; it is only the *undeserved* that calls for that moral transaction which consists of profit to one at the price of disaster to the other. To demand rewards for your virtue is selfish and immoral; it is your *lack of virtue* that transforms your demand into a moral right.

"A morality that holds *need* as a claim, holds emptiness—nonexistence—as its standard of value; it rewards an *absence*, a defeat: weakness, inability, incompetence, suffering, disease, disaster, the lack, the fault, the flaw—the *zero*.

"Who provides the account to pay these claims? Those who are cursed for being non-zeros, each to the extent of his distance from that ideal. Since all values are the product of virtues, the degree of your virtue is used as the measure of your penalty; the degree of your faults is used as the measure of your gain. Your code declares that the rational man must sacrifice himself to the irrational, the independent man to parasites, the honest man to the dishonest, the man of justice to the unjust, the productive man to thieving loafers, the man of integrity to compromising knaves, the man of self-esteem to sniveling neurotics. Do you wonder at the meanness of soul in those you see around you? The man who achieves these virtues will not accept your moral code; the man who accepts your moral code will not achieve these virtues.

"Under a morality of sacrifice, the first value you sacrifice is morality; the next is self-esteem. When need is the standard, every man is both victim and parasite. As a victim, he must labor to fill the needs of others, leaving himself in the position of a parasite whose needs must be filled by others. He cannot approach his fellow men except in one of two disgraceful roles: he is both a beggar and a sucker.

"You fear the man who has a dollar less than you, that dollar is rightfully his, he makes you feel like a moral defrauder. You hate the man who has a dollar more than you, that dollar is rightfully yours, he makes you feel that you are morally defrauded. The man below is a source of your guilt, the man above is a source of your frustrations. You do not know what to surrender or demand, when to give and when to grab, what pleasure in life is rightfully yours and what debt is still unpaid to others—you struggle to evade, as 'theory,' the knowledge that by the moral standard you've accepted you are guilty every moment of your life, there is no mouthful of food you swallow that is not *needed* by someone somewhere on earth—and you give up the problem in blind resentment, you conclude that moral perfection is not to be achieved or *desired*, that you will muddle through by snatching as snatch can and by avoiding the eyes of the young, of those who look at you as if self-esteem were possible and they expected you to have it. Guilt is all that you retain within your soul—and so does every other man, as he goes past, avoiding *your* eyes. Do you wonder why your morality has not achieved brotherhood on earth or the good will of man to man?

"The justification of sacrifice, that your morality propounds, is more corrupt than the corruption it purports to justify. The motive of your sacrifice, it tells you, should be *love*—the love you ought to feel for every man. A morality that professes the belief that the values of the spirit are more precious than matter, a morality that teaches you to scorn a whore who gives her body indiscriminately to all men—this same morality demands that you surrender your soul to promiscuous love for all comers.

"As there can be no causeless wealth, so there can be no causeless love or any sort of causeless emotion. An emotion is a response to a fact of reality, an estimate dictated by your standards. To love is to *value*. The man who tells you that it is possible to value without values, to love those whom you appraise as worthless, is the man who tells you that it is possible to grow rich by consuming without producing and that paper money is as valuable as gold.

"Observe that he does not expect you to feel a causeless fear. When his kind get into power, they are expert at contriving means of terror, at giving you ample cause to feel the fear by which they desire to rule you. But when it comes to love, the highest of emotions, you permit them to shriek at you accusingly that you are a moral delinquent if you're incapable of feeling causeless love. When a man feels fear without reason, you call him to the attention of a psychiatrist; you are not so careful to protect the meaning, the nature and the dignity of love.

"Love is the expression of one's values, the greatest reward you can earn for the moral qualities you have achieved in your character and person, the emotional price paid by one man for the joy he receives from the virtues of another. Your morality demands that you divorce your love from values and hand it down to any vagrant, not as response to his worth, but as response to his *need*, not as reward, but as alms, not as a payment for virtues, but as a blank check on vices. Your morality tells you that the purpose of love is to set you free of the bonds of morality, that love is superior to moral judgment; that true love transcends, forgives and survives every manner of evil in its object, and the greater the love the greater the depravity it permits to the loved. To love a man for his virtues is paltry and human, it tells you; to love him for his flaws is divine. To love those who are worthy of it is self-interest; to love the unworthy is sacrifice. You owe your love to those who don't deserve it, and the less they deserve it, the more love you owe them—the more loathsome the object, the nobler your love—the more unfastidious your love, the greater the virtue— and if you can bring your soul to the state of a dump heap that welcomes anything on equal terms, if you can cease to value moral values, you have achieved the state of moral perfection.

"Such is your morality of sacrifice and such are the twin ideals it offers: to refashion the life of your body in the image of a human stockyard, and the life of your spirit in the image of a dump.

"Such was your goal—and you've reached it. Why do you now moan complaints about man's impotence and the futility of human aspirations? Because you were unable to prosper by seeking destruction? Because you were unable to find joy by worshipping pain? Because you were unable to live by holding death as your standard of value?

"The degree of your ability to live was the degree to which you broke your moral code, yet you believe that those who preach it are friends of humanity, you damn yourself and dare not question their motives or their goals. Take a look at them now, when you face your last choice—and if you choose to perish, do so with full knowledge of how cheaply so small an enemy has claimed your life. . . .

EDITOR'S NOTE: *The following essay was written in 1974 for* The Ayn Rand Letter, *a biweekly journal published between 1971 and 1976. The essay shows the connection between altruism and America's moral decay, one symptom of which is the introduction of "affirmative action" programs. The "National Day of Humiliation" was a 1973 Senate resolution, passed without opposition, calling for America to "humble [itself] before almighty God."*

Moral Inflation

HERE ARE some of the things that men had to evade in order to think up a moral atrocity such as a "National Day of Humiliation."

Self-abasement is the antithesis of morality. If a man has acted immorally, but regrets it and wants to atone for it, it is not self-abasement that prompts him, but some remnant of love for moral values—and it is not self-abasement that he expresses, but a longing to regain his self-esteem. Humility is not a recognition of one's failings, but a rejection of morality. "I am no good" is a statement that may be uttered only in the past tense. To say: "I am no good" is to declare: "—and I never intend to be any better."

One can feel nothing but mistrust, disgust and contempt for a man who spits in his own face. To drag others along into the same degradation and spit in the face of one's own country, is as base an affront to morality as can be imagined. Yet this has been the policy of American intellectuals for many decades. That it is now adopted by a Senator and approved "with no debate or opposition" by the U.S. Senate, is a measure of the extent to which moral proclamations and moral *principles* are not taken seriously by today's public leaders.

One may disapprove of one's country's policies, one may disagree with most or with all of its citizens, one may seek to change, reform or improve particular laws, conditions or trends; and if one finds an entire country so evil that it deserves damnation, one must leave it. But to stay here and to damn this country—*this country!*—on such phony, trashy allegations as "acquiescence [?] to corruption and waste [!!]" is to step out of any moral bounds.

What effect did the sponsors of that resolution expect it to have on the American people?

There still are people in this country who lost loved ones in World War I. There are more people who carry the unhealed wounds of World War II, of Korea, of Vietnam. There are the disabled, the crippled, the mangled of those wars' battlefields. No one has ever told them why they had to fight nor what their sacrifices accomplished; it was certainly not "to make the world safe for democracy"—look at that world now. The American people have borne it all, trusting their leaders, hoping that someone knew the purpose of that ghastly devastation. The United States gained nothing from those wars, except the growing burden of paying reparations to the whole world—the kind of burden that used to be imposed on a defeated nation.

People have borne patiently the unending drain of their wealth, their effort, their standard of living—first, to help the unemployed of the New Deal era, then the war allies, then the former enemies, and now the unemployables of the entire globe. People have seen and read enough to know the subhuman squalor of human existence in other countries and the atrocities to which men submit. In their innocent, foolishly overgenerous benevolence, the American people have been willing to help, knowing that *theirs* is the greatest country on this ravaged earth, a blessed oasis in a desert of bloody savagery.

Then to hear a proclamation of their country's self-abasement—in this day of raucously chauvinistic boasting, when every racist tribe in every backyard of the globe, from Albania to Uganda, is proclaiming the uniquely sanctified value of the non-achievements of its non-culture—to hear that they, the American people, have not done enough and that their reward is a "National Day of Humiliation," is more than human beings should be asked to bear or understand. If, under a leadership of this kind, people are losing respect for morality and crumbling into cynicism, bitterness, helpless anger, or blind hatred—can one blame them?

Yet the altruist morality dictates such policies to the nation's leaders. Even though altruism declares that "it is more blessed to give than to receive," it does not work that way in practice. The givers are never blessed; the more they give, the more is demanded of them; complaints, reproaches and insults are the only response they get for practicing altruism's virtues (or for their *actual* virtues). Altruism cannot permit a recognition of virtue; it cannot permit self-esteem or moral innocence. Guilt is altruism's stock in trade, and the inducing of guilt is its only means of self-perpetuation. If the giver is not kept under a torrent of degrading, demeaning accusations, he might take a look around and put an end to the self-sacrificing.

Altruists are concerned only with those who suffer—not with those who provide relief from suffering, not even enough to care whether they are able to survive. When no actual suffering can be found, the altruists are compelled to invent or manufacture it. Observe their admission that, compared to the rest of the world, people do not suffer from real poverty in this country—they suffer from *relative* poverty (i.e., from envy). Observe that with the inflation of altruism into a government policy—with public cash and legislative favors pouring upon the pressure groups of newly minted sufferers—the proper, basic functions of the government are crumbling, corroded by neglect and "lack of funds" (!). Yet these are the functions required for the survival of the givers, who carry all the rest on their shoulders and are the greatest victims of altruistic exploitation: the middle class.

These basic functions are: the police, the law courts, the military. (These represent the only moral justification for the existence of a government: the protection of individual rights, i.e., the protection of individual citizens from the initiators of physical force.) What is the state of these governmental functions today?

Observe the conditions of an average American's existence. He has lost the most rudimentary form of protection: the safety of city streets. He is in danger on his way to work in the morning, and on his way home; he is in danger if he steps out of the house after dark; his family are in danger if they go shopping, visiting, or walking in a public park. They dare not ride the subway, yet they are threatened with the loss of their safest transportation: their car. Criminal attacks are a daily occurrence, any time, any place: purse-snatching, mugging, burglary, rape, murder. The police are helpless: they have been brought close to impotence by impossible rules, which protect the "*rights*" of the criminals. The policemen struggle on as best they can, but they admit bitterly that there is little they can do: they risk their lives to arrest a thug, but the courts set him free.

The average man cannot seek redress in court, whether in criminal or civil matters: he cannot afford it. The cost, the length of time required, and the unpredictable outcome of non-objective laws, have made him give up the hope of appealing to justice, whether he suffers from a neighbor's petty chiseling or from some major violation of his rights. He has grown stoically—or cynically—indifferent: he knows (or senses) that the main violator is the government, that no muggers can deprive him of the sums which the government seizes at income-tax time.

The moral inflation leaves him unprotected against the financial inflation: he works harder and harder (often in the form of "moonlighting"), but his real income is shrinking, he is not rising in the world, he is not getting anywhere, he is running on a hopeless treadmill. Try to tell his wife—in the midst of her desperate struggle to provide the family with decent meals, which they can't afford—that she must bear "humiliation" for the sin of "waste"!

Just as these people sense that today's leadership does not regard them as worth protecting, so they sense that their country, too, is regarded as not worth defending. The military services have survived, so far—in the midst of an unrelenting campaign of attacks, vilifications, and demands that the defense budget be cut (even though welfare projects, not defense, consume the largest share of the national budget).

To add insult to the American people's injury, *The New York Times* published an editorial (May 25, 1972), entitled "Retreat on Rights," which said: "The Supreme Court decisions permitting criminal convictions by less than unanimous juries and narrowing witnesses' immunity against self-incrimination are disquieting in their practical effects but, even more, as portents of things to come.

"In the United States and other free countries, the drift of history in this century has been toward strengthening the power of government and diminishing the liberties of the individual. One of the few countervailing pressures has been the libertarian tendency of the Supreme Court to construe the Bill of Rights and the Fourteenth Amendment broadly in behalf of accused individuals, racial and religious minorities, the impoverished and ignorant, and political radicals and dissenters. The Court's new majority bloc made up mostly of Nixon appointees may be bringing that tendency to an end." After discussing the possible consequences of the Supreme Court decision—such as: "Prosecutors will find it easier to get convictions in cases which now end in hung juries"—the editorial urges the country to hope that the effects will not prove "destructive of individual rights."

This means that we must fight the world's drift toward statism by protecting the individual rights of criminals.

(Don't remind me that an accused person is not necessarily a criminal and that he must be protected against unjust accusations. The rights of the accused are not a primary—they are a consequence derived from a man's inalienable, individual rights. A consequence cannot survive the destruction of its cause. What good will it do you to be protected in the rare emergency of a false arrest, if you are treated as the rightless subject of an unlimited government in your daily life?)

A mawkish sentimentality toward criminals, coupled with a brutal cruelty toward innocent citizens, is not a new phenomenon. In my review of *The Language of Dissent* by Lowell B. Mason (*The Objectivist Newsletter*, August 1963), I wrote: "Mr. Mason makes a profoundly important observation: whenever a country's criminal laws are more lenient than its civil laws, it means that the country is accepting the basic principle of statism and is moving toward a totalitarian state. (Such a trend means that crimes against individuals are regarded as negligible, while the collectivist concept of 'Crimes against the State' becomes paramount and supersedes all rights.) In Soviet Russia, he points out, criminals were treated 'with tolerance and circumspection. On the other hand, those accused of violating the state's political and economic commands were sentenced to death or exiled to Siberia without any semblance of trial as we know the word here in America.' "

Now observe the odd assortment of individuals whose rights and liberties are singled out by the *Times* editorial for special protection. "Racial and religious minorities," as well as "political radicals and dissenters," should find it offensive to be lumped with "the impoverished and ignorant" and the (probably) criminal. The obvious question is: What about the rights and liberties of the honest, the educated, the self-supporting, the majority? The answer is that the assortment is dictated by and represents a confession of altruism's essence: it is only suffering, weakness, failure, default—real or imaginary, spiritual or material or numerical or moral—that entitle men to rights, liberties and public concern; happiness, strength, success, virtue do not.

In a cultural atmosphere of this sort, who can find any inspiration or desire to preserve his moral integrity? The signs of moral deterioration are all around us. But, to the great credit of this country, most people, so far, have not given up.

The ideologues of altruism have miscalculated in regard to this country. Materially, they have obtained more than they could hope to extort from any other, poorer nation. Spiritually, they have failed: they mistook generosity for guilt; the guilt-infection did not take hold. Men who live on an earned income are not likely to accept an unearned guilt.

Since the inflation of altruism has not breached the American people's basic self-esteem, the altruists are now trying to revive the grotesque, anti-moral absurdity of original sin—i.e., of prenatal guilt—in a secular form. Having failed to induce personal guilt, they are struggling to induce *racial* guilt—by proclaiming that people must suffer and pay for the (alleged) sins of their fathers.

This prehistorical notion requires more than the destruction of morality. It requires the obliteration of all the concepts which centuries of growing civilization struggled to identify: reason, individualism, personal integrity (and *person*), volition, choice, responsibility, language, understanding, and human communication.

The inversion of all standards—the propagation of racism as antiracist, of injustice as just, of immorality as moral, and the reasoning behind it, which is worse than the offenses—is flagrantly evident in the policy of preferential treatment for minorities (i.e., racial quotas) in employment and education. (See my essay on "Racism" in *The Virtue of Selfishness*.) If there is a quicker way to destroy people than by preaching brotherly love while spreading blind, inter-racial hatred, you name it.

The most eloquent example of that policy is the DeFunis case.

In 1971, Marco DeFunis, Jr., a Phi Beta Kappa, *magna cum laude* graduate of the University of Washington in Seattle, was denied admission to the University's Law School. The school accepted 275 out of 1600 applicants (for an eventual class of 150). They were chosen mainly on the basis of special tests which purported to give a student's "Predicted First Year Average," estimating his ability to succeed in law school—and, in part, on the basis of various other considerations. Four racial minority groups—Black, Chicano, American Indian, and Filipino—were singled out for preferential treatment; their applications were processed separately and differently from all the others. I quote from Justice Douglas's opinion in a subsequent Supreme Court decision: "Thirty-seven minority applicants were admitted under this procedure. Of these, 36 had Predicted First Year Averages below DeFunis' 76.23, and 30 had averages below 74.5, and thus would ordinarily have been summarily rejected by the Chairman. . . . What places this case in a special category is the fact that the school did not choose one set of criteria but two, and then determined which to apply to a given applicant on the basis of his race."

DeFunis sued the University of Washington, claiming that he was a victim of "reverse discrimination," that his constitutional rights had been violated and he had been denied the Fourteenth Amendment guarantee of "equal protection of the laws." The Washington trial court upheld his claim and ordered the school to admit him. The school complied, but appealed. The Washington Supreme Court reversed the decision. DeFunis took the case to the U.S. Supreme Court, obtaining a stay which permitted him to attend the Law School until the final disposition of his case.

The case aroused intense public controversy. Various groups and organizations filed friend-of-the-court briefs, supporting DeFunis or opposing him—a greater number of briefs than in any other case in recent history. It was clear to both sides that a crucially important *moral* issue was at stake. The Court announced its decision on April 23, 1974. By that time, DeFunis was completing his last term at the Law School, and the school had agreed to let him graduate, regardless of the Court's decision. This permitted the Supreme Court to avoid judgment on the issue.

It was the Court's *conservative* majority that took advantage of a legal technicality and—in a brief, unsigned opinion—declared the case to be moot, since DeFunis's rights were not affected any longer. The four liberal Justices dissented, objecting to the avoidance of the constitutional issues. Justice Douglas wrote a separate, dissenting opinion of an extremely confusing, inconclusive nature. The moral question was left unanswered.

What is of special significance to this country's public morale and morality, is the kind of argumentation that this case brought forth in advance of the Supreme Court's ruling.

The brief of the B'nai B'rith Anti-Defamation League, filed in support of DeFunis, states: "If the Constitution prohibits exclusion of blacks and other minorities on racial grounds, it cannot permit the exclusion of whites on racial grounds. . . . discrimination on the basis of race is illegal, immoral, unconstitutional, inherently wrong and destructive of democratic society. . . . A racial quota is a device for establishing a status, a caste, determining superiority or inferiority for a class measured by race without regard to individual merit."

This, of course, is unanswerable. The advocates of racial quotas do not attempt to answer it; they ignore it, or worse: they declare that their goal is to end racial discrimination eventually by means of practicing it temporarily. (This is borrowed from the methodology of Marxism, which claims that we can bring the state to wither away eventually by means of establishing a totalitarian dictatorship temporarily. In neither case are we given any indication of *how* such a trick is to be accomplished.)

An article eloquently entitled "Discriminating to end discrimination" (*The New York Times Magazine*, April 14, 1974) presents a good cross section of arguments offered by both sides of the issue. "Advocates of affirmative action [i.e., of preferential treatment] like to compare the racial situation in America to two runners, one of whom has had his legs shackled for 200 years. . . . Removing the shackles doesn't make the two instantly equal in ability to compete. The previously shackled runner has to be given some advantage in order to compete effectively until he gets his legs into condition." (How? By shackling the fast runner, lowering the standards, and slowing down everyone's running? No answer is given. But it must be mentioned that many intelligent blacks regard this type of argument as a racist insult, which it is.)

The article quotes a woman attorney for some anti-DeFunis groups, who said: "It is now well understood, however, that our society cannot be completely color-blind in the short term if we are to have a color-blind society in the long term." She "argues that a racial classification can only be presumed unconstitutional if it disadvantages a group subject to a history of discrimination or held down by special disabilities. She contends that the 14th Amendment was meant to help powerless, oppressed minorities, and that the white majority needs no such help." (This is altruism superseding and rewriting the Constitution: if you have no special disabilities, you have no rights and no protection of the laws.)

The University of Washington, according to the article, "concedes that some white students may be excluded from law school because of the affirmative-action program, but it maintains that its program is 'necessary' to achieve an 'overriding purpose'—i.e., to increase the number of minority lawyers in the state and the nation. . . . And, the university notes, had it not been for the nation's history of racial discrimination, white students would have had far more students to compete with than they do now."

This type of argument, which modern intellectuals permit themselves to use with growing frequency, is a measure of their growing distance from reality: it consists in changing one factor of a complex situation and assuming that all the rest would remain unchanged. In fact, if racial discrimination hampered the intellectual development of black students, the absence of such discrimination would not have brought more competition to white students, but less: it would have created more universities to satisfy a greater demand (assuming a free economy).

But if projected potentialities are to be equated with actuality, if "might have been" is to be the equivalent of "*was*," then I submit the following argument: If my grandfather had come to this country and if he had gone into the oil business, he would have given stiff competition to Nelson A. Rockefeller's grandfather and, therefore, Mr. Rockefeller would not be as rich as he is today and, therefore, I demand my constitutional right to half of Mr. Rockefeller's money.

Absurd? Not by today's standards. The grossness of such absurdity did not prevent the broadcast of an editorial which declared: "WCBS Radio endorses the argument of the University of Washington Law School—had it not been for the nation's history of racial discrimination, white students would have far more students to compete with than they do today. Affirmative-action programs that give preference to qualified minorities over more qualified whites may seem unjust, but that injustice pales beside the monstrosities of two centuries of segregation." (May 1, 1974.)

Dr. Alvin Lashinsky, Vice President of the Jewish Rights Council, who broadcast a reply to that editorial, sounded like a welcome voice of sanity: "We utterly condemn what appears to us to be a call by WCBS for retribution—to have children pay for acts their grandfathers committed, and for innocents of other minorities to also suffer only because their skin is white. . . . Excellence of our professions has always been achieved by high standards and the only way to give minorities self-respect is by improving the ability of the poorly qualified through remedial education beforehand, otherwise the finished product may be a poorly qualified physician or lawyer or a poorly skilled surgeon or even a semi-literate clerk or secretary. Does anyone, WCBS or the minorities, really want this?" (May 3, 1974.)

The answer is: Yes—as far as the ideologues of altruism are concerned—that is precisely what they want. They do not want to lift the poorly qualified, but to tear down the competent; they do not want to help the weak, but to destroy the strong. How many of them would admit such motives, even to themselves, I do not know. Observe that the WCBS editorial did not dare openly to demand the rejection of the qualified in favor of the unqualified; it fudged, it spoke of "*qualified* minorities" versus "more qualified whites," making it a matter of degree—which does not make the injustice any the less vicious.

While the altruists proclaim that the financially or racially handicapped are their chief concern, none of them noticed the fact that DeFunis was doubly handicapped. The admission requirements at the University of Washington Law School (as at most universities) are highly arbitrary: apart from scholastic achievement, the committee considers such factors as "recommendations" from prominent persons or groups (i.e., pull) and a student's "extra-curricular and community activities" (i.e., altruism). "Community activities" are a luxury which DeFunis could not have afforded: his "extra-curricular activity" consisted in working his way through college. And if the persecution suffered by a student's ancestors is grounds for giving him special advantages, DeFunis belongs to the racial minority that suffered the longest, most horrendous record of persecution in history: he is Jewish. So much for the sincerity of the altruists' motives.

Now consider the moral import of their arguments. Observe that the common denominator of their claims is the total absence of the concept of a *person*. An individual and a group are regarded as interchangeable—and it is instructive to observe the switching. A group can be "shackled for 200 years," an individual cannot—but it is individuals who collect reparations, not the group as a whole. A group, the white majority, must pay for their ancestors' racial discrimination, it is alleged—but it is white individuals who pay, by being denied job and education opportunities, not the group as a whole. It is, allegedly, an "overriding purpose" to increase the number of minority lawyers in the nation—but minority lawyers are individuals, and what is being "*overriden*"? The rights of other individuals, who are white.

The crass indifference of all such tribal profiteers to the reality of an individual human life, is their most vicious and shocking characteristic. An individual human life is a brief and fragile period of time. If the goal of "reverse discrimination" is a color-blind society in some indeterminate future, what good will it do to DeFunis (and to thousands like him), who is denied a professional education in the brief, irreplaceable years of his youth and finds his plans, his future, his life-course wrecked? *Who* has the right to do this to him? For the sake of what? For the alleged future benefit of society, i.e., of a large majority of people? But it is for the sake of a *minority* that he has been sacrificed.

There is no such thing as a collective guilt. A country may be held responsible for the actions of its government and it may be guilty of an evil (such as starting a war)—but then it is a public, not a private, matter and the entire country has to bear the burden of paying reparations for it. The notion of random individuals paying for the sins of an entire country, is an unspeakable modern atrocity.

This country has no guilt to atone for in regard to its black citizens. Certainly, slavery was an enormous evil. But a country that fought a civil war to abolish slavery, has atoned for it on such a scale that to talk about racial quotas in addition, is grotesque. However, it is not for injustices committed by the government that the modern racists are demanding reparations, but for *racial prejudice*—i.e., for the personal views of private citizens. How can an individual be held responsible for the views of others, whom he has no power to control, who may be his intellectual enemies, whose views may be the opposite of his own? What can make him responsible for them? The answer we hear is: The fact that his skin is of the same color as theirs. If *this* is not an obliteration of morality, of intellectual integrity, of individual rights, of the freedom of man's mind (and, incidentally, of the First Amendment), you take it from here; I can't—it turns my stomach.

What I am able to discuss is the ancient notion of paying for the sins of one's fathers, and the effect of this notion on morality. Suppose a man leads a decent, responsible life financially: he works hard, lives within his means, plans his future accordingly, and always pays his debts; then, suddenly, he is confronted with a demand that he pay a debt of his father's, contracted before he was born—and he is given to understand that other demands will be sprung on him, for the debts of his grandfather, his great-grandfather, etc. Would he accept it? Would he remain decent, conscientious and hard-working? Or would he blow his savings on one drunken orgy, then drift at the whim of the moment, mooching and chiseling as best he can?

The same is true in the realm of morality. Morality is inseparable from personal choice and personal responsibility. If a man lives conscientiously according to a set of moral principles, then hears that his moral rectitude does not depend on *his* actions, but on the actions of his ancestors, he will not remain moral for long. He will let himself slide into that cynical, senseless, hopeless gray bog which is today's culture, where floating shapes scowl at him menacingly and hoarse voices screech about "affirmative action."

No, men are not evil by nature—and when evil ideas take over a culture, two factors are responsible: the absence of good ideas, and force. Just as financial inflation is caused by the government, so is moral inflation. The government is destroying the people's morality by many forms of injustice, which include such things as forcing racial quotas on schools and business concerns. As the *Times Magazine* article explains in regard to the DeFunis case: "H.E.W. [Department of Health, Education and Welfare] was leaning hard on the university for alleged noncompliance with affirmative action in campus hiring. The university, like 2,500 other institutions of higher learning in the United States, holds Government grants and contracts and thus is required by Federal law to institute 'goals and timetables' for hiring more women and minorities on its faculty." (So much for the notion of the government granting subsidies to education without strings attached, i.e., without affecting the schools' intellectual freedom.)

The next time you hear a politician deplore the moral decline of this country, remember (and, perhaps, remind him) that if one wants to preserve a nation's morality, one must set up conditions of existence in which moral behavior is rewarded, not punished—and that this cannot be done on an altruist basis: after centuries of moral inflation, the balloon of altruism has burst.

EDITOR'S NOTE: *This passage comes from an anthology of essays published under the title* The New Left: The Anti-Industrial Revolution. *(A new, expanded and revised edition, retitled* Return of the Primitive: The Anti-Industrial Revolution *will be published in 1999.) The excerpt identifies the fundamental motive that drives the moralists of altruism.*

The Age of Envy

A CULTURE, like an individual, has a sense of life or, rather, the equivalent of a sense of life—an emotional atmosphere created by its dominant philosophy, by its view of man and of existence. This emotional atmosphere represents a culture's dominant values and serves as the leitmotif of a given age, setting its trends and its style.

Thus Western civilization had an Age of Reason and an Age of Enlightenment. In those periods, the quest for reason and enlightenment was the dominant intellectual drive and created a corresponding emotional atmosphere that fostered these values.

Today, we live in the Age of Envy.

"Envy" is not the emotion I have in mind, but it is the clearest manifestation of an emotion that has remained nameless; it is the only element of a complex emotional sum that men have permitted themselves to identify.

Envy is regarded by most people as a petty, superficial emotion and, therefore, it serves as a semihuman cover for so inhuman an emotion that those who feel it seldom dare admit it even to themselves. Mankind has lived with it, has observed its manifestations and, to various extents, has been ravaged by it for countless centuries, yet has failed to grasp its meaning and to rebel against its exponents.

Today, that emotion is the leitmotif, the sense of life of our culture. It is all around us, we are drowning in it, it is almost explicitly confessed by its more brazen exponents—yet men continue to evade its existence and are peculiarly afraid to name it, as primitive people were once afraid to pronounce the name of the devil.

That emotion is: *hatred of the good for being the good.*

This hatred is not resentment against some prescribed view of the good with which one does not agree. For instance, if a child resents some conventional type of obedient boy who is constantly held up to him as an ideal to emulate, this is not hatred of the good: the child does *not* regard that boy as *good*, and his resentment is the product of a clash between his values and those of his elders (though he is too young to grasp the issue in such terms). Similarly, if an adult does not regard altruism as good and resents the adulation bestowed upon some "humanitarian," this is a clash between his values and those of others, not hatred of the good.

Hatred of the good for being the good means hatred of that which one regards as good by one's own (conscious or subconscious) judgment. It means hatred of a person for possessing a value or virtue one regards as desirable.

If a child wants to get good grades in school, but is unable or unwilling to achieve them and begins to hate the children who do, *that* is hatred of the good. If a man regards intelligence as a value, but is troubled by self-doubt and begins to hate the men *he* judges to be intelligent, *that* is hatred of the good.

The nature of the particular values a man chooses to hold is not the primary factor in this issue (although irrational values may contribute a great deal to the formation of that emotion). The primary factor and distinguishing characteristic is an emotional mechanism set in reverse: a response of hatred, not toward human vices, but toward human virtues.

To be exact, the emotional mechanism is not set in reverse, but is set one way: its exponents do not experience love for evil men; their emotional range is limited to hatred or indifference. It is impossible to experience love, which is a response to values, when one's automatized response to values is hatred.

In any specific instance, this type of hatred is heavily enmeshed in rationalizations. The most common one is: "I don't hate him for his intelligence, but for his conceit!" More often than not, if one asks the speaker to name the evidence of the victim's conceit, he exhausts such generalities as: "He's insolent . . . he's stubborn . . . he's selfish," and ends up with some indeterminate accusation which amounts to: "He's intelligent and he knows it." Well, why shouldn't he know it? Blank out. Should he hide it? Blank out. From whom should he hide it? The implicit, but never stated, answer is: "From people like me."

Yet such haters accept and even seem to admire the spectacle of conceit put on for their benefit by a man who shows off, boasting about his own alleged virtues or achievements, blatantly confessing a lack of self-confidence. This, of course, is a clue to the nature of the hatred. The haters seem unable to differentiate conceptually between "conceit" and a deserved *pride*, yet they seem to know the difference "instinctively," i.e., by means of their automatized sense of life.

Since very few men have fully consistent characters, it is often hard to tell, in a specific instance, whether a given man is hated for his virtues or for his actual flaws. In regard to one's own feelings, only a rigorously conscientious habit of introspection can enable one to be certain of the nature and causes of one's emotional responses. But introspection is the mental process most fiercely avoided by the haters, which permits them a virtually unlimited choice of rationalizations. In regard to judging the emotional responses of others, it is extremely difficult to tell their reasons in a specific case, particularly if it involves complex personal relationships. It is, therefore, in the broad, impersonal field of responses to strangers, to casual acquaintances, to public figures or to events that have no direct bearing on the haters' own lives that one can observe the hatred of the good in a pure, unmistakable form.

Its clearest manifestation is the attitude of a person who characteristically resents someone's success, happiness, achievement or good fortune—and experiences pleasure at someone's failure, unhappiness or misfortune. This is pure, "nonvenal" hatred of the good for being the good: the hater has nothing to lose or gain in such instances, no practical value at stake, no existential motive, no knowledge except the fact that a human being has succeeded or failed. The expressions of this response are brief, casual, as a rule involuntary. But if you have seen it, you have seen the naked face of evil.

Do not confuse this response with that of a person who resents someone's unearned success, or feels pleased by someone's deserved failure. These responses are caused by a sense of justice, which is an entirely different phenomenon, and its emotional manifestations are different: in such cases, a person expresses indignation, not hatred—or relief, not malicious gloating.

Superficially, the motive of those who hate the good is taken to be envy. A dictionary definition of envy is: "1. a sense of discontent or jealousy with regard to another's advantages, success, possessions, etc. 2. desire for an advantage possessed by another" (*The Random House Dictionary*, 1968). The same dictionary adds the following elucidation: "To *envy* is to feel resentful because someone else possesses or has achieved what one wishes oneself to possess or to have achieved."

This covers a great many emotional responses, which come from different motives. In a certain sense, the second definition is the opposite of the first, and the more innocent of the two.

For example, if a poor man experiences a moment's envy of another man's wealth, the feeling may mean nothing more than a momentary concretization of his desire for wealth; the feeling is not directed against that particular rich person and is concerned with the wealth, not the person. The feeling, in effect, may amount to: "I wish I had an income (or a house, or a car, or an overcoat) like his." The result of this feeling may be an added incentive for the man to improve his financial condition.

The feeling is less innocent, if it involves personal resentment and amounts to: "I want to put on a front, like this man." The result is a second-hander who lives beyond his means, struggling to "keep up with the Joneses."

The feeling is still less innocent, if it amounts to: "I want *this man's* car (or overcoat, or diamond shirt studs, or industrial establishment)." The result is a criminal.

But these are still human beings, in various stages of immorality, compared to the inhuman object whose feeling is: "I *hate* this man because he is wealthy and I am not."

Envy is part of this creature's feeling, but only the superficial, semirespectable part; it is like the tip of an iceberg showing nothing worse than ice, but with the submerged part consisting of a compost of rotting living matter. The envy, in this case, is semirespectable because it seems to imply a desire for material possessions, which is a human being's desire. But, deep down, the creature has no such desire: it does not want to be rich, it wants the human being to be poor.

This is particularly clear in the much more virulent cases of hatred, masked as envy, for those who possess personal values or virtues: hatred for a man (or a woman) because he (or she) is beautiful or intelligent or successful or honest or happy. In these cases, the creature has no desire and makes no effort to improve its appearance, to develop or to use its intelligence, to struggle for success, to practice honesty, to be happy (nothing can make it happy). It knows that the disfigurement or the mental collapse or the failure or the immorality or the misery of its victim would not endow it with his or her value. *It does not desire the value: it desires the value's destruction.*

"They do not want to own your fortune, they want you to lose it; they do not want to succeed, they want you to fail; they do not want to live, they want you to die; they desire nothing, they hate existence . . ." (*Atlas Shrugged*).

What endows such a creature with a quality of abysmal evil is the fact that it has an awareness of values and is able to recognize them in people. If it were merely amoral, it would be indifferent; it would be unable to distinguish virtues from flaws. But it does distinguish them—and the essential characteristic of its corruption is the fact that its mind's recognition of a *value* is transmitted to its emotional mechanism as *hatred*, not as love, desire or admiration.

Consider the full meaning of this attitude. Values are that which one acts to gain and/or keep. Values are a necessity of man's survival, and wider: of any living organism's survival. Life is a process of self-sustaining and self-generated action, and the successful pursuit of values is a precondition of remaining alive. Since nature does not provide man with an automatic knowledge of the code of values he requires, there are differences in the codes which men accept and the goals they pursue. But consider the abstraction "value," apart from the particular content of any given code, and ask yourself: What is the nature of a creature in which the sight of a value arouses hatred and the desire to destroy? In the most profound sense of the term, such a creature is a killer, not a physical, but a metaphysical one—it is not an enemy of *your* values, but of *all* values, it is an enemy of anything that enables men to survive, it is an enemy of life as such and of everything living.

A community of values—of some sort of values—is a necessity of any successful relationship among living beings. If you were training an animal, you would not hurt it every time it obeyed you. If you were bringing up a child, you would not punish him whenever he acted properly. What relationship can you have with the hating creatures, and what element do they introduce into social relationships? If you struggle for existence and find that your success brings you, not approval and appreciation, but hatred, if you strive to be moral and find that your virtue brings you, not the love, but the hatred of your fellow-men, what becomes of your own benevolence? Will you be able to generate or to maintain a feeling of good will toward your fellow-men?

The greatest danger in this issue is men's inability—or worse: unwillingness—fully to identify it.

Evil as the hating creatures are, there is something still more evil: those who try to appease them.

It is understandable that men might seek to hide their vices from the eyes of people whose judgment they respect. But there are men who hide their virtues from the eyes of monsters. There are men who apologize for their own achievements, deride their own values, debase their own character—for the sake of pleasing those they know to be stupid, corrupt, malicious, evil. An obsequious pandering to the vanity of some alleged superior, such as a king, for the sake of some practical advantage, is bad enough. But pandering to the vanity of one's inferiors—inferior specifically in regard to the value involved—is so shameful an act of treason to one's values that nothing can be left thereafter of the person who commits it, neither intellectually nor morally, and nothing ever is.

If men attempt to play up to those they admire, and fake virtues they do not possess, it is futile, but understandable, if not justifiable. But to fake vices, weaknesses, flaws, disabilities? To shrink one's soul and stature? To play down—or write down, or speak down, or think down?

Observe just one social consequence of this policy: such appeasers do not hesitate to join some cause or other appealing for mercy; they never raise their voices in the name of justice.

Cowardice is so ignoble an inner state that men struggle to overcome it, in the face of real dangers. The appeaser chooses a state of cowardice where no danger exists. To live in fear is so unworthy a condition that men have died on barricades, defying the tyranny of the mighty. The appeaser chooses to live in chronic fear of the impotent.

Men have died in torture chambers, on the stake, in concentration camps, in front of firing squads, rather than renounce their convictions. The appeaser renounces his under the pressure of a frown on any vacant face. Men have refused to sell their souls in exchange for fame, fortune, power, even their own lives. The appeaser does not sell his soul: he gives it away for free, getting nothing in return.

The appeaser's usual rationalization is: "I don't want to be disliked." By whom? By people he dislikes, despises and condemns.

Let me give you some examples. An intellectual who was recruiting members for Mensa—an international society allegedly restricted to intelligent men, which selects members on the dubious basis of I.Q. tests—was quoted in an interview as follows: "Intelligence is not especially admired by people. Outside Mensa you had to be very careful not to win an argument and lose a friend. Inside Mensa we can be ourselves and that is a great relief" (*The New York Times*, September 11, 1966). A friend, therefore, is more important than the truth. What kind of friend? The kind that resents you for being right.

A professor, the head of a department in a large university, had a favorite graduate student who wanted to be a teacher. The professor had tested him as an instructor and regarded him as exceptionally intelligent. In a private conversation with the young man's parents, the professor praised him highly and declared: "There is only one danger in his future: he is such a good teacher that the rest of the faculty will resent him." When the young man got his Ph.D., the professor did not offer him a job, even though he had the power to do so.

The notion that an intelligent girl should hide her intelligence in order to be popular with men and find a husband, is widespread and well-known. Of what value would such a husband be to her? Blank out.

In an old movie dealing with college life, a boy asks a girl to help him get good grades by means of an actually criminal scheme (it involves the theft of a test from the professor's office). When she refuses, the boy asks scornfully: "Are you some sort of moralist?" "Oh, no, no," she answers hastily and *apologetically*, "it's just my small-town upbringing, I guess."

Do not confuse appeasement with tactfulness or generosity. Appeasement is not consideration for the feelings of others, it is *consideration for and compliance with the unjust, irrational and evil feelings of others*. It is a policy of exempting the emotions of others from moral judgment, and of willingness to sacrifice innocent, virtuous victims to the evil malice of such emotions.

Tactfulness is consideration extended only to rational feelings. A tactful man does not stress his success or happiness in the presence of those who have suffered failure, loss or unhappiness; not because he suspects them of envy, but because he realizes that the contrast can revive and sharpen their pain. He does not stress his virtues in anyone's presence: he takes for granted that they are recognized. As a rule, a man of achievement does not flaunt his achievements, neither among equals nor inferiors nor superiors; he does not evaluate himself—or others—by a comparative standard. His attitude is not: "I am better than you," but: "I am good."

If, however, he encounters an envious hater who gets huffy, trying to ignore, deny or insult his achievements, he asserts them proudly. In answer to the hater's stock question: "Who do you think you are?"—he tells him.

It is the pretentious mediocrity—the show-off, the boaster, the snooty posturer—who seeks, not virtue or value, but *superiority*. A comparative standard is his only guide, which means that he has no standards and that he has a vested interest in reducing others to inferiority. Decent people, properly, resent a show-off, but the haters and enviers do not: they recognize him as a soul mate.

Offensive boasting or self-abasing appeasement is a false alternative. As in all human relationships, the guidelines of proper conduct are: objectivity and justice. But this is not what men are taught or were taught in the past.

"Use your head—but don't let anyone know it. Set your goals high—but don't admit it. Be honest—but don't uphold it. Be successful—but hide it. Be great—but act small. Be happy—but God help you if you are!" Such are the moral injunctions we gather from the cultural atmosphere in which we grow up—as men did in the past, throughout history.

The appeasement of evil—of an unknowable, undefinable, inexplicable evil—has been the undertow of mankind's cultural stream all through the ages. In primitive cultures (and even in ancient Greece) the appeasement took the form of the belief that the gods resent human happiness or success, because these are the prerogatives of the gods to which men must not aspire. Hence the superstitious fear of acknowledging one's good fortune—as, for instance, the ritual of parents wailing that their newborn son is puny, ugly, worthless, for fear that a demon would harm him if they admitted their happy pride in his health and looks. Observe the contradiction: Why attempt to deceive an omnipotent demon who would be able to judge the infant's value for himself? The intention of the ritual, therefore, is not: "Don't let him know that the infant is good," but: "Don't let him know that *you* know it and that you're happy!"

Men create gods—and demons—in their own likeness; mystic fantasies, as a rule, are invented to explain some phenomenon for which men find no explanation. The notion of gods who are so malicious that they wish men to live in chronic misery, would not be conceived or believed unless men sensed all around them the presence of some inexplicable malevolence directed specifically at their personal happiness.

Are the haters of the good that numerous? No. The actual haters are a small, depraved minority in any age or culture. The spread and perpetuation of this evil are accomplished by those who profiteer on it.

The profiteers are men with a vested interest in mankind's psychological devastation, who burrow their way into positions of moral-intellectual leadership. They provide the haters with unlimited means of rationalization, dissimulation, excuse and camouflage, including ways of passing vices off as virtues. They slander, confuse and disarm the victims. Their vested interest is power-lust. Their stock-in-trade is any system of thought or of belief aimed at keeping men *small*.

Observe the nature of some of mankind's oldest legends.

Why were the men of Babel punished? Because they attempted to build a tower to the sky.

Why did Phaëthon perish? Because he attempted to drive the chariot of the sun.

Why was Icarus smashed? Because he attempted to fly.

Why was Arachne transformed into a spider? Because she challenged a goddess to a competition in the art of weaving—and won it.

"Do not aspire—do not venture—do not rise—ambition is self-destruction," drones this ancient chorus through the ages—through all the ages, changing its lyrics, but not its tune—all the way to the Hollywood movies in which the boy who goes to seek a career in the big city becomes a wealthy, but miserable scoundrel, while the small-town boy who stays put wins the girl next door, who wins over the glamorous temptress.

There is and was abundant evidence to show that the curse of an overwhelming majority of men is passivity, lethargy and fear, not ambition and audacity. But men's well-being is not the motive of that chorus.

Toward the end of World War II, newspapers reported the following: when Russian troops moved west and occupied foreign towns, the Soviet authorities automatically executed any person who had a bank account of $100 or a high-school education; the rest of the inhabitants submitted. This is a physical dramatization of the spiritual policy of mankind's moral-intellectual leaders: destroy the tops, the rest will give up and obey.

Just as a political dictator needs specially indoctrinated thugs to enforce his orders, so his intellectual road-pavers need them to maintain their power. Their thugs are the haters of the good; the special indoctrination is the morality of altruism.

It is obvious—historically, philosophically and psychologically—that altruism is an inexhaustible source of rationalizations for the most evil motives, the most inhuman actions, the most loathsome emotions. It is not difficult to grasp the meaning of the tenet that *the good is an object of sacrifice*—and to understand what a blanket damnation of anything living is represented by an undefined accusation of "selfishness."

But here is a significant phenomenon to observe: the haters and enviers—who are the most vociferous shock troops of altruism—seem to be subconsciously impervious to the altruist criterion of the good. The touchy vanity of these haters—which flares up at any suggestion of their inferiority to a man of virtue—is not aroused by any saint or hero of altruism, whose moral superiority they profess to acknowledge. Nobody envies Albert Schweitzer. Whom do they envy? The man of intelligence, of ability, of achievement, of independence.

If anyone ever believed (or tried to believe) that the motive of altruism is compassion, that its goal is the relief of human suffering and the elimination of poverty, the state of today's culture now deprives him of any foothold on self-deception. Today, altruism is running amuck, shedding its tattered rationalizations and displaying its soul.

Altruists are no longer concerned with material wealth, not even with its "redistribution," only with its destruction—but even this is merely a means to an end. Their savage fury is aimed at the destruction of intelligence—of ability, ambition, thought, purpose, justice; the destruction of morality, any sort of morality; the destruction of values qua values.

The last fig leaf of academic pretentiousness is the tag used to disguise this movement: *egalitarianism*. It does not disguise, but reveals.

Egalitarianism means the belief in the equality of all men. If the word "equality" is to be taken in any serious or rational sense, the crusade for this belief is dated by about a century or more: the United States of America has made it an anachronism—by establishing a system based on the principle of individual rights. "Equality," in a human context, is a political term: it means equality before the law, the equality of fundamental, inalienable rights which every man possesses by virtue of his birth as a human being, and which may not be infringed or abrogated by man-made institutions, such as titles of nobility or the division of men into castes established by law, with special privileges granted to some and denied to others. The rise of capitalism swept away all castes, including the institutions of aristocracy and of slavery or serfdom.

But this is not the meaning that the altruists ascribe to the word "equality."

They turn the word into an anti-concept: they use it to mean, not *political*, but *metaphysical* equality—the equality of personal attributes and virtues, regardless of natural endowment or individual choice, performance and character. It is not man-made institutions, but nature, i.e., *reality*, that they propose to fight—by means of man-made institutions.

Since nature does not endow all men with equal beauty or equal intelligence, and the faculty of volition leads men to make different choices, the egalitarians propose to abolish the "unfairness" of nature and of volition, and to establish universal equality *in fact*—in defiance of facts. Since the Law of Identity is impervious to human manipulation, it is the Law of Causality that they struggle to abrogate. Since personal attributes or virtues cannot be "redistributed," they seek to deprive men of their consequences—of the rewards, the benefits, the achievements created by personal attributes and virtues.

It is not equality before the law that they seek, but *inequality*; the establishment of an inverted social pyramid, with a new aristocracy on top—*the aristocracy of non-value.* . . .

3. Man, the Rational Animal

A theory of ethics rests on a view of man's nature. The first two selections, written in 1969 about the Apollo 11 *mission (and its antithesis, Woodstock), capture AR's distinctive view.*

The first of these, from the anthology The Voice of Reason, *conveys her positive vision of man; the second, from* Return of the Primitive, *offers her analysis of man's greatest enemy.*

Apollo 11

"NO MATTER what discomforts and expenses you had to bear to come here," said a NASA guide to a group of guests, at the conclusion of a tour of the Space Center on Cape Kennedy, on July 15, 1969, "there will be seven minutes tomorrow morning that will make you feel it was worth it."

It was.

The tour had been arranged for the guests invited by NASA to attend the launching of Apollo 11. As far as I was able to find out, the guests—apart from government officials and foreign dignitaries—were mainly scientists, industrialists, and a few intellectuals who had been selected to represent the American people and culture on this occasion. If this was the standard of selection, I am happy and proud that I was one of these guests.

The NASA tour guide was a slight, stocky, middle-aged man who wore glasses and spoke—through a microphone, at the front of the bus—in the mild, gentle, patient manner of a schoolteacher. He reminded me of television's Mr. Peepers—until he took off his glasses and I took a closer look at his face: he had unusual, intensely intelligent eyes.

The Space Center is an enormous place that looks like an untouched wilderness cut, incongruously, by a net of clean, new, paved roads: stretches of wild, subtropical growth, an eagle's nest in a dead tree, an alligator in a stagnant moat—and, scattered at random, in the distance, a few vertical shafts rising from the jungle, slender structures of a shape peculiar to the technology of space, which do not belong to the age of the jungle or even fully to ours.

The discomfort was an inhuman, brain-melting heat. The sky was a sunless spread of glaring white, and the physical objects seemed to glare so that the mere sensation of sight became an effort. We kept plunging into an oven, when the bus stopped and we ran to modern, air-conditioned buildings that looked quietly unobtrusive and militarily efficient, then plunging back into the air-conditioned bus as into a pool. Our guide kept talking and explaining, patiently, courteously, conscientiously, but his heart was not in it, and neither was ours, even though the things he showed us would have been fascinating at any other time. The reason was not the heat; it was as if nothing could register on us, as if we were out of focus, or, rather, focused too intently and irresistibly on the event of the following day.

It was the guide who identified it, when he announced: "And now we'll show you what you *really* want to see"—and we were driven to the site of Apollo 11.

The "VIP's" tumbled out of the bus like tourists and rushed to photograph one another, with the giant rocket a few hundred yards away in the background. But some just stood and looked.

I felt a kind of awe, but it was a purely theoretical awe; I had to remind myself: "This is it," in order to experience any emotion. Visually it was just another rocket, the kind you can see in any science-fiction movie or on any toy counter: a tall, slender shape of dead, powdery white against the white glare of the sky and the steel lacing of the service tower. There were sharp black lines encircling the white body at intervals—and our guide explained matter-of-factly that these marked the stages that would be burned off in tomorrow's firings. This made the meaning of the rocket more real for an instant. But the fact that the lunar module, as he told us, was already installed inside the small, slanted part way on top of the rocket, just under the still smaller, barely visible spacecraft itself, would not become fully real; it seemed too small, too far away from us, and, simultaneously, too close: I could not quite integrate it with the parched stubble of grass under our feet, with its wholesomely usual touches of litter, with the psychedelic colors of the shirts on the tourists snapping pictures.

Tomorrow, our guide explained, we would be sitting on bleachers three miles away; he warned us that the sound of the blast would reach us some seconds later than the sight, and assured us that it would be loud, but not unbearable.

I do not know that guide's actual work at the Space Center, and I do not know by what imperceptible signs he gave me the impression that he was a man in love with his work. It was only that concluding remark of his, later, at the end of the tour, that confirmed my impression. In a certain way, he set, for me, the tone of the entire occasion: the sense of what lay under the surface of the seemingly commonplace activities.

My husband and I were staying in Titusville, a tiny frontier settlement—the frontier of science—built and inhabited predominantly by the Space Center's employees. It was just like any small town, perhaps a little newer and cleaner—except that ten miles away, across the bluish spread of the Indian River, one could see the foggy, bluish, rectangular shape of the Space Center's largest structure, the Vehicle Assembly Building, and, a little farther away, two faint vertical shafts: Apollo 11 and its service tower. No matter what one looked at in that town, one could not really see anything else.

I noticed only that Titusville had many churches, too many, and that they had incredible, modernistic forms. Architecturally, they reminded me of the more extreme types of Hollywood drive-ins: a huge, cone-shaped roof, with practically no walls to support it—or an erratic conglomeration of triangles, like a coral bush gone wild—or a fairy-tale candy-house, with S-shaped windows dripping at random like gobs of frosting. I may be mistaken about this, but I had the impression that here, on the doorstep of the future, religion felt out of place and this was the way it was trying to be modern.

Since all the motels of Titusville were crowded beyond capacity, we had rented a room in a private home: as their contribution to the great event, many of the local homeowners had volunteered to help their chamber of commerce with the unprecedented flood of visitors. Our room was in the home of an engineer employed at the Space Center. It was a nice, gracious family, and one might have said a typical small-town family, except for one thing: a quality of cheerful openness, directness, almost innocence—the benevolent, unself-consciously self-confident quality of those who live in the clean, strict, reality-oriented atmosphere of science.

On the morning of July 16, we got up at 3 A.M. in order to reach the NASA Guest Center by 6 A.M., a distance that a car traveled normally in ten minutes. (Special buses were to pick up the guests at that Center, for the trip to the launching.) But Titusville was being engulfed by such a flood of cars that even the police traffic department could not predict whether one would be able to move through the streets that morning. We reached the Guest Center long before sunrise, thanks to the courtesy of our hostess, who drove us there through twisting back streets.

On the shore of the Indian River, we saw cars, trucks, trailers filling every foot of space on both sides of the drive, in the vacant lots, on the lawns, on the river's sloping embankment. There were tents perched at the edge of the water; there were men and children sleeping on the roofs of station wagons, in the twisted positions of exhaustion; I saw a half-naked man asleep in a hammock strung between a car and a tree. These people had come from all over the country to watch the launching across the river, miles away. (We heard later that the same patient, cheerful human flood had spread through all the small communities around Cape Kennedy that night, and that it numbered one million persons.) I could not understand why these people would have such an intense desire to witness just a few brief moments; some hours later, I understood it.

It was still dark as we drove along the river. The sky and the water were a solid spread of dark blue that seemed soft, cold, and empty. But, framed by the motionless black leaves of the trees on the embankment, two things marked off the identity of the sky and the earth: far above in the sky, there was a single, large star; and on earth, far across the river, two enormous sheaves of white light stood shooting motionlessly into the empty darkness from two tiny upright shafts of crystal that looked like glowing icicles; they were Apollo 11 and its service tower.

It was dark when a caravan of buses set out at 7 A.M. on the journey to the Space Center. The light came slowly, beyond the steam-veiled windows, as we moved laboriously through back streets and back roads. No one asked any questions; there was a kind of tense solemnity about that journey, as if we were caught in the backwash of the enormous discipline of an enormous purpose and were now carried along on the power of an invisible authority.

It was full daylight—a broiling, dusty, hazy daylight—when we stepped out of the buses. The launch site looked big and empty like a desert; the bleachers, made of crude, dried planks, seemed small, precariously fragile and irrelevant, like a hasty footnote. Three miles away, the shaft of Apollo 11 looked a dusty white again, like a tired cigarette planted upright.

The worst part of the trip was that last hour and a quarter, which we spent sitting on wooden planks in the sun. There was a crowd of seven thousand people filling the stands, there was the cool, clear, courteous voice of a loudspeaker rasping into sound every few minutes, keeping us informed of the progress of the countdown (and announcing, somewhat dutifully, the arrival of some prominent government personage, which did not seem worth the effort of turning one's head to see), but all of it seemed unreal. The full reality was only the vast empty space, above and below, and the tired white cigarette in the distance.

The sun was rolling up and straight at our faces, like a white ball wrapped in dirty cotton. But beyond the haze, the sky was clear—which meant that we would be able to see the whole of the launching, including the firing of the second and third stages.

Let me warn you that television does not give any idea of what we saw. Later, I saw that launching again on color television, and it did not resemble the original.

The loudspeaker began counting the minutes when there were only five left. When I heard: "Three-quarters of a minute," I was up, standing on the wooden bench, and do not remember hearing the rest.

It began with a large patch of bright, yellow-orange flame shooting sideways from under the base of the rocket. It looked like a normal kind of flame and I felt an instant's shock of anxiety, as if this were a building on fire. In the next instant the flame and the rocket were hidden by such a sweep of dark red fire that the anxiety vanished: this was not part of any normal experience and could not be integrated with anything. The dark red fire parted into two gigantic wings, as if a hydrant were shooting streams of fire outward and up, toward the zenith—and between the two wings, against a pitch-black sky, the rocket rose slowly, so slowly that it seemed to hang still in the air, a pale cylinder with a blinding oval of white light at the bottom, like an upturned candle with its flame directed at the earth. Then I became aware that this was happening in total silence, because I heard the cries of birds winging frantically away from the flames. The rocket was rising faster, slanting a little, its tense white flame leaving a long, thin spiral of bluish smoke behind it. It had risen into the open blue sky, and the dark red fire had turned into enormous billows of brown smoke, when the sound reached us: it was a long, violent crack, not a rolling sound, but specifically a cracking, grinding sound, as if space were breaking apart, but it seemed irrelevant and unimportant, because it was a sound from the past and the rocket was long since speeding safely out of its reach—though it was strange to realize that only a few seconds had passed. I found myself waving to the rocket involuntarily, I heard people applauding and joined them, grasping our common motive; it was impossible to watch passively, one had to express, by some physical action, a feeling that was not triumph, but more: the feeling that that white object's unobstructed streak of motion was the only thing that mattered in the universe. The rocket was almost above our heads when a sudden flare of yellow-gold fire seemed to envelop it—I felt a stab of anxiety, the thought that something had gone wrong, then heard a burst of applause and realized that this was the firing of the second stage. When the loud, space-cracking sound reached us, the fire had turned into a small puff of white vapor floating away. At the firing of the third stage, the rocket was barely visible; it seemed to be shrinking and descending; there was a brief spark, a white puff of vapor, a distant crack—and when the white puff dissolved, the rocket was gone.

These were the seven minutes.

What did one feel afterward? An abnormal, tense overconcentration on the commonplace necessities of the immediate moment, such as stumbling over patches of rough gravel, running to find the appropriate guest bus. One had to overconcentrate, because one knew that one did not give a damn about anything, because one had no mind and no motivation left for any immediate action. How do you descend from a state of pure exaltation?

What we had seen, in naked essentials—but in reality, not in a work of art—was the concretized abstraction of man's greatness.

The meaning of the sight lay in the fact that when those dark red wings of fire flared open, one knew that one was not looking at a normal occurrence, but at a cataclysm which, if unleashed by nature, would have wiped man out of existence—and one knew also that this cataclysm was planned, unleashed, and *controlled* by man, that this unimaginable power was ruled by *his* power and, obediently serving his purpose, was making way for a slender, rising craft. One knew that

this spectacle was not the product of inanimate nature, like some au-
rora borealis, or of chance, or of luck, that it was unmistakably
human—with "human," for once, meaning *grandeur*—that a purpose
and a long, sustained, disciplined effort had gone to achieve this series of moments, and that man was succeeding, succeeding, succeeding! For once, if only for seven minutes, the worst among those who
saw it had to feel—not "How small is man by the side of the Grand
Canyon!"—but "How great is man and how safe is nature when he
conquers it!"

That we had seen a demonstration of man at his best, no one could
doubt—this was the cause of the event's attraction and of the
stunned, numbed state in which it left us. And no one could doubt
that we had seen an achievement of man in his capacity as a rational
being—an achievement of reason, of logic, of mathematics, of total
dedication to the absolutism of reality. How many people would con-
nect these two facts, I do not know.

The next four days were a period torn out of the world's usual context, like a breathing spell with a sweep of clean air piercing
mankind's lethargic suffocation. For thirty years or longer, the newspapers had featured nothing but disasters, catastrophes, betrayals, the
shrinking stature of men, the sordid mess of a collapsing civilization;
their voice had become a long, sustained whine, the megaphone of
failure, like the sound of an oriental bazaar where leprous beggars, of
spirit or matter, compete for attention by displaying their sores. Now,
for once, the newspapers were announcing a human achievement,
were reporting on a human triumph, were reminding us that man still
exists and functions as man.

Those four days conveyed the sense that we were watching a magnificent work of art—a play dramatizing a single theme: the efficacy
of man's mind. One after another, the crucial, dangerous maneuvers
of Apollo 11's fight were carried out according to plan, with what appeared to be an effortless perfection. They reached us in the form of
brief, rasping sounds relayed from space to Houston and from Houston to our television screens, sounds interspersed with computerized
figures, translated for us by commentators who, for once, by conta-
gion, lost their usual manner of snide equivocation and spoke with
compelling clarity.

The most confirmed evader in the worldwide audience could not
escape the fact that these sounds announced events taking place far
beyond the earth's atmosphere—that while he moaned about his

loneliness and "alienation" and fear of entering an unknown cocktail party, three men were floating in a fragile capsule in the unknown darkness and loneliness of space, with earth and moon suspended like little tennis balls behind and ahead of them, and with their lives suspended on the microscopic threads connecting numbers on their computer panels in consequence of the invisible connections made well in advance by man's brain—that the more effortless their performance appeared, the more it proclaimed the magnitude of the effort expended to project it and achieve it—that no feelings, wishes, urges, instincts, or lucky "conditioning," either in these three men or in all those behind them, from highest thinker to lowliest laborer who touched a bolt of that spacecraft, could have achieved this incomparable feat—that we were watching the embodied concretization of a single faculty of man: his rationality.

There was an aura of triumph about the entire mission of Apollo 11, from the perfect launch to the climax. An assurance of success was growing in the wake of the rocket through the four days of its moon-bound flight. No, not because success was guaranteed—it is never guaranteed to man—but because a progression of evidence was displaying the precondition of success: *these men know what they are doing*.

No event in contemporary history was as thrilling, here on earth, as three moments of the mission's climax: the moment when, superimposed over the image of a garishly colored imitation-module standing motionless on the television screen, there flashed the words: "Lunar module has landed"—the moment when the faint, gray shape of the actual module came shivering from the moon to the screen—and the moment when the shining white blob which was Neil Armstrong took his immortal first step. At this last, I felt one instant of unhappy fear, wondering what he would say, because he had it in his power to destroy the meaning and the glory of that moment, as the astronauts of Apollo 8 had done in their time. He did not. He made no reference to God; he did not undercut the rationality of his achievement by paying tribute to the forces of its opposite; he spoke of man. "That's one small step for a man, one giant leap for mankind." So it was.

As to my personal reaction to the entire mission of Apollo 11, I can express it best by paraphrasing a passage from *Atlas Shrugged* that kept coming back to my mind: "Why did I feel that joyous sense of confidence while watching the mission? In all of its giant course, two aspects pertaining to the inhuman were radiantly absent: the causeless and the purposeless. Every part of the mission was an embodied answer to 'Why?' and 'What for?'—like the steps of a life-course chosen by the sort of mind I worship. The mission was a moral code enacted in space."

Now, coming back to earth (as it is at present), I want to answer briefly some questions that will arise in this context. Is it proper for the government to engage in space projects? No, it is not—except insofar as space projects involve military aspects, in which case, and to that extent, it is not merely proper but mandatory. Scientific research as such, however, is not the proper province of the government.

But this is a political issue; it pertains to the money behind the lunar mission or to the method of obtaining that money, and to the project's administration; it does not affect the nature of the mission as such, it does not alter the fact that this was a superlative technological achievement.

In judging the effectiveness of the various elements involved in any large-scale undertaking of a mixed economy, one must be guided by the question: which elements were the result of coercion and which the result of freedom? It is not coercion, not the physical force or threat of a gun, that created Apollo 11. The scientists, the technologists, the engineers, the astronauts were free men acting of their own choice. The various parts of the spacecraft were produced by private industrial concerns. Of all human activities, science is the field least amenable to force: the facts of reality do not take orders. (This is one of the reasons why science perishes under dictatorships, though technology may survive for a short while.)

It is said that without the "unlimited" resources of the government, such an enormous project would not have been undertaken. No, it would not have been—*at this time*. But it would have been, when the economy was ready for it. There is a precedent for this situation. The first transcontinental railroad of the United States was built by order of the government, on government subsidies. It was hailed as a great achievement (which, in some respects, it was). But it caused economic dislocations and political evils, for the consequences of which we are paying to this day in many forms.

If the government deserves any credit for the space program, it is only to the extent that it did not act as a government, i.e., did not use coercion in regard to its participants (which it used in regard to its backers, i.e., the taxpayers). And what is relevant in this context (but is not to be taken as a justification or endorsement of a mixed economy) is the fact that of all our government programs, the space program is the cleanest and best: it, at least, has brought the American citizens a return on their forced investment, it has worked for its money, it has earned its keep, which cannot be said about any other program of the government.

There is, however, a shameful element in the ideological motivation (or the publicly alleged motivation) that gave birth to our space program: John F. Kennedy's notion of a space competition between the United States and Soviet Russia.

A competition presupposes some basic principles held in common by all the competitors, such as the rules of the game in athletics, or the functions of the free market in business. The notion of a competition between the United States and Soviet Russia in any field whatsoever is obscene: they are incommensurable entities, intellectually and morally. What would you think of a competition between a doctor and a murderer to determine who could affect the greatest number of people? Or: a competition between Thomas A. Edison and Al Capone to see who could get rich quicker?

The fundamental significance of Apollo 11's triumph is not political; it is philosophical; specifically, moral-epistemological.

The lunar landing as such was not a milestone of science, but of technology. Technology is an applied science, i.e., it translates the discoveries of theoretical science into practical application to man's life. As such, technology is not the first step in the development of a given body of knowledge, but the last; it is not the most difficult step, but it is the ultimate step, the implicit purpose, of man's quest for knowledge.

The lunar landing was not the greatest achievement of science, but its greatest visible result. The greatest achievements of science are invisible: they take place in a man's mind; they occur in the form of a connection integrating a broad range of phenomena. The astronaut of an earlier mission who remarked that his spacecraft was driven by Sir Isaac Newton understood this issue. (And if I may be permitted to amend that remark, I would say that Sir Isaac Newton was the copilot of the flight; the pilot was Aristotle.) In this sense, the lunar landing was a first step, a beginning, in regard to the moon, but it was a last step, an end product, in regard to the earth—the end product of a long, intellectual-scientific development.

This does not diminish in any way the intellectual stature, power, or achievement of the technologists and the astronauts; it merely indicates that they were the worthy recipients of an illustrious heritage, who made full use of it by the exercise of their own individual ability. (The fact that man is the only species capable of transmitting knowledge and thus capable of progress, the fact that man can achieve a division of labor, and the fact that large numbers of men are required for a large-scale undertaking, do not mean what some creeps are suggesting: that achievement has become collective.)

I am not implying that all the men who contributed to the flight of Apollo 11 were necessarily rational in every aspect of their lives or convictions. But in their various professional capacities—each to the extent that he did contribute to the mission—they had to act on the principle of strict rationality.

The most inspiring aspect of Apollo 11's flight was that it made such abstractions as rationality, knowledge, science perceivable in direct, immediate experience. That it involved a landing on another celestial body was like a dramatist's emphasis on the dimensions of reason's power: it is not of enormous importance to most people that man lands on the moon, but that man *can* do it, is.

This was the cause of the world's response to the flight of Apollo 11.

Frustration is the leitmotif in the lives of most men, particularly today—the frustration of inarticulate desires, with no knowledge of the means to achieve them. In the sight and hearing of a crumbling world, Apollo 11 enacted the story of an audacious purpose, its execution, its triumph, and the means that achieved it—the story and the demonstration of man's highest potential. Whatever his particular ability or goal, if a man is not to give up his struggle, he needs the reminder that success is possible; if he is not to regard the human species with fear, contempt, or hatred, he needs the spiritual fuel of knowing that man the hero is possible.

This was the meaning and the unidentified motive of the millions of eager, smiling faces that looked up to the flight of Apollo 11 from all over the remnants and ruins of the civilized world. This was the meaning that people sensed, but did not know in conscious terms—and will give up or betray tomorrow. It was the job of their teachers, the intellectuals, to tell them. But it is not what they are being told.

A great event is like an explosion that blasts off pretenses and brings the hidden out to the surface, be it diamonds or muck. The flight of Apollo 11 was "a moment of truth": it revealed an abyss between the physical sciences and the humanities that has to be measured in terms of interplanetary distances. If the achievements of the physical sciences have to be watched through a telescope, the state of the humanities requires a microscope: there is no historical precedent for the smallness of stature and shabbiness of mind displayed by today's intellectuals.

In *The New York Times* of July 21, 1969, there appeared two whole pages devoted to an assortment of reactions to the lunar landing, from all kinds of prominent and semi-prominent people who represent a cross-section of our culture.

It was astonishing to see how many ways people could find to utter variants of the same bromides. Under an overwhelming air of staleness, of pettiness, of musty meanness, the collection revealed the naked essence (and spiritual consequences) of the basic premises ruling today's culture: irrationalism—altruism—collectivism.

The extent of the hatred for reason was somewhat startling. (And, psychologically, it gave the show away: one does not hate that which one honestly regards as ineffectual.) It was, however, expressed indirectly, in the form of denunciations of technology. (And since technology is the means of bringing the benefits of science to man's life, judge for yourself the motive and the sincerity of the protestations of concern with human suffering.)

"But the chief reason for assessing the significance of the moon landing negatively, even while the paeans of triumph are sung, is that this tremendous technical achievement represents a defective sense of human values, and of a sense of priorities of our technical culture." "We are betraying our moral weakness in our very triumphs in technology and economics." "How can this nation swell and stagger with technological pride when it is so weak, so wicked, so blinded and misdirected in its priorities? While we can send men to the moon or deadly missiles to Moscow or toward Mao, we can't get foodstuffs across town to starving folks in the teeming ghettos." "Are things more important than people? I simply do not believe that a program comparable to the moon landing cannot be projected around poverty, the war, crime, and so on." "If we show the same determination and willingness to commit our resources, we can master the problems of our cities just as we have mastered the challenge of space." "In this regard, the contemporary triumphs of man's mind—his ability to translate his dreams of grandeur into awesome accomplishments— are not to be equated with progress, as defined in terms of man's primary concern with the welfare of the masses of fellow human beings . . . the power of human intelligence which was mobilized to accomplish this feat can also be mobilized to address itself to the ultimate acts of human compassion." "But, the most wondrous event would be if man could relinquish all the stains and defilements of the untamed mind. . . ."

There was one entirely consistent person in that collection, Pablo Picasso, whose statement, in full, was: "It means nothing to me. I have no opinion about it, and I don't care." His work has been demonstrating that for years.

The best statement was, surprisingly, that of the playwright Eugene Ionesco, who was perceptive about the nature of his fellow intellectuals. He said, in part:

> It's an extraordinary event of incalculable importance. The sign that it's so important is that most people aren't interested in it. They go on discussing riots and strikes and sentimental affairs. The perspectives opened up are enormous, and the absence of interest shows an astonishing lack of goodwill. I have the impression that writers and intellectuals—men of the left—are turning their backs to the event.

This is an honest statement—and the only pathetic (or terrible) thing about it is the fact that the speaker has not observed that "men of the left" are not "most people."

Now consider the exact, specific meaning of the evil revealed in that collection: it is the *moral* significance of Apollo 11 that is being ignored; it is the *moral stature* of the astronauts—and of all the men behind them, and of all achievement—that is being denied. Think of what was required to achieve that mission: think of the unself-pitying effort; the merciless discipline; the courage; the responsibility of relying on one's judgment; the days, nights and years of unswerving dedication to a goal; the tension of the unbroken maintenance of a full, clear mental focus; and the honesty (honesty means: loyalty to truth, and truth means: the recognition of reality). All these are not regarded as virtues by the altruists and are treated as of no moral significance.

Now perhaps you will grasp the infamous inversion represented by the morality of altruism.

Some people accused me of exaggeration when I said that altruism does not mean mere kindness or generosity, but the sacrifice of the best among men to the worst, the sacrifice of virtues to flaws, of ability to incompetence, of progress to stagnation—and the subordinating of all life and of all values to the claims of anyone's suffering.

You have seen it enacted in reality.

What else is the meaning of the brazen presumption of those who protest against the mission of Apollo 11, demanding that the money (which is not theirs) be spent, instead, on the relief of poverty?

This is not an old-fashioned protest against mythical tycoons who "exploit" their workers, it is not a protest against the rich, it is not a protest against idle luxury, it is not a plea for some marginal charity, for money that "no one would miss." It is a protest against science and progress, it is the impertinent demand that man's mind cease to function, that man's ability be denied the means to move forward, that achievement stop—because the poor hold a first mortgage on the lives of their betters.

By their own assessment, by demanding that the public support them, these protesters declare that they have not produced enough to support themselves—yet they present a claim on the men whose ability produced so enormous a result as Apollo 11, declaring that it was done at *their* expense, that the money behind it was taken from *them*. Led by their spiritual equivalents and spokesmen, they assert a private right to public funds, while denying the public (i.e., the rest of us) the right to any higher, better purpose.

I could remind them that without the technology they damn, there would be no means to support them. I could remind them of the pretechnological centuries when men subsisted in such poverty that they were unable to feed themselves, let alone give assistance to others. I could say that anyone who used one-hundredth of the mental effort used by the smallest of the technicians responsible for Apollo 11 would not be consigned to permanent poverty, not in a free or even semi-free society. I could say it, but I won't. It is not their practice that I challenge, but their moral premise. Poverty is not a mortgage on the labor of others—misfortune is not a mortgage on achievement—failure is not a mortgage on success—suffering is not a claim check, and its relief is not the goal of existence—man is not a sacrificial animal on anyone's altar or for anyone's cause—life is not one huge hospital.

Those who suggest that we substitute a war on poverty for the space program should ask themselves whether the premises and values that form the character of an astronaut would be satisfied by a lifetime of carrying bedpans and teaching the alphabet to the mentally retarded. The answer applies as well to the values and premises of the astronauts' admirers. Slums are not a substitute for stars. [. . .]

As far as "national priorities" are concerned, I want to say the following: we do not have to have a mixed economy, we still have a chance to change our course and thus to survive. But if we do continue down the road of a mixed economy, then let them pour all the millions and billions they can into the space program. If the United States is to commit suicide, let it not be for the sake and support of the worst human elements, the parasites-on-principle, at home and abroad. Let it not be its only epitaph that it died paying its enemies for its own destruction. Let some of its lifeblood go to the support of achievement and the progress of science. The American flag on the moon—or on Mars, or on Jupiter—will, at least, be a worthy monument to what had once been a great country.

Apollo and Dionysus

ON JULY 16, 1969, one million people, from all over the country, converged on Cape Kennedy, Florida, to witness the launching of Apollo 11 that carried astronauts to the moon.

On August 15, 300,000 people, from all over the country, converged on Bethel, New York, near the town of Woodstock, to witness a rock music festival.

These two events were news, not philosophical theory. These were facts of our actual existence, the kinds of facts—according to both modern philosophers and practical businessmen—that philosophy has nothing to do with.

But if one cares to understand the meaning of these two events—to grasp their roots and their consequences—one will understand the power of philosophy and learn to recognize the specific forms in which philosophical abstractions appear in our actual existence.

The issue in this case is the alleged dichotomy of *reason versus emotion*.

This dichotomy has been presented in many variants in the history of philosophy, but its most colorfully eloquent statement was given by Friedrich Nietzsche. In *The Birth of Tragedy from the Spirit of Music*, Nietzsche claims that he observed two opposite elements in Greek tragedies, which he saw as metaphysical principles inherent in the nature of reality; he named them after two Greek gods: Apollo, the god of light, and Dionysus, the god of wine. Apollo, in Nietzsche's metaphysics, is the symbol of beauty, order, wisdom, efficacy (though Nietzsche equivocates about this last)—i.e., the symbol of reason. Dionysus is the symbol of drunkenness or, rather, Nietzsche cites drunkenness as his identification of what Dionysus stands for: wild, primeval feelings, orgiastic joy, the dark, the savage, the unintelligible element in man—i.e. the symbol of emotion.

Apollo, according to Nietzsche, is a necessary element, but an unreliable and thus inferior guide to existence, that gives man a superficial view of reality: the illusion of an orderly universe. Dionysus is the free, unfettered spirit that offers man—by means of a mysterious intuition induced by wine and drugs—a more profound vision of a different kind of reality, and is thus the superior. And—indicating that Nietzsche knew clearly what he was talking about, even though he chose to express it in a safely, drunkenly Dionysian manner—Apollo represents the principle of individuality, while Dionysus leads man "into complete self-forgetfulness" and into merging with the "Oneness" of nature. (Those who, at a superficial reading, take Nietzsche to be an advocate of individualism, please note.)

This much is true: reason *is* the faculty of an individual, to be exercised individually; and it is only dark, irrational emotions, obliterating his mind, that can enable a man to melt, merge and dissolve into a mob or a tribe. We may accept Nietzsche's symbols, but *not* his estimate of their respective values, nor the metaphysical necessity of a reason-emotion dichotomy.

It is *not* true that reason and emotion are irreconcilable antagonists or that emotions are a wild, unknowable, ineffable element in men. But this is what emotions become for those who do not care to know what they feel, and who attempt to subordinate reason to their emotions. For every variant of such attempts—as well as for their consequences—the image of Dionysus is an appropriate symbol.

Symbolic figures are a valuable adjunct to philosophy: they help men to integrate and bear in mind the essential meaning of complex issues. Apollo and Dionysus represent the fundamental conflict of our age. And for those who may regard them as floating abstractions, reality has offered two perfect, fiction-like dramatizations of these abstract symbols: at Cape Kennedy and at Woodstock. They were perfect in every respect demanded of serious fiction: they concretized the *essentials* of the two principles involved, in action, in a pure, extreme, isolated form. The fact that the spacecraft was called "Apollo" is merely a coincidence, but a helpful coincidence.

If you want to know fully what the conflict of reason versus irrational emotion means—in fact, in reality, on earth—keep these two events in mind: it means Apollo 11 versus the Woodstock festival. Remember also that you are asked to make a choice between these two—and that the whole weight of today's culture is being used to push you to the side of and into Woodstock's mud. [. . .]

One of the paradoxes of our age is the fact that the intellectuals, the politicians and all the sundry voices that choke, like asthma, the throat of our communications media have never gasped and stuttered so loudly about their devotion to the public good and about the people's will as the supreme criterion of value—and never have they been so grossly indifferent to the people. The reason, obviously, is that collectivist slogans serve as a rationalization for those who intend, not to follow the people, but to rule it. There is, however, a deeper reason: the most profound breach in this country is not between the rich and the poor, but between the people and the intellectuals. In their view of life, the American people are predominantly Apollonian; the "mainstream" intellectuals are Dionysian.

This means: the people are reality-oriented, common-sense-oriented, technology-oriented (the intellectuals call this "materialistic" and "middle-class"); the intellectuals are emotion-oriented and seek, in panic, an escape from a reality they are unable to deal with, and from a technological civilization that ignores their feelings.

The flight of Apollo 11 brought this out into the open. With rare exceptions, the intellectuals resented its triumph. A two-page survey of their reactions, published by *The New York Times* on July 21, was an almost unanimous spread of denigrations and denunciations. (See my article "Apollo 11.") What they denounced was "technology"; what they resented was achievement and its source: reason. The same attitude—with rare exceptions—was displayed by the popular commentators, who are not the makers, but the products and the weather vanes of the prevailing intellectual trends.

Walter Cronkite of CBS was a notable exception. But Eric Sevareid of CBS was typical of the trend. On July 15, the eve of the launching, he broadcast from Cape Kennedy a commentary that was reprinted in *Variety* (July 23, 1969). "In Washington and elsewhere," he said, "the doubts concern future flights, their number, their cost and their benefits, as if the success of Apollo 11 were already assured. We are a people who hate failure. It's un-American. It is a fair guess that failure of Apollo 11 would not curtail future space programs but re-energize them."

Please consider these two sentences: "We are a people who hate failure. It's un-American." (In the context of the rest, this was not intended as a compliment, though it should have been; it was intended as sarcasm.) Who *doesn't* hate failure? Should one love it? Is there a nation on earth that doesn't hate it? Surely, one would have to say that failure is un-British or un-French or un-Chinese. I can think of only one nation to whom this would not apply: failure is *not* un-Russian (in a sense which is deeper than politics).

But what Mr. Sevareid had in mind was not failure. It was the American dedication to success that he was deriding. It is true that no other nation as a whole is as successful as America, which is America's greatest virtue. But success is never automatically immediate; passive resignation is not a typical American trait; Americans seldom give up. It is this precondition of success—the "try, try again" precept—that Mr. Sevareid was undercutting.

He went on to say that if Apollo 11 succeeded, "the pressure to divert these great sums of money to inner space, terra firma and inner man will steadily grow." He went on to discuss the views of men who believe "that this adventure, however majestic its drama, is only one more act of escape, that it is man once again running away from himself and his real needs, that we are approaching the bright side of the moon with the dark side of ourselves. . . . We know that the human brain will soon know more about the composition of the moon than it knows about the human brain . . . [and] why human beings do what they do."

This last sentence is true, and one would think that the inescapable conclusion is that man should use his brain to study human nature by the same *rational* methods he has used so successfully to study inanimate matter. But not according to Mr. Sevareid; he reached a different conclusion: "It is possible that the divine spark in man will consume him in flames, that the big brain will prove our ultimate flaw, like the dinosaur's big body, that the metal plaque Armstrong and Aldrin expect to place on the moon will become man's epitaph."

On July 20, while Apollo 11 was approaching the moon, and the world was waiting breathlessly, Mr. Sevareid found it appropriate to broadcast the following remark: no matter how great this event, he said, nothing much has changed, "man still puts his pants on, one leg at a time, he still argues with his wife," etc. Well, each to his own hierarchy of values and of importance.

On the same day, David Brinkley of NBC observed that since men can now see and hear everything directly on television, by sensory-perceptual means (as he stressed), commentators are no longer needed at all. This implies that perceived events will somehow provide men automatically with the appropriate conceptual conclusions. The truth is that the more men perceive, the more they need the help of commentators, but of commentators who are able to provide a *conceptual* analysis.

According to a fan letter I received from Canada, the U.S. TV-commentaries during Apollo 11's flight were mild compared to those on Canadian television. "We listened to an appalling panel of 'experts' disparage the project as a 'mere technological cleverness by a stupid, pretentious speck of dust in the cosmos.' . . . They were also very concerned about the 'inflated American ego' if the voyage succeeded. One almost got the impression that they would be greatly relieved if the mission failed!"

What is the actual motive behind this attitude—the unadmitted, subconscious motive? An intelligent American newsman, Harry Reasoner of CBS, named it inadvertently; I had the impression that he did not realize the importance of his own statement. Many voices, at the time, were declaring that the success of Apollo 11 would destroy the poetic-romantic glamor of the moon, its fascinating mystery, its appeal to lovers and to human imagination. Harry Reasoner summed it up by saying simply, quietly, a little sadly, that if the moon is found to be made of green cheese, it will be a blow to science; but if it isn't, it will be a blow to "those of us whose life is not so well organized."

And *this* is the whole shabby secret: to some men, the sight of an achievement is a reproach, a reminder that their own lives are irrational and that there is no loophole, no escape from reason and reality. Their resentment is the cornered Dionysian element baring its teeth.

What Harry Reasoner's statement implied was the fact that only the vanguard of the Dionysian cohorts is made up of wild, rampaging irrationalists, openly proclaiming their hatred of reason, dripping wine and blood. The bulk of Dionysus' strength, his grass-roots following, consists of sedate little souls who never commit any major crime against reason, who merely indulge their petty irrational whims once in a while, covertly—and, overtly, seek a "balance of power," a compromise between whims and reality. But reason is an absolute: in order to betray it, one does not have to dance naked in the streets with vine leaves in one's hair; one betrays it merely by sneaking down the back stairs. Then, someday, one finds oneself unable to grasp why one feels no joy at the scientific discoveries that prolong human life or why the naked dancers are prancing all over one's own body. . . .

———————

EDITOR'S NOTE: *How can one live by reason, students often asked, when most people are unreasonable? Here, in part, from* The Virtue of Selfishness *is AR's answer, written in 1962.*

How Does One Lead a Rational Life in an Irrational Society?

I WILL confine my answer to a single, fundamental aspect of this question. I will name only one principle, the opposite of the idea which is so prevalent today and which is responsible for the spread of evil in the world. That principle is: *One must never fail to pronounce moral judgment.*

Nothing can corrupt and disintegrate a culture or a man's character as thoroughly as does the precept of *moral agnosticism*, the idea that one must never pass moral judgment on others, that one must be morally tolerant of anything, that the good consists of never distinguishing good from evil.

It is obvious who profits and who loses by such a precept. It is not justice or equal treatment that you grant to men when you abstain equally from praising men's virtues and from condemning men's vices. When your impartial attitude declares, in effect, that neither the good nor the evil may expect anything from you—whom do you betray and whom do you encourage?

But to pronounce moral judgment is an enormous responsibility. To be a judge, one must possess an unimpeachable character; one need not be omniscient or infallible, and it is not an issue of errors of knowledge; one needs an unbreached integrity, that is, the absence of any indulgence in conscious, willful evil. Just as a judge in a court of law may err, when the evidence is inconclusive, but may not evade the evidence available, nor accept bribes, nor allow any personal feeling, emotion, desire or fear to obstruct his mind's judgment of the facts of reality—so every rational person must maintain an equally strict and solemn integrity in the courtroom within his own mind, where the responsibility is more awesome than in a public tribunal, because *he*, the judge, is the only one to know when he has been impeached.

There is, however, a court of appeal from one's judgments: objective reality. A judge puts himself on trial every time he pronounces a verdict. It is only in today's reign of amoral cynicism, subjectivism and hooliganism that men may imagine themselves free to utter any sort of irrational judgment and to suffer no consequences. But, in fact, a man is to be judged by the judgments he pronounces. The things which he condemns or extols exist in objective reality and are open to the independent appraisal of others. It is his own moral character and standards that he reveals, when he blames or praises. If he condemns America and extols Soviet Russia—or if he attacks businessmen and defends juvenile delinquents—or if he denounces a great work of art and praises trash—it is the nature of his own soul that he confesses.

It is their fear of *this* responsibility that prompts most people to adopt an attitude of indiscriminate moral neutrality. It is the fear best expressed in the precept: "Judge not, that ye be not judged." But that precept, in fact, is an abdication of moral responsibility: it is a moral blank check one gives to others in exchange for a moral blank check one expects for oneself.

There is no escape from the fact that men have to make choices; so long as men have to make choices, there is no escape from moral values; so long as moral values are at stake, no moral neutrality is possible. To abstain from condemning a torturer, is to become an accessory to the torture and murder of his victims.

The moral principle to adopt in this issue, is: "*Judge, and be prepared to be judged.*"

The opposite of moral neutrality is not a blind, arbitrary, self-righteous condemnation of any idea, action or person that does not fit one's mood, one's memorized slogans or one's snap judgment of the moment. Indiscriminate tolerance and indiscriminate condemnation are not two opposites: they are two variants of the same evasion. To declare that "everybody is white" or "everybody is black" or "everybody is neither white nor black, but gray," is not a moral judgment, but an escape from the responsibility of moral judgment.

To judge means: to evaluate a given concrete by reference to an abstract principle or standard. It is not an easy task; it is not a task that can be performed automatically by one's feelings, "instincts" or hunches. It is a task that requires the most precise, the most exacting, the most ruthlessly objective and *rational* process of thought. It is fairly easy to grasp abstract moral principles; it can be very difficult to apply them to a given situation, particularly when it involves the moral character of another person. When one pronounces moral judgment, whether in praise or in blame, one must be prepared to answer "Why?" and to prove one's case—to oneself and to any rational inquirer.

The policy of always pronouncing moral judgment does not mean that one must regard oneself as a missionary charged with the responsibility of "saving everyone's soul"—nor that one must give unsolicited moral appraisals to all those one meets. It means: (a) that one must know clearly, in full, verbally identified form, one's own moral evaluation of every person, issue and event with which one deals, and act accordingly; (b) that one must make one's moral evaluation known to others, when it is rationally appropriate to do so.

This last means that one need not launch into unprovoked moral denunciations or debates, but that one *must* speak up in situations where silence can objectively be taken to mean agreement with or sanction of evil. When one deals with irrational persons, where argument is futile, a mere "I don't agree with you" is sufficient to negate any implication of moral sanction. When one deals with better people, a full statement of one's views may be morally required. But in no case and in no situation may one permit one's own values to be attacked or denounced, and keep silent.

Moral values are the motive power of a man's actions. By pronouncing moral judgment, one protects the clarity of one's own perception and the rationality of the course one chooses to pursue. It makes a difference whether one thinks that one is dealing with human errors of knowledge or with human evil.

Observe how many people evade, rationalize and drive their minds into a state of blind stupor, in dread of discovering that those they deal with—their "loved ones" or friends or business associates or political rulers—are not merely mistaken, but *evil*. Observe that this dread leads them to sanction, to help and to spread the very evil whose existence they fear to acknowledge.

If people did not indulge in such abject evasions as the claim that some contemptible liar "means well"—that a mooching bum "can't help it"—that a juvenile delinquent "needs love"—that a criminal "doesn't know any better"—that a power-seeking politician is moved by patriotic concern for "the public good"—that communists are merely "agrarian reformers"—the history of the past few decades, or centuries, would have been different.

Ask yourself why totalitarian dictatorships find it necessary to pour money and effort into propaganda for their own helpless, chained, gagged slaves, who have no means of protest or defense. The answer is that even the humblest peasant or the lowest savage would rise in blind rebellion, were he to realize that he is being immolated, not to some incomprehensible "noble purpose," but to plain, naked human evil.

Observe also that moral neutrality necessitates a progressive sympathy for vice and a progressive antagonism to virtue. A man who struggles not to acknowledge that evil is evil, finds it increasingly dangerous to acknowledge that the good is the good. To him, a person of virtue is a threat that can topple all of his evasions—particularly when an issue of justice is involved, which demands that he take sides. It is then that such formulas as "Nobody is ever fully right or fully wrong" and "Who am I to judge?" take their lethal effect. The man who begins by saying: "There is some good in the worst of us," goes on to say: "There is some bad in the best of us"—then: "There's *got to* be some bad in the best of us"—and then: "It's the best of us who make life difficult—why don't they keep silent?—who are *they* to judge?"

And then, on some gray, middle-aged morning, such a man realizes suddenly that he has betrayed all the values he had loved in his distant spring, and wonders how it happened, and slams his mind shut to the answer, by telling himself hastily that the fear he had felt in his worst, most shameful moments was right and that values have no chance in this world.

An irrational society is a society of moral cowards—of men paralyzed by the loss of moral standards, principles and goals. But since men have to act, so long as they live, such a society is ready to be taken over by anyone willing to set its direction. The initiative can come from only two types of men: either from the man who is willing to assume the responsibility of asserting rational values—or from the thug who is not troubled by questions of responsibility.

No matter how hard the struggle, there is only one choice that a rational man can make in the face of such an alternative.

PART THREE

Atlas Shrugged

The theme of Atlas Shrugged *is the role of man's mind—and specifically of the men of ability—in human existence. "I set out to show," said AR, "how desperately the world needs prime movers, and how viciously it treats them. And I show it on a hypothetical case—what happens to the world without them" (Journals of Ayn Rand, 1997, p. 392). This is the plot-theme of the novel: what happens when the world's thinkers and producers go on strike against the rule of the mindless.*

The first excerpt (from Chapter VI) presents the anniversary party of a leading steel industrialist, Hank Rearden, who is the greatest victim of the world's mistreatment. Rearden has just created—after ten years of excruciating effort—an invaluable new type of metal. Out of the first heat, he had ordered a special bracelet for his wife, Lillian.

Dagny Taggart, the novel's heroine, is the operating vice president of Taggart Transcontinental Railroad; her brother James is its president. Dagny has been working closely with Rearden to build a new railroad with track made of Rearden Metal. Francisco d'Anconia, a copper baron, is—by all appearances at this point—a worthless playboy who is wasting his great potential along with a huge inherited fortune.

Rearden's Anniversary Party

REARDEN PRESSED his forehead to the mirror and tried not to think. That was the only way he could go through with it, he told himself. He concentrated on the relief of the mirror's cooling touch, wondering how one went about forcing one's mind into blankness, particularly after a lifetime lived on the axiom that the constant, clearest, most ruthless function of his rational faculty was his foremost duty. He wondered why no effort had ever seemed beyond his capacity, yet now he could not scrape up the strength to stick a few black pearl studs into his starched white shirt front.

This was his wedding anniversary and he had known for three months that the party would take place tonight, as Lillian wished. He had promised it to her, safe in the knowledge that the party was a long way off and that he would attend to it, when the time came, as he attended to every duty on his overloaded schedule. Then, during three months of eighteen-hour workdays, he had forgotten it happily—until half an hour ago, when, long past dinner time, his secretary had entered his office and said firmly, "Your party, Mr. Rearden." He had cried, "Good God!" leaping to his feet; he had hurried home, rushed up the stairs, started tearing his clothes off and gone through the routine of dressing, conscious only of the need to hurry, not of the purpose. When the full realization of the purpose struck him like a sudden blow, he stopped.

"You don't care for anything but business." He had heard it all his life, pronounced as a verdict of damnation. He had always known that business was regarded as some sort of secret, shameful cult, which one did not impose on innocent laymen, that people thought of it as of an ugly necessity, to be performed but never mentioned, that to talk shop was an offense against higher sensibilities, that just as one washed machine grease off one's hands before coming home, so one was supposed to wash the stain of business off one's mind before entering a drawing room. He had never held that creed, but he had accepted it as natural that his family should hold it. He took it for granted—wordlessly, in the manner of a feeling absorbed in childhood, left unquestioned and unnamed—that he had dedicated himself, like the martyr of some dark religion, to the service of a faith which was his passionate love, but which made him an outcast among men, whose sympathy he was not to expect.

He had accepted the tenet that it was his duty to give his wife some form of existence unrelated to business. But he had never found the capacity to do it or even to experience a sense of guilt. He could neither force himself to change nor blame her if she chose to condemn him.

He had given Lillian none of his time for months—no, he thought, for years; for the eight years of their marriage. He had no interest to spare for her interests, not even enough to learn just what they were. She had a large circle of friends, and he had heard it said that their names represented the heart of the country's culture, but he had never had time to meet them or even to acknowledge their fame by knowing what achievements had earned it. He knew only that he often saw their names on the magazine covers on newsstands. If Lillian resented his attitude, he thought, she was right. If her manner toward him was objectionable, he deserved it. If his family called him heartless, it was true.

He had never spared himself in any issue. When a problem came up at the mills, his first concern was to discover what error he had made; he did not search for anyone's fault but his own; it was of himself that he demanded perfection. He would grant himself no mercy now; he took the blame. But at the mills, it prompted him to action in an immediate impulse to correct the error; now, it had no effect. . . . Just a few more minutes, he thought, standing against the mirror, his eyes closed.

He could not stop the thing in his mind that went on throwing words at him; it was like trying to plug a broken hydrant with his bare hands. Stinging jets, part words, part pictures, kept shooting at his brain. . . . Hours of it, he thought, hours to spend watching the eyes of the guests getting heavy with boredom if they were sober or glazing into an imbecile stare if they weren't, and pretend that he noticed neither, and strain to think of something to say to them, when he had nothing to say—while he needed hours of inquiry to find a successor for the superintendent of his rolling mills who had resigned suddenly, without explanation—he had to do it at once—men of that sort were so hard to find—and if anything happened to break the flow of the rolling mills—it was the Taggart rail that was being rolled. . . . He remembered the silent reproach, the look of accusation, long-bearing patience and scorn, which he always saw in the eyes of his family when they caught some evidence of his passion for his business—and the futility of his silence, of his hope that they would not think Rearden Steel meant as much to him as it did—like a drunkard pretending indifference to liquor, among people who watch him with the scornful amusement of their full knowledge of his shameful weakness. . . . "I heard you last night coming home at two in the morning, where were you?" his mother saying to him at the dinner table, and Lillian answering, "Why, at the mills, of course," as another wife would say, "At the corner saloon." . . . Or Lillian asking him, the hint of a wise half-smile on her face, "What were you doing in New York yesterday?" "It was a banquet with the boys." "Business?" "Yes." "*Of course*"—and Lillian turning away, nothing more, except the shameful realization that he had almost hoped she would think he had attended some sort of obscene stag party. . . . An ore carrier had gone down in a storm on Lake Michigan, with thousands of tons of Rearden ore—those boats were falling apart—if he didn't take it upon himself to help them obtain the replacements they needed, the owners of the line would go bankrupt, and there was no other line left in operation on Lake Michigan. . . . "That nook?" said Lillian, pointing to an arrangement of settees and coffee tables in their drawing room. "Why, no, Henry, it's not new, but I suppose I should feel flattered that three weeks is all it took you to notice it. It's my own adaptation of the morning room of a famous French palace—but things like that can't possibly interest you, darling, there's no stock market quotation on them, none whatever." . . . The order for copper, which he had placed six months ago, had not been delivered, the promised date had been postponed three times—"We can't help it, Mr. Rearden"—he had to find another company to deal with, the supply of copper was becoming increasingly uncertain. . . . Philip [Rearden's brother] did not smile, when he looked up in the midst of a speech he was making to some friend of their mother's, about some organization he had joined, but there was something that suggested a smile of superiority in the loose muscles of his face when he said, "No, you wouldn't care for this, it's not business, Henry, not business at all, it's a strictly non-commercial endeavor." . . . That contractor in Detroit, with the job of rebuilding a large factory, was considering structural shapes of Rearden Metal—he should fly to Detroit and speak to him in person—he should have done it a week ago—he could have done it tonight. . . . "You're not listening," said his mother at the breakfast table, when his mind wandered to the current coal price index, while she was telling him about the dream she'd had last night. "You've never listened to a living soul. You're not interested in anything but yourself. You don't give a damn about people, not about a single human creature on God's earth." . . . The typed pages lying on the desk in his office were a report on the tests of an airplane motor made of Rearden Metal—perhaps of all things on earth, the one he wanted most at this moment was to read it—it had lain on his desk, untouched, for three days, he had had no time for it—why didn't he do it now and—

He shook his head violently, opening his eyes, stepping back from the mirror.

He tried to reach for the shirt studs. He saw his hand reaching, instead, for the pile of mail on his dresser. It was mail picked as urgent, it had to be read tonight, but he had had no time to read it in the office. His secretary had stuffed it into his pocket on his way out. He had thrown it there while undressing.

A newspaper clipping fluttered down to the floor. It was an editorial which his secretary had marked with an angry slash in red pencil. It was entitled "Equalization of Opportunity." He had to read it: there had been too much talk about this issue in the last three months, ominously too much.

He read it, with the sound of voices and forced laughter coming from downstairs, reminding him that the guests were arriving, that the party had started and that he would face the bitter, reproachful glances of his family when he came down.

The editorial said that at a time of dwindling production, shrinking markets and vanishing opportunities to make a living, it was unfair to let one man hoard several business enterprises, while others had none; it was destructive to let a few corner all the resources, leaving others no chance; competition was essential to society, and it was society's duty to see that no competitor ever rose beyond the range of anybody who wanted to compete with him. The editorial predicted the passage of a bill which had been proposed, a bill forbidding any person or corporation to own more than one business concern.

Wesley Mouch, his Washington man, had told Rearden not to worry; the fight would be stiff, he had said, but the bill would be defeated. Rearden understood nothing about that kind of fight. He left it to Mouch and his staff. He could barely find time to skim through their reports from Washington and to sign the checks which Mouch requested for the battle.

Rearden did not believe that the bill would pass. He was incapable of believing it. Having dealt with the clean reality of metals, technology, production all his life, he had acquired the conviction that one had to concern oneself with the rational, not the insane—that one had to seek that which was right, because the right answer always won—that the senseless, the wrong, the monstrously unjust could not work, could not succeed, could do nothing but defeat itself. A battle against a thing such as that bill seemed preposterous and faintly embarrassing to him, as if he were suddenly asked to compete with a man who calculated steel mixtures by the formulas of numerology.

He had told himself that the issue was dangerous. But the loudest screaming of the most hysterical editorial roused no emotion in him—while a variation of a decimal point in a laboratory report on a test of Rearden Metal made him leap to his feet in eagerness or apprehension. He had no energy to spare for anything else.

He crumpled the editorial and threw it into the wastebasket. He felt the leaden approach of that exhaustion which he never felt at his job, the exhaustion that seemed to wait for him and catch him the moment he turned to other concerns. He felt as if he were incapable of any desire except a desperate longing for sleep.

He told himself that he had to attend the party—that his family had the right to demand it of him—that he had to learn to like their kind of pleasure, for their sake, not his own.

He wondered why this was a motive that had no power to impel him. Throughout his life, whenever he became convinced that a course of action was right, the desire to follow it had come automatically. What was happening to him?—he wondered. The impossible conflict of feeling reluctance to do that which was right—wasn't it the basic formula of moral corruption? To recognize one's guilt, yet feel nothing but the coldest, most profound indifference—wasn't it a betrayal of that which had been the motor of his life-course and of his pride?

He gave himself no time to seek an answer. He finished dressing, quickly, pitilessly.

Holding himself erect, his tall figure moving with the unstressed, unhurried confidence of habitual authority, the white of a fine hand-kerchief in the breast pocket of his black dinner jacket, he walked slowly down the stairs to the drawing room, looking—to the satisfaction of the dowagers who watched him—like the perfect figure of a great industrialist.

He saw Lillian at the foot of the stairs. The patrician lines of a lemon-yellow Empire evening gown stressed her graceful body, and she stood like a person proudly in control of her proper background. He smiled; he liked to see her happy; it gave some reasonable justification to the party.

He approached her—and stopped. She had always shown good taste in her use of jewelry, never wearing too much of it. But tonight she wore an ostentatious display: a diamond necklace, earrings, rings and brooches. Her arms looked conspicuously bare by contrast. On her right wrist, as sole ornament, she wore the bracelet of Rearden Metal. The glittering gems made it look like an ugly piece of dime-store jewelry.

When he moved his glance from her wrist to her face, he found her looking at him. Her eyes were narrowed and he could not define their expression; it was a look that seemed both veiled and purposeful, the look of something hidden that flaunted its security from detection.

He wanted to tear the bracelet off her wrist. Instead, in obedience to her voice gaily pronouncing an introduction, he bowed to the dowager who stood beside her, his face expressionless.

"Man? What is man? He's just a collection of chemicals with delusions of grandeur," said Dr. Pritchett to a group of guests across the room.

Dr. Pritchett picked a canapé off a crystal dish, held it speared between two straight fingers and deposited it whole into his mouth.

"Man's metaphysical pretensions," he said, "are preposterous. A miserable bit of protoplasm, full of ugly little concepts and mean little emotions—and it imagines itself important! Really, you know, that is the root of all the troubles in the world."

"But which concepts are not ugly or mean, Professor?" asked an earnest matron whose husband owned an automobile factory.

"None," said Dr. Pritchett. "None within the range of man's capacity."

A young man asked hesitantly, "But if we haven't any good concepts, how do we know that the ones we've got are ugly? I mean, by what standard?"

"There aren't any standards."

This silenced his audience.

"The philosophers of the past were superficial," Dr. Pritchett went on. "It remained for our century to redefine the purpose of philosophy. The purpose of philosophy is not to help men find the meaning of life, but to prove to them that there isn't any."

An attractive young woman, whose father owned a coal mine, asked indignantly, "Who can tell us that?"

"I am trying to," said Dr. Pritchett. For the last three years, he had been head of the Department of Philosophy at the Patrick Henry University.

Lillian Rearden approached, her jewels glittering under the lights. The expression on her face was held to the soft hint of a smile, set and faintly suggested, like the waves of her hair.

"It is this insistence of man upon meaning that makes him so difficult," said Dr. Pritchett. "Once he realizes that he is of no importance whatever in the vast scheme of the universe, that no possible significance can be attached to his activities, that it does not matter whether he lives or dies, he will become much more . . . tractable."

He shrugged and reached for another canapé. A businessman said uneasily, "What I asked you about, Professor, was what you thought about the Equalization of Opportunity Bill."

"Oh, that?" said Dr. Pritchett. "But I believe I made it clear that I am in favor of it, because I am in favor of a free economy. A free economy cannot exist without competition. Therefore, men must be forced to compete. Therefore, we must control men in order to force them to be free."

"But, look . . . isn't that sort of a contradiction?"

"Not in the higher philosophical sense. You must learn to see beyond the static definitions of old-fashioned thinking. Nothing is static in the universe. Everything is fluid."

"But it stands to reason that if—"

"Reason, my dear fellow, is the most naïve of all superstitions. That, at least, has been generally conceded in our age."

"But I don't quite understand how we can—"

"You suffer from the popular delusion of believing that things can be understood. You do not grasp the fact that the universe is a solid contradiction."

"A contradiction of what?" asked the matron.

"Of itself."

"How . . . how's that?"

"My dear madam, the duty of thinkers is not to explain, but to demonstrate that nothing can be explained."

"Yes, of course . . . only . . ."

"The purpose of philosophy is not to seek knowledge, but to prove that knowledge is impossible to man."

"But when we prove it," asked the young woman, "what's going to be left?"

"Instinct," said Dr. Pritchett reverently.

At the other end of the room, a group was listening to Balph Eubank. He sat upright on the edge of an armchair, in order to counteract the appearance of his face and figure, which had a tendency to spread if relaxed.

"The literature of the past," said Balph Eubank, "was a shallow fraud. It whitewashed life in order to please the money tycoons whom it served. Morality, free will, achievement, happy endings, and man as some sort of heroic being—all that stuff is laughable to us. Our age has given depth to literature for the first time, by exposing the real essence of life."

A very young girl in a white evening gown asked timidly, "What is the real essence of life, Mr. Eubank?"

"Suffering," said Balph Eubank. "Defeat and suffering."

"But . . . but why? People are happy . . . sometimes . . . aren't they?"

"That is a delusion of those whose emotions are superficial."

The girl blushed. A wealthy woman who had inherited an oil refinery, asked guiltily, "What should we do to raise the people's literary taste, Mr. Eubank?"

"That is a great social problem," said Balph Eubank. He was described as the literary leader of the age, but had never written a book that sold more than three thousand copies. "Personally, I believe that an Equalization of Opportunity Bill applying to literature would be the solution."

"Oh, do you approve of that Bill for industry? I'm not sure I know what to think of it."

"Certainly, I approve of it. Our culture has sunk into a bog of materialism. Men have lost all spiritual values in their pursuit of material production and technological trickery. They're too comfortable. They will return to a nobler life if we teach them to bear privations. So we ought to place a limit upon their material greed."

"I hadn't thought of it that way," said the woman apologetically.

"But how are you going to work an Equalization of Opportunity Bill for literature, Ralph?" asked Mort Liddy. "That's a new one on me."

"My name is Balph," said Eubank angrily. "And it's a new one on you because it's my own idea."

"Okay, okay, I'm not quarreling, am I? I'm just asking." Mort Liddy smiled. He spent most of his time smiling nervously. He was a composer who wrote old-fashioned scores for motion pictures, and modern symphonies for sparse audiences.

"It would work very simply," said Balph Eubank. "There should be a law limiting the sale of any book to ten thousand copies. This would throw the literary market open to new talent, fresh ideas and non-commercial writing. If people were forbidden to buy a million copies of the same piece of trash, they would be forced to buy better books."

"You've got something there," said Mort Liddy. "But wouldn't it be kinda tough on the writers' bank accounts?"

"So much the better. Only those whose motive is not moneymaking should be allowed to write."

"But, Mr. Eubank," asked the young girl in the white dress, "what if more than ten thousand people want to buy a certain book?"

"Ten thousand readers is enough for any book."

"That's not what I mean. I mean, what if they *want* it?"

"That is irrelevant."

"But if a book has a good story which—"

"Plot is a primitive vulgarity in literature," said Balph Eubank contemptuously.

Dr. Pritchett, on his way across the room to the bar, stopped to say, "Quite so. Just as logic is a primitive vulgarity in philosophy."

"Just as melody is a primitive vulgarity in music," said Mort Liddy.

"What's all this noise?" asked Lillian Rearden, glittering to a stop beside them.

"Lillian, my angel," Balph Eubank drawled, "did I tell you that I'm dedicating my new novel to you?"

"Why, thank you, darling."

"What is the name of your new novel?" asked the wealthy woman.

"*The Heart Is a Milkman.*"

"What is it about?"

"Frustration."

"But, Mr. Eubank," asked the young girl in the white dress,

blushing desperately, "if everything is frustration, what is there to live for?"

"Brother-love," said Balph Eubank grimly.

Bertram Scudder stood slouched against the bar. His long, thin face looked as if it had shrunk inward, with the exception of his mouth and eyeballs, which were left to protrude as three soft globes. He was the editor of a magazine called *The Future* and he had written an article on Hank Rearden, entitled "The Octopus."

Bertram Scudder picked up his empty glass and shoved it silently toward the bartender, to be refilled. He took a gulp from his fresh drink, noticed the empty glass in front of Philip Rearden, who stood beside him, and jerked his thumb in a silent command to the bartender. He ignored the empty glass in front of Betty Pope, who stood at Philip's other side.

"Look, bud," said Bertram Scudder, his eyeballs focused approximately in the direction of Philip, "whether you like it or not, the Equalization of Opportunity Bill represents a great step forward."

"What made you think that I did not like it, Mr. Scudder?" Philip asked humbly.

"Well, it's going to pinch, isn't it? The long arm of society is going to trim a little off the hors d'oeuvres bill around here." He waved his hand at the bar.

"Why do you assume that I object to that?"

"You don't?" Bertram Scudder asked without curiosity.

"I don't!" said Philip hotly. "I have always placed the public good above any personal consideration. I have contributed my time and money to Friends of Global Progress in their crusade for the Equalization of Opportunity Bill. I think it is perfectly unfair that one man should get all the breaks and leave none to others."

Bertram Scudder considered him speculatively, but without particular interest. "Well, that's quite unusually nice of you," he said.

"Some people do take moral issues seriously, Mr. Scudder," said Philip, with a gentle stress of pride in his voice.

"What's he talking about, Philip?" asked Betty Pope. "We don't know anybody who owns more than one business, do we?"

"Oh, pipe down!" said Bertram Scudder, his voice bored.

"I don't see why there's so much fuss about that Equalization of Opportunity Bill," said Betty Pope aggressively, in the tone of an expert on economics. "I don't see why businessmen object to it. It's to their own advantage. If everybody else is poor, they won't have any market for their goods. But if they stop being selfish and share the goods they've hoarded—they'll have a chance to work hard and produce some more."

"I do not see why industrialists should be considered at all," said Scudder. "When the masses are destitute and yet there are goods available, it's idiotic to expect people to be stopped by some scrap of paper called a property deed. Property rights are a superstition. One holds property only by the courtesy of those who do not seize it. The people can seize it at any moment. If they can, why shouldn't they?"

"They should," said Claude Slagenhop. "They need it. Need is the only consideration. If people are in need, we've got to seize things first and talk about it afterwards."

Claude Slagenhop had approached and managed to squeeze himself between Philip and Scudder, shoving Scudder aside imperceptibly. Slagenhop was not tall or heavy, but he had a square, compact bulk, and a broken nose. He was the president of Friends of Global Progress.

"Hunger won't wait," said Claude Slagenhop. "Ideas are just hot air. An empty belly is a solid fact. I've said in all my speeches that it's not necessary to talk too much. Society is suffering for lack of business opportunities at the moment, so we've got the right to seize such opportunities as exist. Right is whatever's good for society."

"He didn't dig that ore single-handed, did he?" cried Philip suddenly, his voice shrill. "He had to employ hundreds of workers. They did it. Why does he think he's so good?"

The two men looked at him, Scudder lifting an eyebrow, Slagenhop without expression.

"Oh, dear me!" said Betty Pope, remembering.

Hank Rearden stood at a window in a dim recess at the end of the drawing room. He hoped no one would notice him for a few minutes. He had just escaped from a middle-aged woman who had been telling him about her psychic experiences. He stood, looking out. Far in the distance, the red glow of Rearden Steel moved in the sky. He watched it for a moment's relief.

He turned to look at the drawing room. He had never liked his house; it had been Lillian's choice. But tonight, the shifting colors of the evening dresses drowned out the appearance of the room and gave it an air of brilliant gaiety. He liked to see people being gay, even though he did not understand this particular manner of enjoyment.

He looked at the flowers, at the sparks of light on the crystal glasses, at the naked arms and shoulders of women. There was a cold wind outside, sweeping empty stretches of land. He saw the thin branches of a tree being twisted, like arms waving in an appeal for help. The tree stood against the glow of the mills.

He could not name his sudden emotion. He had no words to state its cause, its quality, its meaning. Some part of it was joy, but it was solemn like the act of baring one's head—he did not know to whom.

When he stepped back into the crowd, he was smiling. But the smile vanished abruptly; he saw the entrance of a new guest: it was Dagny Taggart.

Lillian moved forward to meet her, studying her with curiosity. They had met before, on infrequent occasions, and she found it strange to see Dagny Taggart wearing an evening gown. It was a black dress with a bodice that fell as a cape over one arm and shoulder, leaving the other bare; the naked shoulder was the gown's only ornament. Seeing her in the suits she wore, one never thought of Dagny Taggart's body. The black dress seemed excessively revealing—because it was astonishing to discover that the lines of her shoulder were fragile and beautiful, and that the diamond band on the wrist of her naked arm gave her the most feminine of all aspects: the look of being chained.

"Miss Taggart, it is such a wonderful surprise to see you here," said Lillian Rearden, the muscles of her face performing the motions of a smile. "I had not really dared to hope that an invitation from me would take you away from your ever so much weightier concerns. Do permit me to feel flattered."

James Taggart had entered with his sister. Lillian smiled at him, in the manner of a hasty postscript, as if noticing him for the first time.

"Hello, James. That's your penalty for being popular—one tends to lose sight of you in the surprise of seeing your sister."

"No one can match you in popularity, Lillian," he answered, smiling thinly, "nor ever lose sight of you."

"Me? Oh, but I am quite resigned to taking second place in the shadow of my husband. I am humbly aware that the wife of a great man has to be contented with reflected glory—don't you think so, Miss Taggart?"

"No," said Dagny, "I don't."

"Is this a compliment or a reproach, Miss Taggart? But do forgive me if I confess I'm helpless. Whom may I present to you? I'm afraid

I have nothing but writers and artists to offer, and they wouldn't interest you, I'm sure."

"I'd like to find Hank and say hello to him."

"But of course. James, do you remember you said you wanted to meet Balph Eubank?—oh yes, he's here—I'll tell him that I heard you rave about his last novel at Mrs. Whitcomb's dinner!"

Walking across the room, Dagny wondered why she had said that she wanted to find Hank Rearden, what had prevented her from admitting that she had seen him the moment she entered.

Rearden stood at the other end of the long room, looking at her. He watched her as she approached, but he did not step forward to meet her.

"Hello, Hank."

"Good evening."

He bowed, courteously, impersonally, the movement of his body matching the distinguished formality of his clothes. He did not smile.

"Thank you for inviting me tonight," she said gaily.

"I cannot claim that I knew you were coming."

"Oh? Then I'm glad that Mrs. Rearden thought of me. I wanted to make an exception."

"An exception?"

"I don't go to parties very often."

"I am pleased that you chose this occasion as the exception." He did not add "Miss Taggart," but it sounded as if he had.

The formality of his manner was so unexpected that she was unable to adjust to it. "I wanted to celebrate," she said.

"To celebrate my wedding anniversary?"

"Oh, is it your wedding anniversary? I didn't know. My congratulations, Hank."

"What did you wish to celebrate?"

"I thought I'd permit myself a rest. A celebration of my own—in your honor and mine."

"For what reason?"

She was thinking of the new track on the rocky grades of the Colorado mountains, growing slowly toward the distant goal of the Wyatt oil fields. She was seeing the greenish-blue glow of the rails on the frozen ground, among the dried weeds, the naked boulders, the rotting shanties of half-starved settlements.

"In honor of the first sixty miles of Rearden Metal track," she answered.

"I appreciate it." The tone of his voice was the one that would have been proper if he had said, "I've never heard of it."

She found nothing else to say. She felt as if she were speaking to a stranger.

"Why, Miss Taggart!" a cheerful voice broke their silence. "Now *this* is what I mean when I say that Hank Rearden can achieve any miracle!"

A businessman whom they knew had approached, smiling at her in delighted astonishment. The three of them had often held emergency conferences about freight rates and steel deliveries. Now he looked at her, his face an open comment on the change in her appearance, the change, she thought, which Rearden had not noticed.

She laughed, answering the man's greeting, giving herself no time to recognize the unexpected stab of disappointment, the unadmitted thought that she wished she had seen this look on Rearden's face, instead. She exchanged a few sentences with the man. When she glanced around, Rearden was gone.

"So that is your famous sister?" said Balph Eubank to James Taggart, looking at Dagny across the room.

"I was not aware that my sister was famous," said Taggart, a faint bite in his voice.

"But, my good man, she's an unusual phenomenon in the field of economics, so you must expect people to talk about her. Your sister is a symptom of the illness of our century. A decadent product of the machine age. Machines have destroyed man's humanity, taken him away from the soil, robbed him of his natural arts, killed his soul and turned him into an insensitive robot. There's an example of it—a woman who runs a railroad, instead of practicing the beautiful craft of the handloom and bearing children."

Rearden moved among the guests, trying not to be trapped into conversation. He looked at the room; he saw no one he wished to approach.

"Say, Hank Rearden, you're not such a bad fellow at all when seen close up in the lion's own den. You ought to give us a press conference once in a while, you'd win us over."

Rearden turned and looked at the speaker incredulously. It was a young newspaperman of the seedier sort, who worked on a radical tabloid. The offensive familiarity of his manner seemed to imply that he chose to be rude to Rearden because he knew that Rearden should never have permitted himself to associate with a man of his kind.

Rearden would not have allowed him inside the mills; but the man was Lillian's guest; he controlled himself; he asked dryly, "What do you want?"

"You're not so bad. You've got talent. Technological talent. But, of course, I don't agree with you about Rearden Metal."

"I haven't asked you to agree."

"Well, Bertram Scudder said that your policy—" the man started belligerently, pointing toward the bar, but stopped, as if he had slid farther than he intended.

Rearden looked at the untidy figure slouched against the bar. Lillian had introduced them, but he had paid no attention to the name. He turned sharply and walked off, in a manner that forbade the young bum to tag him.

Lillian glanced up at his face, when Rearden approached her in the midst of a group, and, without a word, stepped aside where they could not be heard.

"Is that Scudder of *The Future*?" he asked, pointing.

"Why, yes."

He looked at her silently, unable to begin to believe it, unable to find the lead of a thought with which to begin to understand. Her eyes were watching him.

"How could you invite him here?" he asked.

"Now, Henry, don't let's be ridiculous. You don't want to be narrow-minded, do you? You must learn to tolerate the opinions of others and respect their right of free speech."

"In my house?"

"Oh, don't be stuffy!"

He did not speak, because his consciousness was held, not by coherent statements, but by two pictures that seemed to glare at him insistently. He saw the article, "The Octopus," by Bertram Scudder, which was not an expression of ideas, but a bucket of slime emptied in public—an article that did not contain a single fact, not even an invented one, but poured a stream of sneers and adjectives in which nothing was clear except the filthy malice of denouncing without considering proof necessary. And he saw the lines of Lillian's profile, the proud purity which he had sought in marrying her.

When he noticed her again, he realized that the vision of her profile was in his own mind, because she was turned to him fullface, watching him. In the sudden instant of returning to reality, he thought that what he saw in her eyes was enjoyment. But in the next instant he reminded himself that he was sane and that this was not possible.

"It's the first time you've invited that . . ." he used an obscene word with unemotional precision, "to my house. It's the last."

"How dare you use such—"

"Don't argue, Lillian. If you do, I'll throw him out right now."

He gave her a moment to answer, to object, to scream at him if she wished. She remained silent, not looking at him, only her smooth cheeks seemed faintly drawn inward, as if deflated.

Moving blindly away through the coils of lights, voices and perfume, he felt a cold touch of dread. He knew that he should think of Lillian and find the answer to the riddle of her character, because this was a revelation which he could not ignore; but he did not think of her—and he felt the dread because he knew that the answer had ceased to matter to him long ago.

The flood of weariness was starting to rise again. He felt as if he could almost see it in thickening waves; it was not within him, but outside, spreading through the room. For an instant, he felt as if he were alone, lost in a gray desert, needing help and knowing that no help would come.

He stopped short. In the lighted doorway, the length of the room between them, he saw the tall, arrogant figure of a man who had paused for a moment before entering. He had never met the man, but of all the notorious faces that cluttered the pages of newspapers, this was the one he despised. It was Francisco d'Anconia.

Rearden had never given much thought to men like Bertram Scudder. But with every hour of his life, with the strain and the pride of every moment when his muscles or his mind had ached from effort, with every step he had taken to rise out of the mines of Minnesota and to turn his effort into gold, with all of his profound respect for money and for its meaning, he despised the squanderer who did not know how to deserve the great gift of inherited wealth. There, he thought, was the most contemptible representative of the species.

He saw Francisco d'Anconia enter, bow to Lillian, then walk into the crowd as if he owned the room which he had never entered before. Heads turned to watch him, as if he pulled them on strings in his wake.

Approaching Lillian once more, Rearden said without anger, the contempt becoming amusement in his voice, "I didn't know you knew that one."

"I've met him at a few parties."

"Is he one of your friends, too?"

"Certainly not!" The sharp resentment was genuine.

"Then why did you invite him?"

"Well, you can't give a party—not a party that counts—while he's in this country, without inviting him. It's a nuisance if he comes, and a social black mark if he doesn't."

Rearden laughed. She was off guard; she did not usually admit things of this kind. "Look," he said wearily, "I don't want to spoil your party. But keep that man away from me. Don't come around with introductions. I don't want to meet him. I don't know how you'll work that, but you're an expert hostess, so work it."

Dagny stood still when she saw Francisco approaching. He bowed to her as he passed by. He did not stop, but she knew that he had stopped the moment in his mind. She saw him smile faintly in deliberate emphasis of what he understood and did not choose to acknowledge. She turned away. She hoped to avoid him for the rest of the evening.

Balph Eubank had joined the group around Dr. Pritchett, and was saying sullenly, ". . . no, you cannot expect people to understand the higher reaches of philosophy. Culture should be taken out of the hands of the dollar-chasers. We need a national subsidy for literature. It is disgraceful that artists are treated like peddlers and that art works have to be sold like soap."

"You mean, your complaint is that they *don't* sell like soap?" asked Francisco d'Anconia.

They had not noticed him approach; the conversation stopped, as if slashed off; most of them had never met him, but they all recognized him at once.

"I meant—" Balph Eubank started angrily and closed his mouth; he saw the eager interest on the faces of his audience, but it was not interest in philosophy any longer.

"Why, hello, Professor!" said Francisco, bowing to Dr. Pritchett.

There was no pleasure in Dr. Pritchett's face when he answered the greeting and performed a few introductions.

"We were just discussing a most interesting subject," said the earnest matron. "Dr. Pritchett was telling us that nothing is anything."

"He should, undoubtedly, know more than anyone else about that," Francisco answered gravely.

"I wouldn't have supposed that you knew Dr. Pritchett so well, Señor d'Anconia," she said, and wondered why the professor looked displeased by her remark.

"I am an alumnus of the great school that employs Dr. Pritchett at present, the Patrick Henry University. But I studied under one of his predecessors—Hugh Akston."

"Hugh Akston!" the attractive young woman gasped. "But you couldn't have, Señor d'Anconia! You're not old enough. I thought he was one of those great names of . . . of the last century."

"Perhaps in spirit, madame. Not in fact."

"But I thought he died years ago."

"Why, no. He's still alive."

"Then why don't we ever hear about him any more?"

"He retired, nine years ago."

"Isn't it odd? When a politician or a movie star retires, we read front page stories about it. But when a philosopher retires, people do not even notice it."

"They do, eventually."

A young man said, astonished, "I thought Hugh Akston was one of those classics that nobody studied any more, except in histories of philosophy. I read an article recently which referred to him as the last of the great advocates of reason."

"Just what did Hugh Akston teach?" asked the earnest matron.

Francisco answered, "He taught that everything is something."

"Your loyalty to your teacher is laudable, Señor d'Anconia," said Dr. Pritchett dryly. "May we take it that you are an example of the practical results of his teaching?"

"I am."

James Taggart had approached the group and was waiting to be noticed.

"Hello, Francisco."

"Good evening, James."

"What a wonderful coincidence, seeing you here! I've been very anxious to speak to you."

"That's new. You haven't always been."

"Now you're joking, just like in the old days." Taggart was moving slowly, as if casually, away from the group, hoping to draw Francisco after him. "You know that there's not a person in this room who wouldn't love to talk to you."

"Really? I'd be inclined to suspect the opposite." Francisco had followed obediently, but stopped within hearing distance of the others.

"I have tried in every possible way to get in touch with you," said Taggart, "but . . . but circumstances didn't permit me to succeed."

"Are you trying to hide from me the fact that I refused to see you?"

"Well . . . that is . . . I mean, why did you refuse?"

"I couldn't imagine what you wanted to speak to me about."

"The San Sebastián Mines, of course!" Taggart's voice rose a little.

"Why, what about them?"

"But . . . Now, look, Francisco, this is serious. It's a disaster, an unprecedented disaster—and nobody can make any sense out of it. I don't know what to think. I don't understand it at all. I have a right to know."

"A right? Aren't you being old-fashioned, James? But what is it you want to know?"

"Well, first of all, that nationalization [by Mexico]—what are you going to do about it?"

"Nothing."

"Nothing?!"

"But surely you don't want me to do anything about it. My mines and your railroad were seized by the will of the people. You wouldn't want me to oppose the will of the people, would you?"

"Francisco, this is not a laughing matter!"

"I never thought it was."

"I'm entitled to an explanation! You owe your stockholders an account of the whole disgraceful affair! Why did you pick a worthless mine? Why did you waste all those millions? What sort of rotten swindle was it?"

Francisco stood looking at him in polite astonishment. "Why, James," he said, "I thought you would approve of it."

"Approve?!"

"I thought you would consider the San Sebastián Mines as the practical realization of an ideal of the highest moral order. Remembering that you and I have disagreed so often in the past, I thought you would be gratified to see me acting in accordance with your principles."

"What are you talking about?"

Francisco shook his head regretfully. "I don't know why you should call my behavior rotten. I thought you would recognize it as an honest effort to practice what the whole world is preaching. Doesn't everyone believe that it is evil to be selfless? I was totally selfless in regard to the San Sebastián project. Isn't it evil to pursue a personal interest? I had no personal interest in it whatever. Isn't it evil to work for profit? I did not work for profit—I took a loss. Doesn't everyone agree that the purpose and justification of an industrial enterprise are not production, but the livelihood of its employees? The San Sebastián Mines were the most eminently successful venture in industrial history: they produced no copper, but they provided a livelihood for thousands of men who could not have achieved in a lifetime, the equivalent of what they got for one day's work, which they could not do. Isn't it generally agreed that an owner is a parasite and an exploiter, that it is the employees who do all the work and make the product possible? I did not exploit anyone. I did not burden the San Sebastián Mines with my useless presence; I left them in the hands of the men who count. I did not pass judgment on the value of that property. I turned it over to a mining specialist. He was not a very good specialist, but he needed the job very badly. Isn't it generally conceded that when you hire a man for a job, it is his need that counts, not his ability? Doesn't everyone believe that in order to get the goods, all you have to do is need them? I haven't carried out every moral precept of our age. I expected gratitude and a citation of honor. I do not understand why I am being damned."

In the silence of those who had listened, the sole comment was the shrill, sudden giggle of Betty Pope: she had understood nothing, but she saw the look of helpless fury on James Taggart's face.

People were looking at Taggart, expecting an answer. They were indifferent to the issue, they were merely amused by the spectacle of someone's embarrassment. Taggart achieved a patronizing smile.

"You don't expect me to take this seriously?" he asked.

"There was a time," Francisco answered, "when I did not believe that anyone could take it seriously. I was wrong."

"This is outrageous!" Taggart's voice started to rise. "It's perfectly outrageous to treat your public responsibilities with such thoughtless levity!" He turned to hurry away.

Francisco shrugged, spreading his hands. "You see? I didn't think you wanted to speak to me."

Rearden stood alone, far at the other end of the room. Philip noticed him, approached and waved to Lillian, calling her over.

"Lillian, I don't think that Henry is having a good time," he said, smiling; one could not tell whether the mockery of his smile was directed at Lillian or at Rearden. "Can't we do something about it?"

"Oh, nonsense!" said Rearden.

"I wish I knew what to do about it, Philip," said Lillian. "I've always wished Henry would learn to relax. He's so grimly serious about everything. He's such a rigid Puritan. I've always wanted to see him drunk, just once. But I've given up. What would you suggest?"

"Oh, I don't know! But he shouldn't be standing around all by himself."

"Drop it," said Rearden. While thinking dimly that he did not want to hurt their feelings, he could not prevent himself from adding, "You don't know how hard I've tried to be left standing all by myself."

"There—you see?" Lillian smiled at Philip. "To enjoy life and people is not so simple as pouring a ton of steel. Intellectual pursuits are not learned in the market place."

Philip chuckled. "It's not intellectual pursuits I'm worried about. How sure are you about that Puritan stuff, Lillian? If I were you, I wouldn't leave him free to look around. There are too many beautiful women here tonight."

"Henry entertaining thoughts of infidelity? You flatter him, Philip. You overestimate his courage." She smiled at Rearden, coldly, for a brief, stressed moment, then moved away.

Rearden looked at his brother. "What in hell do you think you're doing?"

"Oh, stop playing the Puritan! Can't you take a joke?"

Moving aimlessly through the crowd, Dagny wondered why she had accepted the invitation to this party. The answer astonished her: it was because she had wanted to see Hank Rearden. Watching him in the crowd, she realized the contrast for the first time. The faces of the others looked like aggregates of interchangeable features, every face oozing to blend into the anonymity of resembling all, and all looking as if they were melting. Rearden's face, with the sharp planes, the pale blue eyes, the ash-blond hair, had the firmness of ice; the uncompromising clarity of its lines made it look, among the others, as if he were moving through a fog, hit by a ray of light.

Her eyes kept returning to him involuntarily. She never caught him glancing in her direction. She could not believe that he was avoiding her intentionally; there could be no possible reason for it; yet she felt certain that he was. She wanted to approach him and convince herself that she was mistaken. Something stopped her; she could not understand her own reluctance.

Rearden bore patiently a conversation with his mother and two ladies whom she wished him to entertain with stories of his youth and his struggle. He complied, telling himself that she was proud of him in her own way. But he felt as if something in her manner kept suggesting that she had nursed him through his struggle and that she was the source of his success. He was glad when she let him go. Then he escaped once more to the recess of the window.

He stood there for a while, leaning on a sense of privacy as if it were a physical support.

"Mr. Rearden," said a strangely quiet voice beside him, "permit me to introduce myself. My name is d'Anconia."

Rearden turned, startled; d'Anconia's manner and voice had a quality he had seldom encountered before: a tone of authentic respect.

"How do you do," he answered. His voice was brusque and dry; but he had answered.

"I have observed that Mrs. Rearden has been trying to avoid the necessity of presenting me to you, and I can guess the reason. Would you prefer that I leave your house?"

The action of naming an issue instead of evading it, was so unlike the usual behavior of all the men he knew, it was such a sudden, startling relief, that Rearden remained silent for a moment, studying d'Anconia's face. Francisco had said it very simply, neither as a reproach nor a plea, but in a manner which, strangely, acknowledged Rearden's dignity and his own.

"No," said Rearden, "Whatever else you guessed, I did not say that."

"Thank you. In that case, you will allow me to speak to you."

"Why should you wish to speak to me?"

"My motives cannot interest you at present."

"Mine is not the sort of conversation that could interest you at all."

"You are mistaken about one of us, Mr. Rearden, or both. I came to this party solely in order to meet you."

There had been a faint tone of amusement in Rearden's voice; now it hardened into a hint of contempt. "You started by playing it straight. Stick to it."

"I am."

"What did you want to meet me for? In order to make me lose money?"

Francisco looked straight at him. "Yes—eventually."

"What is it, this time? A gold mine?"

Francisco shook his head slowly; the conscious deliberation of the movement gave it an air that was almost sadness. "No," he said, "I don't want to sell you anything. As a matter of fact, I did not attempt to sell the copper mine to James Taggart, either. He came to me for it. You won't."

Rearden chuckled. "If you understand that much, we have at least a sensible basis for conversation. Proceed on that. If you don't have some fancy investment in mind, what did you want to meet me for?"

"In order to become acquainted with you."

"That's not an answer. It's just another way of saying the same thing."

"Not quite, Mr. Rearden."

"Unless you mean—in order to gain my confidence?"

"No. I don't like people who speak or think in terms of gaining anybody's confidence. If one's actions are honest, one does not need the predated confidence of others, only their rational perception. The person who craves a moral blank check of that kind, has dishonest intentions, whether he admits it to himself or not."

Rearden's startled glance at him was like the involuntary thrust of a hand grasping for support in a desperate need. The glance betrayed how much he wanted to find the sort of man he thought he was seeing. Then Rearden lowered his eyes, almost closing them, slowly, shutting out the vision and the need. His face was hard; it had an expression of severity, an inner severity directed at himself; it looked austere and lonely.

"All right," he said tonelessly. "What do you want, if it's not my confidence?"

"I want to learn to understand you."

"What for?"

"For a reason of my own which need not concern you at present."

"What do you want to understand about me?"

Francisco looked silently out at the darkness. The fire of the mills was dying down. There was only a faint tinge of red left on the edge of the earth, just enough to outline the scraps of clouds ripped by the tortured battle of the storm in the sky. Dim shapes kept sweeping through space and vanishing, shapes which were branches, but looked as if they were the fury of the wind made visible.

"It's a terrible night for any animal caught unprotected on that plain," said Francisco d'Anconia. "This is when one should appreciate the meaning of being a man."

Rearden did not answer for a moment; then he said, as if in answer to himself, a tone of wonder in his voice, "Funny . . ."

"What?"

"You told me what I was thinking just a while ago . . ."

"You were?"

". . . only I didn't have the words for it."

"Shall I tell you the rest of the words?"

"Go ahead."

"You stood here and watched the storm with the greatest pride one can ever feel—because you are able to have summer flowers and half-naked women in your house on a night like this, in demonstration of your victory over that storm. And if it weren't for you, most of those who are here would be left helpless at the mercy of that wind in the middle of some such plain."

"How did you know that?"

In time with his question, Rearden realized that it was not his thoughts this man had named, but his most hidden, most personal emotion; and that he, who would never confess his emotions to anyone, had confessed it in his question. He saw the faintest flicker in Francisco's eyes, as of a smile or a check mark.

"What would *you* know about a pride of that kind?" Rearden asked sharply, as if the contempt of the second question could erase the confidence of the first.

"That is what I felt once, when I was young."

Rearden looked at him. There was neither mockery nor self-pity in Francisco's face; the fine, sculptured planes and the clear, blue eyes held a quiet composure, the face was open, offered to any blow, unflinching.

"Why do you want to talk about it?" Rearden asked, prompted by a moment's reluctant compassion.

"Let us say—by way of gratitude, Mr. Rearden."

"Gratitude to me?"

"If you will accept it."

Rearden's voice hardened. "I haven't asked for gratitude. I don't need it."

"I have not said you needed it. But of all those whom you are saving from the storm tonight, I am the only one who will offer it."

After a moment's silence, Rearden asked, his voice low with a sound which was almost a threat, "What are you trying to do?"

"I am calling your attention to the nature of those for whom you are working."

"It would take a man who's never done an honest day's work in his life, to think or say that." The contempt in Rearden's voice had a note of relief; he had been disarmed by a doubt of his judgment on the character of his adversary; now he felt certain once more. "You wouldn't understand it if I told you that the man who works, works for himself, even if he does carry the whole wretched bunch of you along. Now *I'll* guess what you're thinking: go ahead, say that it's evil, that I'm self-ish, conceited, heartless, cruel. I am. I don't want any part of that tripe about working for others. I'm not."

For the first time, he saw the look of a personal reaction in Francisco's eyes, the look of something eager and young. "The only thing that's wrong in what you said," Francisco answered, "is that you permit anyone to call it evil." In Rearden's pause of incredulous silence, he pointed at the crowd in the drawing room. "Why are you willing to carry them?"

"Because they're a bunch of miserable children who struggle to remain alive, desperately and very badly, while I—I don't even notice the burden."

"Why don't you tell them that?"

"What?"

"That you're working for your own sake, not theirs."

"They know it."

"Oh yes, they know it. Every single one of them here knows it. But they don't think you do. And the aim of all their efforts is to keep you from knowing it."

"Why should I care what they think?"

"Because it's a battle in which one must make one's stand clear."

"A battle? What battle? I hold the whip hand. I don't fight the disarmed."

"Are they? They have a weapon against you. It's their only weapon, but it's a terrible one. Ask yourself what it is, some time."

"Where do you see any evidence of it?"

"In the unforgivable fact that you're as unhappy as you are."

Rearden could accept any form of reproach, abuse, damnation anyone chose to throw at him: the only human reaction which he would not accept was pity. The stab of a coldly rebellious anger brought him back to the full context of the moment. He spoke, fighting not to acknowledge the nature of the emotion rising within him. "What sort of effrontery are you indulging in? What's your motive?"

"Let us say—to give you the words you need, for the time when you'll need them."

"Why should you want to speak to me on such a subject?"

"In the hope that you will remember it."

What he felt, thought Rearden, was anger at the incomprehensible fact that he had allowed himself to enjoy this conversation. He felt a dim sense of betrayal, the hint of an unknown danger. "Do you expect me to forget what you are?" he asked, knowing that this was what he had forgotten.

"I do not expect you to think of me at all."

Under his anger, the emotion which Rearden would not acknowledge remained unstated and unthought; he knew it only as a hint of pain. Had he faced it, he would have known that he still heard Francisco's voice saying, "I am the only one who will offer it . . . if you will accept it . . . ." He heard the words and the strangely solemn inflection of the quiet voice and an inexplicable answer of his own, something within him that wanted to cry yes, to accept, to tell this man that he accepted, that he needed it—though there was no name for what he needed, it was not gratitude, and he knew that it was not gratitude this man had meant.

Aloud, he said, "I didn't seek to talk to you. But you've asked for it and you're going to hear it. To me, there's only one form of human depravity—the man without a purpose."

"That is true."

"I can forgive all those others, they're not vicious, they're merely helpless. But you—you're the kind who can't be forgiven."

"It is against the sin of forgiveness that I wanted to warn you."

"You had the greatest chance in life. What have you done with it? If you have the mind to understand all the things you said, how can you speak to me at all? How can you face anyone after the sort of irresponsible destruction you've perpetrated in that Mexican business?"

"It is your right to condemn me for it, if you wish."

Dagny stood by the corner of the window recess, listening. They did not notice her. She had seen them together and she had approached, drawn by an impulse she could not explain or resist; it seemed crucially important that she know what these two men said to each other.

She had heard their last few sentences. She had never thought it possible that she would see Francisco taking a beating. He could smash any adversary in any form of encounter. Yet he stood, offering no defense. She knew that it was not indifference; she knew his face well enough to see the effort his calm cost him—she saw the faint line of a muscle pulled tight across his cheek.

"Of all those who live by the ability of others," said Rearden, "you're the one real parasite."

"I have given you grounds to think so."

"Then what right have you to talk about the meaning of being a man? You're the one who has betrayed it."

"I am sorry if I have offended you by what you may rightly consider as a presumption."

Francisco bowed and turned to go. Rearden said involuntarily, not knowing that the question negated his anger, that it was a plea to stop this man and hold him, "What did you want to learn to understand about me?"

Francisco turned. The expression of his face had not changed; it was still a look of gravely courteous respect. "I have learned it," he answered.

Rearden stood watching him as he walked off into the crowd. The figures of a butler, with a crystal dish, and of Dr. Pritchett, stooping to choose another canapé, hid Francisco from sight. Rearden glanced out at the darkness; nothing could be seen there but the wind.

Dagny stepped forward, when he came out of the recess; she smiled, openly inviting conversation. He stopped. It seemed to her that he had stopped reluctantly. She spoke hastily, to break the silence. "Hank, why do you have so many intellectuals of the looter persuasion here? I wouldn't have them in my house."

This was not what she had wanted to say to him. But she did not know what she wanted to say; never before had she felt herself left wordless in his presence.

She saw his eyes narrowing, like a door being closed. "I see no reason why one should not invite them to a party," he answered coldly.

"Oh, I didn't mean to criticize your choice of guests. But . . . Well, I've been trying not to learn which one of them is Bertram Scudder. If I do, I'll slap his face." She tried to sound casual. "I don't want to create a scene, but I'm not sure I'll be able to control myself. I couldn't believe it when somebody told me that Mrs. Rearden had invited him."

"*I* invited him."

"But . . ." Then her voice dropped. "Why?"

"I don't attach any importance to occasions of this kind."

"I'm sorry, Hank. I didn't know you were so tolerant. I'm not."

He said nothing.

"I know you don't like parties. Neither do I. But sometimes I wonder . . . perhaps we're the only ones who were meant to be able to enjoy them."

"I am afraid I have no talent for it."

"Not for this. But do you think any of these people are enjoying it? They're just straining to be more senseless and aimless than usual. To be light and unimportant . . . You know, I think that only if one feels immensely important can one feel truly light."

"I wouldn't know."

"It's just a thought that disturbs me once in a while. . . . I thought it about my first ball. . . . I keep thinking that parties are intended to be celebrations, and celebrations should be only for those who have something to celebrate."

"I have never thought of it."

She could not adapt her words to the rigid formality of his manner; she could not quite believe it. They had always been at ease together, in his office. Now he was like a man in a strait jacket.

"Hank, look at it. If you didn't know any of these people, wouldn't it seem beautiful? The lights and the clothes and all the imagination that went to make it possible . . ." She was looking at the room. She did not notice that he had not followed her glance. He was looking down at the shadows on her naked shoulder, the soft, blue shadows made by the light that fell through the strands of her hair. "Why have we left it all to fools? It should have been ours."

"In what manner?"

"I don't know . . . I've always expected parties to be exciting and brilliant, like some rare drink." She laughed; there was a note of sadness in it. "But I don't drink, either. That's just another symbol that doesn't mean what it was intended to mean." He was silent. She added, "Perhaps there's something that we have missed."

"I am not aware of it."

In a flash of sudden, desolate emptiness, she was glad that he had not understood or responded, feeling dimly that she had revealed too much, yet not knowing what she had revealed. She shrugged, the movement running through the curve of her shoulder like a faint convulsion. "It's just an old illusion of mine," she said indifferently. "Just a mood that comes once every year or two. Let me see the latest steel price index and I'll forget all about it."

She did not know that his eyes were following her, as she walked away from him.

She moved slowly through the room, looking at no one. She noticed a small group huddled by the unlighted fireplace. The room was not cold, but they sat as if they drew comfort from the thought of a non-existent fire.

"I do not know why, but I am growing to be afraid of the dark. No, not now, only when I am alone. What frightens me is night. Night as such."

The speaker was an elderly spinster with an air of breeding and hopelessness. The three women and two men of the group were well dressed, the skin of their faces was smoothly well tended, but they had a manner of anxious caution that kept their voices one tone lower than normal and blurred the differences of their ages, giving them all the same gray look of being spent. It was the look one saw in groups of respectable people everywhere. Dagny stopped and listened.

"But my dear," one of them asked, "why should it frighten you?"

"I don't know," said the spinster. "I am not afraid of prowlers or robberies or anything of the sort. But I stay awake all night. I fall asleep only when I see the sky turning pale. It is very odd. Every evening, when it grows dark, I get the feeling that this time it is final, that daylight will not return."

"My cousin who lives on the coast of Maine wrote me the same thing," said one of the women.

"Last night," said the spinster, "I stayed awake because of the shooting. There were guns going off all night, way out at sea. There were no flashes. There was nothing. Just those detonations, at long intervals, somewhere in the fog over the Atlantic."

"I read something about it in the paper this morning. Coast Guard target practice."

"Why, no," the spinster said indifferently. "Everybody down on the shore knows what it was. It was Ragnar Danneskjöld. It was the Coast Guard trying to catch him."

"Ragnar Danneskjöld in Delaware Bay?" a woman gasped.

"Oh, yes. They say it is not the first time."

"Did they catch him?"

"No."

"Nobody can catch him," said one of the men.

"The People's State of Norway has offered a million-dollar reward for his head."

"That's an awful lot of money to pay for a pirate's head."

"But how are we going to have any order or security or planning in the world, with a pirate running loose all over the seven seas?"

"Do you know what it was that he seized last night?" said the spinster. "The big ship with the relief supplies we were sending to the People's State of France."

"How does he dispose of the goods he seizes?"

"Ah, that—nobody knows."

"I met a sailor once, from a ship he'd attacked, who'd seen him in person. He said that Ragnar Danneskjöld has the purest gold hair and the most frightening face on earth, a face with no sign of any feeling. If there ever was a man born without a heart, he's it—the sailor said."

"A nephew of mine saw Ragnar Danneskjöld's ship one night, off the coast of Scotland. He wrote me that he couldn't believe his eyes. It was a better ship than any in the navy of the People's State of England."

"They say he hides in one of those Norwegian fjords where neither God nor man will ever find him. That's where the Vikings used to hide in the Middle Ages."

"There's a reward on his head offered by the People's State of Portugal, too. And by the People's State of Turkey."

"They say it's a national scandal in Norway. He comes from one of their best families. The family lost its money generations ago, but the name is of the noblest. The ruins of their castle are still in existence. His father is a bishop. His father has disowned him and excommunicated him. But it had no effect."

"Did you know that Ragnar Danneskjöld went to school in this country? Sure. The Patrick Henry University."

"Not really?"

"Oh yes. You can look it up."

"What bothers me is . . . You know, I don't like it. I don't like it that he's now appearing right here, in our own waters. I thought things like that could happen only in the wastelands. Only in Europe. But a big-scale outlaw of that kind operating in Delaware in our day and age!"

"He's been seen off Nantucket, too. And at Bar Harbor. The newspapers have been asked not to write about it."

"Why?"

"They don't want people to know that the navy can't cope with him."

"I don't like it. It feels funny. It's like something out of the Dark Ages."

Dagny glanced up. She saw Francisco d'Anconia standing a few steps away. He was looking at her with a kind of stressed curiosity; his eyes were mocking.

"It's a strange world we're living in," said the spinster, her voice low.

"I read an article," said one of the women tonelessly. "It said that times of trouble are good for us. It is good that people are growing poorer. To accept privations is a moral virtue."

"I suppose so," said another, without conviction.

"We must not worry. I heard a speech that said it is useless to worry or to blame anyone. Nobody can help what he does, that is the way things made him. There is nothing we can do about anything. We must learn to bear it."

"What's the use anyway? What is man's fate? Hasn't it always been to hope, but never to achieve? The wise man is the one who does not attempt to hope."

"That is the right attitude to take."

"I don't know . . . I don't know what is right any more . . . How can we ever know?"

"Oh well, who is John Galt?" [This was a popular expression denoting futility.]

Dagny turned brusquely and started away from them. One of the women followed her.

"But I do know it," said the woman, in the soft, mysterious tone of sharing a secret.

"You know what?"

"I know who is John Galt."

"Who?" Dagny asked tensely, stopping.

"I know a man who knew John Galt in person. This man is an old friend of a great-aunt of mine. He was there and he saw it happen. Do you know the legend of Atlantis, Miss Taggart?"

"What?"

"Atlantis."

"Why . . . vaguely."

"The Isles of the Blessed. That is what the Greeks called it, thousands of years ago. They said Atlantis was a place where hero-spirits lived in a happiness unknown to the rest of the earth. A place which only the spirits of heroes could enter, and they reached it without dying, because they carried the secret of life within them. Atlantis was lost to mankind, even then. But the Greeks knew that it had existed. They tried to find it. Some of them said it was underground, hidden in the heart of the earth. But most of them said it was an island. A radiant island in the Western Ocean. Perhaps what they were thinking of was America. They never found it. For centuries afterward, men said it was only a legend. They did not believe it, but they never stopped looking for it, because they knew that that was what they had to find."

"Well, what about John Galt?"

"He found it."

Dagny's interest was gone. "Who was he?"

"John Galt was a millionaire, a man of inestimable wealth. He was sailing his yacht one night, in mid-Atlantic, fighting the worst storm ever wreaked upon the world, when he found it. He saw it in the depth, where it had sunk to escape the reach of men. He saw the towers of Atlantis shining on the bottom of the ocean. It was a sight of such kind that when one had seen it, one could no longer wish to look at the rest of the earth. John Galt sank his ship and went down with his entire crew. They all chose to do it. My friend was the only one who survived."

"How interesting."

"My friend saw it with his own eyes," said the woman, offended. "It happened many years ago. But John Galt's family hushed up the story."

"And what happened to his fortune? I don't recall ever hearing of a Galt fortune."

"It went down with him." She added belligerently, "You don't have to believe it."

"Miss Taggart doesn't," said Francisco d'Anconia. "I do."

They turned. He had followed them and he stood looking at them with the insolence of exaggerated earnestness.

"Have you ever had faith in anything, Señor d'Anconia?" the woman asked angrily.

"No, madame."

He chuckled at her brusque departure. Dagny asked coldly, "What's the joke?"

"The joke's on that fool woman. She doesn't know that she was telling you the truth."

"Do you expect me to believe that?"

"No."

"Then what do you find so amusing?"

"Oh, a great many things here. Don't you?"

"No."

"Well, *that's* one of the things I find amusing."

"Francisco, will you leave me alone?"

"But I have. Didn't you notice that you were first to speak to me tonight?"

"Why do you keep watching me?"

"Curiosity."

"About what?"

"Your reaction to the things which you don't find amusing."

"Why should you care about my reaction to anything?"

"That is my own way of having a good time, which, incidentally, you are not having, are you, Dagny? Besides, you're the only woman worth watching here."

She stood defiantly still, because the way he looked at her demanded an angry escape. She stood as she always did, straight and taut, her head lifted impatiently. It was the unfeminine pose of an executive. But her naked shoulder betrayed the fragility of the body under the black dress, and the pose made her most truly a woman. The proud strength became a challenge to someone's superior strength, and the fragility a reminder that the challenge could be broken. She was not conscious of it. She had met no one able to see it.

He said, looking down at her body, "Dagny, what a magnificent waste!"

She had to turn and escape. She felt herself blushing, for the first time in years; blushing because she knew suddenly that the sentence named what she had felt all evening.

She ran, trying not to think. The music stopped her. It was a sudden blast from the radio. She noticed Mort Liddy, who had turned it on, waving his arms to a group of friends, yelling, "That's it! That's it! I want you to hear it!"

The great burst of sound was the opening chords of Halley's Fourth Concerto. It rose in tortured triumph, speaking its denial of pain, its hymn to a distant vision. Then the notes broke. It was as if a handful of mud and pebbles had been flung at the music, and what followed was the sound of the rolling and the dripping. It was Halley's Concerto swung into a popular tune. It was Halley's melody torn apart, its holes stuffed with hiccoughs. The great statement of joy had become the giggling of a barroom. Yet it was still the remnant of Halley's melody that gave it form; it was the melody that supported it like a spinal cord.

"Pretty good?" Mort Liddy was smiling at his friends, boastfully and nervously. "Pretty good, eh? Best movie score of the year. Got me a prize. Got me a long-term contract. Yeah, this was my score for *Heaven's in Your Backyard*."

Dagny stood, staring at the room, as if one sense could replace another, as if sight could wipe out sound. She moved her head in a slow circle, trying to find an anchor somewhere. She saw Francisco leaning against a column, his arms crossed; he was looking straight at her; he was laughing.

Don't shake like this, she thought. Get out of here. This was the approach of an anger she could not control. She thought: Say nothing. Walk steadily. Get out.

She had started walking, cautiously, very slowly. She heard Lillian's words and stopped. Lillian had said it many times this evening, in answer to the same question, but it was the first time that Dagny heard it.

"This?" Lillian was saying, extending her arm with the metal bracelet for the inspection of two smartly groomed women. "Why, no, it's not from a hardware store, it's a very special gift from my husband. Oh, yes, of course it's hideous. But don't you see? It's supposed to be priceless. Of course, I'd exchange it for a common diamond bracelet any time, but somehow nobody will offer me one for it, even though it is so very, very valuable. Why? My dear, it's the first thing ever made of Rearden Metal."

Dagny did not see the room. She did not hear the music. She felt the pressure of dead stillness against her eardrums. She did not know the moment that preceded, or the moments that were to follow. She did not know those involved, neither herself, nor Lillian, nor Rearden, nor the meaning of her own action. It was a single instant, blasted out of context. She had heard. She was looking at the bracelet of green-blue metal.

She felt the movement of something being torn off her wrist, and she heard her own voice saying in the great stillness, very calmly, a voice cold as a skeleton, naked of emotion, "If you are not the coward that I think you are, you will exchange it."

On the palm of her hand, she was extending her diamond bracelet to Lillian.

"You're not serious, Miss Taggart?" said a woman's voice.

It was not Lillian's voice. Lillian's eyes were looking straight at her. She saw them. Lillian knew that she was serious.

"Give me that bracelet," said Dagny, lifting her palm higher, the diamond band glittering across it.

"This is horrible!" cried some woman. It was strange that the cry stood out so sharply. Then Dagny realized that there were people standing around them and that they all stood in silence. She was hearing sounds now, even the music; it was Halley's mangled Concerto, somewhere far away.

She saw Rearden's face. It looked as if something within him were mangled, like the music; she did not know by what. He was watching them.

Lillian's mouth moved into an upturned crescent. It resembled a smile. She snapped the metal bracelet open, dropped it on Dagny's palm and took the diamond band.

"Thank you, Miss Taggart," she said.

Dagny's fingers closed about the metal. She felt that; she felt nothing else.

Lillian turned, because Rearden had approached her. He took the diamond bracelet from her hand. He clasped it on her wrist, raised her hand to his lips and kissed it.

He did not look at Dagny.

Lillian laughed, gaily, easily, attractively, bringing the room back to its normal mood.

"You may have it back, Miss Taggart, when you change your mind," she said.

Dagny had turned away. She felt calm and free. The pressure was gone. The need to get out had vanished.

She clasped the metal bracelet on her wrist. She liked the feel of the weight against her skin. Inexplicably, she felt a touch of feminine vanity, the kind she had never experienced before: the desire to be seen wearing this particular ornament.

From a distance, she heard snatches of indignant voices: "The most offensive gesture I've ever seen. . . . It was vicious. . . . I'm glad

Lillian took her up on it. . . . Serves her right, if she feels like throwing a few thousand dollars away. . . ."

For the rest of the evening, Rearden remained by the side of his wife. He shared her conversations, he laughed with her friends, he was suddenly the devoted, attentive, admiring husband.

He was crossing the room, carrying a tray of drinks requested by someone in Lillian's group—an unbecoming act of informality which nobody had ever seen him perform—when Dagny approached him. She stopped and looked up at him, as if they were alone in his office. She stood like an executive, her head lifted. He looked down at her. In the line of his glance, from the fingertips of her one hand to her face, her body was naked but for his metal bracelet.

"I'm sorry, Hank," she said, "but I had to do it."

His eyes remained expressionless. Yet she was suddenly certain that she knew what he felt: he wanted to slap her face.

"It was not necessary," he answered coldly, and walked on.

                    *   *   *

It was very late when Rearden entered his wife's bedroom. She was still awake. A lamp burned on her bedside table.

She lay in bed, propped up on pillows of pale green linen. Her bed-jacket was pale green satin, worn with the untouched perfection of a window model; its lustrous folds looked as if the crinkle of tissue paper still lingered among them. The light, shaded to a tone of apple blossoms, fell on a table that held a book, a glass of fruit juice, and toilet accessories of silver glittering like instruments in a surgeon's case. Her arms had a tinge of porcelain. There was a touch of pale pink lipstick on her mouth. She showed no sign of exhaustion after the party—no sign of life to be exhausted. The place was a decorator's display of a lady groomed for sleep, not to be disturbed.

He still wore his dress clothes; his tie was loose, and a strand of hair hung over his face. She glanced at him without astonishment, as if she knew what the last hour in his room had done to him.

He looked at her silently. He had not entered her room for a long time. He stood, wishing he had not entered it now.

"Isn't it customary to talk, Henry?"

"If you wish."

"I wish you'd send one of your brilliant experts from the mills to take a look at our furnace. Do you know that it went out during the party and Simons had a terrible time getting it started again? . . . Mrs.

Weston says that our best achievement is our cook—she loved the hors d'oeuvres. . . . Balph Eubank said a very funny thing about you, he said you're a crusader with a factory's chimney smoke for a plume. . . . I'm glad you don't like Francisco d'Anconia. I can't stand him."

He did not care to explain his presence, or to disguise defeat, or to admit it by leaving. Suddenly, it did not matter to him what she guessed or felt. He walked to the window and stood, looking out.

Why had she married him?—he thought. It was a question he had not asked himself on their wedding day, eight years ago. Since then, in tortured loneliness, he had asked it many times. He had found no answer.

It was not for position, he thought, or for money. She came from an old family that had both. Her family's name was not among the most distinguished and their fortune was modest, but both were sufficient to let her be included in the top circles of New York's society, where he had met her. Nine years ago, he had appeared in New York like an explosion, in the glare of the success of Rearden Steel, a success that had been thought impossible by the city's experts. It was his indifference that made him spectacular. He did not know that he was expected to attempt to buy his way into society and that they anticipated the pleasure of rejecting him. He had no time to notice their disappointment.

He attended, reluctantly, a few social occasions to which he was invited by men who sought his favor. He did not know, but they knew, that his courteous politeness was condescension toward the people who had expected to snub him, the people who had said that the age of achievement was past.

It was Lillian's austerity that attracted him—the conflict between her austerity and her behavior. He had never liked anyone or expected to be liked. He found himself held by the spectacle of a woman who was obviously pursuing him but with obvious reluctance, as if against her own will, as if fighting a desire she resented. It was she who planned that they should meet, then faced him coldly, as if not caring that he knew it. She spoke little; she had an air of mystery that seemed to tell him he would never break through her proud detachment, and an air of amusement, mocking her own desire and his.

He had not known many women. He had moved toward his goal, sweeping aside everything that did not pertain to it in the world and in himself. His dedication to his work was like one of the fires he dealt with, a fire that burned every lesser element, every impurity out of the white stream of a single metal. He was incapable of halfway concerns. But there were times when he felt a sudden access of desire, so violent that it could not be given to a casual encounter. He had surrendered to it, on a few rare occasions through the years, with women he had thought he liked. He had been left feeling an angry emptiness—because he had sought an act of triumph, though he had not known of what nature, but the response he received was only a woman's acceptance of a casual pleasure, and he knew too clearly that what he had won had no meaning. He was left, not with a sense of attainment, but with a sense of his own degradation. He grew to hate his desire. He fought it. He came to believe the doctrine that this desire was wholly physical, a desire, not of consciousness, but of matter, and he rebelled against the thought that his flesh could be free to choose and that its choice was impervious to the will of his mind. He had spent his life in mines and mills, shaping matter to his wishes by the power of his brain—and he found it intolerable that he should be unable to control the matter of his own body. He fought it. He had won his every battle against inanimate nature; but this was a battle he lost.

It was the difficulty of the conquest that made him want Lillian. She seemed to be a woman who expected and deserved a pedestal; this made him want to drag her down to his bed. To drag her down, were the words in his mind; they gave him a dark pleasure, the sense of a victory worth winning.

He could not understand why—he thought it was an obscene conflict, the sigh of some secret depravity within him—why he felt, at the same time, a profound pride at the thought of granting to a woman the title of his wife. The feeling was solemn and shining; it was almost as if he felt that he wished to honor a woman by the act of possessing her. Lillian seemed to fit the image he had not known he held, had not known he wished to find; he saw the grace, the pride, the purity; the rest was in himself; he did not know that he was looking at a reflection.

He remembered the day when Lillian came from New York to his office, of her own sudden choice, and asked him to take her through his mills. He heard a soft, low, breathless tone—the tone of admiration—growing in her voice, as she questioned him about his work and looked at the place around her. He looked at her graceful figure moving against the bursts of furnace flame, and at the light swift steps of her high heels stumbling through drifts of slag, as she walked resolutely by his side. The look in her eyes, when she watched a heat of steel being poured, was like his own feeling for it made visible to him. When her eyes moved up to his face, he saw the same look, but intensified to a degree that seemed to make her helpless and silent. It was at dinner, that evening, that he asked her to marry him.

It took him some time after his marriage before he admitted to himself that this was torture. He still remembered the night when he admitted it, when he told himself—the veins of his wrists pulled tight as he stood by the bed, looking down at Lillian—that he deserved the torture and that he would endure it. Lillian was not looking at him; she was adjusting her hair. "May I go to sleep now?" she asked.

She had never objected; she had never refused him anything; she submitted whenever he wished. She submitted in the manner of complying with the rule that it was, at times, her duty to become an inanimate object turned over to her husband's use.

She did not censure him. She made it clear that she took it for granted that men had degrading instincts which constituted the secret, ugly part of marriage. She was condescendingly tolerant. She smiled, in amused distaste, at the intensity of what he experienced. "It's the most undignified pastime I know of," she said to him once, "but I have never entertained the illusion that men are superior to animals."

His desire for her had died in the first week of their marriage. What remained was only a need which he was unable to destroy. He had never entered a whorehouse; he thought, at times, that the self-loathing he would experience there could be no worse than what he felt when he was driven to enter his wife's bedroom.

He would often find her reading a book. She would put it aside, with a white ribbon to mark the pages. When he lay exhausted, his eyes closed, still breathing in gasps, she would turn on the light, pick up the book and continue her reading.

He told himself that he deserved the torture, because he had wished never to touch her again and was unable to maintain his decision. He despised himself for that. He despised a need which now held no shred of joy or meaning, which had become the mere need of a woman's body, an anonymous body that belonged to a woman whom he had to forget while he held it. He became convinced that the need was depravity.

He did not condemn Lillian. He felt a dreary, indifferent respect for her. His hatred of his own desire had made him accept the doctrine that women were pure and that a pure woman was one incapable of physical pleasure.

Through the quiet agony of the years of his marriage, there had been one thought which he would not permit himself to consider: the thought of infidelity. He had given his word. He intended to keep it. It was not loyalty to Lillian; it was not the person of Lillian that he wished to protect from dishonor—but the person of his wife.

He thought of that now, standing at the window. He had not wanted to enter her room. He had fought against it. He had fought, more fiercely, against knowing the particular reason why he would not be able to withstand it tonight. Then, seeing her, he had known suddenly that he would not touch her. The reason which had driven him here tonight was the reason which made it impossible for him.

He stood still, feeling free of desire, feeling the bleak relief of indifference to his body, to this room, even to his presence here. He had turned away from her, not to see her lacquered chastity. What he thought he should feel was respect; what he felt was revulsion.

". . . but Dr. Pritchett said that our culture is dying because our universities have to depend on the alms of the meat packers, the steel puddlers and the purveyors of breakfast cereals."

Why had she married him?—he thought. That bright, crisp voice was not talking at random. She knew why he had come here. She knew what it would do to him to see her pick up a silver buffer and go on talking gaily, polishing her fingernails. She was talking about the party. But she did not mention Bertram Scudder—or Dagny Taggart.

What had she sought in marrying him? He felt the presence of some cold, driving purpose within her—but found nothing to condemn. She had never tried to use him. She made no demands on him. She found no satisfaction in the prestige of industrial power—she spurned it—she preferred her own circle of friends. She was not after money—she spent little—she was indifferent to the kind of extravagance he could have afforded. He had no right to accuse her, he thought, or ever to break the bond. She was a woman of honor in their marriage. She wanted nothing material from him.

He turned and looked at her wearily.

"Next time you give a party," he said, "stick to your own crowd. Don't invite what you think are my friends. I don't care to meet them socially."

She laughed, startled and pleased. "I don't blame you, darling," she said.

He walked out, adding nothing else.

What did she want from him?—he thought. What was she after? In the universe as he knew it, there was no answer.

———————

EDITOR'S NOTE: *About a hundred pages later, we witness the first run of the John Galt Line, Dagny Taggart's new railroad, which services the wells of oil baron Ellis Wyatt. The rail and a new bridge, both made of Rearden Metal, have been widely denounced by social critics as unsafe; the critics predict a disastrous crash when the train reaches the bridge.*

The John Galt Line

REARDEN WAS in New York on the day when Dagny telephoned him from her office. "Hank, I'm going to have a press conference tomorrow."

He laughed aloud. "No!"

"Yes." Her voice sounded earnest, but, dangerously, a bit too earnest. "The newspapers have suddenly discovered me and are asking questions. I'm going to answer them."

"Have a good time."

"I will. Are you going to be in town tomorrow? I'd like to have you in on it."

"Okay. I wouldn't want to miss it."

The reporters who came to the press conference in the office of the John Galt Line were young men who had been trained to think that their job consisted of concealing from the world the nature of its events. It was their daily duty to serve as audience for some public figure who made utterances about the public good, in phrases carefully chosen to convey no meaning. It was their daily job to sling words together in any combination they pleased, so long as the words did not fall into a sequence saying something specific. They could not understand the interview now being given to them.

Dagny Taggart sat behind her desk in an office that looked like a slum basement. She wore a dark blue suit with a white blouse, beautifully tailored, suggesting an air of formal, almost military elegance. She sat straight, and her manner was severely dignified, just a shade too dignified.

Rearden sat in a corner of the room, sprawled across a broken armchair, his long legs thrown over one of its arms, his body leaning against the other. His manner was pleasantly informal, just a bit too informal.

In the clear, monotonous voice of a military report, consulting no papers, looking straight at the men, Dagny recited the technological facts about the John Galt Line, giving exact figures on the nature of the rail, the capacity of the bridge, the method of construction, the costs. Then, in the dry tone of a banker, she explained the financial prospects of the Line and named the large profits she expected to make. "That is all," she said.

"All?" said one of the reporters. "Aren't you going to give us a message for the public?"

"That was my message."

"But hell—I mean, aren't you going to defend yourself?"

"Against what?"

"Don't you want to tell us something to justify your Line?"

"I have."

A man with a mouth shaped as a permanent sneer asked, "Well, what I want to know, as Bertram Scudder stated, is what protection do we have against your Line being no good?"

"Don't ride on it."

Another asked, "Aren't you going to tell us your motive for building that Line?"

"I have told you: the profit which I expect to make."

"Oh, Miss Taggart, don't say that!" cried a young boy. He was new, he was still honest about his job, and he felt that he liked Dagny Taggart, without knowing why. "That's the wrong thing to say. That's what they're all saying about you."

"Are they?"

"I'm sure you didn't mean it the way it sounds and . . . and I'm sure you'll want to clarify it."

"Why, yes, if you wish me to. The average profit of railroads has been two per cent of the capital invested. An industry that does so much and keeps so little, should consider itself immoral. As I have explained, the cost of the John Galt Line in relation to the traffic which it will carry makes me expect a profit of not less than fifteen per cent on our investment. Of course, any industrial profit above four per cent is considered usury nowadays. I shall, nevertheless, do my best to make the John Galt Line earn a profit of twenty per cent for me, if possible. That was my motive for building the Line. Have I made myself clear now?"

The boy was looking at her helplessly. "You don't mean, to earn a profit for *you*, Miss Taggart? You mean, for the small stockholders, of course?" he prompted hopefully.

"Why, no. I happen to be one of the largest stockholders of Taggart Transcontinental, so my share of the profits will be one of the largest. Now, Mr. Rearden is in a much more fortunate position, because he has no stockholders to share with—or would you rather make your own statement, Mr. Rearden?"

"Yes, gladly," said Rearden. "Inasmuch as the formula of Rearden Metal is my own personal secret, and in view of the fact that the Metal costs much less to produce than you boys can imagine, I expect to skin the public to the tune of a profit of twenty-five per cent in the next few years."

"What do you mean, skin the public, Mr. Rearden?" asked the boy. "If it's true, as I've read in your ads, that your Metal will last three times longer than any other and at half the price, wouldn't the public be getting a bargain?"

"Oh, have you noticed that?" said Rearden.

"Do the two of you realize you're talking for publication?" asked the man with the sneer.

"But, Mr. Hopkins," said Dagny, in polite astonishment, "is there any reason why we would talk to you, if it weren't for publication?"

"Do you want us to quote all the things you said?"

"I hope I may trust you to be sure and quote them. Would you oblige me by taking this down verbatim?" She paused to see their pencils ready, then dictated: "Miss Taggart says—quote—I expect to make a pile of money on the John Galt Line. I will have earned it. Close quote. Thank you so much."

"Any questions, gentlemen?" asked Rearden.

There were no questions.

"Now I must tell you about the opening of the John Galt Line," said Dagny. "The first train will depart from the station of Taggart Transcontinental in Cheyenne, Wyoming, at four P.M. on July twenty-second. It will be a freight special, consisting of eighty cars. It will be driven by an eight-thousand-horsepower, four-unit Diesel locomotive—which I'm leasing from Taggart Transcontinental for the occasion. It will run non-stop to Wyatt Junction, Colorado, traveling at an average speed of one hundred miles per hour. I beg your pardon?" she asked, hearing the long, low sound of a whistle.

"What did you say, Miss Taggart?"

"I said, one hundred miles per hour—grades, curves and all."

"But shouldn't you cut the speed below normal rather than . . . Miss Taggart, don't you have any consideration whatever for public opinion?"

"But I *do*. If it weren't for public opinion, an average speed of sixty-five miles per hour would have been quite sufficient."

"Who's going to run that train?"

"I had quite a bit of trouble about that. All the Taggart engineers volunteered to do it. So did the firemen, the brakemen and the conductors. We had to draw lots for every job on the train's crew. The engineer will be Pat Logan, of the Taggart Comet, the fireman—Ray McKim. I shall ride in the cab of the engine with them."

"Not really!"

"Please do attend the opening. It's on July twenty-second. The press is most eagerly invited. Contrary to my usual policy, I have become a publicity hound. Really. I should like to have spotlights, radio microphones and television cameras. I suggest that you plant a few cameras around the bridge. The collapse of the bridge would give you some interesting shots."

"Miss Taggart," asked Rearden, "why didn't you mention that I'm going to ride in that engine, too?"

She looked at him across the room, and for a moment they were alone, holding each other's glance.

"Yes, of course, Mr. Rearden," she answered.

                    *   *   *

She did not see him again until they looked at each other across the platform of the Taggart station in Cheyenne, on July 22.

She did not look for anyone when she stepped out on the platform: she felt as if her senses had merged, so that she could not distinguish the sky, the sun or the sounds of an enormous crowd, but perceived only a sensation of shock and light.

Yet he was the first person she saw, and she could not tell for how long a time he was also the only one. He stood by the engine of the John Galt train, talking to somebody outside the field of her consciousness. He was dressed in gray slacks and shirt, he looked like an expert mechanic, but he was stared at by the faces around him, because he was Hank Rearden of Rearden Steel. High above him, she saw the letters TT on the silver front of the engine. The lines of the engine slanted back, aimed at space.

There was distance and a crowd between them, but his eyes moved to her the moment she came out. They looked at each other and she knew that he felt as she did. This was not to be a solemn venture upon which their future depended, but simply their day of enjoyment. Their work was done. For the moment, there was no future. They had earned the present.

Only if one feels immensely important, she had told him, can one feel truly light. Whatever the train's run would mean to others, for the two of them their own persons were this day's sole meaning. Whatever it was that others sought in life, their right to what they now felt was all the two of them wished to find. It was as if, across the platform, they said it to each other.

Then she turned away from him.

She noticed that she, too, was being stared at, that there were people around her, that she was laughing and answering questions.

She had not expected such a large crowd. They filled the platform, the tracks, the square beyond the station; they were on the roofs of the boxcars on the sidings, at the windows of every house in sight. Something had drawn them here, something in the air which, at the last moment, had made James Taggart want to attend the opening of the John Galt Line. She had forbidden it. "If you come, Jim," she had said, "I'll have you thrown out of your own Taggart station. This is one event you're not going to see." Then she had chosen Eddie Willers to represent Taggart Transcontinental at the opening.

She looked at the crowd and she felt, simultaneously, astonishment that they should stare at her, when this event was so personally her own that no communication about it was possible, and a sense of fitness that they should be here, that they should want to see it, because the sight of an achievement was the greatest gift a human being could offer to others.

She felt no anger toward anyone on earth. The things she had endured had now receded into some outer fog, like pain that still exists, but has no power to hurt. Those things could not stand in the face of this moment's reality, the meaning of this day was as brilliantly, violently clear as the splashes of sun on the silver of the engine, all men had to perceive it now, no one could doubt it and she had no one to hate.

Eddie Willers was watching her. He stood on the platform, sur-
rounded by Taggart executives, division heads, civic leaders, and the
various local officials who had been outargued, bribed or threatened,
to obtain permits to run a train through town zones at a hundred
miles an hour. For once, for this day and event, his title of Vice-
President was real to him and he carried it well. But while he spoke to
those around him, his eyes kept following Dagny through the crowd.
She was dressed in blue slacks and shirt, she was unconscious of official duties, she had left them to him, the train was now her sole concern, as if she were only a member of its crew.

She saw him, she approached, and she shook his hand; her smile
was like a summation of all the things they did not have to say. "Well,
Eddie, you're Taggart Transcontinental now."

"Yes," he said solemnly, his voice low. [. . .]

He watched from a distance while the train's crew was lined up in
front of the engine, to face a firing squad of cameras. Dagny and
Rearden were smiling, as if posing for snapshots of a summer vacation. Pat Logan, the engineer, a short, sinewy man with graying hair
and a contemptuously inscrutable face, posed in a manner of amused
indifference. Ray McKim, the fireman, a husky young giant, grinned
with an air of embarrassment and superiority together. The rest of the
crew looked as if they were about to wink at the cameras. A photog-
rapher said, laughing, "Can't you people look doomed, please? I know
that's what the editor wants."

Dagny and Rearden were answering questions for the press. There
was no mockery in their answers now, no bitterness. They were enjoying it. They spoke as if the questions were asked in good faith. Irresistibly, at some point which no one noticed, this became true.

"What do you expect to happen on this run?" a reporter asked one
of the brakemen. "Do you think you'll get there?"

"I think we'll get there," said the brakeman, "and so do you,
brother."

"Mr. Logan, do you have any children? Did you take out any extra
insurance? I'm just thinking of the bridge, you know."

"Don't cross that bridge till I come to it," Pat Logan answered contemptuously.

"Mr. Rearden, how do you know that your rail will hold?"

"The man who taught people to make a printing press," said Rearden, "how did *he* know it?"

"Tell me, Miss Taggart, what's going to support a seven-thousand-ton train on a three-thousand-ton bridge?"

"My judgment," she answered.

The men of the press, who despised their own profession, did not know why they were enjoying it today. One of them, a young man with years of notorious success behind him and a cynical look of twice his age, said suddenly, "I know what I'd like to be: I wish I could be a man who covers *news!*"

The hands of the clock on the station building stood at 3:45. The crew started off toward the caboose at the distant end of the train. The movement and noise of the crowd were subsiding. Without conscious intention, people were beginning to stand still.

The dispatcher had received word from every local operator along the line of rail that wound through the mountains to the Wyatt oil fields three hundred miles away. He came out of the station building and, looking at Dagny, gave the signal for clear track ahead. Standing by the engine, Dagny raised her hand, repeating his gesture in sign of an order received and understood.

The long line of boxcars stretched off into the distance, in spaced, rectangular links, like a spinal cord. When the conductor's arm swept through the air, far at the end, she moved her arm in answering signal.

Rearden, Logan and McKim stood silently, as if at attention, letting her be first to get aboard. As she started up the rungs on the side of the engine, a reporter thought of a question he had not asked.

"Miss Taggart," he called after her, "who is John Galt?"

She turned, hanging onto a metal bar with one hand, suspended for an instant above the heads of the crowd.

"*We* are!" she answered.

Logan followed her into the cab, then McKim; Rearden went last, then the door of the engine was shut, with the tight finality of sealed metal.

The lights, hanging on a signal bridge against the sky, were green. There were green lights between the tracks, low over the ground, dropping off into the distance where the rails turned and a green light stood at the curve, against leaves of a summer green that looked as if they, too, were lights.

Two men held a white silk ribbon stretched across the track in front of the engine. They were the superintendent of the Colorado Division and Nealy's chief engineer, who had remained on the job.

Eddie Willers was to cut the ribbon they held and thus to open the new line.

The photographers posed him carefully, scissors in hand, his back to the engine. He would repeat the ceremony two or three times, they explained, to give them a choice of shots; they had a fresh bolt of ribbon ready. He was about to comply, then stopped. "No," he said suddenly. "It's not going to be a phony."

In a voice of quiet authority, the voice of a vice-president, he ordered, pointing at the cameras, "Stand back—way back. Take one shot when I cut it, then get out of the way, fast."

They obeyed, moving hastily farther down the track. There was only one minute left. Eddie turned his back to the cameras and stood between the rails, facing the engine. He held the scissors ready over the white ribbon. He took his hat off and tossed it aside. He was looking up at the engine. A faint wind stirred his blond hair. The engine was a great silver shield bearing the emblem of Nat Taggart.

Eddie Willers raised his hand as the hand of the station clock reached the instant of four.

"Open her up, Pat!" he called.

In the moment when the engine started forward, he cut the white ribbon and leaped out of the way.

From the side track, he saw the window of the cab go by and Dagny waving to him in an answering salute. Then the engine was gone, and he stood looking across at the crowded platform that kept appearing and vanishing as the freight cars clicked past him.

*   *   *

The green-blue rails ran to meet them, like two jets shot out of a single point beyond the curve of the earth. The crossties melted, as they approached, into a smooth stream rolling down under the wheels. A blurred streak clung to the side of the engine, low over the ground. Trees and telegraph poles sprang into sight abruptly and went by as if jerked back. The green plains stretched past, in a leisurely flow. At the edge of the sky, a long wave of mountains reversed the movement and seemed to follow the train.

She felt no wheels under the floor. The motion was a smooth flight on a sustained impulse, as if the engine hung above the rails, riding a current. She felt no speed. It seemed strange that the green lights of the signals kept coming at them and past, every few seconds. She knew that the signal lights were spaced two miles apart.

The needle on the speedometer in front of Pat Logan stood at one hundred.

She sat in the fireman's chair and glanced across at Logan once in a while. He sat slumped forward a little, relaxed, one hand resting lightly on the throttle as if by chance; but his eyes were fixed on the track ahead. He had the ease of an expert, so confident that it seemed casual, but it was the ease of a tremendous concentration, the concentration on one's task that has the ruthlessness of an absolute. Ray McKim sat on a bench behind them. Rearden stood in the middle of the cab.

He stood, hands in pockets, feet apart, braced against the motion, looking ahead. There was nothing he could now care to see by the side of the track: he was looking at the rail.

Ownership—she thought, glancing back at him—weren't there those who knew nothing of its nature and doubted its reality? No, it was not made of papers, seals, grants and permissions. There it was—in his eyes.

The sound filling the cab seemed part of the space they were crossing. It held the low drone of the motors—the sharper clicking of the many parts that rang in varied cries of metal—and the high, thin chimes of trembling glass panes.

Things streaked past—a water tank, a tree, a shanty, a grain silo. They had a windshield-wiper motion: they were rising, describing a curve and dropping back. The telegraph wires ran a race with the train, rising and falling from pole to pole, in an even rhythm, like the cardiograph record of a steady heartbeat written across the sky.

She looked ahead, at the haze that melted rail and distance, a haze that could rip apart at any moment to some shape of disaster. She wondered why she felt safer than she had ever felt in a car behind the engine, safer here, where it seemed as if, should an obstacle rise, her breast and the glass shield would be first to smash against it. She smiled, grasping the answer: it was the security of being first, with full sight and full knowledge of one's course—not the blind sense of being pulled into the unknown by some unknown power ahead. It was the greatest sensation of existence: not to trust, but to know.

The glass sheets of the cab's windows made the spread of the fields seem vaster: the earth looked as open to movement as it was to sight. Yet nothing was distant and nothing was out of reach. She had barely grasped the sparkle of a lake ahead—and in the next instant she was beside it, then past.

It was a strange foreshortening between sight and touch, she thought, between wish and fulfillment, between—the words clicked sharply in her mind after a startled stop—between spirit and body. First, the vision—then the physical shape to express it. First, the thought—then the purposeful motion down the straight line of a single track to a chosen goal. Could one have any meaning without the other? Wasn't it evil to wish without moving—or to move without aim? Whose malevolence was it that crept through the world, struggling to break the two apart and set them against each other?

She shook her head. She did not want to think or to wonder why the world behind her was as it was. She did not care. She was flying away from it, at the rate of a hundred miles an hour. She leaned to the open window by her side, and felt the wind of the speed blowing her hair off her forehead. She lay back, conscious of nothing but the pleasure it gave her.

Yet her mind kept racing. Broken bits of thought flew past her attention, like the telegraph poles by the track. Physical pleasure?—she thought. This is a train made of steel . . . running on rails of Rearden Metal . . . moved by the energy of burning oil and electric generators . . . it's a physical sensation of physical movement through space . . . but is that the cause and the meaning of what I now feel? . . . Do they call it a low, animal joy—this feeling that I would not care if the rail did break to bits under us now—it won't—but I wouldn't care, because I have experienced this? A low, physical, material, degrading pleasure of the body?

She smiled, her eyes closed, the wind streaming through her hair.

She opened her eyes and saw that Rearden stood looking down at her. It was the same glance with which he had looked at the rail. She felt her power of volition knocked out by some single, dull blow that made her unable to move. She held his eyes, lying back in her chair, the wind pressing the thin cloth of her shirt to her body.

He looked away, and she turned again to the sight of the earth tearing open before them.

She did not want to think, but the sound of thought went on, like the drone of the motors under the sounds of the engine. She looked at the cab around her. The fine steel mesh of the ceiling, she thought, and the row of rivets in the corner, holding sheets of steel sealed together—who made them? The brute force of men's muscles? Who made it possible for four dials and three levers in front of Pat Logan to hold the incredible power of the sixteen motors behind them and deliver it to the effortless control of one man's hand?

These things and the capacity from which they came—was this the pursuit men regarded as evil? Was this what they called an ignoble concern with the physical world? Was this the state of being enslaved by matter? Was this the surrender of man's spirit to his body?

She shook her head, as if she wished she could toss the subject out of the window and let it get shattered somewhere along the track. She looked at the sun on the summer fields. She did not have to think, because these questions were only details of a truth she knew and had always known. Let them go past like the telegraph poles. The thing she knew was like the wires flying above in an unbroken line. The words for it, and for this journey, and for her feeling, and for the whole of man's earth, were: It's so simple and so right!

She looked out at the country. She had been aware for some time of the human figures that flashed with an odd regularity at the side of the track. But they went by so fast that she could not grasp their meaning until, like the squares of a movie film, brief flashes blended into a whole and she understood it. She had had the track guarded since its completion, but she had not hired the human chain she saw strung out along the right-of-way. A solitary figure stood at every mile post. Some were young schoolboys, others were so old that the silhouettes of their bodies looked bent against the sky. All of them were armed, with anything they had found, from costly rifles to ancient muskets. All of them wore railroad caps. They were the sons of Taggart employees, and old railroad men who had retired after a full lifetime of Taggart service. They had come, unsummoned, to guard this train. As the engine went past him, every man in his turn stood erect, at attention, and raised his gun in a military salute.

When she grasped it, she burst out laughing, suddenly, with the abruptness of a cry. She laughed, shaking, like a child; it sounded like sobs of deliverance. Pat Logan nodded to her with a faint smile; he had noted the guard of honor long ago. She leaned to the open window, and her arm swept in wide curves of triumph, waving to the men by the track.

On the crest of a distant hill, she saw a crowd of people, their arms swinging against the sky. The gray houses of a village were scattered through a valley below, as if dropped there once and forgotten; the roof lines slanted, sagging, and the years had washed away the color of the walls. Perhaps generations had lived there, with nothing to mark the passage of their days but the movement of the sun from east to west. Now, these men had climbed the hill to see a silver-headed comet cut through their plains like the sound of a bugle through a long weight of silence.

As houses began to come more frequently, closer to the track, she saw people at the windows, on the porches, on distant roofs. She saw crowds blocking the roads at grade crossings. The roads went sweeping past like the spokes of a fan, and she could not distinguish human figures, only their arms greeting the train like branches waving in the wind of its speed. They stood under the swinging red lights of warning signals, under the signs saying: "Stop. Look. Listen."

The station past which they flew, as they went through a town at a hundred miles an hour, was a swaying sculpture of people from platform to roof. She caught the flicker of waving arms, of hats tossed in the air, of something flung against the side of the engine, which was a bunch of flowers.

As the miles clicked past them, the towns went by, with the stations at which they did not stop, with the crowds of people who had come only to see, to cheer and to hope. She saw garlands of flowers under the sooted eaves of old station buildings, and bunting of red-white-and-blue on the time-eaten walls. It was like the pictures she had seen—and envied—in schoolbook histories of railroads, from the era when people gathered to greet the first run of a train. It was like the age when Nat Taggart moved across the country, and the stops along his way were marked by men eager for the sight of achievement. That age, she had thought, was gone; generations had passed, with no event to greet anywhere, with nothing to see but the cracks lengthening year by year on the walls built by Nat Taggart. Yet men came again, as they had come in his time, drawn by the same response.

She glanced at Rearden. He stood against the wall, unaware of the crowds, indifferent to admiration. He was watching the performance of track and train with an expert's intensity of professional interest, his bearing suggested that he would kick aside, as irrelevant, any thought such as "They like it," when the thought ringing in his mind was "It works!"

His tall figure in the single gray of slacks and shirt looked as if his body were stripped for action. The slacks stressed the long lines of his legs, the light, firm posture of standing without effort or being ready to swing forward at an instant's notice; the short sleeves stressed the gaunt strength of his arms; the open shirt bared the tight skin of his chest.

She turned away, realizing suddenly that she had been glancing back at him too often. But this day had no ties to past or future—her thoughts were cut off from implications—she saw no further meaning, only the immediate intensity of the feeling that she was imprisoned with him, sealed together in the same cube of air, the closeness of his presence underscoring her awareness of this day, as his rails underscored the flight of the train.

She turned deliberately and glanced back. He was looking at her. He did not turn away, but held her glance, coldly and with full intention. She smiled defiantly, not letting herself know the full meaning of her smile, knowing only that it was the sharpest blow she could strike at this inflexible face. She felt a sudden desire to see him trembling, to tear a cry out of him. She turned her head away, slowly, feeling a reckless amusement, wondering why she found it difficult to breathe.

She sat leaning back in her chair, looking ahead, knowing that he was as aware of her as she was of him. She found pleasure in the special self-consciousness it gave her. When she crossed her legs, when she leaned on her arm against the window sill, when she brushed her hair off her forehead—every movement of her body was underscored by a feeling the unadmitted words for which were: Is he seeing it?

The towns had been left behind. The track was rising through a country growing more grimly reluctant to permit approach. The rails kept vanishing behind curves, and the ridges of hills kept moving closer, as if the plains were being folded into pleats. The flat stone shelves of Colorado were advancing to the edge of the track—and the distant reaches of the sky were shrinking into waves of bluish mountains.

Far ahead, they saw a mist of smoke over factory chimneys—then the web of a power station and the lone needle of a steel structure. They were approaching Denver.

She glanced at Pat Logan. He was leaning forward a little farther. She saw a slight tightening in the fingers of his hand and in his eyes. He knew, as she did, the danger of crossing the city at the speed they were traveling.

It was a succession of minutes, but it hit them as a single whole. First, they saw the lone shapes, which were factories, rolling across their windowpanes—then the shapes fused into the blur of streets—then a delta of rails spread out before them, like the mouth of a funnel sucking them into the Taggart station, with nothing to protect

them but the small green beads of light scattered over the ground—
from the height of the cab, they saw boxcars on sidings streak past as
flat ribbons of roof tops—the black hole of the train-shed flew at their
faces—they hurtled through an explosion of sound, the beating of
wheels against the glass panes of a vault, and the screams of cheering
from a mass that swayed like a liquid in the darkness among steel
columns—they flew toward a glowing arch and the green lights hanging in the open sky beyond, the green lights that were like the door-
knobs of space, throwing door after door open before them. Then,
vanishing behind them, went the streets clotted with traffic, the open
windows bulging with human figures, the screaming sirens, and—
from the top of a distant skyscraper—a cloud of paper snowflakes
shimmering on the air, flung by someone who saw the passage of a silver bullet across a city stopped still to watch it.

Then they were out again, on a rocky grade—and with shocking
suddenness, the mountains were before them, as if the city had flung
them straight at a granite wall, and a thin ledge had caught them in
time. They were clinging to the side of the vertical cliff, with the earth
rolling down, dropping away, and giant tiers of twisted boulders
streaming up and shutting out the sun, leaving them to speed
through a bluish twilight, with no sight of soil or sky.

The curves of rail became coiling circles among walls that advanced to grind them off their sides. But the track cut through at
times and the mountains parted, flaring open like two wings at the tip
of the rail—one wing green, made of vertical needles, with whole
pines serving as the pile of a solid carpet—the other reddish-brown,
made of naked rock.

She looked down through the open window and saw the silver side
of the engine hanging over empty space. Far below, the thin thread of
a stream went falling from ledge to ledge, and the ferns that drooped
to the water were the shimmering tops of birch trees. She saw the engine's tail of boxcars winding along the face of a granite drop—and
miles of contorted stone below, she saw the coils of green-blue rail unwinding behind the train.

A wall of rock shot upward in their path, filling the windshield,
darkening the cab, so close that it seemed as if the remnant of time
could not let them escape it. But she heard the screech of wheels on
curve, the light came bursting back—and she saw an open stretch of
rail on a narrow shelf. The shelf ended in space. The nose of the en-

gine was aimed straight at the sky. There was nothing to stop them but two strips of green-blue metal strung in a curve along the shelf.

To take the pounding violence of sixteen motors, she thought, the thrust of seven thousand tons of steel and freight, to withstand it, grip it and swing it around a curve, was the impossible feat performed by two strips of metal no wider than her arm. What made it possible? What power had given to an unseen arrangement of molecules the power on which their lives depended and the lives of all the men who waited for the eighty boxcars? She saw a man's face and hands in the glow of a laboratory oven, over the white liquid of a sample of metal.

She felt the sweep of an emotion which she could not contain, as of something bursting upward. She turned to the door of the motor units, she threw it open to a screaming jet of sound and escaped into the pounding of the engine's heart.

For a moment, it was as if she were reduced to a single sense, the sense of hearing, and what remained of her hearing was only a long rising, falling, rising scream. She stood in a swaying, sealed chamber of metal, looking at the giant generators. She had wanted to see them, because the sense of triumph within her was bound to them, to her love for them, to the reason of the life-work she had chosen. In the abnormal clarity of a violent emotion, she felt as if she were about to grasp something she had never known and had to know. She laughed aloud, but heard no sound of it; nothing could be heard through the continuous explosion. "The John Galt Line!" she shouted, for the amusement of feeling her voice swept away from her lips.

She moved slowly along the length of the motor units, down a narrow passage between the engines and the wall. She felt the immodesty of an intruder, as if she had slipped inside a living creature, under its silver skin, and were watching its life beating in gray metal cylinders, in twisted coils, in sealed tubes, in the convulsive whirl of blades in wire cages. The enormous complexity of the shape above her was drained by invisible channels, and the violence raging within it was led to fragile needles on glass dials, to green and red beads winking on panels, to tall, thin cabinets stenciled "High Voltage."

Why had she always felt that joyous sense of confidence when looking at machines?—she thought. In these giant shapes, two aspects pertaining to the inhuman were radiantly absent: the causeless and the purposeless. Every part of the motors was an embodied answer to "Why?" and "What for?"—like the steps of a life-course chosen by the sort of mind she worshipped. The motors were a moral code cast in steel.

They *are* alive, she thought, because they are the physical shape of the action of a living power—of the mind that had been able to grasp the whole of this complexity, to set its purpose, to give it form. For an instant, it seemed to her that the motors were transparent and she was seeing the net of their nervous system. It was a net of connections, more intricate, more crucial than all of their wires and circuits: the rational connections made by that human mind which had fashioned any one part of them for the first time.

They *are* alive, she thought, but their soul operates them by remote control. Their soul is in every man who has the capacity to equal this achievement. Should the soul vanish from the earth, the motors would stop, because *that* is the power which keeps them going—not the oil under the floor under her feet, the oil that would then become primeval ooze again—not the steel cylinders that would become stains of rust on the walls of the caves of shivering savages—the power of a living mind—the power of thought and choice and purpose.

She was making her way back toward the cab, feeling that she wanted to laugh, to kneel or to lift her arms, wishing she were able to release the thing she felt, knowing that it had no form of expression.

She stopped. She saw Rearden standing by the steps of the door to the cab. He was looking at her as if he knew why she had escaped and what she felt. They stood still, their bodies becoming a glance that met across a narrow passage. The beating within her was one with the beating of the motors—and she felt as if both came from him; the pounding rhythm wiped out her will. They went back to the cab, silently, knowing that there had been a moment which was not to be mentioned between them.

The cliffs ahead were a bright, liquid gold. Strips of shadow were lengthening in the valleys below. The sun was descending to the peaks in the west. They were going west and up, toward the sun.

The sky had deepened to the greenish-blue of the rails, when they saw smokestacks in a distant valley. It was one of Colorado's new towns, the towns that had grown like a radiation from the Wyatt oil fields. She saw the angular lines of modern houses, flat roofs, great sheets of windows. It was too far to distinguish people. In the moment when she thought that they would not be watching the train at that distance, a rocket shot out from among the buildings, rose high above the town and broke as a fountain of gold stars against the darkening sky. Men whom she could not see, were seeing the streak of the train on the side of the mountain, and were sending a salute, a lonely plume of fire in the dusk, the symbol of celebration or of a call for help.

Beyond the next turn, in a sudden view of distance, she saw two dots of electric light, white and red, low in the sky. They were not airplanes—she saw the cones of metal girders supporting them—and in the moment when she knew that they were the derricks of Wyatt Oil, she saw that the track was sweeping downward, that the earth flared open, as if the mountains were flung apart—and at the bottom, at the foot of the Wyatt hill, across the dark crack of a canyon, she saw the bridge of Rearden Metal.

They were flying down, she forgot the careful grading, the great curves of the gradual descent, she felt as if the train were plunging downward, head first, she watched the bridge growing to meet them—a small, square tunnel of metal lace work, a few beams crisscrossed through the air, green-blue and glowing, struck by a long ray of sunset light from some crack in the barrier of mountains. There were people by the bridge, the dark splash of a crowd, but they rolled off the edge of her consciousness. She heard the rising, accelerating sound of the wheels—and some theme of music, heard to the rhythm of wheels, kept tugging at her mind, growing louder—it burst suddenly within the cab, but she knew that it was only in her mind: the Fifth Concerto by Richard Halley—she thought: did he write it for this? had he known a feeling such as this?—they were going faster, they had left the ground, she thought, flung off by the mountains as by a springboard, they were now sailing through space—it's not a fair test, she thought, we're not going to touch that bridge—she saw Rearden's face above her, she held his eyes and her head leaned back, so that her face lay still on the air under his face—they heard a ringing blast of metal, they heard a drum roll under their feet, the diagonals of the bridge went smearing across the windows with the sound of a metal rod being run along the pickets of a fence—then the windows were too suddenly clear, the sweep of their downward plunge was carrying them up a hill, the derricks of Wyatt Oil were reeling before them—Pat Logan turned, glancing up at Rearden with the hint of a smile—and Rearden said, "That's that."

The sign on the edge of a roof read: Wyatt Junction. She stared, feeling that there was something odd about it, until she grasped what it was: the sign did not move. The sharpest jolt of the journey was the realization that the engine stood still.

She heard voices somewhere, she looked down and saw that there were people on the platform. Then the door of the cab was flung open, she knew that she had to be first to descend, and she stepped to the edge. For the flash of an instant, she felt the slenderness of her own body, the lightness of standing full-figure in a current of open air. She gripped the metal bars and started down the ladder. She was halfway down when she felt the palms of a man's hands slam tight against her ribs and waistline, she was torn off the steps, swung through the air and deposited on the ground. She could not believe that the young boy laughing in her face was Ellis Wyatt. The tense, scornful face she remembered, now had the purity, the eagerness, the joyous benevolence of a child in the kind of world for which he had been intended.

She was leaning against his shoulder, feeling unsteady on the motionless ground, with his arm about her, she was laughing, she was listening to the things he said, she was answering, "But didn't you know we would?"

In a moment, she saw the faces around them. They were the bondholders of the John Galt Line, the men who were Nielsen Motors, Hammond Cars, Stockton Foundry and all the others. She shook their hands, and there were no speeches; she stood against Ellis Wyatt, sagging a little, brushing her hair away from her eyes, leaving smudges of soot on her forehead. She shook the hands of the men of the train's crew, without words, with the seal of the grins on their faces. There were flash bulbs exploding around them, and men waving to them from the riggings of the oil wells on the slopes of the mountains. Above her head, above the heads of the crowd, the letters TT on a silver shield were hit by the last ray of a sinking sun.

Ellis Wyatt had taken charge. He was leading her somewhere, the sweep of his arm cutting a path for them through the crowd, when one of the men with the cameras broke through to her side. "Miss Taggart," he called, "will you give us a message for the public?" Ellis Wyatt pointed at the long string of freight cars. "She has."

Then she was sitting in the back seat of an open car, driving up the curves of a mountain road. The man beside her was Rearden, the driver was Ellis Wyatt.

They stopped at a house that stood on the edge of a cliff, with no other habitation anywhere in sight, with the whole of the oil fields spread on the slopes below.

"Why, of course you're staying at my house overnight, both of you," said Ellis Wyatt, as they went in. "Where did you expect to stay?"

She laughed. "I don't know. I hadn't thought of it at all."

"The nearest town is an hour's drive away. That's where your crew has gone: your boys at the division point are giving a party in their honor. So is the whole town. But I told Ted Nielsen and the others that we'd have no banquets for you and no oratory. Unless you'd like it?"

"God, no!" she said. "Thanks, Ellis."

It was dark when they sat at the dinner table in a room that had large windows and a few pieces of costly furniture. The dinner was served by a silent figure in a white jacket, the only other inhabitant of the house, an elderly Indian with a stony face and a courteous manner. A few points of fire were scattered through the room, running over and out beyond the windows: the candles on the table, the lights on the derricks, and the stars:

"Do you think that you have your hands full now?" Ellis Wyatt was saying. "Just give me a year and I'll give you something to keep you busy. Two tank trains a day, Dagny? It's going to be four or six or as many as you wish me to fill." His hand swept over the lights on the mountains. "This? It's nothing, compared to what I've got coming." He pointed west. "The Buena Esperanza Pass. Five miles from here. Everybody's wondering what I'm doing with it. Oil shale. How many years ago was it that they gave up trying to get oil from shale, because it was too expensive? Well, wait till you see the process I've developed. It will be the cheapest oil ever to splash in their faces, and an unlimited supply of it, an untapped supply that will make the biggest oil pool look like a mud puddle. Did I order a pipe line? Hank, you and I will have to build pipe lines in all directions to . . . Oh, I beg your pardon. I don't believe I introduced myself when I spoke to you at the station. I haven't even told you my name."

Rearden grinned. "I've guessed it by now."

"I'm sorry, I don't like to be careless, but I was too excited."

"What were you excited about?" asked Dagny, her eyes narrowed in mockery.

Wyatt held her glance for a moment; his answer had a tone of solemn intensity strangely conveyed by a smiling voice. "About the most beautiful slap in the face I ever got and deserved."

"Do you mean, for our first meeting?"

"I mean, for our first meeting."

"Don't. You were right."

"I was. About everything but you. Dagny, to find an exception after years of . . . Oh, to hell with them! Do you want me to turn on the radio and hear what they're saying about the two of you tonight?"

"No."

"Good. I don't want to hear them. Let them swallow their own speeches. They're all climbing on the band wagon now. *We're* the band." He glanced at Rearden. "What are you smiling at?"

"I've always been curious to see what you're like."

"I've never had a chance to be what I'm like—except tonight."

"Do you live here alone, like this, miles away from everything?"

Wyatt pointed at the window. "I'm a couple of steps away from—everything."

"What about people?"

"I have guest rooms for the kind of people who come to see me on business. I want as many miles as possible between myself and all the other kinds." He leaned forward to refill their wine glasses. "Hank, why don't you move to Colorado? To hell with New York and the Eastern Seaboard! This is the capital of the Renaissance. The Second Renaissance—not of oil paintings and cathedrals—but of oil derricks, power plants, and motors made of Rearden Metal. They had the Stone Age and the Iron Age and now they're going to call it the Rearden Metal Age—because there's no limit to what your Metal has made possible."

"I'm going to buy a few square miles of Pennsylvania," said Rearden. "The ones around my mills. It would have been cheaper to build a branch here, as I wanted, but you know why I can't, and to hell with them! I'll beat them anyway. I'm going to expand the mills—and if she can give me three-day freight service to Colorado, I'll give you a race for who's going to be the capital of the Renaissance!"

"Give me a year," said Dagny, "of running trains on the John Galt Line, give me time to pull the Taggart system together—and I'll give you three-day freight service across the continent, on a Rearden Metal track from ocean to ocean!"

"Who was it that said he needed a fulcrum?" said Ellis Wyatt. "Give me an unobstructed right-of-way and I'll show them how to move the earth!"

She wondered what it was that she liked about the sound of Wyatt's laughter. Their voices, even her own, had a tone she had never heard before. When they rose from the table, she was astonished to notice that the candles were the only illumination of the room: she had felt as if she were sitting in a violent light.

Ellis Wyatt picked up his glass, looked at their faces and said, "To the world as it seems to be right now!"

He emptied the glass with a single movement.

She heard the crash of the glass against the wall in the same instant that she saw a circling current—from the curve of his body to the sweep of his arm to the terrible violence of his hand that flung the glass across the room. It was not the conventional gesture meant as celebration, it was the gesture of a rebellious anger, the vicious gesture which is movement substituted for a scream of pain.

"Ellis," she whispered, "what's the matter?"

He turned to look at her. With the same violent suddenness, his eyes were clear, his face was calm; what frightened her was seeing him smile gently. "I'm sorry," he said. "Never mind. We'll try to think that it will last."

The earth below was streaked with moonlight, when Wyatt led them up an outside stairway to the second floor of the house, to the open gallery at the doors of the guest rooms. He wished them good night and they heard his steps descending the stairs. The moonlight seemed to drain sound as it drained color. The steps rolled into a distant past, and when they died, the silence had the quality of a solitude that had lasted for a long time, as if no person were left anywhere in reach.

She did not turn to the door of her room. He did not move. At the level of their feet, there was nothing but a thin railing and a spread of space. Angular tiers descended below, with shadows repeating the steel tracery of derricks, criss-crossing sharp, black lines on patches of glowing rock. A few lights, white and red, trembled in the clear air, like drops of rain caught on the edges of steel girders. Far in the distance, three small drops were green, strung in a line along the Taggart track. Beyond them, at the end of space, at the foot of a white curve, hung a webbed rectangle which was the bridge.

She felt a rhythm without sound or movement, a sense of beating tension, as if the wheels of the John Galt Line were still speeding on. Slowly, in answer and in resistance to an unspoken summons, she turned and looked at him.

The look she saw on his face made her know for the first time that she had known this would be the end of the journey. That look was not as men are taught to represent it, it was not a matter of loose muscles, hanging lips and mindless hunger. The lines of his face were pulled tight, giving it a peculiar purity, a sharp precision of form, making it clean and young. His mouth was taut, the lips faintly drawn inward, stressing the outline of its shape. Only his eyes were blurred, their lower lids swollen and raised, their glance intent with that which resembled hatred and pain.

The shock became numbness spreading through her body—she felt a tight pressure in her throat and her stomach—she was conscious of nothing but a silent convulsion that made her unable to breathe. But what she felt, without words for it, was: Yes, Hank, yes—now—because it is part of the same battle, in some way that I can't name . . . because it is our being, against theirs . . . our great capacity, for which they torture us, the capacity of happiness . . . Now, like this, without words or questions . . . because we want it . . .

It was like an act of hatred, like the cutting blow of a lash encircling her body: she felt his arms around her, she felt her legs pulled forward against him and her chest bent back under the pressure of his, his mouth on hers.

Her hand moved from his shoulders to his waist to his legs, releasing the unconfessed desire of her every meeting with him. When she tore her mouth away from him, she was laughing soundlessly, in triumph, as if saying: Hank Rearden—the austere, unapproachable Hank Rearden of the monklike office, the business conferences, the harsh bargains—do you remember them now?—I'm thinking of it, for the pleasure of knowing that I've brought you to this. He was not smiling, his face was tight, it was the face of an enemy, he jerked her head and caught her mouth again, as if he were inflicting a wound.

She felt him trembling and she thought that this was the kind of cry she had wanted to tear from him—this surrender through the shreds of his tortured resistance. Yet she knew, at the same time, that the triumph was his, that her laughter was her tribute to him, that her defiance was submission, that the purpose of all of her violent strength was only to make his victory the greater—he was holding her body against his, as if stressing his wish to let her know that she was now only a tool for the satisfaction of his desire—and his victory, she knew, was her wish to let him reduce her to that. Whatever I am, she thought, whatever pride of person I may hold, the pride of my courage, of my work, of my mind and my freedom—*that* is what I offer you for the pleasure of your body, *that* is what I want you to use in your service—and that you want it to serve you is the greatest reward I can have.

There were lights burning in the two rooms behind them. He took her wrist and threw her inside his room, making the gesture tell her that he needed no sign of consent or resistance. He locked the door, watching her face. Standing straight, holding his glance, she extended her arm to the lamp on the table and turned out the light. He approached. He turned the light on again, with a single, contemptuous jerk of his wrist. She saw him smile for the first time, a slow, mocking, sensual smile that stressed the purpose of his action.

He was holding her half-stretched across the bed, he was tearing her clothes off, while her face was pressed against him, her mouth moving down the line of his neck, down his shoulder. She knew that every gesture of her desire for him struck him like a blow, that there was some shudder of incredulous anger within him—yet that no gesture would satisfy his greed for every evidence of her desire.

He stood looking down at her naked body, he leaned over, she heard his voice—it was more a statement of contemptuous triumph than a question: "You want it?" Her answer was more a gasp than a word, her eyes closed, her mouth open: "Yes."

She knew that what she felt with the skin of her arms was the cloth of his shirt, she knew that the lips she felt on her mouth were his, but in the rest of her there was no distinction between his being and her own, as there was no division between body and spirit. Through all the steps of the years behind them, the steps down a course chosen in the courage of a single loyalty: their love of existence—chosen in the knowledge that nothing will be given, that one must make one's own desire and every shape of its fulfillment—through the steps of shaping metal, rails and motors—they had moved by the power of the thought that one remakes the earth for one's enjoyment, that man's spirit gives meaning to insentient matter by molding it to serve one's chosen goal. The course led them to the moment when, in answer to the highest of one's values, in an admiration not to be expressed by any other form of tribute, one's spirit makes one's body become the tribute, recasting it—as proof, as sanction, as reward—into a single sensation of such intensity of joy that no other sanction of one's existence is necessary. He heard the moan of her breath; she felt the shudder of his body, in the same instant.

She looked at the glowing bands on the skin of her arm, spaced like bracelets from her wrist to her shoulder. They were strips of sunlight from the Venetian blinds on the window of an unfamiliar room. She saw a bruise above her elbow, with dark beads that had been blood. Her arm lay on the blanket that covered her body. She was aware of her legs and hips, but the rest of her body was only a sense of lightness, as if it were stretched restfully across the air in a place that looked like a cage made of sunrays.

Turning to look at him, she thought: From his aloofness, from his manner of glass-enclosed formality, from his pride in never being made to feel anything—to this, to Hank Rearden in bed beside her, after hours of a violence which they could not name now, not in words or in daylight—but which was in their eyes, as they looked at each other, which they wanted to name, to stress, to throw at each other's face.

He saw the face of a young girl, her lips suggesting a smile, as if her natural state of relaxation were a state of radiance, a lock of hair falling across her cheek to the curve of a naked shoulder, her eyes looking at him as if she were ready to accept anything he might wish to say, as she had been ready to accept anything he had wished to do.

He reached over and moved the lock of hair from her cheek, cautiously, as if it were fragile. He held it back with his fingertips and looked at her face. Then his fingers closed suddenly in her hair and he raised the lock to his lips. The way he pressed his mouth to it was tenderness, but the way his fingers held it was despair.

He dropped back on the pillow and lay still, his eyes closed. His face seemed young, at peace. Seeing it for a moment without the reins of tension, she realized suddenly the extent of the unhappiness he had borne; but it's past now, she thought, it's over.

He got up, not looking at her. His face was blank and closed again. He picked up his clothes from the floor and proceeded to dress, standing in the middle of the room, half-turned away from her. He acted, not as if she wasn't present, but as if it did not matter that she was. His movements, as he buttoned his shirt, as he buckled the belt of his slacks, had the rapid precision of performing a duty.

She lay back on the pillow, watching him, enjoying the sight of his figure in motion. She liked the gray slacks and shirt—the expert mechanic of the John Galt Line, she thought, in the stripes of sunlight and shadow, like a convict behind bars. But they were not bars any longer, they were the cracks of a wall which the John Galt Line had broken, the advance notice of what awaited them outside, beyond the Venetian blinds—she thought of the trip back, on the new rail, with the first train from Wyatt Junction—the trip back to her office in the

Taggart Building and to all the things now open for her to win—but she was free to let it wait, she did not want to think of it, she was thinking of the first touch of his mouth on hers—she was free to feel it, to hold a moment when nothing else was of any concern—she smiled defiantly at the strips of sky beyond the blinds.

"I want you to know this."

He stood by the bed, dressed, looking down at her. His voice had pronounced it evenly, with great clarity and no inflection. She looked up at him obediently. He said:

"What I feel for you is contempt. But it's nothing, compared to the contempt I feel for myself. I don't love you. I've never loved anyone. I wanted you from the first moment I saw you. I wanted you as one wants a whore—for the same reason and purpose. I spent two years damning myself, because I thought you were above a desire of this kind. You're not. You're as vile an animal as I am. I should loathe my discovering it. I don't. Yesterday, I would have killed anyone who'd tell me that you were capable of doing what I've had you do. Today, I would give my life not to let it be otherwise, not to have you be anything but the bitch you are. All the greatness that I saw in you—I would not take it in exchange for the obscenity of your talent at an animal's sensation of pleasure. We were two great beings, you and I, proud of our strength, weren't we? Well, this is all that's left of us—and I want no self-deception about it."

He spoke slowly, as if lashing himself with his words. There was no sound of emotion in his voice, only the lifeless pull of effort; it was not the tone of a man's willingness to speak, but the ugly, tortured sound of duty.

"I held it as my honor that I would never need anyone. I need you. It had been my pride that I had always acted on my convictions. I've given in to a desire which I despise. It is a desire that has reduced my mind, my will, my being, my power to exist into an abject dependence upon you—not even upon the Dagny Taggart whom I admired—but upon your body, your hands, your mouth and the few seconds of a convulsion of your muscles. I had never broken my word. Now I've broken any oath I gave for life. I had never committed an act that had to be hidden. Now I am to lie, to sneak, to hide. Whatever I wanted, I was free to proclaim it aloud and achieve it in the sight of the whole world. Now my only desire is one I loathe to name even to myself. But it is my only desire. I'm going to have you—I'd give up everything I own for it, the mills, the Metal, the achievement of my whole life. I'm going to have you at the price of more than myself: at the price of my self-esteem—and I want you to know it. I want no pretense, no evasion, no silent indulgence, with the nature of our actions left unnamed. I want no pretense about love, value, loyalty or respect. I want no shred of honor left to us, to hide behind. I've never begged for mercy. I've chosen to do this—and I'll take all the consequences, including the full recognition of my choice. It's depravity—and I accept it as such—and there is no height of virtue that I wouldn't give up for it. Now if you wish to slap my face, go ahead. I wish you would."

She had listened, sitting up straight, holding the blanket clutched at her throat to cover her body. At first, he had seen her eyes growing dark with incredulous shock. Then it seemed to him that she was listening with greater attentiveness, but seeing more than his face, even though her eyes were fixed on his. She looked as if she were studying intently some revelation that had never confronted her before. He felt as if some ray of light were growing stronger on his face, because he saw its reflection on hers, as she watched him—he saw the shock vanishing, then the wonder—he saw her face being smoothed into a strange serenity that seemed quiet and glittering at once.

When he stopped, she burst out laughing.

The shock to him was that he heard no anger in her laughter. She laughed simply, easily, in joyous amusement, in release, not as one laughs at the solution of a problem, but at the discovery that no problem had ever existed.

She threw the blanket off with a stressed, deliberate sweep of her arm. She stood up. She saw her clothes on the floor and kicked them aside. She stood facing him, naked. She said:

"I want you, Hank. I'm much more of an animal than you think. I wanted you from the first moment I saw you—and the only thing I'm ashamed of is that I did not know it. I did not know why, for two years, the brightest moments I found were the ones in your office, where I could lift my head to look up at you. I did not know the nature of what I felt in your presence, nor the reason. I know it now. That is all I want, Hank. I want you in my bed—and you are free of me for all the rest of your time. There's nothing you'll have to pretend—don't think of me, don't feel, don't care—I do not want your mind, your will, your being or your soul, so long as it's to me that you will come for that lowest one of your desires. I am an animal who wants nothing but the sensation of pleasure which you despise—but I want it from you. You'd give up any height of virtue for it, while I—I haven't any to give up. There's none I seek or wish to reach. I am so low that

I would exchange the greatest sight of beauty in the world for the sight of your figure in the cab of a railroad engine. And seeing it, I would not be able to see it indifferently. You don't have to fear that you're not dependent upon me. It's I who will depend on any whim of yours. You'll have me any time you wish, anywhere, on any terms. Did you call it the obscenity of my talent? It's such that it gives you a safer hold on me than on any other property you own. You may dispose of me as you please—I'm not afraid to admit it—I have nothing to protect from you and nothing to reserve. You think that this is a threat to your achievement, but it is not to mine. I will sit at my desk, and work, and when the things around me get hard to bear, I will think that for my reward I will be in your bed that night. Did you call it depravity? I am much more depraved than you are: you hold it as your guilt, and I—as my pride. I'm more proud of it than of anything I've done, more proud than of building the Line. If I'm asked to name my proudest attainment, I will say: I have slept with Hank Rearden. I had earned it."

When he threw her down on the bed, their bodies met like the two sounds that broke against each other in the air of the room: the sound of his tortured moan and of her laughter.

———————

EDITOR'S NOTE: *Shortly after the successful run of the John Galt Line, Rearden and Dagny, while on vacation, happen across a revolutionary discovery—left inside an abandoned factory in a blighted part of the country.*

The Abandoned Factory

THE EARTH went flowing under the hood of the car. Uncoiling from among the curves of Wisconsin's hills, the highway was the only evidence of human labor, a precarious bridge stretched across a sea of brush, weeds and trees. The sea rolled softly, in sprays of yellow and orange, with a few red jets shooting up on the hillsides, with pools of remnant green in the hollows, under a pure blue sky. Among the col-

ors of a picture post card, the car's hood looked like the work of a jeweler, with the sun sparkling on its chromium steel, and its black
enamel reflecting the sky.

Dagny leaned against the corner of the side window, her legs
stretched forward; she liked the wide, comfortable space of the car's
seat and the warmth of the sun on her shoulders; she thought that the
countryside was beautiful.

"What I'd like to see," said Rearden, "is a billboard."

She laughed: he had answered her silent thought. "Selling what
and to whom? We haven't seen a car or a house for an hour."

"That's what I don't like about it." He bent forward a little, his
hands on the wheel; he was frowning. "Look at that road."

The long strip of concrete was bleached to the powdery gray of
bones left on a desert, as if sun and snows had eaten away the traces
of tires, oil and carbon, the lustrous polish of motion. Green weeds
rose from the angular cracks of the concrete. No one had used the
road or repaired it for many years; but the cracks were few.

"It's a good road," said Rearden. "It was built to last. The man who
built it must have had a good reason for expecting it to carry a heavy
traffic in the years ahead."

"Yes . . ."

"I don't like the looks of this."

"I don't either." Then she smiled. "But think how often we've
heard people complain that billboards ruin the appearance of the
countryside. Well, there's the unruined countryside for them to admire." She added, "They're the people I hate."

She did not want to feel the uneasiness which she felt like a thin
crack under her enjoyment of this day. She had felt that uneasiness at
times, in the last three weeks, at the sight of the country streaming
past the wedge of the car's hood. She smiled: it was the hood that had
been the immovable point in her field of vision, while the earth had
gone by, it was the hood that had been the center, the focus, the security in a blurred, dissolving world . . . the hood before her and Rearden's hands on the wheel by her side . . . she smiled, thinking that she
was satisfied to let this be the shape of her world.

After the first week of their wandering, when they had driven at
random, at the mercy of unknown crossroads, he had said to her one
morning as they started out, "Dagny, does resting have to be purposeless?" She had laughed, answering, "No. What factory do you
want to see?" He had smiled—at the guilt he did not have to assume,

at the explanations he did not have to give—and he had answered. "It's an abandoned ore mine around Saginaw Bay, that I've heard about. They say it's exhausted."

They had driven across Michigan to the ore mine. They had walked through the ledges of an empty pit, with the remnants of a crane like a skeleton bending above them against the sky, and someone's rusted lunchbox clattering away from under their feet. She had felt a stab of uneasiness, sharper than sadness—but Rearden had said cheerfully, "Exhausted, hell! I'll show them how many tons and dollars I can draw out of this place!" On their way back to the car, he had said, "If I could find the right man, I'd buy that mine for him tomorrow morning and set him up to work it."

The next day, when they were driving west and south, toward the plains of Illinois, he had said suddenly, after a long silence. "No, I'll have to wait till they junk the Bill. The man who could work that mine, wouldn't need me to teach him. The man who'd need me, wouldn't be worth a damn."

They could speak of their work, as they always had, with full confidence in being understood. But they never spoke of each other. He acted as if their passionate intimacy were a nameless physical fact, not to be identified in the communication between two minds. Each night, it was as if she lay in the arms of a stranger who let her see every shudder of sensation that ran through his body, but would never permit her to know whether the shocks reached any answering tremor within him. She lay naked at his side, but on her wrist there was the bracelet of Rearden Metal.

She knew that he hated the ordeal of signing the "Mr. and Mrs. Smith" on the registers of squalid roadside hotels. There were evenings when she noticed the faint contraction of anger in the tightness of his mouth, as he signed the expected names of the expected fraud, anger at those who made fraud necessary. She noticed, indifferently, the air of knowing slyness in the manner of the hotel clerks, which seemed to suggest that guests and clerks alike were accomplices in a shameful guilt: the guilt of seeking pleasure. But she knew that it did not matter to him when they were alone, when he held her against him for a moment and she saw his eyes look alive and guiltless.

They drove through small towns, through obscure side roads, through the kind of places they had not seen for years. She felt uneasiness at the sight of the towns. Days passed before she realized what it was that she missed most: a glimpse of fresh paint. The houses stood like men in unpressed suits, who had lost the desire to stand straight: the cornices were like sagging shoulders, the crooked porch steps like torn hem lines, the broken windows like patches, mended with clapboard. The people in the streets stared at the new car, not as one stares at a rare sight, but as if the glittering black shape were an impossible vision from another world. There were few vehicles in the streets and too many of them were horsedrawn. She had forgotten the literal shape and usage of horsepower; she did not like to see its return.

She did not laugh, that day at the grade crossing, when Rearden chuckled, pointing, and she saw the train of a small local railroad come tottering from behind a hill, drawn by an ancient locomotive that coughed black smoke through a tall stack.

"Oh God, Hank, it's not funny!"

"I know," he said.

They were seventy miles and an hour away from it, when she said, "Hank, do you see the Taggart Comet being pulled across the continent by a coal-burner of that kind?"

"What's the matter with you? Pull yourself together."

"I'm sorry . . . It's just that I keep thinking it won't be any use, all my new track and all your new furnaces, if we don't find someone able to produce Diesel engines. If we don't find him fast."

"Ted Nielsen of Colorado is your man."

"Yes, if he finds a way to open his new plant. He's sunk more money than he should into the bonds of the John Galt Line."

"That's turned out to be a pretty profitable investment, hasn't it?"

"Yes, but it's held him up. Now he's ready to go ahead, but he can't find the tools. There are no machine tools to buy, not anywhere, not at any price. He's getting nothing but promises and delays. He's combing the country, looking for old junk to reclaim from closed factories. If he doesn't start soon—"

"He will. Who's going to stop him now?"

"Hank," she said suddenly, "could we go to a place I'd like to see?"

"Sure. Anywhere. Which place?"

"It's in Wisconsin. There used to be a great motor company there, in my father's time. We had a branch line serving it, but we closed the line—about seven years ago—when they closed the factory. I think it's one of those blighted areas now. Maybe there's still some machinery left there that Ted Nielsen could use. It might have been overlooked—the place is forgotten and there's no transportation to it at all."

"I'll find it. What was the name of the factory?"

"The Twentieth Century Motor Company."

"Oh, of course! That was one of the best motor firms in my youth, perhaps the best. I seem to remember that there was something odd about the way it went out of business . . . can't recall what it was."

It took them three days of inquiries, but they found the bleached, abandoned road—and now they were driving through the yellow leaves that glittered like a sea of gold coins, to the Twentieth Century Motor Company.

"Hank, what if anything happens to Ted Nielsen?" she asked suddenly, as they drove in silence.

"Why should anything happen to him?"

"I don't know, but . . . well, there was Dwight Sanders. He vanished. United Locomotives is done for now. And the other plants are in no condition to produce Diesels. I've stopped listening to promises. And . . . and of what use is a railroad without motive power?"

"Of what use is anything, for that matter, without it?"

The leaves sparkled, swaying in the wind. They spread for miles, from grass to brush to trees, with the motion and all the colors of fire; they seemed to celebrate an accomplished purpose, burning in unchecked, untouched abundance.

Rearden smiled. "There's something to be said for the wilderness. I'm beginning to like it. New country that nobody's discovered." She nodded gaily. "It's good soil—look at the way things grow. I'd clear that brush and I'd build a—"

And then they stopped smiling. The corpse they saw in the weeds by the roadside was a rusty cylinder with bits of glass—the remnant of a gas-station pump.

It was the only thing left visible. The few charred posts, the slab of concrete and the sparkle of glass dust—which had been a gas station—were swallowed in the brush, not to be noticed except by a careful glance, not to be seen at all in another year.

They looked away. They drove on, not wanting to know what else lay hidden under the miles of weeds. They felt the same wonder like a weight in the silence between them: wonder as to how much the weeds had swallowed and how fast.

The road ended abruptly behind the turn of a hill. What remained was a few chunks of concrete sticking out of a long, pitted stretch of tar and mud. The concrete had been smashed by someone and carted away; even weeds could not grow in the strip of earth left behind. On the crest of a distant hill, a single telegraph pole stood slanted against the sky, like a cross over a vast grave.

It took them three hours and a punctured tire to crawl in low gear through trackless soil, through gullies, then down ruts left by cart wheels—to reach the settlement that lay in the valley beyond the hill with the telegraph pole.

A few houses still stood within the skeleton of what had once been an industrial town. Everything that could move, had moved away; but some human beings had remained. The empty structures were vertical rubble; they had been eaten, not by time, but by men: boards torn out at random, missing patches of roofs, holes left in gutted cellars. It looked as if blind hands had seized whatever fitted the need of the moment, with no concept of remaining in existence the next morning. The inhabited houses were scattered at random among the ruins; the smoke of their chimneys was the only movement visible in town. A shell of concrete, which had been a schoolhouse, stood on the outskirts; it looked like a skull, with the empty sockets of glassless windows, with a few strands of hair still clinging to it, in the shape of broken wires.

Beyond the town, on a distant hill, stood the factory of the Twentieth Century Motor Company. Its walls, roof lines and smokestacks looked trim, impregnable like a fortress. It would have seemed intact but for a silver water tank: the water tank was tipped sidewise.

They saw no trace of a road to the factory in the tangled miles of trees and hillsides. They drove to the door of the first house in sight that showed a feeble signal of rising smoke. The door was open. An old woman came shuffling out at the sound of the motor. She was bent and swollen, barefooted, dressed in a garment of flour sacking. She looked at the car without astonishment, without curiosity; it was the blank stare of a being who had lost the capacity to feel anything but exhaustion.

"Can you tell me the way to the factory?" asked Rearden.

The woman did not answer at once; she looked as if she would be unable to speak English. "What factory?" she asked.

Rearden pointed. "That one."

"It's closed."

"I know it's closed. But is there any way to get there?"

"I don't know."

"Is there any sort of road?"

"There's roads in the woods."

"Any for a car to drive through?"

"Maybe."

"Well, which would be the best road to take?"

"I don't know."

Through the open door, they could see the interior of her house. There was a useless gas stove, its oven stuffed with rags, serving as a chest of drawers. There was a stove built of stones in a corner, with a few logs burning under an old kettle, and long streaks of soot rising up the wall. A white object lay propped against the legs of a table: it was a porcelain washbowl, torn from the wall of some bathroom, filled with wilted cabbages. A tallow candle stood in a bottle on the table. There was no paint left on the floor; its boards were scrubbed to a soggy gray that looked like the visual expression of the pain in the bones of the person who had bent and scrubbed and lost the battle against the grime now soaked into the grain of the boards.

A brood of ragged children had gathered at the door behind the woman, silently, one by one. They stared at the car, not with the bright curiosity of children, but with the tension of savages ready to vanish at the first sign of danger.

"How many miles is it to the factory?" asked Rearden.

"Ten miles," said the woman, and added, "Maybe five."

"How far is the next town?"

"There ain't any next town."

"There are other towns somewhere. I mean, how far?"

"Yeah. Somewhere."

In the vacant space by the side of the house, they saw faded rags hanging on a clothesline, which was a piece of telegraph wire. Three chickens pecked among the beds of a scraggly vegetable garden; a fourth sat roosting on a bar which was a length of plumber's pipe. Two pigs waddled in a stretch of mud and refuse; the stepping stones laid across the muck were pieces of the highway's concrete.

They heard a screeching sound in the distance and saw a man drawing water from a public well by means of a rope pulley. They watched him as he came slowly down the street. He carried two buckets that seemed too heavy for his thin arms. One could not tell his age. He approached and stopped, looking at the car. His eyes darted at the strangers, then away, suspicious and furtive.

Rearden took out a ten-dollar bill and extended it to him, asking, "Would you please tell us the way to the factory?"

The man stared at the money with sullen indifference, not moving, not lifting a hand for it, still clutching the two buckets. If one were ever to see a man devoid of greed, thought Dagny, there he was.

"We don't need no money around here," he said.

"Don't you work for a living?"

"Yeah."

"Well, what do you use for money?"

The man put the buckets down, as if it had just occurred to him that he did not have to stand straining under their weight. "We don't use no money," he said. "We just trade things amongst us."

"How do you trade with people from other towns?"

"We don't go to no other towns."

"You don't seem to have it easy here."

"What's that to you?"

"Nothing. Just curiosity. Why do you people stay here?"

"My old man use to have a grocery store here. Only the factory closed."

"Why didn't you move?"

"Where to?"

"Anywhere."

"What for?"

Dagny was staring at the two buckets: they were square tins with rope handles; they had been oil cans.

"Listen," said Rearden, "can you tell us whether there's a road to the factory?"

"There's plenty of roads."

"Is there one that a car can take?"

"I guess so."

"Which one?"

The man weighed the problem earnestly for some moments. "Well, now if you turn to the left by the schoolhouse," he said, "and go on till you come to the crooked oak, there's a road up there that's fine when it don't rain for a couple of weeks."

"When did it rain last?"

"Yesterday."

"Is there another road?"

"Well, you could go through Hanson's pasture and across the

woods and then there's a good, solid road there, all the way down to the creek."

"Is there a bridge across the creek?"

"No."

"What are the other roads?"

"Well, if it's a car road that you want, there's one the other side of Miller's patch, it's paved, it's the best road for a car, you just turn to the right by the schoolhouse and—"

"But that road doesn't go to the factory, does it?"

"No, not to the factory."

"All right," said Rearden. "Guess we'll find our own way."

He had pressed the starter, when a rock came smashing into the windshield. The glass was shatterproof, but a sunburst of cracks spread across it. They saw a ragged little hoodlum vanishing behind a corner with a scream of laughter, and they heard the shrill laughter of children answering him from behind some windows or crevices.

Rearden suppressed a swear word. The man looked vapidly across the street, frowning a little. The old woman looked on, without reaction. She had stood there silently, watching, without interest or purpose, like a chemical compound on a photographic plate, absorbing visual shapes because they were there to be absorbed, but unable ever to form any estimate of the objects of her vision.

Dagny had been studying her for some minutes. The swollen shapelessness of the woman's body did not look like the product of age and neglect: it looked as if she was pregnant. This seemed impossible, but glancing closer Dagny saw that her dust-colored hair was not gray and that there were few wrinkles on her face; it was only the vacant eyes, the stooped shoulders, the shuffling movements that gave her the stamp of senility.

Dagny leaned out and asked, "How old are you?"

The woman looked at her, not in resentment, but merely as one looks at a pointless question. "Thirty-seven," she answered.

They had driven five former blocks away, when Dagny spoke.

"Hank," she said in terror, "that woman is only two years older than I!"

"Yes."

"God, how did they ever come to such a state?"

He shrugged. "Who is John Galt?"

The last thing they saw, as they left the town, was a billboard. A design was still visible on its peeling strips, imprinted in the dead gray that had once been color. It advertised a washing machine.

In a distant field, beyond the town, they saw the figure of a man moving slowly, contorted by the ugliness of a physical effort beyond the proper use of a human body: he was pushing a plow by hand.

They reached the factory of the Twentieth Century Motor Company two miles and two hours later. They knew, as they climbed the hill, that their quest was useless. A rusted padlock hung on the door of the main entrance, but the huge windows were shattered and the place was open to anyone, to the woodchucks, the rabbits and the dried leaves that lay in drifts inside.

The factory had been gutted long ago. The great pieces of machinery had been moved out by some civilized means—the neat holes of their bases still remained in the concrete of the floor. The rest had gone to random looters. There was nothing left, except refuse which the neediest tramp had found worthless, piles of twisted, rusted scraps, of boards, plaster and glass splinters—and the steel stairways, built to last and lasting, rising in trim spirals to the roof.

They stopped in the great hall where a ray of light fell diagonally from a gap in the ceiling, and the echoes of their steps rang around them, dying far away in rows of empty rooms. A bird darted from among the steel rafters and went in a hissing streak of wings out into the sky.

"We'd better look through it, just in case," said Dagny. "You take the shops and I'll take the annexes. Let's do it as fast as possible."

"I don't like to let you wander around alone. I don't know how safe they are, any of those floors or stairways."

"Oh, nonsense! I can find my way around a factory—or in a wrecking crew. Let's get it over with. I want to get out of here."

When she walked through the silent yards—where steel bridges still hung overhead, tracing lines of geometrical perfection across the sky—her only wish was not to see any of it, but she forced herself to look. It was like having to perform an autopsy on the body of one's love. She moved her glance as an automatic searchlight, her teeth clamped tight together. She walked rapidly—there was no necessity to pause anywhere.

It was in a room of what had been the laboratory that she stopped. It was a coil of wire that made her stop. The coil protruded from a pile of junk. She had never seen that particular arrangement of wires, yet it seemed familiar, as if it touched the hint of some memory, faint and very distant. She reached for the coil, but could not move it: it seemed to be part of some object buried in the pile.

The room looked as if it had been an experimental laboratory—if she was right in judging the purpose of the torn remnants she saw on the walls: a great many electrical outlets, bits of heavy cable, lead conduits, glass tubing, built-in cabinets without shelves or doors. There was a great deal of glass, rubber, plastic and metal in the junk pile, and dark gray splinters of slate that had been a blackboard. Scraps of paper rustled dryly all over the floor. There were also remnants of things which had not been brought here by the owner of that room: popcorn wrappers, a whiskey bottle, a confession magazine.

She attempted to extricate the coil from the scrap pile. It would not move; it was part of some large object. She knelt and began to dig through the junk.

She had cut her hands, she was covered with dust by the time she stood up to look at the object she had cleared. It was the broken remnant of the model of a motor. Most of its parts were missing, but enough was left to convey some idea of its former shape and purpose.

She had never seen a motor of this kind or anything resembling it. She could not understand the peculiar design of its parts or the functions they were intended to perform.

She examined the tarnished tubes and odd-shaped connections. She tried to guess their purpose, her mind going over every type of motor she knew and every possible kind of work its parts could perform. None fitted the model. It looked like an electric motor, but she could not tell what fuel it was intended to burn. It was not designed for steam, or oil, or anything she could name.

Her sudden gasp was not a sound, but a jolt that threw her at the junk pile. She was on her hands and knees, crawling over the wreckage, seizing every piece of paper in sight, flinging it away, searching further. Her hands were shaking.

She found part of what she hoped had remained in existence. It was a thin sheaf of typewritten pages clamped together—the remnant of a manuscript. Its beginning and end were gone; the bits of paper left under the clamp showed the thick number of pages it had once contained. The paper was yellowed and dry. The manuscript had been a description of the motor.

From the empty enclosure of the plant's powerhouse, Rearden heard her voice screaming, "Hank!" It sounded like a scream of terror.

He ran in the direction of the voice. He found her standing in the middle of a room, her hands bleeding, her stockings torn, her suit smeared with dust, a bunch of papers clutched in her hand.

"Hank, what does this look like?" she asked, pointing at an odd piece of wreckage at her feet; her voice had the intense, obsessed tone of a person stunned by a shock, cut off from reality. "What does it look like?"

"Are you hurt? What happened?"

"No! . . . Oh, never mind, don't look at me! I'm all right. Look at this. Do you know what that is?"

"What did you do to yourself?"

"I had to dig it out of there. I'm all right."

"You're shaking."

"You will, too, in a moment. Hank! Look at it. Just look and tell me what you think it is."

He glanced down, then looked attentively—then he was sitting on the floor, studying the object intently. "It's a queer way to put a motor together," he said, frowning.

"Read this," she said, extending the pages.

He read, looked up and said, "Good God!"

She was sitting on the floor beside him, and for a moment they could say nothing else.

"It was the coil," she said. She felt as if her mind were racing, she could not keep up with all the things which a sudden blast had opened to her vision, and her words came hurtling against one another. "It was the coil that I noticed first—because I had seen drawings like it, not quite, but something like it, years ago, when I was in school—it was in an old book, it was given up as impossible long, long ago—but I liked to read everything I could find about railroad motors. That book said that there was a time when men were thinking of it—they worked on it, they spent years on experiments, but they couldn't solve it and they gave it up. It was forgotten for generations. I didn't think that any living scientist ever thought of it now. But someone did. Someone has solved it, now, today! . . . Hank, do you understand? Those men, long ago, tried to invent a motor that would draw static electricity from the atmosphere, convert it and create its own power as it went along. They couldn't do it. They gave it up." She pointed at the broken shape. "But there it is."

He nodded. He was not smiling. He sat looking at the remnant, intent on some thought of his own; it did not seem to be a happy thought.

"Hank! Don't you understand what this means? It's the greatest revolution in power motors since the internal-combustion engine—greater than that! It wipes everything out—and makes everything possible. To hell with Dwight Sanders and all of them! Who'll want to look at a Diesel? Who'll want to worry about oil, coal or refueling stations? Do you see what I see? A brand-new locomotive half the size of a single Diesel unit, and with ten times the power. A self-generator, working on a few drops of fuel, with no limits to its energy. The cleanest, swiftest, cheapest means of motion ever devised. Do you see what this will do to our transportation systems and to the country—in about one year?"

There was no spark of excitement in his face. He said slowly, "Who designed it? Why was it left here?"

"We'll find out."

He weighed the pages in his hand reflectively. "Dagny," he asked, "if you don't find the man who made it, will you be able to reconstruct that motor from what is left?"

She took a long moment, then the word fell with a sinking sound: "No."

"Nobody will. He had it all right. It worked—judging by what he writes here. It is the greatest thing I've ever laid eyes on. It was. We can't make it work again. To supply what's missing would take a mind as great as his."

"I'll find him—if I have to drop every other thing I'm doing."

"—and if he's still alive."

She heard the unstated guess in the tone of his voice. "Why do you say it like that?"

"I don't think he is. If he were, would he leave an invention of this kind to rot on a junk pile? Would he abandon an achievement of this size? If he were still alive, you would have had the locomotives with the self-generators years ago. And you wouldn't have had to look for him, because the whole world would know his name by now."

"I don't think this model was made so very long ago."

He looked at the paper of the manuscript and at the rusty tarnish of the motor. "About ten years ago, I'd guess. Maybe a little longer."

"We've got to find him or somebody who knew him. This is more important—"

"—than anything owned or manufactured by anyone today. I don't think we'll find him. And if we don't, nobody will be able to repeat his performance. Nobody will rebuild his motor. There's not enough of it left. It's only a lead, an invaluable lead, but it would take the sort of mind that's born once in a century, to complete it. Do you see our present-day motor designers attempting it?"

"No."

"There's not a first-rate designer left. There hasn't been a new idea in motors for years. That's one profession that seems to be dying—or dead."

"Hank, do you know what that motor would have meant, if built?"

He chuckled briefly. "I'd say: about ten years added to the life of every person in this country—if you consider how many things it would have made easier and cheaper to produce, how many hours of human labor it would have released for other work, and how much more anyone's work would have brought him. Locomotives? What about automobiles and ships and airplanes with a motor of this kind? And tractors. And power plants. All hooked to an unlimited supply of energy, with no fuel to pay for, except a few pennies' worth to keep the converter going. That motor could have set the whole country in motion and on fire. It would have brought an electric light bulb into every hole, even into the homes of those people we saw down in the valley."

"It would have? It will. I'm going to find the man who made it."

"We'll try."

He rose abruptly, but stopped to glance down at the broken remnant and said, with a chuckle that was not gay, "*There* was the motor for the John Galt Line."

Then he spoke in the brusque manner of an executive. "First, we'll try to see if we can find their personnel office here. We'll look for their records, if there's any left. We want the names of their research staff and their engineers. I don't know who owns this place now, and I suspect that the owners will be hard to find, or they wouldn't have let it come to this. Then we'll go over every room in the laboratory. Later, we'll get a few engineers to fly here and comb the rest of the place."

They started out, but she stopped for a moment on the threshold. "Hank, that motor was the most valuable thing inside this factory," she said, her voice low. "It was more valuable than the whole factory and everything it ever contained. Yet it was passed up and left in the refuse. It was the one thing nobody found worth the trouble of taking."

"That's what frightens me about this," he answered.

The personnel office did not take them long. They found it by the sign which was left on the door, but it was the only thing left. There was no furniture inside, no papers, nothing but the splinters of smashed windows.

They went back to the room of the motor. Crawling on hands and knees, they examined every scrap of the junk that littered the floor. There was little to find. They put aside the papers that seemed to contain laboratory notes, but none referred to the motor, and there were no pages of the manuscript among them. The popcorn wrappers and the whiskey bottle testified to the kind of invading hordes that had rolled through the room, like waves washing the remnants of destruction away to unknown bottoms.

They put aside a few bits of metal that could have belonged to the motor, but these were too small to be of value. The motor looked as if parts of it had been ripped off, perhaps by someone who thought he could put them to some customary use. What had remained was too unfamiliar to interest anybody.

On aching knees, her palms spread flat upon the gritty floor, she felt the anger trembling within her, the hurting, helpless anger that answers the sight of desecration. She wondered whether someone's diapers hung on a clothesline made of the motor's missing wires—whether its wheels had become a rope pulley over a communal well—whether its cylinder was now a pot containing geraniums on the window sill of the sweetheart of the man with the whiskey bottle.

There was a remnant of light on the hill, but a blue haze was moving in upon the valleys, and the red and gold of the leaves was spreading to the sky in strips of sunset.

It was dark when they finished. She rose and leaned against the empty frame of the window for a touch of cool air on her forehead. The sky was dark blue. "It could have set the whole country in motion and on fire." She looked down at the motor. She looked out at the country. She moaned suddenly, hit by a single long shudder, and dropped her head on her arm, standing pressed to the frame of the window.

"What's the matter?" he asked.

She did not answer.

He looked out. Far below, in the valley, in the gathering night, there trembled a few pale smears which were the lights of tallow candles.

*   *   *

"God have mercy on us, ma'am!" said the clerk of the Hall of Records.
"Nobody knows who owns that factory now. I guess nobody will ever
know it."

The clerk sat at a desk in a ground-floor office, where dust lay
undisturbed on the files and few visitors ever called. He looked at the
shining automobile parked outside his window, in the muddy square
that had once been the center of a prosperous county seat; he looked
with a faint, wistful wonder at his two unknown visitors.

"Why?" asked Dagny.

He pointed helplessly at the mass of papers he had taken out of the
files. "The court will have to decide who owns it, which I don't think
any court can do. If a court ever gets to it. I don't think it will."

"Why? What happened?"

"Well, it was sold out—the Twentieth Century, I mean. The Twentieth Century Motor Company. It was sold twice, at the same time
and to two different sets of owners. That was sort of a big scandal at
the time, two years ago, and now it's just"—he pointed—"just a
bunch of paper lying around, waiting for a court hearing. I don't see
how any judge will be able to untangle any property rights out of it—
or any right at all."

"Would you tell me please just what happened?"

"Well, the last legal owner of the factory was The People's Mortgage Company, of Rome, Wisconsin. That's the town the other side
of the factory, thirty miles north. That Mortgage Company was a sort
of noisy outfit that did a lot of advertising about easy credit. Mark
Yonts was the head of it. Nobody knew where he came from and nobody knows where he's gone to now, but what they discovered, the
morning after The People's Mortgage Company collapsed, was that
Mark Yonts had sold the Twentieth Century Motor factory to a
bunch of suckers from South Dakota, and that he'd also given it as
collateral for a loan from a bank in Illinois. And when they took a
look at the factory, they discovered that he'd moved all the machinery out and sold it piece-meal, God only knows where and to whom.
So it seems like everybody owns the place—and nobody. That's how
it stands now—the South Dakotans and the bank and the attorney
for the creditors of The People's Mortgage Company all suing one
another, all claiming this factory, and nobody having the right to
move a wheel in it, except that there's no wheels left to move."

"Did Mark Yonts operate the factory before he sold it?"

"Lord, no, ma'am! He wasn't the kind that ever operates anything. He didn't want to *make* money, only to *get* it. Guess he got it, too— more than anyone could have made out of that factory."

He wondered why the blond, hard-faced man, who sat with the woman in front of his desk, looked grimly out the window at their car, at a large object wrapped in canvas, roped tightly under the raised cover of the car's luggage compartment.

"What happened to the factory records?"

"Which do you mean, ma'am?"

"Their production records. Their work records. Their . . . personnel files."

"Oh, there's nothing left of that now. There's been a lot of looting going on. All the mixed owners grabbed what furniture or things they could haul out of there, even if the sheriff did put a padlock on the door. The papers and stuff like that—I guess it was all taken by the scavengers from Starnesville, that's the place down in the valley, where they're having it pretty tough these days. They burned the stuff for kindling, most likely."

"Is there anyone left here who used to work in the factory?" asked Rearden.

"No, sir. Not around here. They all lived down in Starnesville."

"All of them?" whispered Dagny; she was thinking of the ruins. "The . . . engineers, too?"

"Yes, ma'am. That was the factory town. They've all gone, long ago."

"Do you happen to remember the names of any men who worked there?"

"No, ma'am."

"What owner was the last to operate the factory?" asked Rearden.

"I couldn't say, sir. There's been so much trouble up there and the place has changed hands so many times, since old Jed Starnes died. He's the man who built the factory. He made this whole part of the country, I guess. He died twelve years ago."

"Can you give us the names of all the owners since?"

"No, sir. We had a fire in the old courthouse, about three years ago, and all the old records are gone. I don't know where you could trace them now."

"You don't know how this Mark Yonts happened to acquire the factory?"

"Yes, I know that. He bought it from Mayor Bascom of Rome. How Mayor Bascom happened to own it, I don't know."

"Where is Mayor Bascom now?"

"Still there, in Rome."

"Thank you very much," said Rearden, rising. "We'll call on him."

They were at the door when the clerk asked, "What is it you're looking for, sir?"

"We're looking for a friend of ours," said Rearden. "A friend we've lost, who used to work in that factory."

*   *   *

Mayor Bascom of Rome, Wisconsin, leaned back in his chair; his chest and stomach formed a pear-shaped outline under his soiled shirt. The air was a mixture of sun and dust, pressing heavily upon the porch of his house. He waved his arm, the ring on his finger flashing a large topaz of poor quality.

"No use, no use, lady, absolutely no use," he said. "Would be just a waste of your time, trying to question the folks around here. There's no factory people left, and nobody that would remember much about them. So many families have moved away that what's left here is plain no good, if I do say so myself, plain no good, just being Mayor of a bunch of trash."

He had offered chairs to his two visitors, but he did not mind it if the lady preferred to stand at the porch railing. He leaned back, studying her long-lined figure; high-class merchandise, he thought; but then, the man with her was obviously rich.

Dagny stood looking at the streets of Rome. There were houses, sidewalks, lampposts, even a sign advertising soft drinks; but they looked as if it were now only a matter of inches and hours before the town would reach the stage of Starnesville.

"Naw, there's no factory records left," said Mayor Bascom. "If that's what you want to find, lady, give it up. It's like chasing leaves in a storm now. Just like leaves in a storm. Who cares about papers? At a time like this, what people save is good, solid, material objects. One's got to be practical."

Through the dusty windowpanes, they could see the living room of his house: there were Persian rugs on a buckled wooden floor, a portable bar with chomium strips against a wall stained by the seepage of last year's rains, an expensive radio with an old kerosene lamp placed on top of it.

"Sure, it's me that sold the factory to Mark Yonts. Mark was a nice fellow, a nice, lively, energetic fellow. Sure, he did trim a few corners, but who doesn't? Of course, he went a bit too far. That, I didn't expect. I thought he was smart enough to stay within the law—whatever's left of it nowadays."

Mayor Bascom smiled, looking at them in a manner of placid frankness. His eyes were shrewd without intelligence, his smile good-natured without kindness.

"I don't think you folks are detectives," he said, "but even if you were, it wouldn't matter to me. I didn't get any rake-off from Mark, he didn't let me in on any of his deals, I haven't any idea where he's gone to now." He sighed. "I liked that fellow. Wish he'd stayed around. Never mind the Sunday sermons. He had to live, didn't he? He was no worse than anybody, only smarter. Some get caught at it and some don't—that's the only difference. . . . Nope, I didn't know what he was going to do with it, when he bought that factory. Sure, he paid me quite a bit more than the old booby trap was worth. Sure, he was doing me a favor when he bought it. Nope, I didn't put any pressure on him to make him buy it. Wasn't necessary. I'd done him a few favors before. There's plenty of laws that's sort of made of rubber, and a mayor's in a position to stretch them a bit for a friend. Well, what the hell? That's the only way anybody ever gets rich in this world"—he glanced at the luxurious black car—"as you ought to know."

"You were telling us about the factory," said Rearden, trying to control himself.

"What I can't stand," said Mayor Bascom, "is people who talk about principles. No principle ever filled anybody's milk bottle. The only thing that counts in life is solid, material assets. It's no time for theories, when everything is falling to pieces around us. Well, me—I don't aim to go under. Let them keep their ideas and I'll take the factory. I don't want ideas, I just want my three square meals a day."

"Why did you buy that factory?"

"Why does anybody buy any business? To squeeze whatever can be squeezed out of it. I know a good chance when I see it. It was a bankruptcy sale and nobody much who'd want to bid on the old mess. So I got the place for peanuts. Didn't have to hold it long, either—Mark took it off my hands in two-three months. Sure, it was a smart deal, if I say so myself. No big business tycoon could have done any better with it."

"Was the factory operating when you took it over?"

"Naw. It was shut down."

"Did you attempt to reopen it?"

"Not me. I'm a practical person."

"Can you recall the names of any men who worked there?"

"No. Never met 'em."

"Did you move anything out of the factory?"

"Well, I'll tell you. I took a look around—and what I liked was old Jed's desk. Old Jed Starnes. He was a real big shot in his time. Wonderful desk, solid mahogany. So I carted it home. And some executive, don't know who he was, had a stall shower in his bathroom, the like of which I never saw. A glass door with a mermaid cut in the glass, real art work, and hot stuff, too, hotter than any oil painting. So I had that shower lifted and moved here. What the hell, I owned it, didn't I? I was entitled to get something valuable out of that factory."

"Whose bankruptcy sale was it, when you bought the factory?"

"Oh, that was the big crash of the Community National Bank in Madison. Boy, was that a crash! It just about finished the whole state of Wisconsin—sure finished this part of it. Some say it was this motor factory that broke the bank, but others say it was only the last drop in a leaking bucket, because the Community National had bum investments all over three or four states. Eugene Lawson was the head of it. The banker with a heart, they called him. He was quite famous in these parts two-three years ago."

"Did Lawson operate the factory?"

"No. He merely lent an awful lot of money on it, more than he could ever hope to get back out of the old dump. When the factory busted, that was the last straw for Gene Lawson. The bank busted three months later." He sighed. "It hit the folks pretty hard around here. They all had their life savings in the Community National."

Mayor Bascom looked regretfully past his porch railing at his town. He jerked his thumb at a figure across the street: it was a white-haired charwoman, moving painfully on her knees, scrubbing the steps of a house.

"See that woman, for instance? They used to be solid, respectable folks. Her husband owned the dry-goods store. He worked all his life to provide for her in her old age, and he did, too, by the time he died—only the money was in the Community National Bank."

"Who operated the factory when it failed?"

"Oh, that was some quicky corporation called Amalgamated Service, Inc. Just a puff-ball. Came up out of nothing and went back to it."

"Where are its members?"

"Where are the pieces of a puff-ball when it bursts? Try and trace them all over the United States. Try it."

"Where is Eugene Lawson?"

"Oh, him? He's done all right. He's got a job in Washington—in the Bureau of Economic Planning and National Resources."

Rearden rose too fast, thrown to his feet by a jolt of anger, then said, controlling himself, "Thank you for the information."

"You're welcome, friend, you're welcome," said Mayor Bascom placidly. "I don't know what it is you're after, but take my word for it, give it up. There's nothing more to be had out of that factory."

"I told you that we are looking for a friend of ours."

"Well, have it your way. Must be a pretty good friend, if you'll go to so much trouble to find him, you and the charming lady who is not your wife."

Dagny saw Rearden's face go white, so that even his lips became a sculptured feature, indistinguishable against his skin. "Keep your dirty—" he began, but she stepped between them.

"Why do you think that I am not his wife?" she asked calmly.

Mayor Bascom looked astonished by Rearden's reaction; he had made the remark without malice, merely like a fellow cheat displaying his shrewdness to his partners in guilt.

"Lady, I've seen a lot in my lifetime," he said good-naturedly. "Married people don't look as if they have a bedroom on their minds when they look at each other. In this world, either you're virtuous or you enjoy yourself. Not both, lady, not both."

"I've asked him a question," she said to Rearden in time to silence him. "He's given me an instructive explanation."

"If you want a tip, lady," said Mayor Bascom, "get yourself a wedding ring from the dime store and wear it. It's not sure fire, but it helps."

"Thank you," she said. "Good-bye."

The stern, stressed calm of her manner was a command that made Rearden follow her back to their car in silence.

They were miles beyond the town when he said, not looking at her, his voice desperate and low, "Dagny, Dagny, Dagny . . . I'm sorry!"

"I'm not."

Moments later, when she saw the look of control returning to his face, she said, "Don't ever get angry at a man for stating the truth."

"That particular truth was none of his business."

"His particular estimate of it was none of your concern or mine."

He said through his teeth not as an answer, but as if the single thought battering his brain turned into sounds against his will, "I couldn't protect you from that unspeakable little—"

"I didn't need protection."

He remained silent, not looking at her.

"Hank, when you're able to keep down the anger, tomorrow or next week, give some thought to that man's explanation and see if you recognize any part of it."

He jerked his head to glance at her, but said nothing.

When he spoke, a long time later, it was only to say in a tired, even voice, "We can't call New York and have our engineers come here to search the factory. We can't meet them here. We can't let it be known that we found the motor together. . . . I had forgotten all that . . . up there . . . in the laboratory."

"Let me call Eddie, when we find a telephone. I'll have him send two engineers from the Taggart staff. I'm here alone, on my vacation, for all they'll know or have to know."

They drove two hundred miles before they found a long-distance telephone line. When she called Eddie Willers, he gasped, hearing her voice.

"Dagny! For God's sake, where are you?"

"In Wisconsin. Why?"

"I didn't know where to reach you. You'd better come back at once. As fast as you can."

"What happened?"

"Nothing—yet. But there are things going on, which . . . You'd better stop them now, if you can. If anybody can."

"What things?"

"Haven't you been reading the newspapers?"

"No."

"I can't tell you over the phone. I can't give you all the details. Dagny, you'll think I'm insane, but I think they're planning to kill Colorado."

"I'll come back at once," she said.

———

EDITOR'S NOTE: *This scene, from the middle of the novel, is a meeting of Washington bureaucrats and businessmen who survive on government favors. The participants have come together, in the midst of a national economic crisis, to formulate what they describe as "socially necessary" legislation.*

Wesley Mouch is chief regulator of the economy as a whole. Eugene Lawson works under him. Clem Weatherby is the bureaucrat in charge of the railroads. Floyd Ferris runs the State Science Institute. James Taggart is president of Taggart Transcontinental Railroad, and Orren Boyle—Hank Rearden's chief competitor—is president of Associated Steel.

Directive 10-289

"BUT CAN we get away with it?" asked Wesley Mouch. His voice was high with anger and thin with fear.

Nobody answered him. James Taggart sat on the edge of an armchair not moving, looking up at him from under his forehead. Orren Boyle gave a vicious tap against an ashtray, shaking the ash off his cigar. Dr. Floyd Ferris smiled. Mr. Weatherby folded his lips and hands. Fred Kinnan, head of the Amalgamated Labor of America, stopped pacing the office, sat down on the window sill and crossed his arms. Eugene Lawson, who had sat hunched downward, absentmindedly rearranging a display of flowers on a low glass table, raised his torso resentfully and glanced up. Mouch sat at his desk, with his fist on a sheet of paper.

It was Eugene Lawson who answered. "That's not, it seems to me, the way to put it. We must not let vulgar difficulties obstruct our feeling that it's a noble plan motivated solely by the public welfare. It's for the good of the people. The people need it. Need comes first, so we don't have to consider anything else."

Nobody objected or picked it up; they looked as if Lawson had merely made it harder to continue the discussion. But a small man who sat unobtrusively in the best armchair of the room, apart from the others, content to be ignored and fully aware that none of them could be unconscious of his presence, glanced at Lawson, then at Mouch, and said with brisk cheerfulness, "That's the line, Wesley. Tone it down and dress it up and get your press boys to chant it—and you won't have to worry."

"Yes, Mr. Thompson," said Mouch glumly.

Mr. Thompson, the Head of the State, was a man who possessed the quality of never being noticed. In any group of three, his person became indistinguishable, and when seen alone it seemed to evoke a group of its own, composed of the countless persons he resembled. The country had no clear image of what he looked like: his photographs had appeared on the covers of magazines as frequently as those of his predecessors in office, but people could never be quite certain which photographs were his and which were pictures of "*a mail clerk*" or "*a white-collar worker,*" accompanying articles about the daily life of the undifferentiated—except that Mr. Thompson's collars were usually wilted. He had broad shoulders and a slight body. He had stringy hair, a wide mouth and an elastic age range that made him look like a harassed forty or an unusually vigorous sixty. Holding enormous official powers, he schemed ceaselessly to expand them, because it was expected of him by those who had pushed him into office. He had the cunning of the unintelligent and the frantic energy of the lazy. The sole secret of his rise in life was the fact that he was a product of chance and knew it and aspired to nothing else.

"It's obvious that measures have to be taken. Drastic measures," said James Taggart, speaking, not to Mr. Thompson, but to Wesley Mouch. "We can't let things go the way they're going much longer." His voice was belligerent and shaky.

"Take it easy, Jim," said Orren Boyle.

"Something's got to be done and done fast!"

"Don't look at *me*," snapped Wesley Mouch. "I can't help it. I can't help it if people refuse to co-operate. I'm tied. I need wider powers."

Mouch had summoned them all to Washington, as his friends and personal advisers, for a private, unofficial conference on the national crisis. But, watching him, they were unable to decide whether his manner was overbearing or whining, whether he was threatening them or pleading for their help.

"Fact is," said Mr. Weatherby primly, in a statistical tone of voice, "that in the twelve-month period ending on the first of this year, the rate of business failures has doubled, as compared with the preceding twelve-month period. Since the first of this year, it has trebled."

"Be sure they think it's their own fault," said Dr. Ferris casually.

"Huh?" said Wesley Mouch, his eyes darting to Ferris.

"Whatever you do, don't apologize," said Dr. Ferris. "Make them feel guilty."

"I'm not apologizing!" snapped Mouch. "I'm not to blame. I need wider powers."

"But it *is* their own fault," said Eugene Lawson, turning aggressively to Dr. Ferris. "It's their lack of social spirit. They refuse to recognize that production is not a private choice, but a public duty. They have no right to fail, no matter what conditions happen to come up. They've *got* to go on producing. It's a social imperative. A man's work is not a personal matter, it's a social matter. There's no such thing as a personal matter—or a personal life. *That's* what we've got to force them to learn."

"Gene Lawson knows what I'm talking about," said Dr. Ferris, with a slight smile, "even though he hasn't the faintest idea that he does."

"What do you think you mean?" asked Lawson, his voice rising.

"Skip it," ordered Wesley Mouch.

"I don't care what you decide to do, Wesley," said Mr. Thompson, "and I don't care if the businessmen squawk about it. Just be sure you've got the press with you. Be damn sure about that."

"I've got 'em," said Mouch.

"One editor who'd open his trap at the wrong time could do us more harm than ten disgruntled millionaires."

"That's true, Mr. Thompson," said Dr. Ferris. "But can you name one editor who knows it?"

"Guess not," said Thompson; he sounded pleased.

"Whatever type of men we're counting on and planning for," said Dr. Ferris, "there's a certain old-fashioned quotation which we may safely forget: the one about counting on the wise and the honest. We don't have to consider them. They're out of date."

James Taggart glanced at the window. There were patches of blue in the sky above the spacious streets of Washington, the faint blue of mid-April, and a few beams breaking through the clouds. A monument stood shining in the distance, hit by a ray of sun: it was a tall, white obelisk, erected to the memory of the man Dr. Ferris was quoting, the man in whose honor this city had been named. James Taggart looked away.

"I don't like the professor's remarks," said Lawson loudly and sullenly.

"Keep still," said Wesley Mouch. "Dr. Ferris is not talking theory, but practice."

"Well, if you want to talk practice," said Fred Kinnan, "then let me tell you that we can't worry about businessmen at a time like this. What we've got to think about is jobs. More jobs for the people. In my unions, every man who's working is feeding five who aren't, not counting his own pack of starving relatives. If you want my advice— oh, I know you won't go for it, but it's just a thought—issue a directive making it compulsory to add, say, one-third more men to every payroll in the country."

"Good God!" yelled Taggart. "Are you crazy? We can barely meet our payrolls as it is! There's not enough work for the men we've got now! One-third more? We wouldn't have any use for them whatever!"

"Who cares whether you'd have any use for them?" said Fred Kinnan. "They need jobs. That's what comes first—*need*—doesn't it?—not your profits."

"It's not a question of profits!" yelled Taggart hastily. "I haven't said anything about profits. I haven't given you any grounds to insult me. It's just a question of where in hell we'd get the money to pay your men—when half our trains are running empty and there's not enough freight to fill a trolley car." His voice slowed down suddenly to a tone of cautious thoughtfulness: "However, we do understand the plight of the working men, and—it's just a thought—we could, perhaps, take on a certain extra number, if we were permitted to double our freight rates, which—"

"Have you lost your mind?" yelled Orren Boyle. "I'm going broke on the rates you're charging now, I shudder every time a damn boxcar pulls in or out of the mills, they're bleeding me to death, I can't afford it—and you want to *double* it?"

"It is not essential whether you can afford it or not," said Taggart coldly. "You have to be prepared to make some sacrifices. The public needs railroads. Need comes first—above your profits."

"What profits?" yelled Orren Boyle. "When did I ever make any profits? Nobody can accuse me of running a profit-making business! Just look at my balance sheet—and then look at the books of a certain competitor of mine, who's got all the customers, all the raw materials, all the technical advantages and a monopoly on secret formulas—then tell me who's the profiteer! . . . But, of course, the public does need railroads, and perhaps I could manage to absorb a certain raise in rates, if I were to get—it's just a thought—if I were to get a subsidy to carry me over the next year or two, until I catch my stride and—"

"What? Again?" yelled Mr. Weatherby, losing his primness. "How many loans have you got from us and how many extensions, suspensions and moratoriums? You haven't repaid a penny—and with all of you boys going broke and the tax receipts crashing, where do you expect us to get the money to hand you a subsidy?"

"There are people who aren't broke," said Boyle slowly. "You boys have no excuse for permitting all that need and misery to spread through the country—so long as there are people who aren't broke."

"I can't help it!" yelled Wesley Mouch. "I can't do anything about it! I need wider powers!"

They could not tell what had prompted Mr. Thompson to attend this particular conference. He had said little, but had listened with interest. It seemed as if there was something which he had wanted to learn, and now he looked as if he had learned it. He stood up and smiled cheerfully.

"Go ahead, Wesley," he said. "Go ahead with Number 10-289. You won't have any trouble at all."

They had all risen to their feet, in gloomily reluctant deference. Wesley Mouch glanced down at his sheet of paper, then said in a petulant tone of voice. "If you want me to go ahead, you'll have to declare a state of total emergency."

"I'll declare it any time you're ready."

"There are certain difficulties, which—"

"I'll leave it to you. Work it out any way you wish. It's your job. Let me see the rough draft, tomorrow or next day, but don't bother me about the details. I've got a speech to make on the radio in half an hour."

"The chief difficulty is that I'm not sure whether the law actually grants us the power to put into effect certain provisions of Directive Number 10-289. I fear they might be open to challenge."

"Oh, hell, we've passed so many emergency laws that if you hunt through them, you're sure to dig up something that will cover it."

Mr. Thompson turned to the others with a smile of good fellowship. "I'll leave you boys to iron out the wrinkles," he said. "I appreciate your coming to Washington to help us out. Glad to have seen you."

They waited until the door closed after him, then resumed their seats; they did not look at one another.

They had not heard the text of Directive No. 10-289, but they knew what it would contain. They had known it for a long time, in that special manner which consisted of keeping secrets from oneself and leaving knowledge translated into words. And, by the same method, they now wished it were possible for them not to hear the words of the directive. It was to avoid moments such as this that all the complex twistings of their minds had been devised.

They wished the directive to go into effect. They wished it could

be put into effect without words, so that they would not have to know
that what they were doing was what it was. Nobody had ever announced that Directive No. 10-289 was the final goal of his efforts.
Yet, for generations past, men had worked to make it possible, and for
months past, every provision of it had been prepared for by countless
speeches, articles, sermons, editorials—by purposeful voices that
screamed with anger if anyone named their purpose.

"The picture now is this," said Wesley Mouch. "The economic
condition of the country was better than the year before last than it
was last year, and last year it was better than it is at present. It's obvious that we would not be able to survive another year of the same progression. Therefore, our sole objective must now be to hold the line.
To stand still in order to catch our stride. To achieve total stability.
Freedom has been given a chance and has failed. Therefore, more
stringent controls are necessary. Since men are unable and unwilling
to solve their problems voluntarily, they must be forced to do it." He
paused, picked up the sheet of paper, then added in a less formal tone
of voice, "Hell, what it comes down to is that we can manage to exist
as and where we are, but we can't afford to move! So we've got to
stand still. We've got to stand still. We've got to make those bastards
stand still!"

His head drawn into his shoulders, he was looking at them with the
anger of a man declaring that the country's troubles were a personal
affront to him. So many men seeking favors had been afraid of him
that he now acted as if his anger were a solution to everything, as if
his anger were omnipotent, as if all he had to do was to get angry. Yet,
facing him, the men who sat in a silent semicircle before his desk were
uncertain whether the presence of fear in the room was their own
emotion or whether the hunched figure behind the desk generated
the panic of a cornered rat.

Wesley Mouch had a long, square face and a flat-topped skull,
made more so by a brush haircut. His lower lip was a petulant bulb
and the pale, brownish pupils of his eyes looked like the yolks of eggs
smeared under the not fully translucent whites. His facial muscles
moved abruptly, and the movement vanished, having conveyed no expression. No one had ever seen him smile.

Wesley Mouch came from a family that had known neither
poverty nor wealth nor distinction for many generations; it had
clung, however, to a tradition of its own: that of being college-bred
and, therefore, of despising men who were in business. The family's

diplomas had always hung on the wall in the manner of a reproach to the world, because the diplomas had not automatically produced the material equivalents of their attested spiritual value. Among the family's numerous relatives, there was one rich uncle. He had married his money and, in his widowed old age, he had picked Wesley as his favorite from among his many nephews and nieces, because Wesley was the least distinguished of the lot and therefore, thought Uncle Julius, the safest. Uncle Julius did not care for people who were brilliant. He did not care for the trouble of managing his money, either; so he turned the job over to Wesley. By the time Wesley graduated from college, there was no money to manage. Uncle Julius blamed it on Wesley's cunning and cried that Wesley was an unscrupulous schemer. But there had been no scheme about it; Wesley could not have said just where the money had gone. In high school, Wesley Mouch had been one of the worst students and had passionately envied those who were the best. College taught him that he did not have to envy them at all. After graduation, he took a job in the advertising department of a company that manufactured a bogus corn-cure. The cure sold well and he rose to be the head of his department. He left it to take charge of the advertising of a hair-restorer, then of a patented brassière, then of a new soap, then of a soft drink—and then he became advertising vice-president of an automobile concern. He tried to sell automobiles as if they were a bogus corn-cure. They did not sell. He blamed it on the insufficiency of his advertising budget. It was the president of the automobile concern who recommended him to Rearden. It was Rearden who introduced him to Washington—Rearden, who knew no standard by which to judge the activities of his Washington man. It was James Taggart who gave him a start in the Bureau of Economic Planning and National Resources—in exchange for double-crossing Rearden in order to help Orren Boyle in exchange for destroying Dan Conway. From then on, people helped Wesley Mouch to advance, for the same reason as that which had prompted Uncle Julius: they were people who believed that mediocrity was safe. The men who now sat in front of his desk had been taught that the law of causality was a superstition and that one had to deal with the situation of the moment without considering its cause. By the situation of the moment, they had concluded that Wesley Mouch was a man of superlative skill and cunning, since millions aspired to power, but he was the one who had achieved it. It was not within their method of thinking to know that Wesley Mouch was the zero at the meeting point of forces unleashed in destruction against one another.

"This is just a rough draft of Directive Number 10-289," said Wesley Mouch, "which Gene, Clem and I have dashed off just to give you the general idea. We want to hear your opinions, suggestions and so forth—you being the representatives of labor, industry, transportation and the professions."

Fred Kinnan got off the window sill and sat down on the arm of a chair. Orren Boyle spit out the butt of his cigar. James Taggart looked down at his own hands. Dr. Ferris was the only one who seemed to be at ease.

"In the name of the general welfare," read Wesley Mouch, "to protect the people's security, to achieve full equality and total stability, it is decreed for the duration of the national emergency that—

"Point One. All workers, wage earners and employees of any kind whatsoever shall henceforth be attached to their jobs and shall not leave nor be dismissed nor change employment, under penalty of a term in jail. The penalty shall be determined by the Unification Board, such Board to be appointed by the Bureau of Economic Planning and National Resources. All persons reaching the age of twenty-one shall report to the Unification Board, which shall assign them to where, in its opinion, their services will best serve the interests of the nation.

"Point Two. All industrial, commercial, manufacturing and business establishments of any nature whatsoever shall henceforth remain in operation, and the owners of such establishments shall not quit nor leave nor retire, nor close, sell or transfer their business, under penalty of the nationalization of their establishment and of any and all of their property.

"Point Three. All patents and copyrights, pertaining to any devices, inventions, formulas, processes and works of any nature whatsoever, shall be turned over to the nation as a patriotic emergency gift by means of Gift Certificates to be signed voluntarily by the owners of all such patents and copyrights. The Unification Board shall then license the use of such patents and copyrights to all applicants, equally and without discrimination, for the purpose of eliminating monopolistic practices, discarding obsolete products and making the best available to the whole nation. No trademarks, brand names or copyrighted titles shall be used. Every formerly patented product shall be known by a new name and sold by all manufacturers under the same name, such name to be selected by the Unification Board. All private trademarks and brand names are hereby abolished.

"Point Four. No new devices, inventions, products, or goods of any nature whatsoever, not now on the market, shall be produced, invented, manufactured or sold after the date of this directive. The Office of Patents and Copyrights is hereby suspended.

"Point Five. Every establishment, concern, corporation or person engaged in production of any nature whatsoever shall henceforth produce the same amount of goods per year as it, they or he produced during the Basic Year, no more and no less. The year to be known as the Basic or Yardstick Year is to be the year ending on the date of this directive. Over or under production shall be fined, such fines to be determined by the Unification Board.

"Point Six. Every person of any age, sex, class or income, shall henceforth spend the same amount of money on the purchase of goods per year as he or she spent during the Basic Year, no more and no less. Over or under purchasing shall be fined, such fines to be determined by the Unification Board.

"Point Seven. All wages, prices, salaries, dividends, profits, interest rates and forms of income of any nature whatsoever, shall be frozen at their present figures, as of the date of this directive.

"Point Eight. All cases arising from and rules not specifically provided for in this directive, shall be settled and determined by the Unification Board, whose decisions will be final."

There was, even within the four men who had listened, a remnant of human dignity, which made them sit still and feel sick for the length of one minute.

James Taggart spoke first. His voice was low, but it had the trembling intensity of an involuntary scream: "Well, why not? Why should they have it, if we don't? Why should they stand above us? If we are to perish, let's make sure that we all perish together. Let's make sure that we leave them no chance to survive!"

"That's a damn funny thing to say about a very practical plan that will benefit everybody," said Orren Boyle shrilly, looking at Taggart in frightened astonishment.

Dr. Ferris chuckled.

Taggart's eyes seemed to focus, and he said, his voice louder, "Yes, of course. It's a very practical plan. It's necessary, practical and just. It will solve everybody's problems. It will give everybody a chance to feel safe. A chance to rest."

"It will give security to the people," said Eugene Lawson, his mouth slithering into a smile. "Security—that's what the people want. If they want it, why shouldn't they have it? Just because a handful of rich will object?"

"It's not the rich who'll object," said Dr. Ferris lazily. "The rich drool for security more than any other sort of animal—haven't you discovered that yet?"

"Well, who'll object?" snapped Lawson.

Dr. Ferris smiled pointedly, and did not answer.

Lawson looked away. "To hell with them! Why should we worry about *them*? We've got to run the world for the sake of the little people. It's intelligence that's caused all the troubles of humanity. Man's mind is the root of all evil. This is the day of the heart. It's the weak, the meek, the sick and the humble that must be the only objects of our concern." His lower lip was twisting in soft, lecherous motions. "Those who're big are here to serve those who aren't. If they refuse to do their moral duty, we've got to force them. There once was an Age of Reason, but we've progressed beyond it. This is the Age of Love."

"Shut up!" screamed James Taggart.

They all stared at him. "For Christ's sake, Jim, what's the matter?" said Orren Boyle, shaking.

"Nothing," said Taggart, "nothing . . . Wesley, keep him still, will you?"

Mouch said uncomfortably, "But I fail to see—"

"Just keep him still. We don't have to listen to him, do we?"

"Why, no, but—"

"Then let's go on."

"What is this?" demanded Lawson. "I resent it. I most emphatically—" But he saw no support in the faces around him and stopped, his mouth sagging into an expression of pouting hatred.

"Let's go on," said Taggart feverishly.

"What's the matter with you?" asked Orren Boyle, trying not to know what was the matter with himself and why he felt frightened.

"Genius is a superstition, Jim," said Dr. Ferris slowly, with an odd kind of emphasis, as if knowing that he was naming the unnamed in all their minds. "There's no such thing as the intellect. A man's brain is a social product. A sum of influences that he's picked up from those around him. Nobody invents anything, he merely reflects what's floating in the social atmosphere. A genius is an intellectual scavenger and a greedy hoarder of the ideas which rightfully belong to society, from which he stole them. All thought is theft. If we do away with private fortunes, we'll have a fairer distribution of wealth. If we do away with genius, we'll have a fairer distribution of ideas."

"Are we here to talk business or are we here to kid one another?" asked Fred Kinnan.

They turned to him. He was a muscular man with large features, but his face had the astonishing property of finely drawn lines that raised the corners of his mouth into the permanent hint of a wise, sardonic grin. He sat on the arm of the chair, hands in pockets, looking at Mouch with the smiling glance of a hardened policeman at a shoplifter.

"All I've got to say is that you'd better staff that Unification Board with my men," he said. "Better make sure of it, brother—or I'll blast your Point One to hell."

"I intend, of course, to have a representative of labor on that Board," said Mouch dryly, "as well as a representative of industry, of the professions and of every cross-section of—"

"No cross-sections," said Fred Kinnan evenly. "Just representatives of labor. Period."

"What the hell!" yelled Orren Boyle. "That's stacking the cards, isn't it?"

"Sure," said Fred Kinnan.

"But that will give *you* a stranglehold on every business in the country!"

"What do you think I'm after?"

"That's unfair!" yelled Boyle. "I won't stand for it! You have no right! You—"

"Right?" said Kinnan innocently. "Are we talking about rights?"

"But, I mean, after all, there are certain fundamental property rights which—"

"Listen, pal, you want Point Three, don't you?"

"Well, I—"

"Then you'd better keep your trap shut about property rights from now on. Keep it shut tight."

"Mr. Kinnan," said Dr. Ferris, "you must not make the old-fashioned mistake of drawing wide generalizations. Our policy has to be flexible. There are no absolute principles which—"

"Save it for Jim Taggart, Doc," said Fred Kinnan. "I know what I'm talking about. That's because I never went to college."

"I object," said Boyle, "to your dictatorial method of—"

Kinnan turned his back on him and said, "Listen, Wesley, my boys won't like Point One. If I get to run things, I'll make them swallow it. If not, not. Just make up your mind."

"Well—" said Mouch, and stopped.

"For Christ's sake, Wesley, what about us?" yelled Taggart.

"You'll come to me," said Kinnan, "when you'll need a deal to fix the Board. But I'll run that Board. Me and Wesley."

"Do you think the country will stand for it?" yelled Taggart.

"Stop kidding yourself," said Kinnan. "The country? If there aren't any principles any more—and I guess the doc is right, because there sure aren't—if there aren't any rules to this game and it's only a question of who robs whom—then I've got more votes than the bunch of you, there are more workers than employers, and don't you forget it, boys!"

"That's a funny attitude to take," said Taggart haughtily, "about a measure which, after all, is not designed for the selfish benefit of workers or employers, but for the general welfare of the public."

"Okay," said Kinnan amiably, "let's talk your lingo. Who is the public? If you go by quality—then it ain't you, Jim, and it ain't Orrie Boyle. If you go by quantity—then it sure is *me*, because quantity is what I've got behind me." His smile disappeared, and with a sudden, bitter look of weariness he added, "Only I'm not going to say that I'm working for the welfare of my public, because I know I'm not. I know that I'm delivering the poor bastards into slavery, and that's all there is to it. And they know it, too. But they know that I'll have to throw them a crumb once in a while, if I want to keep my racket, while with the rest of you they wouldn't have a chance in hell. So that's why, if they've got to be under a whip, they'd rather *I* held it, not you—you drooling, tear-jerking, mealy-mouthed bastards of the public welfare! Do you think that outside of your college-bred pansies there's one village idiot whom you're fooling? I'm a racketeer—but I know it and my boys know it, and they know that I'll pay off. Not out of the kindness of my heart, either, and not a cent more than I can get away with, but at least they can count on that much. Sure, it makes me sick sometimes, it makes me sick right now, but it's not me who's built this kind of world—*you* did—so I'm playing the game as you've set it up and I'm going to play it for as long as it lasts—which isn't going to be long for any of us!"

He stood up. No one answered him. He let his eyes move slowly from face to face and stop on Wesley Mouch.

"Do I get the Board, Wesley?" he asked casually.

"The selection of the specific personnel is only a technical detail," said Mouch pleasantly. "Suppose we discuss it later, you and I?"

Everybody in the room knew that this meant the answer *Yes*.

"Okay, pal," said Kinnan. He went back to the window, sat down on the sill and lighted a cigarette.

For some unadmitted reason, the others were looking at Dr. Ferris, as if seeking guidance.

"Don't be disturbed by oratory," said Dr. Ferris smoothly. "Mr. Kinnan is a fine speaker, but he has no sense of practical reality. He is unable to think dialectically."

There was another silence, then James Taggart spoke up suddenly. "I don't care. It doesn't matter. He'll have to hold things still. Everything will have to remain as it is. Just as it is. Nobody will be permitted to change anything. Except—" He turned sharply to Wesley Mouch. "Wesley, under Point Four, we'll have to close all research departments, experimental laboratories, scientific foundations and all the rest of the institutions of that kind. They'll have to be forbidden."

"Yes, that's right," said Mouch. "I hadn't thought of that. We'll have to stick in a couple of lines about that." He hunted around for a pencil and made a few scrawls on the margin of his paper.

"It will end wasteful competition," said James Taggart. "We'll stop scrambling to beat one another to the untried and the unknown. We won't have to worry about new inventions upsetting the market. We won't have to pour money down the drain in useless experiments just to keep up with overambitious competitors."

"Yes," said Orren Boyle. "Nobody should be allowed to waste money on the new until everybody has plenty of the old. Close all those damn research laboratories—and the sooner, the better."

"Yes," said Wesley Mouch. "We'll close them. All of them."

"The State Science Institute, too?" asked Fred Kinnan.

"Oh, no!" said Mouch. "That's different. That's government. Besides, it's a non-profit institution. And it will be sufficient to take care of all scientific progress."

"Quite sufficient," said Dr. Ferris.

"And what will become of all the engineers, professors and such, when you close all those laboratories?" asked Fred Kinnan. "What are they going to do for a living, with all the other jobs and businesses frozen?"

"Oh," said Wesley Mouch. He scratched his head. He turned to Mr. Weatherby. "Do we put them on relief, Clem?"

"No," said Mr. Weatherby. "What for? There's not enough of them to raise a squawk. Not enough to matter."

"I suppose," said Mouch, turning to Dr. Ferris, "that you'll be able to absorb some of them, Floyd?"

"Some," said Dr. Ferris slowly, as if relishing every syllable of his answer. "Those who prove co-operative."

"What about the rest?" said Fred Kinnan.

"They'll have to wait till the Unification Board finds some use for them," said Wesley Mouch.

"What will they eat while they're waiting?"

Mouch shrugged. "There's got to be some victims in times of national emergency. It can't be helped."

"We have the right to do it!" cried Taggart suddenly, in defiance to the stillness of the room. "We need it. We need it, don't we?" There was no answer. "We have the right to protect our livelihood!" Nobody opposed him, but he went on with a shrill, pleading, insistence. "We'll be safe for the first time in centuries. Everybody will know his place and job, and everybody else's place and job—and we won't be at the mercy of every stray crank with a new idea. Nobody will push us out of business or steal our markets or undersell us or make us obsolete. Nobody will come to us offering some damn new gadget and putting us on the spot to decide whether we'll lose our shirt if we buy it, or whether we'll lose our shirt if we don't but somebody else does! We won't have to decide. Nobody will be permitted to decide anything. It will be decided once and for all." His glance moved pleadingly from face to face. "There's been enough invented already—enough for everybody's comfort—why should they be allowed to go on inventing? Why should we permit them to blast the ground from under our feet every few steps? Why should we be kept on the go in eternal uncertainty? Just because of a few restless, ambitious adventurers? Should we sacrifice the contentment of the whole of mankind to the greed of a few non-conformists? We don't need them. We don't need them at all. I wish we'd get rid of that hero worship! Heroes? They've done nothing but harm, all through history. They've kept mankind running a wild race, with no breathing spell, no rest, no ease, no security. Running to catch up with them . . . always, without end . . . Just as we catch up, they're years ahead? . . . They leave us no chance . . . They've never left us a chance? . . ." His eyes were moving restlessly; he glanced at the window, but looked hastily away: he did not want to see the white obelisk in the distance. "We're through with them. We've won. This is our age. Our world. We're going to have security—for the first time in centuries—for the first time since the beginning of the industrial revolution!"

"Well, this, I guess," said Fred Kinnan, "is the anti-industrial revolution."

"That's a damn funny thing for you to say!" snapped Wesley Mouch. "We can't be permitted to say that to the public."

"Don't worry, brother. I won't say it to the public."

"It's a total fallacy," said Dr. Ferris. "It's a statement prompted by ignorance. Every expert has conceded long ago that a planned economy achieves the maximum of productive efficiency and that centralization leads to super-industrialization."

"Centralization destroys the blight of monopoly," said Boyle.

"How's that again?" drawled Kinnan.

Boyle did not catch the tone of mockery, and answered earnestly, "It destroys the blight of monopoly. It leads to the democratization of industry. It makes everything available to everybody. Now, for instance, at a time like this, when there's such a desperate shortage of iron ore, is there any sense in my wasting money, labor and national resources on making old-fashioned steel, when there exists a much better metal that I could be making? A metal that everybody wants, but nobody can get. Now is that good economics or sound social efficiency or democratic justice? Why shouldn't I be allowed to manufacture that metal and why shouldn't the people get it when they need it? Just because of the private monopoly of one selfish individual? Should be sacrifice our rights to his personal interests?"

"Skip it, brother," said Fred Kinnan. "I've read it all in the same newspapers you did."

"I don't like your attitude," said Boyle, in a sudden tone of righteousness, with a look which, in a barroom, would have signified a prelude to a fist fight. He sat up straight, buttressed by the columns of paragraphs on yellow-tinged paper, which he was seeing in his mind:

> "At a time of crucial public need, are we to waste social effort on the manufacture of obsolete products? Are we to let the many remain in want while the few withhold from us the better products and methods available? Are we to be stopped by the superstition of patent rights?"

> "Is it not obvious that private industry is unable to cope with the present economic crisis? How long, for instance, are we going

to put up with the disgraceful shortage of Rearden Metal? There is a crying public demand for it, which Rearden has failed to supply."

"When are we going to put an end to economic injustice and special privileges? Why should Rearden be the only one permitted to manufacture Rearden Metal?"

"I don't like your attitude," said Orren Boyle. "So long as we respect the rights of the workers, we'll want you to respect the rights of the industrialists."

"Which rights of which industrialists?" drawled Kinnan.

"I'm inclined to think," said Dr. Ferris hastily, "that Point Two, perhaps, is the most essential one of all at present. We must put an end to that peculiar business of industrialists retiring and vanishing. We must stop them. It's playing havoc with our entire economy."

"Why are they doing it?" asked Taggart nervously. "Where are they all going?"

"Nobody knows," said Dr. Ferris. "We've been unable to find any information or explanation. But it must be stopped. In times of crisis, economic service to the nation is just as much of a duty as military service. Anyone who abandons it should be regarded as a deserter. I have recommended that we introduce the death penalty for those men, but Wesley wouldn't agree to it."

"Take it easy, boy," said Fred Kinnan in an odd, slow voice. He sat suddenly and perfectly still, his arms crossed, looking at Ferris in a manner that made it suddenly real to the room that Ferris had proposed murder. "Don't let me hear you talk about any death penalties in industry."

Dr. Ferris shrugged.

"We don't have to go to extremes," said Mouch hastily. "We don't want to frighten people. We want to have them on our side. Our top problem is, will they . . . will they accept it at all?"

"They will," said Dr. Ferris.

"I'm a little worried," said Eugene Lawson, "about Points Three and Four. Taking over the patents is fine. Nobody's going to defend industrialists. But I'm worried about taking over the copyrights. That's going to antagonize the intellectuals. It's dangerous. It's a spiritual issue. Doesn't Point Four mean that no new books are to be written or published from now on?"

"Yes," said Mouch, "it does. But we can't make an exception for the book-publishing business. It's an industry like any other. When we say 'no new products,' it's got to mean 'no new products.' "

"But this is a matter of the spirit," said Lawson; his voice had a tone, not of rational respect, but of superstitious awe.

"We're not interfering with anybody's spirit. But when you print a book on paper, it becomes a material commodity—and if we grant an exception to one commodity, we won't be able to hold the others in line and we won't be able to make anything stick."

"Yes, that's true. But—"

"Don't be a chump, Gene," said Dr. Ferris. "You don't want some recalcitrant hacks to come out with treatises that will wreck our entire program, do you? If you breathe the word `censorship' now, they'll all scream bloody murder. They're not ready for it—as yet. But if you leave the spirit alone and make it a simple material issue—not a matter of ideas, but just a matter of paper, ink and printing presses—you accomplish your purpose much more smoothly. You'll make sure that nothing dangerous gets printed or heard—and nobody is going to fight over a material issue."

"Yes, but . . . but I don't think the writers will like it."

"Are you sure?" asked Wesley Mouch, with a glance that was almost a smile. "Don't forget that under Point Five, the publishers will have to publish as many books as they did in the Basic Year. Since there will be no new ones, they will have to reprint—and the public will have to buy—some of the old ones. There are many very worthy books that have never had a fair chance."

"Oh," said Lawson; he remembered that he had seen Mouch lunching with Balph Eubank two weeks ago. Then he shook his head and frowned. "Still, I'm worried. The intellectuals are our friends. We don't want to lose them. They can make an awful lot of trouble."

"They won't," said Fred Kinnan. "Your kind of intellectuals are the first to scream when it's safe—and the first to shut their traps at the first sign of danger. They spend years spitting at the man who feeds them—and they lick the hand of the man who slaps their drooling faces. Didn't they deliver every country of Europe, one after another, to committees of goons, just like this one here? Didn't they scream their heads off to shut out every burglar alarm and to break every padlock open for the goons? Have you heard a peep out of them since? Didn't they scream that they were the friends of labor? Do you hear them raising their voices about the chain gangs, the slave camps, the fourteen-hour workday and the mortality from scurvy in the People's States of Europe? No, but you do hear them telling the whip-beaten wretches that starvation is prosperity, that slavery is freedom, that torture chambers are brother-love and that if the wretches don't understand it, then it's their own fault that they suffer, and it's the mangled corpses in the jail cellars who're to blame for all their troubles, not the benevolent leaders! Intellectuals? You might have to worry about any other breed of men, but not about the modern intellectuals: they'll swallow anything. I don't feel so safe about the lousiest wharf rat in the longshoremen's union: he's liable to remember suddenly that he is a man—and then I won't be able to keep him in line. But the intellectuals? That's the one thing they've forgotten along ago. I guess it's the one thing that all their education was aimed to make them forget. Do anything you please to the intellectuals. They'll take it."

"For once," said Dr. Ferris, "I agree with Mr. Kinnan. I agree with his facts, if not with his feelings. You don't have to worry about the intellectuals, Wesley. Just put a few of them on the government payroll and send them out to preach precisely the sort of thing Mr. Kinnan mentioned: that the blame rests on the victims. Give them moderately comfortable salaries and extremely loud titles—and they'll forget their copyrights and do a better job for you than whole squads of enforcement officers."

"Yes," said Mouch. "I know."

"The danger that I'm worried about will come from a different quarter," said Dr. Ferris thoughtfully. "You might run into quite a bit of trouble on that 'voluntary Gift Certificate' business, Wesley."

"I know," said Mouch glumly. "That's the point I wanted Thompson to help us out on. But I guess he can't. We don't actually have the legal power to seize the patents. Oh, there's plenty of clauses in dozens of laws that can be stretched to cover it—almost, but not quite. Any tycoon who'd want to make a test case would have a very good chance to beat us. And we have to preserve a semblance of legality—or the populace won't take it."

"Precisely," said Dr. Ferris. "It's extremely important to get those patents turned over to us *voluntarily*. Even if we had a law permitting outright nationalization, it would be much better to get them as a gift. We want to leave the people the illusion that they're still preserving their private property rights. And most of them will play along. They'll sign the Gift Certificates. Just raise a lot of noise about its being a patriotic duty and that anyone who refuses is a prince of greed, and they'll sign. But—" He stopped.

"I know," said Mouch; he was growing visibly more nervous. "There will be, I think, a few old-fashioned bastards here and there who'll refuse to sign—but they won't be prominent enough to make a noise, nobody will hear about it, their own communities and friends will turn against them for their being selfish, so it won't give us any trouble. We'll just take the patents over, anyway—and those guys won't have the nerve or the money to start a test case. But—" He stopped.

James Taggart leaned back in his chair, watching them; he was beginning to enjoy the conversation.

"Yes," said Dr. Ferris, "I'm thinking of it, too. I'm thinking of a certain tycoon who is in a position to blast us to pieces. Whether we'll recover the pieces or not, is hard to tell. God knows what is liable to happen at a hysterical time like the present and in a situation as delicate as this. Anything can throw everything off balance. Blow up the whole works. And if there's anyone who wants to do it, he does. He does and can. He knows the real issue, he knows the things which must not be said—and he is not afraid to say them. He knows the one dangerous, fatally dangerous weapon. He is our deadliest adversary."

"Who?" asked Lawson.

Dr. Ferris hesitated, shrugged and answered, "The guiltless man."

Lawson stared blankly. "What do you mean and whom are you talking about?"

James Taggart smiled.

"I mean that there is no way to disarm any man," said Dr. Ferris, "except through guilt. Through that which he himself has accepted as guilt. If a man has ever stolen a dime, you can impose on him the punishment intended for a bank robber and he will take it. He'll bear any form of misery, he'll feel that he deserves no better. If there's not enough guilt in the world, we must create it. If we teach a man that it's evil to look at spring flowers and he believes us and then does it—we'll be able to do whatever we please with him. He won't defend himself. He won't feel he's worth it. He won't fight. But save us from the man who lives up to his own standards. Save us from the man of clean conscience. He's the man who'll beat us."

"Are you talking about Henry Rearden?" asked Taggart, his voice peculiarly clear.

The one name they had not wanted to pronounce struck them into an instant's silence.

"What if I were?" asked Dr. Ferris cautiously.

"Oh, nothing," said Taggart. "Only, if you were, I would tell you that I can deliver Henry Rearden. He'll sign."

By the rules of their unspoken language, they all knew—from the tone of his voice—that he was not bluffing.

"God, Jim! No!" gasped Wesley Mouch.

"Yes," said Taggart. "I was stunned, too, when I learned—what I learned. I didn't expect that. Anything but that."

"I am glad to hear it," said Mouch cautiously. "It's a constructive piece of information. It might be very valuable indeed."

"Valuable—yes," said Taggart pleasantly. "When do you plan to put the directive into effect?"

"Oh, we have to move fast. We don't want any news of it to leak out. I expect you all to keep this most strictly confidential. I'd say that we'll be ready to spring it on them in a couple of weeks."

"Don't you think it would be advisable—before all prices are frozen—to adjust the matter of the railroad rates? I was thinking of a raise. A small but most essentially needed raise."

"We'll discuss it, you and I," said Mouch amiably. "It might be arranged." He turned to the others; Boyle's face was sagging. "There are many details still to be worked out, but I'm sure that our program won't encounter any major difficulties." He was assuming the tone and manner of a public address; he sounded brisk and almost cheerful. "Rough spots are to be expected. If one thing doesn't work, we'll try another. Trial-and-error is the only pragmatic rule of action. We'll just keep on trying. If any hardships come up, remember that it's only temporary. Only for the duration of the national emergency."

"Say," asked Kinnan, "how is the emergency to end if everything is to stand still?"

"Don't be theoretical," said Mouch impatiently. "We've got to deal with the situation of the moment. Don't bother about minor details, so long as the broad outlines of our policy are clear. We'll have the power. We'll be able to solve any problem and answer any question."

Fred Kinnan chuckled. "Who is John Galt?"

"Don't say that!" cried Taggart.

"I have a question to ask about Point Seven," said Kinnan. "It says that all wages, prices, salaries, dividends, profits and so forth will be frozen on the date of the directive. Taxes, too?"

"Oh no!" cried Mouch. "How can we tell what funds we'll need in the future?" Kinnan seemed to be smiling. "Well?" snapped Mouch. "What about it?"

"Nothing," said Kinnan. "I just asked."

Mouch leaned back in his chair. "I must say to all of you that I appreciate your coming here and giving us the benefit of your opinions. It has been very helpful." He leaned forward to look at his desk calendar and sat over it for a moment, toying with his pencil. Then the pencil came down, struck a date and drew a circle around it. "Directive 10-289 will go into effect on the morning of May first."

All nodded approval. None looked at his neighbor.

James Taggart rose, walked to the window and pulled the blind down over the white obelisk.

———

EDITOR'S NOTE: *By the novel's midpoint, the economy is in a state of collapse. Dagny Taggart has quit as operating vice president of Taggart Transcontinental, and has been replaced by Clifton Locey, a man whose sole motive is to avoid responsibility. The Unification Board, created by Directive 10-289, is the government agency that now has total power over employment.*

Thematically, this chapter answers the question "Philosophy: who needs it?"

The Tunnel Disaster

KIP CHALMERS swore as the train lurched and spilled his cocktail over the table top. He slumped forward, his elbow in the puddle, and said:

"God damn these railroads! What's the matter with their track? You'd think with all the money they've got they'd disgorge a little, so we wouldn't have to bump like farmers on a hay cart!"

His three companions did not take the trouble to answer. It was late, and they remained in the lounge merely because an effort was needed to retire to their compartments. The lights of the lounge looked like feeble portholes in a fog of cigarette smoke dank with the odor of alcohol. It was a private car, which Chalmers had demanded and obtained for his journey; it was attached to the end of the Comet

and it swung like the tail of a nervous animal as the Comet coiled
through the curves of the mountains.

"I'm going to campaign for the nationalization of the railroads,"
said Kip Chalmers, glaring defiantly at a small, gray man who looked
at him without interest. "That's going to be my platform plank. I've
got to have a platform plank. I don't like Jim Taggart. He looks like a
soft-boiled clam. To hell with the railroads! It's time we took them
over."

"Go to bed," said the man, "if you expect to look like anything
human at the big rally tomorrow."

"Do you think we'll make it?"

"You've got to make it."

"I know I've got to. But I don't think we'll get there on time. This
goddamn snail of a super-special is hours late."

"You've *got* to be there, Kip," said the man ominously, in that stubborn monotone of the unthinking which asserts an end without concern for the means.

"God damn you, don't you suppose I know it?"

Kip Chalmers had curly blond hair and a shapeless mouth. He
came from a semi-wealthy, semi-distinguished family, but he sneered
at wealth and distinction in a manner which implied that only a top-
rank aristocrat could permit himself such a degree of cynical indifference. He had graduated from a college which specialized in breeding
that kind of aristocracy. The college had taught him that the purpose
of ideas is to fool those who are stupid enough to think. He had made
his way in Washington with the grace of a cat-burglar, climbing from
bureau to bureau as from ledge to ledge of a crumbling structure. He
was ranked as semi-powerful, but his manner made laymen mistake
him for nothing less than Wesley Mouch.

For reasons of his own particular strategy, Kip Chalmers had decided to enter popular politics and to run for election as Legislator
from California, though he knew nothing about that state except the
movie industry and the beach clubs. His campaign manager had done
the preliminary work, and Chalmers was now on his way to face his
future constituents for the first time at an overpublicized rally in San
Francisco tomorrow night. The manager had wanted him to start a
day earlier, but Chalmers had stayed in Washington to attend a cocktail party and had taken the last train possible. He had shown no concern about the rally until this evening, when he noticed that the
Comet was running six hours late.

His three companions did not mind his mood: they liked his liquor. Lester Tuck, his campaign manager, was a small, aging man with a face that looked as if it had once been punched in and had never rebounded. He was an attorney who, some generations earlier, would have represented shoplifters and people who stage accidents on the premises of rich corporations; now he found that he could do better by representing men like Kip Chalmers.

Laura Bradford was Chalmers' current mistress; he liked her because his predecessor had been Wesley Mouch. She was a movie actress who had forced her way from competent featured player to incompetent star, not by means of sleeping with studio executives, but by taking the long-distance short cut of sleeping with bureaucrats. She talked economics, instead of glamour, for press interviews, in the belligerently righteous style of a third-rate tabloid; her economics consisted of the assertion that "we've got to help the poor."

Gilbert Keith-Worthing was Chalmers' guest, for no reason that either of them could discover. He was a British novelist of world fame, who had been popular thirty years ago; since then, nobody bothered to read what he wrote, but everybody accepted him as a walking classic. He had been considered profound for uttering such things as: "Freedom? Do let's stop talking about freedom. Freedom is impossible. Man can never be free of hunger, of cold, of disease, of physical accidents. He can never be free of the tyranny of nature. So why should he object to the tyranny of a political dictatorship?" When all of Europe put into practice the ideas which he had preached, he came to live in America. Through the years, his style of writing and his body had grown flabby. At seventy, he was an obese old man with retouched hair and a manner of scornful cynicism retouched by quotations from the yogis about the futility of all human endeavor. Kip Chalmers had invited him, because it seemed to look distinguished. Gilbert Keith-Worthing had come along, because he had no particular place to go.

"God damn these railroad people!" said Kip Chalmers. "They're doing it on purpose. They want to ruin my campaign. I can't miss that rally! For Christ's sake, Lester, do something!"

"I've tried," said Lester Tuck. At the train's last stop, he had tried, by long-distance telephone, to find air transportation to complete their journey; but there were no commercial flights scheduled for the next two days.

"If they don't get me there on time, I'll have their scalps and their railroad! Can't we tell that damn conductor to hurry?"

"You've told him three times."

"I'll get him fired. He's given me nothing but a lot of alibis about all their messy technical troubles. I expect transportation, not alibis. They can't treat me like one of their day-coach passengers. I expect them to get me where I want to go when I want it. Don't they know that I'm on this train?"

"They know it by now," said Laura Bradford. "Shut up, Kip. You bore me."

Chalmers refilled his glass. The car was rocking and the glassware tinkled faintly on the shelves of the bar. The patches of starlit sky in the windows kept swaying jerkily, and it seemed as if the stars were tinkling against one another. They could see nothing beyond the glass bay of the observation window at the end of the car, except the small halos of red and green lanterns marking the rear of the train, and a brief stretch of rail running away from them into the darkness. A wall of rock was racing the train, and the stars dipped occasionally into a sudden break that outlined, high above them, the peaks of the mountains of Colorado.

"Mountains . . ." said Gilbert Keith-Worthing, with satisfaction. "It is a spectacle of this kind that makes one feel the insignificance of man. What is this presumptuous little bit of rail, which crude materialists are so proud of building—compared to that eternal grandeur? No more than the basting thread of a seamstress on the hem of the garment of nature. If a single one of those granite giants chose to crumble, it would annihilate this train."

"Why should it choose to crumble?" asked Laura Bradford, without any particular interest.

"I think this damn train is going slower," said Kip Chalmers. "Those bastards are slowing down, in spite of what I told them!"

"Well . . . it's the mountains, you know . . ." said Lester Tuck.

"Mountains be damned! Lester, what day is this? With all those damn changes of time, I can't tell which—"

"It's May twenty-seventh," sighed Lester Tuck.

"It's May twenty-eighth," said Gilbert Keith-Worthing, glancing at his watch. "It is now twelve minutes past midnight."

"Jesus!" cried Chalmers. "Then the rally is *today*?"

"Yep," said Lester Tuck.

"We won't make it! We—"

The train gave a sharper lurch, knocking the glass out of his hand. The thin sound of its crash against the floor mixed with the screech of the wheel-flanges tearing against the rail of a sharp curve.

"I say," asked Gilbert Keith-Worthing nervously, "are your railroads safe?"

"Hell, yes!" said Kip Chalmers. "We've got so many rules, regulations and controls that those bastards wouldn't dare not to be safe!... Lester, how far are we now? What's the next stop?"

"There won't be any stop till Salt Lake City."

"I mean, what's the next station?"

Lester Tuck produced a soiled map, which he had been consulting every few minutes since nightfall. "Winston," he said. "Winston, Colorado."

Kip Chalmers reached for another glass.

"Tinky Holloway said that Wesley said that if you don't win this election, you're through," said Laura Bradford. She sat sprawled in her chair, looking past Chalmers, studying her own face in a mirror on the wall of the lounge; she was bored and it amused her to needle his impotent anger.

"Oh, he did, did he?"

"Uh-huh. Wesley doesn't want what's-his-name—whoever's running against you—to get into the Legislature. If you don't win, Wesley will be sore as hell. Tinky said—"

"Damn that bastard! He'd better watch his own neck!"

"Oh, I don't know. Wesley likes him very much." She added, "Tinky Holloway wouldn't allow some miserable train to make him miss an important meeting. They wouldn't dare to hold *him* up."

Kip Chalmers sat staring at his glass. "I'm going to have the government seize all the railroads," he said, his voice low.

"Really," said Gilbert Keith-Worthing, "I don't see why you haven't done it long ago. This is the only country on earth backward enough to permit private ownership of railroads."

"Well, we're catching up with you," said Kip Chalmers.

"Your country is so incredibly naïve. It's such an anachronism. All that talk about liberty and human rights—I haven't heard it since the days of my great-grandfather. It's nothing but a verbal luxury of the rich. After all, it doesn't make any difference to the poor whether their livelihood is at the mercy of an industrialist or a bureaucrat."

"The day of the industrialists is over. This is the day of—"

The jolt felt as if the air within the car smashed them forward while the floor stopped under their feet. Kip Chalmers was flung down to the carpet. Gilbert Keith-Worthing was thrown across the table top, the lights were blasted out. Glasses crashed off the shelves, the steel of the walls screamed as if about to rip open, while a long, distant thud went like a convulsion through the wheels of the train.

When he raised his head, Chalmers saw that the car stood intact and still; he heard the moans of his companions and the first shriek of Laura Bradford's hysterics. He crawled along the floor to the doorway, wrenched it open, and tumbled down the steps. Far ahead, on the side of a curve, he saw moving flashlights and a red glow at a spot where the engine had no place to be. He stumbled through the darkness, bumping into half-clothed figures that waved the futile little flares of matches. Somewhere along the line, he saw a man with a flashlight and seized his arm. It was the conductor.

"What happened?" gasped Chalmers.

"Split rail," the conductor answered impassively. "The engine went off the track."

"Off . . . ?"

"On it's side."

"Anybody . . . killed?"

"No. The engineer's all right. The fireman is hurt."

"Split rail? What do you mean, split rail?"

The conductor's face had an odd look: it was grim, accusing and closed. "Rail wears out, Mr. Chalmers," he answered with a strange kind of emphasis. "Particularly on curves."

"Didn't you know that it was worn out?"

"We knew."

"Well, why didn't you have it replaced?"

"It was going to be replaced. But Mr. Locey cancelled that."

"Who is Mr. Locey?"

"The man who is not our Operating Vice-President."

Chalmers wondered why the conductor seemed to look at him as if something about the catastrophe were his fault. "Well . . . well, aren't you going to put the engine back on the track?"

"That engine's never going to be put back on any track, from the looks of it."

"But . . . it's got to move us!"

"It can't."

Beyond the few moving flares and the dulled sounds of screams,

Chalmers sensed suddenly, not wanting to look at it, the black immensity of the mountains, the silence of hundreds of uninhabited miles, and the precarious strip of a ledge hanging between a wall of rock and an abyss. He gripped the conductor's arm tighter.

"But . . . but what are we going to do?"

"The engineer's gone to call Winston."

"Call? How?"

"There's a phone couple of miles down the track."

"Will they get us out of here?"

"They will."

"But . . ." Then his mind made a connection with the past and the future, and his voice rose to a scream for the first time: "How long will we have to wait?"

"I don't know," said the conductor. He threw Chalmers' hand off his arm, and walked away.

The night operator at Winston Station listened to the phone message, dropped the receiver and raced up the stairs to shake the station agent out of bed. The station agent was a husky, surly drifter who had been assigned to the job ten days ago, by order of the new division superintendent. He stumbled dazedly to his feet, but he was knocked awake when the operator's words reached his brain.

"What?" he gasped. "Jesus! The Comet? . . . Well, don't stand there shaking! Call Silver Springs!"

The night dispatcher of the Division Headquarters at Silver Springs listened to the message, then telephoned Dave Mitchum, the new superintendent of the Colorado Division.

"The Comet?" gasped Mitchum, his hand pressing the telephone receiver to his ear, his feet hitting the floor and throwing him upright, out of bed, "The engine done for? The *Diesel*?"

"Yes, sir."

"Oh God! Oh, God Almighty! What are we going to do?" Then, remembering his position, he added, "Well, send out the wrecking train."

"I have."

"Call the operator at Sherwood to hold all traffic."

"I have."

"What have you got on the sheet?"

"The Army Freight Special, westbound. But it's not due for about four hours. It's running late."

"I'll be right down. . . . Wait, listen, get Bill, Sandy and Clarence down by the time I get there. There's going to be hell to pay!"

Dave Mitchum had always complained about injustice, because, he said, he had always had bad luck. He explained it by speaking darkly about the conspiracy of the big fellows, who would never give him a chance, though he did not explain just whom he meant by "the big fellows." Seniority of service was his favorite topic of complaint and sole standard of value; he had been in the railroad business longer than many men who had advanced beyond him; this, he said, was proof of the social system's injustice—though he never explained just what he meant by "the social system." He had worked for many railroads, but had not stayed long with any one of them. His employers had had no specific misdeeds to charge against him, but had simply eased him out, because he said, "Nobody told me to!" too often. He did not know that he owed his present job to a deal between James Taggart and Wesley Mouch: when Taggart traded to Mouch the secret of his sister's private life, in exchange for a raise in rates, Mouch made him throw in an extra favor, by their customary rules of bargaining, which consisted of squeezing all one could out of any given trade. The extra was a job for Dave Mitchum, who was the brother-in-law of Claude Slagenhop, who was the president of the Friends of Global Progress, who were regarded by Mouch as a valuable influence on public opinion. James Taggart pushed the responsibility of finding a job for Mitchum onto Clifton Locey. Locey pushed Mitchum into the first job that came up—superintendent of the Colorado Division—when the man holding it quit without notice. The man quit when the extra Diesel engine of Winston Station was given to Chick Morrison's Special.

"What are we going to do?" cried Dave Mitchum, rushing, half-dressed and groggy with sleep, into his office, where the chief dispatcher, the trainmaster and the road foreman of engines were waiting for him.

The three men did not answer. They were middle-aged men with years of railroad service behind them. A month ago, they were beginning to learn that things had changed and that it was dangerous to speak.

"What in hell are we going to do?"

"One thing is certain," said Bill Brent, the chief dispatcher. "We can't send a train into the tunnel with a coal-burning engine."

Dave Mitchum's eyes grew sullen: he knew that this was the one thought on all their minds; he wished Brent had not named it.

"Well, where do we get a Diesel?" he asked angrily.

"We don't," said the road foreman.

"But we can't keep the Comet waiting on a siding all night!"

"Looks like we'll have to," said the trainmaster. "What's the use of talking about it, Dave? You know that there is no Diesel anywhere on the division."

"But Christ Almighty, how do they expect us to move trains without engines?"

"Miss Taggart didn't," said the road foreman. "Mr. Locey does."

"Bill," asked Mitchum, in the tone of pleading for a favor, "isn't there anything transcontinental that's due tonight, with any sort of a Diesel?"

"The first one to come," said Bill Brent implacably, "will be Number 236, the fast freight from San Francisco, which is due at Winston at seven-eighteen A.M." He added, "That's the Diesel closest to us at this moment. I've checked."

"What about the Army Special?"

"Better not think about it, Dave. That one has priority over everything on the line, including the Comet, by order of the Army. They're running late as it is—journal boxes caught fire twice. They're carrying munitions for the West Coast arsenals. Better pray that nothing stops them on your division. If you think we'll catch hell for holding the Comet, it's nothing to what we'll catch if we try to stop that Special."

They remained silent. The windows were open to the summer night and they could hear the ringing of the telephone in the dispatcher's office downstairs. The signal lights winked over the deserted yards that had once been a busy division point.

Mitchum looked toward the roundhouse, where the black silhouettes of a few steam engines stood outlined in a dim light.

"The tunnel—" he said and stopped.

"—is eight miles long," said the trainmaster, with a harsh emphasis.

"I was only thinking," snapped Mitchum.

"Better not think of it," said Brent softly.

"I haven't said anything!"

"What was that talk you had with Dick Horton before he quit?" the road foreman asked too innocently, as if the subject were irrelevant. "Wasn't it something about the ventilation system of the tunnel being on the bum? Didn't he say that the tunnel was hardly safe nowadays even for Diesel engines?"

"Why do you bring that up?" snapped Mitchum. "I haven't said anything!" Dick Horton, the division chief engineer, had quit three days after Mitchum's arrival.

"I thought I'd just mention it," the road foreman answered innocently.

"Look, Dave," said Bill Brent, knowing that Mitchum would stall for another hour rather than formulate a decision, "you know that there's only one thing to do: hold the Comet at Winston till morning, wait for Number 236, have her Diesel take the Comet through the tunnel, then let the Comet finish her run with the best coal-burner we can give her on the other side."

"But how late will that make her?"

Brent shrugged. "Twelve hours—eighteen hours—who knows?"

"Eighteen hours—for the Comet? Christ, that's never happened before!"

"None of what's been happening to us has ever happened before," said Brent, with an astonishing sound of weariness in his brisk, competent voice.

"But they'll blame us for it in New York! They'll put all the blame on us!"

Brent shrugged. A month ago, he would have considered such an injustice inconceivable; today, he knew better.

"I guess . . ." said Mitchum miserably, "I guess there's nothing else that we can do."

"There isn't, Dave."

"Oh God! Why did this have to happen to us?"

"Who is John Galt?"

It was half-past two when the Comet, pulled by an old switch engine, jerked to a stop on a siding of Winston Station. Kip Chalmers glanced out with incredulous anger at the few shanties on a desolate mountainside and at the ancient hovel of a station.

"Now what? What in hell are they stopping *here* for?" he cried, and rang for the conductor.

With the return of motion and safety, his terror had turned into rage. He felt almost as if he had been cheated by having been made to experience an unnecessary fear. His companions were still clinging to the tables of the lounge; they felt too shaken to sleep.

"How long?" the conductor said impassively, in answer to his question. "Till morning, Mr. Chalmers."

Chalmers stared at him, stupefied. "We're going to stand here till morning?"

"Yes, Mr. Chalmers."

"*Here?*"

"Yes."

"But I have a rally in San Francisco in the evening!"

The conductor did not answer.

"Why? Why do we have to stand? Why in hell? What happened?"

Slowly, patiently, with contemptuous politeness, the conductor gave him an exact account of the situation. But years ago, in grammar school, in high school, in college, Kip Chalmers had been taught that man does not and need not live by reason.

"Damn your tunnel!" he screamed. "Do you think I'm going to let you hold me up because of some miserable tunnel? Do you want to wreck vital national plans on account of a tunnel? Tell your engineer that I must be in San Francisco by evening and that he's got to get me there!"

"How?"

"That's *your* job, not mine!"

"There is no way to do it."

"Then find a way, God damn you!"

The conductor did not answer.

"Do you think I'll let your miserable technological problems interfere with crucial social issues? Do you know who I am? Tell that engineer to start moving, if he values his job!"

"The engineer has his orders."

"Orders be damned! *I* give the orders these days! Tell him to start at once!"

"Perhaps you'd better speak to the station agent, Mr. Chalmers. I have no authority to answer you as I'd like to," said the conductor, and walked out.

Chalmers leaped to his feet. "Say, Kip . . ." said Lester Tuck uneasily, "maybe it's true . . . maybe they can't do it."

"They can if they have to!" snapped Chalmers, marching resolutely to the door.

Years ago, in college, he had been taught that the only effective means to impel men to action was fear.

In the dilapidated office of Winston Station, he confronted a sleepy man with slack, worn features, and a frightened young boy who sat at the operator's desk. They listened, in silent stupor, to a stream of profanity such as they had never heard from any section gang.

"—and it's not *my* problem how you get the train through the tunnel, that's for *you* to figure out!" Chalmers concluded. "But if you don't get me an engine and don't start that train, you can kiss goodbye to your jobs, your work permits and this whole goddamn railroad!"

The station agent had never heard of Kip Chalmers and did not know the nature of his position. But he knew that this was the day when unknown men in undefined positions held unlimited power—the power of life or death.

"It's not up to us, Mr. Chalmers," he said pleadingly. "We don't issue the orders out here. The order came from Silver Springs. Suppose you telephone Mr. Mitchum and—"

"Who's Mr. Mitchum?"

"He's the division superintendent at Silver Springs. Suppose you send him a message to—"

"I should bother with a division superintendent! I'll send a message to Jim Taggart—that's what I'm going to do!"

Before the station agent had time to recover, Chalmers whirled to the boy, ordering, "You—take this down and send it at once!"

It was a message which, a month ago, the station agent would not have accepted from any passenger; the rules forbade it; but he was not certain about any rules any longer:

> Mr. James Taggart, New York City. Am held up on the Comet at Winston, Colorado, by the incompetence of your men, who refuse to give me an engine. Have meeting in San Francisco in the evening of top-level national importance. If you don't move my train at once, I'll let you guess the consequences.

Kip Chalmers.

After the boy had transmitted the words onto the wires that stretched from pole to pole across a continent as guardians of the Taggart track—after Kip Chalmers had returned to his car to wait for an answer—the station agent telephoned Dave Mitchum, who was his friend, and read to him the text of the message. He heard Mitchum groan in answer.

"I thought I'd tell you, Dave. I never heard of the guy before, but maybe he's somebody important."

"I don't know!" moaned Mitchum. "Kip Chalmers? You see his name in the newspapers all the time, right in with all the top-level boys. I don't know what he is, but if he's from Washington, we can't take any chances. Oh Christ, what are we going to do?"

We can't take any chances—thought the Taggart operator in New York, and transmitted the message by telephone to James Taggart's home. It was close to six A.M. in New York, and James Taggart was awakened out of the fitful sleep of a restless night. He listened to the telephone, his face sagging. He felt the same fear as the station agent of Winston, and for the same reason.

He called the home of Clifton Locey. All the rage which he could not pour upon Kip Chalmers, was poured over the telephone wire upon Clifton Locey. "Do something!" screamed Taggart. "I don't care what you do, it's *your* job, not mine, but see to it that that train gets through! What in hell is going on? I never heard of the Comet being held up! Is that how you run your department? It's a fine thing when important passengers have to start sending messages to *me*! At least, when my sister ran the place, I wasn't awakened in the middle of the night over every spike that broke in Iowa—Colorado, I mean!"

"I'm so sorry, Jim," said Clifton Locey smoothly, in a tone that balanced apology, reassurance and the right degree of patronizing confidence. "It's just a misunderstanding. It's somebody's stupid mistake. Don't worry, I'll take care of it. I was, as a matter of fact, in bed, but I'll attend to it at once."

Clifton Locey was not in bed; he had just returned from a round of night clubs, in the company of a young lady. He asked her to wait and hurried to the offices of Taggart Transcontinental. None of the night staff who saw him there could say why he chose to appear in person, but neither could they say that it had been unnecessary. He rushed in and out of several offices, was seen by many people and gave an impression of great activity. The only physical result of it was an order that went over the wires to Dave Mitchum, superintendent of the Colorado Division:

"Give an engine to Mr. Chalmers at once. Send the Comet through safely and without unnecessary delay. If you are unable to perform your duties, I shall hold you responsible before the Unification Board. Clifton Locey."

Then, calling his girl friend to join him, Clifton Locey drove to a country roadhouse—to make certain that no one would be able to find him in the next few hours.

The dispatcher at Silver Springs was baffled by the order that he handed to Dave Mitchum, but Dave Mitchum understood. He knew that no railroad order would ever speak in such terms as giving an engine to a passenger; he knew that the thing was a show piece, he guessed what sort of show was being staged, and he felt a cold sweat at the realization of who was being framed as the goat of the show.

"What's the matter, Dave?" asked the trainmaster.

Mitchum did not answer. He seized the telephone, his hands shaking as he begged for a connection to the Taggart operator in New York. He looked like an animal in a trap.

He begged the New York operator to get him Mr. Clifton Locey's home. The operator tried. There was no answer. He begged the operator to keep on trying and to try every number he could think of, where Mr. Locey might be found. The operator promised and Mitchum hung up, but knew that it was useless to wait or to speak to anyone in Mr. Locey's department.

"What's the matter, Dave?"

Mitchum handed him the order—and saw by the look on the trainmaster's face that the trap was as bad as he had suspected.

He called the Region Headquarters of Taggart Transcontinental at Omaha, Nebraska, and begged to speak to the general manager of the region. There was a brief silence on the wire, then the voice of the Omaha operator told him that the general manager had resigned and vanished three days ago—"over a little trouble with Mr. Locey," the voice added.

He asked to speak to the assistant general manager in charge of his particular district; but the assistant was out of town for the week end and could not be reached.

"Get me somebody else!" Mitchum screamed. "Anybody, of any district! For Christ's sake, get me somebody who'll tell me what to do!"

The man who came on the wire was the assistant general manager of the Iowa-Minnesota District.

"What?" he interrupted at Mitchum's first words. "At Winston, Colorado? Why in hell are you calling *me*? . . . No, don't tell me what happened, I don't want to know it! . . . No, I said! No! You're not going to frame me into having to explain afterwards why I did or didn't do anything about whatever it is. It's not *my* problem! . . . Speak to some region executive, don't pick on me, what do I have to do with Colorado? . . . Oh hell, I don't know, get the chief engineer, speak to him!"

The chief engineer of the Central Region answered impatiently, "Yes? What? What is it?"—and Mitchum rushed desperately to explain. When the chief engineer heard that there was no Diesel, he snapped, "Then hold the train, of course!" When he heard about Mr. Chalmers, he said, his voice suddenly subdued, "Hm . . . Kip Chalmers? Of Washington? . . . Well, I don't know. That would be a matter for Mr. Locey to decide." When Mitchum said, "Mr. Locey ordered me to arrange it, but—" the chief engineer snapped in great relief, "Then do exactly as Mr. Locey says!" and hung up.

Dave Mitchum replaced the telephone receiver cautiously. He did not scream any longer. Instead, he tiptoed to a chair, almost as if he were sneaking. He sat looking at Mr. Locey's order for a long time.

Then he snatched a glance about the room. The dispatcher was busy at his telephone. The trainmaster and the road foreman were there, but they pretended that they were not waiting. He wished Bill Brent, the chief dispatcher, would go home; Bill Brent stood in a corner, watching him.

Brent was a short, thin man with broad shoulders; he was forty, but looked younger; he had the pale face of an office worker and the hard, lean features of a cowboy. He was the best dispatcher on the system.

Mitchum rose abruptly and walked upstairs to his office, clutching Locey's order in his hand.

Dave Mitchum was not good at understanding problems of engineering and transportation, but he understood men like Clifton Locey. He understood the kind of game the New York executives were playing and what they were now doing to him. The order did not tell him to give Mr. Chalmers a coal-burning engine—just "an engine." If the time came to answer questions, wouldn't Mr. Locey gasp in shocked indignation that he had expected a division superintendent to know that only a Diesel engine could be meant in that order? The order stated that he was to send the Comet through *"safely"*—wasn't a division superintendent expected to know what was safe?—"and without unnecessary delay." What was an *unnecessary* delay? If the possibility of a major disaster was involved, wouldn't a delay of a week or a month be considered necessary?

The New York executives did not care, thought Mitchum; they did not care whether Mr. Chalmers reached his meeting on time, or whether an unprecedented catastrophe struck their rails; they cared only about making sure that they would not be blamed for either. If he held the train, they would make him the scapegoat to appease the anger of Mr. Chalmers; if he sent the train through and it did not reach the western portal of the tunnel, they would put the blame on his incompetence; they would claim that he had acted against their orders, in either case. What would he be able to prove? To whom? One could prove nothing to a tribunal that had no stated policy, no defined procedure, no rules of evidence, no binding principles—a tribunal, such as the Unification Board, that pronounced men guilty or innocent as it saw fit, with no standard of guilt or innocence.

Dave Mitchum knew nothing about the philosophy of law; but he knew that when a court is not bound by any rules, it is not bound by any facts, and then a hearing is not an issue of justice, but an issue of men, and your fate depends not on what you have or have not done, but on whom you do or do not know. He asked himself what chance he would have at such a hearing against Mr. James Taggart, Mr. Clifton Locey, Mr. Kip Chalmers and their powerful friends.

Dave Mitchum had spent his life slipping around the necessity of ever making a decision; he had done it by waiting to be told and never being certain of anything. All that he now allowed into his brain was a long, indignant whine against injustice. Fate, he thought, had singled him out for an unfair amount of bad luck: he was being framed by his superiors on the only good job he had ever held. He had never been taught to understand that the manner in which he obtained this job, and the frame-up, were inextricable parts of a single whole.

As he looked at Locey's order, he thought that he could hold the Comet, attach Mr. Chalmers' car to an engine and send it into the tunnel, alone. But he shook his head before the thought was fully formed: he knew that this would force Mr. Chalmers to recognize the nature of the risk: Mr. Chalmers would refuse; he would continue to demand a safe and non-existent engine. And more: this could mean that he, Mitchum, would have to assume responsibility, admit full knowledge of the danger, stand in the open and identify the exact nature of the situation—the one act which the policy of his superiors was based on evading, the one key to their game.

Dave Mitchum was not the man to rebel against his background or to question the moral code of those in charge. The choice he made was not to challenge, but to follow the policy of his superiors. Bill Brent could have beaten him in any contest of technology, but here was an endeavor at which he could beat Bill Brent without effort. There had once been a society where men needed the particular talents of Bill Brent, if they wished to survive; what they needed now was the talent of Dave Mitchum.

Dave Mitchum sat down at his secretary's typewriter and, by means of two fingers, carefully typed out an order to the trainmaster and another to the road foreman. The first instructed the trainmaster to summon a locomotive crew at once, for a purpose described only as "an emergency"; the second instructed the road foreman to "send the best engine available to Winston, to stand by for emergency assistance."

He put carbon copies of the orders into his own pocket, then opened the door, yelled for the night dispatcher to come up and handed him the two orders for the two men downstairs. The night dispatcher was a conscientious young boy who trusted his superiors and knew that discipline was the first rule of the railroad business. He was astonished that Mitchum should wish to send written orders down one flight of stairs, but he asked no questions.

Mitchum waited nervously. After a while, he saw the figure of the road foreman walking across the yards toward the roundhouse. He felt relieved: the two men had not come up to confront him in person; they had understood and they would play the game as he was playing it.

The road foreman walked across the yards, looking down at the ground. He was thinking of his wife, his two children and the house which he had spent a lifetime to own. He knew what his superiors were doing and he wondered whether he should refuse to obey them. He had never been afraid of losing his job; with the confidence of a competent man, he had known that if he quarreled with one employer, he would always be able to find another. Now, he was afraid; he had no right to quit or to seek a job; if he defied an employer, he would be delivered into the unanswerable power of a single Board, and if the Board ruled against him, it would mean being sentenced to the slow death of starvation: it would mean being barred from any employment. He knew that the Board would rule against him; he knew that the key to the dark, capricious mystery of the Board's contradictory decisions was the secret power of pull. What chance would he have against Mr. Chalmers? There had been a time when the self-interest of his employers had demanded that he exercise his utmost ability. Now, ability was not wanted any longer. There had been a time when he had been required to do his best and rewarded accordingly. Now, he could expect nothing but punishment, if he tried to follow his conscience. There had been a time when he had been expected to think. Now, they did not want him to think, only to obey. They did not want him to have a conscience any longer. Then why should he raise his voice? For whose sake? He thought of the passengers—the three hundred passengers aboard the Comet. He thought of his children. He had a son in high school and a daughter, nineteen, of whom he was fiercely, painfully proud, because she was recognized as the most beautiful girl in town. He asked himself whether he could deliver his children to the fate of the children of the unemployed, as he had seen them in the blighted areas, in the settlements around closed factories and along the tracks of discontinued railroads. He saw, in as-

tonished horror, that the choice which he now had to make was between the lives of his children and the lives of the passengers on the
Comet. A conflict of this kind had never been possible before. It was
by protecting the safety of the passengers that he had earned the security of his children; he had served one by serving the other; there
had been no clash of interests, no call for victims. Now, if he wanted
to save the passengers, he had to do it at the price of his children. He
remembered dimly the sermons he had heard about the beauty of
self-immolation, about the virtue of sacrificing to others that which
was one's dearest. He knew nothing about the philosophy of ethics;
but he knew suddenly—not in words, but in the form of a dark, angry,
savage pain—that if this was virtue, then he wanted no part of it.

He walked into the roundhouse and ordered a large, ancient coal-
burning locomotive to be made ready for the run to Winston.

The trainmaster reached for the telephone in the dispatcher's office, to summon an engine crew, as ordered. But his hand stopped,
holding the receiver. It struck him suddenly that he was summoning
men to their death, and that of the twenty lives listed on the sheet before him, two would be ended by his choice. He felt a physical sensation of cold, nothing more; he felt no concern, only a puzzled,
indifferent astonishment. It had never been his job to call men out to
die; his job had been to call them out to earn their living. It was
strange, he thought; and it was strange that his hand had stopped;
what made it stop was like something he would have felt twenty years
ago—no, he thought, strange, only one month ago, not longer.

He was forty-eight years old. He had no family, no friends, no ties
to any living being in the world. Whatever capacity for devotion he
had possessed, the capacity which others scatter among many random concerns, he had given it whole to the person of his young
brother—the brother, his junior by twenty-five years, whom he had
brought up. He had sent him through a technological college, and he
had known, as had all the teachers, that the boy had the mark of genius on the forehead of his grim, young face. With the same single-
tracked devotion as his brother's, the boy had cared for nothing but
his studies, not for sports or parties or girls, only for the vision of the
things he was going to create as an inventor. He had graduated from
college and had gone, on a salary unusual for his age, into the research
laboratory of a great electrical concern in Massachusetts.

This was now May 28, thought the trainmaster. It was on May 1 that Directive 10–289 had been issued. It was on the evening of May 1 that he had been informed that his brother had committed suicide.

The trainmaster had heard it said that the directive was necessary to save the country. He could not know whether this was true or not; he had no way of knowing what was necessary to save a country. But driven by some feeling which he could not express, he had walked into the office of the editor of the local newspaper and demanded that they publish the story of his brother's death. "People have to know it," had been all he could give as his reason. He had been unable to explain that the bruised connections of his mind had formed the wordless conclusion that if this was done by the will of the people, then the people had to know it; he could not believe that they would do it, if they knew. The editor had refused; he had stated that it would be bad for the country's morale.

The trainmaster knew nothing about political philosophy; but he knew that that had been the moment when he lost all concern for the life or death of any human being or of the country.

He thought, holding the telephone receiver, that maybe he should warn the men whom he was about to call. They trusted him; it would never occur to them that he could knowingly send them to their death. But he shook his head: this was only an old thought, last year's thought, a remnant of the time when he had trusted them, too. It did not matter now. His brain worked slowly, as if he were dragging his thoughts through a vacuum where no emotion responded to spur them on; he thought that there would be trouble if he warned anyone, there would be some sort of fight and it was he who had to make some great effort to start it. He had forgotten what it was that one started this sort of fight for. Truth? Justice? Brother-love? He did not want to make an effort. He was very tired. If he warned all the men on his list, he thought, there would be no one to run that engine, so he would save two lives and also three hundred lives aboard the Comet. But nothing responded to the figures in his mind; "lives" was just a word, it had no meaning.

He raised the telephone receiver to his ear, he called two numbers, he summoned an engineer and a fireman to report for duty at once.

Engine Number 306 had left for Winston, when Dave Mitchum came downstairs. "Get a track motor car ready for me," he ordered, "I'm going to run up to Fairmount." Fairmount was a small station, twenty miles east on the line. The men nodded, asking no questions.

Bill Brent was not among them. Mitchum walked into Brent's office. Brent was there, sitting silently at his desk; he seemed to be waiting.

"I'm going to Fairmount," said Mitchum; his voice was aggressively too casual, as if implying that no answer was necessary. "They had a Diesel there couple of weeks ago . . . you know, emergency repairs or something. . . . I'm going down to see if we could use it."

He paused, but Brent said nothing.

"The way things stack up," said Mitchum, not looking at him, "we can't hold that train till morning. We've got to take a chance, one way or another. Now I think maybe this Diesel will do it, but that's the last one we can try for. So if you don't hear from me in half an hour, sign the order and send the Comet through with Number 306 to pull her."

Whatever Brent had thought, he could not believe it when he heard it. He did not answer at once; then he said, very quietly, "No."

"What do you mean, no?"

"I won't do it."

"What do you mean, you won't? It's an order!"

"I won't do it." Brent's voice had the firmness of certainty unclouded by any emotion.

"Are you refusing to obey an order?"

"I am."

"But you have no right to refuse! And I'm not going to argue about it, either. It's what I've decided, it's my responsibility and I'm not asking for your opinion. Your job is to take my orders."

"Will you give me that order in writing?"

"Why, God damn you, are you hinting that you don't trust me? Are you . . . ?"

"Why do you have to go to Fairmount, Dave? Why can't you telephone them about the Diesel, if you think that they have one?"

"You're not going to tell me how to do my job! You're not going to sit there and question me! You're going to keep your trap shut and do as you're told or I'll give you a chance to talk—to the Unification Board!"

It was hard to decipher emotions on Brent's cowboy face, but Mitchum saw something that resembled a look of incredulous horror; only it was horror at some sight of his own, not at the words, and it had no quality of fear, not the kind of fear Mitchum had hoped for.

Brent knew that tomorrow morning the issue would be his word against Mitchum's; Mitchum would deny having given the order; Mitchum would show written proof that Engine Number 306 had been sent to Winston only "to stand by," and would produce witnesses that he had gone to Fairmount in search of a Diesel; Mitchum would claim that the fatal order had been issued by and on the sole responsibility of Bill Brent, the chief dispatcher. It would not be much of a case, not a case that could bear close study, but it would be enough for the Unification Board, whose policy was consistent only in not permitting anything to be studied closely. Brent knew that he could play the same game and pass the frame-up on to another victim, he knew that he had the brains to work it out—except that he would rather be dead than do it.

It was not the sight of Mitchum that made him sit still in horror. It was the realization that there was no one whom he could call to expose this thing and stop it—no superior anywhere on the line, from Colorado to Omaha to New York. They were in on it, all of them, they were doing the same, they had given Mitchum the lead and the method. It was Dave Mitchum who now belonged on this railroad and he, Bill Brent, who did not.

As Bill Brent had learned to see, by a single glance at a few numbers on a sheet of paper, the entire trackage of a division—so he was now able to see the whole of his own life and the full price of the decision he was making. He had not fallen in love until he was past his youth; he had been thirty-six when he had found the woman he wanted. He had been engaged to her for the last four years; he had had to wait, because he had a mother to support and a widowed sister with three children. He had never been afraid of burdens, because he had known his ability to carry them, and he had never assumed an obligation unless he was certain that he could fulfill it. He had waited, he had saved his money, and now he had reached the time when he felt himself free to be happy. He was to be married in a few weeks, this coming June. He thought of it, as he sat at his desk, looking at Dave Mitchum, but the thought aroused no hesitation, only regret and a distant sadness—distant, because he knew that he could not let it be part of this moment.

Bill Brent knew nothing about epistemology; but he knew that man must live by his own rational perception of reality, that he cannot act against it or escape it or find a substitute for it—and that there is no other way for him to live.

He rose to his feet. "It's true that so long as I hold this job, I cannot refuse to obey you," he said. "But I can, if I quit. So I'm quitting."

"You're *what?*"

"I'm quitting, as of this moment."

"But you have no right to quit, you goddamn bastard! Don't you know that? Don't you know that I'll have you thrown in jail for it?"

"If you want to send the sheriff for me in the morning, I'll be at home. I won't try to escape. There's no place to go."

Dave Mitchum was six-foot-two and had the build of a bruiser, but he stood shaking with fury and terror over the delicate figure of Bill Brent. "You can't quit! There's a law against it! I've got a law! You can't walk out on me! I won't let you out! I won't let you leave this building tonight!"

Brent walked to the door. "Will you repeat that order you gave me, in front of the others? No? Then I will."

As he pulled the door open, Mitchum's fist shot out, smashed into his face and knocked him down.

The trainmaster and the road foreman stood in the open doorway.

"He quit!" screamed Mitchum. "The yellow bastard quit at a time like this! He's a law-breaker and a coward!"

In the slow effort of rising from the floor, through the haze of blood running into his eyes, Bill Brent looked up at the two men. He saw that they understood, but he saw the closed faces of men who did not want to understand, did not want to interfere and hated him for putting them on the spot in the name of justice. He said nothing, rose to his feet and walked out of the building.

Mitchum avoided looking at the others. "Hey, you," he called, jerking his head at the night dispatcher across the room. "Come here. You've got to take over at once."

With the door closed, he repeated to the boy the story of the Diesel at Fairmount, as he had given it to Brent, and the order to send the Comet through with Engine Number 306, if the boy did not hear from him in half an hour. The boy was in no condition to think, to speak or to understand anything: he kept seeing the blood on the face of Bill Brent, who had been his idol. "Yes, sir," he answered numbly.

Dave Mitchum departed for Fairmount, announcing to every yard-man, switchman and wiper in sight, as he boarded the track motor car, that he was going in search of a Diesel for the Comet.

The night dispatcher sat at his desk, watching the clock and the telephone, praying that the telephone would ring and let him hear from Mr. Mitchum. But the half-hour went by in silence, and when there were only three minutes left, the boy felt a terror he could not explain, except that he did not want to send that order.

He turned to the trainmaster and the road foreman, asking hesitantly, "Mr. Mitchum gave me an order before he left, but I wonder whether I ought to send it, because I . . . I don't think it's right. He said—"

The trainmaster turned away; he felt no pity: the boy was about the same age as his brother had been.

The road foreman snapped, "Do just as Mr. Mitchum told you. You're not supposed to think," and walked out of the room.

The responsibility that James Taggart and Clifton Locey had evaded now rested on the shoulders of a trembling, bewildered boy. He hesitated, then he buttressed his courage with the thought that one did not doubt the good faith and the competence of railroad executives. He did not know that his vision of a railroad and its executives was that of a century ago.

With the conscientious precision of a railroad man, in the moment when the hand of the clock ended the half-hour, he signed his name to the order instructing the Comet to proceed with Engine Number 306, and transmitted the order to Winston Station.

The station agent at Winston shuddered when he looked at the order, but he was not the man to defy authority. He told himself that the tunnel was not, perhaps, as dangerous as he thought. He told himself that the best policy, these days, was not to think.

When he handed their copies of the order to the conductor and the engineer of the Comet, the conductor glanced slowly about the room, from face to face, folded the slip of paper, put it into his pocket and walked out without a word.

The engineer stood looking at the paper for a moment, then threw it down and said, "I'm not going to do it. And if it's come to where this railroad hands out orders like this one, I'm not going to work for it, either. Just list me as having quit."

"But you can't quit!" cried the station agent. "They'll arrest you for it!"

"If they find me," said the engineer, and walked out of the station into the vast darkness of the mountain night.

The engineer from Silver Springs, who had brought in Number 306, was sitting in a corner of the room. He chuckled and said, "He's yellow."

The station agent turned to him. "Will *you* do it, Joe? Will you take the Comet?"

Joe Scott was drunk. There had been a time when a railroad man, reporting for duty with any sign of intoxication, would have been re-

garded as a doctor arriving for work with sores of smallpox on his face.
But Joe Scott was a privileged person. Three months ago, he had been
fired for an infraction of safety rules, which had caused a major wreck;
two weeks ago, he had been reinstated in his job by order of the Unification Board. He was a friend of Fred Kinnan; he protected Kinnan's
interests in his union, not against the employers, but against the
membership.

"Sure," said Joe Scott. "I'll take the Comet. I'll get her through, if
I go fast enough."

The fireman of Number 306 had remained in the cab of his engine.
He looked up uneasily, when they came to switch his engine to the
head end of the Comet; he looked up at the red and green lights of
the tunnel, hanging in the distance above twenty miles of curves. But
he was a placid, amicable fellow, who made a good fireman with no
hope of ever rising to engineer; his husky muscles were his only asset.
He felt certain that his superiors knew what they were doing, so he
did not venture any questions.

The conductor stood by the rear end of the Comet. He looked at
the lights of the tunnel, then at the long chain of the Comet's windows. A few windows were lighted, but most of them showed only the
feeble blue glow of night lamps edging the lowered blinds. He
thought that he should rouse the passengers and warn them. There
had been a time when he had placed the safety of the passengers
above his own, not by reason of love for his fellow men, but because
that responsibility was part of his job, which he accepted and felt
pride in fulfilling. Now, he felt a contemptuous indifference and no
desire to save them. They had asked for and accepted Directive
10–289, he thought, they went on living and daily turning away in
evasion from the kind of verdicts that the Unification Board was passing on defenseless victims—why shouldn't he now turn away from
them? If he saved their lives, not one of them would come forward to
defend him when the Unification Board would convict him for dis-
obeying orders, for creating a panic, for delaying Mr. Chalmers. He
had no desire to be a martyr for the sake of allowing people safely to
indulge in their own irresponsible evil.

When the moment came, he raised his lantern and signaled the
engineer to start.

"See?" said Kip Chalmers triumphantly to Lester Tuck, as the
wheels under their feet shuddered forward. "*Fear* is the only practical
means to deal with people."

The conductor stepped onto the vestibule of the last car. No one saw him as he went down the steps of the other side, slipped off the train and vanished into the darkness of the mountains.

A switchman stood ready to throw the switch that would send the Comet from the siding onto the main track. He looked at the Comet as it came slowly toward him. It was only a blazing white globe with a beam stretching high above his head, and a jerky thunder trembling through the rail under his feet. He knew that the switch should not be thrown. He thought of the night, ten years ago, when he had risked his life in a flood to save a train from a washout. But he knew that times had changed. In the moment when he thew the switch and saw the headlight jerk sidewise, he knew that he would now hate his job for the rest of his life.

The Comet uncoiled from the siding into a thin, straight line, and went on into the mountains, with the beam of the headlight like an extended arm pointing the way, and the lighted glass curve of the observation lounge ending it off.

Some of the passengers aboard the Comet were awake. As the train started its coiling ascent, they saw the small cluster of Winston's lights at the bottom of the darkness beyond their windows, then the same darkness, but with red and green lights by the hole of a tunnel on the upper edge of the windowpanes. The lights of Winston kept growing smaller, each time they appeared; the black hole of the tunnel kept growing larger. A black veil went streaking past the windows at times, dimming the lights: it was the heavy smoke from the coal-burning engine.

As the tunnel came closer, they saw, at the edge of the sky far to the south, in a void of space and rock, a spot of living fire twisting in the wind. They did not know what it was and did not care to learn.

It is said that catastrophes are a matter of pure chance, and there were those who would have said that the passengers of the Comet were not guilty or responsible for the thing that happened to them.

The man in Bedroom A, Car No. 1, was a professor of sociology who taught that individual ability is of no consequence, that individual effort is futile, that an individual conscience is a useless luxury, that there is no individual mind or character or achievement, that everything is achieved collectively, and that it's masses that count, not men.

The man in Roomette 7, Car No. 2, was a journalist who wrote that it is proper and moral to use compulsion "for a good cause," who believed that he had the right to unleash physical force upon others—to wreck lives, throttle ambitions, strangle desires, violate convictions, to imprison, to despoil, to murder—for the sake of whatever he chose to consider as his own idea of "a good cause," which did not even have to be an idea, since he had never defined what he regarded as the good, but had merely stated that he went by "a feeling"—a feeling unrestrained by any knowledge, since he considered emotion superior to knowledge and relied solely on his own "good intentions" and on the power of a gun.

The woman in Roomette 10, Car No. 3, was an elderly school teacher who had spent her life turning class after class of helpless children into miserable cowards, by teaching them that the will of the majority is the only standard of good and evil, that a majority may do anything it pleases, that they must not assert their own personalities, but must do as others were doing.

The man in Drawing Room B, Car No. 4, was a newspaper publisher who believed that men are evil by nature and unfit for freedom, that their basic interests, if left unchecked, are to lie, to rob and to murder one another—and, therefore, men must be ruled by means of lies, robbery and murder, which must be made the exclusive privilege of the rulers, for the purpose of forcing men to work, teaching them to be moral and keeping them within the bounds of order and justice.

The man in Bedroom H, Car No. 5, was a businessman who had acquired his business, an ore mine, with the help of a government loan, under the Equalization of Opportunity Bill.

The man in Drawing Room A, Car No. 6, was a financier who had made a fortune by buying "frozen" railroad bonds and getting his friends in Washington to "defreeze" them.

The man in Seat 5, Car No. 7, was a worker who believed that he had "a right" to a job, whether his employer wanted him or not.

The woman in Roomette 6, Car No. 8, was a lecturer who believed that, as a consumer, she had "a right" to transportation, whether the railroad people wished to provide it or not.

The man in Roomette 2, Car No. 9, was a professor of economics who advocated the abolition of private property, explaining that intelligence plays no part in industrial production, that man's mind is conditioned by material tools, that anybody can run a factory or a railroad and it's only a matter of seizing the machinery.

The woman in Bedroom D, Car No. 10, was a mother who had put her two children to sleep in the berth above her, carefully tucking them in, protecting them from drafts and jolts; a mother whose husband held a government job enforcing directives, which she defended by saying, "I don't care, it's only the rich that they hurt. After all, I must think of my children."

The man in Roomette 3, Car No. 11, was a sniveling little neurotic who wrote cheap little plays into which, as a social message, he inserted cowardly little obscenities to the effect that all businessmen were scoundrels.

The woman in Roomette 9, Car No. 12, was a housewife who believed that she had the right to elect politicians, of whom she knew nothing, to control giant industries, of which she had no knowledge.

The man in Bedroom F, Car No. 13, was a lawyer who had said, "Me? I'll find a way to get along under any political system."

The man in Bedroom A, Car No. 14, was a professor of philosophy who taught that there is no mind—*how do you know that the tunnel is dangerous?*—no reality—*how can you prove that the tunnel exists?*—no logic—*why do you claim that trains cannot move without motive power?*—no principles—*why should you be bound by the law of cause-and-effect?*—no rights—*why shouldn't you attach men to their jobs by force?*—no morality—*what's moral about running a railroad?*—no absolutes—*what difference does it make to you whether you live or die, anyway?* He taught that we know nothing—*why oppose the orders of your superiors?*—that we can never be certain of anything—*how do you know you're right?*—that we must act on the expediency of the moment—*you don't want to risk your job, do you?*

The man in Drawing Room B, Car No. 15, was an heir who had inherited his fortune, and who had kept repeating, "Why should Rearden be the only one permitted to manufacture Rearden Metal?"

The man in Bedroom A, Car No. 16, was a humanitarian who had said, "The men of ability? I do not care what or if they are made to suffer. They must be penalized in order to support the incompetent. Frankly, I do not care whether this is just or not. I take pride in not caring to grant any justice to the able, where mercy to the needy is concerned."

These passengers were awake; there was not a man aboard the train who did not share one or more of their ideas. As the train went into the tunnel, the flame of Wyatt's Torch was the last thing they saw on earth.

EDITOR'S NOTE: *Here is one more scene from* Atlas Shrugged—*the very opening of Part III, set in Atlantis, a capitalist oasis hidden from the world in the mountains of Colorado. Dagny, flying alone in Colorado in pursuit of a mysterious stranger, has just crash-landed in a deserted meadow.*

Atlantis

WHEN SHE opened her eyes, she saw sunlight, green leaves and a man's face. She thought: I know what this is. This was the world as she had expected to see it at sixteen—and now she had reached it—and it seemed so simple, so unastonishing, that the thing she felt was like a blessing pronounced upon the universe by means of three words: But of course.

She was looking up at the face of a man who knelt by her side, and she knew that in all the years behind her, *this* was what she would have given her life to see: a face that bore no mark of pain or fear or guilt. The shape of his mouth was pride, and more: it was as if he took pride in being proud. The angular planes of his cheeks made her think of arrogance, of tension, of scorn—yet the face had none of these qualities, it had their final sum: a look of serene determination and of certainty, and the look of a ruthless innocence which would not seek forgiveness or grant it. It was a face that had nothing to hide or to escape, a face with no fear of being seen or of seeing, so that the first thing she grasped about him was the intense perceptiveness of his eyes—he looked as if his faculty of sight were his best-loved tool and its exercise were a limitless, joyous adventure, as if his eyes imparted a superlative value to himself and to the world—to himself for his ability to see, to the world for being a place so eagerly worth seeing. It seemed to her for a moment that she was in the presence of a being who was pure consciousness—yet she had never been so aware of a man's body. The light cloth of his shirt seemed to stress, rather than hide, the structure of his figure, his skin was suntanned, his body had the hardness, the gaunt, tensile strength, the clean precision of a foundry casting, he looked as if he were poured out of metal, but some dimmed, soft-lustered metal, like an aluminum-copper alloy, the color of his skin blending with the chestnut-brown of his hair, the loose strands of the hair shading from brown to gold in the sun, and his eyes completing the colors, as the one part of the casting left undimmed and hardly lustrous: his eyes were the deep, dark green of light glinting on metal. He was looking down at her with the faint trace of a smile, it was not a look of discovery, but of familiar contemplation—as if he, too, were seeing the long-expected and the never-doubted.

This was her world, she thought, this was the way men were meant to be and to face their existence—and all the rest of it, all the years of ugliness and struggle were only someone's senseless joke. She smiled at him, as at a fellow conspirator, in relief, in deliverance, in radiant mockery of all the things she would never have to consider important again. He smiled in answer, it was the same smile as her own, as if he felt what she felt and knew what she meant.

"We never had to take any of it seriously, did we?" she whispered.

"No, we never had to."

And then, her consciousness returning fully, she realized that this man was a total stranger.

She tried to draw away from him, but it was only a faint movement of her head on the grass she felt under her hair. She tried to rise. A shot of pain across her back threw her down again.

"Don't move, Miss Taggart. You're hurt."

"You know me?" Her voice was impersonal and hard.

"I've known you for many years."

"Have I known you?"

"Yes, I think so."

"What is your name?"

"John Galt."

She looked at him, not moving.

"Why are you frightened?" he asked.

"Because I believe it."

PART FOUR

Basic Philosophy

EDITOR'S NOTE: *To create* Atlas Shrugged, AR *had to go beyond ethics; she had to originate a new system of philosophy, identifying the nature of man's means of knowledge and of the universe he seeks to know.* "Without an understanding and statement of the right philosophical principle," *she said in a 1946 note to herself,* "I cannot create the right story; but the discovery of the principle interests me only as the discovery of the proper knowledge to be used for my life purpose . . ." *(Journals of Ayn Rand, 1997, p. 479).*

The first selection, from John Galt's speech in Atlas Shrugged, *identifies the axioms of Objectivism, as against its two opposites: the mystics of spirit and the mystics of muscle.*

1. Reason and Reality

Axioms of Objectivism

"EXISTENCE EXISTS—and the act of grasping that statement implies two corollary axioms: that something exists which one perceives and that one exists possessing consciousness, consciousness being the faculty of perceiving that which exists.

"If nothing exists, there can be no consciousness: a consciousness with nothing to be conscious of is a contradiction in terms. A consciousness conscious of nothing but itself is a contradiction in terms: before it could identify itself as consciousness, it had to be conscious of something. If that which you claim to perceive does not exist, what you possess is not consciousness.

"Whatever the degree of your knowledge, these two—existence and consciousness—are axioms you cannot escape, these two are the irreducible primaries implied in any action you undertake, in any part of your knowledge and in its sum, from the first ray of light you perceive at the start of your life to the widest erudition you might acquire at its end. Whether you know the shape of a pebble or the structure of a solar system, the axioms remain the same: that *it* exists and that you *know* it.

"To exist is to be something, as distinguished from the nothing of non-existence, it is to be an entity of a specific nature made of specific attributes. Centuries ago, the man who was—no matter what his errors—the greatest of your philosophers, has stated the formula defining the concept of existence and the rule of all knowledge: A *is* A. A thing is itself. You have never grasped the meaning of his statement. I am here to complete it: Existence is Identity, Consciousness is Identification.

"Whatever you choose to consider, be it an object, an attribute or an action, the law of identity remains the same. A leaf cannot be a stone at the same time, it cannot be all red and all green at the same time, it cannot freeze and burn at the same time. A is A. Or, if you wish it stated in simpler language: You cannot have your cake and eat it, too.

"Are you seeking to know what is wrong with the world? All the disasters that have wrecked your world, came from your leaders' attempt to evade the fact that A is A. All the secret evil you dread to face within you and all the pain you have ever endured, came from your own attempt to evade the fact that A is A. The purpose of those who taught you to evade it, was to make you forget that Man is Man.

"Man cannot survive except by gaining knowledge, and reason is his only means to gain it. Reason is the faculty that perceives, identifies and integrates the material provided by his senses. The task of his senses is to give him the evidence of existence, but the task of identifying it belongs to his reason; his senses tell him only that something *is*, but *what* it is must be learned by his mind.

"All thinking is a process of identification and integration. Man perceives a blob of color; by integrating the evidence of his sight and his touch, he learns to identify it as a solid object; he learns to identify the object as a table; he learns that the table is made of wood; he learns that the wood consists of cells, that the cells consist of molecules, that the molecules consist of atoms. All through this process, the work of his mind consists of answers to a single question: *What* is it? His means to establish the truth of his answers is logic, and logic rests on the axiom that existence exists. Logic is the art of *non-contradictory identification*. A contradiction cannot exist. An atom is itself, and so is the universe; neither can contradict its own identity; nor can a part contradict the whole. No concept man forms is valid unless he integrates it without contradiction into the total sum of his knowledge. To arrive at a contradiction is to confess an error in one's thinking: to maintain a contradiction is to abdicate one's mind and to evict oneself from the realm of reality.

"Reality is that which exists; the unreal does not exist; the unreal is merely that negation of existence which is the content of a human consciousness when it attempts to abandon reason. Truth is the recognition of reality; reason, man's only means of knowledge, is his only standard of truth.

"The most depraved sentence you can now utter is to ask: *Whose* reason? The answer is: *Yours.* No matter how vast your knowledge or how modest, it is your own mind that has to acquire it. It is only with your own knowledge that you can deal. It is only your own knowledge that you can claim to possess or ask others to consider. Your mind is your only judge of truth—and if others dissent from your verdict, reality is the court of final appeal. Nothing but a man's mind can perform that complex, delicate, crucial process of identification which is thinking. Nothing can direct the process but his own judgment. Nothing can direct his judgment but his moral integrity.

"You who speak of a 'moral instinct' as if it were some separate endowment opposed to reason—man's reason *is* his moral faculty. A process of reason is a process of constant choice in answer to the question: True or False?—*Right or Wrong?* Is a seed to be planted in soil in order to grow—right or wrong? Is a man's wound to be disinfected in order to save his life—right or wrong? Does the nature of atmospheric electricity permit it to be converted into kinetic power—right or wrong? It is the answers to such questions that gave you everything you have—and the answers came from a man's mind, a mind of intransigent devotion to that which is *right.*

"A rational process is a *moral* process. You may make an error at any step of it, with nothing to protect you but your own severity, or you may try to cheat, to fake the evidence and evade the effort of the quest—but if devotion to truth is the hallmark of morality, then there is no greater, nobler, more heroic form of devotion than the act of a man who assumes the responsibility of thinking.

"That which you call your soul or spirit is your consciousness, and that which you call 'free will' is your mind's freedom to think or not, the only will you have, your only freedom, the choice that controls all the choices you make and determines your life and your character.

"Thinking is man's only basic virtue, from which all the others proceed. And his basic vice, the source of all his evils, is that nameless act which all of you practice, but struggle never to admit: the act of blanking out, the willful suspension of one's consciousness, the refusal to think—not blindness, but the refusal to see; not ignorance, but the refusal to know. It is the act of unfocusing your mind and inducing an inner fog to escape the responsibility of judgment—on the unstated premise that a thing will not exist if only you refuse to identify it, that A will not be A so long as you do not pronounce the verdict 'It *is.*' Non-thinking is an act of annihilation, a wish to negate existence, an attempt to wipe out reality. But existence exists; reality is not to be wiped out, it will merely wipe out the wiper. By refusing to say 'It is,' you are refusing to say 'I am.' By suspending your judgment, you are negating your person. When a man declares: 'Who am I to know?'—he is declaring: 'Who am I to live?'

"This, in every hour and every issue, is your basic moral choice: thinking or non-thinking, existence or non-existence, A or non-A, entity or zero. [...]

" 'We know that we know nothing,' they [skeptics] chatter, blanking out the fact that they are claiming knowledge—'There are not absolutes,' they chatter, blanking out the fact that they are uttering an absolute—'You cannot *prove* that you exist or that you're conscious,' they chatter, blanking out the fact that *proof* presupposes existence, consciousness and a complex chain of knowledge: the existence of something to know, of a consciousness able to know it, and of a knowledge that has learned to distinguish between such concepts as the proved and the unproved.

"When a savage who has not learned to speak declares that existence must be proved, he is asking you to prove it by means of non-existence—when he declares that your consciousness must be proved, he is asking you to prove it by means of unconsciousness—he is asking you to step into a void outside of existence and consciousness to give him proof of both—he is asking you to become a zero gaining knowledge about a zero.

"When he declares that an axiom is a matter of arbitrary choice and he doesn't choose to accept the axiom that he exists, he blanks out the fact that he has accepted it by uttering that sentence, that the only way to reject it is to shut one's mouth, expound no theories and die.

"An axiom is a statement that identifies the base of knowledge and of any further statement pertaining to that knowledge, a statement necessarily contained in all others, whether any particular speaker chooses to identify it or not. An axiom is a proposition that defeats its opponents by the fact that they have to accept it and use it in the process of any attempt to deny it. Let the caveman who does not choose to accept the axiom of identity, try to present his theory without using the concept of identity or any concept derived from it—let the anthropoid who does not choose to accept the existence of nouns, try to devise a language without nouns; adjectives or verbs—let the witch-doctor who does not choose to accept the validity of sensory perception, try to prove it without using the data he obtained by sensory perception—let the head-hunter who does not choose to accept the validity of logic, try to prove it without using logic—let the pigmy who proclaims that a skyscraper needs no foundation after it reaches its fiftieth story, yank the base from under *his* building, not yours—let the cannibal who snarls that the freedom of man's mind was needed to *create* an industrial civilization, but is not needed to *maintain* it, be given an arrowhead and bearskin, not a university chair of economics.

"Do you think they are taking you back to dark ages? They are taking you back to darker ages than any your history has known. Their goal is not the era of pre-science, but the era of pre-language. Their purpose is to deprive you of the concept on which man's mind, his life and his culture depend: the concept of an *objective* reality. Identify the development of a human consciousness—and you will know the purpose of their creed.

"A savage is a being who has not grasped that A is A and that reality is real. He has arrested his mind at the level of a baby's, at the state when a consciousness acquires its initial sensory perception and has not learned to distinguish solid objects. It is to a baby that the world appears as a blur of motion, without things that move—and the birth of his mind is the day when he grasps that the streak that keeps flickering past him is his mother and the whirl beyond her is a curtain, that the two are solid entities and neither can turn into the other, that they *are* what they are, that they *exist*. The day when he grasps that matter has no volition is the day when he grasps that *he* has—and this is his birth as a *human* being. The day when he grasps that the reflection he sees in a mirror is not a delusion, that it is real, but it is not himself, that the mirage he sees in a desert is not a delusion, that the air and the light rays that cause it are real, but it is not a city, it is a city's reflection—the day when he grasps that he is not a passive recipient of the sensations of any given moment, that his senses do not provide him with automatic knowledge in separate snatches independent of context, but only with the material of knowledge, which his mind must learn to integrate—the day when he grasps that his senses cannot deceive him, that physical objects cannot act without causes, that his organs of perception are physical and have no volition, no power to invent or to distort, that the evidence they give him is an absolute, but his mind must learn to understand it, his mind must discover the nature, the causes, the full context of his sensory material, his mind must identify the things that he perceives—*that* is the day of his birth as a thinker and scientist.

"*We* are the men who reach that day; you are the men who choose to reach it partly; a savage is a man who never does.

"To a savage, the world is a place of unintelligible miracles where anything is possible to inanimate matter and nothing is possible to *him*. His world is not the unknown, but that irrational horror: the unknowable. He believes that physical objects are endowed with a mysterious volition, moved by *causeless*, unpredictable whims, while *he* is a helpless pawn at the mercy of forces beyond his control. He believes that nature is ruled by demons who possess an omnipotent power and that reality is their fluid plaything, where they can turn his bowl of meal into a snake and his wife into a beetle at any moment, where the A he has never discovered can be any non-A they choose, where the only knowledge he possesses is that he must not attempt to know. He can count on nothing, he can only *wish*, and he spends his life on wishing, on begging his demons to grant him his wishes by the arbitrary power of their will, giving them credit when they do, taking the blame when they don't, offering them sacrifices in token of his gratitude and sacrifices in token of his guilt, crawling on his belly in fear and worship of sun and moon and wind and rain and of any thug who announces himself as their spokesman, provided his words are unintelligible and his mask sufficiently frightening—he wishes, begs and crawls, and dies, leaving you, as a record of his view of existence, the distorted monstrosities of his idols, part-man, part-animal, part-spider, the embodiments of the world of non-A.

"*His* is the intellectual state of your modern teachers and *his* is the world to which they want to bring you.

"If you wonder by what means they propose to do it, walk into any college classroom and you will hear your professors teaching your children that man can be certain of nothing, that his consciousness has no validity whatever, that he can learn no facts and no laws of existence, that he's incapable of knowing an objective reality. What, then, is his standard of knowledge and truth? Whatever others *believe*, is their answer. There is no knowledge, they teach, there's only *faith*: your belief that you exist is an act of faith, no more valid than another's faith in his right to kill you; the axioms of science are an act of faith, no more valid than a mystic's faith in revelations; the belief that electric light can be produced by a generator is an act of faith, no more valid than the belief that it can be produced by a rabbit's foot kissed under a stepladder on the first of the moon—truth is whatever people want it to be, and *people* are everyone except yourself; reality is whatever people choose to say it is, there are no objective facts, there are only people's arbitrary wishes—a man who seeks knowledge in a laboratory by means of test tubes and logic is an old-fashioned, superstitious fool; a true scientist is a man who goes around taking public polls—and if it weren't for the selfish greed of the manufacturers of steel girders, who have a vested interest in obstructing the progress of science, you would learn that New York City does not exist, because a poll of the entire population of the world would tell you by a landslide majority that their *beliefs* forbid its existence.

"For centuries, the mystics of spirit have proclaimed that faith is superior to reason, but have not dared deny the existence of reason. Their heirs and product, the mystics of muscle, have completed their job and achieved their dream: they proclaim that everything is faith, and call it a revolt against believing. As revolt against unproved assertions, they proclaim that nothing can be proved; as revolt against supernatural knowledge, they proclaim that no knowledge is possible; as revolt against the enemies of science, they proclaim that science is superstition; as revolt against the enslavement of the mind, they proclaim that there is no mind.

"If you surrender your power to perceive, if you accept the switch of your standard from the *objective* to the *collective* and wait for mankind to tell you what to think, you will find another switch taking place before the eyes you have renounced: you will find that your teachers become the rulers of the collective, and if you then refuse to obey them, protesting that they are not the whole of mankind, they will answer: 'By what means do you know that we are not? *Are*, brother? Where did you get that old-fashioned term?'

"If you doubt that such is their purpose, observe with what passionate consistency the mystics of muscle are striving to make you forget that a concept such as 'Mind' has ever existed. Observe the twists of undefined verbiage, the words with rubber meanings, the terms left floating in midstream, by means of which they try to get around the recognition of the concept of '*thinking.*' Your consciousness, they tell you, consists of 'reflexes,' 'reactions,' 'experiences,' 'urges,' and 'drives'—and refuse to identify the means by which they acquired that knowledge, to identify the act they are performing when they tell it or the act you are performing when you listen. Words have the power to 'condition' you, they say and refuse to identify the reason why words have the power to change your—blank-out. A student reading a book understands it through a process of—blank-out. A scientist working on an invention is engaged in the activity of—blank-out. A psychologist helping a neurotic to solve a problem and untangle a conflict, does it by means of—blank-out. An industrialist—blank-out—there is no such person. A factory is a 'natural resource,' like a tree, a rock or a mud puddle. . . .

———

EDITOR'S NOTE: AR's *view of reason and of its fundamental role in man's life are indicated in the following excerpt, taken from an introductory talk given at Yale in 1960. The complete talk is published in* Philosophy: Who Needs It.

Faith and Force: The Destroyers of the Modern World

. . . NOW THERE is one word—a single word—which can blast the morality of altruism out of existence and which it cannot withstand— the word: "Why?" *Why* must man live for the sake of others? *Why* must he be a sacrificial animal? *Why* is that the good? There is no earthly reason for it—and, ladies and gentlemen, in the whole history of philosophy no *earthly* reason has ever been given.

It is only *mysticism* that can permit moralists to get away with it. It was mysticism, the *un*earthly, the supernatural, the irrational that has always been called upon to justify it—or, to be exact, to escape the necessity of justification. One does not justify the irrational, one just takes it on faith. What most moralists—and few of their victims—realize is that reason and altruism are incompatible. And *this* is the basic contradiction of Western civilization: reason versus altruism. This is the conflict that had to explode sooner or later.

The real conflict, of course, is reason versus mysticism. But if it weren't for the altruist morality, mysticism would have died when it did die—at the Renaissance—leaving no vampire to haunt Western culture. A "vampire" is supposed to be a dead creature that comes out of its grave only at night—only in the darkness—and drains the blood of the living. The description applied to altruism, is exact.

Western civilization was the child and product of reason—via ancient Greece. In all other civilizations, reason has always been the menial servant—the handmaiden—of mysticism. You may observe the results. It is only Western culture that has ever been dominated—imperfectly, incompletely, precariously and at rare intervals—but still, dominated by reason. You may observe the results of that.

The conflict of reason versus mysticism is the issue of life or death—of freedom or slavery—of progress or stagnant brutality. Or, to put it another way, it is the conflict of consciousness versus unconsciousness.

Let us define our terms. What is reason? Reason is the faculty which perceives, identifies and integrates the material provided by man's senses. Reason integrates man's perceptions by means of forming abstractions or conceptions, thus raising man's knowledge from the *perceptual* level, which he shares with animals, to the *conceptual* level, which he alone can reach. The *method* which reason employs in this process is *logic*—and logic is the art of *non-contradictory identification.*

What is mysticism? Mysticism is the acceptance of allegations without evidence or proof, either apart from or *against* the evidence of one's senses and one's reason. Mysticism is the claim to some non-sensory, non-rational, non-definable, non-identifiable means of knowledge, such as "instinct," "intuition," "revelation," or any form of "just knowing."

Reason is the perception of reality, and rests on a single axiom: the Law of Identity.

Mysticism is the claim to the perception of some other reality—other than the one in which we live—whose definition is only that it is *not* natural, it is supernatural, and is to be perceived by some form of unnatural or supernatural means.

You realize, of course, that *epistemology*—the theory of knowledge—is the most complex branch of philosophy, which cannot be covered exhaustively in a single lecture. So I will not attempt to cover it. I will say only that those who wish a fuller discussion will find it in *Atlas Shrugged.* For the purposes of tonight's discussion, the definitions I have given you contain the *essence* of the issue, regardless of whose theory, argument or philosophy you choose to accept.

I will repeat: *Reason* is the faculty which perceives, identifies and integrates the material provided by man's senses. *Mysticism* is the claim to a non-sensory means of knowledge.

In Western civilization, the period ruled by mysticism is known as the Dark Ages and the Middle Ages. I will assume that you know the nature of that period and the state of human existence in those ages. The Renaissance broke the rule of the mystics. "Renaissance" means "rebirth." Few people today will care to remind you that it was a re-birth of *reason*—of man's mind.

In the light of what followed—most particularly, in the light of the industrial revolution—nobody can now take faith, or religion, or rev-elation, or any form of mysticism as his basic and exclusive guide to existence, not in the way it was taken in the Middle Ages. This does not mean that the Renaissance has automatically converted every-body to rationality; far from it. It means only that so long as a single automobile, a single skyscraper or a single copy of Aristotle's Logic re-mains in existence, nobody will be able to arouse men's hope, eager-ness and joyous enthusiasm by telling them to ditch their mind and rely on mystic faith. This is why I said that mysticism, as a cultural power, is dead. Observe that in the attempts at a mystic revival today, it is not an appeal to life, hope and joy that the mystics are making, but an appeal to fear, doom and despair. "Give up, your mind is im-potent; life is only a foxhole," is not a motto that can revive a culture.

Now, if you ask me to name the man most responsible for the pres-ent state of the world, the man whose influence has almost succeeded in destroying the achievements of the Renaissance—I will name Im-manuel Kant. He was the philosopher who saved the morality of al-truism, and who knew that what it had to be saved from was—reason.

This is not a mere hypothesis. It is a known historical fact that Kant's interest and purpose in philosophy was to save the morality of altruism, which could not survive without a mystic base. His meta-physics and his epistemology were devised for that purpose. He did not, of course, announce himself as a mystic—few of them have, since the Renaissance. He announced himself as a champion of rea-son—of *"pure"* reason.

There are two ways to destroy the power of a concept: one, by an open attack in open discussion—the other, by subversion, from the inside; that is: by subverting the meaning of the concept, setting up a straw man and then refuting it. Kant did the second. He did not attack reason—he merely constructed such a version of what *is* reason that it made mysticism look like plain, rational common sense by comparison. He did not deny the validity of reason—he merely claimed that reason is "limited," that it leads us to impossible contradictions, that everything we perceive is an illusion and that we can never perceive reality or "things as they are." He claimed, in effect, that the things we perceive are not real, *because* we perceive them.

A "straw man" is an odd metaphor to apply to such an enormous, cumbersome, ponderous construction as Kant's system of epistemology. Nevertheless, a straw man is what it was—and the doubts, the uncertainty, the skepticism that followed, skepticism about man's ability ever to know anything, were not, in fact, applicable to human consciousness, because it was not a human consciousness that Kant's robot represented. But philosophers accepted it as such. And while they cried that reason had been invalidated, they did not notice that reason had been pushed off the philosophical scene altogether and that the faculty they were arguing about was *not* reason.

No, Kant did not destroy reason; he merely did as thorough a job of undercutting as anyone could ever do.

If you trace the roots of all our current philosophies—such as Pragmatism, Logical Positivism, and all the rest of the neomystics who announce happily that you cannot *prove* that you exist—you will find that they all grew out of Kant.

As to Kant's version of the altruist morality, he claimed that it was derived from "pure reason," not from revelation—except that it rested on a special instinct for *duty*, a "categorical imperative" which one "just knows." *His* version of morality makes the Christian one sound like a healthy, cheerful, benevolent code of selfishness. Christianity merely told man to love his neighbor as himself; that's not exactly rational—but at least it does not forbid man to love himself. What Kant propounded was full, total, abject selflessness: he held that an action is moral *only* if you perform it out of a sense of duty and derive no benefit from it of any kind, neither material nor spiritual; if you derive any benefit, your action is not moral any longer. *This* is the ultimate form of demanding that man turn himself into a "shmoo"—the mystic little animal of the Li'l Abner comic strip, that went around seeking to be eaten by somebody.

It is Kant's version of altruism that is generally accepted today, not practiced—who can practice it?—but guiltily accepted. It is Kant's version of altruism that people, who have never heard of Kant, profess when they equate self-interest with evil. It is Kant's version of altruism that's working whenever people are afraid to admit the pursuit of any personal pleasure or gain or motive—whenever men are afraid to confess that they are seeking their own happiness—whenever businessmen are afraid to say that they are making profits—whenever the victims of an advancing dictatorship are afraid to assert their "selfish" rights.

The ultimate monument to Kant and to the whole altruist morality is Soviet Russia.

If you want to prove to yourself the power of ideas and, particularly, of morality—the intellectual history of the nineteenth century would be a good example to study. The greatest, unprecedented, undreamed of events and achievements were taking place before men's eyes—but men did not see them and did not understand their meaning, as they do not understand it to this day. I am speaking of the industrial revolution, of the United States and of capitalism. For the first time in history, men gained control over physical nature and threw off the control of men over men—that is: men discovered science and political freedom. The creative energy, the abundance, the wealth, the rising standard of living for *every* level of the population were such that the nineteenth century looks like a fiction-Utopia, like a blinding burst of sunlight, in the drab progression of most of human history. If life on earth is one's standard of value, then the nineteenth century moved mankind forward more than all the other centuries combined.

Did anyone appreciate it? Does anyone appreciate it now? Has anyone identified the causes of that historical miracle?

They did not and have not. What blinded them? The morality of altruism.

Let me explain this. There are, fundamentally, only two causes of the progress of the nineteenth century—the same two causes which you will find at the root of any happy, benevolent, progressive era in human history. One cause is psychological, the other existential—or: one pertains to man's consciousness, the other to the physical conditions of his existence. The first is *reason*, the second is *freedom*. And when I say *"freedom,"* I do not mean poetic sloppiness, such as "freedom from want" or "freedom from fear" or "freedom from the necessity of earning a living." I mean *"freedom from compulsion—freedom from rule by physical force."* Which means: *political* freedom.

These two—reason and freedom—are corollaries, and their relationship is reciprocal: when men are rational, freedom wins; when men are free, reason wins.

Their antagonists are: *faith* and *force*. These, also, are corollaries: every period of history dominated by mysticism, was a period of statism, of dictatorship, of tryanny. Look at the Middle Ages—and look at the political systems of today.

The nineteenth century was the ultimate product and expression of the intellectual trend of the Renaissance and the Age of Reason, which means: of a predominantly Aristotelian philosophy. And, for the first time in history, it created a new economic system, the necessary corollary of political freedom, a system of free trade on a free market: *capitalism.*

No, it was not a full, perfect, unregulated, totally laissez-faire capitalism—as it should have been. Various degrees of government interference and control still remained, even in America—and *this* is what led to the eventual destruction of capitalism. But the extent to which certain countries were free was the exact extent of their economic progress. America, the freest, achieved the most.

Never mind the low wages and the harsh living conditions of the early years of capitalism. They were all that the national economies of the time could afford. Capitalism did not create poverty—it inherited it. Compared to the centuries of precapitalist starvation, the living conditions of the poor in the early years of capitalism were the first chance the poor had ever had to survive. As proof—the enormous growth of the European population during the nineteenth century, a growth of over 300 percent, as compared to the previous growth of something like 3 percent per century. [. . .]

I have said that faith and force are corollaries, and that mysticism will always lead to the rule of brutality. The cause of it is contained in the very nature of mysticism. *Reason* is the only *objective* means of communication and of understanding among men; when men deal with one another by means of reason, reality is their *objective* standard and frame of reference. But when men claim to possess supernatural means of knowledge, no persuasion, communication or understanding are possible. Why do we kill wild animals in the jungle? Because no other way of dealing with them is open to us. And *that* is the state to which mysticism reduces mankind—a state where, in case of disagreement, men have no recourse except to physical violence. And more: no man or mystical elite can hold a whole society subjugated to their arbitrary assertions, edicts and whims, without the use of force. Anyone who resorts to the formula: "It's so, because I say so," will have to reach for a gun, sooner or later. Communists, like all materialists, are neo-mystics: it does not matter whether one rejects the mind in favor of revelations or in favor of conditioned reflexes. The basic premise and the results are the same.

Such is the nature of the evil which modern intellectuals have helped to let loose in the world—and such is the nature of their guilt.

Now take a look at the state of the world. The signs and symptoms of the Dark Ages are rising again all over the earth. Slave labor, executions without trial, torture chambers, concentration camps, mass slaughter—all the things which the capitalism of the nineteenth century had abolished in the civilized world, are now brought back by the rule of the neo-mystics.

Look at the state of our intellectual life. In philosophy, the climax of the Kantian version of reason has brought us to the point where alleged philosophers, forgetting the existence of dictionaries and grammar primers, run around studying such questions as: "What do we mean when we say 'The cat is on the mat'?"—while other philosophers proclaim that nouns are an illusion, but such terms as "if-then," "but" and "or" have profound philosophical significance—while still others toy with the idea of an "index of prohibited words" and desire to place on it such words as—I quote—"entity—essence—mind—matter—reality—thing."

In psychology, one school holds that man, by nature, is a helpless, guilt-ridden, instinct-driven automaton—while another school objects that this is not true, because there is no scientific evidence to prove that man is conscious.

In literature, man is presented as a mindless cripple, inhabiting garbage cans. In art, people announce that they do not paint objects, they paint *emotions*. In youth movements—if that's what it can be called—young men attract attention by openly announcing that they are "beat."

The spirit of it all, both the cause of it and the final climax, is contained in a quotation which I am going to read to you. I will preface it by saying that in *Atlas Shrugged* I stated that the world is being destroyed by mysticism and altruism, which are anti-man, anti-mind and anti-life. You have undoubtedly heard me being accused of exaggeration. I shall now read to you an excerpt from the paper of a professor, published by an alumni faculty seminar of a prominent university.

"Perhaps in the future reason will cease to be important. Perhaps for guidance in time of trouble, people will turn not to human thought, but to the human capacity for suffering. Not the universities with their thinkers, but the places and people in distress, the inmates of asylums and concentration camps, the helpless decision makers in bureaucracy and the helpless soldiers in foxholes—these will be the ones to lighten man's way, to refashion his knowledge of disaster into something creative. We may be entering a new age. Our heroes may not be intellectual giants like Isaac Newton or Albert Einstein, but victims like Anne Frank, who will show us a greater miracle than thought. They will teach us how to endure—how to create good in the midst of evil and how to nurture love in the presence of death. Should this happen, however, the university will still have its place. Even the intellectual man can be an example of creative suffering."

Observe that we are not to question "the helpless decision makers in bureaucracy"—we are not to discover that *they* are the cause of the concentration camps, of the foxholes and of victims like Anne Frank—we are not to help such victims, we are merely to feel suffering and to learn to suffer some more—we can't help it, the helpless bureaucrats can't help it, nobody can help it—the inmates of asylums will guide us, not intellectual giants—suffering is the supreme value, not reason.

This, ladies and gentlemen, is cultural bankruptcy.

Since *"challenge"* is your slogan, I will say that if you are looking for a challenge, you are facing the greatest one in history. A *moral* revolution is the most difficult, the most demanding, the most radical form of rebellion, but that is the task to be done today, if you choose to accept it. When I say "radical," I mean it in its literal and reputable sense: fundamental. Civilization does not have to perish. The brutes are winning only by default. But in order to fight them to the finish and with full rectitude, it is the altruist morality that you have to reject. . . .

2. Mind and Body

Contrary to Plato and Kant, AR's view of reason is emphatically not *otherworldly. Her heroes are men of thought—and of action based on it. They are dryly logical—and intensely passionate; idealistic and practical. In short, they represent the harmony or integration of mind and body. This contradicts and nullifies the age-old belief in a soul-body dichotomy. It denies both "spiritualism" and "materialism."*

This excerpt, from the essay "For the New Intellectual," identifies the influence of the mind-body dichotomy throughout history—and the rational alternative to such an approach. (Attila represents the materialist; the Witch Doctor, the spiritualist; the Producer, the union of mind and body.)

Attila and the Witch Doctor

. . . HISTORICALLY, THE professional intellectual is a very recent phenomenon: he dates only from the industrial revolution. There are no professional intellectuals in primitive, savage societies, there are only witch doctors. There were no professional intellectuals in the Middle Ages, there were only monks in monasteries. In the post-Renaissance era, prior to the birth of capitalism, the men of the intellect—the philosophers, the teachers, the writers, the early scientists—were men without a profession, that is: without a socially recognized position, without a market, without a means of earning a livelihood. Intellectual pursuits had to depend on the accident of inherited wealth or on the favor and financial support of some wealthy protector. And wealth was not earned on an open market, either; wealth was acquired by conquest, by force, by political power, or by the favor of those who held political power. Tradesmen were more vulnerably and precariously dependent on favor than the intellectuals.

The professional businessman and the professional intellectual came into existence together, as brothers born of the industrial revolution. Both are the sons of capitalism—and if they perish, they will perish together. The tragic irony will be that they will have destroyed each other; and the major share of the guilt will belong to the intellectual.

With very rare and brief exceptions, pre-capitalist societies had no place for the creative power of man's mind, neither in the creation of ideas nor in the creation of wealth. Reason and its practical expression—free trade—were forbidden as a sin and a crime, or were tolerated, usually as ignoble activities, under the control of authorities who could revoke the tolerance at whim. Such societies were ruled by faith and its practical expression: force. There were no makers of knowledge and no makers of wealth; there were only witch doctors and tribal chiefs. These two figures dominate every anti-rational period of history, whether one calls them tribal chief and witch doctor— or absolute monarch and religious leader—or dictator and logical positivist.

"The tragic joke of human history"—I am quoting John Galt in *Atlas Shrugged*—"is that on any of the altars men erected, it was always man whom they immolated and the animal whom they enshrined. It was always the animal's attributes, not man's, that humanity worshipped: the idol of instinct and the idol of force—the mystics and the kings—the mystics, who longed for an irresponsible consciousness and ruled by means of the claim that their dark emotions were superior to reason, that knowledge came in blind, causeless fits, blindly to be followed, not doubted—and the kings, who ruled by means of claws and muscles, with conquest as their method and looting as their aim, with a club or a gun as sole sanction of their power. The defenders of man's soul were concerned with his feelings, and the defenders of man's body were concerned with his stomach—but both were united against his mind."

These two figures—the man of faith and the man of force—are philosophical archetypes, psychological symbols and historical reality. As philosophical archetypes, they embody two variants of a certain view of man and of existence. As psychological symbols, they represent the basic motivation of a great many men who exist in any era, culture or society. As historical reality, they are the actual rulers of most of mankind's societies, who rise to power whenever men abandon reason.

The essential characteristics of these two remain the same in all ages: *Attila*, the man who rules by brute force, acts on the range of the moment, is concerned with nothing but the physical reality immediately before him, respects nothing but man's muscles, and regards a fist, a club or a gun as the only answer to any problem—and *the Witch Doctor*, the man who dreads physical reality, dreads the necessity of practical action, and escapes into his emotions, into visions of some mystic realm where his wishes enjoy a supernatural power unlimited by the absolute of nature.

Superficially, these two may appear to be opposites, but observe what they have in common: a consciousness held down to the *perceptual* method of functioning, an awareness that does not choose to extend beyond the automatic, the immediate, the given, the involuntary, which means: an animal's "epistemology" or as near to it as a human consciousness can come.

Man's consciousness shares with animals the first two stages of its development: sensations and perceptions; but it is the third state, *conceptions*, that makes him man. Sensations are integrated into perceptions automatically, by the brain of a man or of an animal. But to integrate perceptions into conceptions by a process of abstraction, is a feat that man alone has the power to perform—and he has to perform it *by choice*. The process of abstraction, and of concept-formation is a process of reason, of *thought*; it is not automatic nor instinctive nor involuntary nor infallible. Man has to initiate it, to sustain it and to bear responsibility for its results. The pre-conceptual level of consciousness is nonvolitional; volition begins with the first syllogism. Man has the choice to think or to evade—to maintain a state of full awareness or to drift from moment to moment, in a semiconscious daze, at the mercy of whatever associational whims the unfocused mechanism of his consciousness produces.

But the living organisms that possess the faculty of consciousness need to exercise it in order to survive. An animal's consciousness functions automatically; an animal perceives what it is able to perceive and survives accordingly, no further than the perceptual level permits and no better. Man cannot survive on the perceptual level of *his* consciousness; his senses do not provide him with an automatic guidance, they do not give him the knowledge he needs, only the *material* of knowledge, which his mind has to integrate. Man is the only living species who has to perceive reality—which means: to be *conscious*—by choice. But he shares with other species the penalty of unconsciousness: destruction. For an animal, the question of survival is primarily physical; for man, primarily epistemological.

Man's unique reward, however, is that while animals survive by adjusting themselves to their background, man survives by adjusting his background to himself. If a drought strikes them, animals perish—man builds irrigation canals; if a flood strikes them, animals perish—man builds dams; if a carnivorous pack attacks them animals perish—man writes the Constitution of the United States. But one does not obtain food, safety or freedom—by instinct.

It is against this faculty, the faculty of *reason*, that Attila and the Witch Doctor rebel. The key to both their souls is their longing for the effortless, irresponsible, automatic consciousness of an animal. Both dread the necessity, the risk and the responsibility of rational cognition. Both dread the fact that "nature, to be commanded, must be obeyed." Both seek to exist, not by conquering nature, but by adjusting to the given, the immediate, the known. There is only one means of survival for those who do not choose to conquer nature: to conquer those who do.

The *physical* conquest of men is Attila's method of survival. He regards men as others regard fruit trees or farm animals: as objects in nature, his for the seizing. But while a good farmer knows, at least, that fruit trees and animals have a specific nature and require a specific kind of handling, the *perceptual* mentality of Attila does not extend to so abstract a level: men, to him, are a natural phenomenon and an irreducible primary, as all natural phenomena are irreducible primaries to an animal. Attila feels no need to understand, to explain, nor even to wonder, *how* men manage to produce the things he covets—"*somehow*" is a fully satisfactory answer inside his skull, which refuses to consider such questions as "how?" and "why?" or such concepts as identity and causality. All he needs, his "urges" tell him, is bigger muscles, bigger clubs or a bigger gang than theirs in order to seize their bodies and their products, after which their bodies will obey his commands and will provide him, somehow, with the satisfaction of any whim. He approaches men as a beast of prey, and the consequences of his actions or the possibility of exhausting his victims never enters his consciousness, which does not choose to extend

beyond the given moment. His view of the universe does not include
the power of production. The power of destruction, of brute force, is,
to him, metaphysically omnipotent.

An Attila never thinks of creating, only of *taking over.* Whether he
conquers a neighboring tribe or overruns a continent, material looting is his only goal and it ends with the act of seizure: he has no other
purpose, no plan, no system to impose on the conquered, no values.
His pleasures are closer to the level of sensations than of perceptions:
food, drink, palatial shelter, rich clothing, indiscriminate sex, contests
of physical prowess, gambling—all those activities which do not demand or involve the use of the conceptual level of consciousness. He
does not originate his pleasures: he desires and pursues whatever
those around him seem to find desirable. Even in the realm of desires,
he does not create, he merely takes over.

But a human being cannot live his life moment by moment; a
human consciousness preserves a certain continuity and demands a
certain degree of integration, whether a man seeks it or not. A human
being needs a frame of reference, a comprehensive view of existence,
no matter how rudimentary, and, since his consciousness *is* volitional,
a sense of being *right*, a moral justification of his actions, which
means: a philosophical code of values. Who, then, provides Attila
with values? The Witch Doctor.

If Attila's method of survival is the conquest of those who conquer
nature, the Witch Doctor's method of survival is safer, he believes,
and spares him the risks of physical conflict. *His* method is the conquest of those who conquer those who conquer nature. It is not men's
bodies that he seeks to rule, but men's souls.

To Attila, as to an animal, the phenomena of nature are an irreducible primary. To the Witch Doctor, as to an animal, the irreducible
primary is the automatic phenomena of his own consciousness.

An animal has no critical faculty; he has no control over the function of his brain and no power to question its content. To an animal,
whatever strikes his awareness is an absolute that corresponds to reality—or rather, it is a distinction he is incapable of making: reality, to
him, is whatever he senses or feels. And *this* is the Witch Doctor's
epistemological ideal, the mode of consciousness he strives to induce
in himself. To the Witch Doctor, emotions are tools of cognition, and
wishes take precedence over facts. He seeks to escape the risks of a
quest for knowledge by obliterating the distinction between consciousness and reality, between the perceiver and the perceived, hop-

ing that an automatic certainty and an infallible knowledge of the universe will be granted to him by the blind, unfocused stare of his eyes turned inward, contemplating the sensations, the feelings, the urgings, the muggy associational twistings projected by the rudderless mechanism of his undirected consciousness. Whatever his mechanism produces is an absolute not to be questioned; and whenever it clashes with reality, it is reality that he ignores.

Since the clash is constant, the Witch Doctor's solution is to believe that what he perceives is another, "higher" reality—where his wishes are omnipotent, where contradictions are possible and A is non-A, where his assertions, which are false on earth, become true and acquire the status of a "superior" truth which *he* perceives by means of a special faculty denied to other, "inferior," beings. The only validation of his consciousness he can obtain on earth is the belief and the obedience of others, when they accept his "truth" as superior to their own perception of reality. While Attila extorts their obedience by means of a club, the Witch Doctor obtains it by means of a much more powerful weapon: he pre-empts the field of *morality*.

There is no way to turn morality into a weapon of enslavement except by divorcing it from man's reason and from the goals of his own existence. There is no way to degrade man's life on earth except by the lethal opposition of the *moral* and the *practical*. Morality is a code of values to guide man's choices and actions; when it is set to oppose his own life and mind, it makes him turn against himself and blindly act as the tool of his own destruction. There is no way to make a human being accept the role of a sacrificial animal except by destroying his self-esteem. There is no way to destroy his self-esteem except by making him reject his own consciousness. There is no way to make him reject his own consciousness except by convincing him of its impotence.

The damnation of this earth as a realm where nothing is possible to man but pain, disaster and defeat, a realm inferior to another, "higher," reality; the damnation of all values, enjoyment, achievement and success on earth as a proof of depravity; the damnation of man's mind as a source of *pride*, and the damnation of reason as a "limited," deceptive, unreliable, impotent faculty, incapable of perceiving the "real" reality and the "true" truth; the split of man in two, setting his consciousness (his soul) against his body, and his moral values against his own interest; the damnation of man's nature, body and *self* as evil; the commandment of self-sacrifice, renunciation, suffering, obedience, humility and faith, as the good; the damnation of life and the worship of death, with the promise of rewards beyond the grave—*these* are the necessary tenets of the Witch Doctor's view of existence, as they have been in every variant of Witch Doctor philosophy throughout the course of mankind's history.

The secret of the Witch Doctor's power lies in the fact that man needs an integrated view of life, a *philosophy*, whether he is aware of his need or not—and whenever, through ignorance, cowardice or mental sloth, men choose not to be aware of it, their chronic sense of guilt, uncertainty and terror makes them feel that the Witch Doctor's philosophy is true.

The first to feel it is Attila.

The man who lives by brute force, at the whim and mercy of the moment, lives on a narrow island suspended in a fog of the unknown, where invisible threats and unpredictable disasters can descend upon him any morning. He is willing to surrender his consciousness to the man who offers him protection against those intangible questions which he does not wish to consider, yet dreads.

Attila's fear of reality is as great as the Witch Doctor's. Both hold their consciousness on a subhuman level and method of functioning: Attila's brain is a jumble of concretes unintegrated by abstractions; the Witch Doctor's brain is a miasma of floating abstractions unrelated to concretes. Both are guided and motivated—ultimately—not by thoughts, but by feelings and whims. Both cling to their whims as to their only certainty. Both feel secretly inadequate to the task of dealing with existence.

Thus they come to need each other. Attila feels that the Witch Doctor can give him what he lacks: a long-range view, an insurance against the dark unknown of tomorrow or next week or next year, a code of moral values to sanction his actions and to disarm his victims. The Witch Doctor feels that Attila can give him the material means of survival, can protect him from physical reality, can spare him the necessity of practical action, and can enforce his mystic edicts on any recalcitrant who may choose to challenge his authority. Both of them are incomplete parts of a human being, who seek completion in each other: the man of muscle and the man of feelings, seeking to exist without *mind*.

Since no man can fully escape the conceptual level of consciousness, it is not the case that Attila and the Witch Doctor cannot or do not think; they can and do—but thinking, to them, is not a means of perceiving reality, it is a means of justifying their escape from the necessity of rational perception. Reason, to them, is a means of defeating their victims, a menial servant charged with the task of rationalizing the metaphysical validity and power of their whims. Just as a bank robber will spend years of planning, ingenuity and effort in order to prove to himself that he can exist without effort, so both Attila and the Witch Doctor will go to any length of cunning, calculation and thought in order to demonstrate the impotence of thought and preserve the image of a pliable universe where miracles are possible and whims are efficacious. The power of *ideas* has no reality for either of them, and neither cares to learn that the proof of that power lies in his own chronic sense of guilt and terror.

Thus Attila and the Witch Doctor form an alliance and divide their respective domains. Attila rules the realm of men's physical existence—the Witch Doctor rules the realm of men's consciousness. Attila herds men into armies—the Witch Doctor sets the armies' goals. Attila conquers empires—the Witch Doctor writes their laws. Attila loots and plunders—the Witch Doctor exhorts the victims to surpass their selfish concern with material property. Attila slaughters—the Witch Doctor proclaims to the survivors that scourges are a retribution for their sins. Attila rules by means of *fear*, by keeping men under a constant threat of destruction—the Witch Doctor rules by means of *guilt*, by keeping men convinced of their innate depravity, impotence and insignificance. Attila turns men's life on earth into a living hell—the Witch Doctor tells them that it could not be otherwise.

But the alliance of the two rulers is precarious: it is based on mutual fear and mutual contempt. Attila is an extrovert, resentful of any concern with consciousness—the Witch Doctor is an introvert, resentful of any concern with physical existence. Attila professes scorn for values, ideals, principles, theories, abstractions—the Witch Doctor professes scorn for material property, for wealth, for man's body, for this earth. Attila considers the Witch Doctor impractical—the Witch Doctor considers Attila immoral. But, secretly, each of them believes that the other possesses a mysterious faculty *he* lacks, that the other is the true master of reality, the true exponent of the power to deal with existence. In terms, not of thought, but of chronic anxiety, it is the Witch Doctor who believes that brute force rules the world—and it is Attila who believes in the supernatural; his name for it is "fate" or "luck."

Against whom is this alliance formed? Against those men whose existence and character both Attila and the Witch Doctor refuse to admit into their view of the universe: the men who produce. In any age or society, there are men who *think* and work, who discover how to deal with existence, how to produce the intellectual and the material values it requires. These are the men whose effort is the only means of survival for the parasites of all varieties: the Attilas, the Witch Doctors and the human ballast. The ballast consists of those who go through life in a state of unfocused stupor, merely repeating the words and the motions they learned from others. But the men from whom they learn, the men who are first to discover any scrap of new knowledge, are the men who deal with reality, with the task of conquering nature, and who, to that extent, assume the responsibility of cognition: of exercising their rational faculty.

A producer is any man who works and knows what he is doing. He may function on a fully human, conceptual level of awareness only some part of his time, but, to that extent, he is the Atlas who supports the existence of mankind; he may spend the rest of his time in an unthinking daze, like the others, and, to that extent, he is the exploited, drained, tortured, self-destroying victim of their schemes.

Men's epistemology—or, more precisely, their *psycho-epistemology*, their method of awareness—is the most fundamental standard by which they can be classified. Few men are consistent in that respect; most men keep switching from one level of awareness to another, according to the circumstances or the issues involved, ranging from moments of full rationality to an almost somnambulistic stupor. But the battle of human history is fought and determined by those who are predominantly consistent, those who, for good or evil, are committed to and motivated by their chosen psycho-epistemology and its corollary view of existence—with echoes responding to them, in support or opposition, in the switching, flickering souls of the others.

A man's method of using his consciousness determines his method of survival. The three contestants are Attila, the Witch Doctor and the Producer—or the man of force, the man of feelings, the man of reason—or the brute, the mystic, the thinker. The rest of mankind calls it expedient to be tossed by the current of events from one of those roles to another, not choosing to identify the fact that those three are the source which determines the current's direction.

The producers, so far, have been the forgotten men of history. With the exception of a few brief periods, the producers have not been the leaders or the term-setters of men's societies, although the degree of their influence and freedom was the degree of a society's welfare and progress. Most societies have been ruled by Attila and the Witch Doctor. The cause is not some innate tendency to evil in human nature, but the fact that reason is a volitional faculty which man has to choose to discover, employ and preserve. Irrationality is a state of default, the state of an unachieved human stature. When men do not choose to reach the conceptual level, their consciousness has no recourse but to its automatic, perceptual, semi-animal functions. If a missing link between the human and the animal species is to be found, Attila and the Witch Doctor are that missing link—the profiteers on men's default. [. . .]

The victim of the [nineteenth-century] intellectuals' most infamous injustice was the businessman.

Having accepted the premises, the moral values and the position of Witch Doctors, the intellectuals were unwilling to differentiate between the businessman and Attila, between the producer of wealth and the looter. Like the Witch Doctor, they scorned and dreaded the realm of material reality, feeling secretly inadequate to deal with it. Like the Witch Doctor's, their secret vision (almost their feared and envied ideal) of a practical, successful man, a true master of reality, was Attila; like the Witch Doctor, they believed that force, fraud, lies, plunder, expropriation, enslavement, murder were *practical.* So they did not inquire into the source of wealth or ever ask what made it possible (they had been taught that causality is an illusion and that only the immediate moment is real). They took it as their axiom, as an irreducible primary, that wealth can be acquired only by force—and that a fortune *as such* is the proof of plunder, with no further distinctions or inquiries necessary.

With their eyes still fixed on the Middle Ages, they were maintaining this in the midst of a period when a greater amount of wealth than had ever before existed in the world was being brought into existence all around them. If the men who produced that wealth were thieves, from whom had they stolen it? Under all the shameful twists of their evasions, the intellectuals' answer was: from those who had *not* produced it. They were refusing to acknowledge the industrial revolution (they are still refusing today). They were refusing to admit into their universe what neither Attila nor the Witch Doctor can afford to admit: the existence of man, the Producer.

Evading the difference between production and looting, they called the businessman a robber. Evading the difference between freedom and compulsion, they called him a slave driver. Evading the difference between reward and terror, they called him an exploiter. Evading the difference between pay checks and guns, they called him an autocrat. Evading the difference between trade and force, they called him a tyrant. The most crucial issue they had to evade was the difference between the *earned* and the *unearned*.

Ignoring the existence of the faculty they were betraying, the faculty of discrimination, the intellect, they refused to identify the fact that industrial wealth was the product of man's mind: that an incalculable amount of intellectual power, of creative intelligence, of disciplined energy, of human genius had gone into the creation of industrial fortunes. They could not afford to identify it, because they could not afford to admit the fact that the intellect is a *practical* faculty, a guide to man's successful existence on earth, and that its task is the study of reality (as well as the production of wealth), not the contemplation of unintelligible feelings nor a special monopoly on the "unknowable."

The Witch Doctor's morality of altruism—the morality that damns all those who achieve success or enjoyment on earth—provided the intellectuals with the means to make a virtue of evasion. It gave them a weapon that disarmed their victims; it gave them an automatic substitute for self-esteem, and a chance at an *unearned* moral stature. They proclaimed themselves to be the defenders of the poor against the rich, righteously evading the fact that the rich were not Attilas any longer—and the defenders of the weak against the strong, righteously evading the fact that the strength involved was not the strength of brute muscles any longer, but the strength of man's mind.

But while the intellectuals regarded the businessman as Attila, the businessman would not behave as they, from the position of Witch Doctors, expected Attila to behave: he was impervious to their power. The businessman was as bewildered by events as the rest of mankind, he had no time to grasp his own historical role, he had no moral weapons, no voice, no defense, and—knowing no morality but the altruist code, yet knowing also that he was functioning against it, that self-sacrifice was *not* his role—he was helplessly vulnerable to the intellectuals' attack. He would have welcomed eagerly the guidance of Aristotle, but had no use for Immanuel Kant. That which today is called "common sense" is the remnant of an Aristotelian influence, and *that* was the businessman's only form of philosophy. The businessman asked for proof and expected things to make sense—an expectation that kicked the intellectuals into the category of the unemployed. They had nothing to offer to a man who did not buy any shares of any version of the "noumenal" world.

To understand the course the intellectuals chose to take, it is important to remember the Witch Doctor's psycho-epistemology and his relationship to Attila: the Witch Doctor expects Attila to be his protector against reality, against the necessity of rational cognition, and, at the same time, he expects to rule his own protector, who needs an *unintelligible* mystic sanction as a narcotic to relieve his chronic guilt. They derive their mutual security, not from any form of strength, but from the fact that each has a hold on the other's secret weakness. It is not the security of two traders, who count on the *values* they offer each other, but the security of two blackmailers, who count on each other's *fear*.

The Witch Doctor feels like a metaphysical outcast in a capitalist society—as if he were pushed into some limbo outside of any universe he cares to recognize. He has no means to deal with innocence; he can get no hold on a man who does not seek to live in guilt, on a businessman who is confident of his ability to earn his living—who takes pride in his work and in the value of his product—who drives himself with inexhaustible energy and limitless ambition to do better and still better and ever better—who is willing to bear penalties for his mistakes and expects rewards for his achievements—who looks at the universe with the fearless eagerness of a child, knowing it to be intelligible—who demands straight lines, clear terms, precise definitions—who stands in full sunlight and has no use for the murky fog of the hidden, the secret, the unnamed, the furtively evocative, for any code of signals from the psycho-epistemology of guilt.

What the businessman offered to the intellectuals was the spiritual counterpart of his own activity, that which the Witch Doctor dreads most: the freedom of the market place of ideas.

To live by the work of one's mind, to offer men the products of one's thinking, to provide them with new knowledge, to stand on nothing but the merit of one's ideas and to rely on nothing but *objective* truth, in a market open to any man who is willing to think and has to judge, accept or reject on his own—is a task that only a man on the conceptual level of psycho-epistemology can welcome or fulfill. It is not the place for a Witch Doctor nor for any mystic "elite."

A Witch Doctor has to live by the favor of a protector, by a special dispensation, by a reserved monopoly, by exclusion, by suppression, by *censorship*.

Having accepted the philosophy and the psycho-epistemology of the Witch Doctor, the intellectuals had to cut the ground from under their own feet and turn against their own historical distinction: against the first chance men had ever had to make a professional living by means of the intellect. When the intellectuals rebelled against the "commercialism" of a capitalist society, what they were specifically rebelling against was the open market of ideas, where *feelings* were not accepted and ideas were expected to demonstrate their validity, where the risks were great, injustices were possible and no protector existed but objective reality.

Just as Attila, since the Renaissance, was looking for a Witch Doctor of his own, so the intellectuals, since the industrial revolution, were looking for an Attila of their own. The altruist morality brought them together and gave them the weapon they needed. The field where they found each other was Socialism.

It was not the businessmen or the industrialists or the workers or the labor unions or the remnants of the feudal aristocracy that began the revolt against freedom and the demand for the return of the absolute state: it was the intellectuals. It was the alleged guardians of reason who brought mankind back to the rule of brute force.

Growing throughout the nineteenth century, originated in and directed from intellectual salons, sidewalk cafés, basement beer joints and university classrooms, the industrial counter-revolution united the Witch Doctors and the Attila-ists. They demanded the right to enforce *ideas* at the point of a gun, that is: through the power of government, and compel the submission of others to the views and wishes of those who would gain control of the government's machinery. They extolled the State as the "Form of the Good," with man as its abject servant, and they proposed as many variants of the socialist state as there had been of the altruist morality. But, in both cases, the variations merely played with the surface, while the cannibal essence remained the same: socialism is the doctrine that man has no right to exist for his own sake, that his life and his work do not belong to *him*, but belong to society, that the only justification of his existence is his service to society, and that society may dispose of him in any way it pleases for the sake of whatever it deems to be its own tribal, collective good.

It is only the Attila-ist, pragmatist, positivist, anti-conceptual mentality—which grants no validity to abstractions, no meaning to principles and no power to ideas—that can still wonder why a theoretical doctrine of that kind had to lead in practice to the torrent of blood and brute, non-human horror of such socialist societies as Nazi Germany and Soviet Russia. Only the Attila-ist mentality can still claim that nobody can prove that these had to be the *necessary* results—or still try to blame it on the "imperfection" of human nature or on the evil of some specific gang who "betrayed a noble ideal," and still promise that its own gang would do it better and make it work—or still mumble in a quavering voice that the motive was love of humanity.

The pretenses have worn thin, the evasions do not work any longer; the intellectuals are aware of their guilt, but are still struggling to evade its cause and to pass it on to the universe at large, to man's metaphysically predestined impotence.

Guilt and fear are the disintegrators of a man's consciousness or of a society's culture. Today, America's culture is being splintered into disintegration by the three injunctions which permeate our intellectual atmosphere and which are typical of guilt: don't look—don't judge—don't be certain.

The psycho-epistemological meaning and implementation of these three are: don't integrate—don't evaluate—give up.

The last stand of Attila-ism, both in philosophy and in science, is the concerted assertion of all the neo-mystics that integration is impossible and unscientific. The escape from the conceptual level of consciousness, the progressive contraction of man's vision down to Attila's range, has now reached its ultimate climax. Withdrawing from reality and responsibility, the neo-mystics proclaim that no entities exist, only relationships, and that one may study relationships without anything to relate, and, simultaneously, that every datum is single and discrete, and no datum can ever be related to any other data—that context is irrelevant, that anything may be proved or disproved in midair and midstream, and the narrower the subject of study, the better—that myopia is the hallmark of a thinker or a scientist.

System-building—the integration of knowledge into a coherent sum and a consistent view of reality—is denounced by all the Attila-ists as irrational, mystical and unscientific. This is Attila's perennial way of surrendering to the Witch Doctor—and it explains why so many scientists are turning to God or to such flights of mysticism of their own as would make even an old-fashioned Witch Doctor blush. No consciousness can accept disintegration as a normal and permanent state. Science was born as a result and consequence of philosophy; it cannot survive without a philosophical (particularly epistemological) base. If philosophy perishes, science will be next to go.

The abdication of philosophy is all but complete. Today's philosophers, *qua* Witch Doctors, declare that nobody can define what *is* philosophy or what is its specific task, but this need not prevent anyone from practicing it as a profession. *Qua* Attila-ists, they declare that the use of wide abstractions or concepts is the prerogative of the layman or of the ignorant or of the man in the street—while a philosopher is one who, knowing all the difficulties involved in the problem of abstractions, deals with nothing but concretes.

The injunction "don't judge" is the ultimate climax of the altruist morality which, today, can be seen in its naked essence. When men plead for forgiveness, for the nameless, cosmic forgiveness of an unconfessed evil, when they react with instantaneous compassion to any guilt, to the perpetrators of any atrocity, while turning away indifferently from the bleeding bodies of the victims and the innocent—one may see the actual purpose, motive and psychological appeal of the altruist code. When these same compassionate men turn with snarling hatred upon anyone who pronounces moral judgments, when they scream that the only evil is the determination to fight against evil—one may see the kind of moral blank check that the altruist morality hands out.

Perhaps the most craven attitude of all is the one expressed by the injunction "don't be certain." As stated explicitly by many intellectuals, it is the suggestion that if nobody is certain of anything, if nobody holds any firm convictions, if everybody is willing to give in to everybody else, no dictator will rise among us and we will escape the destruction sweeping the rest of the world. This is the secret voice of the Witch Doctor confessing that he sees a dictator, an Attila, as a man of confident strength and uncompromising conviction. Nothing but a psycho-epistemological panic can blind such intellectuals to the fact that a dictator, like any thug, runs from the first sign of confident resistance; that he can rise *only* in a society of precisely such uncertain, compliant, shaking compromisers as they advocate, a society that invites a thug to take over; and that the task of resisting an Attila can be accomplished only by men of intransigent conviction and moral certainty—not by chickens hiding their heads in the sand ("ostrich" is too big and dignified a metaphor for this instance).

And, paving the way for Attila, the intellectuals are still repeating, not by conviction any longer, but by rote, that the growth of government power is not an abridgment of freedom—that the demand of one group for an unearned share of another group's income is not socialism—that the destruction of property rights will not affect any other rights—that man's mind, intelligence, creative ability are a *"national resource"* (like mines, forests, waterfalls, buffalo reserves and national parks) to be taken over, subsidized and disposed of by the government—that businessmen are selfish autocrats because they are struggling to preserve freedom, while the "liberals" are the true champions of liberty because they are fighting for more government controls—that the fact that we are sliding down a road which has destroyed every other country, does not prove that it will destroy ours—that dictatorship is not dictatorship if nobody calls it by that *abstract* name—and that none of us can help it, anyway.

Nobody believes any of it any longer, yet nobody opposes it. To oppose anything, one needs a firm set of principles, which means: a philosophy.

If America perishes, it will perish by intellectual default. There is no diabolical conspiracy to destroy it: no conspiracy could be big enough and strong enough. Such cafeteria-socialist conspiracies as do undoubtedly exist are groups of scared, neurotic mediocrities who find themselves pushed into national leadership because nobody else steps forward; they are like pickpockets who merely intended to snatch a welfare-regulation or two and who suddenly find that their victim is unconscious, that they are alone in an enormous mansion of fabulous wealth, with all the doors open and a seasoned burglar's job on their hands; watch them now screaming that they didn't mean it, that they had never advocated the nationalization of a country's economy. As to the communist conspirators in the service of Soviet Russia, they are the best illustration of victory by default: their successes are handed to them by the concessions of their victims. There is no national movement for socialism or dictatorship in America, no "man on horseback" or popular demagogue, nothing but fumbling compromisers and frightened opportunists. Yet we are moving toward full, totalitarian socialism, with worn, cynical voices telling us that such is the irresistible trend of history. History, fate and malevolent conspiracy are easier to believe than the actual truth: that we are moved by nothing but the sluggish inertia of unfocused minds. [. . .]

   The New Intellectual will be the man who lives up to the exact meaning of his title: a man who is guided by his *intellect*—not a zombie guided by feelings, instincts, urges, wishes, whims or revelations. Ending the rule of Attila and the Witch Doctor, he will discard the basic premise that made them possible: the soul-body dichotomy. He will discard its irrational conflicts and contradictions, such as: mind *versus* heart, thought *versus* action, reality *versus* desire, the practical *versus* the moral. He will be an *integrated man*, that is: a thinker who is a man of action. He will know that ideas divorced from consequent action are fraudulent, and that action divorced from ideas is suicidal. He will know that the conceptual level of psycho-epistemology—the volitional level of reason and thought—is the basic necessity of man's survival and his greatest moral virtue. He will know that men need philosophy for the purpose of *living on earth*.
   The New Intellectual will be a reunion of the twins who should never have been separated: the intellectual and the businessman. He can come from among the best—that is: the most rational—men who may still exist in both camps. In place of an involuntary Witch Doctor and a reluctant Attila, the reunion will produce two new types: the practical thinker and the philosophical businessman. . . .

———————

EDITOR'S NOTE: A *brief statement in* Atlas Shrugged, *by Francisco d'Anconia to Hank Rearden, indicates how one's view of the mind-body relationship applies to one's view of sex.*

The Meaning of Sex

. . . "DO YOU remember what I said about money and about the men who seek to reverse the law of cause and effect? The men who try to replace the mind by seizing the products of the mind? Well, the man who despises himself tries to gain self-esteem from sexual adventures—which can't be done, because sex is not the cause, but an effect and an expression of a man's sense of his own value." [. . .]

The men who think that wealth comes from material resources and has no intellectual root or meaning, are the men who think—for the same reason—that sex is a physical capacity which functions independently of one's mind, choice or code of values. They think that your body creates a desire and makes a choice for you—just about in some such way as if iron ore transformed itself into railroad rails of its own volition. Love is blind, they say; sex is impervious to reason and mocks the power of all philosophers. But, in fact, a man's sexual choice is the result and the sum of his fundamental convictions. Tell me what a man finds sexually attractive and I will tell you his entire philosophy of life. Show me the woman he sleeps with and I will tell you his valuation of himself. No matter what corruption he's taught about the virtue of selflessness, sex is the most profoundly selfish of all acts, an act which he cannot perform for any motive but his own enjoyment—just try to think of performing it in a spirit of selfless charity!—an act which is not possible in self-abasement, only in self-exaltation, only in the confidence of being desired and being worthy of desire. It is an act that forces him to stand naked in spirit, as well as in body, and to accept his real ego as his standard of value. He will always be attracted to the woman who reflects his deepest vision of himself, the woman whose surrender permits him to experience—or to fake—a sense of self-esteem. The man who is proudly certain of his own value, will want the highest type of woman he can find, the woman he admires, the strongest, the hardest to conquer—because only the possession of a heroine will give him the sense of an achievement, not the possession of a brainless slut. [. . .]

But the man who is convinced of his own worthlessness will be drawn to a woman he despises—because she will reflect his own secret self, she will release him from that objective reality in which he is a fraud, she will give him a momentary illusion of his own value and a momentary escape from the moral code that damns him. Observe the ugly mess which most men make of their sex lives—and observe the mess of contradictions which they hold as their moral philosophy. One proceeds from the other. Love is our response to our highest values—and can be nothing else. Let a man corrupt his values and his view of existence, let him profess that love is not self-enjoyment but self-denial, that virtue consists, not of pride, but of pity or pain or weakness or sacrifice, that the noblest love is born , not of admiration, but of charity, not in response to *values*, but in response to *flaws*—and he will have cut himself in two. His body will not obey him, it will not respond, it will make him impotent toward the woman he professes to love and draw him to the lowest type of whore he can find. His body will always follow the ultimate logic of his deepest convictions; if he believes that flaws are values, he has damned existence as evil and only the evil will attract him. He has damned himself and he will feel that depravity is all he is worthy of enjoying. He has equated virtue with pain and he will feel that vice is the only realm of pleasure. Then he will scream that his body has vicious desires of its own which his mind cannot conquer, that sex is sin, that true love is a pure emotion of the spirit. And then he will wonder why love brings him nothing but boredom, and sex—nothing but shame. [. . .]

[Y]ou'd never accept any part of their vicious creed. You wouldn't be able to force it upon yourself. If you tried to damn sex as evil, you'd still find yourself, against your will, acting on the proper moral premise. You'd be attracted to the highest woman you met. You'd always want a heroine. You'd be incapable of self-contempt. You'd be unable to believe that existence is evil and that you're a helpless creature caught in an impossible universe. You're the man who's spent his life shaping matter to the purpose of his mind. You're the man who would know that just as an idea unexpressed in physical action is contemptible hypocrisy, so is platonic love—and just as physical action unguided by an idea is a fool's self-fraud, so is sex when cut off from one's code of values. It's the same issue, and you would know it. Your inviolate sense of self-esteem would know it. You would be incapable of desire for a woman you despised. Only the man who extols the purity of a love devoid of desire, is capable of the depravity of a desire devoid of love. But observe that most people are creatures cut in half who keep swinging desperately to one side or to the other. One kind of half is the man who despises money, factories, skyscrapers and his own body. He holds undefined emotions about non-conceivable subjects as the meaning of life and as his claim to virtue. And he cries with despair, because he can feel nothing for the woman he respects, but finds himself in bondage to an irresistible passion for a slut from the gutter. He is the man whom people call an idealist. The other kind of half is the man whom people call practical, the man who despises principles, abstractions, art, philosophy and his own mind. He regards the acquisition of material objects as the only goal of existence—and he laughs at the need to consider their purpose or their source. He expects them to give him pleasure—and he wonders why the more he gets, the less he feels. *He* is the man who spends his time chasing women. Observe the triple fraud which he perpetrates upon himself. He will not acknowledge his need of self-esteem, since he scoffs at such a concept as moral values; yet he feels the profound self-contempt which comes from believing that he is a piece of meat. He will not acknowledge, but he knows that sex is the physical expression of a tribute to personal values. So he tries, by going through the motions of the effect, to acquire that which should have been the cause. He tries to gain a sense of his own value from the women who surrender to him—and he forgets that the women he picks have neither character nor judgment nor standard of value. He tells himself that all he's after is physical pleasure—but observe that he tires of his women in a week or a night, that he despises professional whores and that he loves to imagine he is seducing virtuous girls who make a great exception for his sake. It is the feeling of achievement that he seeks and never finds. What glory can there be in the conquest of a mindless body? . . .

———————

EDITOR'S NOTE: *A speech given by* AR *in the late 1960s, "Of Living Death" (published in* The Voice of Reason), *identifies the connection between the Catholic Church's basic philosophy and its view of sex.*

Of Living Death

THOSE WHO wish to observe the role of philosophy in human existence may see it dramatized on a grand (and gruesome) scale in the conflict splitting the Catholic church today.

Observe, in that conflict, men's fear of identifying or challenging philosophical fundamentals: both sides are willing to fight in silent confusion, to stake their beliefs, their careers, their reputations on the outcome of a battle over the effects of an unnamed cause. One side is composed predominantly of men who dare not name the cause; the other, of men who dare not discover it.

Both sides claim to be puzzled and disappointed by what they regard as a contradiction in the two recent encyclicals of Pope Paul VI. The so-called conservatives (speaking in religious, not political, terms) were dismayed by the encyclical *Populorum Progressio* (*On the Development of Peoples*)—which advocated global statism—while the so-called liberals hailed it as a progressive document. Now the conservatives are hailing the encyclical *Humanae Vitae* (*Of Human Life*)—which forbids the use of contraceptives—while the liberals are dismayed by it. Both sides seem to find the two documents inconsistent. But the inconsistency is theirs, not the pontiff's. The two encyclicals are strictly, flawlessly consistent in respect to their basic philosophy and ultimate goal: both come from the same view of man's nature and are aimed at establishing the same conditions for his life on earth. The first of these two encyclicals forbade ambition, the second forbids enjoyment; the first enslaved man to the physical needs of others, the second enslaves him to the physical capacities of his own body; the first damned achievement, the second damns love.

The doctrine that man's sexual capacity belongs to a lower or animal part of his nature has had a long history in the Catholic church. It is the necessary consequence of the doctrine that man is not an integrated entity, but a being torn apart by two opposite, antagonistic, irreconcilable elements: his body, which is of this earth, and his soul, which is of another, supernatural realm. According to that doctrine, man's sexual capacity—regardless of how it is exercised or motivated, not merely its abuses, not unfastidious indulgence or promiscuity, but *the capacity as such*—is sinful or depraved.

For centuries, the dominant teaching of the church held that sexuality is evil, that only the need to avoid the extinction of the human species grants sex the status of a *necessary* evil and, therefore, only procreation can redeem or excuse it. In modern times, many Catholic writers have denied that such is the church's view. But what is its view? They did not answer.

Let us see if we can find the answer in the encyclical *Humanae Vitae*.

Dealing with the subject of birth control, the encyclical prohibits all forms of contraception (except the so-called "rhythm method"). The prohibition is total, rigid, unequivocal. It is enunciated as a moral absolute.

Bear in mind what this subject entails. Try to hold an image of horror spread across space and time—across the entire globe and through all the centuries—the image of parents chained, like beasts of burden, to the physical needs of a growing brood of children—young parents aging prematurely while fighting a losing battle against starvation— the skeletal hordes of unwanted children born without a chance to live—the unwed mothers slaughtered in the unsanitary dens of incompetent abortionists—the silent terror hanging, for every couple, over every moment of love. If one holds this image while hearing that this nightmare is not to be stopped, the first question one will ask is: *Why?* In the name of humanity, one will assume that some inconceivable, but crucially important reason must motivate any human being who would seek to let that carnage go on uncontested.

So the first thing one will look for in the encyclical, is that reason, an answer to that *Why?*

"The problem of birth," the encyclical declares, "like every other problem regarding human life, is to be considered . . . in the light of an integral vision of man and of his vocation, not only his natural and earthly, but also his supernatural and eternal, vocation." [Paragraph 7]

And:

> A reciprocal act of love, which jeopardizes the responsibility to transmit life which God the Creator, according to particular laws, inserted therein, is in contradiction with the design constitutive of marriage, and with the will of the author of life. To use this divine gift, destroying, even if only partially, its meaning and its purpose, is to contradict the nature both of man and of woman and of their most intimate relationship, and therefore it is to contradict also the plan of God and His will. [13]

And *this* is all. In the entire encyclical, this is the only reason given (but repeated over and over again) why men should transform their highest experience of happiness—their love—into a source of lifelong agony. Do so—the encyclical commands—because it is God's will.

I, who do not believe in God, wonder why those who do would ascribe to him such a sadistic design, when God is supposed to be the archetype of mercy, kindness, and benevolence. What *earthly* goal is served by that doctrine? The answer runs like a hidden thread through the encyclical's labyrinthian convolutions, repetitions, and exhortations.

In the darker corners of that labyrinth, one finds some snatches of argument, in alleged support of the mystic axiom, but these arguments are embarrassingly transparent equivocations. For instance:

> . . . to make use of the gift of conjugal love while respecting the laws of the generative process means to acknowledge oneself not to be the arbiter of the sources of human life, but rather the minister of the design established by the Creator. In fact, just as man does not have unlimited dominion over his body in general, so also, with particular reason, he has no such dominion over his creative faculties as such, because of their intrinsic ordination toward raising up life, of which God is the principle. [13]

What is meant here by the words "man does not have unlimited dominion over his body in general"? The obvious meaning is that man cannot change the *metaphysical* nature of his body; which is true. But man has the power of choice in regard to the *actions* of his body—specifically, in regard to "his creative faculties," and the responsibility for the use of these particular faculties is most crucially his. "To acknowledge oneself not to be the arbiter of the sources of human life" is to evade and to default on that responsibility. Here again, the same equivocation or package deal is involved. Does man have the power to determine the nature of his procreative faculty? No. But granted that nature, is he the arbiter of bringing a new human life into existence? He most certainly is, and he (with his mate) is the *sole* arbiter of that decision—and the consequences of that decision affect and determine the entire course of his life.

This is a clue to that paragraph's intention: if man believed that so crucial a choice as procreation is not in his control, what would it do to his control over his life, his goals, his future?

The passive obedience and helpless surrender to the physical functions of one's body, the necessity to let procreation be the inevitable result of the sexual act, is the natural fate of *animals*, not of men. In spite of its concern with man's higher aspirations, with his soul, with the sanctity of married love—it is to the level of animals that the encyclical seeks to reduce man's sex life, in fact, in reality, on earth. What does this indicate about the encyclical's view of sex?

Anticipating certain obvious objections, the encyclical declares:

> Now, some may ask: In the present case, is it not reasonable in many circumstances to have recourse to artificial birth control if,

thereby, we secure the harmony and peace of the family, and better conditions for the education of children already born? To this question it is necessary to reply with clarity: The church is the first to praise and recommend the intervention of intelligence in a function which so closely associates the rational creature with his Creator; but she affirms that this must be one with respect for the order established by God. [16]

To what does this subordinate man's intelligence? If intelligence is forbidden to consider the fundamental problems of man's existence, forbidden to alleviate his suffering, what does this indicate about the encyclical's view of man—and of reason?

History can answer this particular question. History has seen a period of approximately ten centuries, known as the Dark and Middle Ages, when philosophy was regarded as "the handmaiden of theology," and reason as the humble subordinate of faith. The results speak for themselves.

It must not be forgotten that the Catholic church has fought the advance of science since the Renaissance: from Galileo's astronomy, to the dissection of corpses, which was the start of modern medicine, to the discovery of anesthesia in the nineteenth century, the greatest single discovery in respect to the incalculable amount of terrible suffering it has spared mankind. The Catholic church has fought medical progress by means of the same argument: that the application of knowledge to the relief of human suffering is an attempt to contradict God's design. Specifically in regard to anesthesia during childbirth, the argument claimed that since God intended woman to suffer while giving birth, man has no right to intervene. (!)

The encyclical does not recommend unlimited procreation. It does not object to all means of birth control—only to those it calls "artificial" (i.e., scientific). It does not object to man "contradicting God's will" nor to man being "the arbiter of the sources of human life," provided he uses the means it endorses: *abstinence*.

Discussing the issue of "responsible parenthood," the encyclical states: "In relation to physical, economic, psychological and social conditions, responsible parenthood is exercised, either by the deliberate and generous decision to raise a numerous family, or by the decision, made for grave motives and with due respect for the moral law, to avoid for the time being, or even for an indeterminate period, a new birth." [10] To avoid—by what means? By abstaining from sexual intercourse.

The lines preceding that passage are: "In relation to the tendencies of instinct or passion, responsible parenthood means the necessary dominion which reason and will must exercise over them." [10] How a man is to force his reason to obey an irrational injunction and what it would do to him psychologically, is not mentioned.

Further on, under the heading "Mastery of Self," the encyclical declares:

> To dominate instinct by means of one's reason and free will undoubtedly requires ascetic practices. . . . Yet this discipline which is proper to the purity of married couples, far from harming conjugal love, rather confers on it a higher human value. It demands continual effort yet, thanks to its beneficent influence, husband and wife fully develop their personalities, being enriched with spiritual values. . . . Such discipline . . . helps both parties to drive out selfishness, the enemy of true love; and deepens their sense of responsibility. [21]

If you can bear that style of expression being used to discuss such matters—which I find close to unbearable—and if you focus on the meaning, you will observe that the "discipline," the "continual effort," the "beneficent influence," the "higher human value" refer to the torture of sexual frustration.

No, the encyclical does not say that sex as such is evil; it merely says that sexual abstinence *in marriage* is "a higher human value." What does this indicate about the encyclical's view of sex—and of marriage?

Its view of marriage is fairly explicit. "[Conjugal] love is first of all fully human, that is to say, of the senses and of the spirit at the same time. It is not, then, a simple transport of instinct and sentiment, but also, and principally, an act of the free will, intended to endure and to grow by means of the joys and sorrows of daily life, in such a way that husband and wife become one only heart and one only soul, and together attain their human perfection.

"Then this love is total; that is to say, it is a very special form of personal friendship, in which husband and wife generously share everything, without undue reservations or selfish calculations." [9]

To classify the unique emotion of *romantic love* as a form of *friendship* is to obliterate it: the two emotional categories are mutually exclusive. The feeling of friendship is asexual; it can be experienced toward a member of one's own sex.

There are many other indications of this kind scattered through the encyclical. For instance: "These acts, by which husband and wife are united in chaste intimacy and by means of which human life is transmitted, are, as the council recalled, 'noble and worthy.' " [11] It is not *chastity* that one seeks in sex, and to describe it this way is to emasculate the meaning of marriage.

There are constant references to a married couple's *duties*, which have to be considered in the context of the sexual act—"duties toward God, toward themselves, toward the family and toward society." [10] If there is any one concept which, when associated with sex, would render a man impotent, it is the concept of "duty."

To understand the full meaning of the encyclical's view of sex, I shall ask you to identify the common denominator—the common *intention*—of the following quotations:

> [The church's] teaching, often set forth by the Magisterium, is founded upon the inseparable connection, willed by God and unable to be broken by man on his own initiative, between the two meanings of the conjugal act: the unitive meaning and the procreative meaning. Indeed, by its intimate structure, the conjugal act, while most closely uniting husband and wife, capacitates them for the generation of new lives. [12]

"[The conjugal acts] do not cease to be lawful if, for *causes independent of the will of husband and wife,* they are foreseen to be infecund." [11, emphasis added.]

The church forbids: "every action which, either in anticipation of the conjugal act or its accomplishment, or in the development of its natural consequences, proposes, whether as an end or as a means, to render procreation impossible." [14]

The church does not object to "an impediment to procreation" which might result from the medical treatment of a disease, "*provided such impediment is not, for whatever motive, directly willed,*" [15, emphasis added.]

And finally, the church "teaches that each and every marriage act (*'quilibet matrimonii usus,'*) must remain open to the transmission of life." [11]

What is the common denominator of these statements? It is not merely the tenet that sex as such is evil, but deeper: it is the commandment by means of which sex will *become* evil, the commandment which, if accepted, will divorce sex from love, will castrate man spiritually and will turn sex into a meaningless physical indulgence. That commandment is: *man must not regard sex as an end in itself, but only as a means to an end.*

Procreation and "God's design" are not the major concern of that doctrine; they are merely primitive rationalizations to which man's self-esteem is to be sacrificed. If it were otherwise, why the stressed insistence on forbidding man to impede procreation by his conscious will and choice? Why the tolerance of the conjugal acts of couples who are infecund by nature rather than by choice? What is so evil about that choice? There is only one answer: that choice rests on a couple's conviction that the justification of sex is their own enjoyment. And *this* is the view which the church's doctrine is intent on forbidding at any price.

That such is the doctrine's intention, is supported by the church's stand on the so-called "rhythm method" of birth control, which the encyclical approves and recommends.

> The church is coherent with herself when she considers recourse to the infecund periods to be licit, while at the same time condemning, as being always illicit, the use of means directly contrary to fecundation, even if such use is inspired by reasons which may appear honest and serious. . . . It is true that, in the one and the other case, the married couple are concordant in the positive will of avoiding children for plausible reasons, seeking the certainty that offspring will not arrive; but it is also true that only in the former case are they able to renounce the use of marriage in the fecund periods when, for just motives, procreation is not desirable, while making use of it during infecund periods to manifest their affection and to safeguard their mutual fidelity. By so doing, they give proof of a truly and integrally honest love. [16]

On the face of it, this does not make any kind of sense at all—and the church has often been accused of hypocrisy or compromise because it permits this very unreliable method of birth control while forbidding all others. But examine that statement from the aspect of its intention, and you will see that the church is indeed "coherent with herself," i.e., consistent.

What is the *psychological* difference between the "rhythm method" and other means of contraception? The difference lies in the fact that, using the "rhythm method," a couple cannot regard sexual enjoyment as a right and as an end in itself. With the help of some hypocrisy, they merely sneak and snatch some personal pleasure, while keeping the marriage act "open to the transmission of life," thus acknowledging that childbirth is the only moral justification of sex and that only by the grace of the calendar are they unable to comply.

This acknowledgment is the meaning of the encyclical's peculiar implication that "to renounce the use of marriage in the fecund periods" is, somehow, a virtue (a renunciation which proper methods of birth control would not require). What else but this acknowledgment can be the meaning of the otherwise unintelligible statement that by the use of the "rhythm method" a couple "give proof of a truly and integrally honest love"?

There is a widespread popular notion to the effect that the Catholic church's motive in opposing birth control is the desire to enlarge the Catholic population of the world. This may be superficially true of some people's motives, but it is not the full truth. If it were, the Catholic church would forbid the "rhythm method" along with all other forms of contraception. And, more important, the Catholic church would not fight for anti-birth-control legislation all over the world: if numerical superiority were its motive, it would forbid birth control to its own followers and let it be available to other religious groups.

The motive of the church's doctrine on this issue is, philosophically, much deeper than that and much worse; the goal is not metaphysical or political or biological, but psychological: if man is forbidden to regard sexual enjoyment as an end in itself, he will not regard love or his own happiness as an end in itself; if so, then he will not regard his own life as an end in itself; if so, then he will not attain self-esteem.

It is not against the gross, animal, physicalistic theories or uses of sex that the encyclical is directed, but against the *spiritual* meaning of sex in man's life. (By "spiritual" I mean pertaining to man's consciousness.) It is not directed against casual, mindless promiscuity, but against romantic love.

To make this clear, let me indicate, in brief essentials, a rational view of the role of sex in man's existence.

Sex is a physical capacity, but its exercise is determined by man's mind—by his choice of values, held consciously or subconsciously. To a rational man, sex is an expression of self-esteem—*a celebration of himself and of existence*. To the man who lacks self-esteem, sex is an attempt to fake it, to acquire its momentary illusion.

Romantic love, in the full sense of the term, is an emotion possible only to the man (or woman) of unbreached self-esteem: it is his response to his own highest values in the person of another—an integrated response of mind and body, of love and sexual desire. Such a man (or woman) is incapable of experiencing a sexual desire divorced from spiritual values. [. . .]

In other words, sexual promiscuity is to be condemned not because sex as such is evil, but because it is *good*—too good and too important to be treated casually.

In comparison to the moral and psychological importance of sexual happiness, the issue of procreation is insignificant and irrelevant, except as a deadly threat—and God bless the inventors of the Pill!

The capacity to procreate is merely a potential which man is not obligated to actualize. The choice to have children or not is morally optional. Nature endows man with a variety of potentials—and it is his *mind* that must decide which capacities he chooses to exercise, according to his own hierarchy of rational goals and values. The mere fact that man has the capacity to kill does not mean that it is his duty to become a murderer; in the same way, the mere fact that man has the capacity to procreate does not mean that it is his duty to commit spiritual suicide by making procreation his primary goal and turning himself into a stud-farm animal.

It is only animals that have to adapt themselves to their physical background and to the biological functions of their bodies. Man adapts his physical background and the use of his biological faculties to himself—to his own needs and values. *That* is his distinction from all other living species.

To an animal, the rearing of its young is a matter of temporary cycles. To man, it is a lifelong responsibility—a grave responsibility that must not be undertaken causelessly, thoughtlessly, or accidentally.

In regard to the moral aspects of birth control, the primary right involved is not the "right" of an unborn child, or of the family, or of society, or of God. The primary right is one which—in today's public clamor on the subject—few, if any, voices have had the courage to uphold: *the right of man and woman to their own life and happiness*—the right not to be regarded as the means to any end.

Man is an end in himself. Romantic love—the profound, exalted, lifelong *passion* that unites his mind and body in the sexual act—is the living testimony to that principle.

This is what the encyclical seeks to destroy; or, more precisely, to obliterate, as if it does not and cannot exist.

Observe the encyclical's contemptuous references to sexual desire as "instinct" or "passion," as if "passion" were a pejorative term. Observe the false dichotomy offered; man's choice is either mindless, "instinctual" copulation—or marriage, an institution presented not as a union of *passionate* love, but as a relationship of "chaste intimacy," of "special personal friendship," of "discipline proper to purity," of unselfish duty, of alternating bouts with frustration and pregnancy, and of such unspeakable, Grade-B-movie-folks-next-door kind of boredom that any semi-living man would have to run, in self-preservation, to the nearest whorehouse.

No, I am not exaggerating. I have reserved—as my last piece of evidence on the question of the encyclical's view of sex—the paragraph in which the coils and veils of euphemistic equivocation got torn, somehow, and the naked truth shows through.

It reads as follows:

> Upright men can even better convince themselves of the solid grounds on which the teaching of the church in this field is based, if they care to reflect upon the consequences of methods of artificial birth control. Let them consider, first of all, how wide and easy a road would thus be opened up toward conjugal infidelity and the general lowering of morality. Not much experience is needed in order to know human weakness, and to understand that men—especially the young, who are so vulnerable on this point—have need of encouragement to be faithful to the moral law, so that they must not be offered some easy means of eluding its observance. It is also to be feared that the man, growing used to the employment of anticonceptive practices, may finally lose respect for the woman and, no longer caring for her physical and psychological equilibrium, may come to the point of considering her as a mere instrument of selfish enjoyment, and no longer as his respected and beloved companion. [17]

I cannot conceive of a rational woman who does not want to be precisely *an instrument of her husband's selfish enjoyment.* I cannot conceive of what would have to be the mental state of a woman who could desire or accept the position of having a husband who does *not* derive any selfish enjoyment from sleeping with her. I cannot conceive of anyone, male or female, capable of believing that sexual enjoyment would destroy a husband's love and respect for his wife—but regarding her as a brood mare and himself as a stud, would cause him to love and respect her.

Actually, this is too evil to discuss much further.

But we must also take note of the first part of that paragraph. It states that "artificial" contraception would open "a wide and easy road toward conjugal infidelity." Such is the encyclical's actual view of marriage: that marital *fidelity* rests on nothing better than fear of pregnancy. Well, "not much experience is needed in order to know" that that fear has never been much of a deterrent to anyone.

Now observe the inhuman cruelty of that paragraph's reference to the young. Admitting that the young are "vulnerable on this point," and declaring that they need "encouragement to be faithful to the moral law," the encyclical forbids them the use of contraceptives, thus making it cold-bloodedly clear that its idea of moral encouragement consists of terror—the sheer, stark terror of young people caught between their first experience of love and the primitive brutality of the moral code of their elders. Surely the authors of the encyclical cannot be ignorant of the fact that it is not the young chasers or the teenage sluts who would be the victims of a ban on contraceptives, but the *innocent* young who risk their lives in the quest for love—the girl who finds herself pregnant and abandoned by her boyfriend, or the boy who is trapped into a premature, unwanted marriage. To ignore the agony of such victims—the countless suicides, the deaths at the hands of quack abortionists, the drained lives wasted under the double burden of a spurious "dishonor" and of an unwanted child—to ignore all that in the name of "the moral law" is to make a mockery of morality. [. . .]

This leads us to the encyclical's stand on the issue of abortion, and to another example of inhuman cruelty. Compare the coiling sentimentality of the encyclical's style when it speaks of "conjugal love" to the clear, brusque, military tone of the following: "We must once again declare that the direct interruption of the generative process already begun, and, above all, directly willed and procured abortion, *even if for therapeutic reasons*, are to be absolutely excluded as licit means of regulating birth." [14, emphasis added.]

After extolling the virtue and sanctity of motherhood, as a woman's highest duty, as her "eternal vocation," the encyclical attaches a special risk of death to the performance of that duty—an unnecessary death, in the presence of doctors forbidden to save her, as if a woman were only a screaming huddle of infected flesh who must not be permitted to imagine that she has the right to live.

And *this* policy is advocated by the encyclical's supporters in the name of their concern for "the sanctity of life" and for "rights"—the rights of the embryo. (!)

I suppose that only the psychological mechanism of projection can make it possible for such advocates to accuse their opponents of being *"anti-life."*

Observe that the men who uphold such a concept as "the rights of an embryo," are the men who deny, negate, and violate the rights of a living human being.

An embryo *has no rights.* Rights do not pertain to a *potential*, only to an *actual* being. A child cannot acquire any rights until it is born. The living take precedence over the not yet living (or the unborn).

Abortion is a moral right—which should be left to the sole discretion of the woman involved; morally, nothing other than her wish in the matter is to be considered. Who can conceivably have the right to dictate to her what disposition she is to make of the functions of her own body? The Catholic church is responsible for this country's disgracefully barbarian anti-abortion laws, which should be repealed and abolished.

The intensity of the importance that the Catholic church attaches to its doctrine on sex may be gauged by the enormity of the indifference to human suffering expressed in the encyclical. Its authors cannot be ignorant of the fact that man has to earn his living by his own effort, and that there is no couple on earth—on any level of income, in any country, civilized or not—who would be able to support the number of children they would produce if they obeyed the encyclical to the letter.

If we assume the richest couple and include time off for the periods of "purity," it will still be true that the physical and psychological strain of their "vocation" would be so great that nothing much would be left of them, particularly of the mother, by the time they reached the age of forty.

Consider the position of an *average* American couple. What would be their life, if they succeeded in raising, say, twelve children, by working from morning till night, by running a desperate race with the periodic trips to maternity wards, with rent bills, grocery bills, clothing bills, pediatricians' bills, strained-vegetables bills, school book bills, measles, mumps, whooping cough, Christmas trees, movies, ice cream cones, summer camps, party dresses, dates, draft cards, hospitals, colleges—with every salary raise of the industrious, hardworking father mortgaged and swallowed before it is received—what would they have gained at the end of their life except the hope that they might be able to pay their cemetery bills, in advance?

Now consider the position of the majority of mankind, who are barely able to subsist on a level of prehistorical poverty. No strain, no backbreaking effort of the ablest, most conscientious father can enable him properly to feed one child—let alone an open-end progression. The unspeakable misery of stunted, disease-eaten, chronically undernourished children, who die in droves before the age of ten, is a matter of public record. Pope Paul VI—who closes his encyclical by mentioning his title as earthly representative of "the God of holiness and mercy"—cannot be ignorant of these facts; yet he is able to ignore them. [. . .]

The global state advocated in *Populorum Progressio* is a nightmare utopia where all are enslaved to the physical needs of all; its inhabitants are selfless robots, programmed by the tenets of altruism, without personal ambition, without mind, pride, or self-esteem. But self-esteem is a stubborn enemy of all utopias of that kind, and it is doubtful whether mere economic enslavement would destroy it wholly in men's souls. What *Populorum Progressio* was intended to achieve from without, in regard to the physical conditions of man's existence, *Humanae Vitae* is intended to achieve from within, in regard to the devastation of man's consciousness.

"Don't allow men to be happy," said Ellsworth Toohey in *The Fountainhead*. "Happiness is self-contained and self-sufficient. . . . Happy men are free men. So kill their joy in living. . . . Make them feel that the mere fact of a personal desire is evil. . . . Unhappy men will come to you. They'll need you. They'll come for consolation, for support, for escape. Nature allows no vacuum. Empty man's soul—and the space is yours to fill."

Deprived of ambition, yet sentenced to endless toil; deprived of rewards, yet ordered to produce; deprived of sexual enjoyment, yet commanded to procreate; deprived of the right to live, yet forbidden to die—condemned to this state of living death, the graduates of the encyclical *Humanae Vitae* will be ready to move into the world of *Populorum Progressio*; they will have no other place to go.

"If some man like Hugh Akston," said Hank Rearden in *Atlas Shrugged*, "had told me, when I started, that by accepting the mystics' theory of sex I was accepting the looters' theory of economics, I would have laughed in his face. I would not laugh at him now."

It would be a mistake, however, to suppose that in the subconscious hierarchy of motives of the men who wrote these two encyclicals, the second, *Humanae Vitae*, was merely the spiritual means to the first, *Populorum Progressio*, which was the material end. The motives, I believe, were the reverse: *Populorum Progressio* was merely the material means to *Humanae Vitae*, which was the spiritual end.

". . . with our predecessor Pope John XXIII," says Pope Paul VI in *Humanae Vitae*, "we repeat: no solution to these difficulties is acceptable 'which does violence to man's essential dignity' and is based only *'on an utterly materialistic conception of man himself and of his life.'* " [23, emphasis added.] They mean it—though not exactly in the way they would have us believe.

In terms of reality, nothing could be more *materialistic* than an existence devoted to feeding the whole world and procreating to the limit of one's capacity. But when they say "materialistic," they mean pertaining to man's mind and to this earth; by "spiritual," they mean whatever is anti-man, anti-mind, anti-life, and, above all, anti-possibility of human happiness on earth.

The ultimate goal of these encyclicals' doctrine is not the material advantages to be gained by the rulers of a global slave state; the ultimate goal is the spiritual emasculation and degradation of man, the extinction of his love of life, which *Humanae Vitae* is intended to accomplish, and *Populorum Progressio* merely to embody and perpetuate. The means of destroying man's spirit is *unearned guilt*.

What I said in "Requiem for Man" about the motives of *Populorum Progressio* applies as fully to *Humanae Vitae*, with only a minor paraphrase pertaining to its subject. "But, you say, the encyclical's ideal will not work? It is not intended to work. It is not intended to [achieve human chastity or sexual virtue]; it is intended to induce guilt. It is not intended to be accepted and practiced; it is intended to be accepted and broken—broken by man's 'selfish' desire to [love], which will thus be turned into a shameful weakness. Men who accept as an ideal an irrational goal which they cannot achieve, never lift their heads thereafter—and never discover that their bowed heads were the only goal to be achieved." [. . .]

*   *   *

This issue is not confined to the Catholic church, and it is deeper than the problem of contraception; it is a moral crisis approaching a climax. The core of the issue is Western civilization's view of man and of his life. The essence of that view depends on the answer to two interrelated questions: Is man (man the individual) an end in himself?—and: Does man have the right to be happy on this earth?

Throughout its history, the West has been torn by a profound ambivalence on these questions: all of its achievements came from those periods when men acted as if the answer were "Yes"—but, with exceedingly rare exceptions, their spokesmen, the philosophers, kept proclaiming a thunderous "No," in countless forms.

Neither an individual nor an entire civilization can exist indefinitely with an unresolved conflict of that kind. Our age is paying the penalty for it. And it is our age that will have to resolve it.

━━━━━

EDITOR'S NOTE: *In a 1964* Playboy *interview, AR indicated her views on issues such as the proper relationship between reason and emotion, the connection between career and romance, and the nature of love.*

On Emotions, Including Love

. . . LET'S DEFINE our terms. Reason is man's tool of knowledge, the faculty that enables him to perceive the facts of reality. To act rationally means to act in accordance with the facts of reality. Emotions are not tools of cognition. What you feel tells you nothing about the facts; it merely tells you something about your estimate of the facts. Emotions are the result of your value judgments; they are caused by your basic premises, which you may hold consciously or subconsciously, which may be right or wrong. A whim is an emotion whose cause you neither know nor care to discover. Now what does it mean, to act on whim? It means that a man acts like a zombie, without any knowledge of what he deals with, what he wants to accomplish, or what motivates him. It means that a man acts in a state of temporary insanity. [. . .]

An emotion is an automatic response, an automatic effect of man's value premises. An effect, not a cause. There is no necessary clash, no dichotomy between man's reason and his emotions—provided he observes their proper relationship. A rational man knows—or makes it a point to discover—the source of his emotions, the basic premises from which they come; if his premises are wrong, he corrects them. He never acts on emotions for which he cannot account, the meaning of which he does not understand. In appraising a situation, he knows why he reacts as he does and whether he is right. He has no inner conflicts, his mind and his emotions are integrated, his consciousness is in perfect harmony. His emotions are not his enemies, they are his means of enjoying life. But they are not his guide; the guide is his mind. This relationship cannot be reversed, however. If a man takes his emotions as the cause and his mind as their passive effect, if he is guided by his emotions and uses his mind only to rationalize or justify them somehow—*then* he is acting immorally, he is condemning himself to misery, failure, defeat, and he will achieve nothing but destruction—his own and that of others. [. . .]

The only man capable of experiencing a profound romantic love is the man driven by passion for his work—because love is an expression of self-esteem, of the deepest values in a man's or a woman's character. One falls in love with the person who shares these values. If a man has no clearly defined values, and no moral character, he is not able to appreciate another person. In this respect, I would like to quote from *The Fountainhead*, in which the hero utters a line that has often been quoted by readers: "To say 'I love you' one must know first how to say the 'I.' " [. . .]

When you are in love, it means that the person you love is of great personal, selfish importance to you and to your life. If you were selfless, it would have to mean that you derive no personal pleasure or happiness from the company and the existence of the person you love, and that you are motivated only by self-sacrificial pity for that person's need of you. I don't have to point out to you that no one would be flattered by, nor would accept, a concept of that kind. Love is not self-sacrifice, but the most profound assertion of your own needs and values. It is for your *own* happiness that you need the person you love, and that is the greatest compliment, the greatest tribute you can pay to that person. . . .

3. Theory of Concepts

In 1966, AR *published her seminal (and most technical) work in philosophy,* Introduction to Objectivist Epistemology. *Its purpose is to validate reason on the most fundamental level—by identifying the nature, and the basis in reality, of the human mind's unique form of knowledge: concepts. This book is AR's answer to the nominalists and the "realists" in philosophy, i.e., to the "problem of universals."*

We have included in the following selections some essentials from her theory of concepts—along with a few excerpts from the seminars she gave on the book when it first came out; the seminars were attended mostly by philosophers unfamiliar with her theory.

Concept-Formation

A CONCEPT is a mental integration of two or more units which are isolated according to a specific characteristic(s) and united by a specific definition.

The units involved may be any aspect of reality: entities, attributes, actions, qualities, relationships, etc.; they may be perceptual concretes or other, earlier-formed concepts. The act of isolation involved is a process of *abstraction*: i.e., a selective mental focus that *takes out* or separates a certain aspect of reality from all others (e.g., isolates a certain attribute from the entities possessing it, or a certain action from the entities performing it, etc.). The uniting involved is not a mere sum, but an *integration*, i.e., a blending of the units into a *single*, new *mental* entity which is used thereafter as a single unit of thought (but which can be broken into its component units whenever required).

In order to be used as a single unit, the enormous sum integrated by a concept has to be given the form of a single, specific, *perceptual* concrete, which will differentiate it from all other concretes and from all other concepts. This is the function performed by language. Language is a code of visual-auditory symbols that serves the psycho-epistemological function of converting concepts into the mental equivalent of concretes. Language is the exclusive domain and tool of concepts. Every word we use (with the exception of proper names) is a symbol that denotes a concept, i.e., that stands for an unlimited number of concretes of a certain kind.

(Proper names are used in order to identify and include particular entities in a conceptual method of cognition. Observe that even proper names, in advanced civilizations, follow the definitional principles of *genus* and *differentia*: e.g., John Smith, with "Smith" serving as *genus* and "John" as *differentia*—or New York, U.S.A.)

Words transform concepts into (mental) entities; *definitions* provide them with *identity*. (Words without definitions are not language but inarticulate sounds.) We shall discuss definitions later and at length.

The above is a general description of the nature of concepts as products of a certain mental process. But *the* question of epistemology is: what precisely is the nature of that process? To what precisely do concepts refer in reality?

Let us now examine the process of forming the simplest concept, the concept of a single attribute (chronologically, this is not the first concept that a child would grasp; but it is the simplest one epistemologically)—for instance, the concept *"length."* If a child considers a match, a pencil and a stick, he observes that length is the attribute they have in common, but their specific lengths differ. The *difference is one of measurement.* In order to form the concept "length," the child's mind retains the attribute and omits its particular measurements. Or, more precisely, if the process were identified in words, it would consist of the following: "Length must exist in *some* quantity, but may exist in *any* quantity. I shall identify as 'length' that attribute of any existent possessing it which can be quantitatively related to a unit of length, without specifying the quantity."

The child does not think in such words (he has, as yet, no knowledge of words), but *that* is the nature of the process which his mind performs wordlessly. And that is the principle which his mind follows, when, having grasped the concept "length" by observing the three objects, he uses it to identify the attribute of length in a piece of string, a ribbon, a belt, a corridor or a street.

The same principle directs the process of forming concepts of entities—for instance, the concept *"table."* The child's mind isolates two or more tables from other objects, by focusing on their distinctive characteristic: their shape. He observes that their shapes vary, but have one characteristic in common: a flat, level surface and support(s). He forms the concept "table" by retaining that characteristic and omitting *all* particular measurements, not only the measurements of the shape, but of all the other characteristics of tables (many of which he is not aware of at the time).

An adult definition of "table" would be: "A man-made object consisting of a flat, level surface and support(s), intended to support other, smaller objects." Observe what is specified and what is omitted in this definition: the distinctive characteristic of the shape is specified and retained; the particular geometrical measurements of the shape (whether the surface is square, round, oblong or triangular, etc., the number and shape of supports, etc.) are omitted; the measurements of size or weight are omitted; the fact that it is a material object is specified, but the material of which it is made is omitted, thus omitting the measurements that differentiate one material from another; etc. Observe, however, that the utilitarian requirements of the table set certain limits on the omitted measurements, in the form of "no larger than and no smaller than" required by its purpose. This rules out a ten-foot tall or a two-inch tall table (though the latter may be sub-classified as a toy or a miniature table) and it rules out unsuitable materials, such as non-solids.

Bear firmly in mind that the term "measurements omitted" does not mean, in this context, that measurements are regarded as non-existent; it means that *measurements exist, but are not specified.* That measurements *must* exist is an essential part of the process. The principle is: the relevant measurements must exist in *some* quantity, but may exist in *any* quantity.

A child is not and does not have to be aware of all these complexities when he forms the concept "table." He forms it by differentiating tables from all other objects *in the context of his knowledge.* As his knowledge grows, the definitions of his concepts grow in complexity. (We shall discuss this when we discuss definitions.) But the principle and pattern of concept-formation remain the same.

The first words a child learns are words denoting visual objects, and he retains his first concepts *visually*. Observe that the visual form he gives them is reduced to those *essentials* which distinguish the particular kind of entities from all others—for instance, the universal type of a child's drawing of man in the form of an oval for the torso, a circle for the head, four sticks for extremities, etc. Such drawings are a visual record of the process of abstraction and concept-formation in a mind's transition from the perceptual level to the full vocabulary of the conceptual level.

There is evidence to suppose that written language originated in the form of drawings—as the pictographic writing of the Oriental peoples seems to indicate. With the growth of man's knowledge and of his power of abstraction, a pictorial representation of concepts could no longer be adequate to his conceptual range, and was replaced by a fully symbolic code.

A concept is a mental integration of two or more units possessing the same distinguishing characteristic(s), with their particular measurements omitted.

The element of *similarity* is crucially involved in the formation of every concept; similarity, in this context, is the relationship between two or more existents which possess the same characteristic(s), but in different measure or degree.

Observe the multiple role of measurements in the process of concept-formation, in both of its two essential parts: differentiation and integration. Concepts cannot be formed at random. All concepts are formed by first differentiating two or more existents from other existents. All conceptual differentiations are made in terms of *commensurable characteristics* (i.e., characteristics possessing a common unit of measurement). No concept could be formed, for instance, by attempting to distinguish long objects from green objects. Incommensurable characteristics cannot be integrated into one unit.

Tables, for instance, are first differentiated from chairs, beds and other objects by means of the characteristic of *shape*, which is an attribute possessed by all the objects involved. Then, their particular kind of shape is set as the distinguishing characteristic of tables—i.e., a certain category of geometrical measurements of shape is specified. Then, within that category, the particular measurements of individual table-shapes are omitted.

Please note the fact that a given shape represents a certain category or set of geometrical measurements. Shape is an attribute; differences of shape—whether cubes, spheres, cones or any complex combinations—are a matter of differing measurements; any shape can be reduced to or expressed by a set of figures in terms of *linear measurement*. When, in the process of concept-formation, man observes that shape is a commensurable characteristic of certain objects, he does not have to measure all the shapes involved *nor even to know how to measure them*; he merely has to observe the element of *similarity*.

Similarity is grasped *perceptually*; in observing it, man is not and does not have to be aware of the fact that it involves a matter of measurement. It is the task of philosophy and of science to identify that fact.

As to the actual process of measuring shapes, a vast part of higher mathematics, from geometry on up, is devoted to the task of discovering methods by which various shapes can be measured—complex methods which consist of reducing the problem to the terms of a simple, primitive method, the only one available to man in this field: linear measurement. (Integral calculus, used to measure the area of circles, is just one example.)

In this respect, concept-formation and applied mathematics have a similar task, just as philosophical epistemology and theoretical mathematics have a similar goal: the goal and task of bringing the universe within the range of man's knowledge—by identifying relationships to perceptual data.

Another example of implicit measurement can be seen in the process of forming concepts of colors. Man forms such concepts by observing that the various shades of blue are similar, as against the shades of red, and thus differentiating the range of blue from the range of red, of yellow, etc. Centuries passed before science discovered the unit by which colors could actually be measured: the wavelengths of light—a discovery that supported, in terms of mathematical proof, the differentiations that men were and are making in terms of visual similarities. (Any questions about "borderline cases" will be answered later.)

A commensurable characteristic (such as shape in the case of tables, or hue in the case of colors) is an essential element in the process of concept-formation. I shall designate it as the "Conceptual Common Denominator" and define it as "The characteristic(s) reducible to a unit of measurement, by means of which man differentiates two or more existents from other existents possessing it."

The distinguishing characteristic(s) of a concept represents a specified category of measurements within the "Conceptual Common Denominator" involved.

New concepts can be formed by integrating earlier-formed concepts into wider categories, or by subdividing them into narrower categories (a process which we shall discuss later). But all concepts are ultimately reducible to their base in perceptual entities, which are the base (the given) of man's cognitive development.

The first concepts man forms are concepts of entities—since entities are the only primary existents. (Attributes cannot exist by themselves, they are merely the characteristics of entities; motions are motions of entities; relationships are relationships among entities.)

In the process of forming concepts of entities, a child's mind has to focus on a distinguishing characteristic—i.e., on an attribute—in order to isolate one group of entities from all others. He is, therefore, aware of attributes while forming his first concepts, but he is aware of them *perceptually, not* conceptually. It is only after he has grasped a number of concepts of entities that he can advance to the stage of abstracting attributes from entities and forming separate concepts of attributes. The same is true of concepts of motion: a child is aware of motion *perceptually,* but cannot conceptualize "motion" until he has formed some concepts of that which moves, i.e., of entities.

(As far as can be ascertained, the perceptual level of a child's awareness is similar to the awareness of the higher animals: the higher animals are able to perceive entities, motions, attributes, and certain numbers of entities. But what an animal cannot perform is the process of abstraction—of mentally separating attributes, motions or numbers from entities. It has been said that an animal can perceive two oranges or two potatoes, but cannot grasp the concept "two.")

Concepts of *materials* are formed by observing the differences in the constituent materials of entities. (Materials exist only in the form of specific entities, such as a nugget of gold, a plank of wood, a drop or an ocean of water.) The concept of "gold," for instance, is formed by isolating gold objects from all others, then abstracting and retaining the material, the gold, and omitting the measurements of the objects (or of the alloys) in which gold may exist. Thus, the material is the same in all the concrete instances subsumed under the concept, and differs only in quantity.

Concepts of *motion* are formed by specifying the distinctive nature of the motion and of the entities performing it, and/or of the medium in which it is performed—and omitting the particular measurements of any given instance of such motion and of the entities involved. For instance, the concept "walking" denotes a certain kind of motion performed by living entities possessing legs, and does not apply to the motion of a snake or of an automobile. The concept "swimming" denotes the motion of any living entity propelling itself through water, and does not apply to the motion of a boat. The concept "flying" denotes the motion of any entity propelling itself through the air, whether a bird or an airplane.

Adverbs are concepts of the characteristics of motion (or action); they are formed by specifying a characteristic and omitting the measurements of the motion and of the entities involved—e.g., "rapidly," which may be applied to "walking" or "swimming" or "speaking," etc., with the measurement of what is "rapid" left open and depending, in any given case, on the type of motion involved.

Prepositions are concepts of relationships, predominantly of spatial or temporal relationships, among existents; they are formed by specifying the relationship and omitting the measurements of the existents and of the space or time involved—e.g., "on," "in," "above," "after," etc.

Adjectives are concepts of attributes or of characteristics. *Pronouns* belong to the category of concepts of entities. *Conjunctions* are concepts of relationships among thoughts, and belong to the category of concepts of consciousness.

As to concepts of consciousness, we shall discuss them later and at length. (To anticipate questions such as: "Can you measure love?"— I shall permit myself the very philosophical answer: "And how!")

Now we can answer the question: To what precisely do we refer when we designate three persons as "men"? We refer to the fact that they are living beings who possess the *same* characteristic distinguishing them from all other living species: a rational faculty—though the specific measurements of their distinguishing characteristic *qua* men, as well as of all their other characteristics *qua* living beings, are different. (As living beings of a certain kind, they possess innumerable characteristics in common: the same shape, the same range of size, the same facial features, the same vital organs, the same fingerprints, etc., and all these characteristics differ only in their measurements.)

Two links between the conceptual and the mathematical fields are worth noting at this point, apart from the obvious fact that the concept "unit" is the base and start of both.

1. A concept is not formed by observing every concrete subsumed under it, and does not specify the number of such concretes. A concept is like an arithmetical sequence of *specifically defined units,* going off in both directions, open at both ends and including *all* units of that particular kind. For instance, the concept "man" includes all men who live at present, who have ever lived or will ever live. An arithmetical sequence extends into infinity, without implying that infinity actually exists; such extension means only that whatever number of units does exist, it is to be included in the same sequence. The same principle applies to concepts: the concept "man" does not (and need not) specify what number of men will ultimately have existed— it specifies only the characteristics of man, and means that any number of entities possessing these characteristics is to be identified as "men."

2. The basic principle of concept-formation (which states that the omitted measurements must exist in *some* quantity, but may exist in *any* quantity) is the equivalent of the basic principle of algebra, which states that algebraic symbols must be given *some* numerical value, but may be given *any* value. In this sense and respect, perceptual awareness is the arithmetic, but *conceptual awareness is the algebra of cognition.*

The relationship of concepts to their constituent particulars is the same as the relationship of algebraic symbols to numbers. In the equation $2a = a + a$, any number may be substituted for the symbol "a" without affecting the truth of the equation. For instance: $2 \times 5 = 5 + 5$, or: $2 \times 5,000,000 = 5,000,000 + 5,000,000$. In the same manner, by the same psycho-epistemological method, a concept is used as an algebraic symbol that stands for *any* of the arithmetical sequence of units it subsumes.

Let those who attempt to invalidate concepts by declaring that they cannot find "manness" in men, try to invalidate algebra by declaring that they cannot find "a-ness" in 5 or in 5,000,000.

*   *   *

[. . .] Let us note, at this point, the radical difference between Aristotle's view of concepts and the Objectivist view, particularly in regard to the issue of essential characteristics.

It is Aristotle who first formulated the principles of correct definition. It is Aristotle who identified the fact that only concretes exist. But Aristotle held that definitions refer to metaphysical *essences,* which exist *in* concretes as a special element or formative power, and he held that the process of concept-formation depends on a kind of direct intuition by which man's mind grasps these essences and forms concepts accordingly.

Aristotle regarded "essence" as metaphysical; Objectivism regards it as *epistemological*.

Objectivism holds that the essence of a concept is that fundamental characteristic(s) of its units on which the greatest number of other characteristics depend, and which distinguishes these units from all other existents within the field of man's knowledge. Thus the essence of a concept is determined *contextually* and may be altered with the growth of man's knowledge. The metaphysical referent of man's concepts is not a special, separate metaphysical essence, but the *total* of the facts of reality he has observed, and this total determines which characteristics of a given group of existents he designates as *essential*. An essential characteristic is factual, in the sense that it does exist, does determine other characteristics and does distinguish a group of existents from all others; it is *epistemological* in the sense that the classification of "essential characteristic" is a device of man's method of cognition—a means of classifying, condensing and integrating an ever-growing body of knowledge.

Now refer to the four historical schools of thought on the issue of concepts, which I listed in the foreword to this work—and observe that the dichotomy of "intrinsic or subjective" has played havoc with this issue, as it has with every issue involving the relationship of consciousness to existence.

The extreme realist (Platonist) and the moderate realist (Aristotelian) schools of thought regard the referents of concepts as *intrinsic*, i.e., as "universals" inherent in things (either as archetypes or as metaphysical essences), as special existents unrelated to man's consciousness—to be perceived by man directly, like any other kind of concrete existents, but perceived by some non-sensory or extra-sensory means.

The nominalist and the conceptualist schools regard concepts as *subjective*, i.e., as products of man's consciousness, unrelated to the facts of reality, as mere "names" or notions arbitrarily assigned to arbitrary groupings of concretes on the ground of vague, inexplicable resemblances.

The extreme realist school attempts, in effect, to preserve the primacy of existence (of reality) by dispensing with consciousness—i.e., by converting concepts into concrete existents and reducing consciousness to the perceptual level, i.e., to the automatic function of grasping percepts (by supernatural means, since no such percepts exist).

The extreme nominalist (contemporary) school attempts to establish the primacy of consciousness by dispensing with existence (with reality)—i.e., by denying the status of existents even to concretes and converting concepts into conglomerates of fantasy, constructed out of the debris of other, lesser fantasies, such as words without referents or incantations of sounds corresponding to nothing in an unknowable reality.

To compound the chaos: it must be noted that the Platonist school begins by accepting the primacy of consciousness, by reversing the relationship of consciousness to existence, by assuming that reality must conform to the content of consciousness, not the other way around—on the premise that the presence of any notion in man's mind proves the existence of a corresponding referent in reality. But the Platonist school still retains some vestige of respect for reality, if only in unstated motivation: it distorts reality into a mystical construct in order to extort its sanction and validate subjectivism. The nominalist school begins, with empiricist humility, by negating the power of consciousness to form any valid generalizations about existence—and ends up with a subjectivism that requires no sanction, a consciousness freed from the "tyranny" of reality.

None of these schools regards concepts as *objective*, i.e., as neither revealed nor invented, but as produced by man's consciousness in accordance with the facts of reality, as mental integrations of factual data computed by man—as the products of a cognitive method of classification whose processes must be performed by man, but whose content is dictated by reality.

It is as if, philosophically, mankind is still in the stage of transition which characterizes a child in the process of learning to speak—a child who is using his conceptual faculty, but has not developed it sufficiently to be able to examine it self-consciously and discover that what he is using is *reason*.

Consciousness and Identity

. . . MAN IS neither infallible nor omniscient; if he were, a discipline such as epistemology—the theory of knowledge—would not be necessary nor possible: his knowledge would be automatic, unquestionable and total. But such is not man's nature. Man is a being of volitional consciousness: beyond the level of percepts—a level inadequate to the cognitive requirements of his survival—man has to acquire knowledge by his own effort, which he may exercise or not, and by a process of reason, which he may apply correctly or not. Nature gives him no automatic guarantee of his mental efficacy; he is capable of error, of evasion, of psychological distortion. He needs a *method* of cognition, which he himself has to discover: he must discover how to use his rational faculty, how to validate his conclusions, how to distinguish truth from falsehood, how to set the criteria of *what* he may accept as knowledge. Two questions are involved in his every conclusion, conviction, decision, choice or claim: *What* do I know?—and: *How* do I know it?

It is the task of epistemology to provide the answer to the "How?"—which then enables the special sciences to provide the answers to the "What?"

In the history of philosophy—with some very rare exceptions—epistemological theories have consisted of attempts to escape one or the other of the two fundamental questions which cannot be escaped. Men have been taught either that knowledge is impossible (skepticism) or that it is available without effort (mysticism). These two positions appear to be antagonists, but are, in fact, two variants on the same theme, two sides of the same fraudulent coin: the attempt to escape the responsibility of rational cognition and the absolutism of reality—the attempt to assert the primacy of consciousness over existence.

Although skepticism and mysticism are ultimately interchangeable, and the dominance of one always leads to the resurgence of the other, they differ in the form of their inner contradiction—the contradiction, in both cases, between their philosophical doctrine and their psychological motivation. Philosophically, the mystic is usually an exponent of the *intrinsic* (revealed) school of epistemology; the skeptic is usually an advocate of epistemological *subjectivism*. But, psychologically, the mystic is a subjectivist who uses intrinsicism as a means to claim the primacy of *his* consciousness over that of others. The skeptic is a disillusioned intrinsicist who, having failed to find automatic supernatural guidance, seeks a substitute in the collective subjectivism of others.

The motive of all the attacks on man's rational faculty—from any quarter, in any of the endless variations, under the verbal dust of all the murky volumes—is a single, hidden premise: the desire to exempt consciousness from the law of identity. The hallmark of a mystic is the savagely stubborn refusal to accept the fact that consciousness, like any other existent, possesses identity, that it is a faculty of a specific nature, functioning through specific means. While the advance of civilization has been eliminating one area of magic after another, the last stand of the believers in the miraculous consists of their frantic attempts to regard *identity* as the *disqualifying* element of consciousness.

The implicit, but unadmitted premise of the neo-mystics of modern philosophy, is the notion that only an ineffable consciousness can acquire a valid knowledge of reality, that "true" knowledge has to be causeless, i.e., acquired without any means of cognition.

The entire apparatus of Kant's system, like a hippopotamus engaged in belly-dancing, goes through its gyrations while resting on a single point: that man's knowledge is not valid because his consciousness possesses identity. "His argument, in essence, ran as follows: man is *limited* to a consciousness of a specific nature, which perceives by specific means and no others, therefore, his consciousness is not valid; man is blind, because he has eyes—deaf, because he has ears—deluded, because he has a mind—and the things he perceives do not exist, *because* he perceives them." (*For the New Intellectual.*)

This is a negation, not only of man's consciousness, but of *any* consciousness, of consciousness as such, whether man's, insect's or God's. (If one supposed the existence of God, the negation would still apply: either God perceives through no means whatever, in which case he possesses no identity—or he perceives by some divine means and no others, in which case his perception is not valid.) As Berkeley negated existence by claiming that "to be, is to be perceived," so Kant negates consciousness by implying that to be perceived, is not to be.

What Kant implied through coils of obfuscating verbiage, his more consistent followers declared explicitly. The following was written by a Kantian: "With him [Kant] all is phenomenal [mere appearance] which is relative, and all is relative which is an object to a conscious subject. The conceptions of the understanding as much depend on the constitution of our thinking faculties, as the perceptions of the senses do on the constitution of our intuitive faculties. Both *might* be different, were our mental constitution changed; both probably *are* different to beings differently constituted. The *real* thus becomes identical with the *absolute*, with the object as it is in itself, out of all relation to a subject; and, as all consciousness is a relation between subject and object, it follows that to attain a knowledge of the real we must go out of consciousness." (Henry Mansel, "On the Philosophy of Kant," reprinted in Henry Mansel, *Letters, Lectures and Reviews*, ed. H. W. Chandler, London: John Murray, 1873, p. 171.)

From primordial mysticism to this, its climax, the attack on man's consciousness and particularly on his conceptual faculty has rested on the unchallenged premise that any knowledge acquired by a *process* of consciousness is necessarily subjective and cannot correspond to the facts of reality, since it is "*processed* knowledge."

Make no mistake about the actual meaning of that premise: it is a revolt, not only against being conscious, but against being alive—since in fact, in reality, on earth, every aspect of being alive involves a process of self-sustaining and self-generated action. (This is an example of the fact that the revolt against identity is a revolt against existence. "The desire not to be anything, is the desire not to be." *Atlas Shrugged.*)

All knowledge *is* processed knowledge—whether on the sensory, perceptual or conceptual level. An "unprocessed" knowledge would be a knowledge acquired without means of cognition. Consciousness (as I said in the first sentence of this work) is not a passive state, but an active process. And more: the satisfaction of every need of a living organism requires an act of *processing* by that organism, be it the need of air, of food or of knowledge.

No one would argue (at least, not yet) that since man's body has to *process* the food he eats, no objective rules of proper nutrition can ever be discovered—that "true nutrition" has to consist of absorbing some ineffable substance without the participation of a digestive system, but since man is incapable of "true feeding," nutrition is a subjective matter open to his whim, and it is merely a social convention that forbids him to eat poisonous mushrooms.

No one would argue that since nature does not tell man automatically what to eat—as it does not tell him automatically how to form concepts—he should abandon the illusion that there is a right or wrong way of eating (or he should revert to the safety of the time when he did not have to "trust" objective evidence, but could rely on dietary laws prescribed by a supernatural power).

No one would argue that man eats bread rather than stones purely as a matter of "convenience."

It is time to grant to man's consciousness the same cognitive respect one grants to his body—i.e., the same *objectivity*.

Objectivity begins with the realization that man (including his every attribute and faculty, including his consciousness) is an entity of a specific nature who must act accordingly; that there is no escape from the law of identity, neither in the universe with which he deals nor in the working of his own consciousness, and if he is to acquire knowledge of the first, he must discover the proper method of using the second; that there is no room for the *arbitrary* in any activity of man, least of all in his method of cognition—and just as he has learned to be guided by objective criteria in making his physical tools, so he must be guided by objective criteria in forming his tools of cognition: his concepts.

Just as man's physical existence was liberated when he grasped the principle that "nature, to be commanded, must be obeyed," so his consciousness will be liberated when he grasps that *nature, to be apprehended, must be obeyed*—that the rules of cognition must be derived from the nature of existence and the nature, the *identity*, of his cognitive faculty.

Abstraction from Abstractions

First-Level Concepts

Prof. F: I have a fundamental question about the hierarchy of concepts. On page 22 you say, "The meaning of 'furniture' cannot be grasped unless one has first grasped the meaning of its constituent concepts; these are its link to reality." Now, what about the meaning of "table": can we say that the meaning of "table" cannot be grasped unless one has first grasped the meaning of "dining table," "conference table," "writing table," and so forth? Are these its constituent concepts? Or is the concept "table" a kind of privileged concept that comes at a kind of absolute bottom in the hierarchy of concepts and has a direct relationship to reality?

Or would you say that where a concept comes is determined by the context of one's own learning? For instance, might a person form the concept of "furniture" without having formed the concept of "table" before? Might he form the concept of "living being" before he has formed the concept of "animal"?

AR: In a sense, yes. There is a big problem here, however, whether this applies all the way through the conceptual chain—which I would claim cannot be the case. But, on the level we are discussing, there is a certain element of the optional. Because when you first form your concepts, you might conceivably first form in a very loose way the concepts "living entity" versus "inanimate object," and later subdivide into "man," "animals," "plants," etc. (and "tables," "rocks," "houses," on the other hand). In a loose way, that can be done, but only up to a certain level. Because, suppose you started with the concept "living being." You would then find that that is too generalized a category, and you would have to say, in effect, "By living beings I mean men, animals, and plants."

Therefore, understanding what your original semi-concept "living being" meant would depend on what you mean by the constituents, such as "man," "animal," and "plant."

What then is the ultimate determinant here? What I call the "first level" of concepts are existential concretes—that to which you can *point* as if it were an ostensive definition and say: "I mean *this*." Now, you can point to a table. You cannot point to furniture. You have to say, "By furniture I mean . . ." and you would have to include all kinds of objects.

Prof. F: Why wouldn't one have an equal difficulty when one came, let's say, to the concept of "bird"? Why wouldn't one have to say, "By bird, I mean eagles, penguins, and hummingbirds"?

AR: Because, in fact, one doesn't. And that is the difference between subcategories of concepts and first-level concepts. Because, you see, you could not arrive at the differences between eagles, hummingbirds, etc., unless you had first separated birds from other animals.

Even if chronologically you may learn those concepts in different orders, ultimately when you organize your concepts to determine which are basic-level concepts and which are derivatives (in both directions, wider integration or narrower subdivision), the test will be: which objects you perceive directly in reality and can point to, and which you have to differentiate by means of other concepts.

Prof. F: Then you are suggesting that metaphysically there are certain lowest species or infima species: certain concepts that are directly tied to concretes. Whereas, on top of them, we continually build higher-order concepts, which refer, in turn, to the lower.

AR: Yes, if you mean, by "metaphysical," existential objects—entities which exist qua entities.

Prof. E: I'd like to ask a follow-up question. This is the kind of question I get all the time, which I do not fully know how to answer. I will give the example: "table" is first-level, and then you can go up to "furniture" or down to "living-room table," etc.

AR: That's right.

Prof. E: Then I get this kind of question: Is it theoretically possible for someone to start by first conceptualizing living-room tables (he wouldn't, of course, be able to call it "living-room *table*" since he wouldn't yet have the concept "table") and then "desk," etc. and have separate concepts for all of what *we* call subcategories of "table," and then one day, in effect, grasp in an act of higher integration that they have something uniting them all, and reach the concept "table"?

AR: Theoretically, maybe; existentially, no. By which I mean that in order to do that, if that is how a child starts, he would have to live in a furniture store. He would have to have observed an enormous number of certain kinds of tables so that he isolates them first and then arrives at the overall category, which is "table."

Here, the process is directed by what is available to the child's observation when he begins to form the concept.

Prof. E: Would the state of his ability to discriminate also be relevant to defining what is a first-level concept? In other words, he couldn't perhaps discriminate subtler distinctions before he had the gross category.

AR: Exactly. And he has to have, and this is very essential, a sufficient number of examples of a given category differentiated from other dissimilar entities before he can form a concept.

Prof. E: What do you say about this objection? People say you can't point to table, all you can point to is living-room table, or dining-room table, etc., and, therefore, how do you distinguish "table" from "furniture" in this respect?

AR: The answer is in the Conceptual Common Denominator. If you point to table and you say, "I mean this," what do you differentiate it from? From chairs, cabinets, beds, etc. You do not mean only a dining-room table but not an end table. What is involved here, in the act of pointing, as in everything about concepts, is: from what are you differentiating it?

Prof. B: Isn't the issue then what similarities and differences you are able to be aware of? And wouldn't that be a function of two things: the actual properties of the objects plus the context that you are in?

AR: That's right.

Prof. B: Take the earlier question of whether you could form the concept of "furniture" before the concept "table." In order to do that, you would have to perceive the similarities uniting all items of furniture before you perceived the difference between a table and, say, a bed. And the question is: how could that ever come up?

AR: The difficulty here is that the infant or child would have to have a much wider range of perception than is normal to a beginning consciousness. He would have to consider objects outside of the room, objects moving in the street, and then conclude: by "furniture" I mean the objects in this room. Even subverbally, if this is what he observes, he has already made an enormously wide range of observations, which is not likely as a beginning. In logic, there would be objections to that, because how would he differentiate furniture from, let's say, moving vehicles in the street? How did he get to that wide a range without first observing the immediate differences and similarities around him?

Prof. B: If he looked at a bed and a dresser, let's say, he would have to see them as different before he saw them as similar.

AR: That's right. Also, remember that we use "table" as an example because that is the object most likely to be one of the first perceived by a child in our civilization. But now suppose a child has to grasp the concept "coconut." In our civilization that would be a much later development. He would probably first grasp "food," then maybe "apple" and "pear," until some day he discovers an unusual food—a coconut. But now take a child in a primitive society, in a jungle. He never heard of tables, and he might be bewildered when he first sees a table in the home of the local missionary. But "coconut" might be one of the first concepts he forms because coconuts are all around him.

The overall rule for what is first-level is: those existential concretes which are first available to your consciousness. But they have to be concretes. A first-level concept cannot be one which, in order to indicate what you mean by it, requires other concepts, as is the case with "furniture." "Furniture" is not a term designating concretes directly. It is a term designating different kinds of concretes which all have to be conceptualized, as against another very broad category, such as moving vehicles, let us say.

In other words, if, after you have acquired a conceptual vocabulary, a given concept cannot be understood by you or communicated by you without reference to other concepts, then it is a higher-level concept, even if maybe somehow you grasped it first (and I question the issue of whether you could grasp it first). But the hierarchy that you will establish eventually when you are in the realm of a developed language, the hierarchy of which concept depends on the other, will not be determined by the accidental order in which *you* learned them, because that can have a great deal of the optional element and depends on what is available in your immediate surroundings.

It is after you are in the realm of language, when you can organize your concepts and say what you mean by "table," what you mean by "furniture"—it is at this level, logically and not chronologically, that you can determine which are concepts of the first order and which are derivatives.

Induction

Prof. H: This is a common question relating to induction. Someone is boiling water, and he notices that every time the water gets to a certain temperature, it boils. Now he wants to know: does all water boil at that temperature, or is it only due to some accidental feature about this particular water? How does he determine whether it's accidental or essential?

AR: By whether you can or cannot establish a causal connection between what you have determined to be the essential characteristic of water and the fact that it boils at a certain temperature.

Prof. H: I suppose what I'm asking is: how do you establish the causal connection?

AR: That's a scientific question. But, in essence, what you do is this. Let's say you have to establish the molecular structure of water. How do those molecules act at a certain temperature? And if you see that something happens to the molecules which causes boiling at a certain temperature, you conclude: that's essential to the nature of water, adding the parenthesis: "within the present context of my knowledge." You will later discover that water behaves differently at a different altitude. So you never claim water necessarily, as an absolute, will always and everywhere boil at the same temperature. No, you say, "Within my present context, omitting elements of which I have no knowledge at present, water will always boil at a certain temperature, because boiling is a state depending on certain kind of molecular motions, and water's molecules will always reach that stage at a certain temperature."

Now, with later development, you might discover that maybe there are differences in certain molecules of water when in an impure state. Or with atomic additions, say, something else happens. But then your context has changed. You don't say that water has changed. It's only that your definition of how the essential characteristic of water will function will have to include more: what water will do at sea level, what it will do at higher altitudes, and what it will do under new molecular or atomic influences, or in relation to some scientific phenomenon not yet known to any of us. But the principle there is the same. Does that answer it?

Prof. H: I have to think about it.

AR: Okay, but ask again later, because I don't want to leave you with semi-answers. And that is the rational procedure: think it over, and if a further question occurs to you, then ask me later. This applies to everybody else as well. If any answer is only partial, the right thing to do is to think it over, because one can't discuss it and integrate it at the same time. If you see that there is still an area not covered, then ask me later.

Prof. A: How would you answer this common objection to your answer? In relating the boiling of water to the energy required to break certain molecular bonds, you haven't actually made any progress in regard to the induction, because you've only got the same kind of generalization on the molecular level that you had before on the gross, macroscopic level. You now know, "In a given number of cases, it has always taken a certain amount of energy to break this molecular bond." But that fact has the same sort of status as the fact you started with: "In a given number of cases, I heated the water to 212 degrees, and it always boiled." I know the objection is crazy, because in some way you do have more knowledge when you've gone down to the molecular level. But I can't see what the error is.

AR: But you see, you answered it. When you simply boil water, you do not know that it has molecules, nor what happens to those molecules. When you arrive at that later stage of knowledge, you've discovered something about water and the conditions of its boiling which you didn't know before. And, therefore, within your present context, this is a sufficient explanation, even though it's not the exclusive and final explanation. To reach that you would have to have omniscience. But, if you can say, "It's in the nature of water that it's composed of molecules, and something happens to those molecules at a certain temperature, this explains to me why water boils," that is a causal explanation. It isn't the same thing as saying, "I don't know why it boils, but if I heat it, it bubbles up." That's all that you knew before. And, therefore, your knowledge is now further advanced.

Prof. A: But it seems that the certainty that you were first trying to attach to the idea that water boils under certain conditions is derivative from the degree of certainty you have concerning the idea that a certain amount of energy disrupts the molecules.

AR: If this is supposed to be on the same level, what would the person raising this objection consider to be a different level?

Prof. A: Yes, that's exactly the problem.

AR: That's not the problem. No. That's the method of ruling his objection out. Because you discover that he has no ground for his conclusion that you're on the same level. Look at the facts. You observe that water boils. You discover something in the constituent elements of water that causes it. You know more than you did before. But he tells you, "No, you're at the same place." Then you ask him, "What place do you want to go to? What do you regard as knowledge?"

Prof. E: And then his answer would be that he wants a mystic apprehension of "necessity," which he hasn't yet received. All he has is "contingent" facts.

AR: Yes. And you ask him what does he regard the facts of reality as: a necessity or a contingency? He'll say, "Of course it's a contingency, because God made it this way, and he could have made it another." And you say, "Good-bye."

Prof. F: But I am not clear why it is a significant step when one goes from the macroscopic phenomenon, boiling, to the molecular level. Why does one then say, "Aha! Now, within our present context of knowledge, we've made a satisfactory advance."

AR: Let's ask something wider: what is knowledge? And what is study, what is observation? It's the discovery of properties in the nature of certain objects, existents, entities. All knowledge consists of learning more and more about the nature—the properties and characteristics—of given objects. So first you see only water—just that. Then you observe that it boils at a certain point. Your knowledge is advanced. You know more about water than you did when you only observed it in a lake. Then you discover such a thing as molecules, then you discover the molecular structure of water. Your knowledge about what water is is still greater. Now you observe what happens to those molecules when you apply a certain amount of energy. Your knowledge is still greater. If it isn't, what do you mean by knowledge?

Prof. F: Both you and your positivist opponents would agree that the knowledge is greater. But they would then raise the question of whether one has to go a further step or not—or why one should have made this step in the first place. Why does the breaking of the macroscopic down into the molecular constitute a significant step, whereas the addition of some other type of knowledge—

AR: Such as?

Prof. F: Such as the knowledge of, say, the shape of the water at present, or the electrical charges involved.

AR: All that is knowledge. The knowledge of anything that can happen to water—what temperature it will freeze at, how it reflects light—any characteristic of a given object of study is knowledge. If you can establish that this characteristic pertains to water, you have learned something new about water.

But if the problem here involves the issue of necessity vs. contingency, then it's a prescientific problem, a strictly philosophical problem. What do you mean by "necessity"? By "necessity," we mean that things are a certain way and had to be. I would maintain that the statement "Things are," when referring to non-man-made occurrences, is the synonym of "They had to be." Because unless we start with the premise of an arbitrary God who creates nature, what is had to be. We have to drop any mystical premise and keep the full context in mind. Then, aside from human action, what things are is what they had to be.

The alternative of what "had to be" versus what "didn't have to be" doesn't apply metaphysically. It applies only to the realm of human action and human choice. For instance, will you wear a gray suit or a blue suit? That's up to you. You didn't have to wear either one. Let's assume you have only one suit. Even then you can't say you had to wear it. You chose to wear it rather than be naked. Anything pertaining to actions open to human choice raises the question: "Is it necessary or is it volitional?" But in regard to facts which are metaphysical—that is, not created by a human action—there is no such thing as necessity—or, the fact of existence is the necessity.

Prof. A: I think that was exactly my problem. I was assuming that the fact that a certain entity had always done a certain thing had no significance in itself—that it could be otherwise tomorrow. But actually, something would act differently tomorrow only if a new factor entered in.

AR: Yes.

Prof. A: And by going to the molecular level, you tend to exclude any new factor; you have more awareness of the mechanism operating, so you have more knowledge of what is going to affect it and what isn't; you understand what the process is that's happening. I was assuming exactly what you were saying, that the fact that the energy required was so-and-so today, might change tomorrow, because of God knows what. So the answer lies in the point that necessity is just identity.

AR: Exactly.

Prof. C: On this issue of boiling water and finding out that it must boil because of understanding its molecular structure: isn't it related in some way to the issue of unit-economy in concepts? Because in theory-formation one attempts to condense a vast amount of knowledge into a smaller and smaller number of principles. And when one is able to explain the boiling of water in terms of the electrons and protons, not only does one explain boiling as necessary from these few facts, but also one explains a vast number of other characteristics, properties, and set of behaviors for water and a whole scad of other substances.

AR: Oh yes.

Prof. C: So when you go to that level, you have widened your knowledge to a much larger scope by integrating the data to a few simple laws, such as, in this case, the properties of the electrons.

AR: You mean, it is also applicable to more than water, and if you discover how the molecules of water react to heat, you then open the way to discoveries concerning how other elements react to heat, and you learn a great deal about other elements that way.

Prof. C: Right.

AR: Oh, of course.

Prof. C: So the objection of the logical positivist would be valid only if one learned nothing else relating water at the molecular level to other substances. Then one would say one has additional knowledge, but one doesn't have a more fundamental knowledge.

AR: No, the objection wouldn't be valid even then. To begin with, the supposition is impossible. Everything that you discover about one kind of subject or element opens the way for the same type of inquiry and discovery about other elements.

But let's assume for a moment that it had no other applications. Even then, you learn something about water and how to handle it and what you can obtain from it. If you discover that its molecules move in a certain way and that causes boiling, this can lead you to discover other things you can do with water, such as what happens under a deep freeze or what happens with liquid oxygen—which is all derived from the same type of knowledge, from the same category of science.

And don't forget—it is important here—what the purpose of knowledge is. The purpose is for you to deal with that which you are studying. And if you discover why water boils, you will know something more and will be able to do more things with water than the primitive man who knows only that if he holds it over fire a certain length of time it will boil. By discovering such issues as temperature and molecular structure, you have made yourself infinitely more capable of dealing with water and using it for your purposes than the primitive man who only made the first observation.

PART FIVE

Early Novels and Politics

Editor's Note: *Although AR is widely known as a champion of individualism and capitalism, political themes were her primary concern only in her early works. Her focus changed in the 1930s when she concluded that politics rests on ethics and, ultimately, on basic philosophy.*

Anthem, a novelette published in 1938, is the story of a future collectivist society in which the word "I" has been lost—and of the individual who rediscovers it.

The first excerpt from Anthem presents the young hero on the brink of a scientific invention. The second passage, much later in time, shows the hero offering his invention to the Council of Scholars. The final excerpt is the first three paragraphs of the climactic Chapter Eleven.

1. The Individual vs. the State

Anthem

IT IS A SIN TO WRITE THIS. It is a sin to think words no others think and to put them down upon a paper no others are to see. It is base and evil. It is as if we were speaking alone to no ears but our own. And we know well that there is no transgression blacker than to do or think alone. We have broken the laws. The laws say that men may not write unless the Council of Vocations bid them so. May we be forgiven!

But this is not the only sin upon us. We have committed a greater crime, and for this crime there is no name. What punishment awaits us if it be discovered we know not, for no such crime has come in the memory of men and there are no laws to provide for it.

It is dark here. The flame of the candle stands still in the air. Nothing moves in this tunnel save our hand on the paper. We are alone here under the earth. It is a fearful word, alone. The laws say that none among men may be alone, ever and at any time, for this is the great transgression and the root of all evil. But we have broken many laws. And now there is nothing here save our one body, and it is strange to see only two legs stretched on the ground, and on the wall before us the shadow of our one head.

The walls are cracked and water runs upon them in thin threads without sound, black and glistening as blood. We stole the candle from the larder of the Home of the Street Sweepers. We shall be sentenced to ten years in the Palace of Corrective Detention if it be discovered. But this matters not. It matters only that the light is precious and we should not waste it to write when we need it for that work which is our crime. Nothing matters save the work, our secret, our evil, our precious work. Still, we must also write, for—may the Council have mercy on us!—we wish to speak for once to no ears but our own.

Our name is Equality 7-2521, as it is written on the iron bracelet which all men wear on their left wrists with their names upon it. We are twenty-one years old. We are six feet tall, and this is a burden, for there are not many men who are six feet tall. Ever have the Teachers and the Leaders pointed to us and frowned and said: "There is evil in your bones, Equality 7-2521, for your body has grown beyond the bodies of your brothers." But we cannot change our bones nor our body.

We were born with a curse. It has always driven us to thoughts which are forbidden. It has always given us wishes which men may not wish. We know that we are evil, but there is no will in us and no power to resist it. This is our wonder and our secret fear, that we know and do not resist.

We strive to be like all our brother men, for all men must be alike. Over the portals of the Palace of the World Council, there are words cut in the marble, which we repeat to ourselves whenever we are tempted:

"*We are one in all and all in one.*
There are no men but only the great WE,
One, indivisible and forever."

We repeat this to ourselves, but it helps us not.

These words were cut long ago. There is green mould in the grooves of the letters and yellow streaks on the marble, which come from more years than men could count. And these words are the truth for they are written on the Palace of the World Council, and the World Council is the body of all truth. Thus has it been ever since the Great Rebirth, and farther back than that no memory can reach.

*   *   *

But we must never speak of the times before the Great Rebirth, else we are sentenced to three years in the Palace of Corrective Detention. It is only the Old Ones who whisper about it in the evenings, in the Home of the Useless. They whisper many strange things, of the towers which rose to the sky, in those Unmentionable Times, and of the wagons which moved without horses, and of the lights which burned without flame. But those times were evil. And those times passed away, when men saw the Great Truth which is this: that all men are one and that there is no will save the will of all men together.

All men are good and wise. It is only we, Equality 7-2521, we alone who were born with a curse. For we are not like our brothers. And as we look back upon our life, we see that it has ever been thus and that it has brought us step by step to our last, supreme transgression, our crime of crimes hidden here under the ground.

We remember the Home of Infants where we lived till we were five years old, together with all the children of the City who had been born in the same year. The sleeping halls there were white and clean and bare of all things save one hundred beds. We were just like all our brothers then, save for the one transgression: we fought with our brothers. There are few offenses blacker than to fight with our brothers, at any age and for any cause whatsoever. The Council of the Home told us so, and of all the children of that year, we were locked in the cellar most often.

When we were five years old, we were sent to the Home of the Students, where there are ten wards, for our ten years of learning. Men must learn till they reach their fifteenth year. Then they go to work. In the Home of the Students we arose when the big bell rang in the tower and we went to our beds when it rang again. Before we removed our garments, we stood in the great sleeping hall, and we raised our right arms, and we said all together with the three Teachers at the head:

"We are nothing. Mankind is all. By the grace of our brothers are we allowed our lives. We exist through, by and for our brothers who are the State. Amen."

*   *   *

Then we slept. The sleeping halls were white and clean and bare of all things save one hundred beds.

We, Equality 7-2521, were not happy in those years in the Home of the Students. It was not that the learning was too hard for us. It was that the learning was too easy. This is a great sin, to be born with a head which is too quick. It is not good to be different from our brothers, but it is evil to be superior to them. The Teachers told us so, and they frowned when they looked upon us.

So we fought against this curse. We tried to forget our lessons, but we always remembered. We tried not to understand what the Teachers taught, but we always understood it before the Teachers had spoken. We looked upon Union 5-3992, who were a pale boy with only half a brain, and we tried to say and do as they did, that we might be like them, like Union 5-3992, but somehow the Teachers knew that we were not. And we were lashed more often than all the other children.

The Teachers were just, for they had been appointed by the Councils, and the Councils are the voice of all justice, for they are the voice of all men. And if sometimes, in the secret darkness of our heart, we regret that which befell us on our fifteenth birthday, we know that it was through our own guilt. We had broken a law, for we had not paid heed to the words of our Teachers. The Teachers had said to us all:

"Dare not choose in your minds the work you would like to do when you leave the Home of the Students. You shall do that which the Council of Vocations shall prescribe for you. For the Council of Vocations knows in its great wisdom where you are needed by your brother men, better than you can know it in your unworthy little minds. And if you are not needed by your brother men, there is no reason for you to burden the earth with your bodies."

We knew this well, in the years of our childhood, but our curse broke our will. We were guilty and we confess it here: we were guilty of the great Transgression of Preference. We preferred some work and some lessons to the others. We did not listen well to the history of all the Councils elected since the Great Rebirth. But we loved the Science of Things. We wished to know. We wished to know about all the things which make the earth around us. We asked so many questions that the Teachers forbade it.

We think that there are mysteries in the sky and under the water and in the plants which grow. But the Council of Scholars has said that there are no mysteries, and the Council of Scholars knows all things. And we learned much from our Teachers. We learned that the earth is flat and that the sun revolves around it, which causes the day and the night. We learned the names of all the winds which blow over the seas and push the sails of our great ships. We learned how to bleed men to cure them of all ailments.

We loved the Science of Things. And in the darkness, in the secret hour, when we awoke in the night and there were no brothers around us, but only their shapes in the beds and their snores, we closed our eyes, and we held our lips shut, and we stopped our breath, that no shudder might let our brothers see or hear or guess, and we thought that we wished to be sent to the Home of the Scholars when our time would come.

All the great modern inventions come from the Home of the Scholars, such as the newest one, which we found only a hundred years ago, of how to make candles from wax and string; also, how to make glass, which is put in our windows to protect us from the rain. To find these things, the Scholars must study the earth and learn from the rivers, from the sands, from the winds and the rocks. And if we went to the Home of the Scholars, we could learn from these also. We could ask questions of these, for they do not forbid questions.

And questions give us no rest. We know not why our curse makes us seek we know not what, ever and ever. But we cannot resist it. It whispers to us that there are great things on this earth of ours, and that we can know them if we try, and that we must know them. We ask, why must we know, but it has no answer to give us. We must know that we may know.

So we wished to be sent to the Home of the Scholars. We wished it so much that our hands trembled under the blankets in the night, and we bit our arm to stop that other pain which we could not endure. It was evil and we dared not face our brothers in the morning. For men may wish nothing for themselves. And we were punished when the Council of Vocations came to give us our life Mandates which tell those who reach their fifteenth year what their work is to be for the rest of their days.

The Council of Vocations came on the first day of spring, and they sat in the great hall. And we who were fifteen and all the Teachers came into the great hall. And the Council of Vocations sat on a high dais, and they had but two words to speak to each of the Students. They called the Students' names, and when the Students stepped before them, one after another, the Council said: "Carpenter" or "Doctor" or "Cook" or "Leader." Then each Student raised their right arm and said: "The will of our brothers be done."

Now if the Council has said "Carpenter" or "Cook," the Students so assigned go to work and they do not study any further. But if the Council has said "Leader," then those Students go into the Home of the Leaders, which is the greatest house in the City, for it has three stories. And there they study for many years, so that they may become candidates and be elected to the City Council and the State Council and the World Council—by a free and general vote of all men. But we wished not to be a Leader, even though it is a great honor. We wished to be a Scholar.

So we waited our turn in the great hall and then we heard the Council of Vocations call our name: "Equality 7-2521." We walked to the dais, and our legs did not tremble, and we looked up at the Council. There were five members of the Council, three of the male gender and two of the female. Their hair was white and their faces were cracked as the clay of a dry river bed. They were old. They seemed older than the marble of the Temple of the World Council. They sat before us and they did not move. And we saw no breath to stir the folds of their white togas. But we knew that they were alive, for a finger of the hand of the oldest rose, pointed to us, and fell down again. This was the only thing which moved, for the lips of the oldest did not move as they said: "Street Sweeper."

We felt the cords of our neck grow tight as our head rose higher to look upon the faces of the Council, and we were happy. We knew we had been guilty, but now we had a way to atone for it. We would accept our Life Mandate, and we would work for our brothers, gladly and willingly, and we would erase our sin against them, which they did not know, but we knew. So we were happy, and proud of ourselves and of our victory over ourselves. We raised our right arm and we spoke, and our voice was the clearest, the steadiest voice in the hall that day, and we said:

"The will of our brothers be done."

And we looked straight into the eyes of the Council, but their eyes were as cold blue glass buttons.

So we went into the Home of the Street Sweepers. It is a grey house on a narrow street. There is a sundial in its courtyard, by which the Council of the Home can tell the hours of the day and when to ring the bell. When the bell rings, we all arise from our beds. The sky is green and cold in our windows to the east. The shadow on the sundial marks off a half-hour while we dress and eat our breakfast in the dining hall, where there are five long tables with twenty clay plates and twenty clay cups on each table. Then we go to work in the streets of the City, with our brooms and our rakes. In five hours, when the sun is high, we return to the Home and we eat our midday meal, for which one-half hour is allowed. Then we go to work again. In five hours, the shadows are blue on the pavements, and the sky is blue with a deep brightness which is not bright. We come back to have our dinner, which lasts one hour. Then the bell rings and we walk in a straight column to one of the City Halls, for the Social Meeting. Other columns of men arrive from the Homes of the different Trades. The candles are lit, and the Councils of the different Homes stand in a pulpit, and they speak to us of our duties and of our brother men. Then visiting Leaders mount the pulpit and they read to us the speeches which were made in the City Council that day, for the City Council represents all men and all men must know. Then we sing hymns, the Hymn of Brotherhood, and the Hymn of Equality, and the Hymn of the Collective Spirit. The sky is a soggy purple when we return to the Home. Then the bell rings and we walk in a straight column to the City Theatre for three hours of Social Recreation. There a play is shown upon the stage, with two great choruses from the Home of the Actors, which speak and answer all together, in two great voices. The plays are about toil and how good it is. Then we walk back to the Home in a straight column. The sky is like a black sieve pierced by silver drops that tremble, ready to burst through. The moths beat against the street lanterns. We go to our beds and we sleep, till the bell rings again. The sleeping halls are white and clean and bare of all things save one hundred beds.

Thus we lived each day of four years, until two springs ago when our crime happened. Thus must all men live until they are forty. At forty, they are worn out. At forty, they are sent to the Home of the Useless, where the Old Ones live. The Old Ones do not work, for the State takes care of them. They sit in the sun in summer and they sit by the fire in winter. They do not speak often, for they are weary. The Old Ones know that they are soon to die. When a miracle happens and some live to be forty-five, they are the Ancient Ones, and children stare at them when passing by the Home of the Useless. Such is to be our life, as that of all our brothers and of the brothers who came before us.

Such would have been our life, had we not committed our crime which changed all things for us. And it was our curse which drove us to our crime. We had been a good Street Sweeper and like all our brother Street Sweepers, save for our cursed wish to know. We looked too long at the stars at night, and at the trees and the earth. And when we cleaned the yard of the Home of the Scholars, we gathered the glass vials, the pieces of metal, the dried bones which they had discarded. We wished to keep these things to study them, but we had no place to hide them. So we carried them to the City Cesspool. And then we made the discovery. [. . .]

*   *   *

IT IS DARK HERE IN THE FOREST. The leaves rustle over our head, black against the last gold of the sky. The moss is soft and warm. We shall sleep on this moss for many nights, till the beasts of the forest come to tear our body. We have no bed now, save the moss, and no future, save the beasts.

We are old now, yet we were young this morning, when we carried our glass box through the streets of the City to the Home of the Scholars. No men stopped us, for there were none about from the Palace of Corrective Detention, and the others knew nothing. No men stopped us at the gate. We walked through empty passages and into the great hall where the World Council of Scholars sat in solemn meeting.

We saw nothing as we entered, save the sky in the great windows, blue and glowing. Then we saw the Scholars who sat around a long table; they were as shapeless clouds huddled at the rise of the great sky. There were men whose famous names we knew, and others from distant lands whose names we had not heard. We saw a great painting on the wall over their heads, of the twenty illustrious men who had invented the candle.

All the heads of the Council turned to us as we entered. These great and wise of the earth did not know what to think of us, and they looked upon us with wonder and curiosity, as if we were a miracle. It is true that our tunic was torn and stained with brown stains which had been blood. We raised our right arm and we said:

"Our greeting to you, our honored brothers of the World Council of Scholars!"

The Collective 0-0009, the oldest and wisest of the Council, spoke and asked:

"Who are you, our brother? For you do not look like a Scholar."

"Our name is Equality 7-2521," we answered, "and we are a Street Sweeper of this City."

Then it was as if a great wind had stricken the hall, for all the Scholars spoke at once, and they were angry and frightened.

"A Street Sweeper! A Street Sweeper walking in upon the World Council of Scholars! It is not to be believed! It is against all the rules and all the laws!"

But we knew how to stop them.

"Our brothers!" we said. "We matter not, nor our transgression. It is only our brother men who matter. Give no thought to us, for we are nothing, but listen to our words, for we bring you a gift such as has never been brought to men. Listen to us, for we hold the future of mankind in our hands."

Then they listened.

We placed our glass box upon the table before them. We spoke of it, and of our long quest, and of our tunnel, and of our escape from the Palace of Corrective Detention. Not a hand moved in that hall, as we spoke, nor an eye. Then we put the wires to the box, and they all bent forward and sat still, watching. And we stood still, our eyes upon the wire. And slowly, slowly as a flush of blood, a red flame trembled in the wire. Then the wire glowed.

But terror struck the men of the Council. They leapt to their feet, they ran from the table, and they stood pressed against the wall, huddled together, seeking the warmth of one another's bodies to give them courage.

We looked upon them and we laughed and said:

"Fear nothing, our brothers. There is a great power in these wires, but this power is tamed. It is yours. We give it to you."

Still they would not move.

"We give you the power of the sky!" we cried. "We give you the key to the earth! Take it, and let us be one of you, the humblest among you. Let us all work together, and harness this power, and make it ease the toil of men. Let us throw away our candles and our torches. Let us flood our cities with light. Let us bring a new light to men!"

But they looked upon us, and suddenly we were afraid. For their eyes were still, and small, and evil.

"Our brothers!" we cried. "Have you nothing to say to us?"

Then Collective 0-0009 moved forward. They moved to the table and the others followed.

."Yes," spoke Collective 0-0009, "we have much to say to you."

The sound of their voice brought silence to the hall and to the beat of our heart.

"Yes," said Collective 0-0009, "we have much to say to a wretch who have broken all the laws and who boast of their infamy! How dared you think that your mind held greater wisdom than the minds of your brothers? And if the Councils had decreed that you should be a Street Sweeper, how dared you think that you could be of greater use to men than in sweeping the streets?"

"How dared you, gutter cleaner," spoke Fraternity 9-3452, "to hold yourself as one alone and with the thoughts of the one and not of the many?"

"You shall be burned at the stake," said Democracy 4-6998.

"No, they shall be lashed," said Unanimity 7-3304, "till there is nothing left under the lashes."

"No," said Collective 0-0009, "we cannot decide upon this, our brothers. No such crime has ever been committed, and it is not for us to judge. Nor for any small Council. We shall deliver this creature to the World Council itself and let their will be done."

We looked upon them and we pleaded:

"Our brothers! You are right. Let the will of the Council be done upon our body. We do not care. But the light? What will you do with the light?"

Collective 0-0009 looked upon us, and they smiled.

"So you think that you have found a new power," said Collective 0-0009. "Do all your brothers think that?"

"No," we answered.

"What is not thought by all men cannot be true," said Collective 0-0009.

"You have worked on this alone?" asked International 1-5537.

"Yes," we answered.

"What is not done collectively cannot be good," said International 1-5537.

"Many men in the Homes of the Scholars have had strange new ideas in the past," said Solidarity 8-1164, "but when the majority of their brother Scholars voted against them, they abandoned their ideas, as all men must."

"This box is useless," said Alliance 6-7349.

"Should it be what they claim of it," said Harmony 9-2642, "then it would bring ruin to the Department of Candles. The Candle is a great boon to mankind, as approved by all men. Therefore it cannot be destroyed by the whim of one."

"This would wreck the Plans of the World Council," said Unanimity 2-9913, "and without the Plans of the World Council the sun cannot rise. It took fifty years to secure the approval of all the Councils for the Candle, and to decide upon the number needed, and to re-fit the Plans so as to make candles instead of torches. This touched upon thousands and thousands of men working in scores of States. We cannot alter the Plans again so soon."

"And if this should lighten the toil of men," said Similarity 5-0306, "then it is a great evil, for men have no cause to exist save in toiling for other men."

Then Collective 0-0009 rose and pointed at our box.

"This thing," they said, "must be destroyed."

And all the others cried as one:

"It must be destroyed!"

Then we leapt to the table.

We seized our box, we shoved them aside, and we ran to the window. We turned and we looked at them for the last time, and a rage, such as it is not fit for humans to know, choked our voice in our throat.

"You fools!" we cried. "You fools! You thrice-damned fools!"

We swung our fist through the windowpane, and we leapt out in a ringing rain of glass.

We fell, but we never let the box fall from our hands. Then we ran. We ran blindly, and men and houses streaked past us in a torrent without shape. And the road seemed not to be flat before us, but as if it were leaping up to meet us, and we waited for the earth to rise and strike us in the face. But we ran. We knew not where we were going. We knew only that we must run, run to the end of the world, to the end of our days.

Then we knew suddenly that we were lying on a soft earth and that we had stopped. Trees taller than we had ever seen before stood over us in a great silence. Then we knew. We were in the Uncharted Forest. We had not thought of coming here, but our legs had carried our wisdom, and our legs had brought us to the Uncharted Forest against our will.

Our glass box lay beside us. We crawled to it, we fell upon it, our face in our arms, and we lay still.

We lay thus for a long time. Then we rose, we took our box and walked on into the forest.

It mattered not where we went. We knew that men would not follow us, for they never enter the Uncharted Forest. We had nothing to fear from them. The forest disposes of its own victims. This gave us no fear either. Only we wished to be away, away from the City and from the air that touches upon the air of the City. So we walked on, our box in our arms, our heart empty.

We are doomed. Whatever days are left to us, we shall spend them alone. And we have heard of the corruption to be found in solitude. We have torn ourselves from the truth which is our brother men, and there is no road back for us, and no redemption.

We know these things, but we do not care. We care for nothing on earth. We are tired.

Only the glass box in our arms is like a living heart that gives us strength. We have lied to ourselves. We have not built this box for the good of our brothers. We built it for its own sake. It is above all our brothers to us, and its truth above their truth. Why wonder about this? We have not many days to live. We are walking to the fangs awaiting us somewhere among the great, silent trees. There is not a thing behind us to regret. [. . .]

*   *   *

I AM. I THINK. I WILL.

My hands . . . My spirit . . . My sky . . . My forest . . . This earth of mine. . . .

What must I say besides? These are the words. This is the answer.

I stand here on the summit of the mountain. I lift my head and I spread my arms. This, my body and spirit, this is the end of the quest. I wished to know the meaning of things. I am the meaning. I wished to find a warrant for being. I need no warrant for being, and no word of sanction upon my being. I am the warrant and the sanction.

―――――――

EDITOR'S NOTE: *The theme of* We the Living, *AR's first novel, published in 1936, is the individual versus the state. Set during the Communist Revolution, the story shows how dictatorship—any dictatorship—suffocates human life.*

The following selection, from the middle of the novel, features the heroine, Kira Argounova; Leo Kovalensky, the man she loves; and Andrei Taganov, an officer of the Soviet secret police who loves her.

Kira is studying at the Technological Institute to be a builder; Leo is studying history and philosophy at Petrograd State University. Kira and Leo are both "bourgeois": her father's business has been confiscated by the Soviets; his father was an admiral who had fought for the Czar. Andrei, of course, is pure "proletarian."

We the Living

The Purge

AT FIRST there were whispers.

Students gathered in groups in dark corners and jerked their heads nervously at every approaching newcomer, and in their whispers one heard the words: "The Purge."

In lines at co-operatives and in tramways people asked: "Have you heard about the Purge?"

In the columns of *Pravda* there appeared many mentions of the deplorable state of Red colleges and of the coming Purge.

And then, at the end of the winter semester, in the Technological Institute, in the University and in all the institutes of higher education, there appeared a large notice with huge letters in red pencil:

THE PURGE

The notice directed all students to call at the office, receive questionnaires, fill them out promptly, have their Upravdom certify to the truth of the answers and return them to the Purging Committee. The schools of the Union of Socialist Soviet Republics were to be cleaned of all socially undesirable persons. Those found socially undesirable were to be expelled, never to be admitted to any college again.

Newspapers roared over the country like trumpets: "Science is a weapon of the class struggle! Proletarian schools are for the Proletariat! We shall not educate our class enemies!"

There were those who were careful not to let these trumpets be heard too loudly across the border.

Kira received her questionnaire at the Institute, and Leo—his at the University. They sat silently at their dinner table, filling out the answers. They did not each much dinner that night. When they signed the questionnaires, they knew they had signed the death warrant of their future; but they did not say it aloud and they did not look at each other.

The main questions were:

Who were your parents?
What was your father's occupation prior to the year 1917?
What was your father's occupation from the year 1917 to the year 1921?
What is your father's occupation now?
What is your mother's occupation?
What did you do during the civil war?
What did your father do during the civil war?
Are you a Trade Union member?
Are you a member of the All-Union Communist Party?

Any attempt to give a false answer was futile; the answers were to be investigated by the Purging Committee and the G.P.U. A false answer was to be punished by arrest, imprisonment or any penalty up to the supreme one.

Kira's hand trembled a little when she handed to the Purge Committee the questionnaire that bore the answer:

What was your father's occupation prior to the year 1917?
Owner of the Argounov Textile Factory.

What awaited those who were to be expelled, no one dared to think; no one mentioned it; the questionnaires were turned in and the students waited for a call from the committee, waited silently, nerves tense as wires. In the long corridors of the colleges, where the troubled stream of students clotted into restless clusters, they whispered that one's "social origin" was most important—that if you were of "bourgeois descent," you didn't have a chance—that if your parents had been wealthy, you were still a "class enemy," even though you were starving—and that you must try, if you could, at the price of your immortal soul, if you had one, to prove your "origin from the workbench or the plough." There were more leather jackets, and red kerchiefs, and sunflower-seed shells in the college corridors, and jokes about: "My parents? Why, they were a peasant woman and two workers."

It was spring again, and melting snow drilled the sidewalks, and blue hyacinths were sold on street corners. But those who were young had no thought left for spring and those who still thought were not young any longer.

Kira Argounova, head high, stood before the Purge Committee of the Technological Institute. At the table, among the men of the committee whom she did not know, sat three persons she knew: Comrade Sonia, Pavel Syerov, Andrei Taganov.

It was Pavel Syerov who did most of the questioning. Her questionnaire lay on the table before him. "So, Citizen Argounova, your father was a factory owner?"

"Yes."

"I see. And your mother? Did she work before the revolution?"

"No."

"I see. Did you employ servants in your home?"

"Yes."

"I see."

Comrade Sonia asked: "And you've never joined a Trade Union, Citizen Argounova? Didn't find it desirable?"

"I have never had the opportunity."

"I see."

Andrei Taganov listened. His face did not move. His eyes were cold, steady, impersonal, as if he had never seen Kira before. And suddenly she felt an inexplicable pity for him, for that immobility and what it hid, although he showed not the slightest sign of what it hid.

But when he asked her a question suddenly, even though his voice was hard and his eyes empty, the question was a plea: "But you've always been in strict sympathy with the Soviet Government, Citizen Argounova, haven't you?"

She answered very softly: "Yes."

*　　*　　*

Somewhere, around a lamp, late in the night, amid rustling papers, reports and documents, a committee was holding a conference.

"Factory owners were the chief exploiters of the Proletariat."

"Worse than landowners."

"Most dangerous of class enemies."

"We are performing a great service to the cause of the Revolution and no personal feelings are to interfere with our duty."

"Order from Moscow—children of former factory owners are in the first category to be expelled."

A voice asked, weighing every word: "Any exceptions to that rule, Comrade Taganov?"

He stood by a window, his hands clasped behind his back. He answered: "None."

*   *   *

The names of those expelled were typewritten on a long sheet of paper and posted on a blackboard in the office of the Technological Institute.

Kira had expected it. But when she saw the name on the list: "*Argounova, Kira,*" she closed her eyes and looked again and read the long list carefully, to make sure.

Then she noticed that her brief case was open; she clasped the catch carefully; she looked at the hole in her glove and stuck her finger out, trying to see how far it would go, and twisted an unraveled thread into a little snake and watched it uncoil.

Then she felt that someone was watching her. She turned. Andrei stood alone in a window niche. He was looking at her, but he did not move forward, he did not say a word, he did not incline his head in greeting. She knew what he feared, what he hoped, what he was waiting for. She walked to him, and looked up at him, and extended her hand with the same trusting smile he had known on the same young lips, only the lips trembled a little.

"It's all right, Andrei. I know you couldn't help it."

She had not expected the gratitude, a gratitude like pain, in his low voice when he answered: "I'd give you my place—if I could."

"Oh, it's all right. . . . Well . . . I guess I won't be a builder after all. . . . I guess I won't build any aluminum bridges." She tried to laugh. "It's all right, because everybody always told me one can't build a bridge of aluminum anyway." She noticed that it was harder for him to smile than for her. "And Andrei," she said softly, knowing that he did not dare to ask it, "this doesn't mean that we won't see each other any more, does it?"

He took her hand in both of his. "It doesn't, Kira, if . . ."

"Well, then, it doesn't. Give me your phone number and address, so I can call you, because we . . . we won't meet here . . . any more.

We're such good friends that—isn't it funny?—I've never even known your address. All's for the best. Maybe . . . maybe we'll be better friends now."

* * *

When she came home, Leo was sprawled across the bed, and he didn't get up. He looked at her and laughed. He laughed dryly, monotonously, senselessly.

She stood still, looking at him.

"Thrown out?" he asked, rising on a wavering elbow, his hair falling over his face. "Don't have to tell me. I know. You're kicked out. Like a dog. So am I. Like two dogs. Congratulations, Kira Alexandrovna. Hearty proletarian congratulations!"

"Leo, you've . . . you've been drinking!"

"Sure. To celebrate. All of us did. Dozens and dozens of us at the University. A toast to the Dictatorship of the Proletariat. . . . Many toasts to the Dictatorship of the Proletariat. . . . Don't stare at me like that. . . . It's a good old custom to drink at births, and weddings, and funerals. . . . Well, we weren't born together, Comrade Argounova. . . . And we've never had a wedding, Comrade Argounova. . . . But we might yet see the other. . . . We might . . . yet . . . the other . . . Kira. . . ."

She was on her knees by the bed, gathering to her breast a pale face with a contorted wound of a mouth, she was brushing damp hair off his forehead, she was whispering: "Leo . . . dearest . . . you shouldn't do that. . . . Now's the time you shouldn't. . . . We have to think clearly now. . . ." She was whispering without conviction. "It's not dangerous so long as we don't give up. . . . You must take care of yourself, Leo. . . . You must spare yourself. . . ."

His mouth spat out: "For what?" [. . .]

* * *

Because there was no future, they hung on to the present.

There were days when Leo sat for hours reading a book, and hardly spoke to Kira, and when he spoke his smile held a bitter, endless contempt for himself, for the world, for eternity.

Once, she found him drunk, leaning against the table, staring intently at a broken glass on the floor.

"Leo! Where did you get it?"

"Borrowed it. Borrowed it from our dear neighbor Comrade Marisha. She always has plenty."

"Leo, why do you?"

"Why shouldn't I? Why shouldn't I? Who in this whole damn world can tell me why I shouldn't?"

But there were days when a new calm suddenly cleared his eyes and his smile. He waited for Kira to come home from work and when she entered he drew her hastily into his arms. They could sit through an evening without a word, their presence, a glance, the pressure of a hand drugging them into security, making them forget the coming morning, all the coming mornings.

Arm in arm, they walked through silent, luminous streets in the white nights of spring. The sky was like dull glass glowing with a sun-less radiance from somewhere beyond. The could look at each other, at the still, sleepless city, in the strange, milky light. He pressed her arm close to his, and when they were alone on a long street dawn-bright and empty, he bent to kiss her.

Kira's steps were steady. There were too many questions ahead; but here, beside her, were the things that gave her certainty: his straight, tense body, his long, thin hands, his haughty mouth with the arrogant smile that answered all questions. And, sometimes, she felt pity for those countless nameless ones somewhere around them who, in a feverish quest, were searching for some answer, and in their search crushed others, perhaps even her; but she could not be crushed, for she had the answer. She did not wonder about the future. The future was Leo.

*   *   *

Leo was too pale and he was silent too often. The blue on his temples looked like veins in marble. He coughed, choking. He took cough medicine, which did not help, and refused to see a doctor.

Kira saw Andrei frequently. She had asked Leo if he minded it. "Not at all," he had answered, "if he's your friend. Only—would you mind?—don't bring him here. I'm not sure I can be polite . . . to one of them."

She did not bring Andrei to the house. She telephoned him on Sundays and smiled cheerfully into the receiver: "Feel like seeing me, Andrei? Two o'clock—Summer Garden—the quay entrance."

They sat on a bench, with the oak leaves fighting the glare of the sun above their heads, and they talked of philosophy. She smiled sometimes when she realized that Andrei was the only one with whom she could think and talk about thoughts.

They had no reason for meeting each other. Yet they met, and made dates to meet again, and she felt strangely comfortable, and he laughed at her short summer dresses, and his laughter was strangely happy.

Once, he invited her to spend a Sunday in the country. She had stayed in the city all summer; she could not refuse. Leo had found a job for Sunday: breaking the wooden bricks of pavements, with a gang repairing the streets. He did not object to her excursion.

In the country, she found a smooth sea sparkling in the sun; and a golden sand wind-pleated into faint, even waves; and the tall red candles of pines, their convulsed roots naked to the sand and wind, pine cones rolling to meet the sea shells.

Kira and Andrei had a swimming race, which she won. But when they raced down the beach in their bathing suits, sand flying from under their heels, spurting sand and water at the peaceful Sunday tourists, Andrei won. He caught her and they rolled down together, a whirl of legs, arms and mud, into the lunch basket of a matron who shrieked with terror. They disentangled themselves from each other and sat there screaming with laughter. And when the matron struggled to her feet, gathered her lunch and waddled away, grumbling something about "this vulgar modern youth that can't keep their love-affairs to themselves," they laughed louder.

They had dinner in a dirty little country restaurant, and Kira spoke English to the waiter who could not understand a word, but bowed low and stuttered and spilled water all over the table in his eagerness to serve the first comrade foreigner in their forgotten corner. When they were leaving, Andrei gave him twice the price of their dinner. The waiter bowed to the ground, convinced that he was dealing with genuine foreigners. Kira could not help looking a little startled. Andrei laughed when they went out: "Why not? Might as well make a waiter happy. I make more money than I can spend on myself anyway."

In the train, as it clattered into the evening and the smoke of the city, Andrei asked: "Kira, when will I see you again?"

"I'll call you."

"No. I want to know now."

"In a few days."

"No. I want a definite day."

"Well, then, Wednesday night?"

"All right."

"After work, at five-thirty, at the Summer Garden."

"All right."

When she came home, she found Leo asleep in a chair, his hands dust-streaked, smears of dust on his damp, flushed face, his dark lashes blond with dust, his body limp with exhaustion.

She washed his face and helped him to undress. He coughed.

The two evenings that followed were long, furious arguments, but Leo surrendered: He promised to visit a doctor on Wednesday. [. . .]

*   *   *

Kira had had a restless day. Leo had promised to telephone her at the office and tell her the doctor's diagnosis. He had not called. She telephoned him three times. There was no answer. On her way home, she remembered that it was Wednesday night and that she had a date with Andrei.

She could not keep him waiting indefinitely at a public park gate. She would drop by the Summer Garden and tell him that she couldn't stay. She reached the Garden on time.

Andrei was not there. She looked up and down the darkening quay. She peered into the trees and shadows of the garden. She waited. Twice, she asked a militia-man what time it was. She waited. She could not understand it.

He did not come.

When she finally went home, she had waited for an hour.

She clutched her hands angrily in her pockets. She could not worry about Andrei when she thought of Leo, and the doctor, and of what she still had to hear. She hurried up the stairs. She darted through Marisha's room and flung the door open. On the davenport, her white coat trailing to the floor, Vava was clasped in Leo's arms, their lips locked together.

Kira stood looking at them calmly, an amazed question in her lifted eyebrows.

They jumped up. Leo was not very steady. He had been drinking again. He stood swaying, with his bitter, contemptuous smile.

Vava's face went a dark, purplish red. She opened her mouth, choking, without a sound. And as no one said a word, she screamed suddenly into the silence: "You think it's terrible, don't you? Well, I think so too! It's terrible, it's vile! Only I don't care! I don't care what I do! I don't care any more! I'm rotten? Well, I'm not the only one! Only I don't care! I don't care! I don't care!"

She burst into hysterical sobs and rushed out, slamming the door. The two others did not move.

He sneered: "Well, say it."

She answered slowly: "I have nothing to say."

"Listen, you might as well get used to it. You might as well get used to it that you can't have me. Because you can't have me. You won't have me. You won't have me long."

"Leo, what did the doctor say?"

He laughed: "Plenty."

"What is it you have?"

"Nothing. Not a thing."

"Leo!"

"Not a thing—yet. But I'm going to have it. Just a few weeks longer. I'm going to have it."

"What, Leo?"

He swayed with a grand gesture: "Nothing much. Just—tuberculosis."

*   *   *

The doctor asked: "Are you his wife?"

Kira hesitated, then answered: "No."

The doctor said: "I see." Then, he added: "Well, I suppose you have a right to know it. Citizen Kovalensky is in a very bad condition. We call it incipient tuberculosis. It can still be stopped—now. In a few weeks—it will be too late."

"In a few weeks—he'll have—tuberculosis?"

"Tuberculosis is a serious disease, citizen. In Soviet Russia—it is a fatal disease. It is strongly advisable to prevent it. If you let it start—you will not be likely to stop it."

"What . . . does he need?"

"Rest. Plenty of it. Sunshine. Fresh air. Food. Human food. He needs a sanatorium for this coming winter. One more winter in Petrograd would be as certain as a firing squad. You'll have to send him south."

She did not answer; but the doctor smiled ironically, for he heard the answer without words and he looked at the patches on her shoes.

"If that young man is dear to you," he said, "send him south. If you have a human possibility—or an inhuman one—send him south."

*   *   *

Kira was very calm when she walked home.

When she came in, Leo was standing by the window. He turned slowly. His face was so profoundly, serenely tranquil that he looked younger; he looked as if he had had his first night of rest; he asked quietly: "Where have you been, Kira?"

"At the doctor's."

"Oh, I'm sorry. I didn't want you to know all that."

"He told me."

"Kira, I'm sorry about last night. About that little fool. I hope you didn't think that I . . ."

"Of course, I didn't. I understand."

"I think it's because I was frightened. But I'm not—now. Everything seems so much simpler—when there's a limit set. . . . The thing to do now, Kira, is not to talk about it. Don't let's think about it. There's nothing we can do—as the doctor probably told you. We can still be together—for a while. When it becomes contagious—well . . ."

She was watching him. Such was his manner of accepting his death sentence.

She said, and her voice was hard: "Nonsense, Leo. You're going south."

*   *   *

In the first State hospital she visited, the official in charge told her: "A place in a sanatorium in the Crimea? He's not a member of the Party? And he's not a member of a Trade Union? And he's not a State employee? You're joking, citizen."

In the second hospital, the official said: "We have hundreds on our waiting list, citizen. Trade Union members. Advanced cases. . . . No, we cannot even register him."

In the third hospital, the official refused to see her.

There were lines to wait in, ghastly lines of deformed creatures, of scars, and slings, and crutches, and open sores, and green, mucous patches of eyes, and grunts, and groans, and—over a line of the living—the smell of the morgue.

There were State Medical headquarters to visit, long hours of waiting in dim, damp corridors that smelt of carbolic acid and soiled linen. There were secretaries who forgot appointments, and assistants who said: "So sorry, citizen. Next, please"; there were young executives who were in a hurry, and attendants who groaned: "I tell you he's gone, it's after office hours, we gotta close, you can't sit here all night."

At the end of the first two weeks she learned, as firmly as if it were some mystic absolute, that if one had consumption one had to be a member of a Trade Union and get a Trade Union despatchment to a Trade Union Sanatorium.

There were officials to be seen, names mentioned, letters of recommendation offered, begging for an exception. There were Trade Union heads to visit, who listened to her plea with startled, ironic glances. Some laughed; some shrugged; some called their secretaries to escort the visitor out; one said he could and he would, but he named a sum she could not earn in a year.

She was firm, erect, and her voice did not tremble, and she was not afraid to beg. It was her mission, her quest, her crusade.

She wondered sometimes why the words: "But he's going to *die*," meant so little to them, and the words: "But he's not a registered worker," meant so little to her, and why it seemed so hard to explain.

She made Leo do his share of inquiries. He obeyed without arguing, without complaining, without hope.

She tried everything she could. She asked Victor for help. Victor said with dignity: "My dear cousin, I want you to realize that my Party membership is a sacred trust not to be used for purposes of personal advantage."

She asked Marisha. Marisha laughed. "With all our sanatoriums stuffed like herring-barrels, and waiting lists till the next generation, and comrade workers rotting alive waiting—and here he's not even sick yet! You don't realize reality, Citizen Argounova."

She could not call on Andrei. Andrei had failed her.

For several days after the date he had missed, she called on Lydia with the same question: "Has Andrei Taganov been here? Have you had any letters for me?"

The first day, Lydia said: "No." The second day, she giggled and wanted to know what was this, a romance? and she'd tell Leo, and with Leo so handsome! and Kira interrupted patiently: "Oh, stop this rubbish, Lydia! It's important. Let me know the minute you hear from him, will you?"

Lydia did not hear from him.

One evening, at the Dunaevs', Kira asked Victor casually if he had seen Andrei Taganov at the Institute. "Sure," said Victor, "he's there every day."

She was hurt. She was angry. She was bewildered. What had she done? For the first time, she questioned her own behavior. Had she acted foolishly that Sunday in the country? She tried to remember every word, every gesture. She could find no fault. He had seemed happier than ever before. After a while, she decided that she must trust their friendship and give him a chance to explain.

She telephoned him. She heard the old landlady's voice yelling into the house: "Comrade Taganov!" with a positive inflection that implied his presence; there was a long pause; the landlady returned and asked: "Who's calling him?" and before she had pronounced the last syllable of her name, Kira heard the landlady barking: "He ain't home!" and slamming her receiver.

Kira slammed hers, too. She decided to forget Andrei Taganov.

*   *   *

It took a month, but at the end of a month, she was convinced that the door of the State sanatoriums was locked to Leo and that she could not unlock it.

There were private sanatoriums in the Crimea. Private sanatoriums cost money. She would get the money.

She made an appointment to see Comrade Voronov and asked for an advance on her salary, an advance of six months—just enough to start him off. Comrade Voronov smiled faintly and asked her how she could be certain that she would be working there another month, let alone six.

She called on Doctor Milovsky, Vava's father, her wealthiest acquaintance, whose bank account had been celebrated by many envious whispers. Doctor Milovsky's face got very red and his short, pudgy hands waved at Kira hysterically, as if shooing off a ghost: "My dear little girl, why, my dear little girl, what on earth made you think that I was rich or something? Heh-heh. Very funny indeed. A capitalist or something—heh-heh, Why, we're just existing, from hand to mouth, living by my own toil like proletarians one would say, barely existing, as one would say—that's it—from hand to mouth."

She knew her parents had nothing. She asked if they could try to help. Galina Petrovna cried.

She asked Vasili Ivanovitch. He offered her his last possession—Maria Petrovna's old fur jacket. The price of the jacket would not buy a ticket to the Crimea. She did not take it.

She knew Leo would resent it, but she wrote to his aunt in Berlin. She said in her letter: "I am writing, because I love him so much—to you, because I think you must love him a little." No answer came.

Through mysterious, stealthy whispers, more mysterious and

stealthy than the G.P.U. who watched them sharply, she learned that there was private money to be lent, secretly and on a high percentage, but there was. She learned a name and an address. She went to the booth of a private trader in a market, where a fat man bent down to her nervously across a counter loaded with red kerchiefs and cotton stockings. She whispered a name. She named a sum.

"Business?" he breathed. "Speculation?"

She knew it best to say yes. Well, he told her, it could be arranged. The rates were twenty-five per cent a month. She nodded eagerly. What security did the citizen have to offer? Security? Surely she knew they didn't lend it on her good looks? Furs or diamonds would do; good furs and any kind of diamonds. She had nothing to offer. The man turned away as if he had never spoken to her in his life.

On her way back to the tramway, through the narrow, muddy passages between the market stalls, she stopped, startled; in a little prosperous-looking booth, behind a counter heavy with fresh bread loaves, smoked hams, yellow circles of butter, she saw a familiar face: a heavy red mouth under a short nose with wide, vertical nostrils. She remembered the train speculator of the Nikolaevsky station, with the fur-lined coat and the smell of carnation oil. He had progressed in life. He was smiling at the customers, from under a fringe of salami.

On her way home, she remembered someone who had said: "I make more money than I can spend on myself." Did anything really matter now? She would go to the Institute and try to see Andrei.

She changed tramways for the Institute. She saw Andrei. She saw him coming down the corridor and he was looking straight at her, so that her lips moved in a smile of greeting; but he turned abruptly and slammed the door of an auditorium behind him.

She stood frozen to the spot for a long time.

When she came home, Leo was standing in the middle of the room, a crumpled paper in his hand, his face distorted by anger.

"So you would?" he cried. "So you're meddling in my affairs now? So you're writing letters? Who asked you to write?"

On the table, she saw an envelope with a German stamp. It was addressed to Leo. "What does she say, Leo?"

"You want to know? You really want to know?"

He threw the letter at her face.

She remembered only the sentence: "There is no reason why you should expect any help from us; the less reason since you are living with a brazen harlot who has the impudence to write to respectable people."

*   *   *

On the first rainy day of autumn, a delegation from a Club of Textile Women Workers visited the "House of the Peasant." Comrade Sonia was an honorary member of the delegation. When she saw Kira at the filing cabinet in Comrade Bitiuk's office, Comrade Sonia roared with laughter: "Well, well, well! A loyal citizen like Comrade Argounova in the Red 'House of the Peasant'!"

"What's the matter, comrade?" Comrade Bitiuk inquired nervously, obsequiously. "What's the matter?"

"A joke," roared Comrade Sonia, "a good joke!"

Kira shrugged with resignation; she knew what to expect.

When a reduction of staffs came to the "House of the Peasant" and she saw her name among those dismissed as "anti-social element," she was not surprised. It made no difference now. She spent most of her last salary to buy eggs and milk for Leo, which he would not touch.

*   *   *

In the daytime, Kira was calm, with the calm of an empty face, an empty heart, a mind empty of all thoughts but one. She was not afraid: because she knew that Leo had to go south, and he would go, and she could not doubt it, and so she had nothing to fear.

But there was the night.

She felt his body, ice and moist, close to hers. She heard him coughing. Sometimes in his sleep, his head fell on her shoulder, and he lay there, trusting and helpless as a child, and his breathing was like a moan.

She saw the red bubble on Maria Petrovna's dying lips, and she heard her screaming: "Kira! I want to live! I want to live!"

She could feel Leo's breath in hot, panting gasps on her neck.

Then, she was not sure whether it was Maria Petrovna or Leo screaming when it was too late: "Kira! I want to live! I want to live!"

Was she going insane? It was so simple. She just needed money; a life, *his* life—and money.

"I make more money than I can spend on myself."

"Kira! I want to live! I want to live!"

*   *   *

She made one last attempt to get money.

She was walking down a street slippery with autumn rain, yellow lights melting on black sidewalks. The doctor had said every week counted; every day counted now. She saw a resplendent limousine stopping in the orange cube of light at a theater entrance. A man stepped out; his fur coat glistened like his automobile fenders. She stood in his path. Her voice was firm and clear:

"Please! I want to speak to you. I need money. I don't know you. I have nothing to offer you. I know it isn't being done like this. But you'll understand, because it's so important. It's to save a life."

The man stopped. He had never heard a plea that was a command. He asked, squinting one eye appraisingly: "How much do you need?"

She told him.

"What?" he gasped. "For one night? Why, your sisters don't make that in a whole career!"

He could not understand why the strange girl whirled around and ran across the street, straight through the puddles, as if he were going to run after her.

*　　*　　*

She made one last plea to the State.

It took many weeks of calls, letters, introductions, secretaries and assistants, but she got an appointment with one of Petrograd's most powerful officials. She was to see him in person, face to face. He could do it. Between him and the power he could use stood only her ability to convince him.

The official sat at his desk. A tall window rose behind him, admitting a narrow shaft of light, creating the atmosphere of a cathedral. Kira stood before him. She looked straight at him; her eyes were not hostile, nor pleading; they were clear, trusting, serene; her voice was very calm, very simple, very young.

"Comrade Commissar, you see, I love him. And he is sick. You know what sickness is? It's something strange that happens in your body and then you can't stop it. And then he dies. And now his life— it depends on some words and a piece of paper—and it's so simple when you just look at it as it is—it's only something made by us, ourselves, and perhaps we're right, and perhaps we're wrong, but the chance we're taking on it is frightful, isn't it? They won't send him to a sanatorium because they didn't write his name on a piece of paper with many other names and call it a membership in a Trade Union. It's only ink, you know, and paper, and something we think. You can write it and tear it up, and write it again. But the other—that which happens in one's body—you can't stop that. You don't ask questions about that. Comrade Commissar, I know they are important, those things, money, and the Unions, and those papers, and all. And if one has to sacrifice and suffer for them, I don't mind. I don't mind if I have to work every hour of the day. I don't mind if my dress is old—like this—don't look at my dress, Comrade Commissar, I know it's ugly, but I don't mind. Perhaps, I haven't always understood you, and all those things, but I can be obedient and learn. Only—only when it comes to life itself, Comrade Commissar, then we have to be serious, don't we? We can't let those things take life. One signature of your hand—and he can go to a sanatorium, and he doesn't have to die. Comrade Commissar, if we just think of things, calmly and simply—as they are—do you know what death is? Do you know that death is—nothing at all, not at all, never again, never, no matter what we do? Don't you see why he can't die? I love him. We all have to suffer. We all have things we want, which are taken away from us. It's all right. But—because we are living beings—there's something in each of us, something like the very heart of life condensed—and *that* should not be touched. You understand, don't you? Well, he is that to me, and you can't take him from me, because you can't let me stand here, and look at you, and talk, and breathe, and move, and then tell me you'll take him—we're not insane, both of us, are we, Comrade Commissar?"

The Comrade Commissar said: "One hundred thousand workers died in the civil war. Why—in the face of the Union of Socialist Soviet Republics—can't one aristocrat die?"

Kira walked home very slowly and looked at the dark city; she looked at the glistening pavements built for many thousands of old shoes; at the tramways for men to ride in; at the stone cubes into which men crawled at night; at the posters that cried of what men dreamed and of what men ate; and she wondered whether any of those thousands of eyes around her saw what she saw, and why it had been given her to see.

*   *   *

Because:

In a kitchen on the fifth floor, a woman bent over a smoking stove and stirred cabbage in a kettle, and the cabbage smelt, and the woman blinked, and groaned with the pain in her back, and scratched her head with the spoon,

Because:

In a corner saloon, a man leaned against the bar and raised a foaming glass of beer, and the foam spilled over the floor and over his trousers, and he belched and sang a gay song,

Because:

In a white bed, on white sheets stained with yellow, a child slept and sniveled in its sleep, its nose wet,

Because:

On a sack of flour in the basement, a man tore a woman's pants off, and bit into her throat, and they rolled, moaning, over the sacks of flour and potatoes,

Because:

In the silence of stone walls slowly dripping frozen dampness, a figure knelt before a gilded cross, and raised trembling arms in exaltation, and knocked a pale forehead against a cold stone floor,

Because:

In the roar of machines whirling lightnings of steel and drops of burning grease, men swung vigorous arms, and panted, heaving chests of muscles glistening with sweat, and made soap,

Because:

In a public bath, steam rose from brass pans, and red, gelatinous bodies shook scrubbing themselves with the soap, sighing and grunting, trying to scratch steaming backs, and murky water and soap suds ran down the floor into the drain—

—Leo Kovalensky was sentenced to die.

*   *   *

It was her last chance and she had to take it.

A modest house stood before her, on a modest street that lay deserted in the darkness. An old landlady opened the door and looked at Kira suspiciously: Comrade Taganov did not receive women visitors. But she said nothing and shuffled, leading Kira down a corridor, then stopped, pointed at a door and shuffled away.

Kira knocked.

His voice said: "Come in."

She entered.

He was sitting at his desk and he was about to rise, but he didn't. He sat looking at her, and then rose very slowly, so slowly that she wondered how long she stood there, at the door, while he was rising, his eyes never leaving her.

Then, he said: "Good evening, Kira."

"Good evening, Andrei."

"Take your coat off."

She was suddenly frightened, uncomfortable, uncertain; she lost all the bitter, hostile assurance that had brought her here; obediently, she took off her coat and threw her hat on the bed. It was a large, bare room with whitewashed walls, a narrow iron bed, one desk, one chair, one chest of drawers, no pictures, no posters, but books, an ocean of books and papers and newspapers, running over the desk, over the chest, over the floor.

He said: "It's cold tonight, isn't it?"

"It's cold."

"Sit down."

She sat by the desk. He sat on the bed, his hands clasping his knees. She wished he would not look at her like that, every second of every long minute. But he said calmly: "How have you been, Kira? You look tired."

"I am a little tired."

"How is your job?"

"It isn't."

"What?"

"Reduction of staffs."

"Oh, Kira, I'm sorry. I'll get you another one."

"Thanks. But I don't know whether I need one. How is your job?"

"The G.P.U.? I've been working hard. Searches, arrests. You still aren't afraid of me, are you?"

"No."

"I don't like searches."

"Do you like arrests?"

"I don't mind—when it's necessary."

They were silent, and then she said: "Andrei, if I make you uncomfortable—I'll go."

"No! Don't go. Please don't go." He tried to laugh. "Make me uncomfortable? What makes you say that? I'm just . . . just a little embarrassed . . . this room of mine . . . it's in no condition to receive such a guest."

"Oh, it's a nice room. Big. Light."

"You see, I'm home so seldom, and when I am, I just have time to fall in bed, without noticing what's around me."

"Oh."

They were silent.

"How is your family, Kira?"

"They are fine, thank you."

"I often see your cousin, Victor Dunaev, at the Institute. Do you like him?"

"No."

"Neither do I."

They were silent.

"Victor has joined the Party," said Kira.

"I voted against him. But most of them were eager to admit him."

"I'm glad you voted against him. He's the kind of Party man I despise."

"What kind of Party man don't you despise, Kira?"

"Your kind, Andrei."

"Kira . . ." It began as a sentence, but stopped on the first word.

She said resolutely: "Andrei, what have I done?"

He looked at her, and frowned, and looked aside, shaking his head slowly: "Nothing." Then he asked suddenly: "Why did you come here?"

"It's been such a long time since I saw you last."

"Two months, day after tomorrow."

"Unless you saw me at the Institute three weeks ago."

"I saw you."

She waited, but he did not explain, and she tried to ignore it, her words almost a plea: "I came because I thought . . . because I thought maybe you wanted to see me."

"I didn't want to see you."

She rose to her feet.

"Don't go, Kira!"

"Andrei, I don't understand!"

He stood facing her. His voice was flat, harsh as an insult: "I didn't want you to understand. I didn't want you to know. But if you want to hear it—you'll hear it. I never wanted to see you again. Because . . ." His voice was like a dull whip. "Because I love you."

Her hands fell limply against the wall behind her. He went on: "Don't say it. I know what you're going to say. I've said it to myself again and again and again. I know every word. But it's useless. I know I should be ashamed, and I am, but it's useless. I know that you liked me, and trusted me, because we were friends. It was beautiful and rare, and you have every right to despise me."

She stood pressed to the wall, not moving.

"When you came in, I thought 'Send her away.' But I knew that if you went away, I'd run after you. I thought 'I won't say a word.' But I knew that you'd know it before you left. I love you. I know you'd think kindlier of me if I said that I hate you."

She said nothing; she cringed against the wall, her eyes wide, her glance holding no pity for him, but a plea for his pity.

"You're frightened? Do you see why I couldn't face you? I knew what you felt for me and what you could never feel. I knew what you'd say, how your eyes would look at me. When did it start? I don't know. I knew only that it must end—because I couldn't stand it. To see you, and laugh with you, and talk of the future of humanity—and think only of when your hand would touch mine, of your feet in the sand, the little shadow on your throat, your skirt blowing in the wind. To discuss the meaning of life—and wonder if I could see the line of your breast in your open collar!"

She whispered: "Andrei . . . don't. . . ."

It was not an admission of love, it was the confession of a crime: "Why am I telling you all this? I don't know. I'm not sure I'm really saying it to you. I've been crying it to myself so often, for such a long time! You shouldn't have come here. I'm not your friend. I don't care if I hurt you. All you are to me is only this: I want you."

She whispered: "Andrei . . . I didn't know. . . ."

"I didn't want you to know. I tried to stay away from you, to break it. You don't know what it's done to me. There was one search. There was a woman. We arrested her. She rolled on the floor, in her nightgown, at my feet, crying for mercy. I thought of you. I thought of you there, on the floor, in your nightgown, crying for pity as I have been crying to you so many months. I'd take you—and I wouldn't care if it were the floor, and if those men stood looking. Afterward, perhaps I'd shoot you, and shoot myself—but I wouldn't care—because it would be afterward. I thought I could arrest you—in the middle of the night—and carry you wherever I wanted—and have you. I could do it, you know. I laughed at the woman and kicked her. My men stared at me—they had never seen me do that. They took the woman to jail—and I found an excuse to run away, to walk home alone—thinking of you. . . . Don't look at me like that. You don't have to be afraid that I'd do it. . . . I have nothing to offer you. I cannot offer you my life. My life is twenty-eight years of that for which you feel contempt. And you—you're everything I've always expected to hate. But I want you.

I'd give everything I have—everything I could ever have—Kira—for something you can't give me!"

He saw her eyes open wide at a thought he could not guess. She breathed: "What did you say, Andrei?"

"I said, everything I have for something you can't. . . ."

It was terror in her eyes, a terror of the thought she had seen for a second so very clearly. She whispered, trembling: "Andrei . . . I'd better go. . . . I'd better go now."

But he was looking at her fixedly, approaching her, asking in a voice suddenly very soft and low: "Or is it something you . . . can . . . Kira?"

She was not thinking of him; she was not thinking of Leo; she was thinking of Maria Petrovna and of the red bubble on dying lips. She was pressed to the wall, cornered, her ten fingers spread apart on the white plaster. His voice, his hope were driving her on. Her body rose slowly against the wall, to her full height, higher, on tiptoe, her head thrown back, so that her throat was level with his mouth when she threw at him:

"I can! I love you."

She wondered how strange it was to feel a man's lips that were not Leo's.

She was saying: "Yes . . . for a long time . . . but I didn't know that you, too . . ." and she felt his hands and his mouth, and she wondered whether this was joy or torture to him and how strong his arms were. She hoped it would be quick. . . .

———

EDITOR'S NOTE: *This scene, late in the novel, shows us the type of scum who rise to the top under collectivism. Syerov is a ranking Soviet bureaucrat; Morozov, a private speculator and influence-purchaser. The two are engaged in a large-scale scheme to steal supplies from the state.*

Stepan Timoshenko is a leader in the Red Baltfleet. He is a veteran Communist fighter—once idealistic about the new government, now bitterly disillusioned.

The Profiteers on Collectivism

Pavel Syerov had a drink before he came to his office. He had another drink in the afternoon. He had telephoned Morozov and a voice he knew to be Morozov's had told him that the Citizen Morozov was not at home. He paced up and down his office and smashed an inkstand. He found a misspelled word in a letter he had dictated, and threw the letter, crumpled into a twisted ball, at his secretary's face. He telephoned Morozov and got no answer. A woman telephoned him and her soft, lisping voice said sweetly, insistently: "But, Pavlusha darling, you promised me that bracelet!" A speculator brought a bracelet tied in the corner of a dirty handkerchief, and refused to leave it without the full amount in cash. Syerov telephoned Morozov at the Food Trust; a secretary demanded to know who was calling; Syerov slammed the receiver down without answering. He roared at a ragged applicant for a job that he would turn him over to the G.P.U. and ordered his secretary to throw out all those waiting to see him. He left the office an hour earlier than usual and slammed the door behind him.

He walked past Morozov's house on his way home and hesitated, but saw a militia-man on the corner and did not enter.

At dinner—which had been sent from a communal kitchen two blocks away, and was cold, with grease floating over the cabbage soup—Comrade Sonia said: "Really, Pavel, I've got to have a fur coat. I can't allow myself to catch a cold—you know—for the child's sake. And no rabbit fur, either. I know you can afford it. Oh, I'm not saying anything about anyone's little activities, but I'm just keeping my eyes open."

He threw his napkin into the soup and left the table without eating.

He called Morozov's house and let the telephone ring for five minutes. There was no answer. He sat on the bed and emptied a bottle of vodka. Comrade Sonia left for a meeting of the Teachers' Council of an Evening School for Illiterate Women House Workers. He emptied a second bottle.

Then he rose resolutely, swaying a little, pulled his belt tight across his fur jacket and went to Morozov's house.

He rang three times. There was no answer. He kept his finger on the bell button, leaning indifferently against the wall. He heard no sound behind the door, but he heard steps rising up the stairs and he flung himself into the darkest corner of the landing. The steps died on the floor below and he heard a door opening and closing. He could not let himself be seen waiting there, he remembered dimly. He reached for his notebook and wrote, pressing the notebook to the wall, in the light of a street lamp outside:

MOROZOV, YOU GOD-DAMN BASTARD!

If you don't come across with what's due me before tomorrow morning, you'll eat breakfast at the G.P.U., and you know what that means.

Affectionately,
PAVEL SYEROV.

He folded the note and slipped it under the door.

Fifteen minutes later, Morozov stepped noiselessly out of his bathroom and tiptoed to the lobby. He listened nervously, but heard no sound on the stair-landing. Then he noticed the faint blur of white in the darkness, on the floor.

He picked up the note and read it, bending under the dining-room lamp. His face looked gray.

The telephone rang. He shuddered, frozen to the spot, as if the eyes somewhere behind that ringing bell could see him with the note in his hand. He crammed the note deep into his pocket and answered the telephone, trembling.

It was an old aunt of his and she sniffled into the receiver, asking to borrow some money. He called her an old bitch and hung up.

Through the open bedroom door, Antonina Pavlovna, sitting at her dressing table, brushing her hair, called out in a piercing voice, objecting to the use of such language. He whirled upon her ferociously: "If it weren't for you and that damn lover of yours . . ."

Antonina Pavlovna shrieked: "He's not my lover—yet! If he were, do you think I'd be squatting around a sloppy old fool like you?"

They had a quarrel.

Morozov forgot about the note in his pocket.

*   *   *

The European roof garden had a ceiling of glass panes; it looked like a black void staring down, crushing those below more implacably than a steel vault. There were lights; yellow lights that looked dimmed in an oppressive haze which was cigarette smoke, or heat, or the black abyss above. There were white tables and yellow glints in the silverware.

Men sat at the tables. Yellow sparks flashed in their diamond studs and in the beads of moisture on their red, flushed faces. They ate; they bent eagerly over their plates; they chewed hurriedly, incredulously; they were not out on a carefree evening in a gay night spot; they were *eating*.

In a corner, a yellowish bald head went over a red steak on a white plate; the man cut the steak, smacking his fleshy red lips. Across the table, a red-headed girl of fifteen ate hastily, her head drawn into her shoulders; when she raised her head, she blushed from the tip of her short, freckled nose to her white, freckled neck, and her mouth was twisted as if she were going to scream.

A fierce jet of smoke swayed by a dark window pane; a thin individual, with a long face that betrayed too closely its future appearance as a skull, rocked monotonously on the back legs of his chair, and smoked without interruption, holding a cigarette in long, yellow fingers, spouting smoke out of wide nostrils frozen in a sardonic, unhealthy grin.

Women moved among the tables, with an awkward, embarrassed insolence. A head of soft, golden waves nodded unsteadily under a light, wide eyes in deep blue rings, a young mouth open in a vicious, sneering smile. In the middle of the room, a gaunt, dark woman with knobs on her shoulders, holes under her collar-bones and a skin the color of muddy coffee, was laughing too loudly, opening painted lips like a gash over strong white teeth and very red gums.

The orchestra played "John Gray." It flung brief, blunt notes out into space, as if tearing them off the strings before they were ripe, hiding the gap of an uncapturable gaiety under a convulsive rhythm.

Waiters glided soundlessly through the crowd and bent over the tables, obsequious and exaggerated, and their flabby jowls conveyed expressions of respect, and mockery, and pity for those guilty, awkward ones who made such an effort to be gay.

Morozov did remember that he had to raise money before morning. He came to the European roof garden, alone. He sat at three different tables, smoked four different cigars and whispered confidentially into five different ears that belonged to corpulent men who did not seem to be in a hurry. At the end of two hours, he had the money in his wallet.

He mopped his forehead with relief, sat alone at a table in a dark corner and ordered cognac.

Stepan Timoshenko leaned so far across a white table cloth that he seemed to be lying on, rather than sitting at, the table. His head was propped on his elbow, his fingers on the nape of his broad neck; he had a glass in his other hand. When the glass was empty, he held it uncertainly in the air, wondering how to refill it with one hand; he solved the problem by dropping the glass with a sonorous crash and lifting the bottle to his lips. The maitre d'hotel looked at him nervously, sidewise, frowning; he frowned at the jacket with the rabbit fur collar, at the crumpled sailor cap sliding over one ear, at the muddy shoes flung out onto the satin train of a woman at the next table. But the maitre d'hotel had to be cautious; Stepan Timoshenko had been there before; everyone knew that he was a Party member.

A waiter slid unobtrusively up to his table and gathered the broken glass into a dust-pan. Another waiter brought a sparkling clean glass and slipped his fingers gently over Timoshenko's bottle, whispering: "May I help you, citizen?"

"Go to hell!" said Timoshenko and pushed the glass across the table with the back of his hand. The glass vacillated on the edge and crashed down. "I'll do as I please!" Timoshenko roared, and heads turned to look at him. "I'll drink out of a bottle if I please. I'll drink out of two bottles!"

"But, citizen . . ."

"Want me to show you how?" Timoshenko asked, his eyes gleaming ominously.

"No, indeed, citizen," the waiter said hastily.

"Go to hell," said Timoshenko with soft persuasion. "I don't like your snoot. I don't like any of the snoots around here." He rose, swaying, roaring: "I don't like any of the damn snoots around here!"

He staggered among the tables. The maitre d'hotel whispered gently at his elbow: "If you're not feeling well, citizen . . ."

"Out of my way!" bellowed Timoshenko, tripping over a woman's slippers.

He had almost reached the door, when he stopped suddenly and his face melted into a wide, gentle smile. "Ah," he said. "A friend of mine. A dear friend of mine!"

He staggered to Morozov, swung a chair high over someone's head, planted it with a resounding smash at Morozov's table and sat down.

"I beg your pardon, citizen?" Morozov gasped, rising.

"Sit still, pal," said Timoshenko and his huge tanned paw pressed Morozov's shoulder down, like a sledge hammer, so that Morozov fell back on his chair with a thud. "Can't run away from a friend, Comrade Morozov. We're friends, you know. Old friends. Well, maybe you don't know me. Stepan Timoshenko's the name. Stepan Timoshenko. . . . Of the Red Baltfleet," he added as an after-thought.

"Oh," said Morozov. "Oh."

"Yep," said Timoshenko, "an old friend and admirer of yours. And you know what?"

"No," said Morozov.

"We gotta have a drink together. Like good pals. We gotta have a drink. Waiter!" he roared so loudly that a violinist missed a note of "John Gray."

"Bring us two bottles!" Timoshenko ordered when a waiter bowed hesitantly over his shoulder. "No! Bring us three bottles!"

"Three bottles of what, citizen?" the waiter asked timidly.

"Of anything," said Timoshenko. "No! Wait! What's the most expensive? What is it that the good, fat capitalists guzzle in proper style?"

"Champagne, citizen?"

"Make it champagne and damn quick! Three bottles and two glasses!"

When the waiter brought the champagne, Timoshenko poured it and planted a glass before Morozov. "There!" said Timoshenko with a friendly smile. "Going to drink with me, pal?"

"Yes, co . . . comrade," said Morozov meekly. "Thank you, comrade."

"Your health, Comrade Morozov!" said Timoshenko, solemnly, raising his glass. "To Comrade Morozov, citizen of the Union of Socialist Soviet Republics!"

They clinked their glasses. Morozov glanced around furtively, helplessly, but no help was coming. He drank, the glass trembling at his lips. Then he smiled ingratiatingly: "This was very nice of you, comrade," he muttered, rising. "And I appreciate it very much, comrade. Now if you don't mind. I've got to be going and . . ."

"Sit still," ordered Timoshenko. He refilled his glass and raised it, leaning back, smiling, but his smile did not seem friendly any longer and his dark eyes were looking at Morozov steadily, sardonically. "To the great Citizen Morozov, the man who beat the revolution!" he said and laughed resonantly, and emptied the glass in one gulp, his head thrown back.

"Comrade . . ." Morozov muttered through lips he could barely force open, "comrade . . . what do you mean?"

Timoshenko laughed louder and leaned across the table toward Morozov, his elbows crossed, his cap far back on his head, over sticky ringlets of dark hair. The laughter stopped abruptly, as if slashed off. Timoshenko said softly, persuasively, with a smile that frightened Morozov more than the laughter: "Don't look so scared, Comrade Morozov. You don't have to be afraid of me. I'm nothing but a beaten wretch, beaten by you, Comrade Morozov, and all I want is to tell you humbly that I know I'm beaten and I hold no grudge. Hell, I hold a profound admiration for you, Comrade Morozov. You've taken the greatest revolution the world has ever seen and patched the seat of your pants with it!"

"Comrade," said Morozov with a blue-lipped determination, "I don't know what you're talking about."

"Oh, yes," said Timoshenko ruefully. "Oh, yes, you do. You know more about it than I do, more than millions of young fools do, that watch us from all over the world with worshipping eyes. You must tell them, Comrade Morozov. You have a lot to tell them."

"Honestly, comrade, I . . ."

"For instance, you know how you made us do it. I don't. All I know is that we've done it. We made a revolution. We had red banners. The banners said that we made it for the world proletariat. We had fools who thought in their doomed hearts that we made it for all those downtrodden ones who suffer on this earth. But you and me, Comrade Morozov, we have a secret. We know, but we won't tell. Why tell? The world doesn't want to hear it. We know that the revolution—it was made for you, Comrade Morozov, and hats off to you!"

"Comrade whoever you are, comrade," Morozov moaned, "what do you want?"

"Just to tell you it's yours, Comrade Morozov."

"What?" Morozov asked, wondering if he was going insane.

"The revolution," said Timoshenko pleasantly. "The revolution. Do you know what a revolution is? I'll tell you. We killed. We killed men in the streets, and in the cellars, and aboard our ships. . . . Aboard our ships . . . I remember . . . There was one boy—an officer—he couldn't have been more than twenty. He made the sign of the cross—his mother must've taught him that. He had blood running out of his mouth. He looked at me. His eyes—they weren't frightened any more. They were kind of astonished. About something his mother hadn't taught him. He looked at me. That was the last thing. He looked at me."

Drops were rolling down Timoshenko's jowls. He filled a glass and it tottered uncertainly in his hand, trying to find his mouth, and he drank without knowing that he was drinking, his eyes fixed on Morozov's.

"That's what we did in the year nineteen-hundred-and-seventeen. Now I'll tell you what we did it for. We did it so that the Citizen Morozov could get up in the morning and scratch his belly, because the mattress wasn't soft enough and it made his navel itch. We did it so that he could ride in a big limousine with a down pillow on the seat and a little glass tube for flowers by the window, lilies-of-the-valley, you know. So that he could drink cognac in a place like this. So that he could scramble up, on holidays, to a stand all draped in red bunting and make a speech about the proletariat. We did it, Comrade Morozov, and we take a bow. Don't glare at me like that, Comrade Morozov, I'm only your humble servant, I've done my best for you, and you should reward me with a smile, really, you have a lot to thank me for!"

"Comrade!" Morozov panted. "Let me go!"

"Sit still!" Timoshenko roared. "Pour yourself a glass and drink. Do you hear me? Drink, you bastard! Drink and listen!"

Morozov obeyed; his glass tinkled, shaking, against the bottle.

"You see," said Timoshenko, as if each word were tearing his throat on its way out, "I don't mind that we're beaten. I don't mind that we've taken the greatest of crimes on our shoulders and then let it slip through our fingers. I wouldn't mind it if we had been beaten by a tall warrior in a steel helmet, a human dragon spitting fire. But we're beaten by a louse. A big, fat, slow, blond louse. Ever seen lice? The blond ones are the fattest. . . . It was our own fault. Once, men were ruled with a god's thunder. Then they were ruled with a sword. Now they're ruled with a Primus. Once, they were held by reverence. Then they were held by fear. Now they're held by their stomachs. Men have worn chains on their necks, and on their wrists, and on their ankles. Now they're enchained by their rectums. Only you don't hold heroes by their rectums. It was our own fault."

"Comrade, for God's sake, comrade, why tell it all to me?"

"We started building a temple. Do we end with a chapel? No! And we don't even end with an outhouse. We end with a musty kitchen with a second-hand stove! We set fire under a kettle and we brewed and stirred and mixed blood and fire and steel. What are we fishing now out of the brew? A new humanity? Men of granite? Or at least a good and horrible monster? No! Little puny things that wiggle. Little things that can bend both ways, little double-jointed spirits. Little things that don't even bow humbly to be whipped. No! They take the lash obediently and whip themselves! Ever sat at a social-activity club meeting? Should. Do you good. Learn a lot about the human spirit."

"Comrade!" Morozov breathed. "What do you want? Is it money you want? I'll pay. I'll . . ."

Timoshenko laughed so loudly that heads turned and Morozov cringed, trying not to be noticed. "You louse!" Timoshenko roared, laughing. "You fool, near-sighted, demented louse! Who do you think you're talking to? Comrade Victor Dunaev? Comrade Pavel Syerov? Comrade . . ."

"Comrade!" Morozov roared, so that heads turned to him, but he did not care any longer. "You . . . you . . . you have no right to say that! I have nothing whatever to do with Comrade Syerov! I . . ."

"Say," Timoshenko remarked slowly, "I didn't say you had. Why the excitement?"

"Well, I thought . . . I . . . you . . ."

"I didn't say you had," Timoshenko repeated. "I only said you should have. You and he and Victor Dunaev. And about one million others—with Party cards and stamps affixed. The winners and the conquerors. Those who crawl. That, pal, is the great slogan of the men of the future: those who crawl. Listen, do you know how many millions of eyes are watching us across lands and oceans? They're not very close and they can't see very well. They see a big shadow rising. They think it's a huge beast. They're too far to see that it's soft and brownish and fuzzy. You know, fuzzy, a glistening sort of fuzz. They don't know that it's made of cockroaches. Little, glossy, brown cockroaches, packed tight, one on the other, into a huge wall. Little cockroaches that keep silent and wiggle their whiskers. But the world is too far to see the whiskers. That's what's wrong with the world, Comrade Morozov: they don't see the whiskers!"

"Comrade! Comrade, what are you talking about?"

"They see a black cloud and they hear thunder. They've been told that behind the cloud, blood is running freely, and men fight, and men kill, and men die. Well, what of it? They, those who watch, are not afraid of blood. There's an honor in blood. But do they know that it's not blood we're bathed in, it's pus? Listen, I'll give you advice. If you want to keep this land in your tentacles, tell the world that you're chopping heads off for breakfast and shooting men by the regiment. Let the world think that you're a huge monster to be feared and respected and fought honorably. But don't let them know that yours is not an army of heroes, nor even of fiends, but of shriveled bookkeepers with a rupture who've learned to be arrogant. Don't let them know that you're not to be shot, but to be disinfected. Don't let them know that you're not to be fought with cannons, but with carbolic acid!"

Morozov's napkin was crumpled into a drenched ball in his fist. He wiped his forehead once more. He said, trying to make his voice gentle and soothing, trying to rise imperceptibly: "You're right, comrade. Those are very fine sentiments. I agree with you absolutely. Now if you'll allow . . ."

"Sit down!" roared Timoshenko. "Sit down and drink a toast. Drink it or I'll shoot you like a mongrel. I still carry a gun, you know. Here . . ." he poured and a pale golden trickle ran down the table cloth to the floor. "Drink to the men who took a red banner and wiped their ass with it!"

Morozov drank.

Then he put his hand in his pocket and took out a handkerchief to mop his forehead. A crumpled piece of paper fell to the floor.

It was the swift, ferocious jerk, with which Morozov plunged down for it, that made Timoshenko's fist dart out and seize Morozov's hand. "What's that, pal?" asked Timoshenko.

Morozov's foot kicked the paper out of reach and it rolled under an empty table. Morozov said indifferently, little damp beads sparkling under his wide nostrils: "Oh, that? Nothing, comrade. Nothing at all. Just some scrap of waste paper."

"Oh," said Timoshenko, watching him with eyes that were alarmingly sober. "Oh, just a scrap of waste paper. Well, we'll let it lie there. We'll let the janitor throw it in the waste basket."

"Yes," Morozov nodded eagerly, "that's it. In the waste basket. Very well put, comrade." He giggled, mopping his forehead. "We'll let the janitor throw it in the waste basket. Would you like another drink, comrade? The bottle's empty. The next one's on me. Waiter! Another bottle of the same."

"Sure," said Timoshenko without moving. "I'll have another drink."

The waiter brought the bottle. Morozov filled the glasses, leaning solicitously over the table. He said, regaining his voice syllable by syllable: "You know, comrade, I think you misunderstood me, but I don't blame you. I can see your motives and I sympathize thoroughly. There are so many objectionable—er—shall we say dishonorable?—types these days. One has to be careful. We must get better acquainted, comrade. It's hard to tell at a glance, you know, and particularly in a place like this. I bet you thought I was a—a speculator, or something. Didn't you? Very funny, isn't it?"

"Very," said Timoshenko. "What are you looking down at, Comrade Morozov?"

"Oh!" Morozov giggled, jerking his head up. "I was just looking at my shoes, comrade. They're sort of tight, you know. Uncomfortable. Guess it's because I'm on my feet so much, you know, in the office."

"Uh-huh," said Timoshenko. "Shouldn't neglect your feet. Should take a hot bath when you come home, a pan of hot water with a little vinegar. That's good for sore feet."

"Oh, indeed? I'm glad you told me. Yes, indeed, thank you very much. I'll be sure and try it. First thing when I get home."

"About time you were getting home, isn't it, Comrade Morozov?"

"Oh! . . . well, I guess . . . well, it's not so late yet and . . ."

"I thought you were in a hurry a little while ago."

"I . . . well, no, I can't say that I'm in any particular hurry, and besides, such a pleasant . . ."

"What's the matter, Comrade Morozov? Anything you don't want to leave around here?"

"Who, me? I don't know what that could be, comrade . . . comrade . . . what did you say your name was, comrade?"

"Timoshenko. Stepan Timoshenko. It isn't that little scrap of waste paper down there under the table, by any chance?"

"Oh, that? Why, Comrade Timoshenko, I'd forgotten all about that. What would I want with it?"

"I don't know," said Timoshenko slowly.

"That's just it, Comrade Timoshenko, nothing. Nothing at all. Another drink, Comrade Timoshenko?"

"Thanks."

"Here you are, comrade."

"Anything wrong under the table, Comrade Morozov?"

"Why no, Comrade Timoshenko. I was just bending to tie my shoe lace. The shoe lace is unfastened."

"Where?"

"Well, isn't that funny? It really isn't unfastened at all. See? And I thought it was. You know how it is, these Soviet . . . these shoe laces nowadays. Not solid at all. Not dependable."

"No," said Timoshenko, "they tear like twine."

"Yes," said Morozov, "just like twine. Just, as you would say, like—like twine. . . . What are you leaning over for, Comrade Timoshenko? You're not comfortable. Why don't you move over here like this, you'll be more . . ."

"No," said Timoshenko, "I'm just fine here where I am. With a fine view of the table there. I like that table. Nice legs it has. Hasn't it? Sort of artistic, you know."

"Quite right, comrade, very artistic. Now on the other hand, comrade, there, on our left, isn't that a pretty blonde there, by the orchestra? Quite a figure, eh?"

"Yes, indeed, comrade. . . . It's nice shoes you have, Comrade Morozov. Patent leather, too. Bet you didn't get those in a co-operative."

"No . . . that is . . . to tell you the truth . . . well, you see . . ."

"What I like about them is that bulb. Right there, on the toes. Like a bump on someone's forehead. And shiny, too. Yep, those foreigners sure know how to make shoes."

"Speaking of the efficiency of production, comrade, take for instance, in the capitalistic countries . . . in the . . . in the . . ."

"Yes, Comrade Morozov, in the capitalistic countries?"

It was Morozov who leaped for the letter. It was Timoshenko who caught his wrist with fingers like talons, and for one brief moment they were on their hands and knees on the floor, and their eyes met silently like those of two beasts in deadly battle. Then Timoshenko's other hand seized the letter, and he rose slowly, releasing Morozov, and sat down at the table. He was reading the letter, while Morozov was still on his hands and knees, staring up at him with the eyes of a man awaiting the verdict of a court-martial.

MOROZOV, YOU GOD-DAMN BASTARD!

If you don't come across with what's due me before tomorrow morning, you'll eat breakfast at the G.P.U., and you know what that means,

Affectionately,
PAVEL SYEROV.

Morozov was sitting at the table when Timoshenko raised his head from the letter. Timoshenko laughed as Morozov had never heard a man laugh.

Timoshenko rose slowly, laughing. His stomach shook, and his rabbit fur collar, and the sinews of his bare throat. He swayed a little and he held the letter in both hands. Then his laughter died down slowly, smoothly, like a gramophone record unwinding, to a low, coughing chuckle on a single dry note. He slipped the letter into his pocket and turned slowly, his shoulders stooped, his movements suddenly awkward, humble. He shuffled heavily, uncertainly to the door. At the door, the maitre d'hotel glanced at him sidewise. Timoshenko returned the glance; Timoshenko's glance was gentle.

Morozov sat at the table, one hand frozen in mid-air in an absurd, twisted position, like the hand of a paralytic. He heard Timoshenko's chuckles dropping down the stairway; monotonous, disjoined chuckles that sounded like hiccoughs, like barks, like sobs.

He jumped up suddenly. "Oh my God!" he moaned. "Oh, my God!"

He ran, forgetting his hat and coat, down the long stairs, out into the snow. In the broad, white, silent street, Timoshenko was nowhere in sight.

*   *   *

Morozov did not send the money to Pavel Syerov. He did not go to his own office at the Food Trust. He sat all the following morning and all of the afternoon at home, in his room, and drank vodka. Whenever he heard the telephone or the door bell ringing, he crouched, his head in his shoulders, and bit his knuckles. Nothing happened.

At dinner time, Antonina Pavlovna brought the evening paper and threw it to him, snapping: "What the hell's the matter with you today?"

He glanced through the paper. There were news items on the front page:

In the village Vasilkino, in the Kama region, the peasants, goaded by the counter-revolutionary hoarder element, burned the local Club of Karl Marx. The bodies of the Club president and secretary, Party comrades from Moscow, were found in the charred ruins. A G.P.U. squad is on its way to Vasilkino.

In the village Sverskoe, twenty-five peasants were executed last

night for the murder of the Village Correspondent, a young comrade from the staff of a Communist Union of Youth newspaper in
Samara. The peasants refused to divulge the name of the murderer.

On the last page was a short item:

> The body of Stepan Timoshenko, former sailor of the Baltic
> Fleet, was found early this morning under a bridge, on the ice of
> Obukhovsky Canal. He had shot himself through the mouth. No
> papers, save his Party card, were found on the body to explain the
> reason for his suicide.

Morozov wiped his forehead, as if a noose had been slipped off his
throat, and drank two glasses of vodka.

When the telephone rang, he swaggered boldly to take the receiver,
and Antonina Pavlovna wondered why he was chuckling.

"Morozov?" a muffled voice whispered over the wire.

"That you, Pavlusha?" Morozov asked. "Listen, pal, I'm awfully
sorry, but I have the money and . . ."

"Forget the money," Syerov hissed. "It's all right. Listen . . . did I
leave you a note yesterday?"

"Why, yes, but I guess I deserved it and . . ."

"Have you destroyed it?"

"Why?"

"Nothing. Only you understand what it could . . . Have you destroyed it?"

Morozov looked at the evening paper, grinned and said: "Sure. I
have. Forget about it, pal."

He held the paper in his hand all evening long.

"The fool!" he muttered under his breath, so that Antonina
Pavlovna looked at him inquisitively, chin forward. "The damn fool!
He lost it. Wandered about all night, God knows where, the drunken
fool. He lost it!"

Morozov did not know that Stepan Timoshenko had come home
from the European roof garden and sat at a rickety table in his un-
heated garret and written painstakingly a letter on a piece of brown
wrapping paper, in the light of a dying candle in a green bottle; that
he had folded the letter carefully and slipped it into an old envelope
and slipped another scrap of paper, wrinkled and creased, into the envelope, and written Andrei Taganov's address on it; that he had sealed

the letter and had gone, steadily, unhurriedly, down the creaking stairs into the street.

The letter on the brown wrapping paper said:

DEAR FRIEND ANDREI,

I promised to say good-bye and here it is. It's not quite what I promised, but I guess you'll forgive me. I'm sick of seeing what I see and I can't stand to see it any longer. To you—as my only legacy—I'm leaving the letter you will find enclosed. It's a hard legacy, I know. I only hope that you won't follow me—too soon.

Your friend,

STEPAN TIMOSHENKO.

2. Capitalism vs. Collectivism

In her defense of individualism, AR is neither a "conservative" nor a "libertarian." Rejecting both movements, she describes herself as a "radical for capitalism." In other words, she identifies and defends the intellectual roots of capitalism on the deepest level—as the following, from her 1965 essay "What Is Capitalism?" (published in Capitalism: The Unknown Ideal), *demonstrates.*

What Is Capitalism?

... MANKIND IS not an entity, an organism, or a coral bush. The entity involved in production and trade is *man.* It is with the study of man—not of the loose aggregate known as a "community"—that any science of the humanities has to begin.

This issue represents one of the epistemological differences between the humanities and the physical sciences, one of the causes of the former's well-earned inferiority complex in regard to the latter. A physical science would not permit itself (not yet, at least) to ignore or bypass the nature of its subject. Such an attempt would mean: a science of astronomy that gazed at the sky, but refused to study individual stars, planets, and satellites—or a science of medicine that studied disease, without any knowledge or criterion of health, and took, as its basic subject of study, a hospital as a whole, never focusing on individual patients.

A great deal may be learned about society by studying man; but this process cannot be reversed: nothing can be learned about man by studying society—by studying the inter-relationships of entities one has never identified or defined. Yet that is the methodology adopted by most political economists. Their attitude, in effect, amounts to the unstated, implicit postulate: "Man is that which fits economic equations." Since he obviously does not, this leads to the curious fact that in spite of the practical nature of their science, political economists are oddly unable to relate their abstractions to the concretes of actual existence.

It leads also to a baffling sort of double standard or double perspective in their way of viewing men and events: if they observe a shoemaker, they find no difficulty in concluding that he is working in order to make a living; but as political economists, on the tribal premise, they declare that his purpose (and duty) is to provide society with shoes. If they observe a panhandler on a street corner, they identify him as a bum; in political economy, he becomes "a sovereign consumer." If they hear the communist doctrine that all property should belong to the state, they reject it emphatically and feel, *sincerely*, that they would fight communism to the death; but in political economy, they speak of the government's duty to effect "a fair redistribution of wealth," and they speak of businessmen as the best, most efficient trustees of the nation's "natural resources."

This is what a basic premise (and philosophical negligence) will do; this is what the tribal premise has done.

To reject that premise and begin at the beginning—in one's approach to political economy and to the evaluation of various social systems—one must begin by identifying man's nature, *i.e.*, those essential characteristics which distinguish him from all other living species.

Man's essential characteristic is his rational faculty. Man's mind is his basic means of survival—his only means of gaining knowledge. [. . .]

A process of thought is an enormously complex process of identification and integration, which only an individual mind can perform. There is no such thing as a collective brain. Men can learn from one another, but learning requires a process of thought on the part of every individual student. Men can cooperate in the discovery of new knowledge, but such cooperation requires the independent exercise of his rational faculty by every individual scientist. Man is the only living species that can transmit and expand his store of knowledge from generation to generation; but such transmission requires a process of thought on the part of the individual recipients. As witness, the breakdowns of civilization, the dark ages in the history of mankind's progress, when the accumulated knowledge of centuries vanished from the lives of men who were unable, unwilling, or forbidden to think.

In order to sustain its life, every living species has to follow a certain course of action required by its nature. The action required to sustain human life is primarily intellectual: everything man needs has to be discovered by his mind and produced by his effort. Production is the application of reason to the problem of survival.

If some men do not choose to think, they can survive only by imitating and repeating a routine of work discovered by others—but those others had to discover it, or none would have survived. If some men do not choose to think or to work, they can survive (temporarily) only by looting the goods produced by others—but those others had to produce them, or none would have survived. Regardless of what choice is made, in this issue, by any man or by any number of men, regardless of what blind, irrational, or evil course they may choose to pursue—the fact remains that reason is man's means of survival and that men prosper or fail, survive or perish in proportion to the degree of their rationality.

Since knowledge, thinking, and rational action are properties of the individual, since the choice to exercise his rational faculty or not depends on the individual, man's survival requires that those who think be free of the interference of those who don't. Since men are neither omniscient nor infallible, they must be free to agree or disagree, to cooperate or to pursue their own independent course, each according to his own rational judgment. Freedom is the fundamental requirement of man's mind.

A rational mind does not work under compulsion; it does not subordinate its grasp of reality to anyone's orders, directives, or controls; it does not sacrifice its knowledge, its view of the truth, to anyone's opinions, threats, wishes, plans, or "welfare." Such a mind may be hampered by others, it may be silenced, proscribed, imprisoned, or destroyed; it cannot be forced; a gun is not an argument. (An example and symbol of this attitude is Galileo.)

It is from the work and the inviolate integrity of such minds—from the intransigent innovators—that all of mankind's knowledge and achievements have come. (See *The Fountainhead*.) It is to such minds that mankind owes its survival. (See *Atlas Shrugged*.)

The same principle applies to all men, on every level of ability and ambition. To the extent that a man is guided by his rational judgment, he acts in accordance with the requirements of his nature and, to that extent, succeeds in achieving a human form of survival and well-being; to the extent that he acts irrationally, he acts as his own destroyer.

The social recognition of man's rational nature—of the connection between his survival and his use of reason—is the concept of *individual rights*.

I shall remind you that "rights" are a moral principle defining and sanctioning a man's freedom of action in a social context, that they are derived from man's nature as a rational being and represent a necessary condition of his particular mode of survival. I shall remind you also that the right to life is the source of all rights, including the right to property.

In regard to political economy, this last requires special emphasis: man has to work and produce in order to support his life. He has to support his life by his own effort and by the guidance of his own mind. If he cannot dispose of the product of his effort, he cannot dispose of his effort; if he cannot dispose of his effort, he cannot dispose of his life. Without property rights, no other rights can be practiced.

Now, bearing these facts in mind, consider the question of what social system is appropriate to man.

A social system is a set of moral-political-economic principles embodied in a society's laws, institutions, and government, which determine the relationships, the terms of association, among the men living in a given geographical area. It is obvious that these terms and relationships depend on an identification of man's nature, that they would be different if they pertain to a society of rational beings or to a colony of ants. It is obvious that they will be radically different if men deal with one another as free, independent individuals, on the premise that every man is an end in himself—or as members of a pack, each regarding the others as the means to *his* ends and to the ends of "the pack as a whole."

There are only two fundamental questions (or two aspects of the same question) that determine the nature of any social system: Does a social system recognize individual rights?—and: Does a social system ban physical force from human relationships? The answer to the second question is the practical implementation of the answer to the first.

Is man a sovereign individual who owns his person, his mind, his life, his work and its products—or is he the property of the tribe (the state, the society, the collective) that may dispose of him in any way it pleases, that may dictate his convictions, prescribe the course of his life, control his work and expropriate his products? Does man have the *right* to exist for his own sake—or is he born in bondage, as an indentured servant who must keep buying his life by serving the tribe but can never acquire it free and clear?

This is the first question to answer. The rest is consequences and practical implementations. The basic issue is only: Is man free?

In mankind's history, capitalism is the only system that answers: Yes.

Capitalism is a social system based on the recognition of individual rights, including property rights, in which all property is privately owned.

The recognition of individual rights entails the banishment of physical force from human relationships: basically, rights can be violated only by means of force. In a capitalist society, no man or group may *initiate* the use of physical force against others. The only function of the government, in such a society, is the task of protecting man's rights, *i.e.*, the task of protecting him from physical force; the government acts as the agent of man's right of self-defense, and may use force only in retaliation and only against those who initiate its use; thus the government is the means of placing the retaliatory use of force under *objective control*.

It is the basic, metaphysical fact of man's nature—the connection between his survival and his use of reason—that capitalism recognizes and protects.

In a capitalist society, all human relationships are *voluntary*. Men are free to cooperate or not, to deal with one another or not, as their own individual judgments, convictions, and interests dictate. They can deal with one another only in terms of and by means of reason, *i.e.*, by means of discussion, persuasion, and *contractual* agreement, by voluntary choice to mutual benefit. The right to agree with others is not a problem in any society; it is *the right to disagree* that is crucial. It is the institution of private property that protects and implements the right to disagree—and thus keeps the road open to man's most valuable attribute (valuable personally, socially, and *objectively*): the creative mind.

This is the cardinal difference between capitalism and collectivism.

The power that determines the establishment, the changes, the evolution, and the destruction of social systems is philosophy. The role of chance, accident, or tradition, in this context, is the same as their role in the life of an individual: their power stands in inverse ratio to the power of a culture's (or an individual's) philosophical equipment, and grows as philosophy collapses. It is, therefore, by reference to philosophy that the character of a social system has to be defined and evaluated. Corresponding to the four branches of philosophy, the four keystones of capitalism are: metaphysically, the requirements of man's nature and survival—epistemologically, reason—ethically, individual rights—politically, freedom.

This, in substance, is the base of the proper approach to political economy and to an understanding of capitalism—not the tribal premise inherited from prehistorical traditions.

The "practical" justification of capitalism does not lie in the collectivist claim that it effects "the best allocation of national resources." Man is *not* a "national resource" and neither is his mind—and without the creative power of man's intelligence, raw materials remain just so many useless raw materials.

The *moral* justification of capitalism does not lie in the altruist claim that it represents the best way to achieve "the common good." It is true that capitalism does—if that catch-phrase has any meaning—but this is merely a secondary consequence. The moral justification of capitalism lies in the fact that it is the only system consonant with man's rational nature, that it protects man's survival *qua* man, and that its ruling principle is: *justice*.

Every social system is based, explicitly or implicitly, on some theory of ethics. The tribal notion of "the common good" has served as the moral justification of most social systems—and of all tyrannies—in history. The degree of a society's enslavement or freedom corresponded to the degree to which that tribal slogan was invoked or ignored.

"The common good" (or "the public interest") is an undefined and undefinable concept: there is no such entity as "the tribe" or "the public"; the tribe (or the public or society) is only a number of individual men. Nothing can be good for the tribe as such; "good" and "value" pertain *only* to a living organism—to an individual living organism—not to a disembodied aggregate of relationships.

"The common good" is a meaningless concept, unless taken literally, in which case its only possible meaning is: the sum of the good of *all* the individual men involved. But in that case, the concept is meaningless as a moral criterion: it leaves open the question of what *is* the good of individual men and how does one determine it?

It is not, however, in its literal meaning that that concept is generally used. It is accepted precisely for its elastic, undefinable, mystical character which serves, not as a moral guide, but as an escape from morality. Since the good is not applicable to the disembodied, it becomes a moral blank check for those who attempt to embody it.

When "the common good" of a society is regarded as something apart from and superior to the individual good of its members, it means that the good of *some* men takes precedence over the good of others, with those others consigned to the status of sacrificial animals. It is tacitly assumed, in such cases, that "the common good" means "the good of the *majority*" as against the minority or the individual. Observe the significant fact that that assumption is *tacit:* even the most collectivized mentalities seem to sense the impossibility of justifying it morally. But "the good of the majority," too, is only a pretense and a delusion: since, in fact, the violation of an individual's rights means the abrogation of all rights, it delivers the helpless majority into the power of any gang that proclaims itself to be "the voice of society" and proceeds to rule by means of physical force, until deposed by another gang employing the same means.

If one begins by defining the good of individual men, one will accept as proper only a society in which that good is achieved and *achievable*. But if one begins by accepting "the common good" as an axiom and regarding individual good as its possible but not necessary consequence (not necessary in any particular case), one ends up with such a gruesome absurdity as Soviet Russia, a country professedly dedicated to "the common good," where, with the exception of a minuscule clique of rulers, the entire population has existed in subhuman misery for over two generations.

What makes the victims and, worse, the observers accept this and other similar historical atrocities, and still cling to the myth of "the common good"? The answer lies in philosophy—in philosophical theories on the nature of moral values.

There are, in essence, three schools of thought on the nature of the good: the intrinsic, the subjective, and the objective. The *intrinsic* theory holds that the good is inherent in certain things or actions as such, regardless of their context and consequences, regardless of any benefit or injury they may cause to the actors and subjects involved. It is a theory that divorces the concept of "good" from beneficiaries, and the concept of "value" from valuer and purpose—claiming that the good is good in, by, and of itself.

The *subjectivist* theory holds that the good bears no relation to the facts of reality, that it is the product of a man's consciousness, created by his feelings, desires, "intuitions," or whims, and that it is merely an "arbitrary postulate" or an "emotional commitment."

The intrinsic theory holds that the good resides in some sort of reality, independent of man's consciousness; the subjectivist theory holds that the good resides in man's consciousness, independent of reality.

The *objective* theory holds that the good is neither an attribute of "things in themselves" nor of man's emotional states, but *an evaluation* of the facts of reality by man's consciousness according to a rational standard of value. (Rational, in this context, means: derived from the facts of reality and validated by a process of reason.) The objective theory holds that *the good is an aspect of reality in relation to man*—and that it must be discovered, not invented, by man. Fundamental to an objective theory of values is the question: Of value to whom and for what? An objective theory does not permit context-dropping or "concept-stealing"; it does not permit the separation of "value" from "purpose," of the good from beneficiaries, and of man's actions from reason.

Of all the social systems in mankind's history, *capitalism is the only system based on an objective theory of values.*

The intrinsic theory and the subjectivist theory (or a mixture of both) are the necessary base of every dictatorship, tyranny, or variant of the absolute state. Whether they are held consciously or subconsciously—in the explicit form of a philosopher's treatise or in the implicit chaos of its echoes in an average man's feelings—these theories make it possible for a man to believe that the good is independent of man's mind and can be achieved by physical force.

If a man believes that the good is intrinsic in certain actions, he will not hesitate to force others to perform them. If he believes that the human benefit or injury caused by such actions is of no significance, he will regard a sea of blood as of no significance. If he believes that the beneficiaries of such actions are irrelevant (or interchangeable), he will regard wholesale slaughter as his moral duty in the service of a "higher" good. It is the intrinsic theory of values that produces a Robespierre, a Lenin, a Stalin, or a Hitler. It is not an accident that Eichmann was a Kantian.

If a man believes that the good is a matter of arbitrary, subjective choice, the issue of good or evil becomes, for him, an issue of: *my* feelings or *theirs?* No bridge, understanding, or communication is possible to him. Reason is the only means of communication among men, and an objectively perceivable reality is their only common frame of reference; when these are invalidated (*i.e.*, held to be irrelevant) in the field of morality, force becomes men's only way of dealing with one another. If the subjectivist wants to pursue some social ideal of his own, he feels morally entitled to force men "for their own good," since he *feels* that he is right and that there is nothing to oppose him but their misguided feelings.

Thus, in practice, the proponents of the intrinsic and the subjectivist schools meet and blend. (They blend in terms of their psychoepistemology as well: by what means do the moralists of the intrinsic school discover their transcendental "good," if not by means of special, non-rational intuitions and revelations, *i.e.*, by means of their feelings?) It is doubtful whether anyone can hold either of these theories as an actual, if mistaken, conviction. But both serve as a rationalization of power-lust and of rule by brute force, unleashing the potential dictator and disarming his victims.

The objective theory of values is the only moral theory incompatible with rule by force. Capitalism is the only system based implicitly on an objective theory of values—and the historic tragedy is that this has never been made explicit.

If one knows that the good is *objective*—*i.e.*, determined by the nature of reality, but to be discovered by man's mind—one knows that an attempt to achieve the good by physical force is a monstrous contradiction which negates morality at its root by destroying man's capacity to recognize the good, *i.e.*, his capacity to value. Force invalidates and paralyzes a man's judgment, demanding that he act against it, thus rendering him morally impotent. A value which one is forced to accept at the price of surrendering one's mind, is not a value to anyone; the forcibly mindless can neither judge nor choose nor value. An attempt to achieve the good by force is like an attempt to provide a man with a picture gallery at the price of cutting out his eyes. Values cannot exist (cannot be valued) outside the full context of a man's life, needs, goals, and *knowledge*.

The objective view of values permeates the entire structure of a capitalist society.

The recognition of individual rights implies the recognition of the fact that the good is not an ineffable abstraction in some supernatural dimension, but a value pertaining to reality, to this earth, to the lives of individual human beings (note the right to the pursuit of happiness). It implies that the good cannot be divorced from beneficiaries, that men are not to be regarded as interchangeable, and that no man or tribe may attempt to achieve the good of some at the price of the immolation of others.

The free market represents the *social* application of an objective theory of values. Since values are to be discovered by man's mind, men must be free to discover them—to think, to study, to translate their knowledge into physical form, to offer their products for trade, to judge them, and to choose, be it material goods or ideas, a loaf of bread or a philosophical treatise. Since values are established contextually, every man must judge for himself, in the context of his own knowledge, goals, and interests. Since values are determined by the nature of reality, it is reality that serves as men's ultimate arbiter: if a man's judgment is right, the rewards are his; if it is wrong, he is his only victim.

It is in regard to a free market that the distinction between an intrinsic, subjective, and objective view of values is particularly important to understand. The market value of a product is *not* an intrinsic value, not a "value in itself" hanging in a vacuum. A free market never loses sight of the question: Of value *to whom?* And, within the broad field of objectivity, the market value of a product does not reflect its *philosophically objective* value, but only its *socially objective* value.

By "philosophically objective," I mean a value estimated from the standpoint of the best possible to man, *i.e.*, by the criterion of the most rational mind possessing the greatest knowledge, in a given category, in a given period, and in a defined context (nothing can be estimated in an undefined context). For instance, it can be rationally proved that the airplane is *objectively* of immeasurably greater value to man (*to man at his best*) than the bicycle—and that the works of Victor Hugo are *objectively* of immeasurably greater value than true-confession magazines. But if a given man's intellectual potential can barely manage to enjoy true confessions, there is no reason why his meager earnings, the product of *his* effort, should be spent on books he cannot read—or on subsidizing the airplane industry, if his own transportation needs do not extend beyond the range of a bicycle. (Nor is there any reason why the rest of mankind should be held down to the level of his literary taste, his engineering capacity, and his income. Values are not determined by fiat nor by majority vote.)

Just as the number of its adherents is not a proof of an idea's truth or falsehood, of an art work's merit or demerit, of a product's efficacy or inefficacy—so the free-market value of goods or services does not necessarily represent their philosophically objective value, but only their *socially objective* value, *i.e.*, the sum of the individual judgments of all the men involved in trade at a given time, the sum of what *they* valued, each in the context of his own life.

Thus, a manufacturer of lipstick may well make a greater fortune than a manufacturer of microscopes—even though it can be rationally demonstrated that microscopes are scientifically more valuable than lipstick. But—valuable *to whom?*

A microscope is of no value to a little stenographer struggling to make a living; a lipstick is; a lipstick, to her, may mean the difference between self-confidence and self-doubt, between glamour and drudgery.

This does not mean, however, that the values ruling a free market are *subjective*. If the stenographer spends all her money on cosmetics and has none left to pay for the use of a microscope (for a visit to the doctor) *when she needs it*, she learns a better method of budgeting her income; the free market serves as her teacher: she has no way to penalize others for her mistakes. If she budgets rationally, the microscope is always available to serve her own specific needs *and no more*, as far as she is concerned: she is not taxed to support an entire hospital, a research laboratory, or a space ship's journey to the moon. Within her own productive power, she does pay a part of the cost of scientific achievements, *when and as she needs them*. She has no "social duty," her own life is her only responsibility—and the only thing that a capitalist system requires of her is the thing that *nature* requires: rationality, *i.e.*, that she live and act to the best of her own judgment.

Within every category of goods and services offered on a free market, it is the purveyor of the best product at the cheapest price who wins the greatest financial rewards *in that field*—not automatically nor immediately nor by fiat, but by virtue of the free market, which teaches every participant to look for the *objective* best within the category of his own competence, and penalizes those who act on irrational considerations.

Now observe that a free market does not level men down to some common denominator—that the intellectual criteria of the majority do not rule a free market or a free society—and that the exceptional men, the innovators, the intellectual giants, are not held down by the majority. In fact, it is the members of this exceptional minority who lift the whole of a free society to the level of their own achievements, while rising further and ever further.

A free market is a *continuous process* that cannot be held still, an upward process that demands the best (the most rational) of every man and rewards him accordingly. While the majority have barely assimilated the value of the automobile, the creative minority introduces the airplane. The majority learn by demonstration, the minority is free to demonstrate. The "philosophically objective" value of a new product serves as the teacher for those who are willing to exercise their rational faculty, each to the extent of his ability. Those who are unwilling remain unrewarded—as well as those who aspire to more than their ability produces. The stagnant, the irrational, the subjectivist have no power to stop their betters.

(The small minority of adults who are *unable* rather than unwilling to work, have to rely on voluntary charity; misfortune is not a claim to slave labor; there is no such thing as the *right* to consume, control, and destroy those without whom one would be unable to survive. As to depressions and mass unemployment, they are not caused by the free market, but by government interference into the economy.)

The mental parasites—the imitators who attempt to cater to what they think is the public's known taste—are constantly being beaten by the innovators whose products raise the public's knowledge and taste to ever higher levels. It is in this sense that the free market is ruled, not by the consumers, but by the producers. The most successful ones are those who discover new fields of production, fields which had not been known to exist.

A given product may not be appreciated at once, particularly if it is too radical an innovation; but, barring irrelevant accidents, it wins in the long run. It is in this sense that the free market is not ruled by the intellectual criteria of the majority, which prevail only at and for any given moment; the free market is ruled by those who are able to see and plan long-range—and the better the mind, the longer the range.

The economic value of a man's work is determined, on a free market, by a single principle: by the voluntary consent of those who are willing to trade him their work or products in return. This is the moral meaning of the law of supply and demand; it represents the total rejection of two vicious doctrines: the tribal premise and altruism. It represents the recognition of the fact that man is not the property nor the servant of the tribe, that *a man works in order to support his own life*—as, by his nature, he must—that he has to be guided by his own rational self-interest, and if he wants to trade with others, he cannot expect sacrificial victims, *i.e.*, he cannot expect to receive values without trading commensurate values in return. The sole criterion of what is commensurate, in this context, is the free, voluntary, uncoerced judgment of the traders.

The tribal mentalities attack this principle from two seemingly opposite sides: they claim that the free market is "unfair" both to the genius and to the average man. The first objection is usually expressed by a question such as: "Why should Elvis Presley make more money than Einstein?" The answer is: Because men work in order to support and enjoy their own lives—and if many men find value in Elvis Presley, they are entitled to spend their money on their own pleasure. Presley's fortune is not taken from those who do not care for his work (I am one of them) nor from Einstein—nor does he stand in Einstein's way—nor does Einstein lack proper recognition and support in a free society, on an appropriate intellectual level.

As to the second objection, the claim that a man of average ability suffers an "unfair" disadvantage on a free market—

> Look past the range of the moment, you who cry that you fear to compete with men of superior intelligence, that their mind is a threat to your livelihood, that the strong leave no chance to the weak in a market of voluntary trade. . . . When you live in a rational

society, where men are free to trade, you receive an incalculable bonus: the material value of your work is determined not only by your effort, but by the effort of the best productive minds who exist in the world around you. . . .

The machine, the frozen form of a living intelligence, is the power that expands the potential of yours life by raising the productivity of your time. . . . Every man is free to rise as far as he's able or willing, but it's only the degree to which he thinks that determines the degree to which he'll rise. Physical labor as such can extend no further than the range of the moment. The man who does no more than physical labor, consumes the material value-equivalent of his own contribution to the process of production, and leaves no further value, neither for himself nor others. But the man who produces an idea in any field of rational endeavor—the man who discovers new knowledge—is the permanent benefactor of humanity. . . . It is only the value of an idea that can be shared with unlimited numbers of men, making all sharers richer at no one's sacrifice or loss, raising the productive capacity of whatever labor they perform. . . .

In proportion to the mental energy he spent, the man who creates a new invention receives but a small percentage of his value in terms of material payment, no matter what fortune he makes, no matter what millions he earns. But the man who works as a janitor in the factory producing that invention, receives an enormous payment in proportion to the mental effort that his job requires of *him*. And the same is true of all men between, on all levels of ambition and ability. The man at the top of the intellectual pyramid contributes the most to all those below him, but gets nothing except his material payment, receiving no intellectual bonus from others to add to the value of his time. The man at the bottom who, left to himself, would starve in his hopeless ineptitude, contributes nothing to those above him, but receives the bonus of all of their brains. Such is the nature of the "competition" between the strong and the weak of the intellect. Such is the pattern of "exploitation" for which you have damned the strong.

(*Atlas Shrugged*)

And such is the relationship of capitalism to man's mind and to man's survival.

The magnificent progress achieved by capitalism in a brief span of

time—the spectacular improvement in the conditions of man's existence on earth—is a matter of historical record. It is not to be hidden,
evaded, or explained away by all the propaganda of capitalism's enemies. But what needs special emphasis is the fact that this progress
was achieved by *non-sacrificial* means.

Progress cannot be achieved by forced privations, by squeezing a
"social surplus" out of starving victims. Progress can come only out of
individual surplus, i.e., from the work, the energy, the creative over-
abundance of those men whose ability produces more than their personal consumption requires, those who are intellectually and
financially able to seek the new, to improve on the known, to move
forward. In a capitalist society, where such men are free to function
and to take their own risks, progress is not a matter of sacrificing to
some distant future, it is part of the living present, it is the normal
and natural, it is achieved as and while men live—and *enjoy*—their
lives. . . .

EDITOR'S NOTE: *The defining principle of capitalism, individual
rights, is explained more fully in the following excerpts, from AR's 1963
essay "Man's Rights" (also published in* Capitalism: The Unknown
Ideal).

Man's Rights

IF ONE wishes to advocate a free society—that is, capitalism—one
must realize that its indispensable foundation is the principle of individual rights. If one wishes to uphold individual rights, one must realize that capitalism is the only system that can uphold and protect
them. And if one wishes to gauge the relationship of freedom to the
goals of today's intellectuals, one may gauge it by the fact that the
concept of individual rights is evaded, distorted, perverted and seldom discussed, most conspicuously seldom by the so-called "conservatives."

"Rights" are a moral concept—the concept that provides a logical transition from the principles guiding an individual's actions to the principles guiding his relationship with others—the concept that preserves and protects individual morality in a social context—the link between the moral code of a man and the legal code of a society, between ethics and politics. *Individual rights are the means of subordinating society to moral law.*

Every political system is based on some code of ethics. The dominant ethics of mankind's history were variants of the altruist-collectivist doctrine which subordinated the individual to some higher authority, either mystical or social. Consequently, most political systems were variants of the same statist tyranny, differing only in degree, not in basic principle, limited only by the accidents of tradition, of chaos, of bloody strife and periodic collapse. Under all such systems, morality was a code applicable to the individual, but not to society. Society was placed *outside* the moral law, as its embodiment or source or exclusive interpreter—and the inculcation of self-sacrificial devotion to social duty was regarded as the main purpose of ethics in man's earthly existence.

Since there is no such entity as "society," since society is only a number of individual men, this meant, in practice, that the rulers of society were exempt from moral law; subject only to the traditional rituals, they held total power and exacted blind obedience—on the implicit principle of: "The good is that which is good for society (or for the tribe, the race, the nation), and the ruler's edicts are its voice on earth."

This was true of all statist systems, under all variants of the altruist-collectivist ethics, mystical or social. "The Divine Right of Kings" summarizes the political theory of the first—" *Vox populi, vox dei*" of the second. As witness: the theocracy of Egypt, with the Pharaoh as an embodied god—the unlimited majority rule or *democracy* of Athens—the welfare state run by the Emperors of Rome—the Inquisition of the late Middle Ages—the absolute monarchy of France—the welfare state of Bismarck's Prussia—the gas chambers of Nazi Germany—the slaughterhouse of the Soviet Union.

All these political systems were expressions of the altruist-collectivist ethics—and their common characteristic is the fact that society stood above the moral law, as an omnipotent, sovereign whim worshipper. Thus, politically, all these systems were variants of an *amoral* society.

The most profoundly revolutionary achievement of the United States of America was *the subordination of society to moral law.*

The principle of man's individual rights represented the extension of morality into the social system—as a limitation on the power of the state, as man's protection against the brute force of the collective, as the subordination of *might* to *right*. The United States was the first *moral* society in history.

All previous systems had regarded man as a sacrificial means to the ends of others, and society as an end in itself. The United States regarded man as an end in himself, and society as a means to the peaceful, orderly, *voluntary* co-existence of individuals. All previous systems had held that man's life belongs to society, that society can dispose of him in any way it pleases, and that any freedom he enjoys is his only by favor, by the *permission* of society, which may be revoked at any time. The United States held that man's life is his by *right* (which means: by moral principle and by his nature), that a right is the property of an individual, that society as such has no rights, and that the only moral purpose of a government is the protection of individual rights.

A "right" is a moral principle defining and sanctioning a man's freedom of action in a social context. There is only *one* fundamental right (all the others are its consequences or corollaries): a man's right to his own life. Life is a process of self-sustaining and self-generated action; the right to life means the right to engage in self-sustaining and self-generated action—which means: the freedom to take all the actions required by the nature of a rational being for the support, the furtherance, the fulfillment and the enjoyment of his own life. (Such is the meaning of the right to life, liberty, and the pursuit of happiness.)

The concept of a "right" pertains only to action—specifically, to freedom of action. It means freedom from physical compulsion, coercion or interference by other men.

Thus, for every individual, a right is the moral sanction of a *positive*—of his freedom to act on his own judgment, for his own goals, by his own *voluntary, uncoerced* choice. As to his neighbors, his rights impose no obligations on them except of a *negative* kind: to abstain from violating his rights.

The right to life is the source of all rights—and the right to property is their only implementation. Without property rights, no other rights are possible. Since man has to sustain his life by his own effort, the man who has no right to the product of his effort has no means to sustain his life. The man who produces while others dispose of his product, is a slave.

Bear in mind that the right to property is a right to action, like all the others: it is not the right *to an object*, but to the action and the consequences of producing or earning that object. It is not a guarantee that a man *will* earn any property, but only a guarantee that he will own it if he earns it. It is the right to gain, to keep, to use and to dispose of material values.

The concept of individual rights is so new in human history that most men have not grasped it fully to this day. In accordance with the two theories of ethics, the mystical or the social, some men assert that rights are a gift of God—others, that rights are a gift of society. But, in fact, the source of rights is man's nature.

The Declaration of Independence stated that men "are endowed by their Creator with certain unalienable rights." Whether one believes that man is the product of a Creator or of nature, the issue of man's opinion does not alter the fact that he is an entity of a specific kind—a rational being—that he cannot function successfully under coercion, and that rights are a necessary condition of his particular mode of survival.

"The source of man's rights is not divine law or congressional law, but the law of identity. A is A—and Man is Man. *Rights* are conditions of existence required by man's nature for his proper survival. If man is to live on earth, it is *right* for him to use his mind, it is *right* to act on his own free judgment, it is *right* to work for his values and to keep the product of his work. If life on earth is his purpose, he has a *right* to live as a rational being: nature forbids him the irrational." (*Atlas Shrugged*)

To violate man's right means to compel him to act against his own judgment, or to expropriate his values. Basically, there is only one way to do it: by the use of physical force. There are two potential violators of man's rights: the criminals and the government. The great achievement of the United States was to draw a distinction between these two—by forbidding to the second the legalized version of the activities of the first.

The Declaration of Independence laid down the principle that "to secure these rights, governments are instituted among men." This provided the only valid justification of a government and defined its only proper purpose: to protect man's rights by protecting him from physical violence.

Thus the government's function was changed from the role of ruler to the role of servant. The government was set to protect man from criminals—and the Constitution was written to protect man from the government. The Bill of Rights was not directed against private citizens, but against the government—as an explicit declaration that individual rights supersede any public or social power.

The result was the pattern of a civilized society which—for the brief span of some hundred and fifty years—America came close to achieving. A civilized society is one in which physical force is banned from human relationships—in which the government, acting as a policeman, may use force *only* in retaliation and *only* against those who initiate its use.

This was the essential meaning and intent of America's political philosophy, implicit in the principle of individual rights. But it was not formulated explicitly, nor fully accepted nor consistently practiced.

America's inner contradiction was the altruist-collectivist ethics. Altruism is incompatible with freedom, with capitalism and with individual rights. One cannot combine the pursuit of happiness with the moral status of a sacrificial animal.

It was the concept of individual rights that had given birth to a free society. It was with the destruction of individual rights that the destruction of freedom had to begin.

A collectivist tyranny dare not enslave a country by an outright confiscation of its values, material or moral. It has to be done by a process of internal corruption. Just as in the material realm the plundering of a country's wealth is accomplished by inflating the currency—so today one may witness the process of inflation being applied to the realm of rights. The process entails such a growth of newly promulgated "rights" that people do not notice the fact that the meaning of the concept is being reversed. Just as bad money drives out good money, so these "printing-press rights" negate authentic rights.

Consider the curious fact that never has there been such a proliferation, all over the world, of two contradictory phenomena: of alleged new "rights" and of slave-labor camps.

The "gimmick" was the switch of the concept of rights from the political to the economic realm.

The Democratic Party platform of 1960 summarizes the switch boldly and explicitly. It declares that a Democratic Administration "will reaffirm the economic bill of rights which Franklin Roosevelt wrote into our national conscience sixteen years ago."

Bear clearly in mind the meaning of the concept of "*rights*" when you read the list which that platform offers:

"1. The right to a useful and remunerative job in the industries or shops or farms or mines of the nation.

"2. The right to earn enough to provide adequate food and clothing and recreation.

"3. The right of every farmer to raise and sell his products at a return which will give him and his family a decent living.

"4. The right of every businessman, large and small, to trade in an atmosphere of freedom from unfair and competition and domination by monopolies at home and abroad.

"5. The right of every family to a decent home.

"6. The right to adequate medical care and the opportunity to achieve and enjoy good health.

"7. The right to adequate protection from the economic fears of old age, sickness, accidents and unemployment.

"8. The right to a good education."

A single question added to each of the above eight clauses would make the issue clear: At *whose expense?*

Jobs, food, clothing, recreation (!), homes, medical care, education, etc., do not grow in nature. These are man-made values—goods and services produced by men. *Who* is to provide them?

If some men are entitled *by right* to the products of the work of others, it means that those others are deprived of rights and condemned to slave labor.

Any alleged "right" of one man, which necessitates the violation of the rights of another, is not and cannot be a right.

No man can have a right to impose an unchosen obligation, an unrewarded duty or an involuntary servitude on another man. There can be no such thing as "*the right to enslave.*"

A right does not include the material implementation of that right by other men; it includes only the freedom to earn that implementation by one's own effort.

Observe, in this context, the intellectual precision of the Founding Fathers: they spoke of the right to *the pursuit* of happiness—*not* of the right to happiness. It means that a man has the right to take the actions he deems necessary to achieve his happiness; it does *not* mean that others must make him happy.

The right to life means that a man has the right to support his life by his own work (on any economic level, as high as his ability will carry him); it does *not* mean that others must provide him with the necessities of life.

The right to property means that a man has the right to take the economic actions necessary to earn property, to use it and to dispose of it; it does *not* mean that others must provide him with property.

The right of free speech means that a man has the right to express his ideas without danger of suppression, interference or punitive action by the government. It does *not* mean that others must provide him with a lecture hall, a radio station or a printing press through which to express his ideas.

Any undertaking that involves more than one man, requires the *voluntary* consent of every participant. Every one of them has the *right* to make his own decision, but none has the right to force his decision on the others.

There is no such thing as "a right to a job"—there is only the right of free trade, that is: a man's right to take a job if another man chooses to hire him. There is no "right to a home," only the right of free trade: the right to build a home or to buy it. There are no "rights to a 'fair' wage or a 'fair' price" if no one chooses to pay it, to hire a man or to buy his product. There are no "rights of consumers" to milk, shoes, movies or champagne if no producers choose to manufacture such items (there is only the right to manufacture them oneself). There are no "rights" of special groups, there are no "rights of farmers, of workers, of businessmen, of employees, of employers, of the old, of the young, of the unborn." There are only *the Rights of Man*—rights possessed by every individual man and by *all* men as individuals.

Property rights and the right of free trade are man's only "economic rights" (they are, in fact, *political* rights)—and there can be no such thing as "an *economic* bill of rights." But observe that the advocates of the latter have all but destroyed the former.

Remember that rights are moral principles which define and protect a man's freedom of action, but impose no obligations on other men. Private citizens are not a threat to one another's rights or freedom. A private citizen who resorts to physical force and violates the rights of others is a criminal—and men have legal protection against him.

Criminals are a small minority in any age or country. And the harm they have done to mankind is infinitesimal when compared to the horrors—the bloodshed, the wars, the persecutions, the confiscations, the famines, the enslavements, the wholesale destructions—perpetrated by mankind's governments. Potentially, a government is the most dangerous threat to man's rights: it holds a legal monopoly on the use of physical force against legally disarmed victims. When unlimited and unrestricted by individual rights, a government is man's deadliest enemy. It is not as protection against *private* actions, but against governmental actions that the Bill of Rights was written. . . .

———————

EDITOR'S NOTE: *This selection, written in the early 1960s and published in* The Virtue of Selfishness, *is AR's answer to the notion of "group rights."*

Collectivized "Rights"

RIGHTS ARE a moral principle defining proper social relationships. Just as a man needs a moral code in order to survive (in order to act, to choose the right goals and to achieve them), so a society (a group of men) needs moral principles in order to organize a social system consonant with man's nature and with the requirements of his survival.

Just as a man *can* evade reality and act on the blind whim of any given moment, but can achieve nothing save progressive self-destruction—so a society *can* evade reality and establish a system ruled by the blind whims of its members or its leader, by the majority gang of any given moment, by the current demagogue or by a permanent dictator. But such a society can achieve nothing save the rule of brute force and a state of progressive self-destruction.

What subjectivism is in the realm of ethics, collectivism is in the realm of politics. Just as the notion that "Anything I do is right because *I* chose to do it," is not a moral principle, but a negation of morality—so the notion that "Anything society does is right because *society* chose to do it," is not a moral principle, but a negation of moral principles and the banishment of morality from social issues.

When "*might*" is opposed to "*right*," the concept of "might" can have only one meaning: the power of brute, physical force—which, in fact, is not a "power" but the most hopeless state of impotence; it is merely the "power" to destroy; it is the "power" of a stampede of animals running amuck.

Yet *that* is the goal of most of today's intellectuals. At the root of all their conceptual switches, there lies another, more fundamental one: the switch of the concept of rights from the individual to the collective—which means: the replacement of "The Rights of Man" by "The Rights of Mob."

Since only an individual man can possess rights, the expression "individual rights" is a redundancy (which one has to use for purposes of clarification in today's intellectual chaos). But the expression "collective rights" is a contradiction in terms.

Any group or "collective," large or small, is only a number of individuals. A group can have no rights other than the right of its individual members. In a free society, the "rights" of any group are derived from the rights of its members through their voluntary, individual choice and *contractual* agreement, and are merely the application of these individual rights to a specific undertaking. Every legitimate group undertaking is based on the participants' right of free association and free trade. (By "legitimate," I mean: noncriminal and freely formed, that is, a group which no one was *forced* to join.)

For instance, the right of an industrial concern to engage in business is derived from the right of its owners to invest their money in a productive venture—from their right to hire employees—from the right of the employees to sell their services—from the right of all those involved to produce and to sell their products—from the right of the customers to buy (or not to buy) those products. Every link of this complex chain of contractual relationships rests on individual rights, individual choices, individual agreements. Every agreement is delimited, specified and subject to certain conditions, that is, dependent upon a mutual trade to mutual benefit.

This is true of all legitimate groups or associations in a free society: partnerships, business concerns, professional association, labor unions (*voluntary* ones), political parties, etc. It applies also to all agency agreements: the right of one man to act for or represent another or others is derived from the rights of those he represents and is delegated to him by their voluntary choice, for a specific, delimited purpose—as in the case of a lawyer, a business representative, a labor union delegate, etc.

A group, as such, has no rights. A man can neither acquire new rights by joining a group nor lose the rights which he does possess. The principle of individual rights is the only moral base of all groups or associations.

Any group that does not recognize this principle is not an association, but a gang or a mob.

Any doctrine of group activities that does not recognize individual rights is a doctrine of mob rule or legalized lynching.

The notion of "collective rights" (the notion that rights belong to groups, not to individuals) means that "rights" belong to some men, but not to others—that some men have the "right" to dispose of others in any manner they please—and that the criterion of such privileged position consists of numerical superiority.

Nothing can ever justify or validate such a doctrine—and no one ever has. Like the altruist morality from which it is derived, this doctrine rests on mysticism: either on the old-fashioned mysticism of faith in supernatural edicts, like "The Divine Right of Kings"—or on the social mystique of modern collectivists who see society as a superorganism, as some supernatural entity apart from and superior to the sum of its individual members.

The amorality of that collectivist mystique is particularly obvious today in the issue of *national* rights.

A nation, like any other group, is only a number of individuals and can have no rights other than the rights of its individual citizens. A free nation—a nation that recognizes, respects and protects the individual rights of its citizens—has a right to its territorial integrity, its social system and its form of government. The government of such a nation is not the ruler, but the servant or *agent* of its citizens and has no rights other than the rights *delegated* to it by the citizens for a specific, delimited task (the task of protecting them from physical force, derived from their right of self-defense).

The citizens of a free nation may disagree about the specific legal procedures or *methods* of implementing their rights (which is a complex problem, the province of political science and of the philosophy of law), but they agree on the basic principle to be implemented: the principle of individual rights. When a country's constitution places individual rights outside the reach of public authorities, the sphere of political power is severely delimited—and thus the citizens may, safely and properly, agree to abide by the decisions of a majority vote in this delimited sphere. The lives and property of minorities or dissenters are not at stake, are not subject to vote and are not endangered by any majority decision; no man or group holds a blank check on power over others.

Such a nation has a right to its sovereignty (derived from the rights of its citizens) and a right to demand that its sovereignty be respected by all other nations.

But this right cannot be claimed by dictatorships, by savage tribes or by any form of absolutist tyranny. A nation that violates the rights of its own citizens cannot claim any rights whatsoever. In the issue of rights, as in all moral issues, there can be no double standard. A nation ruled by brute physical force is not a nation, but a horde—whether it is led by Attila, Genghis Khan, Hitler, Khrushchev or Castro. What rights could Attila claim and on what grounds?

This applies to all forms of tribal savagery, ancient or modern, primitive or "industrialized." Neither geography nor race nor tradition nor previous state of development can confer on some human beings the "right" to violate the rights of others.

The right of "the self-determination of nations" applies only to free societies or to societies seeking to establish freedom; it does not apply to dictatorships. Just as an individual's right of free action does not include the "right" to commit crimes (that is, to violate the rights of others), so the right of a nation to determine its own form of government does not include the right to establish a slave society (that is, to legalize the enslavement of some men by others). *There is no such thing as "the right to enslave."* A nation *can* do it, just as a man *can* become a criminal—but neither can do it *by right*.

It does not matter, in this context, whether a nation was enslaved by force, like Soviet Russia, or by vote, like Nazi Germany. Individual rights are not subject to a public vote; a majority has no right to vote away the rights of a minority; the political function of rights is precisely to protect minorities from oppression by majorities (and the smallest minority on earth is the individual). Whether a slave society was conquered or *chose* to be enslaved, it can claim no national rights and no recognition of such "rights" by civilized countries—just as a mob of gangsters cannot demand a recognition of its "rights" and a legal equality with an industrial concern or a university, on the ground that the gangsters *chose* by unanimous vote to engage in that particular kind of group activity.

Dictatorship nations are outlaws. Any free nation had the *right* to invade Nazi Germany and, today, has the *right* to invade Soviet Russia, Cuba or any other slave pen. Whether a free nation chooses to do so or not is a matter of its own self-interest, *not* of respect for the nonexistent "rights" of gang rulers. It is not a free nation's *duty* to liberate other nations at the price of self-sacrifice, but a free nation has the right to do it, when and if it so chooses.

This right, however, is conditional. Just as the suppression of crimes does not give a policeman the right to engage in criminal activities, so the invasion and destruction of a dictatorship does not give the invader the right to establish another variant of a slave society in the conquered country.

A slave country has no *national* rights, but the *individual* rights of its citizens remain valid, even if unrecognized, and the conqueror has no right to violate them. Therefore, the invasion of an enslaved country is morally justified only when and if the conquerors establish a *free* social system, that is, a system based on the recognition of individual rights.

Since there is no fully free country today, since the so-called "Free World" consists of various "mixed economies," it might be asked whether every country on earth is morally open to invasion by every other. The answer is: No. There is a difference between a country that recognizes the principle of individual rights, but does not implement it fully in practice, and a country that denies and flouts it explicitly. All "mixed economies" are in a precarious state of transition which, ultimately, has to turn to freedom or collapse into dictatorship. There are four characteristics which brand a country unmistakably as a dictatorship: one-party rule—executions without trial or with a mock trial, for political offenses—the nationalization or expropriation of private property—and censorship. A country guilty of these outrages forfeits any moral prerogatives, any claim to national rights or sovereignty, and becomes an outlaw.

Observe, on this particular issue, the shameful end-of-trail and the intellectual disintegration of modern "liberals."

Internationalism had always been one of the "liberals' " basic tenets. They regarded nationalism as a major social evil, as a product of capitalism and as the cause of wars. They opposed any form of national self-interest; they refused to differentiate between rational patriotism and blind, racist chauvinism, denouncing both as "fascist." They advocated the dissolution of national boundaries and the merging of all nations into "One World." Next to property rights, "national rights" were the special target of their attacks.

Today, it is "national rights" that they invoke as their last, feeble, fading hold on some sort of moral justification for the results of their theories—for the brood of little statist dictatorships spreading, like a skin disease, over the surface of the globe, in the form of so-called "newly emerging nations," semi-socialist, semi-communist, semi-fascist, and wholly committed only to the use of brute force.

It is the "national right" of such countries to choose their own form of government (any form they please) that the "liberals" offer as a moral validation and ask us to respect. It is the "national right" of Cuba to *its* form of government, they claim, that we must not violate or interfere with. Having all but destroyed the legitimate national rights of free countries, it is for dictatorships that the "liberals" now claim the sanction of "national rights."

And worse: it is not mere nationalism that the "liberals" champion, but *racism*—primordial tribal racism.

Observe the double standard: while, in the civilized countries of the West, the "liberals" are still advocating internationalism and global self-sacrifice—the savage tribes of Asia and Africa are granted the sovereign "right" to slaughter one another in racial warfare. Mankind is reverting to a preindustrial, prehistorical view of society: to racial collectivism.

Such is the logical result and climax of the "liberals' " moral collapse which began when, as a prelude to the collectivization of property, they accepted the collectivization of rights.

Their own confession of guilt lies in their terminology. Why do they use the word *"rights"* to denote the things they are advocating? Why don't they preach what they practice? Why don't they name it openly and attempt to justify it, if they can?

The answer is obvious.

———

EDITOR'S NOTE: *In a pamphlet from the 1940s, "Textbook of Americanism," AR indicates why procapitalists should shun Utilitarianism.*

On Utilitarianism

"THE GREATEST good for the greatest number" is one of the most vicious slogans ever foisted on humanity.

This slogan has no concrete, specific meaning. There is no way to interpret it benevolently, but a great many ways in which it can be used to justify the most vicious actions.

What is the definition of "the good" in this slogan? None, except: whatever is good for the greatest number. Who, in any particular issue, decides what is good for the greatest number? Why, the greatest number.

If you consider this moral, you would have to approve of the following examples, which are exact applications of this slogan in practice: fifty-one percent of humanity enslaving the other forty-nine; nine hungry cannibals eating the tenth one; a lynching mob murdering a man whom they consider dangerous to the community.

There were seventy million Germans in Germany and six hundred thousand Jews. The greatest number (the Germans) supported the Nazi government which told them that their greatest good would be served by exterminating the smaller number (the Jews) and grabbing their property. This was the horror achieved in practice by a vicious slogan accepted in theory.

But, you might say, the majority in all these examples did not achieve any real good for itself either? No. It didn't. Because "the good" is not determined by counting numbers and is not achieved by the sacrifice of anyone to anyone.

The unthinking believe that this slogan implies something vaguely noble and virtuous, that it tells men to sacrifice themselves for the greatest number of others. If so, should the greatest number of men wish to be virtuous and sacrifice themselves to the smallest number who would be vicious and accept it? No? Well, then should the smallest number be virtuous and sacrifice themselves to the greatest number who would be vicious?

The unthinking assume that every man who mouths this slogan places himself unselfishly with the smaller number to be sacrificed to the greatest number of others. Why should he? There is nothing in the slogan to make him do this. He is much more likely to try to get in with the greatest number, and start sacrificing others. What the slogan actually tells him is that he has no choice, except to rob or be robbed, to crush or get crushed.

The depravity of this slogan lies in the implication that "the good" of a majority must be achieved through the suffering of a minority; that the benefit of one man depends upon the sacrifice of another.

If we accept the Collectivist doctrine that man exists only for the sake of others, then it is true that every pleasure he enjoys (or every bite of food) is evil and immoral if two other men want it. But on this basis men cannot eat, breathe or love (all of that is selfish, and what if two other men want your wife?), men cannot live together at all, and can do nothing except end up by exterminating one another.

Only on the basis of individual rights can any good—private or public—be defined and achieved. Only when each man is free to exist for his own sake—neither sacrificing others to himself nor being sacrificed to others—only then is every man free to work for the greatest good he can achieve for himself by his own choice and by his own effort. And the sum total of such individual efforts is the only kind of general, social good possible.

Do not think that the opposite of "the greatest good for the greatest number" is "the greatest good for the smallest number." The opposite is: the greatest good he can achieve by his own free effort, to every man living.

If you are an Individualist and wish to preserve the American way of life, the greatest contribution you can make is to discard, once and for all, from your thinking, from your speeches, and from your sympathy, the empty slogan of "the greatest good for the greatest number." Reject any argument, oppose any proposal that has nothing but this slogan to justify it. It is a booby-trap. It is a precept of pure Collectivism. You cannot accept it and call yourself an Individualist. Make your choice. It is one or the other.

PART SIX

Romanticism and the Benevolent Universe

1. Romanticism

EDITOR'S NOTE: AR *was often asked whether she was primarily a novelist or a philosopher. She gave her answer—and in the process indicated her view of art—in a 1963 speech at Lewis and Clark College,* "The Goal of My Writing" (*published in* The Romantic Manifesto).

The Goal of My Writing

THE MOTIVE and purpose of my writing is *the projection of an ideal man*. The portrayal of a moral ideal, as my ultimate literary goal, as an end in itself—to which any didactic, intellectual or philosophical values contained in a novel are only the means.

Let me stress this: my purpose is *not* the philosophical enlightenment of my readers, it is *not* the beneficial influence which my novels may have on people, it is *not* the fact that my novels may help a reader's intellectual development. All these matters are important, but they are secondary considerations, they are merely consequences and effects, not first causes or prime movers. My purpose, first cause and prime mover is the portrayal of Howard Roark or John Galt or Hank Rearden or Francisco d'Anconia *as an end in himself*—not as a means to any further end. Which, incidentally, is the greatest value I could ever offer a reader.

This is why I feel a very mixed emotion—part patience, part amusement and, at times, an empty kind of weariness—when I am asked whether I am primarily a novelist or a philosopher (as if these two were antonyms), whether my stories are propaganda vehicles for ideas, whether politics or the advocacy of capitalism is my chief purpose. All such questions are so enormously irrelevant, so far beside the point, so much *not* my way of coming at things.

My way is much simpler and, simultaneously, much more complex than that, speaking from two different aspects. The simple truth is that I approach literature as a child does: I write—and read—for the sake of the story. The complexity lies in the task of translating that attitude into adult terms.

The specific concretes, the *forms* of one's values, change with one's growth and development. The abstraction *"values"* does not. An adult's values involve the entire sphere of human activity, including philosophy—most particularly philosophy. But the basic principle—the function and meaning of values in man's life and in literature—remains the same.

My basic test for any story is: Would I want to meet these characters and observe these events in real life? Is this story an experience worth living through for its own sake? Is the pleasure of contemplating these characters an end in itself?

It's as simple as that. But that simplicity involves the total of man's existence.

It involves such questions as: What kind of men do I want to see in real life—and why? What kind of events, that is, human actions, do I want to see taking place—and why? What kind of experience do I want to live through, that is, what are my goals—and why?

It is obvious to what field of human knowledge all these questions belong: to the field of *ethics*. What is the good? What are the right actions for man to take? What are man's proper *values*?

Since my purpose is the presentation of an ideal man, I had to define and present the conditions which make him possible and which his existence requires. Since man's character is the product of his premises, I had to define and present the kind of premises and values that create the character of an ideal man and motivate his actions; which means that I had to define and present a rational code of ethics. Since man acts among and deals with other men, I had to present the kind of social system that makes it possible for ideal men to exist and to function—a free, productive, rational system, which demands and rewards the best in *every* man, great or average, and which is, obviously, laissez-faire capitalism.

But neither politics nor ethics nor philosophy are ends in themselves, neither in life nor in literature. Only Man is an end in himself.

Now observe that the practitioners of the literary school diametrically opposed to mine—the school of Naturalism—claim that a writer must reproduce what they call "real life," allegedly "as it is," exercising no selectivity and no value-judgments. By "reproduce," they mean "photograph"; by "real life," they mean whatever given concretes they happen to observe; by "as it is," they mean "as it is lived by the people around them." But observe that these Naturalists—or the good writers among them—are extremely selective in regard to two attributes of literature: *style* and *characterization*. Without selectivity, it would be impossible to achieve any sort of characterization whatever, neither of an unusual man nor of an average one who is to be offered as statistically typical of a large segment of the population. Therefore, the Naturalists' opposition to selectivity applies to only one attribute of literature: the content or *subject*. It is in regard to his choice of subject that a novelist must exercise no choice, they claim.

Why?

The Naturalists have never given an answer to that question—not a rational, logical, noncontradictory answer. Why should a writer photograph his subjects indiscriminately and unselectively? Because they "really" happened? To record what really happened is the job of a reporter or of a historian, not of a novelist. To enlighten readers and educate them? That is the job of science, not of literature, of nonfiction writing, not of fiction. To improve men's lot by exposing their misery? But *that* is a value-judgment and a moral purpose and a didactic "message"—all of which are forbidden by the Naturalist doctrine. Besides, to improve anything one must know what constitutes an improvement—and to know that, one must know what is the good and how to achieve it—and to know that, one must have a whole system of value-judgments, a system of *ethics*, which is anathema to the Naturalists.

Thus, the Naturalists' position amounts to giving a novelist full esthetic freedom in regard to *means*, but not in regard to *ends*. He may exercise choice, creative imagination, value-judgments in regard to *how* he portrays things, but not in regard to *what* he portrays—in regard to style or characterization, but not in regard to *subject*. Man—the subject of literature—must not be viewed or portrayed selectively. Man must be accepted as the given, the unchangeable, the not-to-be-judged, the status quo. But since we observe that men do change, that they differ from one another, that they pursue different values, who, then, is to determine the human status quo? Naturalism's implicit answer is: everybody except the novelist.

The novelist—according to the Naturalist doctrine—must neither judge nor value. He is not a creator, but only a recording secretary whose master is the rest of mankind. Let others pronounce judgments, make decisions, select goals, fight over values and determine the course, the fate and the soul of man. The novelist is the only outcast and deserter of that battle. His is not to reason why—his is only to trot behind his master, notebook in hand, taking down whatever the master dictates, picking up such pearls or such swinishness as the master may choose to drop.

As far as I am concerned, I have too much self-esteem for a job of that kind.

I see the novelist as a combination of prospector and jeweler. The novelist must discover the potential, the gold mine, of man's soul, must extract the gold and then fashion as magnificent a crown as his ability and vision permit.

Just as men of ambition for material values do not rummage through city dumps, but venture out into lonely mountains in search of gold—so men of ambition for intellectual values do not sit in their backyards, but venture out in quest of the noblest, the purest, the costliest elements. I would not enjoy the spectacle of Benvenuto Cellini making mud-pies.

It is the selectivity in regard to subject—the most severely, rigorously, ruthlessly exercised selectivity—that I hold as the primary, the essential, the cardinal aspect of art. In literature, this means: *the story*—which means: the plot and the characters—which means: the kind of men and events that a writer chooses to portray.

The subject is not the only attribute of art, but it is the fundamental one, it is the end to which all the others are the means. In most esthetic theories, however, the end—the subject—is omitted from consideration, and only the means are regarded as esthetically relevant. Such theories set up a false dichotomy and claim that a slob portrayed by the technical means of a genius is preferable to a goddess portrayed by the technique of an amateur. I hold that *both* are esthetically offensive; but while the second is merely esthetic incompetence, the first is an esthetic crime.

There is no dichotomy, no necessary conflict between ends and means. The end does *not* justify the means—neither in ethics nor in esthetics. And neither do the means justify the end: there is no esthetic justification for the spectacle of Rembrandt's great artistic skill employed to portray a side of beef.

That particular painting may be taken as a symbol of everything I am opposed to in art and in literature. At the age of seven, I could not understand why anyone should wish to paint or to admire pictures of dead fish, garbage cans or fat peasant women with triple chins. Today, I understand the psychological causes of such esthetic phenomena—and the more I understand, the more I oppose them.

In art, and in literature, the end and the means, or the subject and the style, must be worthy of each other.

That which is not worth contemplating in life, is not worth re-creating in art.

Misery, disease, disaster, evil, all the negatives of human existence, are proper subjects of *study* in life, for the purpose of understanding and correcting them—but are not proper subjects of *contemplation* for contemplation's sake. In art, and in literature, these negatives are worth re-creating only in relation to some positive, as a foil, as a contrast, as a means of stressing the positive—but *not* as an end in themselves.

The "compassionate" studies of depravity which pass for literature today are the dead end and the tombstone of Naturalism. If their perpetrators still claim the justification that these things are "true" (most of them aren't)—the answer is that this sort of truth belongs in psychological case histories, not in literature. The picture of an infected ruptured appendix may be of great value in a medical textbook—but it does not belong in an art gallery. And an infected soul is a much more repulsive spectacle.

That one should wish to enjoy the contemplation of *values*, of the *good*—of man's greatness, intelligence, ability, virtue, heroism—is self-explanatory. It is the contemplation of the *evil* that requires explanation and justification; and the same goes for the contemplation of the mediocre, the undistinguished, the commonplace, the meaningless, the mindless.

At the age of seven, I refused to read the children's equivalent of Naturalistic literature—the stories about the children of the folks next door. They bored me to death. I was not interested in such people in real life; I saw no reason to find them interesting in fiction.

This is still my position today; the only difference is that today I know its full philosophical justification.

As far as literary schools are concerned, I would call myself a Romantic Realist.

Consider the significance of the fact that the Naturalists call Romantic art an "escape." Ask yourself what sort of metaphysics—what view of life—that designation confesses. An escape—from what? If the projection of value-goals—the projection of an improvement on the given, the known, the immediately available—is an "escape," then medicine is an "escape" from disease, agriculture is an "escape" from hunger, knowledge is an "escape" from ignorance, ambition is an "escape" from sloth, and life is an "escape" from death. If so, then a hard-core realist is a vermin-eaten brute who sits motionless in a mud puddle, contemplates a pigsty and whines that "such is life." If *that* is realism, then I am an escapist. So was Aristotle. So was Christopher Columbus.

There is a passage in *The Fountainhead* that deals with this issue: the passage in which Howard Roark explains to Steven Mallory why he chose him to do a statue for the Stoddard Temple. In writing that passage, I was consciously and deliberately stating the essential goal of my own work—as a kind of small, personal manifesto: "I think you're the best sculptor we've got. I think it, because your figures are not what men are, but what men could be—and should be. Because you've gone beyond the probable and made us see what is possible, but possible only through you. Because your figures are more devoid of contempt for humanity than any work I've ever seen. Because you have a magnificent respect for the human being. Because your figures are the heroic in man."

Today, more than twenty years later, I would want to change—or, rather, to clarify—only two small points. First, the words "more devoid of contempt for humanity" are not too exact grammatically; what I wanted to convey was "*untouched*" by contempt for humanity, while the work of others was touched by it to some extent. Second, the words "possible only through you" should not be taken to mean that Mallory's figures were impossible metaphysically, in reality; I meant that they were possible only because *he* had shown the way to make them possible.

"Your figures are not what men are, but what men could be—and should be."

This line will make it clear whose great philosophical principle I had accepted and was following and had been groping for, long before I heard the name "Aristotle." It was Aristotle who said that fiction is of greater philosophical importance than history, because history represents things only as they are, while fiction represents them "as they *might be* and *ought to be.*"

Why must fiction represent things "as they might be and ought to be"?

My answer is contained in one statement of *Atlas Shrugged*—and in the implications of that statement: "As man is a being of self-made wealth, so he is a being of self-made soul."

Just as man's physical survival depends on his own effort, so does his psychological survival. Man faces two corollary, interdependent fields of action in which a constant exercise of choice and a constant creative process are demanded of him: the world around him and his own soul (by "soul," I mean his consciousness). Just as he has to produce the material values he needs to sustain his life, so he has to acquire the values of character that enable him to sustain it and that make his life worth living. He is born without the knowledge of either. He has to discover both—and translate them into reality—and survive by shaping the world and himself in the image of his values.

Growing from a common root, which is philosophy, man's knowledge branches out in two directions. One branch studies the physical world or the phenomena pertaining to man's physical existence; the other studies man or the phenomena pertaining to his consciousness. The first leads to abstract science, which leads to applied science or engineering, which leads to technology—to the actual production of material values. The second leads to art.

Art is the technology of the soul.

Art is the product of three philosophical disciplines: metaphysics, epistemology, ethics. Metaphysics and epistemology are the abstract base of ethics. Ethics is the applied science that defines a code of values to guide man's choices and actions—the choices and actions which determine the course of his life; ethics is the engineering that provides the principles and blueprints. Art creates the final product. It builds the model.

Let me stress this analogy: art does not *teach*—it shows, it displays the full, concretized reality of the final goal. Teaching is the task of ethics. Teaching is not the purpose of an art work, any more than it is the purpose of an airplane. Just as one can learn a great deal from an airplane by studying it or taking it apart, so one can learn a great deal from an art work—about the nature of man, of his soul, of his existence. But these are merely fringe benefits. The primary purpose of an airplane is not to *teach* man how to fly, but to give him the actual experience of flying. So is the primary purpose of an art work.

Although the representation of things "as they might be and ought to be" helps man to achieve these things in real life, this is only a secondary value. The *primary* value is that it gives him the experience of living in a world where things are *as they ought to be*. This experience is of crucial importance to him: it is his psychological life line.

Since man's ambition is unlimited, since his pursuit and achievement of values is a lifelong process—and the higher the values, the harder the struggle—man needs a moment, an hour or some period of time in which he can experience the sense of his completed task, the sense of living in a universe where his values have been successfully achieved. It is like a moment of rest, a moment to gain fuel to move farther. Art gives him that fuel. Art gives him the experience of seeing the full, immediate, concrete reality of his distant goals.

The importance of that experience is not in *what* he learns from it, but in *that* he experiences it. The fuel is not a theoretical principle, not a didactic "message," but the life-giving fact of experiencing a moment of *metaphysical* joy—a moment of love for existence.

A given individual may choose to move forward, to translate the meaning of that experience into the actual course of his own life; or he may fail to live up to it and spend the rest of his life betraying it. But whatever the case may be, the art work remains intact, an entity complete in itself, an achieved, realized, immovable fact of reality— like a beacon raised over the dark crossroads of the world, saying: "*This* is possible."

No matter what its consequences, that experience is not a way station one passes, but a stop, a value in itself. It is an experience about which one can say: "I am glad to have reached this in my life." There are not many experiences of that kind to be found in the modern world.

I have read a great many novels of which nothing remains in my mind but the dry rustle of scraps long since swept away. But the novels of Victor Hugo, and a very few others, were an unrepeatable experience to me, a beacon whose every brilliant spark is as alive as ever.

This aspect of art is difficult to communicate—it demands a great deal of the viewer or reader—but I believe that many of you will understand me introspectively.

There is a scene in *The Fountainhead* which is a direct expression of this issue. I was, in a sense, both characters in that scene, but it was written primarily from the aspect of myself as the consumer, rather than the producer, of art; it was based on my own desperate longing for the sight of human achievement. I regarded the emotional meaning of that scene as entirely personal, almost subjective—and I did not expect it to be shared by anyone. But that scene proved to be the one most widely understood and most frequently mentioned by the readers of *The Fountainhead*.

It is the opening scene of Part IV, between Howard Roark and the boy on the bicycle.

The boy thought that "man's work should be a higher step, an improvement on nature, not a degradation. He did not want to despise men; he wanted to love and admire them. But he dreaded the sight of the first house, poolroom and movie poster he would encounter on his way. . . . He had always wanted to write music, and he could give no other identity to the thing he sought. . . . Let me see that in one single act of man on earth. Let me see it made real. Let me see the answer to the promise of that music. . . . Don't work for my happiness, my brothers—show me yours—show me that it is possible—show me your achievement—and the knowledge will give me courage for mine."

This is the meaning of art in man's life.

It is from this perspective that I will now ask you to consider the meaning of Naturalism—the doctrine which proposes to confine men to the sight of slums, poolrooms, movie posters and on down, much farther down.

It is the Romantic or value-oriented vision of life that the Naturalists regard as "superficial"—and it is the vision which extends as far as the bottom of a garbage can that they regard as "profound."

It is rationality, purpose and values that they regard as naive—while sophistication, they claim, consists of discarding one's mind, rejecting goals, renouncing values and writing four-letter words on fences and sidewalks.

Scaling a mountain, they claim, is easy—but rolling in the gutter is a noteworthy achievement.

Those who seek the sight of beauty and greatness are motivated by *fear*, they claim—they who are the embodiments of chronic terror—while it takes courage to fish in cesspools.

Man's soul—they proclaim with self-righteous pride—is a sewer.

Well, they ought to know.

It is a significant commentary on the present state of our culture that I have become the object of hatred, smears, denunciations, because I am famous as virtually the only novelist who has declared that *her* soul is *not* a sewer, and neither are the souls of her characters, and neither is the soul of man.

The motive and purpose of my writing can best be summed up by saying that if a dedication page were to precede the total of my work, it would read: To the glory of Man.

And if anyone should ask me what it is that I have said to the glory of Man, I will answer only by paraphrasing Howard Roark. I will hold up a copy of *Atlas Shrugged* and say: "The explanation rests."

EDITOR'S NOTE: *This excerpt from a 1969 essay, "What is Romanticism?" (published in* The Romantic Manifesto), *offers a fuller statement of AR's view of art—and of its antithesis: naturalism.*

What Is Romanticism?

ROMANTICISM IS a category of art based on the recognition of the principle that man possesses the faculty of volition.

Art is a selective re-creation of reality according to an artist's metaphysical value-judgments. An artist recreates those aspects of reality which represent his fundamental view of man and of existence. In forming a view of man's nature, a fundamental question one must answer is whether man possesses the faculty of volition—because one's conclusions and evaluations in regard to all the characteristics, requirements and actions of man depend on the answer.

Their opposite answers to this question constitute the respective basic premises of two broad categories of art: Romanticism, which recognizes the existence of man's volition—and Naturalism, which denies it.

In the field of literature, the logical consequences of these basic premises (whether held consciously or subconsciously) determine the form of the key elements of a literary work.

1. If man possesses volition, then the crucial aspect of his life is his choice of values—if he chooses values, then he must act to gain and/or keep them—if so, then he must set his goals and engage in purposeful action to achieve them. The literary form expressing the essence of such action is the *plot*. (A plot is a purposeful progression of logically connected events leading to the resolution of a climax.)

The faculty of volition operates in regard to the two fundamental aspects of man's life: consciousness and existence, i.e., his psychological action and his existential action, i.e., the formation of his own character and the course of action he pursues in the physical world. Therefore, in a literary work, both the characterizations and the events are to be created by the author, according to his view of the role of values in human psychology and existence (and according to the code of values he holds to be right). His characters are abstract projections, not reproductions of concretes; they are invented conceptually, not copied reportorially from the particular individuals he might have observed. The specific characters of particular individuals are merely the evidence of their particular value-choices and have no wider metaphysical significance (except as material for the study of the general principles of human psychology); they do not exhaust man's characterological potential.

2. If man does not possess volition, then his life and his character are determined by forces beyond his control—if so, then the choice of values is impossible to him—if so, then such values as he appears to hold are only an illusion, predetermined by the forces he has no power to resist—if so, then he is impotent to achieve his goals or to engage in purposeful action—and if he attempts the illusion of such action, he will be defeated by those forces, and his failure (or occasional success) will have no relation to his actions. The literary form expressing the essence of this view is plotlessness (since there can be no purposeful progression of events, no logical continuity, no resolution, no climax).

If man's character and the course of his life are the product of unknown (or unknowable) forces, then, in a literary work, both the characterizations and the events are not to be invented by the author, but are to be copied from such particular characters and events as he has observed. Since he denies the existence of any effective motivational principle in human psychology, he cannot create his characters conceptually. He can only observe the people he meets, as he observes inanimate objects, and reproduce them—in the implicit hope that some clue to the unknown forces controlling human destiny may be discovered in such reproductions.

These basic premises of Romanticism and Naturalism (the volition or anti-volition premise) affect all the other aspects of a literary work, such as the choice of theme and the quality of the style, but it is the nature of the story structure—the attribute of plot or plotlessness—

that represents the most important difference between them and serves as the main distinguishing characteristic for classifying a given work in one category or the other.

This is not to say that a writer identifies and applies all the consequences of his basic premise by a conscious process of thought. Art is the product of a man's subconscious integrations, of his sense of life, to a larger extent than of his conscious philosophical convictions. Even the choice of the basic premise may be subconscious—since artists, like any other men, seldom translate their sense of life into conscious terms. And, since an artist's sense of life may be as full of contradictions as that of any other man, these contradictions become apparent in his work; the dividing line between Romanticism and Naturalism is not always maintained consistently in every aspect of every given work of art (particularly since one of these basic premises is false). But if one surveys the field of art and studies the works produced, one will observe that the degree of consistency in the consequences of these two basic premises is a remarkably eloquent demonstration of the power of metaphysical premises in the realm of art.

With very rare (and partial) exceptions, Romanticism is nonexistent in today's literature. This is not astonishing when one considers the crushing weight of the philosophical wreckage under which generations of men have been brought up—a wreckage dominated by the doctrines of irrationalism and determinism. In their formative years, young people could not find much evidence on which to develop a rational, benevolent, value-oriented sense of life, neither in philosophical theory nor in its cultural echoes nor in the daily practice of the passively deteriorating society around them.

But observe the psychological symptoms of an unrecognized, unidentified issue: the virulently intense antagonism of today's esthetic spokesmen to any manifestation of the Romantic premise in art. It is particularly the attribute of plot in literature that arouses an impassioned hostility among them—a hostility with deeply personal overtones, too violent for a mere issue of literary canons. If plot were a negligible and inappropriate element of literature, as they claim it to be, why the hysterical hatred in their denunciations? This type of reaction pertains to *metaphysical* issues, i.e., to issues that threaten the foundations of a person's entire view of life (if that view is irrational). What they sense in a plot structure is the implicit premise of volition (and, therefore, of moral values). The same reaction, for the same subconscious reason, is evoked by such elements as heroes or happy endings or the triumph of virtue, or, in the visual arts, beauty. Physical beauty is not a moral or volitional issue—but the *choice* to paint a beautiful human being rather than an ugly one, implies the existence of volition: of choice, standards, values.

The destruction of Romanticism in esthetics—like the destruction of individualism in ethics or of capitalism in politics—was made possible by philosophical default. It is one more demonstration of the principle that that which is not known explicitly is not in man's conscious control. In all three cases, the nature of the fundamental values involved had never been defined explicitly, the issues were fought in terms of non-essentials, and the values were destroyed by men who did not know what they were losing or why.

This was the predominant pattern of issues in the field of esthetics, which, throughout history, has been a virtual monopoly of mysticism. The definition of Romanticism given here is mine—it is not a generally known or accepted one. There is no generally accepted definition of Romanticism (nor of any key element in art, nor of art itself).

Romanticism is a product of the nineteenth century—a (largely subconscious) result of two great influences: Aristotelianism, which liberated man by validating the power of his mind—and capitalism, which gave man's mind the freedom to translate ideas into practice (the second of these influences was itself the result of the first). But while the practical consequences of Aristotelianism were reaching men's daily existence, its theoretical influence was long since gone: philosophy, since the Renaissance, had been retrogressing overwhelmingly to the mysticism of Plato. Thus the historically unprecedented events of the nineteenth century—the Industrial Revolution, the child-prodigy speed in the growth of science, the skyrocketing standard of living, the liberated torrent of human energy—were left without intellectual direction or evaluation. The nineteenth century was guided, not by an Aristotelian philosophy, but by *an Aristotelian sense of life*. (And, like a brilliantly violent adolescent who fails to translate his sense of life into conscious terms, it burned itself out, choked by the blind confusions of its own overpowering energy.)

Whatever their conscious convictions, the artists of that century's great new school—the Romanticists—picked their sense of life out of the cultural atmosphere: it was an atmosphere of men intoxicated by the discovery of freedom, with all the ancient strongholds of tyranny—of church, state, monarchy, feudalism—crumbling around them, with unlimited roads opening in all directions and no barriers set to their newly unleashed energy. It was an atmosphere best expressed by that century's naive, exuberant and tragically blind belief that human progress, from here on, was to be irresistible and *automatic*.

Esthetically, the Romanticists were the great rebels and innovators of the nineteenth century. But, in their conscious convictions, they were for the most part anti-Aristotelian and leaning toward a kind of wild, freewheeling mysticism. They did not see their own rebellion in fundamental terms; they were rebelling—in the name of the individual artist's freedom—not against determinism, but, much more superficially, against the esthetic "Establishment" of the time: against *Classicism*.

Classicism (an example of a much deeper superficiality) was a school that had devised a set of arbitrary, *concretely* detailed rules purporting to represent the final and absolute criteria of esthetic value. In literature, these rules consisted of specific edicts, loosely derived from the Greek (and French) tragedies, which prescribed every formal aspect of a play (such as the unity of time, place and action) down to the number of acts and the number of verses permitted to a character in every act. Some of that stuff was based on Aristotle's esthetics and can serve as an example of what happens when concrete-bound mentalities, seeking to by-pass the responsibility of thought, attempt to transform abstract principles into concrete prescriptions and to replace creation with imitation. (For an example of Classicism that survived well into the twentieth century, I refer you to the architectural dogmas represented by Howard Roark's antagonists in *The Fountainhead*.)

Even though the Classicists had no answer to *why* their rules were to be accepted as valid (except the usual appeal to tradition, to scholarship and to the prestige of antiquity), this school was regarded as the representative of *reason*. (!)

Such were the roots of one of the grimmest ironies in cultural history: the early attempts to define the nature of Romanticism declared it to be an esthetic school based on *the primacy of emotions*—as against the champions of the primacy of reason, which were the Classicists (and, later, the Naturalists). In various forms, this definition has persisted to our day. It is an example of the intellectually disastrous consequences of definitions by non-essentials—and an example of the penalty one pays for a non-philosophical approach to cultural phenomena.

One can observe the misapprehended element of truth that gave rise to that early classification. What the Romanticists brought to art was *the primacy of values*, an element that had been missing in the stale, arid, third- and fourth-hand (and rate) repetitions of the Classicists' formula-copying. Values (and value-judgments) are the source of emotions; a great deal of emotional intensity was projected in the work of the Romanticists and in the reactions of their audiences, as well as a great deal of color, imagination, originality, excitement and all the other consequences of a value-oriented view of life. This emotional element was the most easily perceivable characteristic of the new movement and it was taken as its defining characteristic, without deeper inquiry.

Such issues as the fact that the primacy of values in human life is not an irreducible primary, that it rests on man's faculty of volition, and, therefore, that the Romanticists, philosophically, were the champions of volition (which is the root of values) and not of emotions (which are merely the consequences)—were issues to be defined by philosophers, who defaulted in regard to esthetics as they did in regard to every other crucial aspect of the nineteenth century.

The still deeper issue, the fact that the faculty of *reason* is the faculty of volition, was not known at the time, and the various theories of free will were for the most part of an anti-rational character, thus reinforcing the association of volition with mysticism.

The Romanticists saw their cause primarily as a battle for their right to individuality and—unable to grasp the deepest metaphysical justification of their cause, unable to identify their values in terms of reason—they fought for individuality in terms of *feelings*, surrendering the banner of reason to their enemies.

There were other, lesser consequences of this fundamental error, all of them symptoms of the intellectual confusion of the age. Groping blindly for a metaphysically oriented, grand-scale, exalted way of life, the Romanticists, predominantly, were enemies of capitalism, which they regarded as a prosaic, materialistic, "petty bourgeois" system—never realizing that it was the only system that could make freedom, individuality and the pursuit of values possible in practice. Some of them chose to be advocates of socialism; some turned for inspiration to the Middle Ages and became shameless glamorizers of that nightmare era; some ended up where most champions of the non-rational end up: in religion. All of it served to accelerate Romanticism's growing break with reality.

When, in the later half of the nineteenth century, Naturalism rose to prominence and, assuming the mantle of reason and reality, proclaimed the artists' duty to portray "things as they are"—Romanticism did not have much of an opposition to offer.

It must be noted that philosophers contributed to the confusion surrounding the term "Romanticism." They attached the name "Romantic" to certain philosophers (such as Schelling and Schopenhauer) who were avowed mystics advocating the supremacy of emotions, instincts or *will* over reason. This movement in philosophy had no significant relation to Romanticism in esthetics, and the two movements must not be confused. The common nomenclature, however, is significant in one respect: it indicates the depth of the confusion on the subject of *volition*. The "Romantic" philosophers' theories were a viciously malevolent, existence-hating attempt to uphold volition in the name of whim worship, while the esthetic Romanticists were groping blindly to uphold volition in the name of man's life and values here, on earth. In terms of essentials, the brilliant sunlight of Victor Hugo's universe is the diametrical opposite of the venomous muck of Schopenhauer's. It was only philosophical package-dealing that could throw them in the same category. But the issue demonstrates the profound importance of the subject of volition, and the grotesque distortions it assumes when men are unable to grasp its nature. This issue may also serve as an illustration of the importance of establishing that volition is a function of man's rational faculty.

In recent times, some literary historians have discarded, as inadequate, the definition of Romanticism as an emotion-oriented school and have attempted to redefine it, but without success. Following the rule of fundamentality, it is as a *volition*-oriented school that Romanticism must be defined—and it is in terms of this essential characteristic that the nature and history of Romantic literature can be traced and understood.

The (implicit) standards of Romanticism are so demanding that in spite of the abundance of Romantic writers at the time of its dominance, this school has produced very few pure, consistent Romanticists of the top rank. Among novelists, the greatest are Victor Hugo and Dostoevsky, and, as single novels (whose authors were not always consistent in the rest of their works), I would name Henryk Sienkiewicz's *Quo*

Vadis and Nathaniel Hawthorne's *The Scarlet Letter*. Among play-wrights, the greatest are Friedrich Schiller and Edmond Rostand.

The distinguishing characteristic of this top rank (apart from their purely literary genius) is their full commitment to the premise of vo-lition in *both of its fundamental areas:* in regard to consciousness and to existence, in regard to man's character and to his actions in the physical world. Maintaining a perfect integration of these two as-pects, unmatched in the brilliant ingenuity of their plot structures, these writers are enormously concerned with man's soul (i.e., his con-sciousness). They are *moralists* in the most profound sense of the word; their concern is not merely with values, but specifically with *moral* values and with the power of moral values in shaping human character. Their characters are "larger than life," i.e., they are abstract projections in terms of essentials (not always successful projections, as we shall discuss later). In their stories, one will never find action for action's sake, unrelated to moral values. The events of their plots are shaped, determined and motivated by the characters' values (or trea-son to values), by their struggle in pursuit of spiritual goals and by profound value-conflicts. Their themes are fundamental, universal, timeless issues of man's existence—and they are the only consistent creators of the rarest attribute of literature: the perfect integration of theme and plot, which they achieve with superlative virtuosity.

If philosophical significance is the criterion of what is to be taken seriously, then these are the most serious writers in world literature.

The second rank of Romanticists (who are still writers of consider-able merit, but of lesser stature) indicates the direction of Romanti-cism's future decline. This rank is represented by such writers as Walter Scott and Alexander Dumas. The distinguishing characteris-tic of their work is the emphasis on action, without spiritual goals or significant moral values. Their stories have well-built, imaginative, suspenseful plot structures, but the values pursued by their characters and motivating the action are of a primitive, superficial, emphatically non-metaphysical order: loyalty to a king, the reclaiming of a heritage, personal revenge, etc. The conflicts and story lines are predominantly external. The characters are abstractions, they are not Naturalistic copies, but they are abstractions of loosely generalized virtues or vices, and characterization is minimal. In time, they become a writer's own self-made bromides, such as "a brave knight," "a noble lady," "a vicious courtier"—so that they are neither created nor drawn from life, but picked from a kind of ready-to-wear collection of stock

characters of Romanticism. The absence of any metaphysical meaning (apart from the affirmation of volition implicit in a plot structure)
is evident in the fact that these novels have plots, but no abstract
themes—with the story's central conflict serving as the theme, usually in the form of some actual or fictionalized historical event.

Going farther down, one can observe the breakup of Romanticism,
the contradictions that proceed from a premise held subconsciously.
On this level, there emerges a class of writers whose basic premise, in
effect, is that man possesses volition *in regard to existence, but not to
consciousness,* i.e., in regard to his physical actions, but not in regard
to his own character. The distinguishing characteristic of this class is:
stories of unusual events enacted by *conventional* characters. The stories are abstract projections, involving actions one does not observe in
"real life," the characters are commonplace concretes. The stories are
Romantic, the characters Naturalistic. Such novels seldom have plots
(since value-conflicts are not their motivational principle), but they
do have a form resembling a plot: a coherent, imaginative, often suspenseful story held together by some one central goal or undertaking
of the characters.

The contradictions in such a combination of elements are obvious;
they lead to a total breach between action and characterization, leaving the action unmotivated and the characters unintelligible. The
reader is left to feel: "These people couldn't do these things!"

With its emphasis on sheer physical action and neglect of human
psychology, this class of novels stands on the borderline between serious and popular literature. No top-rank novelists belong to this category; the better-known ones are writers of science fiction, such as H.
G. Wells or Jules Verne. (Occasionally, a good writer of the Naturalistic school, with a repressed element of Romanticism, attempts a novel
on an abstract theme that requires a Romantic approach; the result
falls into this category. For example, Sinclair Lewis's *It Can't Happen
Here.*) It is obvious why the novels of this category are enormously un-
convincing. And, no matter how skillfully or suspensefully their action
is presented, they always have an unsatisfying, uninspiring quality.

On the other side of the same dichotomy, there are Romanticists
whose basic premise, in effect, is that man possesses volition *in regard
to consciousness, but not to existence,* i.e., in regard to his own character and choice of values, but not in regard to the possibility of achieving his goals in the physical world. The distinguishing characteristics
of such writers are grand-scale themes and characters, no plots and an

overwhelming sense of tragedy, the sense of a "malevolent universe." The chief exponents of this category were poets. The leading one is Byron, whose name has been attached to this particular, "Byronic," view of existence: its essence is the belief that man must lead a heroic life and fight for his values even though he is doomed to defeat by a malevolent fate over which he has no control.

Today, the same view is advocated philosophically by the existentialists, but without the grand-scale element and with Romanticism replaced by a kind of sub-Naturalism.

Philosophically, Romanticism is a crusade to glorify man's existence; psychologically, it is experienced simply as the desire to make life interesting.

This desire is the root and motor of Romantic imagination. Its greatest example, in popular literature, is O. Henry, whose unique characteristic is the pyrotechnical virtuosity of an inexhaustible imagination projecting the gaiety of a benevolent, almost childlike sense of life. More than any other writer, O. Henry represents the spirit of youth—specifically, the cardinal element of youth: the expectation of finding something wonderfully unexpected around all of life's corners.

In the field of popular literature, Romanticism's virtues and potential flaws may be seen in a simplified, more obvious form.

Popular literature is fiction that does not deal with abstract problems; it takes moral principles as the given, accepting certain generalized, *common-sense* ideas and values as its base. (Common-sense values and conventional values are not the same thing; the first can be justified rationally, the second cannot. Even though the second may include some of the first, they are justified, not on the ground of reason, but on the ground of social conformity.)

Popular fiction does not raise or answer abstract questions; it assumes that man knows what he needs to know in order to live, and it proceeds to show his adventures in living (which is one of the reasons for its popularity among all types of readers, including the problem-laden intellectuals). The distinctive characteristic of popular fiction is the absence of an *explicitly* ideational element, of the intent to convey intellectual information (or misinformation).

Detective, adventure, science-fiction novels and Westerns belong, for the most part, to the category of popular fiction. The best writers of this category come close to the Scott-Dumas group: their emphasis is on action, but their heroes and villains are abstract projections, and a loosely generalized view of moral values, of a struggle between good and evil, motivates the action. (As contemporary examples of the best in this class: Mickey Spillane, Ian Fleming, Donald Hamilton.)

When we go below the top level of popular fiction, we descend into a kind of no man's land where literary principles are barely applicable (particularly if we include the field of movies and television). Here, the distinctive characteristics of Romanticism become almost indistinguishable. On this level, writing is not the product of subconscious premises: it is a mixture of elements picked by random imitation rather than by sense-of-life creation.

A certain characteristic is typical of this level: it is not merely the use of conventional, Naturalistic characters to enact Romantic events, but worse: the use of characters who are romanticized embodiments of *conventional* values. Such embodiments represent *canned* values, empty stereotypes that serve as an automatic substitute for value-judgments. This method lacks the essential attribute of Romanticism: the independent, creative projection of an individual writer's values—and it lacks the reportorial honesty of the (better) Naturalists: it does not present concrete men "as they are," it presents human pretensions (a collective role-playing or an indiscriminate collective daydream) and palms this off as reality.

Most of the "slick-magazine" fiction popular before World War II belongs to this class, with its endless variations on the Cinderella theme, the motherhood theme, the costume-drama theme, or the common-man-with-a-heart-of-gold theme. (For example, Edna Ferber, Fannie Hurst, Barry Benefield.) This type of fiction has no plots, only more or less cohesive stories, and no discernible characterizations: the characters are false journalistically, and meaningless metaphysically. (It is an open question whether this group belongs to the category of Romanticism; it is usually regarded as Romantic simply because it is far removed from anything perceivable in reality concretely or abstractly.)

As far as their fiction aspects are concerned, movies and television, by their nature, are media suited exclusively to Romanticism (to abstractions, essentials and drama). Unfortunately, both media came too late: the great day of Romanticism was gone, and only its sunset rays reached a few exceptional movies. (Fritz Lang's *Siegfried* is the best among them.) For a while, the movie field was dominated by the equivalent of the slick-magazine Romanticism, with a still less discriminating level of taste and imagination, and an incommunicable vulgarity of spirit.

Partly in reaction against this debasement of values, but mainly in consequence of the general philosophical-cultural disintegration of our time (with its anti-value trend), Romanticism vanished from the movies and never reached television (except in the form of a few detective series, which are now gone also). What remains is the occasional appearance of cowardly pieces, whose authors apologize for their Romantic attempts, by means of comedy—or mongrel pieces, whose authors beg not to be mistaken for advocates of human values (or human greatness), by means of coyly, militantly commonplace characters who enact world-shaking events and perform fantastic feats, particularly in the realm of science. The nature of this type of scenario can best be encapsulated by a line of dialogue on the order of: "Sorry, baby, I can't take you to the pizza joint tonight, I've got to go back to the lab and split the atom."

The next, and final, level of disintegration is the attempt to eliminate Romanticism from Romantic fiction—i.e., to dispense with the element of values, morality and volition. This used to be called the "hard-boiled" school of detective fiction; today, it is plugged as "realistic." This school makes no distinction between heroes and villains (or detectives and criminals, or victims and executioners) and presents, in effect, two mobs of gangsters fighting savagely and incomprehensibly (no motivation is offered) for the same territory, neither side being able to do otherwise.

This is the dead end where, arriving by different roads, Romanticism and Naturalism meet, blend and vanish: deterministically helpless, compulsively evil characters go through a series of inexplicably exaggerated events and engage in purposeful conflicts without purpose.

Beyond this point, the field of literature, both "serious" and popular, is taken over by a genre compared to which Romanticism and Naturalism are clean, civilized and innocently rational: the Horror Story. The modern ancestor of this phenomenon is Edgar Allan Poe; its archetype or purest esthetic expression is Boris Karloff movies.

Popular literature, more honest in this respect, presents its horrors in the form of physical monstrosities. In "serious" literature, the horrors become psychological and bear less resemblance to anything human; this is the literary cult of depravity.

The Horror Story, in either variant, represents the metaphysical projection of a single human emotion: blind, stark, primitive terror. Those who live in such terror seem to find a momentary sense of relief or control in the process of reproducing that which they fear—as savages find a sense of mastery over their enemies by reproducing them in the form of dolls. Strictly speaking, this is not a metaphysical, but a purely psychological projection; such writers are not presenting their view of life; they are not looking at life; what they are saying is that they *feel* as if life consisted of werewolves, Draculas and Frankenstein monsters. In its basic motivation, this school belongs to psychopathology more than to esthetics.

Historically, neither Romanticism nor Naturalism could survive the collapse of philosophy. There are individual exceptions, but I am speaking of these schools as broad, active, creative movements. Since art is the expression and product of philosophy, it is the first to mirror the vacuum at the base of a culture and the first to crumble.

This general cause had special consequences affecting Romanticism, which hastened its decline and collapse. There were also special consequences affecting Naturalism, which were of a different character and their destructive potential worked at a slower rate.

The archenemy and destroyer of Romanticism was the altruist morality.

Since Romanticism's essential characteristic is the projection of values, particularly *moral* values, altruism introduced an insolvable conflict into Romantic literature from the start. The altruist morality cannot be practiced (except in the form of self-destruction) and, therefore, cannot be projected or dramatized convincingly in terms of man's life on earth (particularly in the realm of psychological motivation). With altruism as the criterion of value and virtue, it is impossible to create an image of man at his best—"as he might be and ought to be." The major flaw that runs through the history of Romantic literature is the failure to present a convincing hero, i.e., a convincing image of a virtuous man.

It is the abstract intention—the grandeur of the author's view of man—that one admires in the characters of Victor Hugo, not their actual characterizations. The greatest Romanticist never succeeded in projecting an ideal man or any convincing major characters of a positive nature. His most ambitious attempt, Jean Valjean in *Les Misérables*, remains a giant abstraction that never integrates into a person, in spite of isolated touches of profound psychological perceptiveness on the part of the author. In the same novel, Marius, the young man who is supposed to be Hugo's autobiographical projection, acquires a certain stature only by means of what the author *says* about him, not by means of what he *shows*. As far as characterization is concerned, Marius is not a person, but the suggestion of a person squeezed into a straitjacket of cultural bromides. The best-drawn and most interesting characters in Hugo's novels are the semi-villains (his benevolent sense of life made him unable to create a real villain): Javert in *Les Misérables*, Josiana in *The Man Who Laughs*, Claude Frollo in *Notre-Dame de Paris*.

Dostoevsky (whose sense of life was the diametrical opposite of Hugo's) was a passionate moralist whose blind quest for values was expressed only in the fiercely merciless condemnation with which he presented evil characters; no one has equaled him in the psychological depth of his images of human evil. But he was totally incapable of creating a positive or virtuous character; such attempts as he made were crudely inept (for example, Alyosha in *The Brothers Karamazov*). It is significant that according to Dostoevsky's preliminary notes for *The Possessed*, his original intention was to create Stavrogin as an ideal man—an embodiment of the Russian-Christian-altruist soul. As the notes progressed, that intention changed gradually, in logically inexorable steps dictated by Dostoevsky's artistic integrity. In the final result, in the actual novel, Stavrogin is one of Dostoevsky's most repulsively evil characters.

In Sienkiewicz's *Quo Vadis*, the best-drawn, most colorful character, who dominates the novel, is Petronius, the symbol of Roman decadence—while Vinicius, the author's hero, the symbol of the rise of Christianity, is a cardboard figure.

This phenomenon—the fascinating villain or colorful rogue, who steals the story and the drama from the anemic hero—is prevalent in the history of Romantic literature, serious or popular, from top to bottom. It is as if, under the dead crust of the altruist code officially adopted by mankind, an illicit, subterranean fire were boiling chaotically and erupting once in a while; forbidden to the hero, the fire of self-assertiveness burst forth from the apologetic ashes of a "villain."

The highest function of Romanticism— the projection of moral values—is an extremely difficult task under any moral code, rational or not, and, in literary history, only the top rank of Romanticists were able to attempt it. Given the added burden of an irrational code, such as altruism, the majority of Romantic writers had to avoid that task—which led to the weakness and neglect of the element of characterization in their writing. In addition, the impossibility of applying altruism to reality, to men's actual existence, led many Romantic writers to avoid the problem by escaping into history, i.e., by choosing to place their stories in some distant past (such as the Middle Ages). Thus, the emphasis on action, the neglect of human psychology, the lack of convincing motivation were progressively dissociating Romanticism from reality—until the final remnants of Romanticism became a superficial, meaningless, "unserious" school that had nothing to say about human existence.

The disintegration of Naturalism brought it to the same state, for different reasons.

Although Naturalism is a product of the nineteenth century, its spiritual father, in modern history, was Shakespeare. The premise that man does not possess volition, that his destiny is determined by an innate "tragic flaw," is fundamental in Shakespeare's work. But, granted this false premise, his approach is metaphysical, not journalistic. His characters are not drawn from "real life," they are not copies of observed concretes nor statistical averages: they are grand-scale abstractions of the character traits which a determinist would regard as inherent in human nature: ambition, power-lust, jealousy, greed, etc.

Some of the famous Naturalists attempted to maintain Shakespeare's abstract level, i.e., to present their views of human nature in metaphysical terms (for example, Balzac, Tolstoy). But the majority, following the lead of Emile Zola, rejected metaphysics, as they rejected values, and adopted the method of journalism: the recording of observed concretes.

The contradictions inherent in determinism were obvious in this movement from the start. One does not read fiction except on the implicit premise of volition—i.e., on the premise that some element (some abstraction) of the fiction story is applicable to oneself, that one will learn, discover or contemplate something of value and that this experience will make a difference. If one were to accept the deterministic premise fully and literally—if one were to believe that the characters of a fiction story are as distant and irrelevant to oneself as the unknowable inhabitants of another galaxy and that they cannot affect one's life in any way whatever, since neither they nor the reader have any power of choice—one would not be able to read beyond the first chapter.

Nor would one be able to write. Psychologically, the whole of the Naturalist movement rode on the premise of volition as on an unidentified, subconscious "stolen concept." Choosing "society" as the factor that determines man's fate, most of the Naturalists were social reformers, advocating social changes, claiming that man has no volition, but society, somehow, has. Tolstoy preached resignation and passive obedience to society's power. In *Anna Karenina*, the most evil book in serious literature, he attacked man's desire for happiness and advocated its sacrifice to *conformity*.

No matter how concrete-bound their theories forced them to be, the writers of the Naturalist school still had to exercise their power of abstraction to a significant extent: in order to reproduce "real-life" characters, they had to select the characteristics they regarded as essential, differentiating them from the non-essential or accidental. Thus they were led to substitute statistics for values as a criterion of selectivity: that which is statistically prevalent among men, they held, is metaphysically significant and representative of man's nature; that which is rare or exceptional, is not.

At first, having rejected the element of plot and even of story, the Naturalists concentrated on the element of characterization—and psychological perceptiveness was the chief value that the best of them had to offer. With the growth of the statistical method, however, that value shrank and vanished: characterization was replaced by indiscriminate recording and buried under a catalogue of trivia, such as minute inventories of a character's apartment, clothing and meals. Naturalism lost the attempted universality of Shakespeare or Tolstoy, descending from metaphysics to photography with a rapidly shrinking lens directed at the range of the immediate moment—until the final remnants of Naturalism became a superficial, meaningless, "unserious" school that had nothing to say about human existence. [. . .]

Such is the esthetic state of our day. But so long as men exist, the need of art will exist, since that need is rooted metaphysically in the nature of man's consciousness—and it will survive a period when, under the reign of irrationality run amuck, men produce and accept tainted scraps to satisfy that need.

As in the case of an individual, so in the case of a culture: disasters can be accomplished subconsciously, but a cure cannot. A cure in both cases requires conscious knowledge, i.e., a consciously grasped, explicit philosophy.

It is impossible to predict the time of a philosophical Renaissance. One can only define the road to follow, but not its length. What is certain, however, is that every aspect of Western culture needs a new code of ethics—a *rational ethics*—as a precondition of rebirth. And, perhaps, no aspect needs it more desperately than the realm of art.

When reason and philosophy are reborn, literature will be the first phoenix to rise out of today's ashes. And, armed with a code of rational values, aware of its own nature, confident of the supreme importance of its mission, Romanticism will have come of age.

═══════════

2. The Benevolent Universe

EDITOR'S NOTE: *Because AR advocated reason and reality in basic philosophy, she advocated* rational *values—values based on reason and reality—in ethics, politics, and esthetics. By their nature, such values are achievable by men in reality—i.e., they are achievable here and now, in this world and this life.*

AR, therefore, had no tolerance for the "tragic view of life" (which many Romantic artists before her had endorsed); she rejected this idea both in life and in art. On the contrary, she believed that happiness, not pain—the achievement of values, not their loss—is and should be the human norm. Thus the key statement by one of the heroes of Atlas Shrugged: *"[W]e do not hold the belief that this earth is a realm of misery where man is doomed to destruction. [. . .] It is not happiness, but suffering that we consider unnatural. It is not success, but calamity that we regard as the abnormal exception in human life."*

AR called this attitude the benevolent-universe premise. It is the deepest reason why the heroes of her novels characteristically achieve their goals; their setbacks or losses are merely temporary obstacles to be overcome by decisive thought and action.

AR's 1962 introduction to one of her favorite pieces of fiction—a 1901 novel, Calumet "K"—*discusses one key result of the benevolent-universe premise when it is applied to fiction: the portrayal of man as efficacious.*

Introduction to Calumet "K"

CALUMET "K" is my favorite novel.

It is not a work of great literature—it is a work of light fiction, written by two collaborators, that appeared originally, in the year 1901, in a popular magazine, *The Saturday Evening Post*. Its style is straightforward and competent, but undistinguished. It lacks the most important ingredient of good fiction, a plot structure. But it has one element that I have never found in any other novel: the portrait of an *efficacious* man.

The formal hero of this novel is a grain elevator, called "Calumet 'K'," and the novel tells the story of its construction, nothing more. But if you find yourself held in suspense, reading intently, hoping that the structure will be built on time, if you find that two simple, descriptive paragraphs (in the chapter before last) are a gloriously triumphant experience that makes you want to cheer aloud—it will be, like the grain elevator itself, the achievement of Charlie Bannon.

Bannon is the young superintendent in charge of building Calumet "K." He is described as follows: "He was worn thin as an old knife-blade, he was just at the end of a piece of work that would have entitled any other man to a vacation; but MacBride made no apologies when he assigned him the new task . . ." He is sent to the job because no one else is able to do it: it is virtually impossible to complete the elevator by a certain crucial date. The construction is the story of Bannon's quietly fierce struggle against powerful interests determined to sabotage the work and stop him. Behind the scenes, the fate of countless lives and enormous fortunes rests, not on Bannon's shoulders, but on his brain.

The essence of the story is Bannon's ingenuity in solving unexpected problems and smashing through sudden obstacles, his self-confident resourcefulness, his inexhaustible energy, his dedication. He is a man who takes nothing for granted, who thinks long-range, who assumes responsibility as a matter of course, as a way of life, knowing that there is no such thing as "luck" and if things are to be done, *he* has to do them.

His dominant characteristic is a total commitment to the absolutism of reality. Even though such philosophical abstractions are outside his knowledge and his story, his basic premise is *the primacy of existence*, not of consciousness—i.e., a mind, focus and passionate concern directed *outward* (with its inner concomitant: an unbreached self-esteem). This is why his story and his problems matter to me, as no lesser human problems can.

It is not merely that Bannon is a purposeful man; there have been plenty of purposeful men in fiction, pursuing all sorts of goals, most of them dubious. Bannon is specifically an *efficacious* man: a man able to deal with reality—a man whose characterization features, stresses and dramatizes this particular trait. In this sense, he is an *American* phenomenon which is not typical of any other culture.

Calumet "K" is a good example of the fact that when fiction, even light fiction, contains some element of truth about human existence, it carries philosophical implications wider than its specific theme. This novel is a remarkable historical-social-psychological document. Today, its subtitle ought to be: *This was America.*

Calumet "K" captures the atmosphere—the sense of life—of a free country: what it was like, what it demanded of men, and, indirectly, by whom and why it would be hated. The story is neither pro-business nor pro-labor, but pro-individual, i.e., pro-human ability: the enemies Bannon has to fight are a Clique of Wall Street speculators, on the one hand, and a corrupt labor leader, on the other.

The story is an excellent illustration, in miniature, of the working of a free economy; Bannon is pitted against the biggest evil allegedly inherent in capitalism: an attempt to establish a monopoly, a Wall Street conspiracy to corner the wheat market. The story demonstrates that so long as men are free to act, no one will be able to cut off all avenues of action, that an attempted evil creates its own antidotes, but one must be prepared to find them and to enlist men's legitimate self-interests on one's side. (In a controlled economy, Bannon would be the first victim, and the Clique would be in charge of a government regulatory agency.)

It is interesting to note that Bannon is not an industrial tycoon, but merely an employee of a building contractor; he is presented, not as a rare exception, but as an average man. I doubt that a man of Bannon's stature could be average in any society; and, in a free one, he would not remain an employee for long. But he represents, in its purest form, the characteristic which a free society demands of all men, on all levels of ability: competence.

The story demonstrates in many skillfully subtle ways that that characteristic runs through the whole social pyramid. On the lower levels, it depends on the quality of the leadership involved in a large, cooperative undertaking. Bannon's leadership is the decisive factor in the issue of morale or lethargic indifference on the part of all the workers on the job. His self-confidence, his demanding standards and his strict fairness bring out the best in them: pride in their work, conscientiousness, energy, enthusiasm—qualities they were beginning to lose under his incompetent predecessor. Their potential virtue is like an inert, responsive mechanism that can swing either way; Bannon is the spark plug. They respond when they know that their best will be appreciated.

Bannon's predecessor, Peterson, is given an interesting characterization: he is presented, stressedly, as a man of brawn versus Bannon, the man of brains. Peterson is not a bad person, he has merely ventured beyond his depth and found himself loaded with a weight beyond his capacity, a weight much greater than that of the timbers and sledge hammers he handles with an easy, show-offish prowess. He is on the verge of turning bad, but a job commensurate with his ability brings him back to the status of a valuable worker. "Nobody can blame me," was, in effect, Peterson's first concern in any emergency. "That is irrelevant," is Bannon's answer.

On the higher levels of the pyramid, one senses—like a light flashing behind the scenes once in a while—that Bannon's competence is recognized and appreciated by his bosses. The same recognition greets him whenever he deals with the heads of other companies. If he is resented, at times, it is always by the underlings, never by the big executives. One of my favorite scenes is a small incident in which Bannon presents to a lumber tycoon the solution to a transportation problem the tycoon had regarded as hopeless. The scene goes as follows:

"Sloan made no reply. He had allowed his wrath to boil for a few minutes merely as a luxury. Now he was thinking seriously of the scheme. 'It sounds like moonshine,' he said at last, 'but I don't know as it is. How are you going to get your barges?'

" 'I've got one already. It leaves Milwaukee tonight.'

"Sloan looked him over. 'I wish you were out of a job,' he said."

This is the keynote of the incredibly wonderful quality of that world which was America at the turn of the century: *a world in which ability mattered.*

But, even within the confines of a simple, popular novel, one can see also the ominous touches on the periphery of that world, the seeds of what was to destroy it.

That free, violently joyous torrent of creative energy flooding a continent, was invisible to men: invisible intellectually. Its meaning had no conceptual identification or moral recognition. It was cut off from all the other aspects of men's existence and from the formal code of values by which they lived their lives. And that code was an ancient, ludicrously incongruous straitjacket, deforming an innocent young giant.

The symptoms of that code may be seen in the novel's lesser element: in its love story. Bannon's romance with a young stenographer, the only woman on the construction site, is so timidly, evasively mid-Victorian that the contrast to the rest of the novel is almost unbearable. The spectacle of men who are remaking the face of a continent, yet are supposed to pretend that a fact such as sex does not exist, is what the mystics' old-world morality imposed on a young country, along with all the rest of their "anti-materialistic" doctrines.

Bannon is quite obviously a represser, who has never taken a first-hand look at anything outside his work. His work is his only happiness; everything else is cut off, as alien territory. But even the extent of his love for his work is not given a fully conscious recognition in his mind, nor does he consciously regard his own competence as a virtue; he simply takes both for granted. He is not anti-intellectual, but *un*-intellectual— as a man of action, too busy to conceptualize. In this respect, also, he is the typical representative of American culture—at its best and worst.

The penalty for that particular flaw is indicated in the story—in an ugly little touch that reads as if the authors, who admire Bannon tremendously, felt, nevertheless, obliged to pay lip-service to altruism. The heroine's attitude toward Bannon changes on the day when she discovers that he has been sending small gifts to a hospitalized worker who was hurt in an accident on the construction site. She confesses to Bannon that: "well, some people think you don't think very much about the men, and that if anybody's hurt, or anything happens, you don't care as long as the work goes on"—and she apologizes to him for having thought so, too.

In other words, the feats of productive energy which he was performing were irrelevant (or even made him an object of suspicion), but the fact that he sent tobacco to a man in a hospital, was required to establish his personal virtue.

Today, we can see what that little cloud of altruism, hovering on the edge of a sunlit sky, has grown into—and what that cultural split has accomplished.

But, as far as *Calumet "K"* is concerned, these are only its peripheral elements, its sky is still sunlit, brilliantly sunlit—and that is its paramount value.

Culturally, *Calumet "K"* can serve as a gauge of the distance we have traveled downward. It was written for a wide popular audience, and reflects the dominant sense of life of its time. It was a time when people were capable of admiring productive achievement, when they saw man as strong, confident, cheerfully efficacious—and the universe as a place where victory and fulfillment are possible. Observe the extent to which this novel is "unmodern." It is entirely devoid of neurotic soul-searching, of bitterness, of cynicism, of that maudlin preoccupation with depravity which is characteristic of today's novels. What it projects predominantly is a quality of innocence and of magnificent *health*. If you want to feel frightened—in regard to the nature of today's dominant sense of life—compare *Calumet "K"* to any novel from any current issue of the same magazine, *The Saturday Evening Post*. . . .

——————

EDITOR'S NOTE: *This 1960 answer to a fan included in* Letters of Ayn Rand *is an eloquent summary of the benevolent-universe attitude.*

Letter to a Fan

August 29, 1960

Dear Mr. Williams:

Thank you for your letter of August 10. I will tell you frankly that yours is one of the few letters that I liked very much.

I am glad that *Atlas Shrugged* and *The Fountainhead* have helped you philosophically. I hope that you will understand and accept my philosophy fully, and—if I understand you correctly—that you will never give up the values you had once held.

You ask me about the meaning of the dialogue on page 702 of *Atlas Shrugged*:

" 'We never had to take any of it seriously, did we?' she whispered.
" 'No, we never had to.' "

Let me begin by saying that this is perhaps *the* most important point in the whole book, because it is the condensed emotional summation, the keynote or leitmotif, of the view of life presented in *Atlas Shrugged*.

What Dagny expresses here is the conviction that joy, exaltation, beauty, greatness, heroism, all the supreme, uplifting values of man's existence on earth, are the meaning of life—*not* the pain or ugliness he may encounter—that one must live for the sake of such exalted moments as one may be able to achieve or experience, *not* for the sake of suffering—that happiness matters, but suffering does not—that no matter how much pain one may have to endure, it is never to be taken seriously, that is: never to be taken as the essence and meaning of life—that the essence of life is the achievement of joy, *not* the escape from pain. The issue she refers to is the basic philosophical issue which John Galt later names explicitly in his speech: that the most fundamental division among men is between those who are pro-man, pro-mind, pro-life—and those who are anti-man, anti-mind, anti-life.

It is the difference between those who think that man's life is important and that happiness is possible—and those who think that man's life, by its very nature, is a hopeless, senseless tragedy and that man is a depraved creature doomed to despair and defeat. It is the difference between those whose basic motive is the desire to achieve values, to experience joy—and those whose basic motive is the desire to escape from pain, to experience a momentary relief from their chronic anxiety and guilt.

It is a matter of one's fundamental, overall attitude toward life—not of any one specific event. So you see that your interpretation was too specific and too narrow; besides, the Looters' World had never meant anything to Dagny and she had realized its "sham and hypocrisy" long before. What she felt, in that particular moment, was the confirmation of her conviction that an *ideal* man and an ideal form of existence *are* possible.

EDITOR'S NOTE: *"Don't Let It Go," a 1971 essay published in* Philosophy: Who Needs It *identifies what will happen to America if it does not translate its implicitly benevolent view of life into an explicit, rational philosophy.*

Don't Let It Go

IN ORDER to form a hypothesis about the future of an individual, one must consider three elements: his present course of action, his conscious convictions, and his sense of life. The same elements must be considered in forming a hypothesis about the future of a nation.

A sense of life is a pre-conceptual equivalent of metaphysics, an emotional, subconsciously integrated appraisal of man and of existence. It represents an individual's unidentified philosophy (which can be identified—and corrected, if necessary); it affects his choice of values and his emotional responses, influences his actions, and, frequently, clashes with his conscious convictions. (For a detailed discussion, see "Philosophy and Sense of Life" in my book *The Romantic Manifesto*.)

A nation, like an individual, has a sense of life, which is expressed not in its formal culture, but in its "life style"—in the kinds of actions and attitudes which people take for granted and believe to be self-evident, but which are produced by complex evaluations involving a fundamental view of man's nature.

A "nation" is not a mystic or supernatural entity: it is a large number of individuals who live in the same geographical locality under the same political system. A nation's culture is the sum of the intellectual achievements of individual men, which their fellow-citizens have accepted in whole or in part, and which have influenced the nation's way of life. Since a culture is a complex battleground of different ideas and influences, to speak of a "culture" is to speak only of the *dominant* ideas, always allowing for the existence of dissenters and exceptions.

(The dominance of certain ideas is not necessarily determined by the number of their adherents: it may be determined by majority acceptance, or by the greater activity and persistence of a given faction, or by default, i.e., the failure of the opposition, or—when a country is free—by a combination of persistence and truth. In any case, ideas and the resultant culture are the product and active concern of a minority. Who constitutes this minority? Whoever chooses to be concerned.)

Similarly, the concept of a nation's sense of life does not mean that every member of a given nation shares it, but only that a dominant majority shares its essentials in various degrees. In this matter, however, the dominance is numerical: while most men may be indifferent to cultural-ideological trends, no man can escape the process of subconscious integration which forms his sense of life.

A nation's sense of life is formed by every individual child's early impressions of the world around him: of the ideas he is taught (which he may or may not accept) and of the way of acting he observes and evaluates (which he may evaluate correctly or not). And although there are exceptions at both ends of the psychological spectrum— men whose sense of life is better (truer philosophically) or worse than that of their fellow-citizens—the majority develop the essentials of the same subconscious philosophy. This is the source of what we observe as "national characteristics."

A nation's political trends are the equivalent of a man's course of action and are determined by its culture. A nation's culture is the equivalent of a man's conscious convictions. Just as an individual's sense of life can clash with his conscious convictions, hampering or defeating his actions, so a nation's sense of life can clash with its culture, hampering or defeating its political course. Just as an individual's sense of life can be better or worse than his conscious convictions, so can a nation's. And just as an individual who has never translated his sense of life into conscious convictions is in terrible danger—no matter how good his subconscious values—so is a nation.

This is the position of America today.

If America is to be saved from destruction—specifically, from dictatorship—she will be saved by her sense of life.

As to the two other elements that determine a nation's future, one (our political trend) is speeding straight to disaster, the other (culture) is virtually nonexistent. The political trend is pure statism and is moving toward a totalitarian dictatorship at a speed which, in any other country, would have reached that goal long ago. The culture is worse than nonexistent: it is operating below zero, i.e., performing the opposite of its function. A culture provides a nation's intellectual leadership, its ideas, its education, its moral code. Today, the concerted effort of our cultural "Establishment" is directed at the obliteration of man's rational faculty. Hysterical voices are proclaiming the impotence of reason, extolling the "superior power" of irrationality, fostering the rule of incoherent emotions, attacking science, glorifying the stupor of drugged hippies, delivering apologies for the use of brute force, urging mankind's return to a life of rolling in primeval muck, with grunts and groans as means of communication, physical sensations as means of inspiration, and a club as means of argumentation.

This country, with its magnificent scientific and technological power, is left in the vacuum of a pre-intellectual era, like the wandering hordes of the Dark Ages—or in the position of an adolescent before he has fully learned to conceptualize. But an adolescent has his sense of life to guide his choices. So has this country.

What is the specifically American sense of life?

A sense of life is so complex an integration that the best way to identify it is by means of concrete examples and by contrast with the manifestations of a different sense of life.

The emotional keynote of most Europeans is the feeling that man belongs to the State, as a property to be used and disposed of, in compliance with his natural, metaphysically determined fate. A typical European may disapprove of a given State and may rebel, seeking to establish what he regards as a better one, like a slave who might seek a better master to serve—but the idea that *he* is the sovereign and the government is his servant, has no emotional reality in his consciousness. He regards service to the State as an ultimate moral sanction, as an *honor*, and if you told him that his life is an end in itself, he would feel insulted or rejected or lost. Generations brought up on statist philosophy and acting accordingly, have implanted this in his mind from the earliest, formative years of his childhood.

A typical American can never fully grasp that kind of feeling. An American is an independent entity. The popular expression of protest against "being pushed around" is emotionally unintelligible to Europeans, who believe that to be pushed around is their natural condition. Emotionally, an American has no concept of service (or of servitude) to anyone. Even if he enlists in the army and hears it called "service to his country," his feeling is that of a generous aristocrat who *chose* to do a dangerous task. A European soldier feels that he is doing his duty.

"Isn't my money as good as the next fellow's?" used to be a popular American expression. It would not be popular in Europe: a fortune, to be good, must be old and derived by special favor from the

State; to a European, money earned by personal effort is vulgar, crude or somehow disreputable.

Americans admire achievement; they know what it takes. Europeans regard achievement with cynical suspicion and envy. Envy is not a widespread emotion in America (not yet); it is an overwhelmingly dominant emotion in Europe.

When Americans feel respect for their public figures, it is the respect of equals; they feel that a government official is a human being, just as they are, who has chosen this particular line of work and has earned a certain distinction. They call celebrities by their first names, they refer to Presidents by their initials (like "F.D.R." or "J.F.K."), not in insolence or egalitarian pretentiousness, but in token of affection. The custom of addressing a person as "Herr Doktor Doktor Schmidt" would be impossible in America. In England, the freest country of Europe, the achievement of a scientist, a businessman or a movie star is not regarded as fully real until he has been clunked on the head with the State's sword and declared to be a knight.

There are practical consequences of these two different attitudes.

An American economist told me the following story. He was sent to England by an American industrial concern, to investigate its European branch: in spite of the latest equipment and techniques, the productivity of the branch in England kept lagging far behind that of the parent-factory in the U.S. He found the cause: a rigidly circumscribed mentality, a kind of psychological caste system, on all the echelons of British labor and management. As he explained it: in America, if a machine breaks down, a worker volunteers to fix it, and usually does; in England, work stops and people wait for the appropriate department to summon the appropriate engineer. It is not a matter of laziness, but of a profoundly ingrained feeling that one must keep one's place, do one's prescribed duty, and never venture beyond it. It does not occur to the British worker that he is free to assume responsibility for anything beyond the limits of his particular job. *Initiative* is an "instinctive" (i.e., automatized) American characteristic; in an American consciousness, it occupies the place which, in a European one, is occupied by *obedience*.

As to the differences in the social atmosphere, here is an example. An elderly European woman, a research biochemist from Switzerland, on a visit to New York, told me that she wanted to buy some things at the five-and-ten. Since she could barely speak English, I offered to go with her; she hesitated, looking astonished and disturbed, then asked:

"But wouldn't that embarrass you?" I couldn't understand what she meant: "Embarrass—how?" "Well," she explained, "you are a famous person, and what if somebody sees you in the five-and-ten?" I laughed. She explained to me that in Switzerland, by unwritten law, there are different stores for different classes of people, and that she, as a professional, has to shop in certain stores, even though her salary is modest, that better goods at lower prices are available in the workingmen's stores, but she would lose social status if she were seen shopping there. Can you conceive of living in an atmosphere of that kind? (We did go to the five-and-ten.)

A European, on any social level, lives emotionally in a world made by others (he never knows clearly by whom), and seeks or accepts his place in it. The American attitude is best expressed by a line from a poem: "The world began when I was born and the world is mine to win." ("The Westerner" by Badger Clark.)

Years ago, at a party in Hollywood, I met Eve Curie, a distinguished Frenchwoman, the daughter of Marie Curie. Eve Curie was a best-selling author of non-fiction books and, politically, a liberal; at the time, she was on a lecture tour of the United States. She stressed her astonishment at American audiences. "They are so happy," she kept repeating, "so *happy*. . . ." She was saying it without disapproval and without admiration, with only the faintest touch of amusement; but her astonishment was genuine. "People are not like that in Europe. . . . Everybody is happy in America—except the intellectuals. Oh, the intellectuals are unhappy everywhere."

This incident has remained in my mind because she had named, unwittingly, the nature of the breach between the American people and the intellectuals. The culture of a worn, crumbling Europe—with its mysticism, its lethargic resignation, its cult of suffering, its notion that misery and impotence are man's fate on earth, and that unhappiness is the hallmark of a sensitive spirit—of what use could it be to a country like America?

It was a European who discovered America, but it was Americans who were the first nation to discover this earth and man's proper place in it, and man's potential for happiness, and the world which is man's to win. What they failed to discover is the words to name their achievement, the concepts to identify it, the principles to guide it, i.e., the appropriate philosophy and its consequence: an *American* culture.

America has never had an *original* culture, i.e., a body of ideas derived from her philosophical (*Aristotelian*) base and expressing her profound difference from all other countries in history.

American intellectuals were Europe's passive dependents and poor relatives almost from the beginning. They lived on Europe's drying crumbs and discarded fashions, including even such hand-me-downs as Freud and Wittgenstein. America's sole contribution to philosophy—Pragmatism—was a bad recycling of Kantian-Hegelian premises.

America's best minds went into science, technology, industry—and reached incomparable heights of achievement. Why did they neglect the field of ideas? Because it represented Augean stables of a kind no joyously active man would care to enter. America's childhood coincided with the rise of Kant's influence in European philosophy and the consequent disintegration of European culture. America was in the position of an eager, precocious child left in the care of a scruffy, senile, decadent guardian. The child had good reason to play hooky.

An adolescent can ride on his sense of life for a while. But by the time he grows up, he must translate it into conceptual knowledge and conscious convictions, or he will be in deep trouble. A sense of life is not a substitute for explicit knowledge. Values which one cannot identify, but merely senses implicitly, are not in one's control. One cannot tell what they depend on or require, what course of action is needed to gain and/or keep them. One can lose or betray them without knowing it. For close to a century, this has been America's tragic predicament. Today, the American people is like a sleepwalking giant torn by profound conflicts. (When I speak of "the American people," in this context, I mean every group, including scientists and businessmen—except the intellectuals, i.e., those whose professions deal with the humanities. The intellectuals are a country's guardians.)

Americans are the most reality-oriented people on earth. Their outstanding characteristic is the childhood form of reasoning: common sense. It is their only protection. But common sense is not enough where theoretical knowledge is required: it can make simple, concrete-bound connections—it cannot integrate complex issues, or deal with wide abstractions, or forecast the future.

For example, consider the statist trend in this country. The doctrine of collectivism has never been submitted explicitly to the American voters; if it had been, it would have sustained a landslide defeat (as the various socialist parties have demonstrated). But the welfare state was put over on Americans piecemeal, by degrees, under cover of some undefined "Americanism"—culminating in the absurdity of a President's declaration that America owes its greatness to "the willingness for self-sacrifice." People sense that something has gone wrong; they cannot grasp what or when. This is the penalty they pay for remaining a silent (and deaf) majority.

Americans are anti-intellectual (with good grounds, in view of current specimens), yet they have a profound respect for knowledge and education (which is being shaken now). They are self-confident, trusting, generous, enormously benevolent and innocent. ". . . that celebrated American 'innocence' [is] a quality which in philosophical terms is simply an ignorance of how questionable a being man really is and which strikes the European as alien . . ." declares an existentialist (William Barrett, *Irrational Man*). The word "questionable" is a euphemism for miserable, guilty, impotent, groveling, evil—which is the European view of man. Europeans do believe in Original Sin, i.e., in man's innate depravity; Americans do not. Americans see man as a value—as clean, free, creative, rational. But the American view of man has not been expressed or upheld *in philosophical terms* (not since the time of our first Founding Father, Aristotle; see his description of the "magnanimous man").

Barrett continues: "Sartre recounts a conversation he had with an American while visiting in this country. The American insisted that all international problems could be solved if men would just get together and be rational; Sartre disagreed and after a while discussion between them became impossible. 'I believe in the existence of evil,' says Sartre, 'and he does not.' " This, again, is a euphemism: it is not merely the existence but the *power* of evil that Europeans believe in. Americans do not believe in the power of evil and do not understand its nature. The first part of their attitude is (philosophically) true, but the second makes them vulnerable. On the day when Americans grasp the cause of evil's impotence—its mindless, fear-ridden, envy-eaten smallness—they will be free of all the man-hating manipulators of history, foreign and domestic.

So far, America's protection has been a factor best expressed by a saying attributed to con men: "You can't cheat an honest man." The innocence and common sense of the American people have wrecked the plans, the devious notions, the tricky strategies, the ideological traps borrowed by the intellectuals from the European statists, who devised them to fool and rule Europe's impotent masses. There have never been any "masses" in America: the poorest American is an individual and, subconsciously, an individualist. Marxism, which has conquered our universities, is a dismal failure as far as the people are concerned: Americans cannot be sold on any sort of class war; American workers do not see themselves as a "proletariat," but are among the proudest of property owners. It is professors and businessmen who advocate cooperation with Soviet Russia—American labor unions do not.

The enormous propaganda effort to make Americans fear fascism but not communism, has failed: Americans hate them both. The terrible hoax of the United Nations has failed. Americans were never enthusiastic about that institution, but they gave it the benefit of the doubt for too long. The current polls, however, indicate that the majority have turned against the U.N. (better late than never).

The latest assault on human life—the ecology crusade—will probably end in defeat for its ideological leadership: Americans will enthusiastically clean their streets, their rivers, their backyards, but when it comes to giving up progress, technology, the automobile, and their standard of living, Americans will prove that the man-haters "ain't seen nothing yet."

The sense-of-life emotion which, in Europe, makes people uncertain, malleable and easy to rule, is unknown in America: fundamental guilt. No one, so far, has been able to infect America with that contemptible feeling (and I doubt that anyone ever will). Americans cannot begin to grasp the kind of corruption implied and demanded by that feeling.

But an honest man can cheat himself. His trusting innocence can lead him to swallow sugar-coated poisons—the deadliest of which is *altruism*. Americans accept it—not for what it is, not as a vicious doctrine of self-immolation—but in the spirit of a strong, confident man's overgenerous desire to relieve the suffering of others, whose character he does not understand. When such a man awakens to the betrayal of his trust—to the fact that his generosity has brought him within reach of a permanent harness which is about to be slipped on him by his sundry beneficiaries—the consequences are unpredictable.

There are two ways of destroying a country: dictatorship or chaos, i.e., immediate rigor mortis or the longer agony of the collapse of all civilized institutions and the breakup of a nation into roving armed gangs fighting and looting one another, until some one Attila conquers the rest. This means: chaos as a prelude to tyranny—as was the case in Western Europe in the Dark Ages, or in the three hundred years preceding the Romanoff dynasty in Russia, or under the war lords regime in China.

A European is disarmed in the face of a dictatorship: he may hate it, but he feels that he is wrong and, metaphysically, the State is right. An American would rebel to the bottom of his soul. But this is all that his sense of life can do for him: it cannot solve his problems.

Only one thing is certain: a dictatorship cannot take hold in America today. This country, as yet, cannot be ruled—but it can explode. It can blow up into the helpless rage and blind violence of a civil war. It cannot be cowed into submission, passivity, malevolence, resignation. It cannot be "pushed around." Defiance, not obedience, is the American's answer to overbearing authority. The nation that ran an underground railroad to help human beings escape from slavery, or began drinking *on principle* in the face of Prohibition, will not say "Yes, sir," to the enforcers of ration coupons and cereal prices. Not yet.

If America drags on in her present state for a few more generations (which is unlikely), dictatorship will become possible. A sense of life is not a permanent endowment. The characteristically American one is being eroded daily all around us. Large numbers of Americans have lost it (or have never developed it) and are collapsing to the psychological level of Europe's worst rabble.

This is prevalent among the two groups that are the main supporters of the statist trend: the very rich and the very poor—the first, because they want to rule; the second, because they want to be ruled. (The leaders of the trend are the intellectuals, who want to do both.) But this country has never had an unearned, hereditary "elite." America is still the country of self-made men, which means: the country of the middle class—the most productive and exploited group in any modern society.

The academia–jet set coalition is attempting to tame the American character by the deliberate breeding of helplessness and resignation—in those incubators of lethargy known as "Progressive" schools, which are dedicated to the task of crippling a child's mind by arresting his cognitive development. (See "The Comprachicos" in my book *Rise of the Primitive: The Anti-Industrial Revolution*). It appears, however, that the "progressive" rich will be the first victims of their own social theories: it is the children of the well-to-do who emerge from expensive nursery schools and colleges as hippies, and destroy the remnants of their paralyzed brains by means of drugs.

The middle class has created an antidote which is perhaps the most helpful movement of recent years: the spontaneous, unorganized, grass-roots revival of the Montessori system of education—a system aimed at the development of a child's cognitive, i.e., rational, faculty. But that is a long-range prospect.

At present, even so dismal a figure as President Nixon is a hopeful sign—precisely because he is so dismal. If any other country were in as desperately precarious a state of confusion as ours, a dozen flamboyant Führers would have sprung up overnight to take it over. It is to America's credit that no such Führer has appeared, and if any did, it is doubtful that he would have a chance.

Can this country achieve a peaceful rebirth in the foreseeable future? By all precedents, it is not likely. But America is an unprecedented phenomenon. In the past, American perseverance became, on occasion, too long-bearing a patience. But when Americans turned, *they turned*. What may happen to the welfare state is what happened to the Prohibition Amendment.

Is there enough of the American sense of life left in people—under the constant pressure of the cultural-political efforts to obliterate it? It is impossible to tell. But those of us who hold it, must fight for it. We have no alternative: we cannot surrender this country to a zero—to men whose battle cry is mindlessness.

We cannot fight against collectivism, unless we fight against its moral base: altruism. We cannot fight against altruism, unless we fight against its epistemological base: irrationalism. We cannot fight *against* anything, unless we fight *for* something—and what we must fight for is the supremacy of reason, and a view of man as a rational being.

These are philosophical issues. The philosophy we need is a conceptual equivalent of America's sense of life. To propagate it, would require the hardest intellectual battle. But isn't that a magnificent goal to fight for?

RECOMMENDED READINGS

Ayn Rand's Novels

We the Living (1936). Set in Soviet Russia, this is Ayn Rand's first and most autobiographical novel. Its theme is "the individual against the state, the supreme value of a human life and the evil of the totalitarian state that claims the right to sacrifice it."

Anthem (1938). This novelette depicts a world of the future, a society so collectivized that even the word "I" has vanished from the language. Anthem's theme is the meaning and glory of man's ego.

The Fountainhead (1943). The story of an innovator—architect Howard Roark—and his battle against a tradition-worshiping society. Its theme: "individualism versus collectivism, not in politics, but in man's soul; the psychological motivations and the basic premises that produce the character of an individualist or a collectivist." Ayn Rand presented here for the first time her projection of the ideal man.

Atlas Shrugged (1957). Ayn Rand's complete philosophy, dramatized in the form of a mystery story "not about the murder of a man's body, but about the murder—and rebirth—of man's spirit." The story is set in a near-future United States whose economy is collapsing due to the inexplicable disappearance of the country's leading innovators and industrialists—the "Atlases" on whom the world rests. The theme is "the role of the mind in man's existence—and, as corollary, the demonstration of a new moral philosophy: the morality of rational self-interest."

Ayn Rand's Other Fiction

Night of January 16th (1934). A courtroom play in which the verdict depends on the sense of life of jurors selected from the audience.

The Early Ayn Rand (1984). A collection of stories and plays written by Ayn Rand in the 1920s and 1930s, plus passages cut from *The Fountainhead*.

Ayn Rand's Nonfiction

For the New Intellectual (1961). A collection of the key philosophical passages from her novels. The forty-eight-page title essay sweeps over the history of thought, showing how ideas control the course of history and how philosophy has served for the most part as an engine of destruction.

The Virtue of Selfishness (1964). Ayn Rand's revolutionary concept of egoism. Essays on the morality of rational selfishness and the political and social implications of such a moral philosophy. Essays include "The Objectivist Ethics," "Man's Rights," "The Nature of Government," and "Racism."

Capitalism: The Unknown Ideal (1966). Essays on the theory and history of capitalism demonstrating that it is the only moral economic system, i.e., the only one consistent with individual rights and a free society. Includes: "What is Capitalism?," "The Roots of War," "Conservatism: An Obituary," and "The Anatomy of Compromise."

Introduction to Objectivist Epistemology (1967). The Objectivist theory of concepts, with Ayn Rand's solution to "the problem of universals," identifying the relationship of abstractions to concretes. Includes an essay by Leonard Peikoff, "The Analytic-Synthetic Dichotomy." The second edition (1990) includes transcripts of Ayn Rand's workshops on her theory—containing her answers to questions about her theory raised by philosophers and other academics.

The Romantic Manifesto (1969). Ayn Rand's philosophy of art, with a new analysis of the Romantic school of literature. Essays include "Philosophy and Sense of Life," "The Psycho-Epistemology of Art," and "What Is Romanticism?"

Return of the Primitive: The Anti-Industrial Revolution (1999) [Formerly titled *The New Left: The Anti-Industrial Revolution* (1971)]. Ayn Rand's answer to environmentalism, "progressive" education, and other contemporary antireason movements. The expanded edition includes an introduction and three additional articles by Peter Schwartz on the new tribalist ideologies, including multiculturalism.

Philosophy: Who Needs It (1982). Everybody needs philosophy—that is the theme of this book. It demonstrates that philosophy is essential in each person's life, and shows how those who do not think philosophically are the helpless victims of ideas they accept passively from others. Essays include "Philosophical Detection," "Causality Versus Duty," and "The Metaphysical Versus the Man-Made."

The Ayn Rand Lexicon: Objectivism from A to Z (1986). A miniencyclopedia of Objectivism, containing the key passages from the writings of Ayn Rand and her associates on four hundred topics in philosophy and related fields. Edited by Harry Binswanger.

The Voice of Reason (1989). Philosophy and cultural analysis, including "Who Is the Final Authority in Ethics?" Also "Religion Versus America" by Leonard Peikoff, and "Libertarianism: The Perversion of Liberty" by Peter Schwartz.

The Ayn Rand Column (1991). A collection of Ayn Rand's columns for the *Los Angeles Times*, and other essays.

Ayn Rand's Marginalia (1995). Notes Ayn Rand made in the margins of the works of more than twenty authors, including Barry Goldwater, C. S. Lewis, and Ludwig von Mises. Edited by Robert Mayhew.

Letters of Ayn Rand (1995). This collection of more than five hundred letters written by Ayn Rand offers much new information on her life as philosopher, novelist, political activist, and Hollywood screenwriter. Includes letters to fans, friends and family members, celebrities, business leaders, and philosophers. Edited by Michael S. Berliner.

Journals of Ayn Rand (1997). The *Journals* contains Ayn Rand's notes for her three main novels—along with such items as her first philosophic musings on paper in English, a vigorous essay on why the House Un-American Activities Committee in 1947 did *not* violate the civil rights of the Hollywood Communists, and the notes for Ayn Rand's last projected novel, *To Lorne Dieterling*. Edited by David Harriman.

Periodicals Edited by Ayn Rand

(available in three bound volumes)

The Objectivist Newsletter (1962–1965)
The Objectivist (1966–1971)
The Ayn Rand Letter (1971–1976)

Works about Objectivism by Leonard Peikoff

The Ominous Parallels: The End of Freedom in America (1982). The Objectivist philosophy of history—through an analysis of the philosophical causes of Nazism, and their parallels in contemporary America.

Objectivism: The Philosophy of Ayn Rand (1991). This is the definitive, systematic statement of Ayn Rand's philosophy, based on Dr. Peikoff's thirty years of philosophical discussions with her. All of the key principles of Objectivism—from metaphysics to art—are presented in a logical, hierarchical structure.

The above recommended reading list is an adaptation of a list compiled by, and is reprinted courtesy of, the Ayn Rand Institute.